POLITICAL LEADERS OF CONTEMPORARY WESTERN EUROPE

POLITICAL LEADERS OF CONTEMPORARY WESTERN EUROPE

A Biographical Dictionary

EDITED BY
DAVID WILSFORD

GREENWOOD PRESS
Westport, Connecticut

Library of Congress Cataloging-in-Publication Data

Political leaders of contemporary Western Europe : a biographical dictionary / edited by David Wilsford.
p. cm.
Includes bibliographical references (p.) and index.
ISBN 0–313–28623–X (alk. paper)
1. Statesmen—Europe—Biography—Dictionaries. I. Wilsford, David.
D839.5.P62 1995
920.04—dc20 94–39084

British Library Cataloguing in Publication Data is available.

Library of Congress Catalog Card Number: 94–39084
ISBN: 0–313–28623–X

First published in 1995

Greenwood Press, 88 Post Road West, Westport, CT 06881
An imprint of Greenwood Publishing Group, Inc.

Printed in the United States of America

The paper used in this book complies with the Permanent Paper Standard issued by the National Information Standards Organization (Z39.48–1984).

10 9 8 7 6 5 4 3 2 1

For Pascale Canlorbe Wilsford

CONTENTS

PREFACE

I am extremely gratified by the timeliness and good cheer with which all the scholars who contributed to this book undertook to write these essays. Equally gratifying, these scholars all responded to critiques of their work with energetic and timely revisions.

The result is a reference volume characterized by the highest scholarship, useful to experts and interested individuals alike for many years. In all, it has been an immense learning experience for me, and I thank all of our contributors for making it so.

We should make a special note here of the opportunities and pitfalls inherent in using so many languages in the various stages of writing these essays. Recognized scholars from fifteen countries across Europe and North America have contributed their expertise and intellects to this project, and this has been a rich contribution to the excellence of the volume. They have not all had the same command of the English language—the publication language of this volume—as natives of the so-called Anglo-Saxon countries. Translators and copy editors have labored intensively over the final English-language product. Nonetheless, the attentive reader will note some differences in syntax, locution and even vocabulary. Because diverse languages are in many ways idiosyncratic, that is, somewhat unique, absolute linguistic uniformity is nigh impossible. It is my view that the linguistic diversity that has been part of the creation of this reference work is a major element in the volume's richness. And I thank every single non-Anglophone contributor for his or her understanding and tolerance in seeing their contribution brought to the printed page in English.

My special thanks go to Mildred Vasan and Greenwood Press and to Martin Schain, who first suggested this project. I wish also to give special thanks to my old friend Thomas Koelble and to new friends Gary Prevost, Chris Bourdouvalis and Frank Belloni for labor under very extreme time pressure. I am grateful to Jay Daniell, Todd Cloud, Christopher Annunziata, Jill Weider and Stacy Hayes for providing extremely important research and clerical and production assistance.

As we go to press, we have learned of the deaths of two of our colleagues who have contributed essays to this volume: Prof. Rudolf Wildenmann of the University of Mannheim wrote on Ludwig Erhard. Prof. Mark Bartholomew of the University of Maine wrote on Willy Brandt. We extend our deepest condolences to their families and friends.

Finally, to the host of scholars in Europe and North America who assisted in consulting with me in the selection of leaders to be included in this volume and who assisted in reviewing these many contributions in their areas of expertise, our deepest appreciation, for the volume could not have been completed without them. While they are too numerous to name here, they all know who they are.

DAVID WILSFORD

LEADERS AND LEADERSHIP

In the 20th century, there have been two particularly influential formulations of leadership styles in politics. The first, by the celebrated early 20th-century German sociologist, Max Weber, drew a distinction between charismatic and routine leadership. ''[The charismatic leader] is obeyed by virtue of personal trust in his revelation, his heroism or his exemplary qualities,'' he wrote in *Economy and Society* (1920). Routine leadership, however (which Weber called ''rational''), is based upon the legally established, impersonal order—of institutions, organizations, rules and procedures. These leaders, he writes, ''exercise the authority of office by virtue of the formal legality of their commands and only within the scope of authority of the office.'' Trust brings followers into a close identity with the charismatic leader, often leading to a willingness to go beyond the normal or expected in the act of following. Routine leaders, on the other hand, base their legitimacy on much narrower, usually legal, grounds.

In the second, somewhat similar, formulation, American historian James MacGregor Burns, in his book *Leadership* (1978), draws a distinction between ''transactional'' and ''transformational'' leadership. In the first, the relationship between leader and follower is reduced to a series of incremental transactions between them, usually over lower-order matters. In the second, transformational, the relationship between the leader and follower is raised to a higher order, the collectivity of followers being significantly *transformed* from its current state by virtue of following the leader in new, perhaps higher, directions.

Indeed, one of the great questions of political science is the degree to which individual political leaders can make a difference amid a myriad of complex institutions that surround them, all the while having to face a great deal of uncertainty about the future. For Weber, routine leadership is indeed embedded in the ongoing institutions that frame political interactions. Charismatic leadership, on the other hand, can more easily surmount the constraints of everyday institutions. Indeed, it is probably only charismatic leadership that can create *new* institutions to replace *old* ones. For Burns, transactional leadership is at home in the institutions of regular politics. Transformational leadership lifts followers up above and beyond their everyday political setting.

In both routine (Weber) and transactional (Burns) styles of leadership, individuals *qua* individuals do not matter very much. Institutions frame, shape and channel individual leaders, rendering their actions contingent upon existing structures. But in charismatic (Weber) and transformational (Burns) leadership, the individual *qua* leader matters a great deal, rendering institutions and existing political structures less important, perhaps even irrelevant, to the outcome.

If this question of individuals versus institutions is salient to politics in general, even in authoritarian countries, then it is doubly so for democracies. For in democracies, like all the ones featured in the pages that follow, any single leader enjoys even less leverage, even less autonomy than his or her authoritarian counterpart. After all, one definition of democracy is that a great number of people tend to get involved, and the more people that get involved, the more unpredictable the outcome becomes.

Which type of leadership is *best*, however, is a normative question not easily resolved. Charismatic, transformational leadership may lead to both good and bad collective outcomes. Both Hitler and Gandhi would qualify as this type of leader, but few of us would characterize the outcome of their leadership in the same way.

From all the rich political stories in this volume, can we begin to generate some hypotheses about political leadership, its characteristics, and the conditions for its being effective? In particular, does a charismatic leader make a difference in the face of bureaucratic institutions? This is the question we formulate from Weber. Does transformational leadership really lead to greater results over the long term than incremental, transactional leadership? This is the question we formulate from Burns.

Out of the complex histories in this volume emerge several initial hypotheses:

1. Charismatic leaders can accelerate reform—or delay it—but in the face of long-term structural forces, the future (be it change or continuity) cannot be avoided.
2. Nonetheless, accelerating a desirable reform by, say, ten years, or delaying an undesirable reform by the same period, could be considered an historically significant accomplishment, that is, a big difference, if you are one of the ones to be positively (or negatively) affected by the impact of charismatic leadership. Of course, in democratic politics, what one views as desirable or undesirable is often a matter of personal belief, not absolute truth.
3. And in the absence of charismatic leadership, big change can still occur if there is a conjuncture of all the right structural forces. In this view, Helmut Kohl, for example, made little difference in the outcome of German unification: The same result and timing would have occurred under any German politician's watch given the overwhelming character of the structural and conjunctural forces at play. Claus Hofhansel's essay on Kohl is suggestive in this regard.

4. Sometimes, the presence of the charismatic leader may be the crucial additional ingredient to the coming together of a powerful conjuncture, permitting an otherwise foregone outcome to be different, either for the good or for the bad.

For example, Urho Kekkonen, president of Finland from 1956 to 1981, was clearly the so-called man of the hour for Finland in the very difficult and delicate settling-in of a postwar *modus vivendi* between his country and the Soviet Union, as Dag Anckar's fine essay shows. According to this account, Kekkonen—a remarkable sportsman and statesman into his elder years—was able to institutionalize, by *personalizing* it, a new Finnish foreign policy designed to accommodate an overbearing Soviet neighbor, all the while without falling into the camp of Soviet-dominated Eastern European satellite countries. As the 1990s unfold, it is all too easy to forget that this was absolutely no mean accomplishment.

So, too, Margaret Thatcher, whatever one thinks of her politics, was clearly a charismatic force. By almost any definition, as Candace Hetzner shows in her essay, Thatcher was able to accelerate remarkable conservative reform of a British political and social system widely acknowledged to be at the brink of stalemate and deterioration.

Nonetheless, this volume does not pretend to answer the question about whether leaders make more difference than institutions, but the accounts in the following pages are full of insight relevant to that question. To be sure, the volume's focus on political leaders means perforce that the stories that follow are told predominantly from the individual perspective, what is more, from the subject's (leader's) particular perspective. But each of these leaders, more or less successfully and with more or less contingency, operated within complex institutional contexts. It is by examining carefully the interplay between them—leaders and institutions—that we can begin to assess the evidence that would permit us to evaluate the hypotheses that we have set forth above.

There were, of course, a number of practical problems in the conception and writing of this volume. The very first was the problematic of decision criteria to apply to the selection of countries and leaders to be included. Attentive readers will notice right away that a number of Western European countries, among them Luxembourg, Andorra and Iceland, to name just three, have not been included. The most glaring omission—because it is the biggest, richest and single most influential country of those excluded—is Switzerland. Yet the consensus of a number of Swiss political scientists who were consulted was that no Swiss leader merited treatment in a book of this kind. As one noted, "The whole Swiss political system *is designed* to militate against great individual leadership!" I yield to the experts on such matters.

Perhaps most difficult was the problematic of leader selection: Who should be included? Who is not quite important enough to make it? Moreover, this question had to be asked comparatively: Given very real space constraints, is Leader X of Country A more significant than Leader Y of Country B? Clearly, many apples had to be compared to numerous oranges. Not all experts will agree with the final decisions that had to be made.

Another thorny decision area was the extent to which older leaders should be preferred over younger ones. This equation was considerably complicated by the fact that we have defined "contemporary" political leaders as those from the post-1945 period to the present. Clearly we have assigned ourselves a vast span of time covering an immense amount of political territory. In the main, we have tended to favor including proven leaders, trying to strike a balance between early, middle and later postwar periods. Largely, we have chosen to leave a number of very interesting but "future" stars to later editions, when they will have proved themselves of clearly enduring historical value.

Nonetheless, some obvious candidates have been left out. For example, Winston Churchill was a prime minister in postwar Britain. He was excluded from this volume, however, because I judged that, by far, his major impact on the British political system occurred before and during World War II. Some may disagree. More a matter of happenstance—and revealing of the logistical difficulties in putting such a vast volume together—Amintore Fanfani was omitted from the Italian political leaders included in this volume. Originally, he was to have been included, but even after a long search, it was impossible to find a contributor in a reasonably timely fashion. This is to be regretted.

Unfortunately, of course, given the history of postwar Western European politics, all this has left us with a lineup of mostly white middle-aged and old men! It is quite revealing of gender differences in postwar Western European politics that only three women are included among the leaders of this volume: Petra Karin Kelly of Germany, Gro Harlem Brundtland of Norway and Margaret Thatcher of the United Kingdom.

Naturally, politics in the 1990s, as in any era, is a moving target. Therefore, this volume is as complete and accurate as it can be at the time it goes to press. Yet if politics in any era is a moving target, then perhaps in this post–Cold War period of dramatic and rapid change in many countries all at once politics is now probably a more swiftly moving and unpredictable target than it has been for some time. Inevitably, by the time this volume is published, some previously significant details may seem less so, while other heretofore overlooked or minimized details may have already assumed clear historical importance.

But this volume is about analyzing politics and political leaders at particular historical moments. The more recent these moments have been, the more uncertainty is perforce attached to the analytical task. Nonetheless, while perhaps not perfectly executed, the task that all the contributors have undertaken here is important: Political leadership—its presence or absence, its good intentions or bad intentions, its successes or failures—has made a difference to the lives of people living in its midst. And leadership has often made a difference—for good or bad—for those that follow in time, for it is they who have had to deal with the historical consequences of so many leaders—charismatic, routine, transformational and transactional.

BIBLIOGRAPHY

Aberbach, Joel D., Robert D. Putnam, and Bert Rockman, *Bureaucrats and Politicians in Western Democracies.* Cambridge, Ma.: Harvard University Press, 1981.

Burns, James MacGregor. *Leadership.* New York: Harper and Row, 1978.

Dalton, Russell J. *Citizen Politics in Western Democracies: Public Opinion and Political Parties in the United States, Great Britain, France and Germany.* Chatham, NJ: Chatham House,1988.

———. *Politics in Germany*, 2nd ed. New York: HarperCollins, 1993.

———, Scott Flanagan, and Paul Allen Beck, eds. *Electoral Change in Advanced Industrial Democracies: Realignment or De-alignment?* Princeton, NJ: Princeton University Press, 1984.

Erhmann, Henry W., and Martin Schain. *Politics in France*, 5th ed. New York: HarperCollins, 1993.

Putnam, Robert D. *The Comparative Study of Political Elites.* Englewood Cliffs, NJ: Prentice-Hall, 1976.

Rose, Richard. *Politics in England*, 5th ed. Glenview, Ill.: Scott, Foresman, 1989.

Weber, Max. *Economy and Society*, 2 vols. Berkeley, Ca.: University of California Press, 1978.

A

KONRAD ADENAUER (1876–1967), first chancellor of the Federal Republic of Germany, was one of the most significant leaders of the postwar period. As chancellor he personally conducted his country's foreign policy, moving Germany away from its traditional role as bridge between East and West by integrating the new West German state into the Western Alliance. His most significant foreign policy successes included the restoration of West German sovereignty (1954), the joining of NATO (1955) and collaboration to establish a united Europe, resulting in the Treaty of Rome (1957), which created the European Community (EC). On the domestic front, Adenauer was one of the men responsible for establishing the Christian Democratic Union (CDU) as the major party in West Germany. Adenauer's other domestic successes included integrating ten million refugees into the new West German state in addition to creating a social market economy (with Ludwig Erhard), which led to speedy economic recovery.

Konrad Adenauer was born on January 5, 1876, in Cologne. His father was a minor bureaucrat and a devout Catholic. Thus, religion would become a major variable throughout Adenauer's life. Cognizant of the persecution of the Catholic Church by the Second Empire (1871–1918), Adenauer soon came to despise everything associated with the Prussian regime. He would always feel closer to the Catholic cities of Paris and Brussels than to Protestant Berlin. For him the heart of Christianity was Western Europe, the area between the Loire and the Weser rivers. Everything east of the Weser he considered "Asiatic." Once in the 1920s he even secretly admitted that for him the Asian tundra started beyond the city of Braunschweig. Clearly there was no love lost between Adenauer and Prussia.

Educated at the Universities of Freiburg, Munich and Bonn and early on an active member of the Catholic Center Party, Adenauer started his political career at the age of thirty, as a "Beigeordneter" in Cologne. After losing his father the same year (1906) and his wife in 1916, Adenauer suffered a disfiguring car accident in March 1917. Undaunted by all this, Adenauer turned toward politics for salvation and became the youngest lord mayor in Germany on September 18, 1917.

As lord mayor of Cologne, Adenauer would, in fact, begin to exhibit some of the attributes associated with the Prussian bureaucracy. His style, emphasizing autocracy, ambition and punctuality, would ironically be considered ''Prussian.'' As soon as the German Empire was defeated in 1918, Adenauer's dislike for Prussia resurfaced. Having always associated Prussia with nationalism, militarism, Marxism and materialism—all concepts he despised—he now cautiously advocated that the Rhineland should separate itself from the Prussian state. For him, not France but Prussia was the real enemy of the Rhineland. Thus, as early as 1919 Adenauer advocated the creation of a West German state with Cologne as its capital. This, of course, would have made the mayor of Cologne the new leader of this West German state. However, Adenauer was not able to realize this goal in 1919, because Prussia was still too strong to tolerate such a move. Instead, Adenauer would remain lord mayor of Cologne throughout the Weimar Republic period (1919–1933), establishing the city's university.

Even though he was a prominent man in the Catholic Center Party, being in the inner circle from which the party picked its nominees for the chancellorship, he would never receive this honor. With the demise of the Weimar Republic and the rise of fascism, Adenauer's political career came to a halt. Being opposed to Nazism, Adenauer was barred from office in 1933 and forced into early retirement. Throughout the era of the Third Reich (1933–1945) Adenauer was a political refugee, even being sent to a concentration camp in 1944. When the Allies liberated Germany the following year, Adenauer was released and at the age of sixty-nine started his second political career.

Untarnished by Nazism, Adenauer went back into politics, cofounding the Christian Democratic Union (CDU) in the British zone of occupation in 1945. As the chairman of this new, all-encompassing party, Adenauer set himself up for the leadership of postwar Germany. Soon Adenauer became a favorite of the Western Allies, mainly due to the fact that he was both an anticommunist and free of Nazi associations. As the chairman of a ''Parliamentary Council'' appointed by the German federal states to draw up a new constitution for a West German state in 1948, Adenauer became a ''national'' politician.

In 1949, after the Allies had accepted the new constitution, called the ''Basic Law,'' it was Adenauer and his Christian Democrats—and not the favored Social Democrats—who emerged victorious in the first postwar elections, held on August 16. Thus, at the age of seventy-three, Adenauer became the first chancellor of West Germany, a post he would hold for the next fourteen years.

However, it was the decade from 1949 until 1959 which constituted the heyday of the Adenauer era. During this time, Adenauer set the foundation for West Germany's future political context, especially in the area of foreign policy. His pursuit of policies leading to integration into the West soon paid off. By 1951 the new West German state was allowed to create its own foreign ministry. One year later the first supranational organization in postwar Europe came into existence (the European Coal and Steel Community) and by 1954 West German sovereignty had been finally achieved. With the advent of the European Community (1957), the joining of NATO (1955) and the return of the Saarland to Germany (1958), Adenauer had achieved his objectives of Western integration and European unification.

These foreign policy successes, coupled with a speedy economic recovery at home, contributed to Adenauer's reelection in 1953 and 1957. In the latter year, for the first and only time, the Christian Democrats also achieved an absolute majority in parliament. Adenauer's political career seemed to have reached its zenith. However, in 1959 he would commit a major strategic error, which would lead to the decline of the Adenauer era.

In 1959 the incumbent federal president, Heuss, decided not to run for reelection to a third term. Adenauer's Christian Democrats, having an absolute majority in both houses of parliament, now faced the question of who should succeed Heuss. Adenauer right away perceived this as a chance to nominate a political foe to the largely ceremonial presidency in order to remove him from the political scene.

Adenauer's major challenger within the CDU was Ludwig Erhard, minister of finance and father of the postwar German economic miracle. Knowing that Erhard would very likely be his successor, Adenauer now tried to neutralize him by nominating Erhard to the presidency but without consulting him first. Erhard withdrew his candidacy, whereupon Adenauer—impressed by the powers his friend Charles de Gaulle enjoyed as president of the French Fifth Republic—decided to run himself, on the condition that, first, the powers of the German federal presidency would be increased and, second, the right to pick his own successor would be given to him.

Not only the public, but even his own party opposed this move, leading Adenauer to withdraw his candidacy. Adenauer's formerly supreme position within his party was weakened, his prestige fell and public trust in him decreased. As the end of the Adenauer era began, one debacle after another would follow.

First, there was the building of the Berlin Wall in August 1961, which undermined the credibility of Adenauer's Ostpolitik (his policy toward East Germany) and cost him his absolute majority in the 1961 elections. Only his public pledge to resign by 1963 led the Free Democratic Party to join into a coalition government with Adenauer and his CDU. For the first time, Adenauer had been forced to give in to a demand by a coalition partner. More important, his own party started to split into two wings, namely, an ''Atlanticist'' one, advocating close ties with the United States, and a ''Gaullist'' one, headed by Adenauer himself and seeking closer ties with France.

For the first time since his election as chancellor in 1949, Adenauer was not able to impose his foreign policy views upon West Germany. Disappointed with the foreign policy of the new Kennedy administration, which for Adenauer almost amounted to treason, the old man now shifted closer to the only real friend he had left, Charles de Gaulle. This new collaboration resulted in Adenauer's last great foreign policy triumph, the friendship treaty between Germany and France, signed in January 1963.

Holding to the terms of the compromise worked out with the Free Democrats two years earlier, Adenauer resigned the chancellorship on October 15, 1963, and was replaced by Ludwig Erhard. However, he continued to remain chairman of the Christian Democratic Union and leader of the ''Gaullist'' wing of his party until his death in 1967. In 1966 he even proved powerful enough to sabotage Erhard's policies, forcing him from office. It was only in 1967, when he was ninety-one, that his death would bring an end to the Adenauer era.

Throughout his political life, Adenauer represented the Catholic conservative current of German public opinion. Adenauer's worldview was deeply shaped by his devout Catholicism and upbringing in the Rhineland. While these were qualities he would never abandon and, in addition, they proved to be very conducive toward his goals of Western integration and European unification, his ''Prussian'' qualities soon surfaced after he had taken office in 1949; and for the next fourteen years, he would rule West Germany with an iron fist. Believing that the German people were children who did not know what was good for them, it was he, their father, who made policy on their behalf. Clearly Adenauer had been shaped by the political environment he had been born into, namely, that of the Second Empire (1871–1918).

Thus, Adenauer's political ideology was a mix of Catholic conservatism and Prussian autocracy. On one hand he despised Prussia; on the other he assumed some of the same qualities associated with it. Most important, he believed that the German people were too immature to make rational decisions in the realm of foreign affairs and that foreign policy would thus have to be conducted by himself without the interference of parliament and especially of the public.

To facilitate this process he created the Chancellery in September of 1949. This institution was based on several foundations. First, there was the ''Referenten System,'' referring to the fact that Adenauer would call upon the great minds of Germany, be they political scientists, historians or lawyers, to serve and head agencies within the Chancellery. This provided Adenauer with two advantages. First, he was able to receive advice directly from the best experts in the country. Second, these intellectuals were not professional politicians with a power base, which weakened them in their position toward the chancellor. Being politically powerless, they were totally dependent on the goodwill of the chancellor, who was, of course, aware of that fact. This allowed him to not only fire them at will, but also to play them off against each other and thus to control them.

The Chancellery assumed great importance because it was used to coordinate and control the ministries. Not only did it judge and evaluate policy proposals made by the different ministries, but it also had the function of supervising the implementation of policies by these ministries. Furthermore, especially in the area of foreign and defense policy, it was the Chancellery which replaced the ministries in the policy-making process, thereby excluding both the cabinet and the parliament. Even when the Germans received the right to set up a foreign ministry in 1951, Adenauer would continue to rely upon his chancellery to make foreign policy decisions. (This was simplified by the fact that he had chosen to become his own foreign minister.)

The Chancellery thus preserved for Adenauer the option of not informing—or even misinforming—his cabinet, parliament and the German public, an option he actively employed. Only in the last stages of ongoing negotiations, conducted between the Chancellery and foreign countries, would information be provided, and even then very sparsely and only that which was favorable so that Adenauer's work would not be jeopardized. Clearly, Konrad Adenauer was a true believer in the traditional conservative concepts of secret and quiet diplomacy as well as balance of power theory. His tight control over the Chancellery and over his own political party facilitated this approach.

Throughout the Adenauer era (1949–1963), the Christian Democratic Union (CDU) was too dependent upon the chancellor to mount a credible challenge to his way of governing. Being dependent upon the chancellor at the national level very soon turned the Christian Democrats into Adenauer's personal "Kanzlerverein." Not being a centralized organization, the Christian Democrats did not even constitute a national party until 1950. The party was also factionalized to a very high extent, meaning that the Christian Democrats had to rely upon the chancellor to hold the party together. It was he who, through the Chancellery, raised funds, devised national campaign strategy, conducted polls and even recruited candidates to office. In other words, the Chancellery substituted for the national party during election years, in turn allowing the chancellor to dominate the party. Thus, no challenge to Adenauer's way of handling policy making could come from the party itself, because any move against him would have jeopardized the whole party. In addition, the historical deference of the German public to the leader in the decision-making process facilitated Adenauer's approach to governing.

Throughout his political life Adenauer was painted as extremely dogmatic, a true ideologue, resistant to any kind of change in foreign or domestic policy. However, upon closer inspection, Adenauer clearly demonstrates two sides. One does fit the picture of the rigid ideologue. For example, every time the four powers met to discuss the German question, or even disarmament, Adenauer tried his best to sabotage those meetings, fearing that they would threaten his goal of Western integration. On the other hand, he proved to be extremely pragmatic on issues favoring his overall objectives. Here he would even accept terms overtly unfavorable to West Germany, demonstrating a willingness to override German public opinion in several instances, the best example being the reparations agreement with the state of Israel in 1952.

When analyzing Adenauer's foreign policy moves, it is also imperative to differentiate between the so-called old ideas of Adenauer's, most specifically policies he had already advocated as lord mayor of Cologne, and the new ideas born out of the German defeat in World War II. The former included reconciliation with France and the rest of Catholic Western Europe through economic integration, while the latter centered around the regaining of sovereignty, reunification, the rebuilding of the German economy and especially the readmission of Germany into the world of free nations.

It was, therefore, not mere anticommunism that led him to pursue so vigorously a policy of Western integration and European unification, because in fact all of his foreign policy objectives complemented each other, as demonstrated by his pursuit of Western integration and European unification. For example, as early as 1919 Adenauer had proposed economic integration with France to put the military-industrial complexes of both nations under a common system of supervision, ruling out future wars between the two nations. In his opinion only a common economic interest between France and Germany could guarantee peace in Europe. Thus the foundation of a United States of Europe, according to Adenauer, was to be a Franco-German process of reconciliation.

Another important force favoring European integration was the new Soviet threat Western Europe was facing. Adenauer believed that only a free United States of Europe could muster sufficient resources to face the common threat from the East. Other benefits of a United Europe included markets for German goods, a prevention of a new alliance between all four victorious powers, the readmission of Germany as an equal into the free world and the regaining of German sovereignty. Thus early on Adenauer became one of the staunchest supporters of the European unification movement. Subsequent successes in this area included the establishment of the European Coal and Steel Community in 1952, resulting in the abolition of parts of the occupation statute, the failed European Defense Community in 1954, leading to the regaining of sovereignty and the joining of NATO by 1955 and, of course, the European Economic Community, created in 1957.

In addition, West Germany's integration into the West prevented Germany, for the foreseeable future, from going back to its traditional role of bridge between East and West, which would have led to the German neutrality that Adenauer deemed so dangerous. Where did all this leave the question of reunification? Did Adenauer sacrifice it to achieve Western integration?

According to Adenauer, the two objectives were in fact complementary. Early on he recognized that the Soviet Union was turning its zone of occupation into a Stalinist sphere. With the advent of the Cold War, Adenauer realized that German unification had now been turned into a long-term goal which would have to follow Western integration. To justify his policies, which to the German public appeared harmful to the goal of reunification, he devised a unique political theory, the "policy of strength." According to this theory, any security policies toward the Soviet Union had to be defensive. Soviet expansionism, enforced by nationalism, had to be counterbalanced by a united free world, which due to its superior economic, political and moral system would engage the Soviet Union in a defensive struggle. Eventually the Soviet Union would not be able to cope with Western strength anymore and would have to settle with or fold before the West. Only then would reunification of Germany in peace and freedom be possible.

This theory clearly had a strong anticommunist and antidétente foundation, seeming to turn Adenauer into one of the most dogmatic, anti-Soviet leaders in Western Europe. This commonly held view is, however, not necessarily valid. As soon as Adenauer had achieved sovereignty for Germany, he became quite flexible on the issue of German reunification. As early as 1955 he established diplomatic relations with the Soviet Union and subsequently offered several proposals as to how reunification could be achieved.

Thus, Adenauer's Ostpolitik also had two dimensions: First, there was the political-ideological one, in which Adenauer appeared to be a dogmatic anti-communist, objecting to any kind of détente with the Soviet Union before reunification in peace and freedom had been achieved. With this strong stand against communism, he not only attracted public support, integrating minor right-wing parties and the refugees into his own party, but also established an ideological cohesion with the American foreign policy line under Dulles. Second, there was Adenauer the "Realpolitiker," who personally proposed to the Soviet Union several solutions to the German problem. These solutions, including the "Austria Settlement" (1958) and the "Burgfriedens Plan" (1962), would always place a heavy emphasis on the improvement of basic human rights and living conditions in East Germany. Therefore, it would be wrong to claim that Adenauer had written off the question of reunification. However, reunification was clearly for him only possible after Western integration had been successfully achieved.

The legacy of the Adenauer era can be felt in Germany to the present day. It was Adenauer who implemented "chancellor democracy" into the German system, making the chancellor supreme in the policy-making process. Furthermore, it was he who integrated Germany into the Western Alliance, thus overcoming a century-old tradition of bridging between East and West. It was also Adenauer who was able to reintegrate Germany into the free world and who was a major player in the creation of the European Community. Domestically, it was Adenauer who for the first time in German history brought Catholics and Protestants together into one political party and who was furthermore able to integrate ten million refugees into West German society, while at the same time preventing a new rise of fascism. Last, but not least, there is his greatest accomplishment, namely the overcoming of century-old enmity between the German and French people.

BIBLIOGRAPHY

Works by Adenauer:

Erinnerungen 1945–1953. Stuttgart: Deutsche Verlags Anstalt, 1965.

Erinnerungen 1953–1955. Stuttgart: Deutsche Verlags Anstalt, 1966.

Erinnerungen 1955–1959. Stuttgart: Deutsche Verlags Anstalt, 1967.
Erinnerungen 1959–1963. Stuttgart: Deutsche Verlags Anstalt, 1968.

Other Works:

Baring, Arnulf. *Im Anfang war Adenauer: Die Entstehung der Kanzlerdemokratie*. Munich: Deutscher Taschenbuchverlag Gmbh Co. KG, 1971.
Hanrieder, Wolfram. *The Stable Crisis: Two Decades of German Foreign Policy*. London: Harper and Row, 1970.
Hiscocks, Richard. *The Adenauer Era*. New York: J. B. Lippincott Company, 1966.
Schwarz, Hans-Peter. *Konrad Adenauer und seine Zeit*. Stuttgart: Deutsche Verlags Anstalt, 1976.
———. *Adenauer: Der Aufstieg*. Stuttgart: Deutsche Verlags Anstalt, 1986.
———. *Adenauer: Der Staatsmann 1952–1967*. Stuttgart: Deutsche Verlags Anstalt, 1991.
Stahl, Walter. *The Politics of Postwar Germany*. New York: Praeger Publishers, 1963.
Willis, Roy F. *France, Germany and the New Europe*. Stanford, Calif.: Stanford University Press, 1968.

MARCUS STADELMANN

GIULIO ANDREOTTI (1919–) has been one of the most influential political leaders of postwar Italy. With respect to occupying top-level positions in the Italian government, he has no rival, having served in the cabinet for nearly four decades. This includes seven terms as prime minister and long periods as minister of defense and foreign affairs. As such, he has played a major role in shaping Italy's domestic and foreign policies for the past half century.

Andreotti was born on January 14, 1919, in Rome and raised as a practicing Catholic. He studied jurisprudence at Rome University, specializing in canon law, and was awarded his laureate in 1941. Born into the Church, he has kept close ties with it. Indeed, his political development owes much to his involvement in associations organized under the Church's auspices. For example, as a leader in the Catholic student movement, he first attracted the attention of Aldo Moro, then president of the Federation of Catholic Universities (FUCI), a breeding ground for conservative party leaders. Moro selected Andreotti to direct the association's journal; when Moro left the presidency of FUCI, Pope Pius XII, on Moro's recommendation, named young Andreotti the Federation's president.

As with numerous Catholic political activists in the postfascist era, Andreotti's road to national leadership passed from the Church to Catholic Action to Italy's Catholic Party. In the Vatican library, in fact, he met his political mentor, Alcide De Gasperi, who recruited him to help found Democrazia Cristiana, or Christian Democracy (DC). This collaboration with the architect of Italy's leading postwar party had much to do with Andreotti's early political success. In 1947, during De Gasperi's tenure as prime minister, he selected his protégé to serve as his undersecretary in the Council of Ministers. From that time until De Gasperi left office in 1953, Andreotti was the DC leader's closest aide.

But Andreotti's political success was due to more than simply being well connected. In 1945, prior to his appointment as cabinet undersecretary, he had already been elected to the National Council of the DC, where he served as the party's representative for Catholic youth associations. A year later, at age twenty-seven, he was elected to the Italian Constituent Assembly and shared in the historic task of constructing a new constitution for postfascist Italy. When the first parliamentary elections of the new republic were held in 1948, he won a seat in the Chamber of Deputies, to which he was reelected into the 1990s.

Still, it was his appointment as cabinet undersecretary that linked him directly to the decision-making centers of the government and the ruling party. Moreover, when De Gasperi gave up the premiership, Andreotti stayed on as undersecretary to the new prime minister, Giuseppe Pella. Thus, for seven years (1947–1954), he was at the vortex of power, privy to the making of crucial domestic and international policies which shaped Italy's future for successive decades.

With minor interruptions, Andreotti remained in the government up to the 1990s, serving in no fewer than thirty-three cabinets. His assignments included top posts in the ministries of industry, finance, treasury and budget, in addition to defense, foreign affairs and the prime ministership. (In the last three posts alone, he served a total of twenty years: seven at defense (1959–1966), six as foreign minister (1983–1989) and seven as prime minister (1972–1973, 1976–1979 and 1989–1992).

Any explanation of Andreotti's long tenure in power must begin with two important features of the Christian Democratic Party in the Italian political system: the forty-six-year dominance of Italian politics by the DC, and the faction system that emerged early on as a defining characteristic of the DC's internal organization.

Having emerged as Italy's leading party in the early postfascist period, the DC, with the support of the Italian communists, secured the prime ministership at the end of 1945. The DC's political ascendancy was immediately reinforced by the Cold War. A coalition of forces, including the U.S. government, the Catholic Church and moderate-to-conservative socioeconomic forces, rallied around the DC in opposition to the Communists and Socialists, contributing to a stunning victory for the Christian Democrats in Italy's first postwar national elections in 1948. Thereafter, the DC steadily increased its hold on the country by appointing party loyalists in every part of the state apparatus, creating a highly structured clientele system that not only supported the party's electoral position but extended its influence throughout society.

Nonetheless, since 1953 the DC has been obliged to share power with other parties in order to maintain the parliamentary support required to govern. Thus, to a remarkable extent, the struggle for power has been limited to brokering new coalitions under its leadership. Within the dominant party itself, competition has been and continues to be carried on among organized currents, or factions. No one can expect to become a DC leader without an organized base of support within the party and its electorate and among the myriad interests that have gravitated to this power center over the decades.

Quick to recognize this, early on Andreotti used the perquisites of power at his disposal to reinforce and enlarge his personal electoral following in Lazio—one of Italy's most conservative southern regions—and to organize the provincial committees he controlled. As a consequence, when De Gasperi stepped down from the party's leadership in 1954, Andreotti had a strong base of support in the DC and was prepared to contend in his own right for a place in the power structure. In the struggle for control of the National Council, whose majority selects the party's leadership, he presented his own platform and list of candidates under the label *Primavera.* His list was supported not only by those whose political fortunes depended directly upon him, but also by a large part of the party's old Roman cadres (25 percent of his following), as well as by some of the younger parliamentary deputies. In addition, he benefited from the tactical support of many from the DC's traditional right wing.

However, the real strength of the Primavera current derived from the force of Andreotti's personality. In the 1958 parliamentary elections, for example, he received 227,000 preference votes, the largest of any Christian Democratic candidate. Under his leadership, the faction provided effective expression of the conservative interests of his Lazio constituents, as well as those in other southern regions.

Throughout this period, Andreotti projected both a staunchly conservative and pragmatic political image. For example, a major theme that he articulated was that the struggle against Italian communism had to be the preeminent, if not exclusive, concern of the DC. This required not only a steady reinforcement of the party's organization, but also a willingness to adopt tactical alliances with any and all anti-Communist forces, so long as it did not require ideological concessions from the DC. While this strong anti-Communist posture earned him considerable support among conservative forces, it could also be interpreted in terms of power rather than ideology. That is, Andreotti recognized the PCI as the only real organizational threat to the DC's hegemonic position. Whatever the case, his ideological stance and tactical flexibility earned him the deep distrust of the Social Democrats, who were convinced that he had no ideological scruples.

Equally essential to Andreotti's success was his skill at reconciliation. Italian party leaders constitute an intense, highly competitive system of political and personal interaction. The system is complicated by rather special ideological and institutional constraints, including, until recently, the imperatives of the Cold War. The dominant organizational elements of this system have been the DC and the PCI, the former cast in the role of a permanent governing party, and the latter constituting the (almost) permanent opposition and unacceptable alternative. Within this framework, the primary objective of Andreotti and other Christian Democratic leaders has been to perpetuate the status of the two parties: Keep the DC dominant and the PCI excluded from the governing circle.

To this end, and because the DC after 1948 would never again win a parliamentary majority, the party's ongoing task has been to reconcile the conflicting interests of the smaller, ideologically divided parties (Socialists, Social Democrats, Republicans and Liberals) whose support it has needed to maintain control of the government. In the process, it has also had to reconcile the conflicting attitudes of DC factions toward these subordinate partners, upon whom the party has become dependent.

Forging alliances has, therefore, been central to the maintenance of Christian Democratic power. The posture of Andreotti on this matter has been defining. Throughout the 1950s and into the 1960s he willingly accepted the parliamentary support of right-wing parties—from the Liberals to the Neo-Fascists and Monarchists—defending his position on tactical grounds. While recognizing that the DC was involved in a struggle not only against communism and socialism but also against right-wing totalitarianism, he was convinced that his party stood a better chance of winning voters from the right than from the left. He also argued that it was better to *have* the vote of the right than to *give* it to the right.

In addition, Andreotti's perception of the relative threat of the right and left to the system was changing rapidly. In 1959 he argued that neofascism was on the wane and communism on the rise, with more than one voter out of four supporting the PCI. Under the circumstances, he concluded, the DC had to be willing to accept support even from right-wing parties to ensure DC success against the Communists. But to counter critics on his left, he added the proviso that the DC should give up nothing in exchange. That is, the right would have to accept both the "Christian inspiration" and the programs of the DC.

The alliance question became increasingly problematic as the parliamentary majority of the DC and its allies narrowed. It was made especially so when the Social Democrats and the DC left-wing factions refused to continue joining in coalitions with the right-wing Liberals. This obliged the Christian Democrats collectively to look to the Socialists as an alternative. Yet many DC leaders shared a long-standing antipathy to the PSI based on the latter's previous alliance with the Communists. In the forefront of these was Andreotti, whose value orientation and close ties with the Church could be expected to lead to an aversion to the Socialists. Thus, when the so-called opening to the left was first proposed in 1956, he strongly opposed it, arguing that the Socialists were natural enemies of the political, economic, religious and spiritual values of Christian Democracy.

Nonetheless, as it became clear to Andreotti that opinion within the DC and among the Italian public more generally was becoming relatively more receptive to an opening to the left, his sense of realpolitik led to a change in his position. In 1964 he accepted the concept of a DC-PSI alliance, and by 1979, this alliance had become seemingly unbreakable. It reached its peak in the mid–1980s with the highly personalized political partnership known as CAF, from the last-name initials of Craxi (the PSI leader), Andreotti, and Arnaldo Forlani, then political secretary of the DC.

One of the most intense phases of Andreotti's political career was his government of ''national solidarity'' in the mid–1970s. First, the PCI had distanced itself from both Leninist theory and Soviet policies. Second, there was a rightist coup in Chile which overthrew the leftist regime of Salvador Allende. To avoid similar events in Italy, PCI leader Enrico Berlinguer proposed an ''historic compromise'' which envisioned the sharing of power between Italy's Catholic and Communist parties. As a starter, in 1974 Berlinguer indicated his party's willingness to join the parliamentary majority—even if excluded from formal participation in the government. But while the Moro government (formed in November 1974) did consult the PCI behind the scenes, no change in the PCI's formal status was made.

Yet the issue of Communist participation was made more pressing by the results of the 1975 regional and local elections in which the PCI made striking advances. A jump of 5.1 percent gave it an historic high of 33.4 percent of the vote nationally. Thus the lead of the DC, with 35.1 percent, was cut to less than 2 percent. Moreover, the PCI's new strength enabled it to govern alone or in coalition with the PSI in a number of regions and in most of the country's largest cities. Further, with the PCI's prestige soaring, the Socialists sensed that the country was moving leftward and, claiming their intent to bring the Communists into the government, abandoned their support of the DC-led center-left coalition, causing the collapse of Moro's government in January 1976.

In national elections the following June, the PCI won enough parliamentary seats to restrict coalition options to two formulas: either another DC-led coalition of the center-left (including the PSI) or a government of national solidarity (including the PCI). The DC, along with the American and German governments, but *not* the PSI, preferred the former; the PCI, naturally, pressed for the latter. In the face of this impasse, Italy's president, Giovanni Leone, turned to Andreotti to negotiate a solution and form a new government.

In doing so, Andreotti introduced a novel approach called the ''non–no confidence'' formula. It consisted of a minority government composed of Christian Democrats exclusively, made possible by the *abstention* from confidence votes of all other parties of a so-called constitutional arch, which had been momentarily enlarged to include the PCI.

This change in the Communists' status was vital to Andreotti's scheme. Given their enlarged parliamentary strength, if the Communists were to vote with the opposition, his government would not survive its first parliamentary test. Accordingly, to meet the needs of the DC, the PCI was allowed, in exchange for its support, to move a step closer to legitimacy. Thus, ironically, for the first time since 1947 the Communists were not in the opposition by virtue of an arrangement negotiated by their historical archenemy, Andreotti (in concert with Moro). Of great importance, Andreotti was probably the only Italian leader who could adequately reassure the American government that PCI involvement in the governing process would be handled in such a way as to neutralize any potential damage to U.S. or NATO interests.

Being a shrewd political manager, Andreotti was able to govern with this extraordinary arrangement for eighteen months (July 1976–January 1978), not a small accomplishment by Italian standards. However, it was a period in which terrorist activity and other forms of violence repeatedly threatened disorder in the system and the cohesion of the ''abstainers.'' Their fragile unity finally collapsed when Berlinguer insisted that the PCI be formally included in a government of ''national emergency,'' threatening to withdraw his party's abstention from confidence votes if it continued to be excluded from power. The change he sought was mainly symbolic, since the PCI was already part of the government in that no policy decisions could be made without its approval. Nevertheless, with conservatives horrified at the prospect of the PCI's formal inclusion in the cabinet, Andreotti resigned.

He remained at the front line, however, and after two months of negotiations agreed to head another all–Christian Democratic government backed by the Communists. While the new arrangement did not provide for its participation in the cabinet, the PCI was included as a formal component of the parliamentary majority—as distinct from its previous status as an *external* supporter. This was another important first for the PCI, at least since 1947, and it seemed to mark one more step on its journey to power. But on the very day set for the parliamentary vote of confidence in the new government, Aldo Moro, then the DC president, was kidnapped by the Red Brigade terrorist group, a development that would significantly alter relations between the two major parties.

In the interim, however, the new Andreotti government was confirmed and, with the backing of the Communists, confronted some of the most dramatic crises of Italy's history. The political paralysis gripping the country for two months was finally ended with the tragic assassination of Moro, whose body was left by the Red Brigade in Rome midway between the headquarters of the DC and the PCI.

Throughout the crisis, the PCI, to its credit, demonstrated bedrock solidarity with the government. Despite this, Andreotti and the DC never accorded the Communists the political legitimacy that they so earnestly sought. Instead, by means of innuendo, Andreotti fostered the notion that the Red Brigades were linked to the PCI and that, therefore, it shared responsibility for the Moro tragedy. Moreover, his subsequent management of the government worked very much to the detriment of the Communists, frustrating their programmatic aims and creating disillusion and dissension within the party's rank and file.

With the DC linking the PCI to left-wing terrorism and the PCI accusing the DC of reneging on promised reforms, relations between the two parties became increasingly antagonistic. Finally, under strong pressure from party members and supporters dissatisfied with the PCI's role in supporting the government, in January 1979 Berlinguer again demanded direct Communist participation in the cabinet and immediately withdrew the PCI from the parliamentary majority, forcing the cabinet to resign.

Andreotti's government of ''national solidarity'' during this period marks a watershed in postwar Italian history. Whatever might have been his intentions, the Communists' parliamentary association with his government proved disastrous for them. Having embarked upon the experiment at the very peak of their popularity, they exited it grievously damaged. They never recovered; instead, they entered a period of decline which ended ultimately in the party's dissolution in February 1990 and reconstitution as the Democratic Party of the Left. Certainly, other factors, such as the general decline of communism worldwide, contributed to this result. But it is difficult to avoid the conclusion that Andreotti's tactics toward the Communists at that critical juncture played a role in the demise of the PCI.

When Andreotti next moved front-stage in August 1983, it was as Italy's foreign minister in the first government headed by a Socialist, Bettino Craxi. Andreotti remained in this post for six years in both Socialist- and Christian Democratic–led cabinets. During this period, he reinforced his long-standing ties with the United States, which he always viewed as a cornerstone of Italian foreign policy. He committed himself equally to the process of further integrating and strengthening the European Community and Italy's role in it, and he strongly supported Gorbachev's transformation of relations between the Soviet Union and the Eastern and Central European countries.

At the same time, he worked assiduously to promote Italy's complex economic and political relationships in the Mediterranean and to increase its mediating role in the Middle East. Early in his tenure as foreign minister, Italy participated in the multinational peacekeeping force in Lebanon, providing the force's largest military contingent. Later, Andreotti engaged in intensive, behind-the-scenes shuttle diplomacy aimed at facilitating a settlement of the Iranian-Iraqi war. He was also an outspoken proponent of a Palestinian homeland during this period.

In July 1989, after this long stint as foreign minister, Andreotti was again named prime minister and served until March 1991. Then, despite his party's appreciable losses in the general elections of April 1991, he managed to form another government, which lasted until June 1992. These two governments, likely to be his last, coincided with momentous historical changes in Europe and the international system. These included the unexpected eclipse of Soviet control in Eastern and Central Europe and the collapse of communist regimes there, the historic unification of the two Germanies and the disintegration of Soviet communism and the Soviet empire itself. There was also the successful American-led international response to Iraq's invasion of Kuwait. In all this, Italy was fortunate to have Andreotti at the helm, for he was well acquainted with the most important international leaders and he managed the Italian role in these complicated and overlapping processes in a convincing, professional manner. However, even his considerable diplomatic skill did not spare him from getting caught in the conflicting yet converging domestic and international pressures that emerged out of the Persian Gulf war.

The Gulf crisis was only the most recent in a series of events that have complicated Italy's attempt to simultaneously pursue an independent Mediterranean strategy and maintain its long-standing commitments to the United States, its most powerful ally, whose interests in the Middle East especially have not always coincided with those of Italy. These tensions have been troubling for Andreotti, who has maintained close ties with American leaders for nearly forty years. Beyond serving as the principal linkage between Rome and Washington, he has generally been a staunch supporter of American foreign policy. Some have even accused him of subservience to the United States.

However, others have charged that he has been overly friendly with the former Soviet Union, Libya's Khaddafi and adversaries of the United States in the Middle East. For example, in 1985 the Reagan administration was outraged by Italy's refusal to detain the Palestinian Liberation Front leader, Abu Abbas, in connection with the Achille Lauro hijacking, which involved the slaying of an American citizen. Friction also developed between President George Bush and Andreotti during the Gulf crisis of 1990–1991 because of Andreotti's support of Pope John Paul II's pacifist approach to Saddam Hussein.

To date, Andreotti has served in the Italian national government for almost as long as the life span of the postwar republic itself, becoming a mainstay of both the ruling group in the Christian Democratic Party and Italian politics generally. What is remarkable, his admirers believe, is that he succeeded so well in such a complex political milieu, changing strategies and tactics as necessary, keeping options open, and—consistent with the dependence on others that is an essential part of politics, especially in Italy—maintaining as much autonomy as he could. Moreover, contrary to his stated distaste for the Italian political system, he obviously accommodated himself to it exceptionally well; in fact, many see him as the very epitome of it.

Clearly, his success has been due in large measure to his professional approach to the business of politics and the exercise of power. Andreotti has carefully combined his political abilities with an exceptional knowledge of the mechanisms of power and their inner workings, which he acquired through his long exposure to government and the policymaking process.

Moreover, Andreotti has practiced politics with a degree of emotional detachment, skepticism and cynicism that separates him from Christian Democrats like Giuseppe Dossetti, whose political activism derived from religious, moral and ideological convictions. Avoiding ideological formulas, he has favored a pragmatic, concrete approach, whether in the making of public policy or in the formation of political alliances. In his view, the function of politics and government is to make policy choices that are realistic, that is, feasible and realizable.

Finally, Andreotti's political career has also been characterized by a pronounced aura of "mystery." Far from being averse to this image, he has viewed it as very useful to his leadership. One tactic he has frequently used has been to reveal as little as possible about real or presumed "secrets of state" that he is thought to possess. And when he has been the source of political "revelations,'' they have often involved only half-truths, the remainder of which he has shrewdly kept to himself. As he is always suspected of knowing more than he chooses to reveal and of having ulterior motives for revealing what he does, his revelations only add to the aura of mystery that surrounds him.

The supposed mysteriousness surrounding Andreotti intensified the innumerable rumors and outright accusations against him of corruption, undefined illegal activities, participation in political conspiracies and plots, subservience to foreign entities (American corporations, the CIA, the American government) and connections with the Mafia. However, rather than categorically denying these charges and challenging his accusers for proof of their allegations, Andreotti has tended to turn them aside by suggesting that his behavior has simply been misunderstood or misinterpreted.

Heretofore, the many charges against Andreotti have never been proven and, until recently, he has suffered little political damage. Instead, his success in defusing or deflecting the accusations against him has tended to undermine their credibility and to produce a certain backlash of sympathy for him. However, in 1993, as part of an ongoing investigation of political corruption among Italy's elite known as ''Clean Hands,'' testimony has more convincingly linked Andreotti to the country's system of organized crime. He has, in fact, been accused of serving as the Mafia's political protector and, in this capacity, of having actually ordered the assassination of a top anti-Mafia crusader, General Carlo Alberto Dalla Chiesa, as well as the killing of a journalist who had been reporting on the connections between top-level Christian Democratic politicians and the Mafia. While the investigation of these charges has still to be concluded, it seems clear that Andreotti's active political career and his days as an influential powerbroker have come to an end.

BIBLIOGRAPHY

Work by Andreotti:

Governare con la crisi. Milan: 1991.

Other Works:

Galli, Giorgio. *Storia della Democrazia Cristiana.* Rome and Bari: Laterza, 1978.
——— . *Mezzo Secoli di DC.* Milan: Rizzoli, 1993.
Rizzo, Franco. *Andreotti, Moro . . . e gli altri.* Rome: Editrice Ianua, 1987.

FRANK BELLONI

CLEMENT ATTLEE (1883–1967) was prime minister of Britain from 1945 to 1951. ''Mr. Attlee is a modest man. But then, he has a great deal to be modest about.'' Such was Winston Churchill's assessment of the man who was his World War II deputy and his principal opponent in the early postwar years. Attlee was often the butt of jocular, slighting comments. When not joking, however, Churchill accorded Attlee considerably more praise.

In appearance and manner, Attlee *was* unremarkable. He resembled a Labour

Party version of the Conservatives' Stanley Baldwin—phlegmatic and plodding. A small, bald man with a sizable, well-trimmed mustache and round, steel-rimmed spectacles, Attlee contrasted sharply with the rotund and rambunctious Churchill, his immediate predecessor as prime minister. Although he was not colorful, his laconic manner of speaking led to many anecdotes. After his first meeting with Attlee, for example, King George VI commented to his private secretary, "I gather they call the prime minister 'Clem.' 'Clam' would be more appropriate!"

Appearances to the contrary, Attlee was quick-witted and decisive, not so much innocuous as ruthless. He could lay claim to being the most influential peacetime British prime minister of the 20th century and the most successful leader the British Labour Party has ever had. So much was accomplished while Attlee was in office that Peter Hennessey, a leading expert on the British executive, regards the period as a benchmark against which all subsequent British administrations must be measured. Harold Macmillan, himself prime minister six years after Attlee and leader of the Conservative Party, rated Attlee so highly as a party leader that he could not think of a better one.

Attlee's father was a well-off lawyer who supported the Liberal Party. His mother, however, favored the Conservatives. As did most children from the prosperous middle class, Attlee went to a private school. Despite his commitment to social reform, he valued this form of elitism. Subsequently, for his political accomplishments, Attlee was made a Knight of the Garter, one of the highest honors a British monarch can bestow. When Attlee died, the Garter Flag was given to his old school to hang with his portrait in the dining room.

Attlee went to university at Oxford, and although he did not join any political club there, he later characterized his views while an undergraduate as very conservative. After graduating from Oxford, he was called to the bar, apparently intending to duplicate his father's career. Like many upper-middle-class families, his had a tradition of social service. Since his old school operated a boys' club in the London slums, he decided to do volunteer work there. He soon became manager, which required him to live on the premises. Upon his father's death, Attlee received a small inheritance that enabled him to quit his brief legal career and become a full-time social worker. Except for his service in World War I, he lived in the London slums for a decade and a half.

The poverty he witnessed quickly turned him into a socialist. Important as he felt his social work to be, however, Attlee feared that he could only ameliorate the symptoms of poverty. Eliminating the causes, he thought, would require collective political action. He joined the Fabian Society, the group of prominent middle-class intellectuals who greatly influenced the Labour Party. But their patronizing, elitist attitudes so disgusted him that he joined the Independent Labour Party (ILP), a much more working-class movement. The ILP was one of the founding groups of the Labour Representation Committee (LRC) in 1900; the LRC six years later changed its name to the Labour Party, becoming one of Britain's major parties.

Despite strong pacifism within the ILP, Attlee was determined to fight when war broke out. Although too old at thirty-one for the army, he eventually managed to get a commission. He served with distinction both at Gallipoli and on the Western Front, rising to the rank of major. When World War I was over, he returned to the slums to resume his social work and political activity. Having served as both mayor and alderman, he stood for Parliament in 1922. He won and was reelected nine times, serving more than a third of a century before retiring.

In 1931 Labour prime minister Ramsay MacDonald deserted his party, forming a right-wing government to deal with the country's financial crisis. The split made that year's election a disaster for the Labour Party. All its former cabinet ministers but one lost their seats in the House of Commons. The sole survivor, George Lansbury, became the party's leader and Attlee was chosen as deputy. To many, this event epitomized Attlee's career; his advance seemed not so much merited as merely fortuitous. True, Attlee was fortunate; had his party not suffered an electoral disaster, he would have had little prospect of being elected deputy and, as a result, never would have become prime minister.

On the other hand, Attlee cannot be dismissed as a nonentity. He had a distinguished war record, notable service in local government, and nine years of experience in the House of Commons during which he had been the party's spokesman on various issues. Perhaps most important, he had lived with and worked for the poor. He was not a middle-class intellectual familiar with poverty only through statistics in books. Devoid of personal ambition, he, unlike MacDonald, never would be seduced by the glamour of power. He was in politics not to advance a career but to achieve social reform. Few among the other fifty who survived the 1931 election had all these qualities. That they chose Attlee as their deputy leader was more than an accident.

When Lansbury was stricken ill in 1934, Attlee was placed in charge of the parliamentary Labour Party for most of that year. The following year, Mussolini invaded Abyssinia. Attlee favored sanctions, while Lansbury, who was a committed pacifist, did not. The strength of trade union support for action against aggression forced Lansbury to resign as party leader. Two weeks later, in part to capitalize on Labour's division, the Conservative prime minister, Baldwin, called an election. Attlee was the obvious choice to lead the Labour Party's campaign.

In this election, Labour nearly tripled its strength in the House of Commons. Some of the credit had to be given to Attlee. On the other hand, he had not seemed more than an interim leader and with prominent figures who had been defeated in 1931 back in Parliament, it was thought that he would likely be replaced. However, personal conflict and factional maneuvering prevented an alternative candidate to Attlee from emerging, and Attlee was elected leader, although two ballots were required. Much of his support came from those Labour legislators who had been part of the 1931–1935 rump, when he was deputy leader.

Before the next general election, Britain found itself at war. When Churchill replaced Neville Chamberlain as prime minister, he formed a coalition government which included the Labour Party. Attlee, who held various positions during the war, was the only person other than Churchill to serve continuously as a member of the war cabinet. Moreover, early in 1942, he was designated deputy prime minister.

Elections were postponed each year during the war, so that ten years passed before the British voters went to the polls. The 1945 election then produced a landslide for Labour. Despite being led by Churchill, the Conservatives were routed. And whereas the Labour governments of the 1920s had been minority ones, this time Attlee became the first Labour prime minister to command a majority in the House of Commons, thus being able to plan on a full five years in power.

Following Labour's narrow victory in 1950, Attlee formed his second government, one usually dismissed as a mere epilogue, twenty months of drift presided over by geriatric, ill leaders. The Conservative victory of 1951—the first of three straight that would keep them in power for thirteen years—seemed to repudiate Attlee's leadership.

The irony, however, is that in that election Labour not only won *more* votes than did the Conservatives, but *more than any other party* in British history. (In the British political system, plurality voting in single-member districts means that a minority of the overall national vote can lead to a majority of the parliamentary seats.) This vote record stood for forty years. Not until 1992 did any party receive more votes than Labour did in the election which drove Attlee from office. Labour may have lost its way by 1950–1951, but millions of British voters were not ready to reject the party and the prime minister that had transformed Britain, as they had done to Churchill and the Conservatives in 1945.

Although he never again served as prime minister, Attlee continued as party leader for a few more years. When he retired several months after the 1955 election, he had led the Labour Party for twenty years, longer than any other British party leader in the 20th century. Given events from 1935 to 1955, that record of longevity by itself suggests a good deal of leadership skill. He recognized, as some of his successors failed to do, that the Labour Party had to be led from the left of center. Although Attlee probably should have retired as leader sooner than he did, he stayed on to ensure that Herbert Morrison, who he feared could not hold the party together, would not become leader.

When he retired as party leader, he also resigned from the House of Commons. As was the custom, Attlee was then made an earl, and he was enough of a traditionalist not to reject the offer of an hereditary peerage. Although he received a small pension as a former prime minister, Attlee had to write and lecture for money, much as had the former American president Grant. When Attlee died, his estate was worth less than $20,000; clearly, he had made no financial gain out of public service.

Attlee's reputation rests primarily on the extraordinary number and scope of actions initiated during his first government. As far as the average person was concerned, establishing the welfare state was the greatest achievement of those years. The new order that had been promised, but not delivered, to those who had fought in World War I was finally put into place for their successor generation. A comprehensive national insurance system covering the population replaced the existing limited social benefits. In it, people were protected against the financial burdens of workplace injury, sickness, unemployment, maternity, old age and death. The insurance system was buttressed by a national assistance program to aid any who fell below minimum standards. Most innovative was comprehensive government-operated health care (''socialized medicine'' to Americans). Initially free or imposing only nominal charges, the National Health Service (NHS) provided medical care to everyone.

Over the years, the detailed provisions of the British welfare state have changed. It remains, however, fundamentally as it was enacted under Attlee. Subsequent Conservative governments neither dismantled it nor cut back its benefits. In the 1980s, Prime Minister Margaret Thatcher sought to roll back government and reverse the public's attitudes of dependency. However, even she was compelled to promise the electorate in the 1987 election that the NHS was safe in the Conservatives' hands. In the campaign, she bragged about how much money the Conservatives had spent on the NHS.

Another Labour program of great importance to the public was housing. Britain long had had public housing, but only in 1927 and 1938 did government build as many as 100,000 units. Labour expanded the program both to rebuild after the damage of World War II bombing and to improve living conditions for lower-income families. Although local governments implemented the program and owned the houses, the national government provided the bulk of the finance and directed the program. In 1948 the government built 171,000 units. In each of the next three years, about 140,000 were built.

So successful was this program that the Conservatives felt compelled to promise that when they were returned to office 300,000 new homes would be built. They argued that reducing economic controls and aiding private builders would stimulate more rapid construction. Nonetheless, when under a subsequent Conservative government more than 300,000 units *were* built, two-thirds of them were constructed by government. Subsequently, the Thatcher governments drastically cut back spending on housing. Thatcher also launched a major initiative to permit those living in public housing to buy their homes on favorable terms. The proportion of owner-occupiers increased by about 25 percent during the 1980s. Nonetheless, when she left office a quarter of British households still lived in public housing. The programs of Attlee's governments continued to shape British society.

Of less immediate importance to the average Briton than either the welfare state or housing, though perhaps Labour's most major change, was nationalization. Many major enterprises were nationalized by the government. Coal, aviation, telecommunications, electricity, the railways and other transportation, gas and iron and steel all became publicly owned. These enterprises employed about a tenth of the British workforce and accounted for about a fifth of the British economy. Except for iron and steel and long-distance road haulage, the Conservatives did not denationalize these enterprises when they returned to power. Labour's actions were accepted as part of the postwar consensus for a third of a century; only in the mid-1980s did the Conservatives under Thatcher begin an extensive program of privatization.

In the area of foreign affairs and security policy, an action of major importance was the program to develop a British atomic bomb. This initiative was mainly Attlee's personal decision, since he did not consult the cabinet. Only some time later did he even inform his colleagues. Nuclear weapons was only one of several matters causing some disagreements with the United States. Nonetheless, ties remained close and President Truman and Attlee felt affinity with each other as plain men who had risen higher than most would have expected them to do. Attlee's governments firmly supported the Western Alliance against the Soviet Union. In all these matters—in contrast to domestic policy—a Conservative government would have behaved similarly. Nonetheless, that a Labour government took these actions is important. Had it not done so, international affairs would have evolved quite differently following World War II.

On another international matter, however, a Conservative government would not have implemented the same policy. In 1947 Britain granted independence to India. Attlee is widely agreed to have played the major role in this action. As early as the late 1920s, he had been a member of a fact-finding commission that had gone to India. Thus, he had some expertise on the country. Not only was he willing to accept independence, but he constantly forced the pace. Compared to the dismantling of other countries' empires—compared, indeed, to Britain's own decolonization of several other territories—Indian independence was achieved with limited bitterness and recrimination. India has continued to be a major member of the British Commonwealth, whereas the other country of the subcontinent, Pakistan, eventually did choose to leave.

Significant as were establishing the British welfare state and expanding government ownership, Attlee did not regard either as his most memorable accomplishment. Asked several years after he had left office for what he would most be remembered, he replied, "Don't know. If anything, India, possibly." It was an astute reply, because India was most clearly the policy on which he made a difference, the action which would not have been taken—or, at least not accomplished as effectively—had he not been prime minister.

The reply also suggests why evaluations of Attlee vary so greatly. He did not possess an elaborate vision that he wished his government to implement. He is not particularly identified with a set of policies that he advocated. He was not charismatic; he did not galvanize others to follow his lead. When introducing an item on the cabinet's agenda, he would comment with a couple of sentences and then ask for the opinions of others. Some characterize him as a cipher, a ditherer unable to make his own decisions, who simply went with the flow of colleagues' opinions. The Labour government took many important, innovative actions from 1945 to 1950; only the nuclear bomb and India, however, were clearly attributable to Attlee himself.

At issue, however, is leadership style as well as policy initiation. The charge against Attlee implicitly assumes that only a mobilizer—only a Churchill or a Thatcher—can be a significant prime minister. A prime minister can be credited only with those policies that are on his or her personal agenda. This view fails to recognize that the ''normal'' leadership style for British prime ministers is consensus building rather than mobilizing. Although the consensus builder is much less dramatic than the mobilizer, those performing this role skillfully can also be great prime ministers.

In so doing, Attlee led a group of exceptionally strong-willed, talented colleagues of diverse views. All but two of his first cabinet had been in office in the wartime coalition, so they were experienced as well. Five or six members of the cabinet were major figures in 20th-century British politics. Attlee's talent was to hold such a group together while it transformed British society. His own lack of identification with particular policy positions gave him maneuverability to crystallize the common core in his colleagues' views. He was able to integrate a variety of measures into a coordinated program of reform that was widely acceptable. His concern with practical effectiveness in preference to achieving some ideological vision embodied perfectly the basic values of British political culture. To dismiss his role as that of mere presiding officer, therefore, is to embrace a constricted view of leadership.

Although he did not try to impose his views on the cabinet, neither did he permit rambling discussions and discursive interventions. Under his guidance cabinet meetings were shorter than they had been for a quarter of a century. A civil servant who worked directly with him and four other prime ministers asserted that Britain never was as well governed—as to effective, decisive decision making—as it was under Attlee. He refused to permit intrusions to distract him from completing his work. When someone entered his office, he would stare at them, saying nothing, thus forcing them to come to the point or feel so uncomfortable that they would quickly depart. Should they need additional encouragement to go, he would lift himself slightly out of his chair, look across at the clock, and grunt.

Attlee's prominent colleagues might overshadow him, but they could not intimidate him. Plots to replace him as leader were endemic, yet he survived them all. Part of the reason was his well-known lack of personal ambition. Attlee was willing to leave without a fight whenever the party no longer wanted him; he would not, however, step aside merely to gratify the personal ambitions of others. While he remained in charge, he squelched any challenge to his authority.

Harold Laski, an internationally known political scientist active in the Labour Party, chaired the party's powerful National Executive Committee. Prior to the 1945 general election, he told Attlee to resign as leader in favor of someone of more impressive appearance and abilities. Attlee simply dismissed the idea. Following Labour's election victory, Laski continued to pronounce on public issues as though he were running the government. Attlee tolerated such behavior for less than a month after becoming prime minister before admonishing Laski, "You have no right whatever to speak on behalf of the Government. Foreign Affairs are in the capable hands of Ernest Bevin [the Foreign Secretary]. His task is quite sufficiently difficult without the embarrassment of irresponsible statements of the kind which you are making . . . a period of silence on your part would be welcome."

Attlee's leadership style was a major factor in implementing one of the most major reform programs in 20th-century Britain. His first government determined the nature of British society for the succeeding quarter of a century. Only in the mid-1970s did questions about the applicability of Keynesian economics, the role of economic interests (especially the trade unions) in governmental decision making and the scope of governmental social and economic action begin to be questioned. The Thatcher governments of the 1980s did depart from much of the consensus that the Attlee governments had established. Nonetheless, British life today owes at least as much to Attlee's six years as prime minister nearly half a century ago as it does to Thatcher's more than a decade in office a quarter of a century later. Unlike her, he did not have a personal policy agenda. Nonetheless, playing to perfection the role of consensus builder, he was as responsible for his governments' accomplishments as she, in the role of mobilizer, was for hers.

BIBLIOGRAPHY

Works by Attlee:

As It Happened. New York: Viking, 1954.
The Labour Party in Perspective. London: Gollancz, 1937.

Other Works:

Burridge, Trevor. *Clement Attlee: A Political Biography.* London: Cape, 1985.
Harris, Kenneth. *Attlee.* London: Weidenfeld and Nicolson, 1982.
Hennessy, Peter. "The Attlee Governments, 1945–51," in Peter Hennessy and Anthony Seldon (eds.), *Ruling Performance: British Governments from Attlee to Thatcher.* Oxford: Basil Blackwell, 1987.
Morgan, Kenneth. *Labour in Power 1945–1951.* Oxford: Clarendon Press, 1984.
Pelling, Henry. *The Labour Governments, 1945–51.* New York: St. Martin's Press, 1984.
Williams, Francis. *A Prime Minister Remembers.* London: Heineman, 1961.

JÖRGEN RASMUSSEN

B

BAUDOUIN I (1930–1993) was one of the longest-reigning monarchs of the 20th century, having been sworn in as the fifth king of Belgium in 1951, occupying the throne for forty-two years. Not only was he a popular, well-respected figure abroad, but he was also widely regarded as a symbol of unity within his own country.

While Belgium has been a parliamentary constitutional monarchy since its independence from Holland in 1830, the monarch exercises limited political power by virtue of the Belgian constitution. Baudouin I did, however, exercise a tremendous political influence over his country during his reign. The independence of the Belgian Congo in 1960, the long process of devolution undertaken during the 1970s and 1980s and, recently, Baudouin's unwillingness to countersign a ministerial act liberalizing abortion laws are some of the major opportunities seized by him which reveal what might be referred to as the "presidential powers" behind the Belgian throne.

Baudouin's childhood was marked by several tragic events which most certainly had an impact on molding his personality as well as his perception of the role of the monarchy. Born in Brussels on September 7, 1930, into the de Saxe Cobourg Gotha royal family, Baudouin was the first son of the then–Crown Prince Léopold and Crown Princess Astrid. Baudouin's birth year coincided with the Belgian centennial celebration of independence from Holland. The royal couple also had a daughter, Josephine Charlotte, born in 1927, and another son, Albert, in 1934. Baudouin's full name was Baudouin Albert Charles Léopold Axel Marie Gustave, Duke of Hainaut and Prince of Belgium. Prince Baudouin's sister, Josephine Charlotte, being the first child, was given the title Princess of Belgium. His younger brother, Albert, now the Belgian king, was the Prince of Liège.

At the age of three, Prince Baudouin became heir apparent to the throne when his grandfather, King Albert, was killed in a rock-climbing accident in the Ardennes, a mountainous region in the southwest of Belgium. His father Léopold became the fourth king of Belgium, Léopold III, and his mother Astrid became the queen. The title of Belgian Crown Prince, Duke of Brabant, was then bestowed upon Baudouin. Two years after the tragic death of King Albert, when Baudouin was not quite five years old, tragedy struck the royal family once more: Queen Astrid, deeply loved by the Belgians, died in an automobile accident in Switzerland in August 1935.

Prince Baudouin was trained for kingship at an early age. His private schooling began at age seven, and to prepare the future king to rule a bilingual (French-Flemish) country, half his schooling took place in French and half in Flemish. Prince Baudouin became a familiar figure to the Belgian people very early on. He often accompanied his father at military reviews and other public ceremonies.

While the 1930s brought much tragedy and mourning to the Belgian royal family, the political and economic situation of Europe caused further worry and concern. On the domestic front, Léopold III was dealing with government instability. On the international scene, the rise of national socialism in Germany, Belgium's eastern neighbor, and Hitler's expansionist moves into Central and Eastern Europe contributed to a very somber political climate. The treaties of Locarno and the League of Nations, symbols of peace after World War I, were soon regarded as ineffective in dealing with the growing threat of the new German power. By 1936, Belgium declared its foreign policy to be one of nonalignment and independence, hoping thereby to avoid being immersed in another world conflict. This formal declaration of neutrality was recognized by France, Britain and Germany.

On May 10, 1940, however, German troops invaded Belgium. King Léopold III headed the Belgian army during an eighteen-day defensive military campaign, then unconditionally surrendered to the enemy. The Belgian government fled to London and actively participated in the Allies' efforts to contain the enemy. Nonetheless, King Léopold and the royal family stayed in Belgium during the Nazi occupation. In June 1944, Léopold III, his new wife, Princess Liliane, whom he had married in 1941, and the royal children were deported to Germany, then to Austria. Their deportation lasted ten months until May 1945, when they were liberated by the American army. However, the royal family was prevented from returning to Brussels upon its liberation because popular opposition to Léopold III had become increasingly evident during the course of the war.

After the war, this opposition to Léopold's return developed into a major political issue known as the "royal question." This crisis of confidence in him threatened both the monarchy and the unity of the country. The main political party supporting the king's return was the Social Christian majority party, while the opposition was led by Paul-Henri Spaak's Socialist Party. The conflict also split along ethnic, cultural and linguistic lines in that the Flemish population of the north favored the king's return, while the French-speaking Walloons in the south opposed it.

The "royal question" centered on the role of the king during wartime. Those opposed to his return accused Léopold of pro-Nazi leanings. To justify their opposition, they cited several factors such as the king's unconditional surrender to the Nazis after only eighteen days of military campaign, his appearance as a guest of Hitler at Berchtesgaden, his marriage in 1941 (while the country was occupied) to Liliane Baels, a commoner whose father was known to be a pro-Nazi, his refusal to join the government-in-exile in London and his lack of support for the Allies' counteroffensive efforts. The royal question divided both the government and parliament and created chaos and protests at the popular level. As a result, Léopold, Liliane and the royal children took up residence in Switzerland until 1950; in the meantime, on September 20, 1944, the Belgian parliament established a regency to govern the country with Prince Charles, Léopold's brother, as regent.

From exile, Léopold III made known his strong desire to resume the Belgian throne. However, a law had been passed by parliament on July 19, 1945, which required a parliamentary majority vote in favor of the king's return prior to Léopold's resumption of constitutional powers. A popular referendum was held on the royal question in March 1950, in which 57.6 percent of the Belgian population voted in favor of the king's return. The necessary parliamentary majority vote followed, but only after a governmental crisis and more political unrest in the country. Léopold III was recalled to the throne on June 4, 1950, by a slim cabinet majority under Social Christian leadership. Nonetheless, facing protests and demonstrations in the streets, Léopold was forced to abdicate on September 7, 1951, transferring power to Prince Baudouin.

Baudouin I was sworn in as chief of state before a joint session of the Belgian parliament on August 15, 1951, two months prior to his twenty-first birthday. The circumstances of his accession to the throne were, at best, extremely difficult. The monarchy had been threatened from within, and Baudouin I would have to prove that he could govern with his ministers. There was also a fresh sense of urgency in rebuilding trust in the institution of the monarchy. Nonetheless, Baudouin I's accession to the throne was marked by a large showing of popular support which was echoed in governmental and parliamentary circles.

Nine years after becoming the fifth king of Belgium, Baudouin I was engaged to Doña Fabiola de Mora y Aragon, a Spanish princess. The royal couple was married in Brussels on December 15, 1960. Fabiola was adopted by the Belgians as their own queen and has from that time enjoyed broad popular support.

From a political perspective, Baudouin I acceded to the throne of Belgium without much experience in running a country. The years of occupation and especially exile in Germany, then in Switzerland, prevented the then-prince from attending England's Eton College, where his father had once been a student. Baudouin's nonresidence in Belgium for six of the formative years of his youth were an additional obstacle to overcome. Unlike previous kings, Baudouin had received no formal military training and had no senatorial experience. (In Belgium it is customary for a royal prince to be given a Senate seat at age eighteen.) Finally, the circumstances of Léopold III's reign and particularly his forced abdication were probably not the most promising training grounds for the new king.

Perhaps it is precisely because of this lack of formal training and preparedness that some of the established leadership in Belgium foresaw in Baudouin a monarch they could easily manipulate and who would perform mostly the ceremonial functions traditionally reserved to the crown. Forty-two years of reign proved them wrong.

Constitutionally, the role and functions of the Belgian monarch have not changed since 1830. The framers of the Belgian constitution established a unitary state with a parliamentary government. In such an institutional arrangement, the parliament expresses the will of the people and the monarchy's role is limited to that of an occasional "coactor" in governing the country, sharing some legislative powers with parliament and some executive powers with the cabinet government. The king is not responsible to parliament; instead, the government—made up of a prime minister and his cabinet—is. All acts of the monarch are encompassed by this ministerial responsibility. The government must submit to a confidence vote of parliament before it can assume office, and it may lose the parliament's confidence at any time if that body wishes to withhold its support for legislation proposed by the executive. Hence a "government crisis" results from votes of no confidence.

However, it is precisely in the formation of a cabinet government in Belgium that the "power" of the monarch is revealed. First, the king chooses a *formateur* whose role is to bring together a majority coalition capable of sustaining a parliamentary vote of confidence on a detailed political program. Of course, election results are an important input into the monarch's choice, especially in determining the party affiliation of the *formateur*.

Most often, the political party with the strongest electoral support is likely to assume the key responsibility of forming a governing coalition. But the complexity of Belgian politics and its multiparty system do not often present a clear picture of what a "winning coalition" might be for future governing. More important, the role assumed by the *formateur* is an advisory one to the king and an attempt at bridging the major political differences among potential coalition partners. The *formateur*, in his attempts to build support among political parties which would guarantee a majority cabinet, develops a detailed political program for the future government. And he does this in close consultation with the monarch. The latter traditionally meets with the party presidents, leaders of the unions and representatives of major economic and financial interest groups in the country. The meetings led by the *formateur* or those initiated by the king occur behind closed doors. The process of forming a government coalition in Belgium is a very complex one.

One of Baudouin's first official acts as monarch in 1951 was to formally approve a majority Social Christian cabinet. This majority one-party government was not only short-lived, but proved to be an exception in Belgian national politics. No single party has benefited from such majority support in over thirty-five years. Between 1951 and 1960, five government coalitions were to be formed, providing the young king with ample opportunities for learning about Belgian politics.

Dominating the debates in parliamentary and governmental arenas during that decade was the issue of state subsidies to public and private (mostly Catholic) schools. The education issue deeply divided the country along its clerical-anticlerical cleavage. After several governmental crises, marathon negotiations and heated debates in parliament, the school issue was resolved by a government agreement known as the "School Pact of 1958." The major elements of this pact were recognition of parental freedom to choose between public and private school systems and the extension of state subsidies to both public and Catholic schools at primary and secondary levels.

During these debates, Baudouin was not only a well-informed participant behind the scenes, but also made it a custom to hold extensive meetings with all parties concerned. Early on in his reign, Baudouin revealed an acute sense of diplomacy and an awareness of the politics of governing. It was clearly he who chose *formateurs* for new coalitions. For example, the king demonstrated respect for the Socialists by always attempting to include them in government coalitions. The king's strategy in this regard was no doubt the result of a calculated risk. Inside the government, the Socialists could be tamed. In an opposition role, they were to be less trusted.

By the early 1960s, and for the next thirty years, the domestic political agenda in Belgium was dominated by the multidimensional issue of devolution. The transformation of the Belgian unitary state into a federal state was to take more than three decades. While ministers, prime ministers and political parties saw their electoral fortunes sometimes enhanced and at other times threatened by this lengthy, complex regionalization process, King Baudouin and the institution of the monarchy remained largely untouched by federalism. Few monarchs or heads of state have been able to maintain—much less assert—their power while their country undergoes such drastic transformation.

Central to Baudouin I's political resilience was his ability to choose the right people at the right time and to dismiss those who presented a threat to the viability of the country. Wilfried Martens, who led nine coalition governments, was an example of the king's choice. While some accused Martens of being a blind servant of the king, Baudouin found in the Christian Democratic party leader a man in whom he could confide and trust. While the devolution process could have proven extremely problematic for the monarch, Martens saw to it that the country's move toward federalism largely preserved the prerogatives of the crown.

Baudouin I's expertise and vision of the role of the monarchy was demonstrated in foreign affairs as well. By the late 1950s, the crisis of decolonization was at the forefront of international politics. For Belgium, decolonization centered around independence movements in its colony, the Congo. King Léopold II, the second monarch of Belgium, had created an independent state of the Congo of which he was sovereign. The Congo became the Belgian Congo in

1908. The Belgians governed this central African country, eighty times its size, for over fifty years. Starting in 1955, demands for independence became more vocal in the Belgian Congo, led by black African leaders such as Lumumba and Kasavubu.

In 1959, King Baudouin addressed the Belgian nation and for the first time recognized that independence of the Congo was imminent. Black leaders continued to organize and criticize the colonial power; they envisioned a presidential, autonomous system of government for the Congo. Baudouin I, however, still viewed the colony as an "inheritance" and favored a "Belgian-Congolese" community where he would be maintained as king both of Belgium and of the Congo. Nonetheless, in the midst of great political turmoil, the colony was granted independence on June 1, 1960. Lumumba and Kasavubu, however, would soon be eliminated by a new emerging leader, Mobutu.

For over twenty-five years, King Baudouin personally dictated Belgium's foreign policy toward the Congo (renamed Zaire in 1971). These policies reflected the close friendship between Mobutu and Baudouin, as well as the personal political agenda of Mobutu. The Belgian government and especially the foreign ministry appeared to implement Mobutu's wishes as conveyed by the king in areas of foreign aid, assistance in maintaining order and economic development. Until the late 1980s, policies toward Zaire were thus dictated from above. When the "marriage of reason" between Baudouin and Mobutu finally ended, the Belgian foreign ministry was once again able to take more autonomous initiatives in its relations with the former colony.

No account of Baudouin I and Belgian politics would be complete without referring to one important incident which left the Belgians without a king—although only for a thirteen-hour period. In early 1990, the Belgian parliament had enacted new legislation liberalizing the abortion laws that had been in effect since 1867. Prior to this, Belgium and Ireland were the only remaining Western European countries in which abortion was illegal under any circumstances. The 1990 legislation changed the Belgian law to legalize abortion under very strict circumstances.

Before this, Baudouin I, a devout Catholic, had often expressed in public speeches his concern for human life. On April 4, 1990, in a totally unexpected development, he refused to sign the abortion legislation enacted by parliament. In Belgium, the king must sign all legislation before it becomes official. Baudouin declared that he could not, in good conscience and as a Roman Catholic, sign a law permitting abortion. Confronted with what amounted to a veto by the king, the government acted to suspend Baudouin I from power and declared him "unable to govern." The cabinet government (a coalition of Socialists and Christian Democrats) then assumed the king's powers and promulgated the abortion legislation. Then on April 5, 1990, the Belgian parliament was called into special session. By a vote of 245 to 0, with 94 abstentions, King Baudouin I was reinstated as the reigning monarch of Belgium.

Critics complained that the king and the cabinet had misused the "unable to govern'' clause of the Belgian constitution. Indeed, the clause was probably meant to cover inability to govern due to illness or insanity rather than dissent. Although constitutional scholars still debate the incident, it is revealing that no member of parliament—as indicated by the vote—chose to oppose the return of Baudouin I.

While the events surrounding the abortion legislation were unprecedented in Belgian history, the assertion of the king's powers are not. Following these events some Belgian political leaders believe that the power of the monarchy in Belgium should be curtailed, reducing the king's role to a completely symbolic one. Such changes did not, however, occur during Baudouin I's reign.

Baudouin and Fabiola earned the overwhelming respect, indeed love, of their country. They endured throughout the transformation of the Belgian state from a unitary to a federal one. Moreover, many argue that, in a deeply divided society, Baudouin played an extremely constructive role in these changes. For four decades, he received the overwhelming support of Belgian politicians.

In his later years, Baudouin was in poor health due to a heart ailment. On July 31, 1993, while vacationing with Fabiola at their Spanish residence, he was stricken at his desk by a heart attack and died. The royal couple had no children.

In light of Baudouin's assertion of power and his personal popularity in a highly divided Belgium, the question of Baudouin's successor takes on added importance. After his death, the Belgian parliament named his younger brother, Albert, as king. Indeed, Baudouin's reign was an extraordinary one and his impact on Belgian politics—both morally and practically—went far beyond the constitutional description of his duties. Upon his death, there was a vast outpouring of grief in Belgium and thousands upon thousands of Belgians attended his funeral. Whether Albert, or eventually his oldest son, Philippe, can gain the level of popular acceptance in Belgium and provide continuity to the legacy of Baudouin is yet to be seen.

BIBLIOGRAPHY

Illegems, Danny, and Jan Willems. ''De Kroon ontbloot,'' *Panorama*, August–September 1991.

Mabille, Xavier. ''Le Débat politique d'avril 1990 sur la sanction et la promulgation de la loi,'' *Courier hebdomadaire du Crisp*, Brussels, no. 1275, 1990.

Molitor, André. *Souvenirs*. Paris and Gembloux: Editions Duclot, 1984.

MARTINE M. DERIDDER

ENRICO BERLINGUER (1922–1984) and **BETTINO CRAXI** (1934–) have been among the most important political leaders of the Italian left since the formation of that country's democratic regime in the aftermath of World War II. Berlinguer served as the secretary of the Italian Communist Party (PCI)—once the largest and most sophisticated nonruling communist party in the world—from 1972 until his death in June 1984. His memory is revered among many Italians to this day. Craxi became the leader of the Italian Socialist

Party (PSI) in 1976, after the Socialists had suffered a significant electoral setback. He held that post until he was forced to resign in 1993 in the midst of a serious financial scandal that threatened to do severe, permanent damage to his party's already tarnished reputation. In addition to his party position, Craxi also served the longest consecutive term of any prime minister in the history of the Italian republic (1983–1986).

Despite Craxi's considerable achievements, the likelihood of his being remembered in the way Berlinguer has been does not appear very high. However, it is their interrelationship as leaders of parties in competition with one another for dominance of the Italian left that makes a joint account of their politics and careers quite compelling. In effect, while Craxi proved to be a lasting nemesis to Berlinguer, playing an important part in keeping the latter from ever participating in an Italian government, it was Berlinguer who would prove to have a much greater lasting impact on Italian politics, well beyond his death.

Enrico Berlinguer was born on May 25, 1922, in the provincial city of Sassari on the island of Sardinia. His family was neither of peasant nor working-class background; although not particularly wealthy, the Berlinguers were part of Sardinia's nobility, references to the family first appearing in archives toward the end of the 17th century. Berlinguer's relatives included the Christian Democratic politician Francesco Cossiga, who became a prime minister and, later, president of Italy.

Berlinguer's father Mario, a lawyer, was active politically for many years. He was elected to parliament at the age of thirty-three as an opponent of fascism. When Mussolini's dictatorship collapsed in 1943, Mario Berlinguer resumed his political career as a member of the ardently antifascist Action Party. The family apartment in Sassari was also filled with books. Enrico and his younger brother Giovanni grew up reading many of them. Bakunin, Marx, Mazzini and Antonio Labriola were among the favorites.

In addition to growing up in a family critical of the fascist regime and absorbing the views of Marx and other political thinkers through his reading, Berlinguer came into much contact with various workers, artisans, ex–political prisoners and others who were willing to express procommunist and anarchist views. He became politically conscious as an adolescent in the late 1930s, forming an identity for himself that went somewhat beyond his father's liberal antifascism. Berlinguer enrolled in the jurisprudence faculty of the University of Sassari in 1941 (not an auspicious year for academic pursuits), did some more reading (especially Lenin and Stalin during this period), then became a member of the still clandestine Communist Party. After the collapse of the fascist regime on the mainland, Berlinguer led a public protest of young Communists against conditions prevailing on the island. He was jailed for this effort but later released toward the end of April 1944.

Later in that year Berlinguer left Sassari for Salerno, on the mainland, in order to meet Palmiro Togliatti, the PCI secretary. Togliatti, recently returned from the Soviet Union, was in the process of constructing a ''party of a new type.'' He wanted the PCI, having just emerged from years of clandestine activity, to become a respectable mass party with broad popular support across the country instead of a revolutionary vanguard organization whose cadres were preparing the proletariat for revolution. As a handsome young man with nearly impeccable bourgeois credentials, Berlinguer was precisely the kind of person that Togliatti wished to see active in party work. Accordingly, the PCI secretary wrote a letter instructing that Berlinguer be given a job at the party's new headquarters in Rome. Thus, at the age of twenty-two, Berlinguer began what proved to be a lifelong career as a Communist functionary.

After a brief period at the party's temporary national headquarters, he was sent to Milan to help reorganize the PCI in the immediate aftermath of the war. Berlinguer was unusual among the young Communists working for the party in that city, for he was one of the few who had not fought in the Resistance. He had neither served a long term in a fascist prison nor been a slave laborer in a Nazi concentration camp. Despite this ''limitation,'' he impressed many with the patience and tenacity with which he approached the tasks he was assigned.

The PCI held its fifth party congress, the first open one after twenty years in hiding, in Rome around the 1946 new year. The congress, dominated by Togliatti and the Resistance leaders Luigi Longo and Pietro Secchia, selected a new party central committee. Berlinguer, at the age of twenty-four, was chosen as a ''candidate'' member of this important body. The quality of his work in Milan had impressed others as had his obvious personal charm. The fact that he was a young man of aristocratic origins did nothing to harm his prospects. In effect, Berlinguer became a protégé of Togliatti, seemingly marked for high party office.

After his election to the PCI central committee, Berlinguer was chosen to serve as leader of youth organizations. At first he headed the Fronte della Gioventù (Youth Front), an organization designed to draw its membership from the young members of all the parties that had participated in the antifascist Resistance. However, when Berlinguer took on this responsibility, Cold War tensions had risen to such a point that the Front's membership was largely, though not exclusively, Communist. Hardworking, handsome, dashing (he drove around Rome on a Harley-Davidson motorcycle), Berlinguer continued to impress Togliatti and other PCI leaders. Thus at the party's next congress he was elevated from the central committee to the PCI's Direzione, a singular honor for someone not yet twenty-six. Later, in 1949, at the height of the Cold War, the PCI abandoned the idea of a Youth Front, considering it a relic of the Popular Front period. In its place a Federation of Young Italian Communists (FGCI) was created and Berlinguer was chosen its first leader. During these years and despite his later reputation, Berlinguer appeared to be an ardent Stalinist. At the FGCI's first congress, he lavished praise on the Soviet ruler.

In 1951 Berlinguer became leader of the World Federation of Communist Youth, an organization of some hundreds of thousands of members worldwide with headquarters in Budapest. During his work on behalf of the federation,

Berlinguer delivered speeches announcing the imminent collapse of capitalism and celebrating the Soviet Union's immense social and economic achievements; he expressed particular satisfaction at the wisdom of Stalin's peace policy.

After some years leading these youth organizations, the inevitable occurred as Berlinguer became too old to play such a role. This period of personal transformation, as he began a search for new responsibilities, coincided with a time of crisis within the PCI itself. Not only did Stalin die in 1953, but in 1956 the new Soviet leader, Nikita Khrushchev, disclosed Stalin's enormous crimes. Meanwhile, Soviet forces had intervened in Hungary to prevent the reform-minded government of Imre Nagy from leading his country out of the Warsaw Pact.

Togliatti had spent most of his career as a loyal Stalinist, and the PCI was thrown into crisis by the events of 1956. The party's working-class base remained loyal, but there were serious defections among the PCI's numerous supporters among the intellectuals. Berlinguer, however, was not one of these. His intervention at the PCI congress of December 1956 was devoted to the dangers of reformism. He condemned the illusion that "capitalist society could be improved."

After 1956, Togliatti gingerly led the PCI in a different direction. He became the leading advocate of the idea of "polycentrism" in the international communist movement. After the Hungarian crisis and during the widening Sino-Soviet split, Togliatti stressed the desirability of the world's communist parties each pursuing their own road to socialism and taking national traditions into account along the way. Accordingly, Togliatti advanced an "Italian way" to socialism, calling attention to the distinctive Marxist writings of Antonio Gramsci, whose *Prison Notebooks* became a sacred text to Italian intellectuals.

While the PCI was evolving, Berlinguer's career did not advance. No longer in the party's Direzione, he spent the second half of the 1950s as the head of a party training school and then on assignment to help revive the party organization back on Sardinia. By now he was married to a woman of middle-class origins, Letizia Laurenti: She continued to attend Catholic Mass on a regular basis. Together they had two daughters and a son. Berlinguer's ascent to power then resumed in the 1960s. Pleased by his organizational work on Sardinia, Togliatti and Luigi Longo, the vice-secretary, chose him to replace Giorgio Arnendola, a longtime and highly visible leader, as head of the PCI's nationwide organization in 1960. The following year he was reelected to the central committee.

During these years Italy was undergoing fundamental transformation. From a poor country with a weak industrial base and a large agricultural sector, Italy was becoming a relatively prosperous industrialized society with an increasingly urban population. Against this background, Berlinguer demonstrated considerable skill in adapting the PCI to these new circumstances. Party membership increased, the PCI proving especially attractive to immigrants from the Mezzogiorno (southern Italy) in search of industrial jobs in Turin, Milan and other northern cities.

Berlinguer was rewarded for his work. By the time he was forty (in 1964), he was reelected to the Direzione and also became a member of the party secretariat. Although he had yet to be elected to parliament, and as a consequence was still largely unknown to the general public, Berlinguer had become one of only a handful of individuals with posts in the party's two leading decision-making organs.

In 1964, Togliatti died, and his place was taken by Luigi Longo, the aging leader of the World War II Resistance movement. Under Longo's tutelage, Berlinguer was appointed to lead the PCI delegations that visited the Soviet Union and North Vietnam over the next few years. Berlinguer was thereby adding foreign policy experience to his domestic organizational activities. If ever there was someone who had been groomed for leadership, it was he.

The 1960s were also a time of Communist growth. These were the years of the "opening to the left," as the Christian Democratic–led ruling coalition expanded to include the Italian Socialists (PSI), thereby forming a center-left alliance governing Italy. Contrary to widely held expectations, however, this arrangement did little to enhance the Socialists' popularity or to isolate the PCI. Instead, the PSI lost strength, being widely perceived as having been corrupted by its alliance with the scandal-ridden Christian Democrats. As a consequence, the PCI increasingly became a pole of attraction for many Italians, middle- as well as working-class, who were fed up with corruption and stalemated efforts at reform. In all this, the Italian Communists presented themselves as honest, businesslike and trustworthy alternatives to the Christian Democrats.

For Berlinguer and his party, 1968 proved to be an important year. After Longo suffered a stroke, Berlinguer was elected PCI vice-secretary. He was also elected to the Chamber of Deputies for the first time. Partially paralyzed, Longo continued on as the PCI's leader for some years, but from 1968 onward, Berlinguer appeared as the increasingly visible spokesman for the Italian party. In this capacity he had a number of interesting things to say about domestic and international political developments.

In international affairs, both he and Longo strongly condemned the 1968 Soviet-led Warsaw Pact intervention in Czechoslovakia. In Prague, Dubcek's effort to create "socialism with a human face" was an example of what the PCI hoped could be accomplished in Italy. Along these lines, Berlinguer, through his speeches, interviews and writings emphasized the PCI's strong commitment to peaceful change in the context of its support for pluralism and constitutional government. In the following years these views, plus a desire to act with increasing independence from the Soviet Union, placed Berlinguer and the PCI well ahead of other Western European communist parties (the French and Spanish ones in particular) in a movement that became known as Eurocommunism.

The PCI's evident commitment to pluralism and Eurocommunist ideas was not without its critics on the Italian left. In 1969, Luigi Pintor, Rossana Rossanda and other members of the Manifesto group were expelled from the party for the heresy of demanding that it adopt a more radical line in view of the changing circumstances of political life.

These circumstances involved a dramatic escalation in the level of mass involvement in Italian politics by university students, northern industrial workers and others during the whole period from 1968–1969 to the mid–1970s. Mass protest and political violence became commonplace, as millions of Italians took to the streets of Milan, Turin, Rome and other major cities to demand, among other things, not only better wages and improved working conditions but fundamental changes in labor-management relations. Extraparliamentary leftist groups (for example, Potere Operaio and Lotta Continua) surfaced, proclaiming their desire to overthrow capitalism by revolutionary means. On the right, various neo-fascist groups were mobilized for purposes of violent confrontation with the extraparliamentary leftists. Talk of a right-wing coup d'état was in the air.

In 1972 Longo's age and health dictated that he accept the largely ceremonial post of party president, and, in this exceptionally heated political atmosphere, Berlinguer became PCI secretary. While some on the left defined the situation as potentially revolutionary, Berlinguer's reaction was the "historic compromise" proposal. The long-term solution to Italy's manifold problems, he argued, would involve an alliance between the PCI and the two other forces in Italian politics with deep roots among the masses: the Socialists and the Christian Democrats. Instead of revolution or simply seeking an alternative to Christian Democratic rule, Berlinguer appealed for collaboration and national unity. Later, he cited the military coup against Allende in Chile as a justification for such a position.

Under Berlinguer's leadership, the PCI achieved the greatest electoral successes in the party's history. In the 1975 regional elections, the party not only received more than 30 percent of the vote but came within a few percentage points of overtaking the Christian Democrats as Italy's largest single party. In fact this electoral "earthquake" (as some analysts described it) stimulated fear in Washington and among many anti-Communist Italians that the results of the next parliamentary elections would compel a Communist presence in the national government. Before the June 1976 vote, Berlinguer went out of his way to assure all of Italy that the PCI, should it win, had no malevolent intentions. He even went so far as to say that his party supported continued Italian participation in NATO.

The PCI's electoral results did not achieve the *sorpasso* ("overtaking") that many in the party had expected. Nonetheless, with more than 34 percent of the vote, the Communists were a force that could not be ignored in the formation of subsequent governments.

During this period, Italy was beset with a "galloping" inflation rate, not unrelated to rapid wage increases, and a serious problem involving political terrorism. Political leaders discussed the possibility of creating a coalition government to be supported by all parties within the so-called constitutional arc. If not exactly the ''historic compromise'' that Berlinguer sought, he did achieve some of his goals. In exchange for leadership posts in parliament, an expression of willingness on the government's part to consult the PCI on all important policy matters, plus a few lesser considerations, Berlinguer agreed not to oppose the all–Christian Democratic government of Giulio Andreotti. In addition, in order to slow inflation, the PCI leader agreed to encourage the country's major labor union federation to limit its wage demands.

The direction in which Berlinguer led the PCI in the few years following the 1976 election, however, did not endear him to important elements within his own party. Many Marxist intellectuals were critical of his willingness to support the continuation of corrupt Christian Democratic rule in a situation, they believed, where it should be replaced. Second, union leaders and spokesmen for other working-class organizations complained that their members were being asked to sacrifice quite a bit in exchange for a very modest Communist role in government decision making.

In March 1978 one of the principal architects of the rapprochement between the PCI and the Christian Democrats, Aldo Moro, was kidnapped and subsequently killed by Red Brigade terrorists. This event stunned the Italian public, while the episode dragged on for almost two months before his captors murdered Moro. Berlinguer condemned the Red Brigades in the strongest possible terms and opposed any negotiations with them, but the fact that the terrorist group and the PCI both called themselves ''communist''—while also using the same Marxist-Leninist vocabulary—inevitably left the impression that the revolutionary terrorists and the PCI had something in common.

To make matters worse, Berlinguer and the rest of the PCI leadership were then confronted by another ideological challenge. Bettino Craxi, who had become the PSI's leader after the 1976 elections, launched a campaign to distinguish the philosophical roots of his party from those of the PCI. Craxi and his followers in the PSI emphasized their party's origins within the traditions of democratic socialism, as against the PCI's links to Lenin, Stalin and the totalitarian regimes of Eastern Europe.

By the late 1970s, Berlinguer and his party were caught in a bind. Despite his expressions of support for democratic pluralism, his leadership of the Eurocommunist movement and his willingness to criticize Soviet conduct in very strong terms (with regard to the intervention in Afghanistan, for example), the PCI's very name and its ideological roots seemed to place limits on its appeal to reform-minded but moderate voters. On the other hand, there were clearly forces at work within the party—both at the top and at the grassroots level—who viewed Berlinguer as having erred in promoting a collaboration with the despised Christian Democrats.

In this context, Berlinguer led the PCI back into opposition. The ''historic compromise'' had failed before it could be fully realized. But it was too late.

The PCI lost votes in the 1979 parliamentary elections. Membership figures began to decline as well. Berlinguer labored mightily to prevent these setbacks from becoming a trend. In 1981 he reacted to the Jaruzelski coup in Poland by expressing support for the Solidarity movement there and by saying that the Russian Revolution of October 1917 had "lost its propulsive spin." In other words, he proclaimed that the historic role of the Soviet Union had come to an end.

Also in 1981 the Christian Democrats were forced to loosen their grip on power by relinquishing control of the prime ministership. But this development was not the result of Berlinguer's efforts. A scandal concerning the involvement of high-level Christian Democratic politicians in the secretive Masonic lodge, Propaganda Due, was the immediate cause. The Republican Party leader, Giovanni Spadolini, headed the new government. He was then succeeded by Craxi in 1983.

Voter support for the PCI continued to decline during the 1983 elections. Under Craxi, the Socialists appeared aggressive and dynamic, with new plans to stabilize the economy and reform state institutions. Berlinguer and the PCI sought to regain the initiative they had lost by becoming vigorous defenders of the *scala mobile*, the escalator clause in union contracts that pegged increases in workers' wages to the inflation rate. When in the name of fighting inflation, Prime Minister Craxi issued a decree suspending this practice, Berlinguer led the PCI and the PCI-backed Italian labor confederation in staging work stoppages and mass demonstrations against Craxi's decision. The challenge did not succeed, and the Communists appeared defeated.

In the spring of 1984 Berlinguer launched a speaking tour in connection with the PCI's campaign for the European Parliament elections of that year. In June he suffered a cerebral hemorrhage while making a speech in Padova. He lapsed into a coma and four days later, on June 22, he died. Sandro Pertini, the president of Italy, accompanied Berlinguer's body back to Rome. More than one million people participated in the funeral ceremony. Political leaders from all parties paid their respects. Even the Vatican expressed its condolences.

If 1976 was the high point in the PCI's electoral performance and in Berlinguer's reputation as a party leader, then that same year was clearly a low point in the history of Italian socialism. The PSI received as small a percentage of the vote (9.6 percent) as it had at any time since 1953, when the party had resumed running lists of candidates independently of the Communists. Moreover, the Socialist parliamentary delegation was the smallest it had ever been in the history of republican Italy. And, while the PCI under Berlinguer enjoyed the reputation of having exceptionally astute leadership, almost the opposite was widely believed with respect to the PSI. Often torn by factional conflict, the PSI had been led in the postwar decades by such figures as Rodolfo Morandi, Pietro Nenni and Francesco De Martino, individuals with sincere commitments to socialism, a sense of inferiority vis-à-vis the Communists, and very limited skills as political tacticians.

Among the socialist parties of Western Europe, or indeed the industrialized democracies in general, the Italian Socialist Party had become unique. By the mid–1970s it was the only such party with less support in the electorate than a communist rival. (The leadership seemed so inept that it led to speculation that the Communists had been able to plant ''moles'' inside the PSI whose bungling was deliberate rather than accidental!) In any case, given the growing sophistication of the Italian electorate and the country's increasing prosperity, the situation seemed unnatural.

In the aftermath of the 1976 elections, there were demands at all levels of the party for De Martino's resignation. Refusing to resign, De Martino was removed from his post at a special meeting of the PSI central committee. At the same gathering, the members elected a new national directorate, one composed of ''young colonels,'' a new generation of Socialist leaders charged with the responsibility of reinvigorating the old party. On July 16, 1976, the directorate chose the forty-two-year-old Bettino Craxi to be the PSI's new leader.

Although physically and temperamentally it would be hard to imagine two individuals more different than Berlinguer and Craxi, their early lives actually bear some resemblance to each other. Like Berlinguer, Craxi came from a political family of provincial origins. His father, Vittorio, was a Sicilian who left the island for Milan in 1929 after receiving a law degree and refusing to join the Fascist Party. After practicing law in Milan for a few years, the elder Craxi married a local woman, Maria Ferrari. Bettino, their first child, was born on February 24, 1934.

Craxi's father was a Socialist who became active in the antifascist Resistance movement during World War II. Such prominent Socialist figures as Sandro Pertini and Lelio Basso were frequent visitors to his office. Craxi, like Berlinguer, became politicized at an early age. At eleven, so the story goes, he led a group of friends on an attack of a neighborhood Fascist Party office.

After the war, Pietro Nenni, the PSI leader, chose Craxi's father to run as a Popular Front candidate in the important 1948 parliamentary elections. (PSI and PCI candidates ran on the same list.) Young Bettino campaigned on his father's behalf. Later, at the age of seventeen, he formally joined the PSI youth organization in 1951. Both of these experiences served to make Craxi an anti-Communist. As a leader of Socialist youth in Milan, he became acutely aware of the PCI's efforts to manipulate and control the Socialist organization for its own ends. If Berlinguer grew up reading Lenin and Stalin, Craxi devoured R. H. S. Crossman's *The God That Failed*, with its accounts of how various European intellectuals were deceived by and had become disenchanted with their lives as communist party members. And it was the works of Filippo Turati, the early PSI reformist, rather than those of Gramsci, that provided Craxi with his political direction.

At the same time as joining the PSI, Craxi also enrolled in the jurisprudence faculty of Milan's Statale, the state university. Although he never finished his degree program, he founded and then led the university's Socialist student organization. Craxi's organizational work, as well as his writings in various leftist publications (critical of the Soviet Union), called him to the attention of Milan's PSI federation secretary. He, in turn, called Craxi's efforts to the attention of Pietro Nenni.

If Berlinguer was a protégé of Togliatti, it is fair to describe Nenni as playing an analogous role in Craxi's career. The old PSI leader's help was indispensable in winning Craxi election to the party central committee at the age of twenty-three. In these years, the mid-to-late 1950s, internal Socialist Party politics was being shaped by recent events in the Soviet bloc: Khrushchev's secret speech in which he disclosed Stalin's crimes, and the Soviet repression of the Hungarian uprising in October 1956. In this context, there were still strong forces at work in the party who defended Soviet conduct and who argued that the PSI should retain its ties to the PCI. Nenni, on the other hand, led the *autonomisti*, the party faction that favored a course independent of the Communists while also supporting the ''opening to the left,'' defined as a reform-minded ruling coalition with the Christian Democrats. Given his background, it should come as no surprise that Craxi became identified with Nenni's current within the party.

Despite the eventual triumph of Nenni's position, Craxi failed to win reelection to the central committee in 1959. He had, however, become a professional politician, and over the next years he devoted most of his time to organizational work for the PSI in Milan. His first assignment in this capacity was in the industrial suburb of Sesto San Giovanni. Known as the ''Stalingrad'' of Italy because of the PCI's intense support in this working-class community, Sesto San Giovanni proved to be another place where Craxi came into conflict with the Communists—to the point of having fistfights with some of the local PCI cadres.

In this and other situations, however, Craxi proved to be an exceptionally effective organizer. In fact, by 1964 he had become provincial party secretary in Milan. Over the following years, Craxi clearly came to dominate Milanese Socialism. He assembled a brain trust of advisers including Antonio Natali, Carlo Tognoli, Claudio Martelli and his brother-in-law, Paolo Pillitteri, and housed them at a new party headquarters in the Piazza del Duomo. A strikingly handsome man, Martelli would later follow Craxi to Rome, where he would serve as a cabinet minister in various governments. The others would serve terms as mayors of Milan. Eventually all four members of this brain trust would be implicated in the largest bribery scandal in Italian history. And, according to the magistrates involved in investigating the scandal, the Piazza del Duomo headquarters was one location, among several, where Milanese contractors and other businessmen allegedly came to provide *tangenti* (kickbacks) to these and other Socialist politicians.

Of course, these disclosures would occur many years in the future. In the 1960s, Craxi and his followers appeared to be the rising stars of the PSI, a party that from 1963 forward had become a full-fledged coalition partner of the ruling

Christian Democratic Party in a political system where patronage and clientelism were viewed as normal ways of doing business.

Like Berlinguer, Craxi was elected to parliament for the first time in 1968. He moved his base of operations, accordingly, from Milan to Rome, though he continued to exert control over the Milanese PSI through the brain trust. In Rome he developed close ties to other *autonomisti* in the party, and in 1970, when a vacancy appeared, Nenni recommended that Craxi become one of the PSI's three vice secretaries. In this post Craxi developed an interest in foreign policy, a relatively rare concern for Italian politicians. He became the PSI representative to the Socialist International, where he was elected its vice president after a few years, and he also served as a strongly pro-NATO member of the Chamber of Deputies' foreign affairs committee. But it was from his position as PSI vice-secretary that Craxi ascended to national leadership in 1976.

Despite the PSI's poor showing at the polls in 1976, the cards that Craxi was dealt were not all bad ones. The Christian Democrats did not do well enough to rule Italy by themselves or even in coalition with the small parties of the center. And while they could have entered into a long-term agreement with the Communists, the Americans objected. There were also strong pressures within the Christian Democracy (DC) itself against pursuing such an arrangement. If the DC wished to retain power, it had few choices other than seeking the PSI's help. The question for Craxi was: At what price should this help be forthcoming?

In fact, the new PSI leader also had the option—advocated by his own predecessor—of reaching an accommodation with the PCI. But such an arrangement would most likely have ensured that his party would become permanently subordinate to the Communists. And not only was Craxi an anti-Communist, but he also aspired to play a role analogous to that of François Mitterrand in France. Like Mitterrand, Craxi's ambition was to make the PSI the dominant party of the Italian left. To accomplish this objective, he sought to create an alternative "pole of attraction" between the PCI and the DC which would involve the Socialists dominating an alliance with the small "laical" parties to the left of center in the party spectrum. (These latter were the Republicans and the Social Democrats.) In this context, there was little possibility of close ties with the Communists.

Over the next few years, Craxi consolidated his control over the PSI by defeating challenges emanating from the party's left wing, mainly from the followers of Enrico Manca and Claudio Signorile. Outside this arena, the new PSI secretary launched an audacious campaign to upset the PCI's near-hegemonic position in Italian cultural life. Craxi, along with like-minded Socialists, wrote articles in such party-controlled journals as *Mondoperaio* attacking the PCI's totalitarian roots. And during the 1978 crisis brought on by the kidnapping of Aldo Moro, he managed to distinguish the PSI from the PCI by encouraging the government to enter into a dialogue with the Red Brigades. Also in 1978, the president of Italy, a member of the DC, resigned as the result of still another bribery scandal. Craxi seized the moment. Although he was not able to win sufficient support for his first choice, he succeeded in promoting the PSI veteran Alessandro Pertini for the post. Elected president at the age of eighty-two, the latter was the first Socialist to become head of state in the history of republican Italy.

In the 1979 national elections, the PSI showed only modest gains as against its 1976 showing. Nonetheless, President Pertini called upon Craxi to form the next government. As the leader of a party representing a little under 10 percent of the electorate, Craxi did not succeed in putting together the requisite parliamentary majority. Nonetheless, the PSI did rejoin the subsequent government, still led by the DC. On this occasion and at Craxi's insistence, the PSI received more major cabinet posts, nine portfolios altogether, than it had previously. In fact, the party was no longer subordinate to the DC.

Not only did Craxi seek an expanded role for his party in the Italian government but he also sought to achieve an expanded role for his country in the world arena. Among other things, he led the Socialists in advocating a greater Italian influence in the Mediterranean. An opponent of Berlinguer on most matters, he shared with the PCI secretary a strong favoritism for the Palestinian cause in the Arab-Israeli conflict. In the early 1980s, in the wake of the Soviet Union's modernization of its intermediate-range weapons, Craxi also became a strong proponent of the deployment of Pershing II and Cruise missiles. As a result, Craxi was able to earn some credit with the Americans, never a bad idea for an aspiring Italian politician.

When the Propaganda Due scandal became public in 1982, the government of DC leader Arnaldo Forlani was forced to resign. Craxi sought to succeed him, but the Christian Democrats resisted the initiative and Forlani's post was assumed by Giovanni Spadolini, leader of the Republican Party (PRI). Craxi's chance at the premiership finally came after the 1983 parliamentary elections. Not only did the results of the balloting buoy the PSI (it won over 11 percent of the vote) but the DC suffered a substantial loss of support, while the PCI declined as well. On the basis of this outcome, Craxi was able to put together a five-party—*pentipartiti*—governing coalition with himself as prime minister. Not only did Craxi thus become Italy's first Socialist head of government, but he served as prime minister during the same time as Sandro Pertini, the fellow Socialist, continued to serve out his term as Italy's president. For a party with less than 12 percent of the vote, the PSI, thanks largely to Craxi's political acumen, had come to play a crucial role in the political system.

As prime minister, Craxi cultivated a style of leadership labeled *decisionismo*. Unlike many of his extremely cautious and circumspect DC predecessors, he appeared to be a leader prepared to act quickly and decisively as the situation warranted. He went out of his way to convey a sense of action and movement, so much so that the graffito ''Bettino = Benito'' began to appear on the walls of many Italian cities—equating, obviously, his style to Mussolini's. For the Communists, the similarity with the fascist dictator was not confined simply to the style of Craxi's leadership, it applied to the substance of his policy as well.

His anti-Communist rhetoric, along with his 1984 decree blocking cost of living increases through the *scala mobile*, permitted PCI leaders (including Berlinguer until his death in June) to portray Craxi as a man of the right and an enemy of the working class.

The PCI's anti-Craxi campaign did not succeed. In 1985 the Communists' attempt to get the decree abrogated in a national referendum fell far short of the majority required. In effect, Craxi won a posthumous victory over Berlinguer, whose party continued to decline at the polls. And, if anything, Craxi and the PSI were gaining strength as reflected by local election results.

Nineteen eighty-five was also the year of the Achille Lauro incident, the takeover of an Italian cruise ship by a Palestinian terrorist band. While a full account is not possible here, it is important to note that it was Craxi's decision to permit the group's leader, Abul Abbas, to escape prosecution by permitting him to leave Italy for a safe haven after he had been captured by American forces (along with his followers) and taken to a NATO base in Sicily. Craxi defended his action in parliament by comparing the PLO's struggle to that of Mazzini's campaign to create a united Italy in the last century. Despite the resignation of his defense minister in the wake of Craxi's decision, the prime minister was able to weather the mild storm of protest it caused.

Bettino Craxi was able to stay in office long enough to carry out some reforms of the legal system and the Italian welfare state that he had long advocated. Eventually he resigned the premiership during the summer of 1986 as the result of a long-simmering dispute with Ciriaco Di Mita, the DC's national secretary. Craxi was then able to constitute a second government, one which lasted into 1987. But after the spring parliamentary elections of that year, the DC regained its control of the prime minister's office.

In the years immediately following his term as head of government, Craxi, who continued to be the dominant figure in the PSI, became identified with the cause of institutional reform. Efforts were mounted by various groups and organizations to reform and streamline the cumbersome Italian system. Craxi became a champion of a constitutional amendment to create a directly elected and powerful president, after the French system, to replace the weak executive arrangement that had produced so many revolving governments since the constitution had first gone into effect in 1948. Critics were quick to point out that Craxi himself hoped to serve as the first incumbent of the office whose creation he now advocated.

At the end of 1989, the PCI began to come apart. The collapse of communist regimes in Eastern Europe and the end of the Berlin Wall caused Achille Occhetto, the new PCI leader, to advocate the formation of a completely new party to take the place of the old one. Over the next year, the old PCI underwent a period of turmoil as a new party, the Democratic Party of the Left (PDS), emerged to take the place of the defunct Communist one. Against this background, Craxi paraphrased Gorbachev by repeatedly referring to a "common house of the left." Since communism had manifestly failed, it was time to reunify the entire socialist movement in Italy. It was not hard to identify the particular individual Craxi hoped would lead such a newly reunited political entity. But the hostility to Craxi within the PDS—among leaders as well as rank-and-file members—was such as to make such an arrangement a very unlikely possibility.

In fact, unless Craxi proves to be the Italian equivalent of China's Deng Xiaoping, the prospects of his becoming the leader of any political institution do not appear bright. In 1992 investigators in Milan began to uncover a vast bribe and kickback scandal involving businessmen, city officials and party politicians. The Socialist Party was especially hard hit by these investigations. One after another of its Milanese leaders was taken into custody as the scandal spread, eventually reaching nationwide dimensions. Craxi himself was also implicated, and in February 1993 he was forced to resign as PSI secretary. Parliament then voted to lift his immunity so that he could be prosecuted for criminal activity associated with the scandal. His career as a political leader appears to have come to an end.

The Italian left is now clearly in shambles. The PCI's sixty-year-long history has come to an end. While prospects for the PDS, its successor, are uncertain, the fact that the PCI never officially participated in a government has insulated the communist PDS from much of the unfolding scandal, all this while many speculate that the PSI will disintegrate completely as a result of a scandal in which almost all of its national leaders have been directly implicated. It is true that Craxi proved to be a more adroit political strategist than Berlinguer. In their conflict for political power and for control over the Italian left, Craxi emerged for a time as the winner. The Communists were kept from power and then marginalized. But Craxi's victory has proven Pyrrhic, whereas it is Berlinguer's name that is identified with the cause of democratic change, Eurocommunism and demands for an end to Soviet repression in Eastern Europe. On balance, this is not such a bad legacy after all.

BIBLIOGRAPHY

Works on Berlinguer:

Corsini, Paolo, and Massimo DeAngelis (eds.). *Berlinguer òggi*. Rome: Editrice L'Unità, 1987.

Fiori, Giuseppe. *Vita di Enrico Berlinguer*. Bari: Laterza, 1989.

Gorressio, Vittorio. *Berlinguer*. Milan: Feltrinelli, 1976.

Valentine, Chiara. *Il Compagno Berlinguer*. Milan: Mondadori, 1985.

———. *Berlinguer, Il Segretario*. Milan: Mondadori, 1987.

Works on Craxi:

Di Scala, Spencer. *Renewing Italian Socialism*. New York: Oxford University Press, 1988.

Ghirelli, Antonio. *L'Effeto Craxi*. Milan: Rizzoli Editore, 1982.

Scalfari, Eugenio. *L'Anno di Craxi*. Milan: Mondadori, 1984.

Statera, Gianni. *Il Caso Craxi*. Milan: Mondadori, 1987.

LEONARD WEINBERG

WILLY BRANDT (1913–1992) was a prominent leader occupying critical positions at critical moments in German history: mayor of Berlin (1957–1966), vice-chancellor and foreign minister of the Federal Republic of Germany (1966–1969), chancellor (1969–1974) and president of the Socialist International (1976–1992). Moreover, Brandt was the key actor in establishing West Germany's Ostpolitik, the policy of rapprochement with East Germany, Eastern Europe and the Soviet Union. This policy was predicated upon expanding contacts with the East in order to improve West German–Eastern European relations and as a step toward paving the way for German reunification.

As a senior statesman, Brandt was a relentless advocate and actor in the cause of building a European and global ''security order'' based upon controlled and monitored demilitarization, extensive global economic aid, and a restructuring of international institutions to give greater voice to the Third World.

Willy Brandt was born on December 18, 1913, in Lübeck, Germany, the son of an unmarried working-class mother. His real name was Herbert Frahm but he adopted the name Willy Brandt when, at nineteen, he fled Nazi Germany for Scandinavia. He kept that name afterward. During his years in exile in Scandinavia (primarily in Norway), he would see firsthand the fruits of the social democracy he had already come to embrace. Equally important, he would develop a web of contacts and friendships that would well serve him and the social democratic movement over the years. Here he developed his lifelong friendship with Bruno Kreisky (who would become chancellor of Austria) and Olof Palme (who would become prime minister of Sweden). These three leaders were sometimes referred to as the ''Little International'' by their friends or as the ''Nordic Mafia'' by their detractors. They and others often met in the home of Gunnar and Alva Myrdal in Sweden.

In his adopted home of Norway, Brandt would meet and marry his first two wives, he would become more comfortable in the Norwegian language than in German, and he would acquire the remoteness and almost shyness that one finds in rural Norway.

Brandt returned to Germany in 1946; he first became a newspaper reporter in Berlin, then was soon elected to the city's Chamber of Deputies. He would become lord mayor in 1957. From that time until 1989, Berlin would often be the focal point of the Cold War; being mayor therefore implied that Brandt would be party to the various Berlin crises.

The Berlin blockade and the Berlin Wall crisis were perhaps most instrumental to Brandt in illustrating the situation of Germany—and of Europe—in the superpower confrontation. Neither Berlin, nor West Germany nor even Western Europe could stand alone against Soviet power and influence. American goodwill and an American presence were indispensable in balancing Soviet power. Yet to a socialist like Brandt, the American presence should not be too great nor should Europe expect U.S. support forever. If Germany was often the glacis of the Cold War, Germany itself should play a particularly active role in overcoming its situation.

Serving as mayor of Berlin placed Brandt in the limelight of West German politics and gave him the experience and the contacts to reach for the leadership of his party. At the 1960 Social Democratic Party (SDP) convention, Brandt was chosen the party's candidate for chancellor, leading the party in the national elections. During the 1960s, the SDP would score impressive gains which would pave the way for the ''Grand Coalition'' government, comprised of the Christian Democratic Union (and its Bavarian sister party, the Christian Social Union) and the Social Democratic Party. In this government, the Christian Democrat Kurt Georg Kiesinger would become chancellor and Brandt would become minister for foreign affairs and vice-chancellor.

The Grand Coalition government (1966–1969) would affect Brandt, the Social Democrats and West Germany in many profound ways. First, the creation of the coalition broadcast to Germany that the Social Democrats had indeed given up most of their more radical beliefs, as they had claimed to have done at the 1959 Bad Godesberg convention. Their inclusion in the Grand Coalition illustrated that they were now ''fit to govern.'' The Bad Godesberg convention and the Grand Coalition alienated many in the left wing of the SDP who feared that the party was sacrificing its ideals in exchange for respectability and power.

Second, the Grand Coalition once again propelled Brandt into the national limelight and in short order the very charismatic Brandt eclipsed Chancellor Kiesinger in national prestige and influence.

Third, as foreign minister, Brandt was able to refine and begin implementation of his ''Ostpolitik'' (literally, ''eastern policy''): the step-by-step rapprochement between the two Germanies, between West Germany and Eastern Europe, and between West Germany and the Soviet Union. The policy of Ostpolitik was enormously controversial in the SDP, as well as in West Germany as a whole. Nonetheless, the person of Brandt and the policies he pursued were so attractive that by the 1969 national elections, Brandt's Social Democrats won a plurality of the vote and were able to form a ruling coalition with the small Free Democratic Party.

As chancellor, Brandt continued his Ostpolitik. In 1969 he would take the very bold and equally controversial step of announcing that there were two German states within one German nation. Supporters of Ostpolitik saw this as a necessary first step on the path toward rapprochement and eventual reunification. Opponents tended to see it as a nearly treasonous act. Until that time Germany had subscribed to the Hallstein Doctrine (named for one of Adenauer's state ministers) that stated there is only one Germany and Bonn represented it. The two states/one nation declaration removed obstacles to direct negotiation between West and East Germany and, just as important, mitigated Soviet animosity toward West Germany so as to make such direct contacts politically more acceptable. Brandt notes in his memoirs that he was willing to recognize the *territorial* status quo so that he could change the *political* status quo.

Integral to the recognition of the two states/one nation concept was the acceptance of the Oder-Neisse line as constituting the legal and inviolable border between East Germany and Poland. Without a clarification of this important issue, Eastern European and Soviet authorities would have been far less likely to engage in any rapprochement that might have ultimately resulted in German reunification.

As a result of the recognition of the Oder-Neisse line many German conservatives felt betrayed. Refugees from east of the line, lands now held largely by Poland, felt particularly deserted as their homelands, the former eastern provinces of Germany, were renounced.

In 1970, Brandt traveled to Moscow, East Germany and Poland for meetings with the respective heads of government. In each of these venues a treaty was signed renouncing the use of force against one another, and with Poland it was formally agreed that the existing borders (Oder-Neisse line) were inviolable if not immutable.

The so-called Basic Treaty (signed in 1972) with East Germany was particularly divisive in West Germany. Many conservative West Germans, such as Franz-Josef Strauss and his Bavarian Christian Social Union, felt that for Brandt even to meet with East German authorities lent the latter an aura of legitimacy and could be construed as a legal recognition of the communist regime. Nonetheless, the Basic Treaty was ratified in 1973 after very long and stormy parliamentary consideration. In 1972 Brandt had received a vote of no confidence on this issue in the Bundestag, and his chancellorship was saved only by the West German requirement of a ''constructive vote of no confidence'' whereby, in order to dismiss a government, the Bundestag must also simultaneously agree on the composition of a successor government. In 1973, conservatives in the CDU/CSU challenged the legality of the Basic Treaty in West Germany's supreme court but the court ruled the treaty to be legal. Brandt's Ostpolitik was now well under way, becoming deeply rooted.

While Brandt was a strong supporter of NATO and of the continued United States presence in Europe and in the Federal Republic, he continually supported a deeper and more comprehensive structure for peace in Europe. Deeply influenced by his confidant Egon Bahr, Brandt called for a ''European peace order.'' Such an order would be created by settling outstanding disputes and shifting from a defense policy to a security policy. One primary mechanism by which such a ''peace order'' could be constructed was the Conference on Security and Cooperation in Europe (CSCE). This thirty-five-nation conference (including the United States and Canada, the Soviet Union and all of the European countries except Albania) had been promoted by European social democrats as well as by others and was convened in Helsinki in 1973. It produced a ''Final Act'' two years later. These ''Helsinki Accords'' underwrote many of the major points promoted in Brandt's Ostpolitik: the inviolability of borders, increased trade, increased human contact between East and West and the promotion of human rights.

Willy Brandt's attitude toward European integration was unusually ambiguous. While he was a staunch supporter of integration per se, his conception of a United Europe was not synonymous with the European Community. Clearly, Brandt envisaged a wider Europe somehow including the East. While he often promoted such a concept of Europe, its precise contours were never clearly defined.

Brandt's extremely active foreign policy had several overarching goals including German reunification, stabilization of the European security environment and, certainly not least, the rehabilitation of Germany's international image. When visiting Warsaw in 1970, Brandt dropped to his knees at the memorial to those who had died in the Warsaw ghetto. When visiting Israel in 1973 (the first postwar chancellor to do so), Brandt laid a wreath at Yad Vashem and read eight verses of Psalm 103. Both of these acts were received with mixed feelings at home but were welcomed abroad as indicators of atonement and of an even more deeply seated democratic culture in West Germany that was committed to creating and living in a more peaceful world. Perhaps this is symbolized most clearly by the fact that Brandt was awarded the Nobel Peace Prize in 1971.

Brandt abruptly resigned as chancellor in April 1974 when it was learned that one of his confidants, Günter Guillaume, was an East German spy. In retrospect, however, Brandt stated that he should not have resigned over the ''Guillaume affair.''

During his years as foreign minister, vice-chancellor and chancellor, Brandt ushered in, won widespread approval for and institutionalized Ostpolitik. He was able to maintain good relations across the Atlantic while at the same time pursuing a security policy far more daring than that which Washington favored. He was able to cast himself, and his nation, as a ''good European'' even though he worked for a far broader and more ambitious conception of Europe than that entertained in Brussels. Finally, he was largely successful in rehabilitating the international image of Germany.

In domestic policy, Brandt had a more mixed record. While he always appealed to youth and to leftist intellectuals, the period of Grand Coalition in which the CDU and SDP shared power tended to make the SDP left feel ignored or even betrayed. Some joined the ranks of the ''extraparliamentary opposition,'' taking their battle to the streets. Others promised to take the ''long march through the institutions,'' aiming to use the institutions of the state to radically transform it. Still others deserted the party altogether and formed antisystem parties, the best example being the Greens.

Brandt's resignation as chancellor in no way marked a withdrawal from politics. He would stay on and repeatedly win reelection to the Bundestag. He would serve three years in the European Parliament (1979–1982). He would remain president of the SDP until 1987. He would continue to be a powerful moral force and senior statesman in German politics.

Freed from the demands of being chancellor, Brandt was willing to accept the presidency of the Socialist International in 1976 and would serve in that capacity until 1992. In this, Brandt was an extraordinary leader who was committed to breaking the Socialist International free from "the ghetto of Europe." Under his leadership the International dramatically expanded its membership to include all of the major social democratic parties of the developing countries. The Socialist International expanded its agenda as well. Brandt's old friend Bruno Kreisky was charged with investigating and seeking solutions to the Israeli-Arab situation and his old friend Olof Palme was similarly charged with working with the African "Front Line States" to increase pressure against apartheid. Brandt himself and the Jamaican social democratic leader, Michael Manley, each chaired a commission to investigate and draw up a plan of action to address the international North-South divide. Palme chaired a commission to propose a similar action plan to build "common security" in Europe.

Under Brandt's leadership, the Socialist International overcame its old image of being a European gentlemen's club and, instead, became a serious actor and moral force in world politics. As a result of Brandt's constant high-level pressure upon international leaders to work for a dramatically reformed and more just world order, he was awarded the Third World Prize at the United Nations in 1985.

Throughout a long career—as mayor of Berlin, West German foreign minister and chancellor and president of the Socialist International—Brandt was both ceaselessly innovative and very often controversial, never flinching from challenging the status quo or prevailing orthodoxies.

BIBLIOGRAPHY

Works by Brandt:

My Road to Berlin. New York: Doubleday, 1960.

A Peace Policy for Europe. New York: Holt, Rinehart and Winston, 1969.

In Exile. Philadelphia: University of Pennsylvania Press, 1971.

Common Crisis: North-South Cooperation for World Recovery. Cambridge: MIT Press, 1983.

Arms and Hunger. New York: Pantheon, 1986.

Willy Brandt Erinnerungen. Berlin: Verlag Ullstein, 1989.

Other Works:

Bartholomew, Mark. "The Foreign Policy of Willy Brandt's Socialist International," *Coexistence*, Vol. 26, No. 4, 1989.

Binder, David. *The Other German: Willy Brandt's Life and Times*. Washington, D.C.: New Republic Books, 1975.

Drath, Viola H. *Willy Brandt: Prisoner of His Past*. Radnor, Pa.: Chilton Book Co., 1975.

Prittie, Terence. *Willy Brandt: Portrait of a Statesman*. New York: Schocken Books, 1974.

MARK BARTHOLOMEW

GRO HARLEM BRUNDTLAND (1939–) is Norwegian Labor Party leader, three-time prime minister of Norway, and former minister of the environment who is probably best-known for her role as chair of the influential World Commission on Environment and Development (WCED). The Commission's report, *Our Common Future*, has put the issue of sustainable development on the international agenda.

Gro Harlem Brundtland has been one of the most influential figures on the Norwegian political scene in the last decade. She is widely perceived as the only person capable of governing a society known for its fragmentation and inconclusive electoral results. While she has proven herself to be an adept politician, she has also been quite controversial. On the home front, record unemployment has plagued her government. Internationally, a recent decision permitting the hunting of the minke whale has tarnished her reputation as a world environmental advocate. Further, she currently faces one of her biggest political challenges, steering Norway into the European Community fold.

Brundtland was born on April 20, 1939, in Oslo. Because her parents, Gudmund and Inga Harlem, were active in the Norwegian Resistance during World War II, she was forced twice as a child to flee Norway to Sweden. Her father later served Labor governments as minister of defense and of social affairs. Her mother was a secretary of the Labor Party's secretariat.

Gro met and married her husband, Arne Olav Brundtland, while a medical student at the University of Oslo, from which she graduated in 1963. She also holds a master's degree from Harvard's School of Public Health which she earned in 1965 while Arne was a visiting scholar at Harvard's Center for International Affairs.

Although her involvement in the Labor Party began when she entered the party's youth movement at the age of seven, her rise within it was nonetheless meteoric. She worked as a consultant in the Ministry of Health and Social Affairs and as the associate director of school health services in Oslo until 1974, when she was appointed minister of the environment by then–Prime Minister Trygve Bratteli. In 1975, she became deputy chairman of the Labor Party and entered the Storting (parliament) in 1977. In the Storting she served on the Finance Committee, chaired the Foreign Affairs Committee and, in 1979, became the deputy leader of Labor's parliamentary group.

She had just four years of parliamentary experience when she became Norwegian prime minister in February 1981. At the age of forty-one, she was not only the country's first female premier, but also the youngest person to ever serve as Norway's head of government. Her election as Labor leader, replacing Odvar Nordli, was almost unanimous, and she was widely perceived as the only one who could unite the party in order to successfully contend the upcoming general elections. When she assumed the leadership, the party's popularity was plummeting. Nordli's lackluster leadership, inflation, high tax levels and a split in the party over Norway's future in NATO were thought to be the root causes.

Despite the loss of eleven seats in the Storting, Brundtland's 1981 campaign enhanced her stature as a politician. Opinion polls before she took over the party's leadership showed Labor running neck and neck with the opposition

Conservative Party. On election day, the party had moved ahead to garner 42.3 percent of the vote as opposed to the Conservatives' 31.6 percent share. Following these elections, her government, which had commanded a parliamentary majority only with the support of members of the Socialist Left, was forced to resign. A minority Conservative government took office on October 14, 1981.

Brundtland returned to the premiership again in May 1986, when Kåre Willoch's government, a three-party center-right coalition, collapsed after his economic program failed by one vote to win parliamentary support. Many believed Norway at that time to be ungovernable. The political left held 77 of parliament's 157 seats. And, although the bourgeois parties had a one-seat majority, considerable differences existed among them. Norway's 1814 constitution prohibits dissolving parliament and calling elections more frequently than every four years. Further, Norway's oil-dependent economy was reeling in the wake of the 1986 collapse in oil prices.

Against this backdrop, some argued that it was inadvisable for Labor to attempt to form a government. When Brundtland accepted King Olav V's invitation to form a minority cabinet, pundits predicted a quick return of the center-right coalition.

Brundtland proved herself worthy of the challenge, however. She adroitly exploited differences among the opposition parties to maintain her position. Further, her austerity package put the country back on the road to economic recovery. Economists praised her efforts, while she was able to win the grudging respect of Norwegian business. But her economic measures were not without their critics.

Her first move was controversial. Bruntland decided to voluntarily comply with the Organization of Petroleum Exporting Countries' (OPEC) quotas, reducing Norwegian oil output in order to help stabilize world oil prices. This decision drew criticism from members of the opposition, who accused her of compromising Norway's independent oil policy.

Brundtland's government narrowly survived a no-confidence vote in June 1987, when the Conservative Party attempted to bring down the government by opposing Labor's limits on income transfers within the agricultural sector. In the event, the maverick Progress Party, with a mere two seats in the Storting, sustained the government, and the Conservatives appeared to have made a grab for power for power's sake. Brundtland's political stock again rose.

In 1988, the Brundtland government passed a stiff incomes policy with penal sanctions, capping the growth rate of wages at 4 percent. Brundtland also devalued the currency and tightened consumer credit. Although these moves succeeded in holding down inflation and bringing current accounts back into balance by 1989, unemployment rose to nearly 4 percent, the highest rate in Norway since the 1930s depression. While this rate of joblessness compared favorably to the European average at the time, it was viewed in Norway as intolerable by a population accustomed to nearly full employment. Moreover, for Labor, full employment had always been a centerpiece of its economic program. The rise in unemployment under a Labor government constituted a blow to the party's credibility.

Voter discontent with the jobless rate manifested itself in the 1989 general elections, in which the Labor Party had its worst showing since 1930. Labor's presence in the Storting shrank by another eight seats. But the electoral winner of these shifting voter allegiances was not the Conservative Party. Voters moved from the center to both the left—to the Left Socialists—and to the extreme right—to the Progress Party, led by the charismatic Carl Hagen. The opposition coalition, led by Conservative Jan Syse, held one less seat than Labor.

Brundtland resigned the premiership, however, in October 1989, when it became apparent that the center-right coalition would win a vote of no confidence against her with the support of Hagen's Progress Party. Again, however, the opposition did not prove to be a viable alternative to a Brundtland government. Internal inconsistencies within the coalition regarding Norway's membership in the European Community (EC) proved fatal to it just thirteen months later. The Center Party, vehemently anti-EC, refused to compromise on allowing European investors greater access to Norwegian markets. The center-right government fell.

Brundtland returned to the premiership for a third time in November 1990, depending on an issue-by-issue coalition of support. The priorities of her third government include full employment, child care and the environment. She has increased maternity leave, built more kindergartens and established a number of nature reserves.

However, the government's 1992 budget also ran a record deficit in an effort to curb the country's unemployment rate, which has continued to rise to a level above 7.5 percent. The government's increased spending has consumed revenue from North Sea oil, in a departure from past governments, which emphasized the need to save oil revenues for future generations, recognizing that reserves would one day be depleted.

Overall, Bruntland has had her greatest long-term impact on Norwegian politics in three areas: increasing participation of women in government and politics, pursuit of a vigorous environmental policy and cautious approval of Norway's proposed membership in the European Community.

All the Brundtland cabinets have been characterized by a high percentage of women appointments. Her 1981 government included three women besides herself; her 1986 government, seven. The 1986 level of women's representation in government office, 43 percent, was a world record and reflected Labor's implementation of a positive discrimination measure adopted in 1983 requiring that both sexes have at least 40 percent—and neither one more than 60 percent—representation at all levels of government.

Labor's providing political opportunities for women has also meant that opposition parties have been under increasing pressure to elect and appoint more women. This bold move has perhaps forever changed the Norwegian political landscape. Further, the success of women in gaining access to political channels in Norway has encouraged women in the rest of Europe and in other parts of the world by demonstrating that it is possible for women to achieve political office.

Perhaps because of a focus on personal attributes such as gender in the selection of ministers, or perhaps because of her own gender, Gro Harlem Brundtland has contributed to an increased personalization of Norwegian politics. A growing emphasis on the individual candidates themselves was first evident in the 1981 debates between Brundtland and Willoch, referred to as the ''Gro-Kåre'' debates. The contrast between the candidates' styles as well as their policies was at issue. In addition, the Norwegian media have long been preoccupied with Brundtland's personal life. Political satirists have particularly relished the fact that Arne Olav Brundtland, an international affairs expert, is an active member of the Conservative Party.

It is as a champion of green politics that Brundtland is most known internationally. After having served on both the Brandt Commission, formed in 1977, and the Palme Commission, launched in 1980, Brundtland was asked by United Nations Secretary General Javier Pérez de Cuéllar to lead the World Commission on Environment and Development (WCED), commonly known as the Brundtland Commission. The charge of the commission, as outlined in its inaugural meeting in 1984, was to examine and formulate new methods of development and environmental cooperation while at the same time raising the global community's level of understanding and commitment to action.

The Brundtland Commission's report, *Our Common Future,* was never adopted by the United Nations General Assembly. Nonetheless, it has become extremely influential. To the international debate on the environment, the report has added the concept of ''sustainable development''—that is, progress which meets the needs of the present generation while not compromising future ones. The commission has called for a redefinition of the concept of security to include environmental security and has provided stark evidence of a world on the brink of ecological disaster. It has argued that there are vital links between poverty, demographics and environmental degradation. In particular, Brundtland has encouraged cost sharing of development among industrialized nations. She has urged industrialized nations to contribute 0.7 percent of GNP to developing countries. Norway has given at least at this level for more than a decade, currently donating 1.1 percent of its GNP to such countries.

One of the most distinct results of the commission's work was the convening of the United Nations Conference on Environment and Development, the Earth Summit in Rio in June 1992. Brundtland was one of the principal architects of this meeting. Results of the Earth Summit included a new Commission on Sustainable Development, part of the UN Economic and Social Council, a treaty on global warming, a convention on biodiversity, a statement on forest principles and Agenda 21, detailing global goals and strategies.

Brundtland's work with her commission has received a great deal of recognition and praise. She has been awarded a number of prizes, including the Delphi Prize for Man and the Environment (1992), the Indira Gandhi Award for Peace,

Disarmament, and Development (1988), the Third World Foundation Prize (1989), the United Earth's Environmental Award (1991) and the International Environmental Bureau's Prize (1988). In addition, Brundtland has been inducted into the 1991 Hall of Fame of the International Women's Forum.

Well respected internationally, she was seriously considered for United Nations general secretary upon the retirement of Javier Pérez de Cuéllar in 1991, a position which eventually went to the Egyptian diplomat, Bhoutros Bhoutros-Ghali. She also participates in the International Negotiation Network, founded by former U.S. president Jimmy Carter to attempt to mediate intranational conflicts, an area outside the purview of the United Nations.

Ironically, because of Brundtland's leadership of the WCED, her domestic environmental policy has come under extremely close scrutiny both from the international community and the country's own extensive network of environmental groups.

On the one hand, Brundtland's government has implemented the toughest standards in the world on carbon dioxide emissions, and Norwegians are heavily taxed at the gas pump to discourage consumption of fossil fuels. Moreover, the government has announced plans to cut the emission of CO_2 from oil platforms in the North Sea by 40 percent in an effort to meet its pledge to stabilize Norway's contribution of greenhouse gases to the atmosphere at 1989 levels by the year 2000. But whether or not the government will remain committed to these goals or abandon them in favor of establishing some gas-based industries (Norway is currently exclusively hydropowered) is debatable. The installation of a gas-line to Norway and the creation of gas-powered industry would generate substantially greater amounts of carbon dioxide. But they would also generate many more jobs, making gas-driven industry attractive to a Brundtland government eager to curb unemployment.

Perhaps no action of the Brundtland government has drawn as much criticism from environmentalists as its 1992 decision to resume whaling. Norway halted whaling after the 1987 season in order to comply with an international ban on it. International environmental activists, including members of Greenpeace, have not understood the action, given Brundtland's reputation for promoting responsible use of environmental resources. But the Norwegian government has insisted that it has a legal right to harvest minke whales, given that it had filed an objection to the moratorium and to the minke's protected status.

In its defense, the Norwegian government has argued that there are scientific reasons for the resumption of whaling, providing evidence that stocks of the minke whale are substantial enough to permit some harvesting. The government has actively lobbied the International Whaling Commission (IWC) to accept its estimates of the minke population, claiming that previous IWC estimates were unrealistically low. In a victory for the government, the IWC accepted the Norwegian estimates. But Norway has not waited for the IWC to establish a quota for acceptable levels of minke harvesting. Instead, in 1992 the government allowed the harvesting of minke to begin for scientific purposes and announced that it would not wait for the IWC quota before allowing whaling to resume for commercial purposes in 1993. The government's decision has been criticized as much for its diplomatic insensitivity as for its content.

Environmentalists have argued that the government's handling of the issue has underestimated the depth of sentiment in much of the industrialized world for the whale. But Brundtland has always dismissed such sentimentality, arguing that no animal should be elevated to the level of a human, exempt from hunting. Her government insists that whaling is an important part of the Norwegian heritage, its importance as much cultural as commercial. Critics respond, however, that there is nothing traditional—or humane—about the way whaling is conducted, launching grenade-tipped harpoons at the mammals from high-powered fishing boats.

Some have suggested that the government's decision to resume whaling is connected to the eventuality of Norway's entering the European Community. The fishing industry is divided on the question of whether or not Norway should join Finland, Sweden and Austria in applying for Community membership, being well aware that Community membership implies fishing quotas. Brundtland, who has endorsed the idea of EC membership for Norway, has been accused of pandering to these interests in order to win their support. The government adamantly denies this accusation, however.

As the country reevaluates the question of whether or not Norway should seek membership in the EC, Brundtland's political abilities will be challenged. The 1972 Norwegian referendum on entrance into the European Community was acrimonious. Families, friends and political parties—including Labor—were polarized. Brundtland has been cautious about initiating a discussion of the issue within her party and did not explicitly endorse the idea of membership until early 1992, when it became apparent that the new European Economic Area was not going to be a viable alternative.

Now that Finland, Sweden and Austria have applied for EC membership, many argue that it will be increasingly difficult for Norway to stay out. Support for membership, however, has declined in the wake of Denmark's initial rejection of the Maastricht Treaty on European monetary and political union. Resistance within the country has been mobilized around a slogan of the People's Movement, "Norway for the Norwegians." Moreover, results from the 1991 local elections, in which gains were posted by parties firmly opposed to EC membership, have been widely interpreted as suggesting opposition to the government's support for Community membership. In these elections, the Labor Party's showing was its worst in the entire postwar period. Many predict a continued decline in electoral support for Labor as a result of endorsing EC membership. Indeed, voters rejected the EC once again in 1994.

Gro Harlem Brundtland has led the Norwegian Labor Party at a time in which the welfare state has been under attack not only in Norway, but throughout the industrialized world. Although she has never successfully contended any of the general elections that have occurred during her tenure (1981, 1985, 1989), it is to her credit that the party's electoral strength has not suffered more. She has also managed the Norwegian government during a time of increasing factionalism. Although Brundtland has not endeared herself to the Norwegian public, she is widely respected. Many question whether or not there is a viable alternative to her. Nonetheless, her political mettle will be put to the ultimate test as she attempts to finesse the question of EC membership, the one issue which has divided Norwegians like no other.

BIBLIOGRAPHY

Work by Brundtland:

Our Common Future. New York: Oxford University Press, 1987.

Other Works:

Bjørklund, Tor. ''The 1987 Norwegian Local Elections: A Protest Election with a Swing to the Right, '' *Scandinavian Political Studies* 11(3): 211–34 (1988).

Rokkan, Stein. ''Geography, Religion, and Social Class: Crosscutting Cleavages in Norwegian Politics,'' in Seymour M. Lipset and Stein Rokkan (eds.), *Party Systems and Voter Alignments: Cross-National Perspectives.* New York: The Free Press, 1967.

Skjeie, Hege. ''From Movements to Governments: Two Decades of Norwegian Feminist Influences,'' *New Left Review* 187 (1991).

Strøm, Kåre and Jørn Y. Leipart, ''Ideology, Strategy and Party Competition in Postwar Norway,'' *European Journal of Political Research* 17(3): 263–88 (1990).

Valen, Henry. ''The Storting Election of 1989: Polarization and Protest,'' *Scandinavian Political Studies* 13(3): 277–90 (1990).

REBECCA DAVIS

C

SANTIAGO CARRILLO (1913–) has been one of the most outspoken and controversial communist leaders in postwar Western Europe. He stepped down from his position as secretary general of the Spanish Communist Party (PCE) in 1982. For more than twenty years he had struggled to change the ideology of the PCE and thus make it a major political force within Spain and Western Europe in general. His criticism of the Soviet Union and encouragement of interclass mobilization stimulated widespread debate among postwar Marxists about the proper relationship between the communist movement and liberal democracy. His conciliatory politics toward bourgeois parties facilitated the democratic transition in post-Franco Spain. His moderation, however, also troubled many communists who believed the PCE was losing its revolutionary spirit.

Carrillo was born in 1915 in the mining region of Asturias in northern Spain. His father was a labor organizer and a member of the Spanish Socialist Party's executive committee who was elected to the Spanish parliament in 1936. At the age of thirteen, Santiago had joined a Socialist youth organization, and as a teenager, he participated in the famous Asturian workers' uprising, for which he was arrested. After he was released in 1936, he visited the Soviet Union and became convinced that the international communist movement offered the best chance to improve the condition of Spain's working classes. He and several other young labor organizers helped Spain's Socialist and Communist youth organizations merge into a single association with more than 200,000 members. He became secretary general of this new organization. In the meantime, he joined the Spanish Communist Party, despite his father's opposition.

In 1936, several units of the Spanish army, under the leadership of General Francisco Franco, rebelled against the democratically elected Socialist government of Spain. The subsequent Civil War lasted three years. Instructed by the Comintern to pursue a popular front strategy, the Spanish Communist Party cooperated with middle-class parties and avoided revolutionary projects. In contrast, many anarchists and left-wing socialists viewed the military uprising as an opportunity to transform property relations in Spain and therefore supported invasions of estates and experiments in collectivized production.

During the war, Carrillo served on the defense committee for Madrid. Some Spanish conservatives maintain that he engineered the systematic execution (often without trial) of more than a thousand captured military officers and suspected insurgents. Carrillo has repeatedly denied these charges. In addition, numerous Spanish radicals (especially anarchists and Trotskyists) have denounced Carrillo for sabotaging revolutionary projects by workers and peasants and pandering both to bourgeois parties in Spain and to Western capitalist nations. Carrillo has responded by arguing that only a multiclass alliance could have defeated Franco's rebel forces, and that the ad hoc revolutionary projects by peasants and workers did not effectively end exploitation in Spain. Instead, the revolutionary experiments dissuaded liberal democracies from aiding the Spanish Republic and thus sealed the government's fate.

After Franco's troops defeated the government's forces, Carrillo went into exile. During the next two decades, he traveled to numerous countries and held a number of offices within the international communist movement. By shrewdly siding with alternate factions within the PCE, Carrillo steadily rose within the party, despite older militants' distrust of the Young Turk. To many observers' surprise, he became secretary general in 1960.

Carrillo long had believed that in order to become a major force in Spanish politics, the PCE had to broaden its working-class base and revise its insurrectionary strategy. Once he became secretary general, Carrillo wrote numerous tracts and speeches explaining and defending his new strategies for Spanish communism, gradually articulating a relatively coherent political theory that became known throughout Europe as Eurocommunism.

Carrillo's reasoning rested on the assumption that postwar European capitalism had developed in directions that Marx and Lenin could not foresee. Today, Carrillo argued, the survival of modern capitalism requires that national governments constantly help their nation's largest and most technologically advanced firms by selectively limiting foreign competition, routinizing labor conflict, educating workers to an adequate level of technological sophistication and diverting scarce material resources away from small, inefficient businesses toward large monopolistic firms.

According to Carrillo, state-supported capitalism therefore only benefits the monopoly sector of the capitalist class. Smaller capitalists, family farmers and what Carrillo has called "forces of culture" (scientists, technicians, lawyers, journalists and other professionals) are heavily taxed; they lack access to relatively inexpensive imported goods; and they have their businesses and employment opportunities constantly threatened by ever-expanding monopolies. Because they suffer in multiple ways, citizens from almost every class, save the *haute bourgeoisie*, instinctively support greater government control of private monopolies and greater socialization of the means of production. A communist party in a liberal democracy can thus win support from a vast majority of voters by appealing overtly to their dissatisfaction with monopoly-run capitalism. The party can then use parliament to pass socialist legislation and rely on its electoral majority to legitimize change. The overthrow of capitalism in Western Europe therefore no longer requires armed struggle. There can be, in Carrillo's opinion, a nonviolent and liberal-democratic road to communism.

Communists in Spain, however, faced an additional task, for Franco's dictatorship had suspended almost all freedoms of association, speech and press, and thus made the electoral road to communism seemingly impossible. Carrillo argued that these roadblocks could be overcome through a strategy of large-scale mass mobilizations. After all, the regime ruthlessly repressed workers and pursued foolish economic policies, such as autarky, that excluded Spain from the world economy and perpetuated poverty. A majority of Spaniards, Carrillo believed, were so troubled by the economic and political status quo that they would participate in a nationwide general strike organized by the PCE. A gigantic mobilization would thereby scare the few economically motivated supporters of Franco's regime into deserting it. The dictatorship would then quickly collapse, to be replaced by a constituent assembly and thereafter a liberal democracy. The PCE then could use the multiclass electoral strategy to begin a peaceful transition to socialism and, ultimately, communism.

Carrillo further reasoned that in order to attract allies for both an immediate general strike within Spain and for subsequent elections, the PCE must assuage the fears of middle-class activists and distance itself from the Soviet Union. Criteria for party membership, therefore, should be relaxed so that nonworkers could join. In addition, members of the PCE should more strongly criticize the continuing legacy of Stalinism within the Soviet Union and denounce the Soviet Union's repeated repression of democratic experiments throughout Eastern Europe.

Numerous observers have questioned the sincerity of Carrillo's commitment to democratic norms, partly because of his sometimes heavy-handed treatment of challengers within the PCE. A commonly cited example of Carrillo's autocratic leadership is his struggles with the writer Jorge Semprún and the social theorist Fernando Claudín. Semprún and Claudín, who were members of the PCE's executive committee, questioned Carrillo's thesis that the Spanish economy was faltering under Franco's regime. As they saw it, the Spanish economy during the 1960s had been integrated into the world capitalist economy and was expanding rapidly. Furthermore, standards of living were rising for most citizens, including urban workers and professionals. Consequently, very few Spaniards were so unhappy with the workings of the Francoist system that they would participate in a general strike sponsored by the PCE. Repeated calls for strikes, on the other hand, could enrage the regime and lead to repression of labor organizers who were working underground.

The Communists' repeatedly unsuccessful attempts to ignite general strikes during the late 1950s and early 1960s seemed to corroborate Semprún and Claudín's analysis. Carrillo nonetheless considered their line of reasoning excessively bleak and feared that a postponement of a national general strike into the far future would demoralize Communist militants working underground. Semprún and Claudín, however, continued to request that the executive committee reconsider Carrillo's general-strike strategy. Carrillo responded by arranging their expulsion from the party and allowing them almost no opportunity to respond to charges of conspiring to undermine party unity and morale.

Shortly after Semprún and Claudín were expelled, Carrillo visited communist leaders in Eastern Europe who had resisted Moscow's directives. He also emphatically denounced the Siniavsky and Daniel trial of 1966, as well as the 1968 invasion of Czechoslovakia. Many members of the PCE, however, still believed that the Soviet Union was an evolving socialist society that deserved respect, aid and emulation. Pro-Soviet factions within the PCE began to oppose Carrillo's increasingly hostile pronouncements toward the Soviet Union. Letters questioning Carrillo's revolutionary and ideological credentials began to circulate. Once again, Carrillo dealt with intraparty dissent through a mixture of demotions and expulsions, while promoting younger militants who agreed with his Eurocommunist ideas.

Despite the often bitter factional struggles among the party's leaders, the PCE had gained considerable stature among anti-Franco forces throughout the late 1960s and early 1970s. Carrillo directed Spanish Communists to infiltrate all associations chartered by the state, such as state-sponsored neighborhood and parent associations and factory grievance committees. Within these state-regulated institutions, party members worked alongside nonparty reformers, such as Catholic labor activists, for the expansion of citizens' day-to-day rights and improvements in their standards of living. Carrillo also organized unusually broad-based recruitment drives that brought numerous intellectuals, students and Catholic social activists into the party. Membership no longer required extensive participation in plant-level cells. Local organizations now included neighborhood, housewife and professional units, all of which went beyond the party's traditional working-class base. As a result of the PCE's ubiquitous grassroots activism and relatively nonsectarian methods of recruitment, when Franco died in 1975 the PCE arguably had become the most active and broadly based antiregime organization within Spain.

Carrillo continued to advocate a nationwide general strike as the best method for achieving democracy, even after Franco's death. He noted that numerous large-scale demonstrations, solidarity strikes and citywide riots occurred in Spain during the first half of 1976. But these protests were aimed primarily at redressing specific, short-term grievances, such as incidents of police brutality. A sustained, nationwide general strike against the authoritarian regime per se never transpired.

The Spanish political system was changing rapidly, however. Shortly after Franco's death, King Juan Carlos de Borbón and Premier Adolfo Suárez sought support from various opposition groups for a peaceful transition to democracy. The king and prime minister promised to hold fair elections for parliament but with the understanding that the PCE and other radical left groups could not be legalized. Legalization of the Communists might frighten conservatives and ignite another military coup, or so it was argued. But in the meantime, the government increasingly tolerated the PCE, the police observing PCE-sponsored rallies and meetings, but seldom arresting known Communist leaders.

Fearing that the PCE would be excluded from the first parliamentary elections held in Spain since the Civil War, Carrillo illegally entered Spain in 1977 and held a dramatic press conference in Madrid. Pressured by conservative forces, the government arrested Carrillo, an action that led to numerous demonstrations by pro-Carrillo and anti-Carrillo groups. (Many of the latter wanted him tried for his alleged complicity in mass executions during the civil war.) The government offered to drop charges against Carrillo, if he would leave the country; but Carrillo refused. After a few weeks, he was granted provisional liberty. In the meantime, he secretly negotiated the legalization of the PCE with Suárez and assured government officials that, if legalized, the PCE would not encourage interclass strife.

Subsequently, Carrillo acted in strikingly nonrevolutionary ways. He refrained from attacking centrist parties during the 1977 election campaigns and later pledged loyalty to the government's austerity program, known as the Moncloa pact, which included limitations on wage increases. In 1978 he arranged for references to ''dictatorship of the proletariat'' and ''Leninism'' to be dropped from the party's program. He also invited leaders of the French and Italian communist parties to meet in Madrid and to sign a Eurocommunist declaration of independence from the Soviet Union.

Several commentators argue that given the risks inherent in establishing a new democratic regime in Spain, Carrillo's political behavior was appropriately cautious and ultimately contributed to the consolidation of Spain's new democratic order. Carrillo's behavior, however, also generated new divisions and exacerbated older divisions within the PCE. Many younger militants wanted more sweeping social and political reforms than Suárez was willing to concede and believed that Carrillo's moderation was excessive and counterproductive.

Similarly, many trade union activists, who had supported Carrillo in his earlier battles with pro-Soviet factions, strongly disapproved of his endorsement of the Moncloa pact. They argued that given Spain's rising unemployment and high inflation rate, the party should be supporting working-class mobilizations, not helping the government restrict wages. Finally, numerous PCE militants remained troubled by Carrillo's continuing criticisms of the Soviet Union and by his constant courting of unaffiliated Catholic voters and social activists, middle-class ''forces of culture'' and other nonproletarian constituencies.

The PCE's poor showing in early parliamentary elections exacerbated intra-party disgruntlement. Most Communist candidates, following Carrillo's instructions, avoided combative rhetoric when discussing the economic and social policies of the incumbent government. They also eschewed pronouncements about a possible transition to socialism and instead discussed the need to restore the confidence of small and medium-sized entrepreneurs. Partly because of the party's bland campaigning and futile courting of largely anticommunist middle-class voters, the vote shares going to the PCE were disappointingly small: 9.2 percent in 1977 and 10 percent in 1979. There were, of course, regions within Spain where the PCE did much better. But to Carrillo's chagrin, these were often places, such as Catalonia, where regional sections of the PCE did not fully support Carrillo's Eurocommunist declarations, instead voicing more explicitly revolutionary and pro-Soviet promises. In the meantime, the Communists' chief rivals on the Left, the Spanish Socialist Party, were receiving over a quarter of all ballots cast.

Discouraged by the party's failure to become a significant parliamentary power, tens of thousands of activists abandoned the PCE between 1977 and 1980. In addition, by 1980 several younger leaders began to advocate more democratic procedures within the party, so that the party's policies could be more openly discussed and, when necessary, reconsidered. They also asked for greater regional autonomy within the party, so that electorally favorable alliances with local forces and modifications in the party platform could be attempted. In 1981 Carrillo dealt with the rising tide of discontent in his customary way: He expelled several so-called renovators, most of whom then formed or joined rival left-wing organizations.

After these purges, the electoral fortunes of the PCE plummeted further. The party received only 3.9 percent of the vote in the 1982 parliamentary elections, and Carrillo was obliged to step down as secretary general. The post-Carrillo PCE leadership advocated a new strategy for the party, which included "constructive" opposition to the government's austerity policies, greater PCE involvement in Spain's new ecological, feminist and antinuclear movements and closer ties with the now hegemonic Socialist Party. Carrillo opposed all these changes and began to use his personal influence to prevent local implementation of the leadership's directives. In 1985, after being repeatedly warned about obstructionist behavior, Carrillo was expelled from the party.

Since his separation from the PCE, Carrillo has been unable to join any other major left-wing party. For a while, he tried to join the Spanish Socialist Party. "A good Socialist is no different from a good Communist," he once said. But several leaders within the Socialist Party, such as Jorge Semprún, had earlier been members of the PCE, feared Carrillo's highly autocratic leadership style, and blocked his admission.

Carrillo's efforts to create a strong communist party in Spain clearly failed. Nonetheless, he had a lasting impact on European politics. His Eurocommunist ideas fed debates within the international communist movement over the strategic value of liberal democracy and over the appropriate limits of party loyalty to the Soviet Union. Within Spain, Carrillo contributed to an atmosphere of ideological tolerance that made Spain's liberal-democratic transition possible. Finally, his repeated calls for moderation during the late 1970s, his cooperation with Suárez's attempts to limit wages and his repeated repression of intraparty debate jointly contributed to a fatal hemorrhaging within what at one time was the most prestigious anti-Franco organization in Spain. And by contributing to the PCE's electoral demise, Carrillo inadvertently enabled Spain's first post-Franco Socialist government to pursue a program of free trade and privatization without facing a unified challenge from the left.

BIBLIOGRAPHY

Work by Carrillo:

Eurocommunism and the State. Westport, Conn.: Lawrence Hill & Co., 1978.

Other Works:

Mujal-León, Eusebio. *Communism and Political Change in Spain*. Bloomington: Indiana University Press, 1983.

———. ''Decline and Fall of Spanish Communism,'' *Problems of Communism* 32:1–27 (March–April 1986).

Preston, Paul. ''The Dilemma of Credibility: The Spanish Communist Party, the Franco Regime and After,'' *Government and Opposition* 11:65–83 (Winter 1976).

———. ''The PCE in the Struggle for Democracy in Spain,'' in Howard Machin (ed), *National Communism in Western Europe: A Third Way for Socialism?* London: Methuen, 1983.

Semprún, Jorge. *The Autobiography of Federico Sánchez and the Communist Underground in Spain*. New York: Karz, 1977.

CYRUS ERNESTO ZIRAKZADEH

JACQUES CHIRAC (1932–) has been a key player in the development of stable democratic institutions in France under the Fifth Republic. As the leader of the Gaullist party since 1974, Chirac transformed the party from a loose political movement into a tightly organized party and, in the 1970s and 1980s, led efforts to unify the French right against the reconsolidation of the left. Chirac has consequently been a driving force in the emergence of a stable political party system in the 1980s. As prime minister from 1974 to 1976 and from 1986 to 1988, Chirac also helped to better delineate the division of powers between the president and the prime minister left ambiguous by the 1958 constitution.

His major elected mandates as mayor of Paris (1976–) and deputy of the Corrèze department (1967–) have further enhanced his prominence in French politics. However, Chirac has failed to translate his local power base into national electoral success in his two bids for the presidency in 1981 and 1988. These failures reflect the central paradox of Jacques Chirac's political career: The skills and expertise which have made him a renowned figure in French party politics have prevented him from becoming a leading statesman.

Jacques Chirac was born in Paris in 1932. He was the only child of François and Marie-Louise Chirac, who were both from the rural department of the Corrèze in the south of France, a bastion of Third Republic radicalism. The Radical Party dominated politics in France from the late 19th century until World War II because it represented prodemocratic, anticlerical beliefs while at the same time catering to *la France profonde,* or the local and rural France mostly populated by small shopkeepers, peasants, independent farmers and winegrowers. Although Chirac's father had rejected his past, Jacques Chirac was deeply influenced by his rural and radical origins and never lost his contacts with the Corrèze. He learned to speak the local dialect, or *patois,* in order to better relate to local interests, and in 1969 he bought a chateau in the Corrèze for his family. Not only did he develop a clientelistic network through his local offices, but his pragmatic, take-charge approach to decision making and coalition building can be directly attributed to his rural background.

Chirac spent most of his youth in Paris, although he did seek refuge from the German occupation with his family in the Corrèze. The war years were the only time in Chirac's life when he faced economic hardship and social dislocation. Throughout his childhood Chirac was spoiled by a devout mother. In addition to regular schooling, his parents hired a personal tutor for the young Chirac. It was during this period that Chirac developed his intellectual side, which included a passion for reading and writing poetry.

Chirac's education followed the typical trajectory of a French-born male from an aspiring upper-middle-class family of that period: mathematics in high school, college at the Institute of Political Studies in Paris (known as Sciences Po) in order to prepare for the entrance exam for the prestigious National School of Administration (Ecole Nationale d'Administration, or ENA), a generalist training at ENA preparing him to serve in the upper echelons of the French government bureaucracy. His skills, training and dynamism launched him into a meteoric political career which began with a position on the prime minister's personal staff at the unusually young age of thirty.

Before devoting his life to government service, however, Chirac went through a period of rebellion and uncertainty in his late teens and early twenties. At the same time that he was being trained to be a member of the French political elite, Chirac was developing another side of his multifaceted and often contradictory personality, namely his love of adventure. At eighteen, Chirac ran away from home to work on an iron ship off the northern coast of France. At twenty-one, he worked as a dishwasher in Cambridge, Massachusetts, in order to pay for a trip across the United States.

The young Chirac's adventurous nature also extended into his politics. Unable to accept his father's conservative values and intrigued by the social radicalism of his grandfathers, Chirac was attracted to the left during his early years primarily because he believed that government should have a role in assuring certain levels of social equality. In 1949, Chirac sold political tracts on the streets of Paris for a week for the French Communist Party (PCF). In 1951, he was invited by Michel Rocard (Socialist prime minister from 1988 to 1991) to join the Socialist student group at Sciences Po, but he turned Rocard down. The young Chirac also joined the Gaullist movement, Rally of the French People (RPF), for a year in 1947. His membership in the RPF was a youthful whim, for he did not become a self-proclaimed Gaullist until the 1960s.

In general, the young Chirac was not interested in becoming involved with political parties because of what he regarded as the irresponsible behavior of them under the Fourth Republic (1944–1958). It was his aversion to Fourth Republic politicking and his belief in an interventionist state that eventually led Chirac to Gaullism. However, Chirac's own political convictions were never locked into a specific ideological framework. Throughout his career he would oscillate between a *dirigiste*, prostatist approach and a neo-liberal, antistatist approach to public policy. Chirac's youthful political meandering, therefore, foreshadowed the manner in which the older Chirac would embrace ideas more for their political expediency than for their ideological purity.

Before finishing his education, Chirac discovered his passion for the military while serving his mandatory military service as a second lieutenant in the Algerian war. In a television interview in 1987, Chirac proudly admitted that he was a *fana-militaire*, or great fan of the military. While this wartime experience contributed to Chirac's strong sense of loyalty to Fifth Republic political institutions, to his political mentors and to the Gaullist party, his love for the military also earned him the nickname of "Chirac the Fascist" from his political opponents. Nonetheless, it was this unique combination of intellectual, political and personal qualities that brought the young Chirac to the attention of Georges Pompidou (heir apparent to General de Gaulle) and other key figures in the Gaullist movement as he assumed his first government post.

From 1962 until President Pompidou's death in 1974, Chirac was groomed to become a major political leader by Pompidou and his entourage. In 1967, at the age of thirty-five, Chirac was given his first ministerial post in Pompidou's government. As deputy minister of social affairs, Chirac demonstrated his skills in mediation along with his loyalty to Pompidou by playing a key role in the successful negotiations between management and labor, known as the Grenelle Agreements, that followed the general strikes of May 1968. Chirac was also put in charge of campaign finances for Pompidou's successful bid for the presidency in 1969 following President de Gaulle's resignation the same year.

The string of prestigious ministerial portfolios that Chirac was given during the Pompidou presidency was clear evidence that the Gaullist leadership had chosen him to be a key figure in the future of France and the Gaullist party. As deputy finance minister, Chirac showed his talent in fiscal reform. As agriculture minister, Chirac applied his clientelist approach to consensus building and won the support of the powerful farming unions. During this apprenticeship period, Chirac used his office as minister of the interior (in charge of the national police) to consolidate his power within the Gaullist party and, especially, to demonstrate his authority to its old guard (known as "the barons").

The French press nicknamed Chirac the *poulain de Pompidou*, literally "Pompidou's colt," and the power base that he was able to build up under Pompidou's tutelage enabled him to successfully fill the power vacuum left within the party by Pompidou's unexpected death from cancer in 1974. Chirac displayed his profound loyalty to Pompidou when he announced on the evening prior to the president's death that Pompidou was on the road to recovery. While at age forty-one Chirac was considered too young to run for the presidency, he nonetheless took control over the fading Gaullist movement by refusing to endorse the Gaullist baron Jacques Chaban-Delmas for the presidential elections. Instead, he led a dissident group of Gaullists to endorse the center-right presidential candidate, Valéry Giscard d'Estaing.

Chirac's gamble paid off when Chaban-Delmas failed to make it beyond the first ballot in France's two-round presidential election system and when Giscard then beat his Socialist opponent François Mitterrand on the second ballot. The Gaullist barons had no choice but to recognize Chirac as their new party leader. His position within the party was further reinforced when President Giscard d'Estaing nominated him to be prime minister. With the right-wing majority in the National Assembly diminished (in 1973 the right had lost 117 seats) and the majority of right-wing seats still belonging to Gaullists (183 out of 268 seats), Giscard needed the support of the Gaullists to get his ambitious political reform program through parliament.

Chirac accepted the prime ministership on the premise that this would clear the way for him to revitalize the Gaullist movement. Appointing himself secretary general of the remnants of the movement in 1974, he reorganized the party structure by assuming broad executive powers and purging nearly two-thirds of the old Gaullist leadership at all levels of the party. Chirac's goal was to convert the party into a major right-wing political force so as to effectively compete with the rising Socialist Party (PS) and eventually win back the presidency.

However, President Giscard d'Estaing gave his new prime minster little control over the composition or the running of his government. For example, Giscard forced Chirac to include in his cabinet Françoise Giroud, publisher of the weekly newsmagazine *L'Express*, who was a centrist and known Mitterrand sympathizer (she had cast her vote for Mitterrand in the presidential elections). She was made deputy secretary of women's status. With Giscard's entourage in all the top ministerial positions, Chirac was given little latitude to be an effective prime minister. Chirac resigned in August of 1976, publicly stating that Giscard had not allowed him to do his job. He was the first Fifth Republic prime minister to resign publicly rather than be privately dismissed by the president. Chirac's resignation established a precedent for future presidents. Henceforth, a president could not completely usurp the prime minister's duty to run the government on a day-to-day basis.

After his resignation, Chirac devoted his full attention to transforming the Gaullist movement into a full-fledged, politically viable party, and in 1976 he became president of the new Rally for the Republic (RPR), thus creating a new force in French politics, *le chiraquisme*. His success in creating a strong party forced the other parties dispersed across the center-right of the political spectrum to reorganize themselves into a loose coalition called the Union for French Democracy (UDF). These two factors prevented the left from winning a majority of seats in the 1978 legislative elections. From this point on, the RPR would be the dominant political party of the right and would continue to overshadow the less organized centrist groupings. The birth of the *chiraquiste* RPR, therefore, contributed to the development of stable democratic structures in France, which necessarily included strong political parties capable of governing and being in the opposition.

In the 1970s, the new RPR also began to formulate a clearly conservative platform. General de Gaulle had always sought to cut across partisan lines by emphasizing themes of national solidarity, *dirigisme*, and French prominence in world affairs. In contrast, under Chirac's leadership, the RPR put forward a more traditional conservative platform that stressed less government, law and order, and the defense of traditional values in France. Chirac's conversion to these so-called neo-liberal ideas appeared to occur almost overnight. As late as 1978, in his book *La Lueur de l'espérance*, Chirac had outlined the role of the government in guiding France through difficult economic times. By 1980, in opposition to François Mitterrand, Chirac was denouncing the evils of big government as the RPR's candidate for the presidency. Rather than a fundamental shift in Chirac's personal thinking, this ideological reversal was a result of a political calculation that the French would vote for neo-liberal ideas in the same way as voters in the United States and Great Britain had.

Unlike in 1974, Chirac's political gamble in 1981 did not pay off. The French electorate clearly rejected neo-liberalism in favor of the social reform platform of the Socialist leader, François Mitterrand. In the first round of the 1981 presidential election, Chirac received only 17.9 percent of the votes cast, forcing him to endorse his rival Giscard on the second ballot. When Giscard lost the final round and the victorious Mitterrand called new parliamentary elections, the RPR suffered great losses, winning only 24 more seats than the UDF. Since 1968 the number of Gaullist legislative seats had been reduced from 293 to 87 (out of a total of 490 seats).

Unlike Giscard, Chirac did not choose to withdraw from political life after this electoral disaster. Instead, he became the primary leader of the opposition in the National Assembly. He also attempted to unify the right by working with the UDF to win electoral contests throughout the 1980s and to ultimately win the majority back from the Socialists in the National Assembly. Despite Socialist government efforts to prevent the UDF and the RPR from winning and despite the election of thirty-five extreme right-wing National Front (FN) deputies, the UDF and the RPR successfully cooperated to win a majority of seats in the 1986 legislative elections.

The presence of the extremist National Front in the National Assembly and in a number of local councils across France, and its emphasis on the volatile issue of immigration, compelled the RPR to rethink its stance on immigration in particular in order to recapture the votes it had lost to the FN. In this, Chirac was instrumental in reworking the neo-liberal themes of his party to more strongly focus on illegal immigration as well as general issues of law and order.

With a new right-wing majority in parliament (excluding the National Front) and two years before the next scheduled presidential election, President Mitterrand chose what many believed to be his most prudent option: He asked Jacques Chirac to become prime minister. The years from 1986 to 1988, known as "cohabitation," were an historic moment in the life of the Fifth Republic, as the French constitution was not at all clear about the exact division of government responsibilities between the prime minister and the president in the event of a parliamentary majority hostile to the incumbent president.

Mitterrand's decision to name Chirac prime minister allowed the president to pull away from domestic policy and enjoy the heights of power without getting directly involved in the fray of day-to-day controversial issues. For the most part, cohabitation between the two leaders went smoothly: Mitterrand approved all of Chirac's cabinet appointments, and only once was there an open conflict between the two leaders, when Chirac insisted on going to a major summit meeting along with Mitterrand.

The major reason for Mitterrand's apparent acquiescence was that Chirac had to deal with the worst outbreak of social unrest in France since May 1968. Pursuing his neo-liberal agenda, Chirac oversaw the privatization of many major industries nationalized under the Socialists in 1981. The government also proposed legislation that aimed to improve the quality of education at the universities through a series of reforms which included a first-ever tuition charge for all students.

Perceived by the majority of French students as an attack by the right on the sacrosanct guarantee to a higher education, Paris was stormed by thousands and thousands of high school and college students. After several weeks of fierce resistance, the government was finally forced to unconditionally withdraw the proposed university reform. Then immediately following these student demonstrations, public transport workers went on strike throughout France, paralyzing the country during one of its worst winters. While French public opinion recognized Chirac's problems as partially due to bad luck, it nonetheless linked the prime minister, his party and his neo-liberal policies to continuing social unrest during this period of cohabitation.

In the 1988 presidential elections, out of a field of nine candidates and with 19.9 percent of the vote in the first round, Chirac proved to be the incumbent Mitterrand's major challenger. Once again, however, Chirac was unable to convert his past political success into votes for the presidency. His loss to Mitterrand in these elections must be seen as a triple loss for himself, his party and the right. Having secured the presidency for an unprecedented second term, Mitterrand called new parliamentary elections in order to defeat the right-wing legislative majority. Although these 1988 legislative elections produced a slim left-wing majority dependent on center-left deputies, the outcome showed that the RPR and Jacques Chirac were incapable of capturing the support of a majority of French electors in the way that the Gaullist movement had done in the 1960s.

As the 1990s unfold, Jacques Chirac and the RPR continue to face an uncertain future. On the one hand, the RPR still confronts both a nettlesome National Front on its extreme right, while continuing to lose some votes to the more moderate parties of the center-right regrouped around the UDF. On the other hand, in the 1993 legislative elections, the RPR led the right and center-right to a smashing electoral victory over the Socialists. President Mitterrand was once again forced to choose a prime minister from a new legislative majority hostile to him. In the event, he appointed Edouard Balladur, one of Chirac's most trusted confidants, to the post.

Within the RPR, Chirac faced some important rifts over the French referendum to ratify the Maastricht Treaty on European Community monetary and political integration. Two weeks prior to the referendum in September 1992, Chirac made a public call for the French to ratify the treaty. But according to a public opinion poll taken before the referendum, 63 percent of RPR voters planned to vote against ratification. This faction of the party was being energetically mobilized against the treaty by two of the RPR's major figures, Philippe Séguin and Charles Pasqua. Moreover, the breakdown of the political party system in the late 1980s and early 1990s—as manifested by the rise of the National Front, the decline of the Communist Party and a rising abstention rate—suggests that the stability of French political institutions established in the 1970s and 1980s may not necessarily endure.

Clearly, the original hope of Gaullist leaders in the 1960s that Jacques Chirac would be the future leader of the party and of the right in France generally was realized. But the assertion that he would become a leading statesman has yet to be demonstrated. The skills that Chirac has fine-tuned throughout his life and which have made him an accomplished policy maker, coalition builder and party reformer have prevented him from establishing a useful distance from day-to-day politicking (what the French refer to as *la politique politicienne*). His almost symbiotic relationship with the RPR and his pragmatic, hands-on approach to politics appear to continue to turn off the majority of French voters. Nonetheless, Jacques Chirac's political leadership was crucial during the early period of the Fifth Republic when government institutions and political parties were weak. In the final analysis, Jacques Chirac will more likely be remembered for his loyalty to the Fifth Republic and the Gaullist party than for his ability to lead the French nation.

BIBLIOGRAPHY

Work by Chirac:

La Lueur de l'espérance: Réflexion du soir pour le matin. Paris: La Table Ronde, 1978.

Other Works:

Desjardins, Thierry. *Un Inconnu nommé Chirac*. Paris: La Table Ronde, 1983.

Ehrmann, Henry W., and Martin A. Schain. *Politics in France*. New York: HarperCollins, 1992.

Giesbert, Franz-Olivier. *Jacques Chirac*. Paris: Editions du Seuil, 1987.
Tuppen, John. *Chirac's France, 1986–1988*. New York: St. Martin's Press, 1991.

AMY G. MAZUR

ANDRÉ COOLS (1927–1991) played for many years a leading role in Belgian politics and in his native French-speaking region of Wallonia. Throughout an illustrious political career that included service as Belgian minister of state, vice prime minister, minister of the budget and economic affairs and president of the Belgian Socialist Party, Cools came to symbolize the transformation of labor movement politics in the Belgian political system, redefining the struggle of the working class in Belgium. While he was feared and hated by some, and respected by others—leaving no one indifferent—Cools's impact as a socialist leader is unquestioned, as is the fact that his influence in Belgian politics went far beyond just socialism. André Cools was sixty-three years old when brutally assassinated on July 18, 1991, a death whose circumstances are still surrounded by mystery.

Born in Flémalle-Grande, a commune near the city of Liège, on August 1, 1927, Cools became a union activist early on in his political career. His origins in the working class were deeply rooted: His grandfather was a coal miner, his father a steelworker. At a very early age, Cools was introduced to the Belgian socialist world by his father. The young Cools spent much time at the local headquarters of the party and the socialist union. Cools's father was also involved in local politics as a city councilman prior to his deportation from Belgium during World War II. He died in the Mauthausen concentration camp in 1942.

André Cools's background and his strong links to and activism within the Socialist Party defined him and his mission and gave him a sense of belonging to a strong "political" family. He was a man forever tied to these origins and to the town in which he was born and grew up. The pride of being a member of the working class never left Cools.

Some political scientists have described Belgian sociopolitical life as consisting of three subcultures, or "pillars"—Catholic, socialist and liberal. In this view, an individual is born into a pillar, and the major events of one's life are defined by the pillar. Typically, a member of the socialist pillar, like André Cools, would live and die a socialist, belonging to socialist organizations and engaging in socialist activities throughout a lifetime.

Cools's public and private life exemplies this traditional Belgian pillar-based sociopolitical environment. After the liberation, Cools joined the General Federation of Belgian Workers (FGTB). He became actively involved in the local Socialist Party, first through the Socialist youth movement, then in 1947 joining the ranks of the Socialist Party bureaucracy. In 1948, Cools secured the post of secretary of the local commission of public assistance, holding this position until 1964. In 1948, as well, he married Thérèse Josin, with whom he would have two children.

In 1954, Cools entered the regional organization of the Socialist Party and was named acting deputy in the national parliament. It was not until 1958, however, that Cools truly appeared on the Belgian national political scene by being elected deputy to the Chamber of Representatives, the lower house of the Belgian parliament. For the next thirty years, each parliamentary election would guarantee Cools a parliamentary seat in the lower house.

As a young representative, Cools collaborated very closely with another young Socialist leader, Freddy Terwagne, who became deputy at the same time as Cools. Both men would lead many battles in favor of immigrant workers and the working class. In his early years as a politician, Cools also became a passionate admirer and follower of André Renard, a prominent leader of the working-class movement. He regarded Renard as his ideological father. From Renard, Cools learned that the most important battles in politics lay in defending the working class and prioritizing its demands. Cools and Renard both grew up in a world largely defined by the superiority of the owner over the worker. Renard's ideology, enthusiastically shared by his young follower, was based upon the conviction that workers were to be a cornerstone of the Socialist political program and placed at the center of national political debate.

Actively involved in the FGTB, where Renard led the steelworkers' section, André Cools participated in the "big strikes" of 1960–1961. These strikes were organized to protest national legislation designed to curtail working-class demands. When Renard founded the Walloon Popular Movement (MPW), Cools also joined its ranks. On the parliamentary bench, Cools fought with passion and tenacity for the "great causes" of socialism. In 1963, for example, he became known as one of the party "rebels" when he refused to vote along party lines in support of legislation which sought to maintain order by limiting the right to strike. Cools also departed from the party line over legislation establishing the linguistic border between the Flemish- and French-speaking communities in Belgium.

As a young national deputy, André Cools was a spokesman for the FGTB. In conjunction with Renard, Terwagne and other Socialists, he played a dominant role in what was known as the "common action" program. In the executive bureau of the Liège regional party federation, Cools represented both the party and the Walloon Popular Movement (MPW).

After the 1965 electoral defeat of the Belgian Socialist Party (PSB), Cools supported an opposition role for the Socialists and proceeded actively to reform the structures of the PSB. He favored greater autonomy in party structures along linguistic lines, allowing more independence to the Walloon, Brussels and Flemish federations of the PSB. Cools also worked energetically toward the formation of a common workers' front, in part by pursuing closer relationships with the Christian Workers Movement.

André Cools's first opportunity to hold an official post in a coalition cabinet government came in 1968, when he was offered the position of budget minister in the Eyskens-Merlot government, a coalition of Socialists and Social Christians. When vice prime minister Merlot died in a car accident in 1969, Cools assumed that post as well.

The late 1960s and early 1970s were good years for Belgium: The economy grew, the budget was balanced and the prosperous economic situation allowed the government to cut taxes. Despite favorable economic conditions, however, tensions grew between Cools and the leadership of the labor unions. These tensions became even more apparent in 1971, when, as budget minister, Cools declared that new taxes would have to be levied if the government were to meet union demands for higher workers' salaries and benefits. The growing disagreements between Cools and the unions were to last throughout the 1970s and would eventually lead to Cools's resignation as Socialist Party leader in 1981.

While Cools continued to hold the vice premiership, in 1971 he also became minister of economic affairs, succeeding in this post another prominent Socialist leader, Edmond Leburton. While holding the budget and economic affairs portfolios, Cools implemented reforms on price controls and the value added tax. Moreover, a constitutional review was begun in 1970 which subsequently led to the recognition and the granting of cultural autonomy to the three Belgian cultural communities: Flemish-speaking Flanders, French-speaking Wallonia, and the small German-speaking area along Belgium's eastern border. This reform was implemented in 1971 and was to set the stage for much broader and deeper devolution of political authority from the Belgian state toward the regions, eventually culminating in the formal institution of federalism in 1993.

After the November 1971 elections, Cools was once again named vice prime minister and given the budget portfolio. This government was, however, short-lived, as the linguistic status of the Fourons—a community along the linguistic border claimed by both the Flemish and French speakers—caused a government crisis. In the caretaker government that followed, Cools headed the economic affairs ministry.

Learning very quickly from his national political roles, Cools soon became an experienced politician and statesman. Many acknowledged that both as a cabinet member and as a member of parliament, Cools was well-informed, knew his dossiers and came to realize that management and compromise were essential ingredients in national politics. He learned these lessons from seasoned politicians, such as Gaston Eyskens. Although they did not share a common ideology—Eyskens was indeed a prominent Flemish-speaking leader of the CVP (Christelijke Volkspartij, or Christian Democrats, literally Christian People's Party)—Cools admired Eyskens's sense of state and learned from him that Belgian politics was deeply rooted in party strength. In this, Cools began to see the importance of political action based on a powerful party, such as the CVP, and he envisioned similar foundations for the PSB in Wallonia.

During this period in the early 1970s, Cools became ideologically more and more convinced that the Belgian economy should be managed with state intervention. As minister of the economy, Cools actively pursued an interventionist strategy regarding the steel industry in Wallonia. Then, as Belgium entered the period of constitutional reforms aimed at devolving authority to the regions, Cools's mission became one of developing and managing industrial politics which would ensure continued economic development of his own native region, Wallonia.

In 1973, at age forty-six, André Cools left his government posts to run for the presidency of the PSB, a position which he held until 1981. During this period, Cools, a Francophone, shared the party presidency with three Flemish-speaking Socialists: Jos Van Eynde until 1975, Willy Claes until 1977 and Karel Van Miert until 1978. Then in 1978, the Flemish and Francophone wings of the Belgian Socialist Party split into two independent political parties. The French-speaking party remained under Cools's leadership until 1981.

Cools's primary objective as president of the PSB was to "reunite" the party in order to assure the PSB a dominant role in the economic regionalization of Wallonia and thereby fulfill the aspirations of the Liège union movement. Willy Claes, copresident of the PSB and minister of economic affairs in the national government, was an important ally in this endeavor. Both men shared a vision of socialism in which the party was representative of and spokesman for the labor movement.

Cools and Claes led the national government's adoption of major economic legislation to restructure the steel industry in Wallonia, centered in the Liège-Charleroi industrial basin. The reforms were far-reaching, as they guaranteed a prominent role to the state in the steel industry and named Socialist public administrators to industry's management. This legislation also created a national committee for the planning, control and financing of industrial renewal. In tandem, Cools and Claes ensured that the Socialists would exercise a leadership role in industrial politics at the national level for many years to come.

With this major victory in hand, the Socialist Party proceeded to play a key role in the processes of devolving authority to the regions in Belgium. As party president, Cools participated closely in the efforts of the Leburton coalition government to implement regionalization. He became a member of the parliamentary commission on regionalization in 1973. However, after the fall of Leburton's coalition government in 1974, the Socialists, under Cools's leadership, opted out of government participation. Instead, they played a strong opposition role, proposing a host of laws relating mostly to social and economic affairs.

Socialist leaders also remained active on the regionalization issue, actively debated in all governmental and parliamentary arenas. The Cools-Claes leadership team pursued a series of secret meetings with the so-called "community parties." The most important of these were the FDF (the party of French-speaking Brussels), the RW (the Walloon-Rally Party, representing the Walloon region) and the VU (Volksunie, representing the Flemish-speaking populations of Brussels and Flanders). At the time, however, regional status for Flanders, Wallonia and Brussels had not yet been granted. Formal recognition of these regions was to be at the center of the political agenda for some years to come.

After the 1977 elections, Cools and Claes refused to enter into a grand coalition composed of Social Christians, Socialists and Liberals, but negotiated instead the formation of a coalition government which included two of the community parties, the FDF and the VU, and was headed by the Christian Democrat, Leo Tindemans. These negotiations over forming a government led to the signing of the Egmont Pact in May 1977. This agreement was designed to become the cornerstone of the transformation of the Belgian unitary state into a federal one composed of autonomous regions.

Initially, the various party leaders of a very diverse coalition government collaborated closely. Soon, however, typical disagreements emerged all around as to the interpretation of the Egmont Pact. French-speaking parties defended a process wherein three regions—Flanders, Wallonia and Brussels—would become autonomous, while the Flemish-speaking parties insisted on the recognition of only two regions. Even the Flemish Christian Democrats disavowed their own leader (and prime minister), Tindemans, claiming that the agreement constituted an unacceptable concession to the Francophones. The status of Brussels was at the heart of all these disagreements.

The Belgian Socialist Party was in its turn victim of the controversy and polemic surrounding the implementation of the Egmont Pact when the party's Flemish wing began promoting the idea that cultural community should coincide with economic region. The so-called Stuyvenberg conclave, attempting to reconcile diverse party interpretations over the implementation of the Egmont Pact, revealed that the Belgian Socialist Party was as deeply and intractably divided on the regionalization issue as other Belgian parties were.

On October 28, 1978, Cools formalized the split between the Flemish- and French-speaking wings of the party, dividing it into two autonomous units. Karel Van Miert headed the Flemish-speaking Socialists, while André Cools remained the president of the PS (Parti Socialiste—Socialist Party, French-speaking) until 1981.

During this period, Cools reaffirmed his commitment to pursue economic federalism for Wallonia. The late 1970s also saw a definite break between the PS and the labor federation. Because this was a time of economic downturn in Belgium, union members viewed the Socialists, as a part of the governing coalition, as responsible for the implementation of an economic austerity plan. Social and economic tensions in many Wallonian industries grew steadily, especially in the steel industry. During this turbulent period, Cools intervened directly to settle disputes between the Liège and Charleroi federations of the union. The Liège federation saw in these efforts an attempt to make politics the primary concern of the party, relegating union activity to a secondary position. (Recall that the party had been originally conceived to be the representative of and spokesman for the labor movement.) For these actions, Cools was severely criticized.

On the political front, the 1978 electoral results constituted a rude awakening for Cools. In Belgium, a system of proportional representation is coupled with a preferential voting scheme: A voter is able to either vote for a party slate or indicate a preference for a particular individual candidate. As party leader, the endorsement Cools enjoyed from Socialist voters had always been reflected in a high proportion of individual preference votes. In the 1978 election, however, Cools lost many preference votes. It was therefore obvious that the PS leader could no longer count on a level of popular support sufficient to maintain him as the uncontested leader of the party. The many disputes between the unions and Cools certainly contributed to his poor showing.

By 1980, it was apparent that Cools no longer enjoyed the support of a majority within his own party. He resigned as party leader in 1981 and was replaced by Guy Spitaels. Endorsing Cools's approach, Spitaels made it clear that political action through the Socialist Party was and should be independent from union action. The break between the union movement and the PS became permanent.

Cools and Spitaels sought to reaffirm their strategy for the PS by focusing primarily on a campaign to promote ''radical federalism.'' In the early 1980s, the PS played a leading role in transforming the unitary structures of the Belgian state into a federalist system. The transformation was largely accomplished by 1989 and completely formalized in 1993. By then the PS had also recaptured its dominant position in Wallonia and regained a level of electoral support as high as it had once enjoyed in the late 1950s.

André Cools, after resigning from the PS leadership in 1981, remained politically active within the party and within the Walloon region, but he stepped aside from the Belgian national political scene. In 1983, he was given the title of minister of state by the king and continued to serve in a series of important positions in Wallonian politics. In 1981, he was elected to the presidency of the Walloon Regional Council for a four-year term. After the 1988 elections, Cools became the Wallonian minister of public works and used his power to reinforce the influence of the increasingly powerful regional executive over the communes and municipalities, thereby reinforcing the role of the government in all aspects of the regional economy. In his Liège region, André Cools took on the role of a ''super manager,'' attempting to demonstrate government's capacities to manage and to compete with the private sector in exercising a primary role in the regional economy. In so doing, Cools sought, at any cost, new investment for the region of Wallonia, which put him paradoxically in the midst of a world he so often criticized, that of the banking and financial sectors of the economy.

In some ways, Cools returned to his native region, Wallonia, and turned socialism upside down. Socialism for him was no longer a means to an end. It became an end in and of itself. Management of the economy by the state was the primary goal in order to ensure the control of ''service socialism.''

In 1990, Cools retired from his ministerial and parliamentary posts. He remained mayor of the town, Flémalle, in which he was born, and a member of the Liège federation of the Socialist Party until his tragic murder in 1991. Although criticized by many for ''sleeping with the enemy,'' André Cools's political career and his contributions to Belgium and ''his'' Wallonia were uncontestably substantial.

BIBLIOGRAPHY

Francq, Bernard. ''Cools, la passion du politique,'' *La Revue nouvelle,* pp. 86–93 (Brussels: November 1991).

Meynaud, Jean, Jean Ladrière, and François Perin. *La Décision politique en Belgique.* Paris: Librairie Armand Colin, 1965.

MARTINE M. DERIDDER

D

ALCIDE DE GASPERI (1881–1954) was an extremely important figure in the Italian Catholic movement and one of the greatest statesmen that united Italy has known. In the ten years from 1944 to 1954, his influence on the political, economic and social affairs of the country was so great that this period is now known as the ''age'' of De Gasperi.

De Gasperi was already a nationally known politician in the interwar period. He had hardly time to confirm his leadership of the Italian Popular Party (PPI), of which he became secretary in 1924, when the fascist dictatorship banned all antifascist parties in 1926. He returned to the political scene in August 1943, a few weeks after the fall of Mussolini, and immediately became an important figure. De Gasperi became the recognized head of the Christian Democratic Party (DC), building it upon the foundations of the PPI, which he had been active in reorganizing beginning in 1941.

In this role, De Gasperi faced many difficult problems. In the immediate postwar period it fell mainly to the Catholics to pick up from the fascists and assume greater responsibility for governing the country. Certainly, the credit that De Gasperi had gained from the governments in London and Washington for his role in the Italian Resistance favored his rise to power after the Liberation to the highest post, prime minister. He held the premiership from December 1945 to August 1952, a feat unequaled in the postwar period for Italy. Furthermore, De Gasperi did not depend simply on the high esteem in which he was held internationally, especially in the United States. More fundamental reasons for his success are found in his political style—capable, prudent and pragmatic.

Of course, the judgment of his contemporaries was quite varied. After a brief period of collaboration with the Communists and the Socialists from 1943 to 1947, the left considered him a man of ''order'' pursuing a policy of restoration. He was depicted as a politician willing to sacrifice the general needs of the country to the particular interests of Italian and American capitalists, to American imperialism and to the Catholic Church. On the other hand, De Gasperi's political allies hailed him as a genuine reformer, indeed, as a patriotic hero, for having wisely guided the country from fascism to democracy and for having saved the country from communism.

De Gasperi's historical reputation has been heavily influenced by these contradictory views. Yet today, as much of the Cold War context has been transformed and new documentary sources have become available, the scholarly view of De Gasperi has undergone revision. Even the most critical scholars now recognize that his achievements were political and economic masterpieces. Notwithstanding the fact that many serious problems remain for Italy (especially the gap between the North and the South, the inefficiencies of the state bureaucracy and administration, and grave economic and social inequalities), under De Gasperi's leadership, the country laid the foundations for a successful economic takeoff. Italy is distinguished as being the southern European country most integrated into the economic, political and military structure of the West.

Alcide De Gasperi was born on April 3, 1881, at Pieve Tesino in Trentino. His family lived in relatively well-off economic circumstances, and his father was a civil servant in the Austro-Hungarian Empire, to which this predominantly Italian region then belonged. Catholicism was deeply ingrained in every aspect of life and found particular expression in a philosophy of social duty. De Gasperi grew up in this environment and it was there that he had his first political and administrative experiences.

After finishing the lyceum, De Gasperi moved to Vienna, where he took a university degree in philology. In 1902, he became president of the Trent Catholic students and in 1905 the director of the Catholic newspaper, *Il Trentino*. He held this position until 1925. In 1909 he was elected to the municipal council of Trent and two years later to the Viennese Reichsrat. He fought for the establishment of an Italian university in Trent and for the defense of the cultural identity of Italians in the region. However, his activism on these questions was not based on any radical irredentist idea that Trentino should be joined to Italy, but rather was part of an autonomy reform policy being implemented within the Austro-Hungarian Empire. It was not until 1918 at the end of World War I and upon the defeat of the Austro-Hungarians that De Gasperi stated that he was in favor of an Italian Trentino.

In the period immediately after World War I, De Gasperi continued to be involved in issues concerning his region. The fact that he had completed his political apprenticeship in such a particular context under quite different circumstances than those found in the rest of Italy was to immunize him from the vices of nationalism and provincialism which were so common to Italian politicians of his generation. His situation was to give him a clear, European vision of Italy's internal and international problems.

Furthermore, De Gasperi was not personally involved in the predicament shared by Italian Catholics, who for many years had been prohibited from entering politics by the pope's interdiction of their participation in elections and in political parties, the *non expedit* which resulted from the still-unresolved "Roman question." De Gasperi's background, far removed from the Italian

Catholic movement, freed him of many historical and cultural constraints, allowing him to work out a new relationship between his politics and his religion. De Gasperi was convinced that Catholicism was the moral and spiritual source of humanity, but also believed that faith as such should not interfere with politics. A good Catholic could be respectful of Church dogma, including such issues as the pope's infallibility, while still seeking a balance within his conscience between duties owed to God and those owed to the state.

As leader of the Christian Democrats and head of government of an overwhelmingly Catholic country, De Gasperi tried to maintain this secular relationship as much as the historical circumstances of the period permitted. Furthermore, this was a country where the Church had exercised its power and influence for centuries. During the period from 1941 to 1947, when he was guiding his party toward democracy along with other antifascist movements, including Marxist and atheist ones, De Gasperi sought to avoid implicating the organizational help of the Church in politics. However, during the Cold War, he believed that the threat of communism was particularly dangerous for democracy in Italy, and he saw the antagonism between East and West in terms of a conflict between civilization and barbarism. In this, he did not hesitate to call upon the assistance of the Church to the Christian Democratic Party and proved willing to waive his principles of a nonconfessional party and of separation of politics from religion.

In 1920, De Gasperi joined the Italian Popular Party (PPI), believing in the secular and democratic program of Luigi Sturzo, the priest who had founded the party in March 1919. In 1921 he was elected to the Chamber of Deputies representing the people of Trentino, who were voting as Italians for the first time. This was the end of the first phase of his political career, for from then on he would pass from the regional to the national level of politics.

In 1921–1922, the crisis that was to put an end to liberal rule and bring Mussolini to power had already begun. For the first time, De Gasperi was to take a different position from that of the party secretary, Sturzo, in assessing Mussolini. Sturzo initially believed that fascism was a stabilizing factor for democracy against the threats of Bolshevism. For this reason, he pushed for the PPI to enter into the first Mussolini government after the march on Rome of October 28, 1922. Soon, however, Sturzo realized fascism's true subversive and antidemocratic nature and tried to lead the PPI toward an intransigent opposition. He was hindered in this, not only by the Vatican hierarchy, but also by the "possibilist" faction of the PPI—of which De Gasperi was a part.

Sturzo was forced to abandon his position as party secretary in 1923 and to leave Italy. De Gasperi, who continued to support Mussolini, emerged as the most influential person within the Popular Party. He was elected secretary in May 1924. It was not until the following June that De Gasperi finally distanced himself from fascism, upon the kidnapping and murder of a reformist Socialist member of parliament, Giacomo Matteotti.

In these circumstances, he was to prove his consistency and autonomy, given the fact that without worrying about contradicting the considerably more cautious position of the Church and a large part of the Catholic movement itself, he took part in the so-called Aventine succession. This was a protest movement organized by antifascist elements hoping to persuade the king to dismiss Mussolini from the government. The approach failed, leading to a strengthening of fascism and a final dismantling of democratic institutions between 1925 and 1926. During this period, all political parties were outlawed; their leaders and activists were persecuted.

The members of the Popular Party recognized defeat and ceased all types of political activity. Yet they were able, together with thousands of Catholics involved in religious organizations, to find some limited freedoms within the totalitarian system and maintain their own cultural identity. They were assisted in this by the Lateran Pact, signed on February 11, 1929, by Mussolini and Cardinal Pietro Gasparri. De Gasperi considered the pact to be a good one because it put an end to the conflict between church and state begun in 1870, in spite of the fact that he was preoccupied with the possibility that it reflected well on the fascist regime in terms of image and consensus.

In 1927, De Gasperi was arrested and tried on the pretext of having tried to leave the country secretly. He was to spend four months in prison. In March 1929, he was appointed to a post at the Vatican library. From this period on, he was able to lead an almost normal life. He dedicated himself to his studies and, under a pseudonym, wrote for the newspaper *L'Illustrazione Vaticana*. From this position, he was able to follow national and international events and to form critical opinions. He remained in contact with his former party colleagues and developed deep ties of friendship and respect with key figures in the Vatican hierarchy—for example, with Giovanni Montini, the future Pope Paul VI. From these years at the Vatican, De Gasperi gained experience and knowledge that would serve him well in the future.

As soon as fascism showed signs of losing its consensual base in 1941, De Gasperi threw himself into the reconstruction of a Catholic party. He acted as a vital link between his own generation which had been active in the Popular Party and the younger generation which had nurtured their faith in organizations such as Azione Cattolica or the Federation of Italian Catholic University Students. This younger generation had never believed in Mussolini's regime.

The new party would be called the Christian Democrats and its program was made public in August 1943. It reflected De Gasperi's ideas regarding the structure of the state, which in his view should be pluralistic, parliamentary and decentralized. In economics, the party program called for the capitalist model, respecting, however, the solidarity principles of Catholic social doctrine. The Christian Democratic Party declared itself to be Catholic but nonconfessional, interclass but with a special regard for the middle class and peasants. De Gasperi did not want his party to stake out a clear position on the monarchy versus a republic, as he knew the Catholic world to be divided on the issue. By maintaining neutrality in this controversy, he sought above all to guarantee room for the DC to maneuver politically.

After the declaration of armistice on September 8, 1943, the DC was among the six antifascist parties who were the force behind the National Committee of Liberation. It was also instrumental in the flight of the king, with the Badoglio government, south toward the territories liberated by the Allies. The NCL proclaimed itself to be the sole legitimate government, a position imposed by the left-wing parties (Communists, Socialists and the Action Party), and De Gasperi endorsed the NCL in spite of its clear antimonarchical implications. However, he acted in such a way as to strengthen the position of the DC as the central axis of the antifascist front, and he tried to partially lessen the antagonism between the NCL and the Badoglio government.

In this, De Gasperi had three objectives: to improve relations with the Allies, to avoid alienating the Italian South, which still supported the semiauthoritarian legitimacy of the monarch, and to not leave too much initiative in the hands of a left seeking radical changes in the postfascist period.

Aiming to achieve a dominant position for the party, De Gasperi realized that solid Church support for the DC had to be secured on these terms and acted accordingly. Fortuitously, he was also able to use the unexpected help of Palmiro Togliatti, the Italian Communist leader, to reach this goal. Togliatti had returned to Italy from the Soviet Union at the end of March 1944, announcing his intention to create a united antifascist front together with the moderate and monarchist factions and solemnly expressing his respect for democracy and due legal process. Furthermore, Togliatti said that he was willing to participate in a long-term alliance with the popular mass-based parties—Christian Democrats, Socialists and Communists—to guarantee liberty, peace and progress for Italy. De Gasperi agreed to Togliatti's proposal and joined the antifascist coalition, in which the DC, the PCI and PSI played the most prominent roles. The coalition lasted for another two years after the Liberation. In it, De Gasperi initially served as foreign minister, then as prime minister.

In this delicate historical moment, Italy's modern destiny was to be decided. Once the country's independence and freedom were reestablished, a number of pressing issues came to the fore: Italians had to choose between a monarchy and a republic. The constitution had to be worked out. The new institutions of a democracy had to be built. The economic infrastructure of the country had to be repaired and expanded. The conditions of the peace treaty had to be discussed. Italy's position in the new international order had to be defined.

For these critical processes to take place, but without jeopardizing civil peace, De Gasperi recognized that trust had to be won from large segments of the population which supported the PCI and PSI. Especially from the moment he became head of the government in December 1945, he was able to strengthen the position of the DC in the center of the political spectrum and was able to fend off the most dangerous problems facing the nascent Italian democracy from both the right and the left.

Indeed, having emerged from fascism, the country still necessarily bore some of the signs of fascist mentality and culture, including the structure and bureaucracy of the state. Moreover, much of the Church was still influenced by the Lateran Pact. There was great risk that these political embers could burst into flame because of a longing for the past or for sympathies with other authoritarian-clerical regimes such as Franco's Spain or Salazar's Portugal.

However, De Gasperi also believed that there was the possiblity that the hopes for renewal developed by many Italians during the Resistance could turn into a demand for overly radical or ambitious reforms which went beyond the country's real need for peace, order and normality in the postwar period. Insurrection was not out of the question. Because of this, during his first three years as prime minister (until May 1947), De Gasperi maintained a unity government made up of all the NCL parties, including those of the left.

Nonetheless, it should be pointed out that De Gasperi always considered the alliance with the PCI and PSI to be a choice imposed by circumstances at an extremely difficult moment. He often expressed his views about the complete ideological incompatibility between the DC and the leftist coalition partners. As time passed, the initial reasons for this choice became less valid: Both Italian industry and the Vatican applied increasing pressure on the DC to put an end to what was viewed as an unholy marriage. Moreover, the international situation was changing radically. With the declaration of the Truman Doctrine and the formation of the Cominform—which Togliatti's PCI promptly joined—the Cold War between the United States and the Soviet Union had begun.

Following his own counsel, De Gasperi decided to irrevocably break up the coalition with the left. In January 1947, during a visit to the United States, he expressed these intentions to the American administration, receiving its support and encouragement. The following May, he carried out his intention to drive the Socialists and Communists from power. He reached agreement with the Republican Party, the Liberal Party, and the Social Democratic Party (which had split off from the PSI), all parties more or less ideologically compatible with the DC, to govern the country. This formula, called "centrism," would characterize Italian politics throughout the 1950s, well after its originator had died.

The 1948 elections, against this backdrop of the previous year's political changes, were held in an atmosphere of great tension. The Christian Democrats, openly supported by the Church and, indirectly, by the United States, organized a propaganda crusade against the PCI and the PSI, allied together as the Popular Front. The result was a landslide victory for the DC: 48.5 percent of the electorate voted for the Christian Democrats in a smashing personal triumph for De Gasperi.

Anticommunism became the dominant theme in De Gasperi's politics. He sincerely feared that Italy could share the same fate as the Eastern European countries. For this reason, he did not hesitate to lead Italy into NATO in April 1949, thus anchoring it firmly in the Western Alliance.

During the last phase of his political life, De Gasperi showed ever more conservative tendencies. He supported the idea that Italy needed a "protected" form of democracy, in which certain rights, such as those of association and freedom of speech, should be limited in order to contain subversion. Many political activists in leftist parties and members of the Socialist and Communist labor unions suffered under his governments. Nonetheless, De Gasperi respected the main outlines of the constitution, always denying more or less explicit appeals to ban the PCI.

Even if international affairs and political stability were always his prime concerns, he did not abandon a moderate reformist approach in domestic affairs. Agrarian reforms and legislation to establish a fund for southern Italy were approved, and a new taxation system was introduced. In 1953, De Gasperi tried to have parliament approve a new electoral law which would have awarded a substantial bonus of two-thirds of parliamentary seats to any coalition of parties winning an absolute majority of the votes. He intended this to reinforce forever the centrist tendencies of any government. He did not foresee the reaction this was to produce, not only in the opposition, but also among some of his own coalition partners, such as the Liberals, the Republicans and the Social Democrats.

The Italian electorate voted against the proposed law, marking the political demise of De Gasperi. Designated by the president to form a new government in 1953, he suffered the humiliation of a vote of no confidence in the Chamber of Deputies. Even within the DC, his leadership was questioned. With great dignity, De Gasperi announced his retirement from politics. He returned to his native Trentino, living his last days in solitude and dying there on August 16, 1954.

BIBLIOGRAPHY

Works by De Gasperi:

Discorsi politici. Rome: Cinque Lune, 1956.
Discorsi parlamentari. Rome: Colombo, 1973.
Scritti politici di Alcide De Gasperi. Pier Giorgio Zunino, ed. Milan: Feltrinelli, 1979.

Other Works:

Andreotti, Guilio. *De Gasperi e il suo tempo.* Milan: Mondadori, 1964.
Baget Bozzo, Gianni. *Il Partito cristiano al potere.* Florence: Vallecchi, 1974.
Carillo, Elisa. *Alcide De Gasperi: The Long Apprenticeship.* Notre Dame, Ind.: Notre Dame Press, 1965.
Catti De Gasperi, Maria Romana. *De Gasperi uomo solo.* Milan: Mondadori, 1965.
Harper, L. John. *America and Reconstruction of Italy, 1945–48.* Cambridge: Cambridge University Press.
Kogan, Norman. *Italy and Allies.* Cambridge: Harvard University Press, 1956.
Scoppola, Pietro. *La Proposta politica di De Gasperi.* Bologna: Il Mulino, 1974.
Woolf, J. Stuart. *The Rebirth of Italy, 1945–50.* New York: Humanities Press, 1972.

MARINA TESORO

CHARLES DE GAULLE (1890–1970) has been France's most influential and controversial leader since World War II. During the war, he organized and inspired France's resistance to the German occupation and briefly headed its first postwar government. Recalled to power in 1958, he put an end to the Fourth Republic's unstable governance, rooted in shifting party coalitions and a powerful legislature, by inaugurating the Fifth Republic with a strong presidency that enabled greater continuity and stability in French political life. Externally, he guided France into the postcolonial era by accepting independence for former colonies and Algeria.

A vigorous proponent of French independence and leadership in Europe, de Gaulle resisted supranational development in the European Community (EC), opposed what he saw as U.S. hegemony in Europe and elsewhere, established a French stance autonomous from the North Atlantic Treaty Organization (NATO) and worked toward an easing of East-West tensions. While de Gaulle was viewed widely as an impediment to Atlantic and European unity, except on his own terms, his robust advocacy of the nation-state as the fundamental unit in world politics bespoke a realism that could not be ignored.

Charles de Gaulle was born in Lille, France, on November 22, 1890, and from his early years showed an avid interest in history and military affairs. In 1912 he graduated from the Ecole Militaire at Saint-Cyr, France's foremost military academy, and subsequently joined an infantry regiment. During World War I, de Gaulle was wounded and captured at the battle of Verdun in 1916, and spent more than two and a half years as a prisoner of war. Between the two world wars, he rose in rank and prominence, being appointed to the staff of France's Supreme War Council in 1925, seeing duty in Poland, the Rhineland and the Middle East, and later serving on the secretariat of the National Defense Council. In the 1930s de Gaulle wrote and lectured extensively on military strategy, arguing the then unpopular thesis that France's defense should rely on mechanized and highly mobile army units to meet an attack by Germany, rather than on static linear positions as typified by the Maginot Line.

After the outbreak of World War II, de Gaulle was promoted to brigadier general, a rank he held for the rest of his life, and in June 1940 he was appointed undersecretary of state for war by Premier Paul Reynaud. When Reynaud was replaced as premier by Marshal Pétain, who planned to seek an armistice with Germany, de Gaulle went to London, where, on June 18, he broadcast the first of his appeals to the French people to reject the armistice and continue the fight under his leadership. He was later convicted of treason in absentia by a French military court and sentenced to death.

Though initially de Gaulle had but a small following and was little known within or outside of France, by 1942 his Free French movement was becoming the major focal point of resistance to the German occupation and the French collaborationist regime at Vichy. In 1943, de Gaulle organized the French Committee of National Liberation and the following year transformed it into a provisional government.

After the war, de Gaulle became president of the provisional government pending the adoption of a new constitution. Yet he resigned abruptly in January 1946, while the constitution was still being debated, expressing dissatisfaction with the divisive bickering among the political parties forming the coalition. He opposed the constitution of the Fourth Republic, adopted in October 1946, because of its subordination of the executive to the legislature, which de Gaulle believed would render French governance vulnerable to the vagaries and instabilities of multiparty coalition politics that had afflicted France before the war. De Gaulle tried to reenter political life in 1947 by organizing the Rassemblement du Peuple Français (Rally of the French People) which he viewed as a national coalition above traditional parties. Though the RPF won 120 seats in the National Assembly elections of 1951, de Gaulle soon became discouraged with its prospects and in 1953 withdrew again from politics, devoting his time to the completion of his World War II memoirs.

In 1958, political crisis threatened the French Fourth Republic with civil war as some army leaders and French settlers in Algeria opposed concessions to the demands of Algerian nationalists. In an effort to ease the crisis and restore order and confidence in the government, the National Assembly approved the appointment of de Gaulle as prime minister in June and granted him emergency powers and authority to revise the constitution. In September the constitution of the new Fifth Republic, which featured a strong presidential system, was approved by 83 percent of voters in a national referendum and de Gaulle was elected president of the republic in December.

Nevertheless, he became dissatisfied with this constitution, which provided for the president to be chosen by an electoral college of mostly local officials. In 1962, de Gaulle pushed through a constitutional amendment providing for election of the president by direct popular vote.

In 1965, he was reelected president for a seven-year term, though the need for a second ballot revealed growing discontent with de Gaulle's nationalist policies, his imperious style of rule, and the failure of his government to control inflation. During 1967–1968, France faced growing domestic unrest that culminated in massive student demonstrations demanding educational reform. By May 1968, this student agitation had triggered the largest wave of labor strikes in French history as workers demanded greater benefits from the nation's economic growth and protection from the scourge of inflation that had eroded purchasing power.

Much as in 1958, de Gaulle used a situation of domestic instability to call for a national mandate to reaffirm popular support for his governance. Effectively exploiting widespread fears of societal upheaval following the student and worker protests, as well as the alleged risk of a communist takeover, de Gaulle's Union for the New Republic Party won a landslide victory in the 1968 parliamentary elections.

Yet de Gaulle was unable to convert this urge for order into sustained support for his leadership. In an apparent effort to address domestic grievances by widening participation in governance, he proposed a constitutional reform which would have reduced the authority of the Senate and granted additional powers to regional councils. Following the proposal's defeat in a national referendum in April 1969, de Gaulle resigned from the French presidency, retiring from political life to complete the final volume of his memoirs. He died on November 9, 1970.

Charles de Gaulle's advent to power in 1958 was precipitated by the Algerian crisis, yet the deeper circumstances were rooted in the Fourth Republic's political party factionalism, frequent changes of government and a sense of France's decline as a great power, symbolized by its defeat in Indochina in 1954, the Suez debacle in 1956, the insurgency in Algeria, and the loss of the French empire in Africa in the wake of national independence movements.

This domestic crisis of authority and the deterioration of France's external position combined to produce a general malaise. Yet both appeared conducive to remedy by de Gaulle, who had long advocated strong executive authority and the vigorous promotion of France's role as an independent European and world power. Notwithstanding the initial ambiguity of his position, de Gaulle moved gradually to resolve the conflict over Algeria by agreeing to its independence through the Evian accords in 1962.

However, despite his initial focus on constitutional reform and achieving an Algerian settlement, foreign policy was always de Gaulle's central preoccupation. His long-term aim was to promote the breakdown of European and global Cold War bipolarity which had subordinated most states and issues to the paradigm of East-West confrontation managed by the main protagonists—the United States and the Soviet Union. In his view, the superpowers actually benefited from the Cold War, since it legitimized and reinforced their own hegemonic roles and positions. With an easing and eventual ending of bipolar confrontation, other states would recover increased freedom of maneuver, regional issues could be addressed on their own terms, more flexible issue-specific alignments and coalitions could be arranged and a more decentralized and presumably more stable multipolar system would emerge.

De Gaulle's most controversial actions were in the areas of European, Atlantic and East-West relations. He was unyielding in his insistence on the preservation of state sovereignty and independence, especially for France, and pressured other members of the European Community (EC) to acquiesce to a requirement of unanimity when important national interests were at stake. Suspicious of Britain's close ties with the United States, de Gaulle blocked British membership in the EC during the 1960s. He also tried unsuccessfully to promote a plan for European political union that failed due to its strictly intergovernmental (rather than supranational) character, as well as because of de Gaulle's unconcealed dislike of the EC and his ambitions to build a Europe independent of the United States.

In Atlantic relations, de Gaulle initially sought to establish a tripartite (U.S., Britain, France) leadership group of the Atlantic Alliance and, when this failed, he gradually reduced French military involvement in NATO and withdrew France from NATO's integrated military command in 1966 (although France did not withdraw from NATO's political institutions). Earlier he had required that foreign NATO forces on French territory, mainly American, leave the country. Nevertheless, France remained a member of the Atlantic Alliance and de Gaulle authorized contingency plans for possible cooperation between French and NATO forces in the event of war. In parallel with his disengagement from NATO, de Gaulle developed an independent French nuclear deterrence force which symbolized France's responsibility for its own defense and its claim to great power status, while manifesting de Gaulle's skepticism in the reliability of U.S. nuclear protection.

In East-West relations, de Gaulle tried to advance his goal of a Europe from the Atlantic to the Urals, which envisaged an ending of the hegemony of the United States and the Soviet Union and a concomitant knitting together of Europe as a whole in a pan-European ensemble of states. Several carefully orchestrated French diplomatic overtures to Eastern Bloc states, including an eleven-day visit to the Soviet Union by de Gaulle himself in 1966, were designed to encourage wide acceptance of his vision of Europe. France's withdrawal from the NATO military command was intended to encourage national assertiveness within the Warsaw Pact, though the Soviet Union's invasion of Czechoslovakia in 1968, to reverse Prague's burgeoning political reforms, demonstrated Moscow's firm determination to preserve its Eastern Bloc intact.

Assessments of de Gaulle have varied widely. Whereas most U.S. administrations, beginning with Franklin Roosevelt's presidency during World War II, regarded de Gaulle as arrogant, pompous, uncooperative and stubbornly nationalist, in 1969 President Nixon, who was seeking to improve relations with France, effusively praised de Gaulle as the greatest leader of the time. Indeed, while de Gaulle's single-minded and unyielding pursuit of French interests—and what he regarded as Europe's interests—provoked much criticism, he articulated (albeit often in an extreme form) sentiments of European independence and for the ending of superpower predominance that found wide if more restrained resonance elsewhere in Europe in his own time and later.

During World War II, de Gaulle was not an easy ally to live with. His Free French forces played only a minor military role in the war, and de Gaulle's assertions and expectations on behalf of France—insisting that France be restored to its traditional great power role—were often annoying to Roosevelt and Churchill, whose countries were bearing the major Allied burden of the war against Germany.

During his leadership of the Fifth Republic, not unlike the earlier period, de Gaulle was widely viewed, especially by American policy makers, as a source of discord and obstruction within the West. His proposal for a leadership triumvirate of the Atlantic Alliance to manage global strategy, at a time when France was not yet a nuclear power, was seen as pretentious and divisive to the Alliance as a whole. De Gaulle's open disdain for NATO as an American dominated coalition, and his withdrawal of France from its military structure, were criticized as weakening the West during the Cold War era of East-West confrontation.

The Kennedy administration also regarded the French nuclear force as unnecessary, lacking in credibility as a deterrent, harmful to the strategic unity of the West and likely to encourage the spread of nuclear weapons ambitions to other countries, which could provoke in turn new instabilities. De Gaulle's rejection of the 1963 Limited Nuclear Test Ban Agreement and the 1968 Nuclear Non-Proliferation Treaty further marked France's independent posture. And de Gaulle's vocal criticism of American policy in Southeast Asia during the Vietnam War was yet another irritant to U.S. administrations.

In European affairs, de Gaulle's veto of British membership in the EC delayed the EC's enlargement for a decade. His resistance to a supranational EC, and his insistence on a national veto power over important decisions in the EC Council of Ministers, retarded the EC's progress toward economic integration. De Gaulle's attempt to elevate French policy to a European level by promoting an intergovernmental West European political union, with an independent foreign and defense policy, was viewed by many as disruptive to Western unity as a whole, as potentially threatening to progress within the EC, and as a thinly disguised vehicle for advancing French ambitions for European leadership.

Indeed, de Gaulle's insistence upon independence for France and his parallel aspirations for Europe to play a larger and more influential world role, were hardly compatible. Because if Europe were to mean more than just France, it would require meaningful transfers of economic, political and even military sovereignty from the European states to a centralized policy-making authority. Yet de Gaulle consistently resisted this, since it directly collided with his cherished notion of national independence. For example, de Gaulle refused to make a clear commitment that the French nuclear force would serve as more than a national deterrent, a position that undercut his own advocacy of an independent European defense policy.

Yet if one takes a longer view of history, a more positive assessment of de Gaulle's foreign policy emerges. Together with West German Chancellor Konrad Adenauer, de Gaulle took a major step toward ending the traditional pattern of hostility between France and Germany and provided a framework for their future collaboration by concluding the Franco-German Treaty of Friendship and Cooperation in January 1963. While the treaty had little more than symbolic significance at the time, because of differing French and West German policies toward NATO, the EC and the United States, nevertheless it later became much more important as a basis for achieving closer Franco-German solidarity on a range of European, Atlantic and East-West issues, including intensified cooperation in defense.

Even though de Gaulle's efforts to promote a West European political union came to naught in his own time, the concept on which it was based—intergovernmental cooperation rather than a supranational authority—provided the basis for regularized and expanding political cooperation among the member states of the EC beginning in the early 1970s. De Gaulle's nuclear policy eventually received a measure of Allied endorsement when a 1974 NATO statement came to terms with the French position by acknowledging that the French and British nuclear forces made a contribution to the overall deterrent strength of the Alliance.

Regarding North-South relations, even though Algeria was constitutionally an integral part of the French metropole and not a French colony, de Gaulle recognized that this was a distinction without a difference for a Third World national force which, like many others in the 1950s and 1960s, aspired to independence. Insisting upon independence for France on the world stage, he could hardly deny it to others. Moreover, de Gaulle's acceptance of Algerian independence, though approved by a national referendum, was done at considerable personal and political risk, including attempts on his life by disgruntled French army factions that wanted Algeria to remain part of France. Consistent with the Algerian settlement, de Gaulle then provided for the transformation of France's African territories to the status of independent states.

In the sphere of East-West relations, de Gaulle consistently held that the division of Europe resulting from World War II and the Cold War could not be allowed to stand. He criticized the 1945 Yalta conference agreements (undeservedly, in this author's view) as having in effect divided Europe into spheres of influence entailing U.S. and Soviet hegemony in Western and Eastern Europe respectively, later consolidated by their NATO and Warsaw Pact alliances. Yet whatever its causes, ending the division of Europe remained a central Gaullist preoccupation and the long-range vision that inspired many of his policies. In his World War II memoirs, written in the 1950s, de Gaulle foresaw presciently that one day the will of nations would win out over alien ideologies—hence anticipating the eventual collapse of communism in Eastern Europe that would facilitate movement toward a pan-European reassociation of states.

Thus by withdrawing France from NATO's integrated military command structure in 1966, de Gaulle was doing more than simply manifesting French independence from what he viewed as an American-dominated alliance. He was trying to set in motion a process that would lead to the loosening of Europe's bipolar bloc structure, the ending of U.S. and Soviet predominance in the West and East and eventually the ending of Europe's division—enabling a pan-European reconciliation of states through a process of détente, entente and cooperation.

Yet that goal required a roughly balanced erosion of superpower influence in Europe which the Soviet Union at that time was not prepared to accept. Thus, de Gaulle's vision of a mellowing Cold War and a gradual softening of European divisions was met, to the contrary, with protestations of loyalty to Moscow and the Warsaw Pact by most East European leaders and by the Soviet Union's outright rejection of such an evolution, as it demonstrated with its invasion of Czechoslovakia in 1968. Indeed, during the Cold War period France's influence on the larger issues of alliance and East-West relations was limited, as de Gaulle was unable to persuade his partners in the West or his adversaries in the East to support his views.

Nevertheless, de Gaulle's vision, while premature in his own time, anticipated in broad terms the collapse of communist power in Europe and the ending of the Cold War beginning in the late 1980s. Moreover, his advocacy of a devolution of the structure of global power relationships, from bipolarity to multipolarity, anticipated later superpower retrenchment and the rising prominence of new centers of economic and political influence in Europe and Asia. However, his stubborn insistence on the primacy of the nation-state and national independence was at odds with the logic of interdependence as compelled by the regional and global nature of issues that increasingly defined public policy agendas in the latter half of the 20th century. Hence, somewhat paradoxically, de Gaulle was ahead of his time in some respects, yet wedded to increasingly outmoded notions in others.

BIBLIOGRAPHY

Works by de Gaulle:

The Army of the Future. New York: J. B. Lippincott, 1941.

The Complete War Memoirs of Charles de Gaulle, 3 vols. New York: Simon and Schuster, 1964.

Memoirs of Hope: Renewal and Endeavor. New York: Simon and Schuster, 1971.

Other Works:

Cerny, Philip G. *The Politics of Grandeur: Ideological Aspects of de Gaulle's Foreign Policy*. New York: Cambridge University Press, 1980.

Crozier, Brian. *De Gaulle*. New York: Charles Scribner's Sons, 1973.

Kohl, Wilfrid L. *French Nuclear Diplomacy*. Princeton, N.J.: Princeton University Press, 1971.

Kolodziej, Edward A. *French International Policy under de Gaulle and Pompidou*. Ithaca, N.Y.: Cornell University Press, 1974.

Lacouture, Jean. *De Gaulle: The Ruler, 1945–1970*. New York: Norton, 1992.

WILLIAM C. CROMWELL

EAMON DE VALERA (1882–1975) is the most famous 20th-century Irish politician and statesman. Known colloquially, but not necessarily affectionately, as "Dev," he was head of government for a total of twenty-two years (1932–1948, 1951–1954, and 1957–1959). Then from 1959 until 1973 he was president of Ireland—an almost entirely ceremonial position. De Valera's retirement from active politics marked the end of an era that bore his name. In the 1960s, unprecedented social and economic change swept the country. Thereafter, the frugality, austerity, conservatism and rigid Catholicism of "De Valera's Ireland" seemed as remote as the Middle Ages.

De Valera was nothing short of responsible for fashioning independent Ireland's political system. In 1926 he founded Fianna Fail, the country's largest and most successful political party. A decade later he wrote a new constitution, which remains substantially unaltered. But De Valera failed to achieve his declared and deeply held objective of a united, Gaelic Ireland. Indeed, De Valera's social, economic and foreign policies in the 1930s and 1940s, especially his adroit pursuit of neutrality, made Irish unification increasingly unlikely. For De Valera, neutrality and isolation—albeit an isolation less extreme than during the war years—were to underpin in the postwar period the kind of autarky, self-reliance and cultural distinctiveness to which he was instinctively and emotionally attached. The inevitable consequence for Ireland was mass emigration and a perpetuation of partition.

De Valera first became prominent during the 1916 Easter Rebellion, in which he led a detachment of Irish Volunteers at Boland's Mills in Dublin. After the insurrection, the execution of fifteen other rebel leaders left De Valera the oldest surviving commander. His age (at thirty-five, he seemed old and wise by revolutionary standards), education (graduate of University College, Dublin), profession (teacher), ethos (Irish-Irelander), sound leadership during the rebellion (his unit of Volunteers surrendered last), commuted death sentence (because he had been born in America) and subsequent imprisonment (fourteen months) provided an enviable base for a political career in the radically different Ireland to which he returned in 1917.

There is a photograph, celebrated in Ireland, of De Valera under arrest after the rebellion, surrounded by armed British soldiers. The photograph symbolizes the struggle for Irish independence, the coercive nature of Anglo-Irish relations in the early years of the century, and the politicization of De Valera's generation. At the time the photograph was taken, the Volunteers were depised in Ireland. Their insurrection had caused hundreds of deaths and enormous destruction of property. Coming at the height of the Great War, the rebellion was dismissed by most Irish people as an act of treachery.

Within a matter of months, however, there was a sea change in Irish opinion. Britain's draconian response to the rebellion (atrocities, executions and mass imprisonment), swung popular support behind the Volunteer's separatist ends, if not their extremist means. Britain mistakenly called the insurrection the "Sinn Fein Rebellion." In fact, before the rebellion Sinn Fein was a small, moderate nationalist faction. After the rebellion, Sinn Fein quickly turned into what the British thought it already was: a disciplined, well-organized independence party. Capitalizing on his record as a senior rebel leader, in 1917 De Valera became head of both Sinn Fein and the Irish Volunteers, thus uniting the political and military wings of the separatist movement.

The political situation in Ireland remained extremely fluid. Sinn Fein and the Irish Volunteers were large and influential organizations, but their eventual triumph was far from inevitable. On the contrary, the old Parliamentary Party, which had won "home rule" for Ireland in 1914, only to see its implementation delayed by the outbreak of the Great War, struggled desperately to regain a monopoly of nationalist support. The Parliamentary Party might have succeeded, but British policy ensured that a majority of nationalists stayed in the Sinn Fein camp. A hugely unpopular threat of conscription, and an inept effort to discredit De Valera and others by fabricating the so-called German Plot, were grist to Sinn Fein's mill. In the December 1918 general election, Sinn Fein won 73 of the 105 Irish seats in the House of Commons. (Unionist candidates in Northern Ireland constituencies won most of the remainder.)

Sinn Fein had fought the election on an abstentionist platform. Accordingly, successful Sinn Fein candidates refused to take their seats in London, but met instead in Dublin to constitute Ireland's first independent parliament. Only twenty-eight Sinn Fein M.P.'s attended; the rest, including De Valera, who had been arrested during the "German Plot" fiasco, were either in prison or in hiding. De Valera escaped in February 1919 and attended a private session of parliament on April 1, where he was elected head of the newly constituted, but illegal, Irish government.

De Valera's immediate objective was to win formal independence and international recognition. By that time "home rule" was not enough. The rebellion and its aftermath had so radicalized Irish politics that the hallowed "republic," proclaimed by the martyred dead of 1916, was what a majority of nationalists wanted. President Wilson's endorsement of "self-determination" raised hopes in Ireland of American support, but Irish delegates at the Versailles peace conference came up against insuperable British opposition. The question of Irish independence was by then especially explosive in Britain, where the 1918 general election had increased Unionist leverage. A minority of Irish nationalists forced the issue by attacking police patrols and barracks in Ireland; the British more than obliged by taking retaliatory measures. Terrorism and counterterrorism, insurgency and counterinsurgency, escalated into what was grandiloquently called the "War of Independence" of 1919–1921.

As in any guerrilla campaign, the leadership's main problem was to maintain direction and control. Despite his record in the 1916 rebellion and his unassailable political position, De Valera did not run the war effort. Michael Collins, a young, brilliant, and ruthless organizer, directed military operations. De Valera chose instead to spend his time raising badly needed funds in the United States. His sojourn there for sixteen months, during the height of the War of Independence, seemed excessive and even cowardly. But De Valera's record of rebellion and imprisonment testified to his physical courage, while his fund-raising success more than justified a prolonged absence from Ireland. Incidentally, De Valera's bruising battles with Irish-American politicians honed some invaluable survival skills.

As in 1917, De Valera returned to a radically different Ireland in 1921. A vicious urban and rural guerrilla war seemed destined to continue indefinitely. The Volunteers (now called the Irish Republican Army—the IRA) were too few and ill equipped to win outright, while domestic and international opinion constrained the British government from saturating the country with troops and stamping out the IRA and its sympathizers. Yet a decisive development in the previous year made it politically possible for Britain to call a truce. In 1920 Ireland was partitioned, with the six predominantly Protestant northeastern counties acquiring their own parliament, still within the United Kingdom. British concern about the fate of Irish Protestants/Unionists in an autonomous Ireland had hitherto precluded the possibility of independence. With the vast majority of Protestants/Unionists now safely cocooned in ''Northern Ireland,'' it became politically feasible for the British government to negotiate a settlement with Sinn Fein.

Lloyd George, the wily British prime minister, called the truce and invited De Valera to London for exploratory talks. It was an extraordinary turn of events for the leader of one of the world's great powers to have formal discussions with the ''president'' of a self-styled breakaway republic. The exchange between them was a prelude to an arduous bargaining session between representatives of both sides. It also revealed the impossibility of winning British recognition of the coveted ''Irish Republic.'' As he had in the United States, where he called for a British-style ''Monroe Doctrine for the two neighboring islands,'' De Valera displayed extreme sensitivity in his talks with Lloyd George for British security concerns. Equally aware of the importance Britain attached to maintaining a link between Ireland and the crown, De Valera floated the idea of ''external association,'' that is, reciprocal citizenship and republican status for Ireland within the British Commonwealth.

De Valera's decision not to participate personally in the ensuing negotiations for a treaty continues to perplex historians. Did he stay at home because he knew that the British government would offer only dominion status within the commonwealth? Had he gone, could he have pushed harder for external association? Why did he insist that Collins, the most feared and (to the British) least-known Irish leader, go to London and, inevitably, ''blow his cover.'' It is a measure of De Valera's enigmatic and, some would say, devious character that such questions are still hotly debated in Ireland to this day.

The Irish delegation brought the best deal possible back from London. Predictably, the British had balked at a republic and offered instead a ''free state.'' The key issue for Irish M.P.'s, who debated the proposed treaty in December 1921 and January 1922, was semantic and symbolic. The word *republic* was by then sacrosanct to Irish nationalists. Some ''intransigent'' and ''irreconcilable'' M.P.'s and guerrilla fighters wanted to continue the war until Britain recognized the Irish Republic. Moreover, dominion status necessarily involved a constitutional link to the crown and an oath of allegiance to the British monarch.

''Republicans'' rejected the treaty outright. Pragmatic nationalists, on the other hand, argued that dominion status was the best possible offer on the table, and would give the ''free state'' the diplomatic and constitutional latitude to achieve, in time, the much-desired republic. Lloyd George's undoubtedly real threat to relaunch hostilities in Ireland strengthened the pragmatists' case for accepting the treaty.

During the pivotal debate in the Irish parliament, De Valera developed his earlier ideas on external association and proposed "Document Number Two" as an alternative treaty. De Valera's formula for an oath merely "recognized the King of Great Britain as head of the Associated States." That was more than the Irish Republicans and less than the British imperialists would or could accept. On January 7, 1923, the parliament voted sixty-four to fifty-seven for the treaty. Some of the defeated deputies and a sizable number of IRA volunteers vowed to fight against the new, "free state" government until the cherished republic came into being. As R. F. Foster, one of Ireland's leading historians, has observed, "The break with the irreconcilables came on a form of words."

De Valera's decision to join the antitreaty side in the resulting civil war (1922–1923) was one of the most controversial and momentous events in 20th-century Irish history. It had no impact on the civil war itself (the Republicans were ruthlessly defeated), but profoundly affected the party system in independent Ireland because it led directly to the founding of Fianna Fail. After the civil war, on his release from prison, De Valera was in the political wilderness. He was still president of Sinn Fein, which by then was synonymous with the defeated Republicans. Accepting the reality of the Free State's existence, in 1926 De Valera established Fianna Fail, and cleverly called it "the Republican Party." Large numbers of disaffected Sinn Feiners (defeated Republicans in the civil war) and disillusioned Free Staters soon joined. Intransigent Sinn Feiners remained marginalized, as do their ideological descendants in Ireland today.

Having won forty-four seats in the 1927 election, De Valera and his Fianna Fail colleagues had to take the detested oath in order to enter parliament. They did so—but, in a feat of ethical athleticism hardly unique to Ireland, announced that the oath was merely "an empty formula." Five years later, after another general election and with the support of the small Labor Party, Fianna Fail formed its first government. It was more than ironic that De Valera, who ten years earlier had rejected the treaty on which the Free State was based and who fought against it in a bloody civil war, in 1932 became president (head of government) of the Free State's Executive Council.

De Valera's political resurrection in 1926 and electoral victory in 1932 raise important questions about his renunciation of the treaty in 1922 and its implications for the Irish party system. A majority in parliament had accepted the treaty, yet De Valera joined the democratically defeated minority in taking up arms against it. If he did so for reasons of principle, how, five years later, could he sign the despised oath? And how, ten years later, could he head the government of the regime against which he had taken up arms? De Valera's principled stand had produced a rich political dividend. No wonder that his numerous detractors detected in his actions a strong undercurrent of opportunism.

As for the party system, De Valera's entry into parliament polarized the politics of independent Ireland along pro- and antitreaty lines, although the issue had lost all practical meaning after the civil war. Fianna Fail, "the Republican Party," represented the antitreaty side; Fine Gael, heir to the pragmatic nationalists of 1921–1922, represented the protreaty side. In "De Valera's Ireland"—

the Ireland of the 1930s, 1940s and 1950s—that distinction remained uppermost in Irish politics.

De Valera was to be head of government for the next sixteen years. Like his eyesight, his political vision was myopic. De Valera wanted a united (thirty-two-county) Gaelic Ireland. Yet his triumphalist nationalism made unification increasingly remote. "Gaelic" and "national" were synonyms in De Valera's lexicon for the adjectives peasant, autarkic and Catholic. Those were not values that Northern Ireland Unionists espoused.

As it was, De Valera's predecessors had laid the foundation for a sectarian Free State. De Valera built on it, thereby widening the already deep divide between North and South. De Valera's constitution (1937), the crowning glory of his first period in office, institutionalized the confessional nature of Irish politics by officially recognizing the "special position" of the Catholic Church (Article 44). It alienated northern Unionists further by enshrining southern irredentism (Article 2).

De Valera's policy toward Britain similarly made unification less likely to happen. As head of government, De Valera did exactly what his opponents on the protreaty side had promised during the 1921–1922 parliamentary debate on ratification: He manipulated dominion status to win greater freedom for Ireland. By shrewdly exploiting the 1936 British abdication crisis (when Edward left the British throne to marry the American divorcée Wallis Simpson), De Valera removed all references to the king and governor-general in the Free State constitution and moved far down the road toward his earlier treaty alternative of external association. A year later, when he introduced the new constitution, De Valera could proclaim that Ireland was a republic "in all but name."

De Valera did not use the sacred word *republic* in the constitution because Ireland was still partitioned. Yet his policies helped to ensure that unification grew more remote than ever before. In reality, as De Valera surely knew, unification would have polluted Gaelic Ireland with a massive influx of Protestants, hence his rhetoric of inclusion alongside the politics of exclusion. Hence also his continuing preoccupation with words and symbols. On one celebrated occasion, De Valera entered parliament with an armful of encyclopedias to prove that, in fact if not in word, Ireland was a republic. De Valera's bemused opponents dubbed the country a "dictionary republic."

De Valera's immensely popular pursuit of neutrality during World War II drove another wedge between North and South. As part of the United Kingdom, the North of Ireland participated fully in the British war effort. Northern Unionists saw the war as an opportunity to proclaim their loyalty to the crown, and as further evidence of southern perfidy. Neutrality for the South was practicable because in 1938 the British decided to abandon the three strategically important ports that they had occupied in the South under the terms of the 1921 treaty. Handing over the "treaty ports," at a time when war with Germany was imminent, demonstrated Britain's confidence in De Valera's continuing sensitivity to its security concerns. Notwithstanding Churchill's famous excoriation of Irish neutrality in a V-E Day broadcast, De Valera steered Irish neutrality firmly in favor of the Allies, even before the United States entered the war.

De Valera had opted for neutrality for domestic and international reasons. Domestically, it would have caused another civil war to ally in 1939 with a country that, twenty years earlier, had brutally suppressed Irish independence. The other side of that coin was the degree to which neutrality healed the civil war's wounds. Both sides, pro- and antitreaty, supported Irish neutrality. Only Sinn Fein and the IRA, by then a small minority, supported Germany. Surviving ''irreconcilables'' and some young disciples used the opportunity to launch a military campaign in the North. It was a dismal failure. De Valera dealt ruthlessly with his erstwhile comrades in the IRA, allowing some to die on hunger strike and sentencing others to death.

De Valera lost the 1948 election because voters wanted a change, and a motley coalition of new and existing parties, along with a few independent M.P.'s, offered it to them. The opposition attacked De Valera for a dismal record in office: persistent recession and perpetual partition. The new government took the fateful step in 1949 of declaring Ireland a republic. Paradoxically, the British government's retaliatory ''Ireland Act'' copper-fastened partition by guaranteeing that ''in no event will Northern Ireland or any part thereof cease to be part of . . . the United Kingdom without the consent of the parliament of Northern Ireland.'' De Valera could claim that his circumspection in not declaring Ireland a republic had been warranted. But the policies he pursued during sixteen years in office had done more than anything else to reinforce the divide between North and South.

As if to emphasize his Republican credentials, De Valera used his years in opposition between 1948 and 1951 to embark on an international antipartition campaign. At a time when the world was preoccupied with postwar reconstruction, De Valera's antics probably provided much-needed comic relief. At home, however, his campaign had an important effect, but not on partition. Instead, by stressing in his speeches that Ireland's wartime neutrality was a tenet of republicanism and by arguing that Ireland could not abandon neutrality and join the recently established North Atlantic Treaty Organization as long as Britain ''occupied'' the six counties, De Valera helped to frustrate the alliance-minded tendencies of his opponents.

By the time De Valera returned to office in 1951, the link between nonmembership in NATO and the continuation of partition had been forged in the Irish nationalist mind. De Valera did not dwell on the value of neutrality in the wider context of international relations. On the contrary, he saw it purely as a means toward the ends of full sovereignty for the twenty-six counties, noninvolvement in a future international conflict and isolation from the unspirituality of the postwar world.

But De Valera could only delay temporarily the inevitable onslaught in Ireland of materialism, consumerism and secularism. He succeeded until his resignation from active politics in 1959. In the meantime, De Valera believed that Ireland's economic underdevelopment nurtured a happiness and holiness unobtainable elsewhere. Arguably the tens of thousands of Irish men and women who emigrated during that time in search of a livelihood abroad did not share De Valera's vision.

BIBLIOGRAPHY

Bowman, John. *De Valera and the Ulster Question*. Oxford: Clarendon, 1982.

Edwards, Owen Dudley. *Eamon De Valera*. Washington, D.C: Catholic University of America Press, 1987.

Fisk, Robert. *In Time of War: Ireland, Ulster, and the Price of Neutrality*. Philadelphia: University of Pennsylvania Press, 1983.

FitzGibbon, Constantine. *The Life and Times of Eamon De Valera*. New York: Macmillan, 1974.

Lee, Joseph. *Ireland, 1912–1985*. Cambridge: Cambridge University Press, 1989.

Longford, Earl of. *Eamon De Valera*. Boston: Houghton Mifflin, 1970.

DESMOND DINAN

MICHEL DEBRÉ (1912–) has had a record of distinguished service to the French Republic and the French state that dates to 1934. His career, spanning fifty of his country's most turbulent years, includes a wide variety of administrative and political posts ranging from local councilor to prime minister. Debré was instrumental in founding, defining, nurturing and maintaining the French Fifth Republic. He attacked this pivotal task as he did others: with intensity, fervent nationalism and self-proclaimed tenacity. He is perhaps best-known for his total (some would say blind) devotion to Charles de Gaulle and is credited (some would say blamed) for the general's return to lead the Fifth Republic.

Throughout his career, Debré has been an outspoken political writer and prolific journalist, making nearly constant and always controversial contributions to French public debates since the 1940s. While less apparent, his work in institution building through his nearly single-handed creation of both the prestigious Ecole Nationale d'Administration (ENA) and the 1958 Fifth Republic constitution will doubtless have a more permanent and constructive impact on French political and administrative life than did his own politics.

Debré is a member of a prominent family of scientists and humanists. His mother was one of the first women to intern in a Paris hospital and his father was widely acclaimed as a brilliant professor and a pioneering pediatrician. All of the Debré children became accomplished, his sister in medicine, his brother in art and he in politics and administration. Michel Debré was a diligent student at the prestigious Lycée Louis-le-Grand in Paris, going on to study law, public administration and politics in the capital. Later, his reflections on the inadequacies of this standard Third Republic preparation for public life shaped his reform of French civil service training.

Debré completed his obligatory military service in 1932, briefly considering a military career, but he was drawn instead into government by the turmoil of

French and European politics. Becoming an auditor with the Conseil d'Etat in 1934, Debré then served as a *chargé de mission* in Paul Reynaud's cabinet from November 1938 until he was drafted for World War II. In 1943, following brief service in the military and the Vichy governmenet, Debré began his active role in the French Resistance under the *nom de guerre* of Jacquier.

When asked to become part of the movement's General Studies Committee, Debré gained his first experience in constitutional design while working on plans for postwar political institutions. Convinced that Resistance leaders must act quickly to take advantage of a unique historical moment and to reject the prewar status quo, Debré aimed to prevent foreign (mainly American) intervention in French politics and to reestablish stability and order in the institutions underpinning de Gaulle's government. His main contribution during this period was to organize and recruit prefectoral personnel to replace those of the Vichy regime, including himself as regional prefect of Angers in his native Loire valley. It was in this capacity that Debré first met de Gaulle in August 1944; he remained prefect until the general called him to join the provisional cabinet in April 1945 with the task of initiating administrative reform.

Vichy and Resistance leaders alike advocated massive reforms in the French traditions of educating and recruiting administrators as well as in the organization of the public bureaucracy. Traditionally, the normal path to high public service required three years at the state Faculty of Law followed by three years at the private Institute of Political Science in preparation for exams specific to each government agency. This system, many believed, produced a weak, fragmented and compartmentalized administration which they blamed in part for France's humiliating defeat in World War II.

As de Gaulle's "Constitutional and Electoral Counselor," Debré undertook in October 1945 the design of a new system to train public servants which would fundamentally revamp education in social, economic and administrative sciences throughout the country. As the core of the new system, he established ENA, a state-run *grande école*, with the intention that students would attend the school after three years at the newly nationalized Institute for Political Studies. Rejecting his own training as too "bookish," legalistic and theoretical, Debré's plan for ENA's curriculum emphasized practical experience and ideological neutrality.

To broaden significantly the demographic composition of French administration, Debré instituted a two-pronged admissions path: a general entrance exam which was also open to women (he also admitted the first women to the elite Ecole Polytechnique in 1974) with a second "internal" path to allow a certain number of state employees without the usual political science background to attend ENA as well. For three years, the ENA program would train students with an alternating sequence of classroom instruction and a variety of internships in state agencies. ENA's general exit exams were meant to replace individual agency exams. The well-rounded experience of an ENA education would thus allow *énarques* (the name given to the school's graduates) to develop a network of colleagues across government agencies, thereby creating human ties between previously segregated administrative corps.

Debré's system is today a much-criticized success. Clearly, the current arrangement produces more generally competent administrators than the prewar system did. ENA is the most envied and most often imitated French institution abroad, and the Institute for Political Studies is considered one of the world's best schools in the discipline. While respected for the high caliber of its training, however, ENA is also denounced for producing an elitist technocracy disconnected from French citizens' real needs. Critics consider graduates spoiled, groomed for high stations in life from which they are unlikely to endorse change in the system that produced and nourishes them. Detractors call ENA a great computer that programs the "big heads" of the French administrative, political and economic apparatus. Even some of its own former students regret ENA's close identification with the Fifth Republic's political and institutional status quo. However, Debré remains unfazed by the charge that *énarques* constitute a power elite which monopolizes the centralized French state, for this is as he intended it to be.

From their first meeting in 1944, Debré was firmly convinced that only Charles de Gaulle could lead France back to greatness. When the general abruptly retreated from politics in 1946, Debré was obviously disillusioned, and he watched with disdain as Socialists and Communists reinstigated a "regime of parties" that he deemed incapable of running the country. Despite his disenchantment, however, Debré agreed to serve in the postwar Saar Economic Mission and then as commissioner of German and Austrian affairs. In both positions, he proceeded upon the conviction that France must protect its national interest as the first among European states. This theme would become the consistent leitmotif of Debré's future involvement in foreign affairs.

Soon discontented with France's German policy, Debré refused further administrative posts and threw himself into politics, aiming for nothing less than to replace the contemporary regime of parties with Charles de Gaulle. He joined the Radical Party, losing his first legislative campaign under its banner in 1946. In 1948, he was elected senator as a candidate of the Rassemblement du Peuple Français (Rally of the French People), the party formed around de Gaulle as a reluctant leader. Thus Debré began some forty years as an elected official, a political career that entailed two Senate races, seven National Assembly contests, five municipal and department council races, one European Parliament election (1979) and a presidential bid (1981).

Between 1948 and 1958, with de Gaulle isolated from the national political scene, Debré was the Gaullist spokesman in the Senate. "Debré has reform in his blood," fellow Gaullist Georges Pompidou remarked in the 1950s. On several occasions, Debré submitted plans for a new constitution to de Gaulle, urging the general to change the course of French history with a proposed republic as his institutional base. A ferocious critic of the Fourth Republic regime, Debré launched unrelenting attacks on the governments of the day via every possible means, whether on the chamber floor, on radio or in the several political publications he founded for this purpose. Fighting for the general's return to lead the country to its fated greatness, he berated Fourth Republic leaders for their vision of France as a small, defeated country ready to ''give up'' its Algerian ''province'' in a ''politics of abandonment'' and for subordinating France's national interests to a supranational Europe. As recognized leader of the group known as the ''Ultras,'' Debré pursued with intransigence the objective of ''creating the event'' which would provoke the governing regime to call back the general.

When, in 1958, the Fourth Republic collapsed amid the Algerian crisis and de Gaulle was called back to power, Debré became an integral member of the new regime, moving quickly from virulent opponent of the Fourth Republic to creator and unqualified supporter of the general's Fifth Republic. As keeper of the seals charged with writing a new constitution, Debré appeared unusually serene as he designed the institutional infrastructure France needed to restore domestic strength and international prominence under the general's control. De Gaulle, relatively indifferent to juridical details, left the drafting almost entirely to Debré, who had prepared for the occasion so thoroughly that he could produce a complete document in a matter of months with little advice from others.

Debré's constitutional work brought to concrete culmination his long-standing critique of the ''assembly system'' of previous regimes. France's political experience in the first half of the 20th century proved, Debré thought, that the British practice of parliamentary sovereignty was not viable in his country. Multipartyism and proportional electoral systems in France's past had produced governments lacking legitimacy, too unstable to deal with the crushing economic and social problems of the 1920s, 1930s and the early postwar period. In 1958, the new French constitution needed three elements to overcome past weaknesses: an authoritative executive, a genuine parliamentary system with a cabinet responsible to elected deputies, and a nonproportional electoral system to ensure a stable government majority. In all this, Debré aimed to establish a set of institutions whose legitimacy would outlast his leader's personal authority.

While ''Debré's Constitution,'' as de Gaulle sometimes called it, followed French parliamentary tradition with its two-headed executive and a two-chambered parliament, it was also a hybrid system which considerably strengthened the presidency. Debré intended the legislature to have its own defined sphere of activity but virtually no ability to interfere with the executive. This division of powers evolved in practice toward firm presidentialism under de Gaulle's hand, and the 1962 referendum on direct popular election of the president was designed to further buffer the president from the country's political class, including parties and legislators.

As the Fifth Republic solidified, de Gaulle successfully insulated himself at the center of a supposedly parliamentary system, leaving his prime minister to take the brunt of day-to-day executive unpopularity. Debré denies that he wrote the constitution specifically for de Gaulle, although he admits that it was designed to keep the general in power for as long as necessary to ''restore'' France. Considering himself to be a parliamentarist, he was deeply disturbed by de Gaulle's bold assertions of presidential power and independence, for Debré believed he had created a system congruent with the French people's preference for an executive branch responsible to an active parliament through the cabinet and prime minister. At the same time, out of his personal devotion to the general and his hatred of multipartyism in the French legislature, Debré himself opened the door for highly personalized presidential power. Having equated de Gaulle with French *grandeur*, he could not deny power to the first without threatening the second.

Paradoxically, the Fifth Republic's stability during its first decade resulted less from its institutions as Debré had designed them and more from the loyal Gaullist parliamentary party majority which crystallized in the Union for the New Republic Party (UNR). Even though both Debré and de Gaulle derided political parties, Debré was for years a leader and key player in the UNR and de Gaulle clearly benefited from its organizational strength and its members' loyalty.

To say that the Fifth Republic evolved in ways its ''impassioned founder'' did not intend is not to diminish Debré's contribution. He forged the legal basis of a state which both citizens and leaders could support; his constitution set the rules that gave France a firm political foundation without which the economy and society could not have achieved their postwar successes. The *dirigiste*, executive-centered state he created guided and promoted the country's modernization throughout much of the period known as ''*les trente glorieuses*,'' or ''the thirty glorious years'' of rapid growth following World War II. The Fifth Republic's political institutions have also proven flexible enough to weather a number of challenges (the decolonization of Algeria, for instance) and to adapt to a number of unforeseen modifications (such the ''cohabitation'' of a president and prime minister from opposing political sides). These are no small achievements in a country with France's legacy of political turbulence and dissensus and are due in large part to Debré's careful and prodigious work.

Michel Debré became the Fifth Republic's first prime minister in 1959, remaining in office for over three years, although he reportedly threatened to resign many times. Ultimately, de Gaulle forced him to leave office against his will. The relationship between Debré and the general, obviously the center of the former's political life, was intense and troubled; it became increasingly so during the course of Debré's premiership. On the one hand, Debré demonstrated a pure and total personal and public devotion to the man he had helped to make the country's most powerful leader. The general once referred to Debré as more Gaullist than he. Debré believed that de Gaulle could save France from itself—or at least from the likes of the Fourth Republic's political leaders. The general, for his part, sought out Debré because they shared a vision of a strong central state closely identified with the office and, at least for de Gaulle, the person of the president.

On the other hand, once the Fifth Republic moved from the realm of constitutional theory to political practice, Debré became an accomplice to de Gaulle's desire to accumulate personal along with institutional power. In office, Debré defined the premiership as secondary to the presidency even though he approached his role with remarkable diligence and devotion to "eternal France," for he proved unable to oppose effectively the general's will or to sway him through argument. For instance, Debré clearly believed that the prime minister should choose his own cabinet, but de Gaulle immediately took over this power, controlling cabinet appointments throughout his presidency and leaving Debré on the sidelines.

Those around him saw Debré as a servant who made continuous selfless sacrifices for de Gaulle's glory, even to the point of reversing his own positions, most notably on Algeria. Debré faithfully undertook mundane domestic policy obligations while leaving the pomp of governing to the president, especially in de Gaulle's preferred realm of foreign affairs. Asked once why he did not move France toward a purely presidential regime, de Gaulle replied, "Do you see me going to Parliament every time we have to fix the price of milk?" In Debré, de Gaulle had found the prime minister most willing to assume the bothersome burdens he intended for the position.

Nevertheless, Debré's domestic policy legacy from those years was not insignificant. Due in part to de Gaulle's disinterest in domestic affairs and in part to the period's political stability resulting from both the constitution and the Gaullist parliamentary majority, Debré was able to exercise real executive power in some areas and to pursue an aggressive agenda. He presided over the longest-lasting government (three years and three months) of any French prime minister in a hundred years.

During this time, Debré and other ministers guided France through a period of relatively well planned and coordinated economic growth, accompanied by budgetary discipline and healthy national account balances. His government rebuilt France's foreign exchange reserves, maintained a healthy external trade balance and secured a relatively stable franc. In this heyday of indicative planning, Debré's government completed the proposal to move the huge Parisian food market from the central city to suburban Rungis; it created the first regional rail system (RER) in and around Paris; and it began building the huge ultramodern office and residential complex in the capital's western fringes at La Défense, which was to become the largest single concentration of multinational firms in Europe. Under Debré's watch, the Jacobin state formulated and passed through parliament significant social legislation that provided French workers with what is now considered essential social protection in the form of pensions, health insurance and other benefits.

However, Debré's foreign policy legacy, at least that resulting from his years as prime minister, is relatively minor and largely negative. He took controversial stands on vital issues, but seemed to lack the realism necessary to pursue a constructive postwar role for his country. Blinded by his preoccupation with

French *grandeur* in the world, he proved completely out of step with the march toward both European supranationality and decolonization.

Debré consistently opposed French participation in European organizations ranging from the European Coal and Steel Community (ECSC) immediately after the war to Euratom and the European Economic Community in the 1950s. He resisted the ECSC because it returned to Germany the power it had lost by losing the war. He was against Euratom because the organization would prevent France from pursuing an independent atomic policy. Debré's feelings toward the economic ties proposed in the European Community (EC) were more complex. He declared himself against intra-European protectionism and thus in favor of a free trade area. At the same time, he stood firmly in support of French farmers' demands for protection against unfair competition.

When accused of being reactionary on Europe, Debré responded that he favored a commitment to international cooperative efforts when they were in line with French institutions and respectful of French integrity. He vehemently opposed any plan which would sacrifice his country's sovereignty to the benefit of other European "partners," particularly Germany. If France were to be involved in Europe at all, Debré favored membership in a more confederal *Europe des patries*, with France as leader by virtue of its military and economic strength.

His opposition to Europe went beyond rhetoric and into the realm of action. In the early 1950s, he created a "Committee for the Independence and Unity of France," launching a multifront war against all things European. He came unhinged at the idea of a European army, accusing those who supported the European Defense Community of being "traitors" and "criminals." The French parliament refused to ratify the Defense Community Treaty in 1953 due in part to his efforts. Although his continued opposition to Europe was clearly out of step with French elite opinion supporting stronger European union in the 1980s, popular ambivalence in France toward the 1992 Maastricht Treaty for greater European monetary and political union may vindicate Debré's early mistrust.

The other foreign policy issue which haunted Debré, and every other politician of the time for that matter, was the "Algerian drama." He saw Algeria as a French creation: France built Algeria and in World War II Algerians defended France. When the colonial independence movement began, Debré sided with those in Algeria who wanted to remain French. In particular, he openly supported the French military from 1954 to 1958 and, according to some, plotted with officers there to stage a coup against the Fourth Republic, hoping thereby to precipitate de Gaulle's return.

In 1959, when he was first named prime minister, Debré publicly declared that Algeria was part of France (legally it was) and that there would be no negotiations on this point. Moreover, he promised that France would hold onto Algeria even if, for political reasons, de Gaulle changed his mind—in the event, precisely what happened as French public opinion turned against the war. De Gaulle seems to have realized that it was time for the French to cut their losses and to leave in as orderly and honorable a fashion as possible. De Gaulle apparently recognized that in the postwar world, France would in fact be stronger politically and more respected by other major powers if it withdrew. Seeing that he could not convince the general otherwise, from roughly September 1959, Debré publicly defended de Gaulle's decision to allow Algerians to determine their own fate.

Debré suffered greatly over this change in course on the Algerian question. He offered to resign the premiership, reportedly several times, but the general was not ready to accept his resignation. French civilians and officers in Algeria also felt that Debré had betrayed them. Perhaps the lowest point in his premiership came in 1961 after the French generals' putsch in Algeria when he appeared on French television, strained and haggard, urging citizens to go to the airports to defend their beloved France in case of attack by dissident paratroopers.

Finally, de Gaulle demanded Debré's resignation in April 1962 when it became evident that Debré's well-known position on the Algerian question was bankrupt. The so-called Evian accords, ending French control of Algeria, had been signed and then overwhelmingly approved by the French public in a referendum (90 percent of those casting ballots approved the agreement), and the military officers connected to the putsch and to the terrorist Organisation de l'Armée Secrète (OAS) had been tried, found guilty and imprisoned. What Debré would call the ''loss'' of Algeria was a source of profound disagreement between him and de Gaulle and constituted his greatest political defeat.

Debré left the premiership under what were for him highly unsatisfactory conditions. Article 8 of the constitution did not clearly state that the prime minister served at the pleasure of the president. (De Gaulle later had his premiers sign undated letters of resignation.) Though Debré felt he could still be effective, de Gaulle wanted to signal a new departure with a new political team under Georges Pompidou, who had never previously held elective office. De Gaulle also wished to show the French people that he, too, rebuked Debré for his position on Algeria, which is why the general fired him the day after the referendum.

Debré was defeated in his bid for a National Assembly seat in 1962. In the next year, however, he retumed to the lower house representing the overseas department of Réunion, a somewhat uncomfortable constituency given his position on Algeria. Although politically marginalized in the early and middle 1960s, he eventually returned to Gaullist cabinets as minister of economic affairs and finance (1966–1968), foreign affairs (1968–1969), and defense (under Pompidou, 1969–1973). In the 1970s, in the face of the world oil crisis, Debré pressed the government to pursue economic and budgetary austerity. More recently, consistent with his faith in French greatness, Debré has urged his countrymen to ''roll up their sleeves'' and rise to Asian competition in the business world. In the 1980s, he naturally opposed many Socialist policies under the presidency of François Mitterrand, particularly the move to cut back working hours and increase vacations, arguing that the French needed to work more, not less. An unmodified Jacobin, he also fought Mitterrand's move to decentralize the state, arguing that the policy would tear the country apart and create tremendous waste.

A man of firm convictions who rarely compromised, Michel Debré is known as one of France's most tenacious politicians. Few are indifferent to him. His admirers believe that France would have had to invent Debré if he did not already exist. Once he devoted himself to a task, a cause or a position, he was intense and immovable. Showing neither fear nor hesitation in political conflict, he was respected for his courage and feared for his ferocity. Debré's detractors say his extremism ultimately hurt his country, that behind his Jacobin rhetoric of French unity lay a politics of divisiveness and exclusion.

Undeniably, the contemporary French Fifth Republic would not stand in its present form without the work of Michel Debré. His greatest contributions to its stability and progress came through his construction of its institutions and his dedication to the idea and the reality of the French state. If his political positions were sometimes extreme, if his political rhetoric was usually uncompromising, it was because he had "a certain idea of France," one which he refused to abandon and would only entrust to his hero, Charles de Gaulle.

BIBLIOGRAPHY

Work by Debré:

Trois républiques pour une France, 3 vols. Paris: Albin Michel, 1984, 1988.

Other Works:

Andrews, William, and Stanley Hoffmann (eds.). *The Fifth Republic at Twenty.* Albany, N.Y.: State University of New York Press, 1981.

Gordon, David. *The Passing of French Algeria.* London: Oxford University Press, 1966.

LYNNE LOUISE BERNIER

J. M. (JOOP) DEN UYL (1919–1987) led the Dutch Labor Party (PvdA) from 1967 until 1986 and was premier of the Netherlands from 1973 to 1977. Den Uyl was one of the most influential figures in postwar Dutch social democracy. His importance stems from both the influence he exerted on Labor Party programs and policy as director of the party's research bureau in the 1950s and his leadership of the party in the late 1960s and 1970s, a period of considerable transition not only in Labor but also in the Dutch political system as a whole. Part of a generation which came of age during or immediately after World War II, den Uyl came to embody the demands of a younger generation for redistribution of wealth, knowledge and power. The cabinet which den Uyl led from 1973 to 1977 was unusual not only because of its energy but also because of its distinctively progressive stance and dedication to change.

Johannes Marten den Uyl was born in Hilversum on August 19, 1919. Although raised in a Calvinist milieu and educated in Christian primary and secondary schools, den Uyl studied economics at the Municipal University of

Amsterdam, a secular institution. After completing his studies in 1942, den Uyl worked briefly for the Ministry of Economic Affairs. During the war, den Uyl abandoned Calvinism and became involved in socialist intellectual circles, which operated despite the German occupation.

In 1945, den Uyl served briefly as domestic editor of *Het Parool*, a prosocialist newspaper which emerged from the resistance movement, and then became the editor of *Vrij Nederland*, a progressive weekly with similar origins. As a journalist, den Uyl was closely involved with political questions and often had to tread a delicate path between support for and criticism of a cabinet with which *Vrij Nederland* sympathized. Den Uyl remained at *Vrij Nederland* until 1949, when he became the director of the Wiardi Beckman Foundation (WBS), the Labor Party's research bureau.

At this time, the Wiardi Beckman Foundation was a fledgling organization whose reputation had yet to be established. Den Uyl assembled a young staff, which he constantly challenged and prodded, establishing the WBS as an independent think tank within the PvdA. As the foundation's director, den Uyl wrote numerous articles and was involved in the preparation of two major restatements of party policy, as well as the redrafting of the PvdA's statement of principles.

''De Weg naar vrijheid'' (The Way to Freedom), published in 1951, embodied the doubts which den Uyl and others still harbored about the potential of a market economy. Later, den Uyl and the PvdA began to take account of economic growth, affluence and prospects for full employment. Proposals for economic planning gave way to an emphasis on equality of opportunity and cultural socialism, both already present in the 1951 report.

''Om het kwaliteit van het bestaan'' (On the Quality of Existence), published in 1963, was an attempt to come to grips with the consequences of full employment and the welfare state for social democracy. Paralleling John Kenneth Galbraith, den Uyl argued that neither affluence nor full employment was sufficient to eliminate inequality in a class-divided society. Instead, reflecting elements already present in the 1951 report, the state had to ensure equal access to education and provide a high level of public services.

In addition to directing the Wiardi Beckman Foundation, den Uyl was a member of the Amsterdam City Council beginning in 1953 and a member of the Second Chamber (lower house) of the Dutch parliament beginning in 1956. Den Uyl left the foundation in 1962 and became an alderman (municipal cabinet member) in Amsterdam in 1963, assuming several major economic portfolios.

However, circumstances quickly drew den Uyl into national politics. In 1965, a breakup of the confessional-Liberal coalition, in office since 1959, enabled the Socialists to return to power in a center-left coalition with the Catholics and the Anti-Revolutionaries. Den Uyl was tapped to serve as minister of economic affairs and played an active role both in the closure of the coal mines in Limburg (and their replacement by other industries) and in the design of arrangements for the exploitation of gas reserves in the north. However, the center-left Cals cabinet collapsed in October 1966, triggering new elections in 1967. Fearing that the waning popularity of finance minister and party leader Anne Vondeling would harm the party, the PvdA brought Joop den Uyl forward as caucus chairman and party leader.

Den Uyl assumed the party leadership at a time of considerable tumult in the PvdA and the Dutch political system. The PvdA was in electoral decline and its opportunities to govern were blocked by the preference of the Catholic and Protestant parties for coalitions with the Liberals. Dissident factions and new parties had appeared, demanding return to or renewal of party principles, more political and social democratization, and a party system more sharply demarcated between left and right. The PvdA was doubly challenged by these developments: Internally, den Uyl and others were confronted with a vocal dissident group, New Left, which argued that party leaders had abandoned socialist principles and had been too willing to compromise in order to govern. Externally, the PvdA faced competition from a new party, Democrats '66 (D'66), whose demands for an elected prime minister and a two-party system were attracting the support of younger voters.

Although New Left's attacks rankled the party's leaders and narrowly skirted party rules, den Uyl was determined to keep the dissident faction within the party. Den Uyl opened a dialogue with the dissidents, incorporated some of their demands for further participation and democratization into his own thinking, and eventually won their support and loyalty. However, this exercise was not without its costs: In the process, New Left gained influence within the party organization, achieved modified rules and recruitment processes and rendered the party leadership vulnerable to further attacks from dissident and "anti-establishment" elements long after New Left had been successfully incorporated into the party.

Both to satisfy New Left and take advantage of the changing political situation, the PvdA adopted a strategy of polarization, demanding that prior to elections, political parties state publicly with whom and on what terms they would form coalitions. Designed to align the PvdA with kindred parties, while emphasizing differences with others, the intent was to force voters to choose between progressive and conservative alternatives and increase the PvdA's leverage in cabinet making. In practical terms, this meant forming alliances with Democrats '66 and the Radical Political Party (PPR—a small progressive party which had splintered off from the Catholic Party) in opposition to the confessional parties (who were considering a merger into a single Christian Democratic Party) and the Liberals.

When first deployed in 1971, this polarization strategy kept the PvdA and its allies in the opposition. However, a breakup of the five-party Biesheuvel cabinet resulted in new elections in 1972. The PvdA, D'66 and the PPR contested the election on the basis of a detailed common program, "Keerpunt" (Turning Point), which was to form the foundation of a cabinet if they gained a majority.

In the meantime, the three confessional parties agreed to govern or oppose together.

Although the PvdA and its allies won only 36.9 percent of the vote in the 1972 elections, these ''progressive three'' formed the largest block in parliament. In the subsequent cabinet formation, the PvdA, D'66 and the PPR refused to negotiate with other parties and demanded instead that they be allowed to form a minority government. This resulted in deadlock, broken only when mediators enlisted individual Catholics and Protestants into a progressive cabinet with den Uyl as premier. This arrangement was supported not only by the PvdA and its allies, who regarded the cabinet as their own, but also the Catholics and Anti-Revolutionaries. In contrast to its predecessors, the new cabinet had a distinctively progressive cast: Ten of the sixteen ministers came from the progressive bloc.

The den Uyl cabinet was committed to carrying out the redistribution of wealth, knowledge and power presaged not only in ''Turning Point'' but also den Uyl's 1963 report, ''On the Quality of Existence.'' However, although the den Uyl cabinet was able to take some steps in this direction, neither economic nor political circumstances were favorable to its broader redistributive agenda. Den Uyl's cabinet had barely assumed office before it was confronted with the 1973 OPEC oil embargo. Although the immediate consequences were dealt with by a special enabling act, which permitted the government to restrict wage and price increases, long-term dislocations caused a number of problems. Spiraling inflation forced the government to intervene frequently in wage negotiations. In addition, after 1975 the cabinet was forced to restrict increases in public spending to 1 percent of national income, limiting the extent to which government spending could be used to improve the quality of life or ensure greater equality.

Despite adverse circumstances, the den Uyl cabinet retained its redistributive commitments. In order to reduce income differentials, public sector salaries and benefits were indexed to increases in average private sector wages, and the proportion of the budget devoted to foreign aid was increased. However, the cabinet's legislative program required the support of the Catholic and Anti-Revolutionary parties and, after 1976, of the Christian Democratic Appeal (CDA, formed by the merger of the Catholic and Anti-Revolutionary parties with the Christian Historical Union). Initially, the pace of reform was slow, but by 1977 legislation on the expropriation of private land, increased codetermination in industry, the sharing of ''excess'' profits and the regulation of investment was ready. PvdA strategists made passage of these four measures a test for further cooperation with the Christian Democrats. However, vice premier van Agt and other Catholic ministers rejected the provisions for land expropriation, which led to the resignation of the cabinet's Christian Democratic ministers two months before the 1977 elections.

Despite the split, it was widely assumed that the 1977 elections would result in a new den Uyl government which would continue the agenda of the first. Campaigning on the theme ''Choose the Minister-President,'' the PvdA won

33.8 percent of the vote and an additional ten seats (largely at the expense of smaller parties to the left). However, the confessional bloc, competing for the first time with a single Christian Democratic list, won 31.9 percent of the vote. Acting on an updated version of the polarization strategy, the PvdA demanded that it be given eight of the sixteen portfolios, including the premiership.

The subsequent cabinet negotiations lasted six and a half months. Agreement was secured first on policy orientations and then, with greater difficulty, on the distribution of portfolios. However, attempts to form a center-left cabinet stranded when the PvdA tried to prevent Andreas van Agt, leader of the new Christian Democratic Appeal, from resuming his position as minister of justice. The initiative shifted to van Agt, who then formed a government with the Liberal Party on much the same programmatic basis as had already been agreed to with the PvdA. Van Agt assumed the premiership, while den Uyl returned to the Second Chamber and resumed his position as PvdA caucus chairman.

This van Agt cabinet survived a full four years. In the 1981 elections, however, the Christian Democrats and Liberals lost their majority; Socialists, Democrats '66, and Christian Democrats then formed a new coalition with van Agt as premier. In this government, den Uyl reluctantly agreed to serve as vice premier and minister of social affairs and employment. Nonetheless, this cabinet was ill-fated from the start. It had barely assumed office before quarrels erupted over jobs programs and interpretation of the government's program. These differences were bridged temporarily by mediators, yet PvdA ministers resigned from the government eight months later.

Den Uyl's brief tenure at social affairs proved to be his last opportunity to hold ministerial office. New elections in 1982 produced a Christian Democratic—Liberal majority. A center-right cabinet under Ruud Lubbers, committed to slashing deficits and trimming the public sector, assumed office. Den Uyl continued to lead the PvdA, giving voice to Socialists' opposition to austerity measures and deployment of the cruise missile. In 1986, the PvdA gained five new seats, but this was insufficient to dislodge the Lubbers government. Following these elections, den Uyl resigned the party leadership, designating Wim Kok, the former chairman of the Federation of Dutch Trade Unions (FNV), as his successor. Den Uyl remained in parliament until his death, in December 1987, from an inoperable brain tumor.

Joop den Uyl was a major presence in Dutch politics during both the twenty years he led the PvdA and in his earlier career. His importance stems from an unusual combination of energy, political skill and intellectual ability. Den Uyl was an indefatigable reader who, no matter how busy he was, always managed to keep up with the latest developments. However, den Uyl was not interested in ideas for their own abstract sake, but rather for the ways in which they could be applied in politics. For den Uyl, that meant using ideas in the quest toward a constant goal—a fairer, more equal, less class-divided, more democratic society.

Den Uyl was not only an intellectual, but also an accomplished administrator and political leader. His success stemmed from his grasp of issues, including both details and the large picture, and from an ability to energize, inspire and capture the loyalty of both the smaller circles immediately around him as well as larger (but admittedly partisan) crowds. Problems were invariably solved by gathering information, marshaling arguments and then arguing them through until agreement could be reached, or, failing that, opponents would become exhausted and differences thereby minimized. During den Uyl's premiership, cabinet meetings often began late and lasted well into the night, ignoring the needs of others for sleep.

Del Uyl's ability to listen and persuade helped to maintain the cohesion of his cabinet and to keep his party together. However, den Uyl's ability to persuade was not uniformly successful. Although he could assert himself when he chose to, den Uyl was not fully in control of his party. Nor was he able to develop or maintain a good working relationship with Andreas van Agt, his minister of justice and vice premier. Den Uyl's relationship with van Agt not only brought his cabinet to an end, but rendered further cooperation with the Christian Democrats problematic.

Ultimately, den Uyl's skills were used more as leader of the opposition than in government. Den Uyl's long tenure in opposition reflected both his incomplete control of the party and the inherent contradictions of a strategy which assumed progressive majorities when these did not exist. The accommodation which den Uyl reached with New Left opened the PvdA to dissident elements anxious to control their own leaders and increase the PvdA's leverage vis-à-vis the confessional bloc. PvdA activists constantly forced new versions of the polarization strategy on den Uyl. The presumption was that such strategies would divide the confessionals, force voters to choose between the two blocs, and produce a progressive majority. However, PvdA electoral strength never exceeded 33.8 percent of the vote. Despite its success in 1972, the polarization strategy often tied leaders' hands, antagonized rivals (especially the Christian Democrats) with whom the PvdA would eventually have to cooperate if they were to govern and reduced PvdA influence over government policy. Den Uyl, of course, might have used his authority to resist or reverse such strategy but, at least in public, preferred not to do so.

Nonetheless, Joop den Uyl was both an effective premier and leader of the opposition. The cabinet which he led coped competently with numerous crises, including the OPEC oil boycott, revelations about involvement of Prince Bernhard with the Lockheed Corporation, and hostage-taking incidents by disgruntled South Moluccans. Yet his cabinet's redistributive agenda was a constant source of controversy. Though disappointed that more was not achieved, the PvdA and its allies lauded the cabinet, while business bitterly opposed it, claiming that the government's policies discouraged investment.

On balance, the den Uyl cabinet was able to do little more than take small steps toward his ultimate goals. This was of little surprise to den Uyl, who realized that the period of sustained economic growth—which would have made it easier to devote more resources to reducing inequalities—had ended. In den Uyl's view, though, the economic dislocations of the 1970s did not mean abandoning the struggle. To the contrary, more public steering and guidance of the economy was needed. This was precisely what he attempted to do as premier.

Whether these were optimal measures for the time is a matter of dispute. In light of record levels of unemployment in the early 1980s, more attention to questions of production might have been in order in the mid–1970s. However, the den Uyl cabinet was no more remiss than its immediate successor in failing to perceive the trend toward deindustrialization in the 1970s. How a den Uyl cabinet might have coped with rising unemployment in the 1980s is not clear. After 1982, center-right governments committed to austerity and market-led recovery reversed some of the small steps taken by the den Uyl cabinet, such as the narrowing of income differentials.

In all, politics for den Uyl was a struggle to use the narrow margins of parliamentary democracy to reduce inequalities. His most durable legacy is not any specific policy or piece of legislation, but rather the way in which he used knowledge and ideas in order to advance toward his goal.

BIBLIOGRAPHY

Work by den Uyl:

Inzicht en uitzicht: Opstellen over economie en politiek. Amsterdam: Bert Bakker, 1988.

Other Work:

Kwant, Aat de, Evert Mathies. *Twee dingen: Joop den Uyl geportretteerd door tijdgenoten.* Utrecht: Het Spectrum, 1981.

STEVEN B. WOLINETZ

WILLEM DREES (1886–1988) was the most prominent political figure in the postwar Netherlands. Indeed, his active political career spanned most of the 20th-century, and he reached the heights of political power at a time when the country underwent some of the most profound changes the century was to offer. Serving in every cabinet from 1945 to 1958, often as prime minister, Drees was in the thick of it during the loss of the colonial empire, the rebuilding of the war-ravaged economy and the creation of the European Economic Community.

Curiously, Drees is not remembered as a major player in many of these events. Though he spent most of the 1950s as prime minister, or sharing the office with a coalition partner, he had little interest in or knowledge of foreign affairs. As a politician more focused on domestic policy issues, he is most remembered for two things. One is serving as leader of the Labor Party when it got its first chance as a governing party. The other is his legacy as a founding figure in the development of the Dutch welfare state, where his role was equivalent to the one played by Bismarck, Beveridge or Roosevelt in the development of other Western welfare states.

For a man who was a modest figure in world politics, it is perhaps appropriate that Drees's political career began somewhat accidentally. Following his graduation from a business trade school, where he specialized in stenography, he took a job as a bank teller. Three years later, in 1906, he left this post to establish a freelance stenography agency, and it was to his good fortune that one of his first commissions was with the lower house of the Dutch parliament (Tweede Kamer). This position provided him with an introduction to parliamentary life and sparked his particular interest in the arguments of the Social Democratic Labor Party (SDAP). He joined the party and by 1910 had become chairman of the SDAP in The Hague. By the time World War II broke out, he had risen to national prominence as leader of the party's parliamentary faction.

After German forces conquered the Netherlands in 1940, many political figures fled to London, where they set up an exile government. Drees, however, was foiled in his attempt to escape and therefore spent the duration of the war on the continent, where he suffered for his continued political activism. After the government-in-exile in London declared war on Germany, Dutch forces arrested Germans residing in Indonesia, then a Dutch colony. In reprisal, German occupation forces conducted a roundup of prominent political leaders, including Drees, who were sent to prison. Although socialists and communists were special targets of the Gestapo forces, these prisoners spanned the entire political spectrum.

Drees was released early due to poor health. His liberty, however, was not to mean rest and recuperation. He immediately became involved in the antifascist movement and served as coordinator for a number of underground activities. This forced him to live in hiding throughout the war while he served as an important liaison between the government-in-exile and the Resistance. Moreover, he continued to associate with other Resistance figures who shared a desire to rewrite the terms of political discourse once the country was liberated.

It was his wartime experience that made Drees a logical choice to set a new course for postwar Dutch politics. Before the war, Dutch socialists had been relegated to perpetual opposition. The country had been dominated by a shaky coalition between Catholic and Protestant political parties, which occasionally cooperated with the Liberal Party but vowed never to share office with the socialists. This polarization produced political gridlock, a situation that was partly responsible for the country's weak response to German aggression. The ironic benefit of the war was that it created a watershed for change in this situation by fostering a great deal of contact between leaders from various political groupings. Both in prison and in the Resistance, Drees discovered other prominent Dutch politicians who also desired to avoid the stalemate that had characterized Dutch politics in the interbellum.

Drees's wartime activities explain much about his postwar political concerns. He was a central figure in shaping the notion among the political elite that the prewar state of divisiveness needed to give way to a new spirit of cooperation. His dominating personality enhanced his ability to bridge the traditional distance between parties. It was this cooperative spirit and ability to gain the respect of even his political rivals that made him a logical choice for co–prime minister (along with the Liberal Party leader, W. Schermerhorn) in forming the first postwar government.

Drees was a key figure in helping to construct a political system in the Netherlands that the American political scientist Arend Lijphart would later call a ''consociational democracy.'' Unlike interbellum politics, where divisions between ideologically opposed social groups (Catholics, Protestants, socialists and Liberals) led to divisiveness and gridlock, Drees and others of like mind sought to established channels of elite cooperation across the ideological ''pillars.'' This elite consultation was based on two important preconditions: that pillar elites were willing to negotiate and reach consensus, and that a generally passive public refrained from challenging these elite decisions. The latter precondition, a passive public, was already a given in the Netherlands. Drees helped nurture along the first precondition, the elite consensus that made the system work.

It was this transformation in the nature of Dutch politics that made possible the Labor Party's participation in postwar government. No longer ostracized from the political establishment, the Dutch Labor Party was accorded a legitimate status by the major parties, although they did so grudgingly. This ''breakthrough,'' as it is known in Labor Party circles, allowed the party to become a major player. From the end of the war until 1958, all six governing coalitions were to include Labor. Drees held office in all six, and in the four coalitions where Labor was the senior governing partner, he served as prime minister.

Though it was hoped that the socialist breakthrough would inaugurate a new era of stability in Dutch politics, the 1950s was, in fact, a rocky period. Part of the reason was that the spirit of elite accord had not been adopted by the entire political elite. Many political leaders, who had neither fled to London during the war, nor suffered persecution at the hands of the Nazis, still exhibited a penchant for the ideological apartheid of the interbellum. Within the Catholic Party, for example, the tension between these two persuasions was so pronounced as to cause periodic crises within the party. Cabinet discussions tended to reflect this discord, since Labor's main coalition partner throughout this period was the Catholic Party. Known as Red-Roman coalitions, these uneasy pacts between the Catholic and Labor parties followed a series of policy lines that totally defy characterization on a left-right ideological scale.

Foreign policy during this period is one example. In 1948, the country became embroiled in a conflict in Indonesia, then a Dutch colony. Fighting was started by guerrilla forces seeking liberation. Dutch forces were then dispatched twice, in 1947 and again in 1948, in a vain attempt to retain control of the islands. Though the Labor Party, and especially Drees, were sympathetic to self-determination, there were great reservations about the type of country the Indonesian resistance was proposing. Drees's fear—a fear borne out by history—was that a single state dominated by the Javanese would rule at the expense of other ethnic groups on the islands. Drees echoed his party's concern by advocating a federal system for a free Indonesia, or even dividing the territory into four separate states. It was the Javanese rejection of these suggestions that permitted Drees to justify efforts to suppress the rebellion. The conflict, and the way it was handled by the Dutch government, was criticized by Britain, the United States and the United Nations. Moreover, Drees's role in the conflict gave him the dubious honor of being one of the few socialist prime ministers to fight a colonial war.

Governments often follow a foreign policy designed to promote a domestic political agenda. Indeed, for Drees's Labor Party, support of the conflict with Indonesia had much to do with maintaining the party's position in the government. There was a real fear that the Catholic Party, which favored a hard line against the rebellion, would withdraw and form a center-right government that would be more diligent in retaining colonial control of Indonesia. Drees concluded that since Labor could not change the outcome of the Indonesian conflict, the issue was not worth risking a collapse of the government.

If his pragmatic attitude in matters of foreign policy sounds unlike a socialist, it may have been because Drees was less dogmatic in the way he viewed the ideals of socialism. At the end of World War I, when the Netherlands was gripped by the same fear of socialist revolution that affected the entire continent, Drees worked to dissuade his fellow partisans from fomenting revolution in Holland. His conciliatory attitude in dealing with other parties stems from his rejection at an early age of the party's revolutionary emphasis.

Despite his rejection of revolutionary ideas, however, Drees was committed to reforming capitalism into a more socialist political economy. In a memo written during the war, he laid out his major ideas for social and economic reform. Central to this was social security, which he defined as full employment, job security and universal guarantee of a minimum standard of living. Realization of these as public goals, Drees believed, would require that the private sector give up some of its cherished autonomy. To this end, he advocated extensive nationalization of utilities, transportation and selected monopoly industries. Other industries, he argued, should hand themselves over to substantial government supervision. Taxes were to have a heavy redistributive component, falling hardest on income earned from nonproductive, speculative activities.

And though he focused on converting private capital to public uses, Drees was not a great advocate of labor rights. Indeed one of the remarkable characteristics of Drees's tenure in government, and the source of much criticism of him from the left, was the fact that in the 1950s the Netherlands became known as the country run by a social democrat who took a harsh stance against strikers. Though he rejected suggestions by Catholic Party ministers to ban strikes, he accused the unions of moral wrongheadedness for putting self-interested concerns ahead of the greater good of Dutch society, especially at a time when reconstruction required a concerted effort by all groups. Though he was a socialist, he was deeply imbued with the typically Dutch Calvinist principles of thrift and sobriety, and he felt that unions should exhibit the same modesty and restraint.

Indeed, Drees lived by the values he espoused. He spent virtually his entire adult life in the same small home in a modest neighborhood in The Hague. He owned no automobile and rarely traveled. His appearance was not ostentatious, but stoic. Even on occasional excursions to the beach he dressed in suits and ties that were slightly out of fashion. Drees was, in his own words, a democrat before he was a socialist, and his conception of democratic governance left an imprint on the system. In Drees's political game, the rules required cooperation and willingness to reach consensus. Those who abided by the rules could play; those who relied on conflict and competition were ejected from the game.

Yet there should be rewards in society for those who held themselves to proper standards of conduct, Drees felt. This conviction compelled him to initiate numerous reforms in economic relations that would reward those responsible for prosperity. Two of the most significant reforms introduced in economic relations during the 1950s created the institutions of Dutch corporatism and provided labor some voice in setting the course for postwar economic development.

One of these, the Industrial Reorganization Act of 1950, made it mandatory for workers to belong to an industrial organization. As more than trade unions, these industrial organizations were bipartite associations representing labor and management interests. They were responsible primarily for administering occupational security programs, such as disability and pensions. By making participation in the associations mandatory, Drees was able to vastly expand the scope of the workforce covered by social security programs, guaranteeing a greater degree of uniformity in the benefits workers received. Prior to this law, such bipartite institutions existed, but they were spontaneous associations, usually resulting from collusion between confessional (Protestant or Catholic) unions and employer federations. These earlier voluntary associations often locked out socialist and nonunion workers, a situation that was rectified by the new system.

The other important change in industrial relations was the establishment of the Social Economic Council in 1952. Known by its Dutch acronym, SER, this council is a tripartite association of management, labor and the state that is responsible for advising the government on all aspects of economic and social policy. Although the council's advisory status does not make its advice binding on the government, throughout the 1950s and 1960s both government and parliament largely refrained from passing laws that differed from the SER's position.

Reform in industrial relations was a huge success for the Labor Party, but Drees's initiatives did not end there. Indeed, social policy was his real passion, and he was instrumental in laying the groundwork for what would later become a drastic expansion in the Dutch welfare state. While minister of social affairs, a post he held from 1946 to 1948, he initiated two programs dramatically extending social welfare benefits. One of these focused on expanding the existing worker insurance programs into universal entitlement, thereby making all Dutch citizens eligible for public support. The other involved transforming the old charity-based system of poor relief into a state-administered system of public assistance. Though conflict with Catholic Party members of the government prevented Drees from making real progress on the second of these issues, he was quite successful in establishing universal entitlements for social insurance.

Drees's big legislative success took the form of an Emergency Retirement Pension Act. Passed with lightning speed in 1947, the act granted all Dutch citizens over the age of sixty-five a right to a public pension. The emergency provision was only a temporary measure, however, and was not formalized until 1958. In addition, controversy over the universal entitlement principle prevented its introduction into other social insurance programs until the 1960s. Nonetheless, the initiatives taken by Drees opened a debate that eventually led to a dramatic expansion of the Dutch welfare state along the principles laid out in his Emergency Act.

Passage of the Emergency Act was met with such huge popular support that it made Drees into a national hero. In a society where two decades of economic depression and war were still fresh memories, the new entitlement provided assurance that those who suffered in the past would not continue to do so. But though he was a staunch advocate of universal entitlement, Drees did not believe it was the state's place to provide for the fulfillment of individual wants. The old age pension was a minimum subsistence allotment, intended to save the elderly from situations of privation. Drees still believed that those who desired comfortable retirements needed to make provisions on their own.

Moreover, there were more personal reasons for Drees's passionate commitment to social reform. Like many of the major figures in the development of the Dutch welfare state, Drees's concerns with expanding social welfare provisions were largely informed by the experiences of his youth. When he was only five years old, his father died of tuberculosis, leaving behind a wife and three children, but no means to provide for them. The Twentsche Bank, where the elder Drees had worked as a teller, provided a pension to the widow Drees on the condition that she pledge her son's future services to the bank, as was then the custom. Drees fulfilled this obligation, working for three years with the bank after graduation. This period of servitude delayed his own career goals, all because the enterprise where his father had labored during his life continued to dictate family decisions after the man's death. This experience stirred in Drees the desire to ensure that no one should suffer from circumstances not of his or her own making.

Regardless of the real motive for his conviction to social reform, Drees himself lived to appreciate the benefits of the retirement system he had established. In 1958, at the age of seventy-two, he retired. But he was to live another thirty years before his death in 1988. He claimed his decision to retire from politics was due to his age. As he put it, if seventy years was the proper age for the retirement of university professors, it should also be appropriate for politicians.

But for a man still in good health and very influential politically, perhaps

Drees's real impetus for retiring was a disdain for the prospect of returning to polarizing partisan politics. Disintegration of the governing coalition in 1958 returned Labor to the opposition benches. One tradition of Dutch politics is that the cabinet be above partisanship. Though partisan affiliation influences cabinet appointments, once in office ministers are not directly responsible to their party. After thirteen years of being above the fray, Drees did not want to return to it. In the 1960s he remained active as an adviser to the Labor Party, but quickly became disenchanted as the party disintegrated into a gaggle of bickering factions, some of which split off to form new parties. By the 1970s, Drees came to stand out as a figure who represented an older, outmoded class of politician.

BIBLIOGRAPHY

Works by Drees:

Zestig Jaar Levenservaring. Amsterdam: Arbeiderspers, 1962.

Marx en het democratisch socialisme. Amsterdam: Arbeiderspers, 1979.

Other Works:

Cox, Robert H. *Between Bismarck and Beveridge: The Development of the Dutch Welfare State*. Pittsburgh: University of Pittsburgh Press, 1993.

Galen, John Jansen van, and Herman Vuisje. *100 jaar Drees: Wethouder van Nederland*. Alphen aan den Rijn: Sijthoff, 1988.

Messer, Eduard. *Dr. Willem Drees*. Amsterdam: Broekman and De Meris, 1961.

Wijnen, H. A. van. *Willem Drees: Democrat*. Weesp: van Holkema and Warendorf, 1984.

ROBERT H. COX

E

LUDWIG ERHARD (1897–1977) is known chiefly for his major contribution in placing the postwar West German economy on a stable path of development according to free market principles. As longtime finance minister under Adenauer, he is believed by many to have been the principal architect of the West German economic miracle.

In Germany, Erhard was widely regarded as having found the solution to the question of how to reconstruct a devastated postwar economy, and as one who, in spite of many crises and the seeming successes of socialism in neighboring countries, held firmly to his belief in free enterprise. When the ultimate vindication of his beliefs came—with the fall of the Berlin Wall and the demise of Eastern Bloc socialism and Marxist materialism—he had died; by then, everyone, it seemed, was moving toward a free market economy, or at least paying lip service to it.

The son of a small German middle-class family, Erhard began with a somewhat uninspiring career as an economist. As an economist, however, he was deeply influenced by his teacher, Oppenheimer, in Frankfurt, and Oppenheimer's ideas in the 1920s of the "mobility of land," meaning its deregulation, as an instrument to overcome the injustices of property distribution. Later on, Erhard became the political spokesman of what was known as the "neoliberal school of economics," comprising such figures as Hayek, Mises, Rüstow, Röpke, Böhm, Eucken and others.

During the Nazi era, Erhard went intellectually underground. He spent 1944, for example, at work on his position paper outlining how to reconstruct the German economy after the war. This treatise became the major document for building the new *Wirtschaftsordnung*. Amazing stories exist from this period about how Erhard carried his manuscript around Berlin in a paper bag impervious to the threats on his life after the unsuccessful attempt of military officers to assassinate Hitler on July 20, 1944.

Initially, in the aftermath of the war, Erhard found it difficult to convince officers of the American army and the occupation authorities in Munich and

Frankfurt of the importance of establishing the basis for a new economy. In addition, he had to compete with the Social Democratic Party (SPD) and its program, replete with strong socialist ideas as put forth at the party convention in Hannover in 1946.

During this whole period, Adam Smith's free market philosophy acquired an almost religious quality for Erhard, although with some important corrective elements. As Alexander Rüstow has pointed out, the imposition of the free market belief system on society in the first half of the 19th century (especially in the form of ''Manchester liberalism''), with its hierarchical and feudal structures, literally created the ''proletariat.'' In turn, free market liberalism thereby became the basis of societal conflict for over a hundred years subsequently.

A ''neo-liberal'' movement at the end of the 1920s and through the Great Depression years tried to avoid the mistakes of so-called pagan liberalism. The core of the *Ordnungspolitiks* was still the market as the basic operating instrument of the economy. But in addition to the market, a relatively strong government was required to regulate the irregular conditions of a market economy, especially in regard to breaking up monopolies. To the neo-liberals, it also seemed necessary to lessen the wide gulf between rich and poor in society. In Germany, the defeat in World War I contributed a great deal to this condition.

An independent central bank to regulate monetary policy also assumed great importance to the postwar German neo-liberals, who aimed to place monetary policy under the control of nonpartisan experts. (''Get the hands of the politicians off the money,'' said one of them at the close of the war.) The experience of both Weimar and Nazi monetary policy—both subject to overtly political decision making and the first, in particular, leading to disastrous inflationary results—contributed to postwar neo-liberal thinking in Germany.

After World War II, these neo-liberal ideas spread extensively throughout Germany. People were—after the years of the *Zwangswirtschaft*—quite receptive to the basic notions of neo-liberalism. For some, Hayek and Mises were the theoretical ''trumpets'' of liberal thought. Schumpeter had paved the way for the incorporation of the market idea into the concept of ''state.'' Rüstow had founded his cultural sociology on the idea of neo-liberalism. Böhm and Röpke incorporated the notion into their work on economic law and economic theory. Eucken and his school produced many scholars who diffused the idea widely. But it was Ludwig Erhard who was the political spokesman of this trend. It was he who understood how to match economic theory to the political desires of the people.

Immediately after the war, there were only a few scholars left at German universities who worked on developing socialist ideas. In the business world, ''managers'' (who acquired this title from Burnham's book *The Managerial Revolution*) were easily inclined to practice free market economics. The West German central bank also acted in accordance with this doctrine to create stable money, often in opposition to the government's policy. The big landowners (the ''Junkers'') of East Germany's Prussia were either gone or expropriated by

Russia, so the idea of deregulating the market for land was put into practice in the West.

All these factors certainly created a very favorable situation for neo-liberalism. However, it took many years for Ludwig Erhard and his staff to carry out through government policy the full implementation of their understanding of neo-liberalism. Moreoever, they had to do so in the face of a number of ups and downs in international politics, especially against the backdrop of the Cold War. In retrospect, only Erhard's decision in 1949 to yield to the farmers, creating a highly protected agricultural market, proved subsequently to be a far-reaching mistake.

Over all these years, Ludwig Erhard held to the belief that socialist economies of the Eastern Bloc would be finally doomed because no single man or planning staff could master the information necessary to control economic processes. For Erhard, this was the basic error of socialist economics.

Erhard's speeches are full of remarks indicating his belief that central decision making, in the end, always redounds to the detriment of consumers and finally to the expense of the economy as such. These speeches earned him the image of a ''socialist hater,'' which in fact he was not. But he was convinced that the socialists were wrong. The ideological fight between him and the socialists was characterized by strong stubbornness on his side.

On the other hand, Erhard did not appreciate, and even disregarded, some elements which were to prove very decisive for the success of a market economy. One of these was so-called tariff autonomy, according to which business associations and trade unions would negotiate the terms and conditions of work without interference from government authorities. Adenauer and some trade union leaders put into place such a system of industrial relations in the early 1950s. (Some scholars have called this system ''neo-corporatism,'' but in doing so they risk confusing Latin American experiences with the development of a multidimensional public/private governmental structure.)

Erhard also underestimated traditional German economic development policy, which—since the middle of the 19th century—had created a highly developed social and economic infrastructure, educated a strong, skilled labor force and was based on a sophisticated law of inheritance. This approach provided, at least in the western part of the former Germany, a higher flexibility of wealth and property than was usually the case in other countries like Great Britain, France or Italy. For example, the region in Germany with the highest productivity, namely the south, enjoys few natural resources with the exception of salt, but possesses a sophisticated law of inheritance, an educational system of the highest standards and a highly developed infrastructure.

The argument could be made that without such traditions managers could hardly make decisions to invest in economic enterprises which for a long time would be without profit. In spite of its devastating results, the war and the defeat of 1945 had not destroyed this basic social and economic infrastructure. One celebrated professor of economics said early in 1948, as German industry was being dismantled by the occupying forces, ''Emotionally I can understand the protests [by Germans], but all the new industrial structure of Germany needs is 'good' money and confidence.'' By 1948–1949, both good money and confidence were in place. (Many years later a British ambassador, giving a speech at a German university, ''congratulated'' the audience for having lost the war, thereby being able to build a ''modern'' economy.)

Erhard's blind spots are especially important in view of the societal problems in East Germany and Eastern Europe. It is now quite clear that, without such deep-seated traditional economic and social development, the likelihood of synergy is very small indeed, and the liberal idea alone, based on the free market, is not enough for Poland, Rumania, Bulgaria and other former communist regimes.

Finally, and not the least of his quarrels with Chancellor Adenauer, Ludwig Erhard also overlooked the importance of governmental stability for economic reconstruction, and it was Adenauer who had created this stability. A politician with his roots in 19th-century thinking, Konrad Adenauer was very often the master of the day. Nonetheless, Erhard proved to be the man with the far wider, longer-term vision. It was not an economy alone he had in mind; it was a new society.

Erhard replaced Adenauer as chancellor in 1963 when the latter resigned under the terms of an earlier coalition agreement with the Free Democrats. By summer 1965, Ludwig Erhard was at the very peak of his political popularity. When he brought his national election campaign to northern Germany, literally hundreds of thousands of people would wait in the streets to cheer him. ''Everybody knows who I am,'' he would begin his campaign speeches, referring to himself as a known and trusted quantity. A charismatic leader, he was universally acknowledged as the symbol of West Germany's economic success. By the 1960s, many years of bitter disputes with Konrad Adenauer over the Chancellery had been forgotten, and the electoral situation of his opponent, the Social Democrat Willy Brandt, seemed quite hopeless. He led the CDU to a great electoral victory.

Somewhat paradoxically, Erhard often claimed that he was not a ''politician.'' For instance, in 1965 after the CDU victory, he said on the occasion of a party in his honor that he would rather escape to his Bavarian home than participate in the processes of coalition formation. He despised the bargaining inherent in such processes (as well as personally disliking the FDP's negotiators; the latter claimed that they had achieved many more concessions than they had ever dreamed of!).

Certainly, such traits were a part of his very character. After he had become chancellor, for example, he used to walk the streets shopping and talking with people—much to the dismay of his security police. Naturally, he enjoyed his personal popularity as much as he enjoyed a cigar or a glass of whiskey. He was a ''citizen'' as he understood it.

However, as chancellor he eventually fell victim to his own political misjudgments, illustrating that perhaps he was not, as indeed he claimed, a politician. Perhaps most important of these misjudgments, he grossly overestimated the support of his own party. This miscalculation was one of the chief reasons for his downfall one year after his greatest electoral success. (The other reason was a change of allegiance on the part of the Free Democrats, his coalition partners). Yet in spite of the withdrawal of the FDP from his government, he could have stayed on as chancellor within the terms of German constitutional law. But the night before he resigned, he said that he would not carry out this power play "behind the backs of the people." Because of the lack of support within his party (and because of some "king's murderers" within the party, as well), Erhard became the first "charismatic loser" in German postwar politics. (The other politician during this period who could be characterized as a charismatic loser is Helmut Schmidt, who in a crucial period was also left without support by his SDP party. In both cases, the chancellor did not hold the chairmanship of his party. During Erhard's tenure, Adenaur still chaired the CDU; during Schmidt's tenure, Willy Brandt still chaired the SPD.)

Erhard committed another mistake with his policy of *formierte Gesellschaft*. Some of his advisers—strongly influenced by the writings of Carl Schmitt, a very conservative German *Staatslehrer* and teacher of famous scholars—had convinced Erhard that an end should be put to "interest struggles" by creating a highly structured, hierarchical society. This was, of course, the revival of a kind of *Standestaat* and detrimental to the modernization that neo-liberalism was aiming for. Erhard favored the idea for different reasons than his advisers: He wanted to reduce conflict in society, an old German bourgeois notion.

Setting out such a policy put Erhard into opposition not only against the intellectuals, but also against those persons who had hoped that he would go on with a strong policy of modernization. Erhard lost some of his popularity because he contradicted the better part of himself: His vision for a new society was the new hope, whereas the *formierte Gesellschaft* was an old idea.

Another arena of politics which caused him considerable headache was foreign policy. First, Adenauer never ceased to interfere in this domain, even after leaving the chancellorship, believing that only he was qualified to conduct foreign policy, not Erhard. For instance, in 1964 when Charles de Gaulle came to West Germany for a state visit, it was Adenauer whom he first saw. Inspired by his personal relationship with Adenauer, de Gaulle offered to conduct negotiations with the Soviet Union on Germany's behalf, provided Erhard agreed to cover some of the cost of the *force de frappe*, France's nuclear strike force. Erhard nearly lost his temper at the insult of this offer, and never was the Franco-German relationship at a lower ebb than after this incident. In addition, Erhard favored an open European market outside of the European Community, which he thought would be ruled by a bureaucracy from Brussels.

Erhard's second major area of difficulty in foreign policy was his unstinting faith in his personal friend, Lyndon Johnson, a faith he exhibited without hesitation, whatever the latter did or did not do, including his Vietnam policy. The most celebrated instance in this respect was Erhard's visit to the United States shortly after the 1965 election. He seemed highly impressed by the show Johnson put on for him, playing with Johnson's grandchildren on his knees and enjoying the Texas barbecue. But the visit was a disaster, including as it did promoting business interests in deals that later turned out to be negotiated by non-German businessmen.

After that visit, criticism became rather harsh inside Germany. Soon voices arose in his own party arguing for the use of the "constructive vote of no confidence" against Erhard as a result of such "stupidity." Clearly, Erhard's strength was in his vision of a liberal society for the future; his grave weakness lay in conducting the daily business of politics. There were many instances which demonstrated this weakness, and it made Erhard very dependent on his ministers and advisers. As long as these were loyal, like Gerhard Schröder, his foreign minister after 1963, almost nothing went wrong. When, however, disloyalty developed, as in the case of Franz Josef Strauss, his government faced great difficulties.

The whole year of 1966, against the backdrop of a slight recession, was characterized by constant threats to Erhard's power. As early as March and April 1966, his government's support was eroding in both parliament and in public opinion. After Erhard lost his temper during an election rally in the Ruhr district during the summer of that year—the famous *pinscher* speech in Gelsenkirchen—many blamed him directly for the CDU's election defeat in North Rhine–Westphalia, even though there were other causes for the loss as well. This period marked the beginning of Erhard's end as chancellor. His government was succeeded by the Grand Coalition from 1966 to 1969, with the CDU's Kurt Kiesinger serving as chancellor and the SDP's Willy Brandt serving as vice-chancellor and minister of foreign affairs.

Many of his former enemies attended Erhard's funeral many years later in Bavaria, where he was buried. Many of these were of a far different political type than Erhard, street tough in politics, so to speak. Some, but not all of them, were finally ashamed of their former intrigues against him. But there were only a few at his funeral who fully appreciated Erhard's role in firmly establishing the notion of a market economy in Europe, a notion that would subsequently wash all over the continent and other parts of the world. It was the burial of a man whose economic policies had illuminated the next century, perhaps finally defeating "dialectic and historical materialism."

BIBLIOGRAPHY

Work by Erhard:

Kriegsfinanzierung und Schuldenkonsolidierung. Berlin: Propyläen, 1944.

Other Works:

Hildebrand, Klaus. *Von Erhard zur Grossen Koalition, 1963–69*. Stuttgart: Deutsche-Verlagsanstalt, 1984.

Ludwig-Erhard-Stiftung. *Ludwig Erhard und seine Politik*. Stuttgart: G. Fischer, 1985.

RUDOLF WILDENMANN

TAGE ERLANDER (1901–1985) was prime minister of Sweden without interruption for twenty-three years from 1946 until 1969, a record for parliamentary democracies. Erlander's tenure in office coincided with the maturation of what has been called the "Swedish model": an extensive tax-financed welfare system, peaceful labor-management relations, a brand of politics marked by consensus and the ability to anticipate future needs and, finally, an ambition to pursue a foreign policy of nonalignment leading to neutrality in case of war.

The selection of forty-five-year-old Tage Erlander in October 1946 as leader of the Social Democratic Party—the king designating him shortly thereafter prime minister—came as a total surprise to Sweden. Four days earlier, the country had been shocked by the sudden death of Per Albin Hansson, prime minister since 1932. In earlier speculations about possible successors to Hansson, Erlander's name had never been mentioned. That he now unexpectedly—and after a few days of hectic discussions—emerged as the choice of the majority of the Social Democratic caucus in parliament was due to many circumstances. He belonged to a new, younger generation of politicians than the deceased prime minister, and during his two years as a member of the Social Democratic cabinet he had dealt with both social and education policy, two key issue areas for a Social Democratic Party determined to continue transforming Swedish society. He was also considered to be efficient and hardworking, yet also a man of vision. Finally, he was seen as a personable man with the ability to establish contact and cooperate with others.

Tage Erlander had grown up in an idyllic part of Värmland, close to the Norwegian border. His father was an elementary school teacher and cantor and his paternal grandfather, Erland Andersson, had been a smith at a nearby ironworks who, despite a hard life, had nonetheless succeeded in helping his son enter the normal school of the province capital. Tage Erlander's mother was a farmer's daughter. This boyhood environment was in many ways a classic one for a Swedish politician: ambitious, lower-middle-class, temperate, a nonconformist religion, liberal, and firsthand experience with labor.

At the age of nineteen Erlander enrolled at the University of Lund. He began his studies in natural sciences but shifted after a while to social sciences; he soon got engaged in various student activities and obtained his first regular job in the editorial offices of a major Swedish encyclopedia—more than a decade after his matriculation at the university. There was something of the perpetual student about Tage Erlander.

He did not apply for membership in the Swedish Social Democratic Party until 1928. Prior to that time he had read socialist works, had been shocked by the graphic picture of class struggle presented when striking agricultural workers on the rich plains of Skåne were thrown out of their homes and had established contacts with trade unionists and young Social Democrats outside his own academic environment. Erlander was elected a member of the Lund City Council in 1930 and a member of the Riksdag in 1932. In the late 1930s he moved from

Lund to Stockholm, being appointed undersecretary in the Ministry of Social Affairs; in the fall of 1944 he was appointed minister without portfolio and in the summer of 1945 education minister.

Erlander's foremost mentor in the Social Democratic movement was Gustav Möller, minister of social affairs. Möller was regarded, besides the prime minister Per Albin Hansson, as the main creator of the Swedish welfare state that began to take form during the years before World War II. The irony and tragedy was that Möller in 1946 regarded himself as the natural successor to the deceased Per Albin Hansson, letting his name be presented as an alternative to that of the twenty-years-younger Tage Erlander. The older man lost by a fairly narrow margin. For Tage Erlander, this contest against a friend and benefactor added to the unhappiness and uncertainty that he felt after his sudden and unexpected elevation to the premiership of Sweden.

Erlander's situation in the fall of 1946 resembled that of Harry S Truman in the spring of 1945. Both had suddenly been thrown into offices previously held by men looked upon as father figures of their respective countries; both lacked, to begin with, the breadth, stature and authority of their predecessors; both were in some quarters looked upon with clear disdain, the Swede being regarded as an old student politician of limited academic success and the American as a failed businessman and a product of a corrupt political machine. Furthermore, Tage Erlander also shared Truman's fate of being bitterly attacked and criticized during his first years in office. He replied with an intensive campaign of information and activity leading up to the first general elections he had to face as prime minister, those to the Second Chamber of the Riksdag in September 1948. The Social Democrats, generally expected to lose, retained their hold on the Chamber as Harry Truman, likewise expected to lose two months later, regained the presidency. Erlander, like Truman, survived a baptism of fire.

Erlander felt throughout his twenty-three years in power that it was important to combine the dual functions of party leader and prime minister, thereby minimizing the risk of tensions developing between the cabinet and the party and between the government chancery and party headquarters. A pattern stands out in the way he balanced and combined these two central roles.

To Erlander, as well as to most other Social Democrats, the party as such was in a sense superior to its Riksdag caucus and the cabinet. The tasks of the party leader were multiple: to keep the party from committing itself to positions that the cabinet found difficult to accept, to be an explainer of cabinet decisions, to be a listener and take the party's pulse, to be a preacher and activist. Erlander was intensely loyal to his party at the same time as he was intellectually prone to systematically consider the pros and cons of any issue.

Two concerns were uppermost in Erlander's mind as a party leader. First, the party had to be kept together: A united Social Democratic party was seen as a precondition for electoral success, as well as for the party's continued ability to serve as an agent of reform in society and to enable the government to rule effectively. Erlander succeeded in this undertaking. The party did not split into factions under his charge; the potentially explosive issue of the late 1950s over whether or not the Swedish military force should be armed with nuclear weapons was neutralized by a series of postponements. The unity between the party and the trade union movement was also preserved.

The second central concern of Tage Erlander as party leader was winning elections. There were no fewer than eleven election campaigns, including 1948, during his years as party leader. His own activities during the week preceding election day in September were largely the same from one campaign to another. Among other things he made a habit of driving around some part of the country for a week in August before schools were back in session, with his wife Aina, a schoolteacher, serving as his chauffeur.

In his combination of compassion, humor, banter and seriousness, Erlander was an effective campaigner. A balance was often struck between painting a vision of how the future would be better if the Social Democrats were to remain in power and reminding voters of everything the party had achieved in the past. Most of these election campaigns, but not all, were won. While gauging the effects of his personal activities on these results is of course difficult, the remarkable victory of his very last election campaign, in the fall of 1968 when the Social Democrats scored more than 50 percent of the vote, is often attributed to Erlander personally.

Tage Erlander's opponents in Swedish politics criticized him from time to time for being too much of a party tactician and for devoting too much of his time to party affairs. Erlander, naturally enough, had a totally different perspective. To him a successful Social Democratic Party would lead to a successful Sweden, since the well-being of the one implied the well-being of the other. A party the size of the Social Democrats must necessarily feel a special responsibility for the nation and it could not involve itself, as could the smaller parties, in shortsighted tactical maneuvers only for its own benefit. Moreover, the Social Democratic Party was made up of the less well-to-do and thus had to be especially concerned with the well-being of the nation, for it is the less well-to-do who suffer most when times are bad. Finally, in a Sweden characterized by a strong business community, in Erlander's view a suitable balance of power was obtained only when a strong labor movement dominated the government.

Despite the attention given to his duties as party leader, most of Erlander's time was taken up by being prime minister. Early on, he developed an often reaffirmed parliamentary doctrine. A government in a parliamentary democracy should be "strong" and this desirable strength was only obtained when the government both had the support of a parliamentary majority and was held together by common values. Such a government was able to achieve many things: articulate and realize the desires of large segments of the population, resist special interests, make unpopular decisions, engage in long-range planning and avoid having to compromise unduly.

Naturally Erlander's philosophy was influenced by the fact that in the Swedish multiparty context the Social Democrats had the best chances of creating the conditions necessary for this kind of government. Throughout the Erlander era, they held an absolute majority in the First Chamber of the Swedish parliament, although not in the Second Chamber (with the exception of a few years) even though they were very close to it. For most of Erlander's tenure the cabinet consisted exclusively of Social Democrats, except for six years from 1951 to 1957, when they governed in coalition with the Agrarian Party (whose name was changed to the Center Party in 1956).

On a daily basis, an air of aloofness characterized Erlander's leadership. He was well-informed on political issues, an early riser who read newspapers and memoranda extensively and who listened to radio news many times a day. He also met with many people. He steadfastly maintained, however, that a prime minister must to a certain extent remove himself from day-to-day administrative worries. He should not try to be an active coordinator of governmental affairs. Such direct involvement would subject him to endless machinations with others, thereby distracting his attention from other duties and necessitating the establishment of an extensive staff that would duplicate the whole ministerial structure. In fact, Erlander's own staff was almost nonexistent; in 1953 the twenty-six-year-old Olof Palme was appointed his personal secretary and remained such for a decade until being appointed minister without portfolio.

The cabinet members of Erlander governments were therefore left with a great deal of room in which to maneuver. The main coordinating work of day-to-day operations was carried out by the minister of finance and his subordinates, simply because they were charged with determining the size of the budget and raising the revenue necessary to implement the government's policy measures. This distribution of functions between Erlander and his minister of finance was once compared to that between the chairman of the board and the president of a large corporation.

Although Tage Erlander as head of the government remained somewhat aloof from the cabinet's everyday work, many tasks remained for him to fulfill. Foremost, of course, he chose the members of the cabinet; in selecting these he often consulted with others. Furthermore, despite his reluctance to involve himself deeply in day-to-day policy issues, he had to take the lead when issues in one way or other had become politically urgent. He also had to resolve conflicts occurring in his government due to clashes of personality or opinion. Erlander seems to have dealt with conflicts within the cabinet in the same way as he carried out his other functions in the government: to delay matters rather than force decisions, to talk things over further with those most closely involved, to use ambiguous language and perhaps a little humor to coax and compromise, rather than dictate.

As prime minister Erlander more than anyone was responsible for maintaining the necessary relations between the cabinet and the Riksdag. He served as chairman both of the Social Democratic caucus in the Riksdag and its steering committee; cohesion was thereby ensured between the cabinet and the caucus. He was an active defender of his government's policy in the plenary debates of the Riksdag, making as many as seventy statements in the Riksdag during a year. Usually, when defending and explaining the government's policies, Erlander was well-informed and genuinely supportive of actions taken. It did, however, also occur that he had to defend decisions which he had not been involved in shaping nor been informed about in advance. But his sense of loyalty to the cabinet necessitated his solidarity with other members of the cabinet in support of decisions made in the government's name.

The twenty-three years during which Tage Erlander served as leader of the Social Democrats and as prime minister was a period of dramatic change in Sweden. The country had emerged from the war years with its industrial capacity unscathed and with access to rich natural resources that were essential to the reconstruction of Europe. On average, the GNP increased at a rate of 2.5 per cent, with the greatest increases being achieved during what has been referred to as the "record-breaking years" of the early 1960s. Reforms were piled, one upon the other, in this wealthy and dynamic society. The influence of Tage Erlander on this incessant activity was both indirect and direct.

Indirectly he influenced policies by his shaping of public debate through innumerable talks and addresses, both before and after decisions were taken, giving inspiration to the often gray and rather plodding day-to-day work of politics.

Tage Erlander was, however, no great theoretician. In his youth he had read Marx but could hardly be regarded as a Marxist. He looked upon himself as a "socialist" but he was not willing—as his political opponents often charged—to equate his brand of socialism with nationalization. Yet, he could be considered an ideologue. His ideology consisted of a belief in a series of fundamental values and a readiness to utilize the public sector—the state and municipalities—to realize these values while holding capitalism in check. He also had a faith in the rationality of man and in a future that would be better than the past or the present. Further, Erlander was convinced that ideology continued to affect—and should affect—everyday politics; he did not subscribe to the fashionable 1950s thesis of the death of ideology. Politics must be something more than the simple administering of existing society. Ideology, on the other hand, should not, in its influence on daily politics, be allowed to be too specific and detailed. Some vagueness was advisable.

In one respect, Erlander as an ideologue was original. He promoted the idea of the "strong society" as closely connected to his idea of a "strong government." People were said to need more, rather than less, from the public sector as their standard of living rose. Demands of society therefore increase, rather than decrease. Erlander was indefatigable in reciting all the goals that were too much for an individual to achieve alone and that thus remained to the public sector: better schools and more scientific research, better health care and urban housing, better roads and more electricity, expanded and improved labor market policies and so on. Nor did he accept the view of his opponents that private business and private initiative in general were constrained by new public sector initatives. Quite the opposite, in his view, the expanding public sector provided business with the necessary organizational basis. Good roads, a mobile workforce, well-educated citizens, all benefited private enterprise. No limit should be set on the expansion of the public sector. This promotion of the ''strong society'' was clearly tied to Erlander's and the Social Democratic Party's belief in the state as a useful instrument in the hands of the citizenry.

Erlander, of course, also influenced the development of Swedish politics in a very direct way, despite his reluctance to be drawn into day-to-day decision making. Like most heads of government, he gave special attention to questions of foreign, defense and economic policy because of their inherent importance. In the area of foreign and defense policy his task was in large measure to help maintain unity among the political parties and, to a certain extent, also to maintain unity within his own party. He played a particularly active role in the negotiations concerning Scandinavian defense cooperation in 1948–1949. In the area of economic policy, where disagreement often occurred between government and opposition, he was involved, year after year, in often difficult parliamentary debates with the distinguished leader of the Liberal Party, Bertil Ohlin, a professor of economics and future Nobel laureate. The economic issues of the day were the classic ones of employment, wages, interest rates, taxes, inflation and the balance of payments. Early on, Erlander supported an ''active labor market policy,'' which among other things meant governmental support for retraining and relocation of the workforce.

Matters that had become burning political issues—regardless of what kind of issues they were—always demanded his attention. Many of these issues were ''affairs'' or scandals exploding for a short time in public but seeming rather trifling or meaningless in hindsight. Others were of a far more central kind. The best-known of them was the issue of supplementary pensions, which led both to a referendum in the fall of 1957 and a dissolution of the Second Chamber the following spring. Erlander and the Social Democrats supported a supplementary pension system that was obligatory, that is, all citizens were guaranteed by the state a pension in relation to the income they had previously earned. Employers had to finance this obligatory supplementary pension system through contributions to a number of funds. The position advocated by Erlander and the Social Democrats carried the day.

Another central political issue, debated through almost all the Erlander years, concerned reform of the Swedish constitution. The agreement finally reached at the end of Erlander's tenure and with his active involvement constituted a compromise between political parties: The bicameral legislature was replaced by a unicameral one, the term was shortened to three years, the electoral system was to be based on absolute proportionality for all parties obtaining more than 4 percent of the vote, elections to the Riksdag were to be held concurrently with elections to the municipal and county councils.

Tage Erlander's decision-making style was distinctive. He had a very quick intellect; when briefed, he grasped substantive issues and saw where problems lay. He was eager to discuss; arguments were to be presented for and against, and when he felt the arguments were weak or one-sided he would sometimes adopt an extreme position in order to provoke the necessary counterarguments. He was a great worrier; Olof Palme once described this aspect of Erlander's character as a tendency toward "worst-case analysis." His remarks during discussions and meetings were often characterized by vagueness; he was prone to keeping options open for a long time, avoiding language that might commit him to a specific position too soon. All this does not mean, however, that he had difficulty making decisions. Politics was, in his way of thinking, a process with its own laws and its own rhythm that could only be tamed and channeled in certain situations. The clever politician is one who does not hurry, but who also does not wait too long, lest time make the decision for him. One has to take full advantage of the strategic moment, acting when the time is ripe. On many occasions when central political issues were at stake, Tage Erlander showed that he had these capacities.

Erlander turned out to be quite a different party leader and prime minister than many had thought he would be when he unexpectedly was elected to these positions in 1946. Instead of being a temporary solution, he remained in office for twenty-three years, developing into a very popular leader. He was not primarily an administrator, as might have been expected from his earlier work experience in the chancery, but rather turned out to be an activist who spent most of his time outside the chancery, giving speeches, participating in debates and traveling. He did not, with his background in social and educational issues, spend most of his time on these policy areas, but on many other matters, including especially foreign policy. While remaining a fighter, polemicist and effective defender of Social Democratic values throughout his tenure, he also gradually emerged as a skillful compromiser between conflicting views and interests and as a well-liked senior politician.

Tage Erlander seems not to have been preoccupied with a desire to wield power, even though he was certainly stimulated by seeing that his words and actions carried weight and had effect. His path to the chairmanship of the party and to the premiership had not been marked by conscious calculation. Suddenly, simply, he found himself there with fear in his heart. His style of leadership did not correspond to that of a politician who is only concerned about protecting and expanding his power; he never removed strong personalities from around him in an attempt to establish his own dominance. Nor did he, as many power-hungry politicians are wont to do, hesitate to seek advice and comments from those around him. He questioned, listened and argued continuously. Finally, he did not, as many who wish to maintain their power often do, try to build up an administrative apparatus to guarantee his control and ensure that important issues would always be brought to him before a final decision was made.

There was something paradoxical about Erlander's relationship to power and to its excercise. Although he appeared uninterested in power for its own sake and was even inclined to deemphasize his ability to exercise the power available to him as leader of the Social Democratic Party and as prime minister, much of his thought and many of his actions concerned power relationships in society. The citizenry, he always said, derives benefit from the existence of a "strong government" and from the fact that the government is determined to expand the "strong society." It is reasonable to assume that someone who led both the labor movement and a government with a strong parliamentary position was himself "powerful." But that was something Erlander was very unwilling to admit. The power and influence which undeniably lay in the positions he held for such a long time were counterbalanced by his lack of interest in exercising power for the sake of power and by the fact that he appeared unaffected by actually having power.

His personality was a surprising and complex mix: Erlander was speculative, yet he also had a great interest in things that were practical and down to earth. He was inquisitive and critical, yet very loyal to the labor movement and demanded such loyalty of others. He was humorous and expansive, yet easily became very serious. He was somewhat bohemian, yet also dutiful and orderly. He was friendly and warm, yet he could become very angry and caustic in debate. And underlying all the surprising combinations of Erlander's personality was an element directly corresponding to the most utopian of the values toward which the Swedish welfare state during his time was said to strive, namely, equality. Tage Erlander remained surprisingly unspoiled by his twenty-three years in power. He was egalitarian, indeed nearly classless, genuinely lacking pretensions.

Tage Erlander lived for a decade and a half after resigning as party leader and prime minister. He withdrew to a house built by the Social Democratic Party for him and his wife on an estate, Bomersvik, outside Stockholm, owned by the Social Democratic youth organization. He published his memoirs in five volumes; he continued to be involved both in discussions and meetings with old friends from his long political life and to establish new contacts among all the young party workers who attended courses and seminars at Bomersvik. He remained a very central figure in Swedish life and gained popularity and prestige among people who had never even voted for him. His death in June 1985 was a national event, and the transportation of his coffin to his native village Ransäter in Värmland, where he is buried, was transformed into a kind of postmortem triumphal tour.

BIBLIOGRAPHY

Ruin, Olaf. *Tage Erlander: Serving the Welfare State, 1946–1969.* Pittsburgh, Pa.: Unversity of Pittsburgh Press, 1990.

OLOF RUIN

F

THORBJÖRN FÄLLDIN (1926–) led the Center Party from 1971 to 1985 and was the first nonsocialist prime minister of Sweden since 1936. He headed three governments (1976–1978, 1979–1981, 1981–1982). The decades of his political career were particularly tumultuous for Sweden. Constitutional reform created a unicameral parliament in the 1970s, a change that helped the Center, Liberal and Conservative parties win the 1976 parliamentary election but that also led to less stable governments. The three parties formed the first nonsocialist coalition government since 1905. Three of the most significant issues of modern Swedish political history headed the agenda of the Fälldin years: nuclear power, wage earner funds and the most serious incident in Swedish foreign policy since the early postwar period. Economic problems also became more dominant.

Thorbjörn Fälldin is a self-made man and proud of his peasant roots, sensitive, and principled to the point of stubbornness. These traits would later give him a populist political appeal that first charmed and then disappointed the Swedish nation. Fälldin grew up in rural northern Sweden with parents actively involved in political and civic associations promoting the cause of agriculture. Civic associations played an important role in Fälldin's childhood. He climbed rapidly and successfully up the career ladder within the youth organization of the Agrarian Party. By age twenty-five he was a municipal councilman and chairman of the regional party youth association.

In the 1950s, Fälldin represented a new generation of up-and-coming political leaders. Young activists within the Agrarian Party questioned the ties between their party and the Social Democrats; both had governed in coalition from 1936 to 1939 and again from 1951 to 1957. These activists wanted to renew the party by changing its name to the Center Party and mobilizing supporters from urban areas. A particular characteristic of Fälldin that distinguished him from older party comrades was his skeptical attitude toward social democracy and trade unions.

He was elected to the lower chamber of parliament in 1958 as its youngest member. Fälldin took his work as M.P. seriously and even showed his independence by disagreeing with the party leader in closed party sessions. He continued to hold municipal office and remained a leader of the farmers' union and other civic associations while in office. His main political theme in these years was demographic change, especially depopulation of the countryside.

He devoted more time to party matters after he was forced to leave parliament in 1964. He was elected to the party's governing board and spent time getting acquainted with local party organizations. Various party members began in these years to consider him the party's crown prince. In 1966 he became an M.P. in the upper chamber, where he became good friends with a future leader of the Liberal Party. Cooperation between the two parties began in the early 1960s. Fälldin returned to the lower chamber in 1968.

In 1969 Fälldin became vice-chairman of the Center Party without the support of Gunnar Hedlund, the rather cantankerous leader of the party. Fälldin's capacity for work, leadership qualities and television-friendly ways weighed heavily in his favor. The last quality explained in part his rise to national prominence. He was known as ''the young M.P. with the beautiful voice'' in the early days of televised news. This quality combined well with another important trait, his calm but clear leadership style. Fälldin was a primary agent of change in his party's professionalization and democratization.

The question on everyone's mind was *when* he would become party leader. This occurred in 1971, when Hedlund finally decided to resign after twenty-three years at the post. Fälldin's important political concerns as party leader were decentralization of political authority to local government, the environment (in particular the issue of nuclear power) and cooperation with the Liberal and Conservative parties to create a true nonsocialist bloc. His leadership style seemed ideal for this last task, and he was a much more formidable opponent of the Social Democrats than his predecessor.

Fälldin was also one of the first national politicians in Sweden to promote women to political office, as shown by the role that he gave to Karin Söder in televised political debates and by appointing her first minister of foreign affairs and then minister of health and social affairs. Söder later replaced Fälldin as party leader in 1985.

Fälldin's political strategy worked well. Opinion polls confirmed that he was a political sensation. Everything about him interested journalists and therefore the public. Fälldin captured the sentiments of different segments of the population with his personal charm, populism and farmer sensibilities. Even the urban, cynical Stockholm press liked him, and thanks to them, he grew to mythical proportions. Yet not everyone was happy with this new Swedish folk hero. There was considerable competition between Olof Palme and Thorbjörn Fälldin, two new and relatively young party leaders, representing different political traditions with respect to both style and ideology.

The results of the 1973 parliamentary election were very close, but the nonsocialist parties did not receive sufficient support to take office. It was the Center Party's best election ever; it received 25.1 percent of the vote and became the largest of the three nonsocialist parties. It was Fälldin's first and greatest triumph, but the results were also disappointing at the same time because he was very eager to head a new government. This psychological setback made him more cautious politically.

A second setback shortly afterward was his inability to negotiate a merger of the Center and Liberal parties, a move designed to counter the growing strength of the Conservative Party. The way Fälldin dealt with the issue shows how his personality traits influenced his leadership style. Fälldin was so sure that he was right that he misjudged party attitude on the issue. He reacted to this setback by becoming deeply depressed for almost one year. Later he explained that his disappointment over his failure to merge the parties led to a personality change. He became less outspoken, put less trust in his political instincts, lost his political self-confidence and became overly concerned with political details.

The issue of nuclear power reinvigorated him politically. In 1974 he became a leading spokesperson against nuclear power. Fälldin argued his position with, as he put it, the stubbornness of a donkey. Enthusiasm over the issue led to a new bonding between party leader and cadre. Electoral researchers conclude that the party would have suffered a larger loss in the 1976 parliamentary election had it not been for the mobilizing potential of its anti–nuclear power stance. Part of the attraction was the new political style Fälldin offered voters. Unlike other politicians, he spoke categorically and morally: ''I will not enter a government that brings more nuclear power plants on line,'' he declared. ''Let me say in order to avoid any misunderstanding: No ministerial post can be so attractive that I would be prepared to compromise my conviction.'' The closer it came to election night, the more Fälldin articulated his position in uncompromising detail. Some party activists warned him about this, but he dismissed them as the same people who opposed his election as party leader. The other nonsocialist parties maintained a very low profile on the issue in the election campaign.

As leader of the largest nonsocialist party, Fälldin was called upon to form a new government after the 1976 parliamentary election. Negotiations among the three coalition parties were not an easy affair: They disagreed on many crucial issues including the phasing out of nuclear power. Moreover, the leaders of the Conservative and Liberal parties were not on speaking terms. Yet Fälldin made a serious political mistake by not demanding that negotiations begin with the nuclear power issue. Two weeks of tedious but successful negotiations on all other major subjects had passed before Fälldin specified his demands regarding nuclear power. Meanwhile, political time was running out for the formation of a new government. The Conservative and Liberal leaders gave him an ultimatum, forcing him to accept both the starting up of a new nuclear power plant and the so-called compromise law requiring that plants be put on line only if the nuclear power industry could ensure that spent fuel could be safely stored in solid rock.

Fälldin handled this controversial and symbolic political issue very poorly.

Opinion polls showed a growing disappointment with him and his Center Party. Accusations of political betrayal hurt his sensitive nature, for he believed himself to be ethically purer than most other Swedish politicians. Privately Fälldin complained, "Do I have to endure this hell just because I am prime minister?" Yet clearly he had committed a serious political blunder. His statements had led voters to expect drastic and rapid reform of Swedish energy policy, and, since this could not be fulfilled, severe disappointment with the Center Party and its leader as well as distrust in the political system itself had set in. In fact, the party's commitment to phasing out nuclear power was not even backed up with a comprehensive, detailed plan. Fälldin seriously considered resigning as prime minister, but his plans were stymied by the decision of the Liberal Party leader, vice prime minister in his government, to resign for personal reasons.

His principled stand on the issue of nuclear power in combination with his sensitive nature and bullheadedness explains Fälldin's decision not to drop the issue. It led to protracted, often fruitless discussions and finally a government crisis. Fälldin was taken aback when the apolitical justice minister declared that the compromise law did not legally prohibit the government from granting permits to bring nuclear power plants on line. What is most surprising is that he and his party had never bothered to check the law's validity. Fälldin had backed himself into a corner and lacked the necessary political skills to find a successful way out of it.

The nuclear power issue brought down Fälldin's government. He justified his resignation by stating that there was a limit to how much a party could compromise its soul. A minority Liberal Party government then ruled until the parliamentary election in 1979. Once out of office, Fälldin devoted his time to mobilizing support for a national referendum on nuclear power. In this, the disaster at the Three Mile Island nuclear plant in the United States in the spring of 1979 convinced a parliamentary majority that a referendum was necessary.

At this point, the Swedish public was more negative toward nuclear power than ever before, but this did not help the Center Party in the fall 1979 parliamentary election. Nevertheless, a new nonsocialist coalition government was created with Thorbjörn Fälldin as prime minister. He was much less popular, but this time the nuclear power issue did not complicate interparty negotiations. This Fälldin government was criticized for its weak economic policy. In the end, Fälldin could not hold his coalition together after a tax policy agreement made with the Social Democrats so outraged the Conservative Party that it pulled out. Fälldin's lack of political resolve on the issue was satirized in a political cartoon: In one balloon he was shown thinking, "I haven't done anything wrong"; in another one he was shown thinking, "I haven't done anything."

A minority government consisting of the Center and Liberal parties with Fälldin as prime minister governed Sweden from May 1981 to the fall 1982 election. This was his third government. This time he was more comfortable with his political role: The tax agreement was a feather in his prime ministerial cap, and he traveled abroad more frequently. Fälldin, however, lacked the international reputation of other Swedish politicians, and his proficiency in foreign languages was quite poor. Opinion polls, nonetheless, showed that Swedish citizens once again began to show him their trust.

A very serious and delicate international incident for Sweden in 1981 showed, indeed, that Fälldin was a very capable national leader. The incident, jokingly called "Whiskey on the Rocks," involved the stranding of a Soviet Whiskey-class submarine with the designation U–137 in a military zone in the southern Swedish archipelago. The issue involved both Swedish-Soviet bilateral relations and the credibility of Swedish neutrality policy. It did not help matters that a fisherman—and not the rather expensive Swedish military defense system—found the submarine. The crisis lasted ten days.

Fälldin was a reserve military officer and enjoyed the company of top military commanders, and his rather legalistic perspective of politics was well suited for this problem. At the beginning, his political judgment was not very sound, as witnessed by his lax attitude toward the defense minister, who misunderstood the gravity of the incident, remaining in Norway during its first crucial days, and by Fälldin's own decision to go home to his farm on the second day of crisis. But thereafter his involvement became firmer and more active once it was ascertained that the submarine carried nuclear arms. Fälldin took charge of the issue, in contrast to his usual proclivity to let his ministers take care of their own spheres of responsibility. He followed carefully the advice of the Swedish military, as well as his foreign and security policy staff. His outward calm, nonetheless, belied an inward insecurity about how the Social Democratic leader and his main political opponent, Olof Palme, would react to his handling of the affair.

Fälldin's political intuition told him that the Soviets should not be given an ultimatum, but that Swedish national interests could neither be jeopardized nor compromised. The country's international reputation was at stake. He firmly rejected all proposals for drastic measures, and his slow, cautious political style proved to be the best approach. Yet he was, in fact, prepared to risk war to prevent further violations of Sweden's territorial waters. Also, he was acutely aware that the issue could not be allowed to turn into a domestic political issue, giving any party political points. He even played the mass media well, as witnessed by the way he publicly announced that the submarine was armed with nuclear weapons. A seasoned foreign policy expert considered Fälldin's appearance at this press conference to be the most sensationally successful of his tenure in office. Fälldin placed four demands before the Soviets, and in the end they accepted each one of them. Clearly, Fälldin deserves much credit for successfully resolving the crisis.

Part of Fälldin's problem as a statesman was that he found it difficult to combine the roles of prime minister and party leader. Usually he gave government priority over party, an action not followed by other coalition leaders. One exception is the 1982 election campaign, when journalists nicknamed Fälldin "the Hulk" (after an American television series shown in Sweden) because of his aggressive, partisan behavior in a debate pitting him against a flu-strickened Olof Palme. His debating skills here secured him several more years as party leader. Yet criticism of his style of party leadership was getting stronger. He could no longer mobilize support as he had in the 1976 campaign. The nonsocialist parties lost the 1982 election. It was Fälldin's third electoral loss: The party was now down to 15.5 percent of the popular vote.

Newspapers speculated about his resignation from the party leadership. His leave of absence for illness (1983–1984) added more fuel to this tabloid fire. Fälldin had a serious ulcer and thought seriously of leaving politics. His illness and unsure, indecisive leadership style did not help the internal disarray in which the Center Party found itself after the 1982 election. Younger members of the party criticized him, but Fälldin was nonetheless reelected at the 1985 party assembly. Yet his authority as party leader was challenged by the election of critics to the party's board. Also, Fälldin was becoming somewhat authoritarian, and his respect for procedural democracy was diminishing. The question was now how long he could remain as party leader.

Fälldin's ability to communicate via television decreased greatly once he became older and tired, and was labeled a political loser. The results of the 1985 parliamentary election underscored the need to reinvigorate the party; it received only 12.4 percent of the vote, with 2.6 percent going to its election partner, the small Christian Democratic Party. During his term of leadership, the Center Party had lost over half of its voters. At a closed party meeting, Fälldin expressed disappointment with himself as party leader: "What bothers me the most is not the election outcome but that I could not keep the party together. The party has never been so ideologically split as it is today, and I bear a large part of the responsibility." He resigned on December 5, 1985, althought it is more correct to say that he was pushed out of office. Today, however, Fälldin accepts political assignments as a respected elder statesman.

What kind of leader was Thorbjörn Fälldin? His failure with the nuclear power issue dominates this assessment, but other leadership qualities should be noted. He listened attentively to the demands of youth and women's associations throughout most of his tenure as party leader, a progressive attitude for the time. He put trust in his ministers, allowing them to work independently and develop their own political skills. Yet some ministers should not have been given so much political trust, and their independence made coordination of the coalition governments difficult. Sweden's budget deficit grew enormously under his rule. He was also a political loner and had more detailed knowledge of public policy than most other Swedish prime ministers. This kept his ministers and political appointees alert. His background led him to ask down-to-earth questions about how policy proposals would really affect the little folk; sometimes this would lead to unnecessary political delays.

Fälldin dedicated himself to making the government work but often devoted too much attention to these political details. He was aware of this and frequently explained that his governments spent more time on time-consuming tedious tasks than formulating a nonsocialist vision of politics. His tendency toward indecisiveness did not combine well with the general complications created by administrative inexperience and political discord which characterized his governments. He had endless patience for government problems and believed that discussion would eventually lead to objectively correct decisions. This explains his aversion to pork barrel and political compromise as well as his view that the pace of government was too hectic.

Fälldin does not bear the entire blame for the problems of governability during his rule or for the inability to realize nonsocialist goals. National economic problems, as well as ideological differences among the three parties, blocked fulfillment of long-term political aims. Yet as a politician he was ill equipped to be an agent of visionary political change. He symbolized the political confusion of the 1970s and 1980s: Swedes were identifying less with social democracy, but no new political alternative had yet taken form.

One leadership quality that raised Fälldin to national esteem was his ability to mobilize support for latent political issues, for example, nuclear power and decentralization of political authority to local government. His popularity and honesty were important here. Yet they were not the leadership qualities necessary to deal successfully with political power plays in the artificial alliance of nonsocialist coalition governments. They were inadequate for tough political negotiations, as witnessed so well in the cases of nuclear power and tax policies. Fälldin was a good political entrepreneur, but unfortunately was less than successful as a political executive.

BIBLIOGRAPHY

Childs, Marquis. "The Sheep Farmer and the Nuclear Option: The Political Cost," in Marquis Childs (ed.), *Sweden: The Middle Way on Trial*. New Haven, Conn.: Yale University Press, 1980.

Elmbrant, Björn. *Fälldin*. Stockholm: Fisher & Co., 1991.

Petersson, Olof. *Regeringsbildningen 1979*. Stockholm: Rabén & Sjögren, 1979.

———. "The Government Crisis in Sweden," *Scandinavian Political Studies* 2(2):171–78 (1979).

Stern, Eric K. *The U–137 Incident: A Study in Swedish Crisis Management*. Stockholm: University of Stockholm, International Graduate School, Stockholm International Studies 90(1), 1990.

Strand, Dieter. *Palme mot Fälldin: Rapporter från vägen till nederlaget*. Stockholm: Rabén & Sjögren, 1977.

Vedung, Evert. *Kärnkraften och regeringen Fälldins fall*. Stockholm: Rabén & Sjögren, 1979.

MICHELE MICHELETTI

GARRET FITZGERALD (1926–   ) has been one of the most influential Irish political leaders in recent decades. As president of the Fine Gael (League of the Gaels) Party (1977–1987) and during his two terms as prime minister (1981–1982 and 1982–1987), he was a principal proponent of Anglo-Irish cooperation to achieve a negotiated settlement to the ongoing ''troubles'' in Northern Ireland.

Garret FitzGerald was born on February 9, 1926, in Dublin. His father, Desmond FitzGerald, had been a participant in the abortive Easter Uprising against the British in 1916 and later served as both external affairs minister (1922–1927) and defense minister (1927–1932) in the Irish Free State. His mother, Mabel FitzGerald (née McConnell), who also participated in the Easter Uprising, was from an upper-class Presbyterian family in Belfast. After early education at St. Brigid's School in Bray, Colaiste na Rinne in Waterford, and Belvedere College in Dublin, FitzGerald attended University College Dublin (UCD) and received a legal education at the King's Inns, after which he was called to the bar in 1947.

For the next eleven years, FitzGerald worked as a research analyst for the national airline, Aer Lingus, where he developed economic analysis skills that would prove useful in his subsequent political career. After leaving the airline in 1958, he spent a year at Trinity College Dublin before assuming a lecturer's position in the Department of Political Economy at UCD, which he held from 1959 until 1987. During the 1960s, FitzGerald was also active as a journalist, writing a weekly economic column for the *Irish Times*, and serving as an Irish correspondent for the BBC, the *Economist*, and the *Financial Times*.

During the mid–1960s, FitzGerald became involved in national politics, joining the Fine Gael Party and winning a seat in the Seanad (the upper house of the Irish parliament) in 1965. The smaller of Ireland's two ''catch-all'' parties, Fine Gael was attractive to FitzGerald for several reasons. First, more than its principal opposition, Fianna Fail (or ''Soldiers of Destiny''), it was the party of the middle class. And as the Irish middle class had grown and modernized in the postwar years, Fine Gael had evolved from a right-of-center, proclerical platform to a secular, center-left party. Second, as the heir to the Cummann na nGaedheal (''Clan of the Gaels'') Party, which had accepted the 1921 Anglo-Irish Treaty that partitioned the island into the Irish Free State and the province of Northern Ireland (which remained in the union with Great Britain), it had never been as stridently antipartition or anti-Unionist as Fianna Fail. As the son of a northern, Protestant mother, FitzGerald believed that opportunities for reunification would be enhanced if the Irish Republic became less sectarian and more sympathetic to the concerns of the Unionist majority in Northern Ireland.

In 1969, FitzGerald gave up his seat in the Seanad and won election to the more powerful lower house (the Dail Eireann), representing southeast Dublin. Advocating both structural and policy changes, he attempted to wrest control of Fine Gael from party leader Liam Cosgrave in 1972. Despite the strained relations that resulted from this attempt, which failed, Cosgrave named FitzGerald minister for foreign affairs when a Fine Gael–Labour coalition government was formed following the 1973 elections.

The decision to name FitzGerald to the foreign affairs post was undoubtedly assisted by the deterioration of the political situation in Northern Ireland during this period. In the late 1960s, the civil rights movement turned violent as the provisional wing of the Irish Republican Army (IRA) and the Protestant Ulster Defense Association (UDA) battled each other and the civil authorities in offsetting campaigns of terror. Striving to control the violence, the British government dispatched troops to Ulster in 1969, suspended the Northern Irish parliament in 1972, and instituted direct rule from London in 1973.

The situation revived the "national question" in the Irish Republic, and politicians in Dublin struggled to respond to both the escalating political violence and the British presence in the North. Garret FitzGerald was among those who advocated constitutional changes, such as the successful 1972 referendum to delete references in Article 44 to "the special position of the Holy Catholic Apostolic and Roman Church." His 1972 book, *Towards a New Ireland*, outlined the case for a more pluralistic, less sectarian Irish state that would be more appealing to Ulster Unionists and make possible a reunified Ireland based on the consent of all relevant communities; the book would form the basis for Fine Gael policy as FitzGerald assumed increasing power within the party.

Capitalizing on his intellect, eloquence and keen grasp of economic dynamics, FitzGerald excelled in the foreign ministry post, increasing his stature within the party and gaining a European-wide reputation for deft diplomacy, especially during his tenure as president of the European Community's Council of Ministers between January and June 1975.

In the general election of 1977, the Fine Gael–Labour coalition collapsed following a bout of high inflation and political embarrassments over a family planning bill, and a Fianna Fail government returned to power. Promising to work for greater party professionalization and policy changes, FitzGerald was chosen to replace Cosgrave as Fine Gael leader. He immediately overhauled the party staff, established a research office, refurbished the composition of the party's front bench, and undertook a nationwide tour of party branch offices. It is ironic that the academic FitzGerald, whom some called "Garret the Good" and whose cerebral, antipolitical demeanor sometimes made him seem out of place in the coarse, patronage-driven world of partisan politics, would be the leader to modernize his party and prepare it for a return to power in the 1980s.

During FitzGerald's tenure as opposition leader, economic recession and ongoing intraparty feuds within Fianna Fail brought about the retirement of Prime Minister Jack Lynch in late 1979. He was replaced by Charles Haughey, whose political struggles with FitzGerald would define Irish politics during most of the 1980s. In terms of their personalities and positions on the "national question," the two could hardly have been more different and as a result they neither liked nor respected one another. The well-bred FitzGerald, with his academic background, was open, unassuming, engaging and basically a political outsider. Haughey, in contrast, was a self-made entrepreneur who had been active in Fianna Fail politics since the 1940s; he was regarded as cunning, personally distant and less than scrupulous in both his private and public affairs. More nationalistic than FitzGerald, Haughey had been tried and acquitted in 1970 on charges of illegally conspiring to smuggle weapons into Northern Ireland, and he believed that the key to reunification was not constitutional change in the Irish Republic, but the withdrawal of British support for the Unionists in Ulster.

The June 1981 general elections were contested against the background of continued economic stagnation and public outrage over the hunger strike deaths of IRA prisoners being held by the British. Support for Fianna Fail ebbed, and FitzGerald was able to piece together a coalition agreement with the Labour Party that gave him the bare majority necessary to form a new government. One of the his first priorities as prime minister was the initiation of a ''constitutional crusade'' designed to amend the constitution further to accommodate Unionist fears. Specifically, the crusade called for changes in Articles 2 and 3 of the Irish Republic's constitution; these articles claim the republic's sovereignty over the six counties of Northern Ireland.

Building upon earlier summit meetings between Haughey and British Prime Minister Margaret Thatcher in 1980, FitzGerald met with Thatcher in November 1981 and reiterated the Irish government's position that unification ''would require the consent of a majority of the people in Northern Ireland.'' But FitzGerald interpreted these words differently than his predecessor had. For Haughey, Northern Ireland was illegitimate, ''a failed political entity'' that could be sustained only by extraordinary British subvention. If the British would withdraw that external support, then the Unionists would perforce ''consent'' to a negotiated reunification. A peaceful, consensual solution could not be reached so long as the British continued to sponsor Unionist intransigence.

While he stopped short of granting the Unionist position ''legitimacy,'' FitzGerald recognized that the British—especially a Thatcher-led government—were unlikely to abandon Northern Ireland as long as the Unionists steadfastly opposed reunification. For FitzGerald, Unionist ''consent'' was a prerequisite for, not a likely result of, British withdrawal. As a result, in the short term, FitzGerald accepted plans for more extensive Anglo-Irish cooperation (including the creation of an Anglo-Irish Intergovernmental Council to provide an institutional basis for continued negotiations on the status of Ulster); in the long term, he believed that internal changes within the Irish Republic would be necessary.

Before FitzGerald could capitalize on the momentum generated by his summit with Thatcher, his coalition majority disintegrated over the 1982 budget proposals, and a Fianna Fail–led coalition briefly returned to power after the February elections. When Haughey's new coalition, too, proved unstable, FitzGerald led Fine Gael to a strong showing in the November elections, and constructed a more stable coalitional arrangement with Labour that lasted until 1987.

Upon his return to government, FitzGerald lent his support to a plan originated by John Hume, the leader of Northern Ireland's Social Democratic and Labour Party, for an unprecedented meeting of political, religious and social leaders from both sides of the border to discuss the future of Ireland. The New Ireland Forum convened on May 30, 1983, and produced its report the following year. Although the Forum produced no major breakthroughs, it did explore a number of alternative political arrangements (specifically unification, confederation, joint authority), and it endorsed, in vague terms, FitzGerald's call for a more pluralistic, less sectarian state. At first it appeared as though the Forum's report would have little impact. Meeting with FitzGerald at Chequers under the structure of the Anglo-Irish Intergovernmental Council, Thatcher ruled out all of the Forum's options as unacceptable ''derogation[s] from sovereignty.''

The highlight of FitzGerald's political career was his ability to move beyond Thatcher's ''out, out, out'' rejection of the Forum's options and negotiate with the British government the Hillsborough Agreement of 1985. Meeting outside of Belfast in November, Thatcher and FitzGerald signed an accord that acknowledged that the status of Northern Ireland could only be altered with the consent of the majority, recognized nationalist aspirations to a unified Ireland, and called for a reconciliation between the two cultural traditions on the island.

The agreement also established institutions for greater cooperation between the British and Irish governments, specifically calling for the establishment of an Intergovernmental Conference where a ''Permanent Irish Ministerial Representative'' would be consulted on security, justice and political matters in Northern Ireland. The agreement granted the Dublin government the right to propose legislation of special interest to the Catholic community in the North and committed it to work in close cooperation with British officials in the capture and prosecution of IRA terrorists. In short, FitzGerald had negotiated a treaty that gave the Irish Republic something more than a consultative role—yet less than an executive one—in Ulster.

Although the Hillsborough Agreement was enthusiastically received by large majorities in both Britain and Ireland, it did little to stabilize the situation in Northern Ireland. Perhaps ironically, Unionists had long distrusted FitzGerald more than Haughey, believing that his more moderate stance on the national question might lead Westminster to sell out their interests. In the Unionists' view, the Hillsborough pact was one-sidedly nationalistic in its structure and provided concrete evidence that London was prepared to force them into some sort of political union with the Irish Republic. Unionist leaders resigned their seats in Parliament, organized large-scale strikes and called for a ''suspension'' of the agreement at a minimum.

In the spirit of Hillsborough and to test the waters for possible changes in Articles 2 and 3, FitzGerald called for a constitutional referendum in June 1986 to legalize divorce in the Irish Republic, couching his argument in terms of improved relations with the North. Despite early public opinion polls that had shown a firm majority in favor of such an amendment, the measure failed by a two-to-one margin, to the chagrin of both Dublin and London. Unionists, of course, interpreted the result as conclusive evidence of the sectarian nature of the Irish state and, in the wake of the vote, British pressure on them subsided.

FitzGerald's failure in the divorce referendum also presaged the end of his political career. Unable to effect major constitutional changes and with only limited economic success (e.g., foreign borrowing had not decreased, and inflation had been cut, but at the expense of higher unemployment and emigration), Fine Gael's coalition collapsed in January 1987 over proposed cuts in government spending. After a general election in which Fine Gael's vote plummeted to its lowest level in thirty years, FitzGerald resigned as the leader of his party and retired to private life.

Throughout his political life, Garret FitzGerald represented a moderate, modernizing force in Irish politics. He refurbished the Fine Gael Party following its 1977 defeats, injected a more personal/presidential style of campaigning into politics, championed constitutional revisions to pluralize and secularize Irish society and made significant strides toward better North-South and Anglo-Irish relations.

But Garret FitzGerald will be marked by history as a man whose ultimate accomplishments were ironic: Despite his party-building efforts, Fine Gael was weaker electorally when he left than when he assumed its leadership; despite his ''crusade,'' the 1986 referendum entrenched rather than displaced Catholic moral teaching in the constitution; and despite his best intentions, his greatest diplomatic success did more to harden the Unionists' resolve than to convince them of the benefits of reunification.

Intelligent, eloquent and moderate, Garret FitzGerald represented a break with the past in Irish politics. He wanted to move the political debate beyond the ancient polemic between nationalists and loyalists to a new level, where a dialogue could be held on the nature and future of Irish society. His limited success in achieving this goal says less about him than it does about the limiting context of Irish politics.

BIBLIOGRAPHY

Works by FitzGerald:

Towards a New Ireland. London: Charles Knight, 1972.

All in a Life: An Autobiography. London: Macmillan, 1991.

Other Works:

Aughey, Arthur. *Under Siege: Ulster Unionism and the Anglo-Irish Agreement.* London: Hurst and Company, 1989.

Kenny, Anthony. *The Road to Hillsborough: The Shaping of the Anglo-Irish Agreement.* Oxford: Pergamon Press, 1986.

O'Malley, Padraig. *The Uncivil Wars: Ireland Today.* Belfast: Blackstaff Press, 1983.

Penniman, Howard, and Brian Farrell (eds.). *Ireland at the Polls 1981, 1982, and 1987: A Study of Four General Elections.* Durham, N.C.: Duke University Press/American Enterprise Institute, 1987.

Townshend, Charles (ed.). *Consensus in Ireland: Approaches and Recessions.* Oxford: Clarendon Press.

L. MARVIN OVERBY

HARILAOS FLORAKIS (1914–) has been the leading figure in the Communist Party of Greece (KKE) since 1972. Still an active politician with considerable influence in Greek political life, Florakis was a major participant in political events which shaped the history of both the Greek communist movement and post–World War II Greece, exercising his most significant influence during the last two decades.

If for nothing else, Florakis will be remembered for two things: first, for establishing the dominance of the KKE over any other organized version of the Greek communist left, and second, for his flexibility in helping to form a unique government alliance between the Communists and the Conservatives. In the first, the KKE's dominance of the left, Florakis was particularly influential during the years of dictatorship in Greece (1967–1974) and immediately after (1974–1981), a period when more than one ideology competed for preeminence on the Greek left. In the second, an alliance between Communists and Conservatives was put together in the late 1980s with the purpose of strengthening Greece's democratic institutions, which were seen to be suffering during the late 1980s at the hands of a populist Socialist government.

Harilaos Florakis's political influence must be considered at the intersection of two relatively independent factors. First, there are the authoritarian traditions of communist political culture inherited from the Greek communist movement and constantly reinforced during the post–World War II period through the interaction between the Greek communists and their Soviet comrades. Second, there is the process of post–World War II capitalist modernization in a country like Greece with a very particluar identity: that is, Balkan but not Slavic, European but not Western, and Middle Eastern but not Muslim. If nothing else, it was this particularity that determined the fate of Greece when the victors of World War II were working to shape and share spheres of influence.

Harilaos Florakis, son of Ioannis Florakis, was born on July 20, 1914, in Rahoula, a small village near the city of Karditsa in the Thessaly region of central Greece. He completed his secondary education and graduated from a technical school as a telegraphist. In conjunction with his technical training he enrolled in the law school at the University of Athens. His first involvement with the Communist Party dates back to the 1930s, when, as a high school student, he became an associate of the Federation of the Communist Youth of Greece (OKNE). Later, while working as a telegraphist, he engaged in union activities and served as secretary for the union of telegraphists.

In September 1941, the KKE created the National Liberation Front (EAM), which in turn shortly gave birth to the Greek Liberation Army (ELAS). EAM focused on two major goals. The first was resistance to German fascist occupation; the second was the establishment of a democratic political system after the end of the war. In the period just prior to World War II (1936–1940), Greece was governed by an unpopular military dictatorship in conjunction with an equally unpopular monarch. EAM's agenda met with broad support among the population, soon being embraced by the vast majority of Greeks. During this period, the EAM program made no reference of any kind to the establishment of a socialist society in Greece—not even as a long-term strategic goal. Therefore, it is clear that the KKE, through EAM, dominated the nation, especially the Greek middle class, with its leadership but not with its entire ideology. By 1943 EAM's membership had reached approximately two million out of a total population of seven million people.

As the end of the war neared, two visions for the postwar Greek political order were quite clear, one supported by EAM and one by the British. Given that the middle class had already endorsed EAM's vision, the British at first had no significant allies besides the king and a small number of Greek troops which during the war had remained in the Middle East under British command. It was only after the end of the civil war in 1949, and because of that war, that class and strong state institutions united against the KKE.

Florakis became a member of the Greek Communist Party in 1941. It was a period of restructuring for the KKE along lines of new strictures imposed upon politics by the Nazi occupation of Greece. During the Nazi reign, Florakis led his union in the infamous 1942 strike. This strike was one of the first in Nazi-occupied Europe, and the first of any major importance. For his activities he was repeatedly arrested. At the beginning of 1943, he joined the Greek Liberation Army (ELAS). He fought the Germans as an officer of the fifth and eleventh divisions. In 1945 he was elected to the KKE leadership in Athens.

The KKE's activities after the war stalled during a long period of indecisiveness and passive political maneuvering, due most likely to Stalin's intention of complying with Churchill's demand that the West should predominate over Greece. The tremendous advantage in power that the Communists enjoyed in 1944 gradually disappeared. By 1947 the British had already established governing mechanisms around increasingly reactionary positions unified by the emerging ideology of anticommunism. In particular, the middle class no longer sided with the KKE.

In the meantime, the United States succeeded the British as Greece's protector. In 1947, possibly with Stalin's encouragement, the Communists, under the leadership of Nicos Zahariadis, decided to start a civil war. Stalin encouraged such a war because he could use it as leverage in negotiations with the West. Zahariadis's authoritarian style of Communist leadership resulted, however, in a number of fatal mistakes and contributed to the KKE loss in the civil war. During these civil war years (1947–1949), Florakis was the leader of a sizable military unit in the first division of the Communist army, passing under a pseudonym. In 1949 he was elected for the first time to the KKE's central committee.

The end of the civil war found Greece in a state of economic disaster. But what would have far greater impact on Greek political development was the victors' intention to define social and political life by extreme reactionary positions. During the 1950s, an extreme anticommunism became the official ideology of the Greek state, and a number of antidemocratic institutions and centers of autonomous political authority evolved. The army, the police and the monarchy constituted a state mechanism that would, in the end, turn itself against any commitment for the democratic modernization of Greek politics. After serving as prime minister for ten years, the Conservative leader Konstantinos Karamanlis, disappointed with his inability to control this reactionary state, abandoned politics and emigrated to Paris.

At the end of the civil war Florakis was among tens of thousands of Communist fighters who sought asylum in Eastern Europe. As a leader of an illegal party, he later slipped across the Greek border on a mission to instruct and direct the implementation of the party's politics. During this period, in 1954, he was arrested, taken to court and given a life sentence. As a result, he spent eighteen years in concentration camps and prisons around Greece.

In the 1960s, the political center reemerged in Greek politics, seeking to take the task of modernizing and unifying the nation out of the hands of the Conservative Party. George Papandreou became the leader and unifying figure of the center parties. Gradually, however, parts of the center became radicalized under the guidance of Papandreou's son, Andreas, thus threatening the reactionary state with defeat. It is because of this political turbulence that a military dictatorship (1967–1974) can be explained: Dictatorship represented the temporary victory of a reactionary state against rational capitalist forces that were working for the modernization and democratization of Greece. In other words, the momentum of twenty years of anticommunism was strong enough to carry the country to what seemed to be an irrational political system.

The Greek leftist movement had entered the 1950s at its weakest strength. Between 50,000 and 60,000 members of the Communist Party fled to locations throughout Eastern Europe, along with most of the leadership. The most active Communists who remained were jailed. It was in the midst of this specter of total defeat for the Communist movement that an interesting experiment took place. In August 1951 the few Communist leaders who had managed to maintain their freedom joined forces with leaders of the small non-Communist political left to form the Greek Democratic Left (EDA). Following EAM's earlier example, the EDA focused on an agenda of democratization and mutual forgiveness from the traumas of the civil war. This new agenda quickly succeeded in meeting with the approval of a large number of Greeks. Prior to the resurgence of the political center, the EDA had become the second strongest political party in Greece, behind the governing Conservatives.

Of course, the success of the EDA constituted a serious challenge for that part of the Communist leadership that had fled to exile outside Greece. If nothing else, it was evident that the decision-making center for the left had shifted back inside Greece. For some KKE leaders, this shift was perceived to be highly problematic. First, it threatened the degree of control that the KKE's leaders had over the leftist movement. Second, it could produce unpleasantness with the Soviet Union, for the EDA followed a policy of significant independence from the Soviets and had in more than one instance refused to support policies of the Soviet Communists simply because they were Soviet.

Khrushchev's succession to Stalin at the head of the Soviet Communist Party kept these disagreements with the EDA from evolving into open conflict. In fact, the EDA enjoyed considerable support from the Soviets for some time. It was also during this period that Zahariadis was removed from his post as secretary of the Greek Communist Party and replaced by Kostas Koligiannis. Despite the apparent symbolism of this change—the leadership most associated with defeat in the civil war being replaced by a new generation—the new secretary maintained the same style of authoritarian leadership. Of course, Koligiannis was by no means elevated to the party leadership by any form of internal democratic procedure. Rather, he was selected by a small, closed circle of Greek Communist leaders with the support of their Soviet comrades.

In 1968, under a combination of both internal and external pressures, the KKE split. The Soviet Union had intervened in Hungary and Czechoslovakia, new subjects of political struggle had appeared in the form of social movements in the Western capitalist democracies and the Khrushchevian experiment in the Soviet Union had ended. The EDA ''experiment'' was not to be forgiven by the majority of Greek communist leaders who lived outside Greece. Even though, for a while, the debate took the form of a split over the geographic location of leadership (to the interior or exterior of Greece), it would be misleading to blame the schism on anything but the combination of factors just mentioned.

In fact, similar debates took place within all the major Western European Communist parties about the same time. The tradition of absolute dependence of the KKE on the USSR in the previous period and the conditions of dictatorship in Greece may be the crucial factors that led to a more dramatic conclusion in the Greek case than in other Western European countries. As a result of the schism, in 1968 the KKE split into two parties. One was the KKE/Interior, with most of its power among the members and leaders of the party within Greek territory. The other KKE was stronger among the Greek Communists of the Eastern diaspora and it enjoyed the blessing of the Soviet party.

In 1972, the KKE replaced Koligiannis with Florakis in an attempt to disassociate the party from a leadership charged with negative acts during the split. In June 1972, at the sixteeth plenary session of the KKE central committee, Harilaos Florakis became a member of the KKE's political office. In October of the same year, while still serving time in prison, he became the first secretary of the central committee. He was elected general secretary of the central committe of the KKE by the ninth, tenth, eleventh and twelfth conventions.

In 1974, the long overdue project of modernization reappeared on the political scene. Karamanlis was called from Paris to rescue the country before absolute national disaster struck. Among his first acts was legalization of the KKE. Under Karamanlis's leadership, Greece was linking itself both to Europe and to the European Community, finally seeking a place among the Western democracies. With the restoration of democracy and the legalization of the KKE in Greece, Florakis was elected to parliament as a representative of the second district of the city of Athens. He was reelected to the parliament in six elections from 1974 to 1990.

Yet, despite the relatively enlightened face of Karamanlis's conservative rule, it soon became evident that the Conservative version of modernization was limited. In the beginning of the 1980s, the Conservative Party was replaced in government by Andreas Papandreou's party, the Panhellenic Socialist Movement (PASOK). This party was a unique combination that had started in the 1980s as a populist party of social change, located at the center-left of the political spectrum and employing heavy rhetorical references to the historical Greek left. However, PASOK finished the decade as a populist party with a mixed record; Papandreou's governments were finally voted out of office in 1989 due to a number of scandals and amid accusations of economic mismanagement, although his PASOK was returned to power in 1993.

Under Florakis's leadership, the KKE definitively prevailed over the KKE/Interior—but not before the latter 1980s. The consequences of this defeat of the KKI/Interior's ideas of Eurocommunism in Greece and the resulting dominance by the KKE and its more traditional approach to communism have yet to be fully assessed by historians. Nevertheless, both parties were incapable of playing any significant role in shaping either the PASOK agenda or in forcing PASOK into a government coalition. Papandreou's movement, on the other hand, managed to gain for itself a large part of the traditional Greek sympathy for the leftist cause.

Under Florakis's leadership, the KKE supported PASOK's politics even when those politics were far from being socialist. Once again the reasons for this support were centered in the KKE's sensitivity to Moscow's foreign policy priorities. Papandreou seemed to satisfy the Soviets as long as his international politics followed a line rather independent of NATO and the United States. This independent line was exchanged for the KKE's uncritical support of PASOK. In the realm of theory, the KKE was operating under the doctrine of the "stage transition to socialism," and Papandreou's promise of change seemed to be the first of these stages. In July 1989 Florakis was elected president of the KKE—a position created especially for him. During that period, he was also named president of the Coalition of the Left and Progressive Parties (SYN), the organization formed by the KKE and its allies in the late 1980s.

The end of the 1980s was a period of rapid change in socialist countries. With the advent of Gorbachev's transformations, which allowed a greater degree of flexibility, the KKE undertook a number of suprising political initiatives. It developed a political alliance, the SYN, with the noncommunist remnants of KKE/Interior. But even more important, Florakis led the SYN into an alliance with the Conservatives in an effort to form a transitional government that would bring to justice those who were involved in economic scandals during Papandreou's tenure. Finally free in practice from any external limitations or restrictions, Florakis showed an amazing talent for political maneuvering, negotiation and decisiveness. It is doubtful that this government alliance between the right and left would ever have taken place in a country like Greece without Florakis and his ability for high-level political diplomacy.

The KKE hoped that this alliance would ultimately result in the empowerment of the left. Such an empowered left would be the future government partner to a purified and weakened PASOK. However, in the event, the Conservative government finally managed to win a very weak majority of the electoral vote. Papandreou then not only managed to establish his innocence of corruption charges in court, but he also reestablished himself as the chief alternative to Conservative rule.

In the meantime, these new initiatives exacted a heavy price on the KKE. Along with the final collapse of socialism in Eastern Europe, they opened for the KKE the familiar road of internal disagreement. The KKE split once again in 1991. This time the schism was between those who believed that communist parties had exhausted their historical role as agents of social change and those who tried to maintain the name, symbols, institutions and traditions of the KKE. Despite his role as initiator of the previous period of unusual political experimentation, Harilaos Florakis suprised everyone by throwing his support to the hard-line communist side. At the fourteenth convention of the KKE, he was unanimously elected to the new position of honorary president of the party. For his contributions to the communist movement, Florakis has also been given numerous awards established to honor prominent communist figures in Eastern European countries.

From his earlier partnership with the Conservatives to his very recent position on the future of communist parties, one is left with the ultimate question: Having always acted in the interests of communist orthodoxy, what surprises does the aging communist leader still hold in store for Greek politics?

BIBLIOGRAPHY

Elefantis, Angelos. *Under the Constellation of Populism*. Athens: Politis, 1991.
Tsoukalas, Konstantinos. *The Greek Tragedy*. New York: Penguin, 1969.

ARISTOTLE TYMPAS

FRANCISCO FRANCO (1892–1975) was general and leader of the Nationalist forces that overthrew the Spanish Republic in the Spanish Civil War (1936–1939). From the end of the Civil War until he died in 1975 Franco was the dominant political figure in Spain. As a dictator who long outlived his contemporaries, Adolf Hitler and Benito Mussolini, Franco left an indelible mark on Spanish society, which has only succeeded in firmly establishing democratic norms within the last ten years.

He was born Francisco Paulino Hermenegildo Teodulo Franco y Bahamonde in El Ferrol, province of Galicia, on December 4, 1892. His upbringing was harsh at the hands of a pious Catholic mother and a father who was an officer in the Spanish Naval Administrative Corps. He entered the Infantry Academy at Toledo at the age of fourteen, having been denied the opportunity to follow four generations of his family to the Naval Academy by cutbacks in the naval service. After graduation he volunteered for service in the colonial campaigns in Spanish Morocco and gained a commission at age twenty. At twenty-one he was the youngest captain in the Spanish army. By 1920 he was second in command in the newly formed Spanish Foreign Legion.

During the crucial campaign against the Moroccan rebels, the legion played a decisive role in bringing the revolt to an end. Franco became a national hero, and at the age of thirty-three was promoted to brigadier general, the youngest in Spanish history. The establishment of the Republic in 1931 put Franco's career on hold as he was placed on the inactive list due to a sharply antimilitary policy. However, in 1933 a new conservative government restored him to active command and in 1934 he was promoted to major general. In October 1934, he gained new prominence among the rightist elements in the country when he led the crushing of a rising by the Asturian miners. In May 1935 he was appointed chief of the army's general staff and he worked to restore discipline to the military institutions which had been weakened earlier by the Republic.

The year 1936 was crucial for the Spanish Republic as political parties regrouped into two hostile camps, the rightist National Bloc and the leftist Popular Front. The left won elections in February, but the right refused to accept the results, beginning a campaign to bring down the government.

Franco, who had been sent by the Republican government to an obscure post in the Canary Islands, joined in the military rebellion on July 18, 1936. His forces gained control of the Moroccan protectorate and soon afterward landed in Spain on a troop transport plane sent by Mussolini. They then marched toward Madrid. As the Nationalist forces approached the capital in anticipation of an easy victory, Franco was named commander in chief and head of the rebel Nationalist government. Franco was chosen because of his military prestige and his lack of previous involvement in politics. Franco also benefited from the death in a mysterious plane crash of General Emilio Mola, who had a similar claim on power.

On October 1, 1936, Franco, ranking survivor of the insurgent generals, was invested at Burgos with the title of El Caudillo and became head of the national government. Franco had failed to take Madrid, however, so, supported and encouraged by Hitler and Mussolini, he began a campaign of attrition. He also realized that even a military dictatorship needed some measure of popular support, leading him to court the anticommunist middle class through the Falange (the Spanish fascist movement) which he coopted and reorganized in 1937. This represented a significant political transformation for Franco, who was not known to have definite ideological convictions. The Falange, however, never developed into a mass fascist party similar to those existing in Germany and Italy. This failure stemmed in part from Franco's neglect of the movement in later years and his general lack of affinity with the core of fascist ideas.

Franco was a cautious and relatively unimaginative military leader, but he triumphed largely because of the superior quality of his army and continuing German and Italian assistance. Republican forces put up a brave fight against difficult odds, but with the lack of support from Western democracies, they were forced into an unconditional surrender on April 1, 1939.

Franco had led the Nationalist cause with the intent of creating a Spain where leftist views would be eliminated. He considered these ideas to be imported phenomena and therefore un-Spanish. He wanted to root out leftist ideas in much the same way that the Allies wished to eliminate fascist ideas from Germany. The "Law of Political Responsibilities" in February 1939 outlined the political repression that was to follow the Nationalist victory. Anyone judged to have contributed to the country's political troubles between 1934 and 1936, or who opposed the Nationalists during the Civil War, was guilty of an offense. All parties who had any part in the government and all their members were guilty except rank-and-file unionists who were not politically active. Any Spaniard who had been abroad and had viewed the conflict as a neutral was treated as a subversive, as were all Freemasons.

The range of punishments prescribed for these offenses varied from death to imprisonment to exile to a remote part of Spain. Prison terms ranged from a minimum of six months to a maximum of fifteen years. Prison sentences were often accompanied by large fines, and in some instances fines were imposed on relatives of prisoners who were executed. In 1941 the prison population of mostly political offenders numbered 233,000. The net effect of Franco's repression of his political enemies was the destruction of a political opposition in Spain for close to two decades. The anarcho-syndicalist National Workers Confederation (CNT), the socialist General Workers Union (UGT), the Communist Party (PCE), and the Socialist Workers Party (PSOE) were all destroyed within Spain, relegated to establishing exile organizations which had little impact within Spain for a number of years. In general these organizations would only begin to reorganize again in Spain in the 1960s.

Having defeated the Republican forces on the eve of World War II, Franco used the war years to consolidate his power, while carefully avoiding Spanish involvement in the war. While remaining clearly sympathetic to the Axis, he made no military or diplomatic commitments to Hitler, remaining officially neutral. Nevertheless, Franco maintained close contact with the Axis powers throughout the war. In 1940 Franco met with Hitler at Hendaye but fended off the German leader's attempts to bring Spain into the war on Germany's side. In February of 1941 he met with Mussolini and later with Pétain, the French Nazi collaborator, and Franco did eventually provide some Spanish troops for Germany's Soviet front.

However, as the inevitability of the Axis defeat began to emerge by 1943, Franco slowly disassociated himself from Mussolini and Hitler and in August 1944 he proposed an Anglo-Spanish understanding to Churchill. Nevertheless, Franco suffered through severe diplomatic isolation at the end of the war. Initially he was viewed by most world leaders as the last surviving fascist dictator and not worthy of full diplomatic recognition. The United Nations General Assembly passed a motion in 1946 calling for Spain's diplomatic isolation. In spite of its obvious needs, including widespread hunger, Spain was not included in the American Marshall Plan of post–World War II assistance.

However, the onset of the Cold War and rising East-West tensions resulted in a dramatic reversal of his stature among Western leaders. Almost overnight he became a prominent "anticommunist head of state" rather than a "fascist dictator." By 1948 most Western nations had reestablished normal diplomatic relations with Spain, and in 1950 the United Nations revoked its earlier position of ostracizing his government. Franco gained the biggest breakthrough for Spain with the signing of a bilateral agreement between the United States and Spain in 1953 and in the same year the completion of a pact with the Vatican.

The U.S.-Spanish agreement provided the United States with access to naval and air bases on Spanish territory. In return the Spanish government received significant U.S. economic aid, which contributed substantially to the stability of the regime. Psychologically, it also represented a very important victory for Franco because recognition from the United States, acknowledged leader of the world's democratic states, meant that Franco's government had found a new international respectability without making any concessions on the nature of its internal political processes, which went unreformed. The relationship was further underscored during a visit to Franco by President Eisenhower in 1959 during which the dictator received a warm embrace from the American president. It should be noted that U.S. recognition and aid to the Franco government gained the United States long-term animosity from Franco's political opposition. To this day anti-Franco activists blame the U.S. government for prolonging the existence of his regime.

The subsequent twenty years of Franco's rule in Spain after the U.S. agreement saw dramatic changes in the character of Spanish society, although the political dictatorship would remain firmly in power until after his death. Franco consolidated his official hold on the Spanish government through a variety of actions. With his political opponents largely imprisoned, killed or driven into exile, Franco staged a referendum in 1947 that made Spain into a monarchy but entrusted political leadership to himself for the remainder of his life. Twenty years later in 1967, Franco permitted the election of a small number of deputies to parliament and in 1969, Juan Carlos, eldest son of the pretender to the Spanish throne, was named Franco's official successor. Franco relinquished the position of premier in 1973 but retained his authority as head of state and commander in chief of the armed forces. In his later years, as his policies moderated, Franco came to be viewed by some as an elder statesman. But for a significant segment of Spanish society he remained a tyrant who imposed a brutal military regime on a deeply divided society.

Franco survived for the long haul by demonstrating an ability to adapt to changing times. During the 1950s Spanish society was dramatically transformed by a rapid growth in industry and simultaneous migration of large numbers of people from the countryside to the city. Franco did not resist these changes and provided government support to certain infrastructure projects. This willingness to change contrasted sharply with the unflexibility of the Portuguese dictator Antonio Salazar and resulted in a much higher level of industrial development in Spain. In addition, these rapid changes were accompanied by the rebirth of labor struggles and subsequently the reemergence of leftist political activity. The Franco regime never legalized the unions nor did it grant recognition to the political opposition on the left, but from the 1960s onward, these groups and organizations were largely tolerated by the regime.

Franco succeeded in holding on to power for thirty-six years, far longer than most political observers would have guessed. He accomplished this through a variety of means and with the aid of a number of factors. Initially, as we have seen, he ruled in large measure through harsh repression. Initially, as well, he ruled through the Falange State Party which he had resurrected during the Civil War. However, the party was downgraded in the 1940s and largely not used as a mass fascist party. His regime was always based on a strong core of support from the Spanish upper classes and from those sectors of Spanish society that were conservative and fiercely anticommunist. But Franco was not a truly popular ruler and did not turn to the masses for support.

Instead, Franco played off potential opponents from within the elite against one another. His political style was not heavy-handed but rather stressed a delegation of tasks to his political appointees. Franco used this approach in order to be an arbiter of disputes and to deflect criticisms of unpopular programs onto his subordinates.

When Franco died in 1975, political and economic elites realized that the continuation of Franco's dictatorial system was not possible. In order to better integrate Spain into the European market and reap the full benefits of its modernization, Spain had to adopt democratic values and repudiate what had come before. What may be most remarkable about Spain is that between 1975 and 1977 Franco's closest associates succeeded in transforming themselves into democrats who carried out the fundamental dismantling of the dictatorship, all the while working to establish democratic rule.

BIBLIOGRAPHY

Amsden, Jon. *Collective Bargaining and Class Conflict in Spain*. London: Redwood Press, 1972.

Fusi, J. P. *Franco: A Biography*. New York: Harper and Row, 1987.

Hills, George. *Franco: The Man and His Nation*. New York: Macmillan, 1967.

Payne, Stanley, *Franco's Spain*. New York: Thomas Crowell, 1967.

Trythall, J. W. D. *El Caudillo: A Political Biography of Franco*. New York: McGraw-Hill, 1970.

GARY PREVOST

G

HANS-DIETRICH GENSCHER (1927–) served as the Federal Republic of Germany's foreign minister for eighteen years, from 1974 to 1992, after serving almost five years as interior minister, setting a remarkable record for cabinet longevity. During the same period of almost a quarter of a century, as leader of the Free Democratic Party, Genscher was also a leading player in the party and coalition politics that determined the balance of power in Bonn.

By the time of his retirement in May 1992, Genscher had earned universal respect as Germany's most important foreign minister in the twentieth century, or at least since Gustav Stresemann of the Weimar Republic. Genscher's international reputation rested above all on his role in promoting a peaceful end to the Cold War, which had deeply divided both Germany and Europe. He had not foreseen the sudden collapse of communist rule that made German unification possible, but the attainment of national unity in 1990 nevertheless can be regarded as the capstone of his political career.

Just a few years earlier, Genscher's reputation had been more controversial. Some conservative critics regarded "Genscherism" as appeasement of the Soviet Union. It seems likely, however, that future historians will continue to award Genscher high marks for his adroit handling of foreign affairs in a dramatic period of European and German transformation. But these historians may well differ in their assessment of whether his masterful diplomacy included much creative planning and strategic shaping of developments, or whether it lay primarily in a shrewd pursuit of opportunities that happened to arise on his watch.

Genscher's power base was the Free Democratic Party (FDP). Since the founding of the Federal Republic in 1949, this small liberal party has maneuvered between its much larger counterparts on the moderate right and left, the Christian Democrats (CDU/CSU) and the Social Democrats (SPD) respectively. With its tiny base of electoral support, the FDP has had to make special effort to ensure that it attracts the minimum 5 percent of the popular vote necessary for parliamentary representation. As a small "third" party, however, the FDP often plays the pivotal role of kingmaker and balancer in coalition politics. Since

1969, when Genscher first became a cabinet member, the FDP has virtually decided which of the two major parties would remain in power, by forming an alliance first with the SPD and then, in 1982, by switching to a coalition with the CDU/CSU. In this, Genscher and his party have presented themselves to German voters as a ''corrective'' force, acting sometimes as a brake, at other times as an accelerator, offsetting tendencies toward either ''excess'' or ''inertia'' in the larger coalition partner.

Genscher led the FDP for over a decade, from 1974 to 1985, and he continued in some ways to be their most important politician until his retirement from the cabinet. His independent base of political support usually strengthened his hand within the government, but there were also times when the role of party leader limited his room to maneuver. He was inevitably drawn into coalition wrangles, and he had to be concerned about his small party's electoral vulnerability. Nevertheless, Genscher could also look back on his career in party politics with satisfaction. After leading the FDP through a dangerous electoral setback during the early 1980s, Genscher played a crucial role in the party's later revival among German voters both before and after unification.

Genscher's life has spanned much of the turmoil of Germany's recent political history. Like many other politicians, he has rarely been inclined to self-reflection, and he has given few clues about how events and experiences may have shaped his personality and politics. The only major exception has been his frequent reference (especially in later years) to his own roots in East Germany as a source for his strong sense of responsibility for both parts of the divided nation. Close German observers have explained his relentless drive as a compensation for several years of severe illness and forced inactivity as a young man. Among other influences, it seems likely that Genscher's early encounters with Nazism and communism reinforced his pragmatic discomfort with political extremism and ideological rigidity.

Genscher was born on March 21, 1927, near the industrial city of Halle, in what is today the state of Saxony-Anhalt. He grew up as the only child in a family that was conventionally Protestant, like most others in this homeland of Martin Luther. His parents both came from farmer families. After military service in World War I, his father studied law and became legal adviser to an agrarian association. His politics were those of a patriotic conservative, while Genscher's mother appears to have been wholly apolitical. In 1937, the family's life was jarred when the father died suddenly of blood poisoning. The ten-year-old son took on many family responsibilities and came to occupy a central place in his mother's life. She would later follow him to West Germany, where they remained close until her death in 1988.

Genscher's boyhood included the customary membership in the Hitler Youth. The war disrupted his high school education at a gymnasium in Halle, when he and his classmates were recruited in 1943 to serve as antiaircraft helpers, while continuing to receive sporadic schooling. Genscher entered full military service in early 1945. At the end of the war, in early May, the U.S. Army took the eighteen-year-old Genscher prisoner. He was turned over to the British forces, who released him a few weeks later. By July, he had returned home to Halle, in what was now the Soviet Occupied Zone of Germany.

In summer 1946, after a short stint as an unskilled construction worker and some additional course work to achieve his high school diploma, Genscher began to study law in Halle. A few months later, his life changed abruptly when he fell ill with tuberculosis. The following year and a half were spent in a hospital and sanatorium, where Genscher continued his studies as best he could. After recuperating, he transferred to the University of Leipzig, completed his first law exam in October 1949, and began the long legal internship that precedes the second German law exam.

This was the year when the division of Germany became formalized with the establishment of two rival German states. Communist controls on life in the German Democratic Republic (GDR) led Genscher to flee with two other law clerks to West Germany in August 1952. He immediately found work in a law office in Bremen, where he completed his legal training and became a lawyer in 1954. Soon thereafter, Genscher went through another year-long bout with tuberculosis. The life-threatening disease afflicted him once more, before a successful operation in 1957 finally made a full cure possible.

By then Genscher had already taken steps that would lead to a career in the FDP. His interest in party politics dated back to the immediate postwar period in Halle, where he had joined the Liberal Democratic Party (LDP) in 1946 at the age of nineteen. The Liberal Democrats had a stronghold in his home region, and the middle-class party fit well with Genscher's own background. Even though he remained a fairly inactive member, his political choice involved an early rejection of both the apolitical and socialist alternatives. Membership also gave the young man an opportunity to observe how the LDP rapidly lost its original political independence. Within a few years, it had become one of several East German ''bloc'' parties that received special privileges in return for loyal subordination to the ruling Communists.

In Bremen, Genscher was drawn to the FDP, a West German counterpart to the early LDP. His party work brought quick recognition of his political energy and skills. In April 1956, he was hired as assistant to the FDP's parliamentary leader in Bonn. He climbed rapidly in the party organization, reaching the position of federal manager in 1962. From there, his political connections led to a safe candidacy and election in 1965 to the Bundestag (the lower house of parliament), where he became the FDP's parliamentary whip. He seemed ideally suited for this role, with his talent for bargaining and his grasp of power relationships.

Between 1966 and 1969, West Germany was ruled by a ''Grand Coalition'' of both the CDU and the SDP. Alone in parliamentary opposition, the FDP used the opportunity to go through a major change in leadership, program and strategy, usually known as its ''opening to the left.'' Apart from adopting some ideas for modern educational and legal reform, the FDP came to favor a policy of dialogue and détente toward the Soviet Union and other countries in Eastern Europe, similar to an approach that was finding support in the SPD. An important component of the new ''Ostpolitik'' was a willingness to normalize relations with the GDR, thereby reducing the consequences of Germany's division.

Genscher was not the originator of these ideas, but he was on record as an early supporter of the FDP's reform course. In 1968 a party conference chose him as deputy to the new leader, Walter Scheel. A year later, the FDP entered a governing coalition with the SPD. The chancellor of this government, Willy Brandt (SPD), took a leading hand in shaping and legitimizing the new Ostpolitik that bound the two coalition parties together. As the FDP's two most important cabinet members, Scheel occupied the foreign ministry, while Genscher took over the ministry of the interior.

During the next few years, Bonn laid the foundation in foreign affairs on which Genscher would later build. West Germany normalized relations with Eastern Europe in a remarkable series of bilateral treaties. This breakthrough made possible the Conference on Security and Cooperation in Europe (CSCE), which convened in 1973 and turned out to be the first in a continuing series of meetings that would later become a main arena for Genscher's initiatives for a pan-European security order.

Genscher's political skills had long been recognized by insiders in Bonn, but he operated largely behind the scenes until he entered the cabinet in 1969. As minister of the interior, his crumpled figure soon became familiar in numerous public appearances, and he established a reputation as an omnipresent problem solver. He did remarkably little, however, to promote his ministry's share of the ''internal reforms'' that the government also had included on its ambitious agenda. Instead, his energies were absorbed by the wave of political terrorism by far-left radicals which afflicted West Germany in the early 1970s.

As the federal cabinet member in charge of such problems, Genscher concentrated on strengthening several internal security agencies. In the tense atmosphere of those years, West Germany went far beyond just apprehending terrorists, implementing widespread loyalty checks in the public service. Critics of this practice, for which Genscher was coresponsible, assailed it as a major infringement on civil liberties. But the interior minister viewed it as the legitimate self-defense of a threatened democratic order.

In May 1974 Genscher was drawn into the controversy over Willy Brandt's resignation, after the chancellor's personal assistant, Günter Guillaume, was arrested as an East German spy. Genscher had received a security tip about Guillaume almost a year earlier and brought the matter to Brandt's attention. Both appear to have treated it lightly, and Guillaume subsequent enjoyed access to secret NATO documents.

Genscher himself could also have been damaged by this serious security lapse, but instead he survived and even advanced politically. A major reason lay in the political need to keep him in the government, since Genscher was a key element in an intricate combination of arrangements designed to undergird the continuation of the SPD-FDP coalition. Scheel had just been elected federal president, and the government partners had agreed that Genscher would replace him as both foreign minister and vice-chancellor. It was already a foregone conclusion that the FDP would elect Genscher to take over from Scheel as party leader as well.

Although he had only minimal preparation, Genscher quickly gained a firm grasp of international politics. In one of his first major public appearances as foreign minister, he explained to the Bundestag that the provisions of the Helsinki Final Act, agreed to by the thirty-five participating nations in the CSCE, could be the basis for overcoming the division of both Europe and Germany. The international agreement provided for arms control, economic cooperation and the protection of human rights. Genscher would often return to these provisions as a pan-European framework that should be extended and institutionalized.

The new chancellor, Helmut Schmidt (SPD), received more attention than his foreign minister as an assertive West German voice in the international arena. Under the leadership of Schmidt, who had expertise and interest in both economic matters and security policy, Bonn again shifted its main attention to ''Westpolitik.'' Both he and Genscher were less active than their predecessors in Ostpolitik, partly because they were constrained by a general deterioration in superpower relations. This ''second Cold War'' arose from Soviet initiatives abroad that Washington, from its global perspective, found destabilizing. As an alliance partner, the Federal Republic participated in counterinitiatives, including the symbolic boycott of the Moscow Olympics in 1980. From its Central European position, however, West Germany did try its best to preserve the newly found *modus vivendi* with Eastern Europe. Under Genscher's management, Bonn was able to continue a ''mini-détente'' of its own by broadening its ties to the GDR.

Genscher's interest in saving détente was balanced by a strong commitment to military deterrence. In the early 1980s, he and the FDP became key players in the debate about intermediate nuclear forces (INF), the most divisive security controversy in West German politics since the rearmament question of the 1950s. The issue concerned the response by NATO to the military imbalance created by a Soviet missile buildup in Eastern Europe during the late 1970s. Schmidt and Genscher both supported a ''dual track'' strategy of restoring military parity by either negotiating a removal of the new Soviet weapons or, if that should fail, stationing new American medium-range nuclear missiles in West Germany. As deployment of the American missiles drew near in the early 1980s, Chancellor Schmidt ran into fierce opposition from many members of his own party, who regarded the NATO countermove as risky and unnecessary. Genscher quelled resistance within the FDP by threatening to resign as party leader if not supported on the INF issue.

In the fall of 1982, Genscher took it upon himself to lead his party out of its thirteen-year-old partnership with the SPD. It was a difficult political divorce, because just two years before, the FDP had waged a successful electoral campaign as a loyal partner of Helmut Schmidt. Since then, however, the two parties had become increasingly estranged over fiscal and defense strategies, at a time when the economy was sagging and the missile issue was coming to culmination.

But electoral considerations played the biggest role in the FDP's decision to leave the partnership. The government's standing in public opinion polls had plummeted, and the small FDP appeared to be in mortal danger from voter defections, whether it stayed with the SPD or broke away. After some awkward testing of the political winds, Genscher finally braved charges of betrayal and led the FDP into a new government coalition with the CDU/CSU, headed by Helmut Kohl, in October 1982. The political gamble paid off. In a subsequent Bundestag election, the FDP survived with 7 percent of the vote, in large part because it presented itself as a guarantor of responsible moderation and continuity in the new government's foreign policy.

Genscher continued as party leader for another two years, perhaps the most difficult ones in the entire history of the FDP. He seemed unable to shake off the label of political opportunism or shield his party's reputation from additional damage, including an embarrassing political finance scandal. As a consequence, the Free Democrats recorded disastrous results in elections to several West German state legislatures and to the European Parliament in Strasbourg.

In what turned out to be a well-timed move, Genscher stepped down from the FDP leadership at the beginning of 1985. He remained the most prominent member of the party, but he now was freed to concentrate fully on foreign policy. The removal from the day-to-day wrangles of party politics also had a tonic effect on his reputation. From 1987 on, opinion polls consistently rated him the most popular politician in the Federal Republic. The party used Genscher as its main drawing card to make an impressive advance in the Bundestag election of 1987 (9.1 percent of the vote).

It was in the CDU-FDP government during these years that Genscher put his distinctive mark on Bonn's foreign policy and emerged as something of a pacesetter in East-West relations. He had more room to maneuver than previously, in part because Chancellor Kohl had far less experience and interest in international affairs than his SPD predecessors Brandt and Schmidt. Moreover, Kohl had been among the early Christian Democratic converts to the new Ostpolitik, and he initially found Genscher and the FDP to be a useful brake on the remaining hawks in the CDU/CSU—much as Schmidt earlier had used Genscher and the FDP as a counterweight to the left wing of his own SPD. Moreover, Genscher himself, as the longest-serving foreign minister in the West, had gained in international experience and stature. He purposefully used all these assets in his moves to counteract tensions emanating from the military buildup in the 1980s.

Genscher had continued to support the INF decision after 1983, despite enormous West German demonstrations against the new missile deployment, but he stressed the concomitant need for arms negotiations and arms control agreements. As the Reagan administration pushed for larger military budgets within the NATO alliance, Genscher increasingly stood out with his advocacy of confidence-building relationships between East and West through the CSCE process. The Strategic Defense Initiative (SDI, popularly known as Star Wars) received only limited support from Genscher and his party, partly because of doubts concerning its technological assumptions, but also because of misgivings about a possibly harmful impact on arms control. When Genscher welcomed the resumption of arms control negotiations between the United States and the Soviet Union in early 1985, he also suggested that West Germany could now play a more active role in a new phase of Ostpolitik.

Although Genscher continued to regard conventional and nuclear deterrence as the necessary elements of an ultimate military security, he spoke and acted increasingly in terms of a broader concept of security that emphasized economic, political and cultural cooperation between the divided halves of Europe. He seemed tireless in promoting such "cooperative structures." The nonmilitary aspects of Genscher's security concept were intended to produce a web of interdependence that would reduce the likelihood of resorting to arms. Genscher habitually presented such initiatives as steps that would serve gradually to overcome the division of Europe and Germany.

A decisive turn came with the emergence of Mikhail Gorbachev as a Soviet reformer. Genscher was among the first and most determined Western leaders to recognize and explore the possibility of working closely with Gorbachev for an improvement in East-West relations. His view was best presented in a widely noticed speech, given in Davos, Switzerland, on February 1, 1987, just a few months after Helmut Kohl had committed the gaffe of comparing Gorbachev's skills at public relations to those of Joseph Goebbels, the Nazi propaganda minister. Genscher spoke instead of the Soviet leader's new thinking as presenting a unique opportunity for a turning point in East-West relations after four decades of Cold War confrontation. He warned that it would be a mistake of historic dimensions if the West passed up this chance to bridge the division of Europe and Germany. Genscher's argument was broadly popular in West Germany, where the deterioration in superpower relations had met with little understanding.

Some observers from the larger Allied powers reacted skeptically to "Genscherism." One major concern centered on the foreign minister's apparent modification of the bipolar view of Europe, which had been the cornerstone of the Atlantic Alliance since shortly after the end of World War II. Another reason for unease stemmed from the impression that Genscher's initiatives presaged a West German bid for a major international role. Genscher consequently had to perform a careful balancing act in these years, as Bonn acted less than before like a follower in the Alliance. He always presented his activities on behalf of détente as being in the shared interest of overcoming the dangerous division imposed by the Cold War. Germany, he stated frequently, had a special historical responsibility for bringing together a Europe which it had done so much to divide.

Genscher in some ways turned out to be in the vanguard of a second period of general détente, which began with Reagan and Gorbachev's superpower summit at Reykjavik in 1986. An arms control breakthrough at the end of the following year, which included the medium-range missiles (INF) stationed in Europe, seemed finally to vindicate NATO's dual track policy. Genscher and the FDP had been pivotal in making possible the original deployment of missiles despite resistance from the SPD. In an important example of their role as balancer, the foreign minister and his party now pressured a somewhat reluctant CDU/CSU into accepting INF removal from German territory.

It was not inconsistent for Genscher at this point to put pressure on Chancellor Kohl to resist NATO plans to modernize short-range nuclear weapons (SNF). The planned move was intended to balance the continuing Soviet superiority in conventional arms, but Genscher feared that it would prompt the Soviet military to override Gorbachev's disarmament efforts. His resistance to SNF modernization was also driven by a special German perspective on such weapons. Genscher continued to support an ultimate nuclear deterrent, but he had misgivings about short-range nuclear arms that had potential use as war-fighting weapons in a limited conflict area, such as Germany. The foreign minister spoke for many other Germans in voicing his apprehensions about the special vulnerability of his divided country, and he was successful in delaying any action on the matter in the late 1980s. With the disintegration of the Warsaw Pact, NATO moved by 1991 to adopt a "new strategic concept" that resembled in several respects Genscher's ideas for an overarching European security order. By then the SNF issue had become moot.

Genscher envisaged a reintegration of the divided continent through a long process of bridge building between Western and Eastern Europe. Like others, he therefore was taken aback by the sudden collapse of the communist systems in 1989–1990. Although the dislocation really did not fit neatly into his more evolutionary vision of change, he adjusted to the new situation with his usual talent for recognizing opportunities in shifting power relationships. He played a key role in the negotiations that led Hungary and Czechoslovakia to permit East German refugees to travel to the West in 1989.

After the Berlin Wall was opened in November 1989, Chancellor Kohl moved to take the lead on the question of German unification with a plan for early confederation of the two German states that he did not discuss in advance with his foreign minister. In the aftermath, when a rapid and complete merger became possible, Kohl stayed more involved in international politics than he ever had previously. But Genscher continued to play an indispensable role in the rapid series of negotiations which in 1990 led to a removal of the last obstacles to national reunification. One of his primary achievements was to allay anxieties among many neighboring countries about a politically and economically stronger Germany. In particular, he insisted unequivocally that the border with Poland be declared permanent at a time when Kohl, apparently for electoral reasons, still spoke ambiguously on that subject.

Genscher labored valiantly to calm fears about the possibly destabilizing impact of the new Germany. He stressed repeatedly that the Federal Republic would be embedded within a number of supranational institutions, such as NATO, the CSCE framework, and the European Community (EC). He was among the strongest promoters of a further economic and political integration (or "deepening") of the EC, but he also advocated a "broadening" of this "Little Europe" through the inclusion of new member countries from Central and northern Europe. And he emphasized the positive role that Germany could play in the economic and political reconstruction of central and Eastern Europe after the collapse of communism.

Although national unification came in a form and with a speed that Genscher had not expected, his long-term work on behalf of a new pan-European security structure had helped create the international setting in which Gorbachev felt it prudent to play his "German card." Without Moscow's willingness to abandon the right it had claimed to intervene on behalf of foreign communist regimes, developments in the GDR would have taken a different course in 1989. In the aftermath, Genscher could plausibly be presented by the FDP as "the architect of German unity." The first Bundestag election after unification, in December 1990, resulted in a triumph for Genscher's small party. The FDP received 11 percent of the total popular vote, its best result in almost three decades. In Genscher's home town of Halle, East German voters went much further by placing his party ahead of both the CDU and the SPD.

In the last year and a half before his resignation as foreign minister, Genscher seemed at times less surefooted than before. He had become a master at working within the network of deliberation and crisis consultation that he had helped build up during his many years in office. But he now seemed less nimble or comfortable in dealing with the new disorders that followed upon the end of the Cold War. Genscher's situation was not helped by his impaired health, which on occasion had forced him to interrupt his relentless work pace in the late 1980s. Politically, the Bonn coalition appeared to be overwhelmed by the dislocations that accompanied the crash of the old Eastern European order. The position of Genscher's FDP as balancer once again appeared to be endangered, as the German party system came under pressure from electoral discontent and the rise of protest groups on the radical right.

When Genscher suddenly announced his decision to leave office on the completion of his eighteenth year as foreign minister, in May 1992, he mentioned the need for a generational political change as one of his motives. His stunned party, after initial confusion, selected Klaus Kinkel to be his successor. Although Kinkel had joined the FDP less than two years earlier, he had worked closely with Genscher since the early 1970s. Throughout the German foreign ministry, Genscher's almost two decades of direction had left a mark not only by way of organizational memory but also through numerous personnel appointments.

Genscher's resignation nevertheless closed a major chapter in the Federal Republic's history. The new German foreign minister now speaks for a united Germany that, alone among the European powers, has emerged more powerful at the end of the Cold War than it was during it. Yet in facing the unexpected economic, social and political problems of reconstruction after the collapse of communism, Germany appears tempted to turn inward at the very time its effort and initiatives are needed to build a more stable European framework. Genscher often has echoed Thomas Mann's preference for a European Germany rather than a German Europe, an outlook the successor generation shares. Ironically, however, Genscher's agenda for a unified Europe as a setting for German unification has been reversed and only half fulfilled by recent developments. His successors will have to define a role for a unified Germany in a more ambiguous European setting than he had anticipated or wanted.

BIBLIOGRAPHY

Works by Genscher:

''Toward an Overall Western Strategy for Peace, Freedom and Progress,'' *Foreign Affairs* 6(1) (February 1982).

Unterwegs zur Einheit: Reden und Dokumente aus bewegter Zeit. Berlin: Siedler Verlag, 1991.

Other Works:

Blechman, Barry M., and Cathleen Fisher. *The Silent Partner: West Germany and Arms Control.* Cambridge, Mass.: Ballinger Publishing House, 1988.

Fritsch-Bournazel, Renata. *Europe and German Unification.* New York: Berg Publishers, Inc., 1992.

Hanrieder, Wolfram F. *Germany, America, Europe: Forty Years of German Foreign Policy.* New Haven, Conn.: Yale University Press, 1989.

Kirchner, Emil J. ''Genscher and What Lies Behind Genscherism,'' *West European Politics* 13(2): 159–72 (April 1990).

Szabo, Stephen F. *The Changing Politics of German Security.* London: Pinter Publishers, 1990.

CHRISTIAN SØE

EINAR GERHARDSEN (1897–1987) was the dominant political leader in postwar Norway. For twenty years he was the ''national father,'' an image accorded him by his opponents as well as his supporters. ''The Gerhardsen period'' is used to this day, by laymen and scholars alike, to describe this era. More than anyone else, Gerhardsen outlined the main political lines to be followed by Norway in the early postwar period.

During a very long political career, Gerhardsen held many positions. From 1923 to 1969 he was a member of the central committee of the Norwegian Labor Party, first serving as its secretary beginning in 1923, then elected deputy chairman in 1939. He took over as de facto chairman starting in 1940, being formally named to the post in 1945. He remained in the top leadership position of the party until he resigned in 1965. From 1945 to 1969, he was continually elected to the Norwegian parliament (Storting), although when serving as prime minister he did not take his seat there. He was Norwegian prime minister (head of government), first from 1945 to 1951, then again from 1955 to 1965. After his retirement in 1969, Gerhardsen continued to be deeply influential in Labor Party politics as an ''elder statesman.''

In addition to these formal positions, Gerhardsen was an active leader in the Norwegian Resistance during the German occupation. During the war, he was a political prisoner for four years.

As prime minister in the postwar years, Gerhardsen formed four different governments. The first one, an all-party coalition, lasted from June to October 1945. When Labor won its decisive victory in the October election, gaining 76 of the 150 seats in the Storting, the all-party coalition resigned, leaving its place to a one-party Labor government under Gerhardsen. Surprisingly, Gerhardsen then resigned the premiership in 1951, subsequently forming his third government in 1955. After having lost its Storting majority in 1961, the Labor government fell to a vote of no confidence in September 1963, but a nonsocialist coalition which replaced it was short-lived. In October of that year, Gerhardsen again formed a government, now for the fourth time. His final exit from the premiership followed the electoral defeat of October 1965.

A prime minister for fifteen years, Gerhardsen dominated Norwegian politics as much as a single man can ever do in any political system. Even when he resigned in 1951, he handpicked his own successor and carried out the whole operation alone and in secret. Some called it Gerhardsen's ''coup d'état with the sign reversed.''

Most probably, this period around 1951 represents the apex of Gerhardsen's political career. Even upon leaving the premiership, he kept the chairmanship of the party. In 1955 he undertook the reverse operation, reclaiming the premiership, all the while retaining the party leadership. But by this year, Gerhardsen exercised somewhat less power than before, for some events were no longer his alone to control. From then until the mid–1960s, his overwhelming dominance of Norwegian and Labor Party politics slowly eroded, until he was defeated by the Norwegians at the polls in the 1965 election.

Nonetheless, the early 1960s constitute a watershed in Norwegian postwar politics, testifying amply to Gerhardsen's central role in contemporary Norwegian political history.

Above all, Gerhardsen formulated the line to be followed by Norway in the general reconstruction of its society and economy in the first two decades after the war. These lines were laid out in an all-parties ''common program,'' drawn up as a full-fledged scheme during the German occupation. Its hallmark was a state-led economy building upon the cooperation of industrial and labor organizations, with goals of increased production, particularly within the export industries, full employment, price controls and negotiated wages, and the safeguarding of basic democratic political values. Within a very short time, this approach not only succeeded in reconstructing the devastated parts of the country, but had also set Norway well along the road toward growth and affluence. However, this state-controlled economy was much more motivated—even within the hard core of the Labor Party—by postwar necessity than by classical socialist ideology. From the beginning of the 1950s, economic control was systematically liberalized, paving the way for a typical mixed system, characterized by closely structured but free corporatism.

The political system that thus developed in Norway was constructed less upon political conflict than upon negotiations between all parties involved. Polarizing ideologies, therefore, tended to be replaced by a belief that conflicts could be solved in a perspective of all-embracing common interests. Within this framework, the main pillars of the Norwegian welfare system were deeply embedded. Its main traits were social reforms, societal leveling and human justice, and an ideology of common challenges and solidarity beyond the usual election rhetoric.

This ''social democratizing'' of Norwegian society occurred in parallel with the development of a new attitude toward foreign and security politics. The experience of World War II had definitively undermined any belief in the possibility of neutrality. Similarly, the Cold War put an end to any notions of ''bridge building'' between East and West. In particular, the communist coup in Czechoslovakia in 1948 forced Norway's Labor Party to choose sides. After negotiations for a Nordic alliance failed, Norway joined the North Atlantic Treaty Organization (NATO), reinforcing the close relationship between domestic and foreign policies. The Labor Party also further strengthened its dominant position thereby, for it now held the front against the communists and was able to portray itself as the party for common national interests. Alliance with the West paid rich electoral dividends to the party in the early postwar period, although by 1961, the party fragmented and lost its parliamentary majority.

Clearly, however, the Labor Party dominated Norwegian politics for the first two decades after the war, its position firmly established within a traditional multiparty democratic parliamentary system. The procedures and values of democracy were beyond dispute. With strong electoral support and a very close relationship to the trade union movement, the Labor Party leadership was successful during this period at transforming the party from one of revolutionary class warfare to one based on moderate social reform.

Indeed, Gerhardsen belonged to that generation of socialists who gradually evolved from revolutionary origins the basic attitudes of reformism. Resistance against the Nazi threat to democratic as well as fundamental national values was a deeply felt experience. This experience remained for many years the motivating force in his personality. The road to what Gerhardsen still called ''socialism'' was paved with true respect for democratic procedures, especially regular and free elections as the central feature. It is most telling that the party under Gerhardsen never exploited great electoral victories by redistributing property and power relations in society. Electoral support was never interpreted as a socialist mandate. On the contrary, the reformist way and its public appeal explained electoral success. Vaguely, and with great success, Gerhardsen defined "socialism" as "the good life," never really embracing the classical socialist criterion of state ownership of the means of production.

Consequently, Gerhardsen was never a "true believer" of socialism in the typical radical, nondemocratic sense. While he could wax rhetorical, he was primarily a pragmatist, trained in the handicraft of practical politics. Theory was never particularly relevant to him. His strength was in being an interpreter of the people, seeking their common values, more than it was in being leader who broke down barriers and blazed new trails.

Any politican tends to perceive the interests of his party as synonomous with the interests of the nation, and Gerhardsen was no exeption to this rule. But to a remarkable degree, he achieved wide popular acceptance of his vision: The 1945 program, the values of Labor, the national interest, all were one and the same. When he spoke with great fervor of cooperating to build society, this vision was also his party program, adjusted to contextual necessities.

In this way, Gerhardsen quite naturally assumed the role of "national father," and along with it, he exercised the right to define Norway's national interest. Thus a striking trait of his leadership was his ability to cast political decisions in nonpolitical terms. In this perspective, Gerhardsen symbolized "the social democratic order." The main key to it and to his thinking was the term *compromise*. Cooperation and community meant overcoming dogmas. Compromise became the basic democratic criterion.

From his beginnings as a politician, Gerhardsen was always closely identified with the labor movement. He was born inside the party and lived both with it and within it, personally, ideologically and organizationally. He had the most intimate knowledge of its functioning, and as leader he remained personally acquainted with the rank and file. His book *The Committee Representative* was a "must" for young recruits. The party was the foundations upon which he built both his own power and the future of Norwegian society.

The party's health and unity, therefore, was always a paramount concern to Gerhardsen at every crossroads. This leitmotif dominated both his general and more specific policy decisions. The labor movement had been seriously split after World War I. This experience remained a vivid memory to Gerhardsen and affected his attitude toward compromise solutions regarding the party's internal affairs. This line was a brilliant success until the birth of the Socialist People's Party in 1961. Gerhardsen considered this split in the labor movement to be his most serious defeat as a leader.

Emphasizing compromise, Gehardsen's leadership consisted much more of efforts to look for common solutions than to defy the opposition. He was permanently seeking to find the least common denominator. His leadership form therefore relied on persuasion more than on dictates, negotiation rather than orders from above. He did not, of course, totally lack a sometimes brutal capacity for decision making, often in small elitist power groups. His tactical cards even encompassed the threat of resigning: a final trump for a leader without successors. But it remained a permanent trait of his political style to hesitate, showing a lack of decisiveness which often left his colleagues bewildered. Nonetheless, the totality of his leadership style and his formal positions giving him authority supplemented by strength of personality, moral and political incorruptibility, personal contacts and political intuition all added up to an indubitable and effective leadership charisma.

To the formidable resource of his leadership style might be added his electoral strength, the party apparatus, a team of clever coworkers and weak opponents. There was no challenger within the party, no serious threat from a parliamentary opposition that remained splintered and fragmented. These were all potential resources yielding influence to the extent they were efficiently used. Influence can also be exerted through ''nondecisions,'' a kind of vetoing of the political agenda, and by the tacit playing on fears and expectations. Gerhardsen mastered all dimensions of the political game.

Influence is impossible to measure beyond approximation. Perhaps the best evidence of influence remains the degree of success in achieving stated goals. Gerhardsen's score in this regard is definitively positive. Beyond doubt, his influence was great, more often than not it was decisive. But such an assessment does not mean that Gerhardsen won every battle. In fact, his influence follows a complex pattern.

In 1949, for example, he clearly preferred a Nordic defense alliance before finally coming out in favor of a NATO solution—and only after he nearly resigned. His initiative in the 1957 NATO Council aroused great attention. But this attempt to reduce the arms race and create a more fruitful international atmosphere probably gave the domestic left-wing opposition a stimulus more than it affected international politics. In 1961 he was not able to prevent his party from splintering. In 1963 he could not solve the parliamentary crisis, get rid of the party secretary or handpick his successor. His government was the first to apply for Norwegian membership in the European Community. It thus put into motion the process which led to the political earthquake of 1972, when Norwegian voters in a referendum rejected EC membership outright.

Defeats such as these were no minor ones. His survival in the face of them, in fact, is the most telling illustration of his strength.

Einar Gerhardsen's long-term impact on Norwegian politics and the economy was substantial. He remains the very symbol of the social democratic welfare state model. This model was constructed upon an activist state, a mixed economy, social leveling and increased feeling of human security within a solidarist community.

Functionally, Gerhardsen was *primus inter pares* among an elite who structured the postwar Norwegian political system along corporative lines. Democratic corporatism was built into the common program of 1945, and Gerhardsen's emphasis on ''cooperation'' was extremely well suited for furthering democratic corporatism.

As a partisan, he was the undisputed leader of an organization which was transformed from class war attitudes into a sort of all-encompassing "people's" party. The development of the Labor Party during this period was both a cause of and a condition for the breaking down of traditional class conflicts in Norwegian society. Election campaigns in these years were of course noisy ones, all about who was most fit to govern on the basis of common national values. The antagonism between socialism and nonsocialism—put forth by electioneering politicians—was mere rhetoric, lacking any real substance. Gerhardsen's national appeal had a rather astonishing penetrating effect.

In an even larger perspective, he gave capitalism a "human face." The economic system survived, to some extent was reformed, but without any serious revolutionary challenge from the party and the elites in power.

In a long-term perspective, two vital problems nonetheless emerge, indicating a serious negative aspect to Gerhardsen's leadership. First, Gerhardsen was a leading exponent, ideologically and politically, for a philosophy of material growth. By the last phase of his reign, this growth had indeed clearly materialized. But "lifestyle illnesses" were also unveiled as part and parcel of the social democratic model. A whole "dessert generation" was indoctrinated with expectations and demands; when society proved incapable of fulfilling them, frustrated reaction followed. The ecological crisis, threatening life itself, is a consequence of the overtaxing of the globe's material resources. For this, a leader like Gerhardsen, along with his party and all those who profited by it, must share responsibility.

Second, one might ask whether social democracy implies a psychology which is basically untenable. Gerhardsen gave the people bread to eat, but evidently "the good life" is not achieved by bread alone. Given optimal material conditions of life, how do individuals behave? Likewise, where does one draw the line between basic necessities of life and socially conditioned wants? In fact, perhaps one should credit Einar Gerhardsen for creating the material and mental surplus which permits these questions to be raised.

By the 1960s, Gerhardsen was no longer the all-powerful party leader. He was growing older, and for some time politics had been an uphill fight. Significantly, he had hinted about his forthcoming resignation. Around him, succession skirmishes were evident, the strongest indication yet that he was on his way out.

In addition, these intraparty skirmishes indicated his lack of control of developments inside the party. Consistently Gerhardsen contradicted the very man who eventually succeeded him. Trygve Bratteli's succession as chairman and later as prime minister is the most telling testimony to Gerhardsen's decline at this stage.

The "Gerhardsen period" is a label indicating good years for society and for the Norwegian people at large. Most likely, both his supporters and opponents would agree. From his younger days and to the end of his life, Gerhardsen always lived as a very modest man. He had no education beyond the elementary level, and he was never tempted to yield to the temptations of power and fame.

He lived in a small private flat, and as prime minister he would queue up with the public for a cinema ticket or take his camping vacations abroad. Behavior like this was inborn; Gerhardsen astutely made it politically advantageous against the backdrop of a people known for their basically egalitarian attitudes.

BIBLIOGRAPHY

Works by Gerhardsen:

Fellesskap i krig og fred: Erindringer 1940–45. Oslo: Tiden Norsk Forlag, 1970.
Samarbeid og strid: Erindringer 1945–55. Oslo: Tiden Norsk Forlag, 1971.
I medgang og motgang: Erindringer 1955–65. Oslo: Tiden Norsk Forlag, 1972.
Mennesker og politik: Erindringer 1965–78. Oslo: Tiden Norsk Forlag, 1978.

Other Works:

Furre, Berge. *Vårt hundreår: Norsk historie 1905–90*. Oslo: Det Norske Samlaget, 1991.
Nyhamar, Jostein. *Einar Gerhardsen 1897–1945*. Oslo: Tiden Norsk Forlag, 1982.
———. *Einar Gerhardsen 1945—1983*. Oslo: Tiden Norsk Forlag, 1983.
Wyller, Thomas Chr. "Einar Gerhardsen som politisk leder." Et fragment. *Norsk statsvitenskapelig tidsskrift* 2(1989).

THOMAS C. WYLLER

VALÉRY GISCARD D'ESTAING (1926–), the third (and youngest) president of the French Fifth Republic, was born on February 2, 1926, in Koblenz, Germany, where his father was an official with the French occupying forces in the Rhineland. The Giscards were a family of lawyers from the Auvergnat region in central France, very active in conservative politics. In 1923 Valéry's father, Edmond, an inspector of finances, and his uncle René, seeking a title of nobility, were granted (in response to a somewhat questionable claim) the patronymic *d'Estaing* by decree of the Council of State.

After moving with his family to Paris in 1935, Giscard attended two prestigious lycées, Janson-de-Sailly and Louis-le-Grand, where he performed brilliantly in preparing for entry to the *grandes écoles.* Toward the end of the war he served briefly in the army. Upon his demobilization in 1945, he enrolled in the Ecole Polytechnique; after graduation (and a brief stay in North America) he continued his studies at the Ecole Nationale d'Administration. Thereafter he entered the higher civil service, where he rose rapidly as a specialist in economics and finance.

Giscard's political career began in 1956, when he was elected as deputy of a constituency in the Puy-de-Dôme (part of the Auvergne) that he had "inherited" from his uncle. In the National Assembly he identified himself with the Party of Independents and Peasants (CNIP). At the apex of the Algerian crisis in 1958, he voted for the investiture of General Charles de Gaulle as prime minister and subsequently supported the new Fifth Republic constitution as well as the election of de Gaulle as president of the new regime.

In November 1958 Giscard was reelected to the National Assembly under the label of Independent Republican. He abandoned his parliamentary seat soon thereafter, however, having been appointed junior minister (*secrétaire d'État*) for the budget under finance minister Antoine Pinay and his successor, Wilfrid Baumgartner. In 1962 Giscard became minister of finance in his own right, a position he kept for four years. At the end of that year he broke with the CNIP because that group had been too close to the proponents of "Algérie Française" and had lost most of its deputies in the December 1962 parliamentary elections. At the same time Giscard and his friends helped to transform the (pro-government) Independent Republicans (RI) into a separate parliamentary party. Soon after de Gaulle's reelection in 1965 (which Giscard supported) he was removed by Premier Georges Pompidou from his cabinet post. He then reentered the higher civil service as inspector of finances.

He did not, however, abandon his political ambitions. He worked for both the creation of a national federation of Independent Republicans as well as that of "Perspectives et Réalités," half political club, half think tank. In 1967 he reentered the National Assembly, becoming the leader of the forty-two deputies belonging to the RI parliamentary group. Concurrently, in the usual French political tradition, he continued to serve as a member of the municipal council of Chamalières, a suburb of Clermont-Ferrand, and was mayor of that town from 1967 until 1974.

As a deputy proclaiming himself a *Gaullien* rather than a *Gaulliste*, Giscard embraced a *oui mais* (yes, but) position: one of qualified and selective support of de Gaulle's policies. For instance, while endorsing the foreign policies and most of the domestic policies of de Gaulle, Giscard criticized the general's "solitary exercise of power." After the events of May–June 1968 and encouraged by his own increasing popularity in public opinion polls, especially in comparison with that of Premier Pompidou, Giscard demanded that Pompidou resign. (He did not.)

In April 1969, Giscard publicly advocated a "no" vote on de Gaulle's referendum to reform the Senate and grant somewhat greater autonomy to the regions. When the referendum failed (with Giscard's help) and de Gaulle resigned, Giscard thought of running for the presidency. However, when polls suggested that he would get only half the votes that Pompidou could expect, he decided to supported the latter; Pompidou, upon being elected, rewarded Giscard by reappointing him minister of finance.

Pompidou's death in 1974 was a God-sent opportunity for Giscard. When Jacques Chaban-Delmas (a former prime minister under Pompidou) became the official Gaullist candidate for the presidency, Giscard set to work putting together his own coalition. Using the Independent Republicans (a party strongly identified with big business, technocrats and the independent professions) as his main vehicle, Giscard argued that "France must be governed at the center." In doing so, he succeeded in obtaining the support of those who rejected both the Bonapartist nationalism of the Gaullists and the "collectivism" of the Socialists and their left-wing allies. In particular, Giscard enjoyed the support of both the pro-Catholic Democratic Center and the main body of anticlerical Radical-Socialists who had refused to ally themselves with the Socialist Party.

Giscard's candidacy was in some respects reminiscent of that of John Kennedy in the United States some fourteen years earlier: He was youthful, modern and *sportif,* and made the most of his photogenic looks in his constant appeals to "my dear television viewers." Unlike the Gaullists, he was outward looking and pro-European and had no complexes about the "Anglo-Saxons." He spoke English well (unlike Pompidou and Mitterrand, who knew little English, or de Gaulle, who refused to speak it in public), and he approached his campaign in a nonideological, pragmatic fashion, making effective use of marketing experts and polling specialists.

As president, Giscard demonstrated a commitment to pluralism and to the loosening *(décrispation)* of interinstitutional relations between the private sector and the public authorities and between the executive and legislative branches. Many of his ideas about political pluralism are articulated in his book, *La Démocratie française* (1976). The title of that book was then appropriated for the establishment of the Union pour la Démocratie Française (UDF), an electoral alliance (or federation) that was used to unite the "Giscardians" for the purpose of winning the 1978 parliamentary elections and of helping Giscard to win a second presidential term in 1981. This alliance was composed of the Independent Republicans (now known simply as the Republicans [Parti Républicain]), the Democratic Center (Centre des Démocrates Sociaux), the Radical Socialists, the club Perspectives et Réalités and a few smaller groups.

Giscard's commitment to pluralism did not mean that he was prepared to abandon the idea of presidential dominance in policy making. On the contrary, he significantly expanded the president's so-called reserved domain by closely involving himself in socioeconomic policy making, a domestic arena most often left to the prime minister under the Gaullists. When Jacques Chirac, a Gaullist who had been appointed prime minister by Giscard as a reward for his support of Giscard in the presidential campaign, demanded a greater decision-making role, Giscard refused, forcing Chirac to resign.

For his policy initiatives, Giscard relied heavily on *énarques* (the high-flying graduates of the Ecole Nationale d'Administration), who accounted for more than half of his presidential advisers. But he also relied on a number of relatives and friends, including several princes and barons (Michel Poniatowski, Olivier Guichard, Jean de Broglie), whom he appointed to important positions. Nevertheless, and somewhat paradoxically, Giscard moved to expand the powers of parliament (permitting it to set up commissions of inquiry) and granted more rights to opposition parties in it (giving them half the time during question periods). He also initiated a constitutional amendment (ratified in 1974) that permitted any sixty deputies or senators to challenge a bill before the Constitutional Council, thus enlarging the avenue of redress to this body. He also initiated legislation to lower the voting age to eighteen, to grant women greater legal equality, to liberalize the divorce laws, and to legalize contraception and abortion. He enlarged the presence of women in the government, and he created a Ministry for the Condition of Women.

Although steeped in traditional aristocratic and elitist values, Giscard was sympathetic both to the views of business and to the demands of the underprivileged masses for expanded social legislation. This attitude was reflected in his economic policy of "advanced liberalism," an ideological commitment to the market under which the state, instead of *directing* the economy, would limit its role to *facilitating* economic concentration, respecting competition and helping firms to conquer foreign markets. Price controls were gradually abolished; tax concessions were offered to job-creating businesses; trade unions were encouraged to seek wage increases and fringe benefits through collective bargaining; nationalized industries were urged to achieve financial self-reliance.

However, Giscard's neo-liberalism had to be periodically modified in response to economic exigencies and electoral pressures. Thus the government bailed out the insolvent social security funds, increased minimum wages, family-income subsidies and unemployment compensation, granted subsidies to public as well as private firms, maintained farm price supports, and reintroduced selective price controls and surtaxes on high incomes. Some of these emergency measures (known as the "Barre plan" after Raymond Barre, an economist who was appointed in 1976 to succeed Chirac as prime minister) were introduced alongside—and modified—the multiannual national economic plan, which had in any case become little more than a statistical forecasting and general "orientation" device.

The tone of Giscard's foreign policy was more flexible and less acerbic than that of de Gaulle, but it was not much different in substance. While proclaiming adherence to the Atlantic Alliance, France refused to rejoin the integrated military command of NATO. Moreover, France continued to rely on its own *force de frappe,* which—so it was pretended—would be used as an enlarged shield (*sanctuarisation élargie*) to protect West Germany as well as France against any Soviet threat.

Giscard was more enthusiastic than orthodox Gaullists in favoring European integration and greater rapprochement with West Germany, and he maintained a close personal relationship with Helmut Schmidt, the Federal Republic's chancellor. He lacked the (often articulated) Gaullist hostility to the United States, but he had a strained relationship with President Carter. Like the Gaullists, he pursued détente with the communist regimes of Eastern Europe and cultivated a closer rapprochement with the Third World, especially Africa. This rapprochement was to be reflected in an enlarged "North-South dialogue," envisaged as a triangular relationship between Western Europe, the developing countries and the oil-producing states of the Middle East, with France playing the role of privileged interlocutor. This was to be complemented by a "trilateral" harmonization of global monetary policy involving Europe, the United States and Japan.

Gradually, Giscard's foreign policies became noticeably more Gaullist. This was particularly true with respect to the Middle East: His position regarding the Arab-Israeli conflict came to reflect that of the Arabs, a position embodied in the Venice Declaration of 1980, in which France successfully pressured its European Community partners to accept the policies of the Palestine Liberation Organization. Giscard also tended to give in to Arab terrorists; thus in 1977, when Abu Daoud, a terrorist implicated in the massacre of Israeli Olympic athletes in Munich five years earlier, was apprehended in France, Giscard refused to extradite him to Germany or Israel and had him released.

Traditional Gaullism was also in evidence in Giscard's presidential manner. As his presidential term continued, he behaved in an increasingly detached if not imperial fashion. On the one hand, he took an ever more personal hand in the appointment of public officials and the direction of domestic policy; on the other hand, he showed a growing disdain for parliament, parties and even public opinion. This was reflected in his involvement in several scandals (including the acceptance of rare diamonds from Bokassa, the self-proclaimed ''emperor'' of the Central African Republic), his government's continued control over the programs of the electronic media, its opposition to the existence of private radio stations, its prosecution of newspapers (such as *Le Monde*) that were critical of him, and his waning interest in institutional democratization.

Although publicly committed to the growth of local democracy, he did little to promote decentralization (except for his restoration of the position of mayor of Paris, a position that had been eliminated a century earlier). Although opposed to the death penalty in principle, he did nothing to abolish it. And although favoring the modernization and democratization of the penal code, he initiated the passage of the ''Security and Liberty'' bill, which made criminal indictments easier and penalties for certain crimes more stringent. Finally, although expressing a desire to reduce the presidential term of office to five years, he did not pursue the matter as president, arguing that he wished to leave institutions to his successor in the same form he had found them.

Despite his obvious successes, Giscard's popularity had declined steeply during the last year of his presidential term. He came to be judged in increasingly negative terms—as a person who behaved more like a monarch than an elected president, one who incompletely identified with the people because (as Edgard Pisani put it) ''he never had to suffer'' and who, in the words of Raymond Aron, pursued ''an Orleanist philosophy and a Bonapartist behavior.''

When he ran for a second term in 1981, Giscard campaigned on the theme of ''change and continuity.'' His narrow defeat by François Mitterrand in the second round was in part the result of a growing popular conviction that Giscard had lost his reformist momentum and that he was too conservative to solve crucial problems, including unemployment, socioeconomic inequalities and growing urban violence. But his defeat must be attributed in part also to the fact that Chirac, the first-round Gaullist candidate, refused to issue an unambiguous call to his supporters to vote for Giscard in the second round.

Since leaving the presidency in 1981, Giscard has not retired from active politics. In the 1980s, he toyed with the idea of becoming president of a politically united Europe, but as that goal became illusory, he concentrated on national politics. In 1984, after winning a by-election, he returned to the National Assembly (concurrently occupying local and regional elective offices); in 1988 he assumed the formal leadership of the UDF, which, he continued to hope, would serve as an instrument for his eventual reelection to the presidency. A year later, he headed a combined list of UDF-Gaullist candidates to the European Parliament and was elected to that institution.

Giscard's prospects of returning to the presidency of the French Republic have been clouded by the ambiguities of the relationship between the UDF and the Gaullist Rally for the Republic Party (RPR), a relationship that parallels the uneasy marriage between Giscard and Chirac, who continues himself to be interested in the presidency. Both political camps usually renew their (somewhat unreliable) collaboration during each election.

But while Giscard has agreed publicly with Chirac on the desirability of unity between the UDF and the RPR, he has differed with the Gaullist leader on the nature of that unity. Whereas Chirac has favored a fusion of the two camps, Giscard has preferred an electoral alliance in which each of the components retains its organizational autonomy. Thus, for the presidential election of 1988 the UDF and RPR officially supported Chirac as the joint candidate of the republican right, but it is probable that Chirac's election was surreptitiously sabotaged by Giscard's less than enthusiastic support of him. For the Assembly elections the same year, the two groups put up common candidates in many constituencies under the label of Union pour la Nouvelle Majorité, but that unity did not bring them the parliamentary control for which they had hoped. Since then, the Giscard and Chirac forces renewed their commitment to field joint parliamentary candidates for the March 1993 parliamentary elections, in which the RPR-UDF coalition won a vast majority, and to a single candidate for the next presidential election, scheduled for 1995.

Nonetheless, UDF-RPR collaboration has been impeded by the continued rivalry between Giscard and Chirac, by policy differences regarding European unification and by confusing approaches to the problem of dealing with the extreme-right Front National and its leader, Jean-Marie Le Pen. Publicly, Giscard has agreed with Chirac that any alliance with the Front National (FN) be avoided, yet he has permitted UDF politicians to make deals with that party on local levels. And in 1991 he appealed to the racism of the FN electorate by writing an article in *Figaro Magazine* deploring the "invasion" of France by foreigners and advocating a more stringent approach to the acquisition of French citizenship (one based on blood ties).

In 1992, while Chirac (reflecting divisions within the RPR) adopted a qualified, hesitant position regarding the referendum to approve the Maastricht Treaty to move the European Community closer to unity, Giscard agreed with the overwhelming majority of Socialists in a clearly pro-Maastricht position and even appeared in public together with Socialist ministers to promote a favorable vote. Finally, although Giscard had agreed with Chirac that the choice of a common conservative standard-bearer in the next presidential elections would be decided by a "primary" vote, he circumvented that agreement by announcing (in October 1992) that he was ready to become the presidential candidate—with the understanding that if he won, he would step down after a five-year tenure.

BIBLIOGRAPHY

Works by Giscard d'Estaing:

La Democratie française. Paris: Fayard, 1976.
L'Etat de la France. Paris: Fayard, 1981.
Deux Français sur trois. Paris: Flammarion, 1984.
Le Pouvoir et la vie. Paris: Compagnie 12, 1988.

Other Works:

Cohen, Samy, and Marie-Claude Smouts. *La Politique extérieure de Valéry Giscard d'Estaing.* Paris: Presses de la Fondation Nationale des Sciences Politiques, 1985.
Conte, Arthur. *L'Homme Giscard.* Paris: Plon, 1981.
Frears, J. R. *France in the Giscard Presidency.* London: Allen & Unwin, 1981.
"Le Giscardisme," *Pouvoirs* 9 (1979).
Lecomte, Bernard, and Christian Sauvage. *Les Giscardiens.* Paris: Albin Michel, 1978.
Noury, Anne, and Michel Louvois. *Le Combat singulier.* Paris: Denoel, 1980.
Pol, Bruno. *La Saga des Giscard.* Paris: Editions Ramsay, 1980.

WILLIAM SAFRAN

FELIPE GONZÁLEZ (MÁRQUEZ) (1942–) has been Spain's prime minister since October 1982. As leader of both the government and the country's largest political party, the Spanish Socialist Party (PSOE), he has dominated domestic politics during the 1980s and into the 1990s. Under his leadership the Socialist Party has steered away from Marxism and toward a pragmatic, pro-growth version of social democracy. As prime minister González has strengthened Spain's new democracy and stimulated economic modernization. He has also sought to bring Spain as a full partner into the movement toward European unity. Since leading his country into the European Community in 1986, he has been one of the Community's champions for further integration.

Yet after a decade in power, González remains controversial. In recent years, he has displayed little of the populist style and zest for public appearances characteristic of him during the early 1980s. According to some observers, González has become increasingly bored with domestic politics, preferring to project his energies and influence into foreign, especially European, affairs. Moreover, he has long alienated many of his initial supporters, especially within the labor movement, who denounce his "betrayal" of socialist ideals. During the late 1980s and early 1990s, his administration (though not González personally) suffered charges of corruption and influence peddling. Despite this loss of luster, he remains his country's dominant politician, in part because the opposition has been weak and divided and in part because he remains the most popular and magnetic leader on the political scene.

González was born on March 5, 1942, the second of four children born to Felipe González Helguera and Juana Márquez Domínguez in Puebla del Río, near Seville. There, with the father working as a livestock handler and dairy farmer, the González family lived in modest, though not impoverished, conditions. In his high school years, the young Felipe joined the Young Christian Workers, a prolabor, Church-sponsored youth group. Excelling in his studies, he later enrolled at the University of Seville, becoming the first member of his family to attend college.

At Seville, he studied with a progressive Catholic professor, Manuel Jiménez Fernández, who further reinforced a growing interest in the affinities between left-leaning Catholicism and socialism. In 1964, toward the end of his studies, he joined the then-banned PSOE. After graduating that same year with a law degree, González spent the following year studying labor law at Catholic University in Louvain, Belgium, where he became influenced by Paul-Henri Spaak and other moderate socialists. There he was also able to read freely about the internal struggles of the Spanish Communist Party (PCE), including the 1964 expulsion of two prominent intellectuals, Jorge Semprún and Fernando Claudín. González later credited the struggles of these two with having influenced his decision to join the Socialists and not the PCE. Within a year of returning to Spain, he had become a crusading labor lawyer in Seville, and, in the next years, became increasingly active and prominent in the Socialist Party.

During the late Franco period, from 1966 to 1975, González gradually emerged as the undisputed leader of the PSOE, a Marxist party that had been founded in 1879 by Pablo Iglesias. Crushed and outlawed at the end of the Civil War (1936–1939), the PSOE survived during the Franco period largely as a party of exiles, most of whom were living in France and Mexico. During the last decade of Franco's rule, however, a domestic Socialist movement began to revive, leading to a growing split between the *históricos,* or the exiled leadership grouped around Rodolfo Llopis, and the *renovadores,* the Spain-based faction that advocated a ''renovation'' of PSOE leadership and ideology.

Operating from his Seville base, González led the latter in attacking the old guard, claiming that the PSOE needed to appeal to new groups (e.g., progressive Catholics and Communists) and classes (e.g., emerging middle strata). This internal struggle reached its apex in 1972, when the ''renovators'' wrested power from the exile group (which then split off to form a separate party) . Two years later, the reconstituted PSOE, holding its twelfth congress in exile in Suresnes, France (political parties still being illegal in Spain), elected González its secretary general. At this congress the delegates endorsed a *ruptura democrática*—a campaign of popular mobilization designed to sweep away the Franquist dictatorship and usher in a democratic state.

In the crucial years following Franco's death in November 1975, however, González and the PSOE (along with the Communist Party and the major labor unions) took a more moderate path, supporting the gradual democratic reforms sponsored by King Juan Carlos and Prime Minister Adolfo Suárez that culminated in a new constitution in 1978. Subsequent electoral results confirmed the wisdom of this approach. In the general elections of 1977 (the first in Spain since 1936), González, capitalizing on his youthful, charismatic appeal, led the Socialists in capturing 29 percent of the vote, a result second only to the 34 percent of Suárez's Union of the Democratic Center (UCD), a coalition of centrist and moderately rightist parties. In elections two years later, the PSOE advanced to 31 percent, although it still remained five points behind the UCD. Along with votes came adherents, as the PSOE grew from less than 4,000 members in 1974 to more than 100,000 by 1980.

During these "transition" years, González tightened his control over a factionalized PSOE while moving it toward ideological moderation. The key events in this evolution were two party congresses in May and September 1979. In the first one, the twenty-eighth party congress, González sought to abolish the party's formal affiliation with Marxism but was defeated, whereupon he resigned as party leader. However, during this same congress, delegates approved changes in internal election rules that ultimately strengthened González's own loyalists' power at the expense of the "critical sector," the party's pro-Marxist wing. In the second "extraordinary" congress, called to select a new leader, González employed his enhanced power to obtain both his reelection as leader and the party's abandonment of Marxism.

In October 1982, firmly controlling the PSOE and challenging a divided, unpopular UCD government (now under Suárez's successor Leopoldo Calvo Sotelo), González led his party in capturing 48 percent of the popular vote and 202 of 350 Cortes seats. Since then, the Socialists have twice retained their parliamentary majority, albeit with declining support (44 percent of the vote and 184 seats in 1986, and 40 percent of the vote and 175 seats in 1989). Because the new constitution gives the prime minister relatively broad powers for a parliamentary system, González has been able to shape policies to an unusual degree.

As an opposition candidate vying for power in 1982, González promised important reforms, including the creation of 800,000 public sector jobs and a reconsideration of Spain's recent membership in NATO. Once in power, however, his policies, both domestic and foreign, have stressed caution over risk and continuity over *ruptura*. Indeed, in key respects González, far from reversing the policies of his UCD predecessors, has extended them.

González's preference for moderation may be explained by at least four factors. The first is his personal style, which, although it plays on his image as a populist progressive, is actually highly pragmatic, elitist and therefore disdainful of radical change initiated or supported by the grass roots. Second, the political context has induced caution, for González has faced the task of completing the post-Franco transition to democracy. At the outset, operating under a four-year-old constitution and mindful of a military coup attempt in February 1981, the

Socialists had to worry about the political fallout that drastic reforms might trigger.

Third, Spain's economic situation has discouraged radical measures. The economy had been racked by the 1979 oil shock—for example, growth averaged only 0.3 percent per year while unemployment leaped from 8.4 percent to 13.8 percent between 1979 and 1981—and the government's first priority was recovery. (González, having taken power in October 1982, was also mindful of the fate of the "Mitterrand experiment," the failed attempt by French Socialists in 1981–1982 to stimulate the economy and redistribute income in the midst of a world recession.) Moreover, as Spain prepared for, and then entered, the European Community in January 1986, the government had to prepare businesses to compete, which meant modernizing small-scale agriculture, an ill-adapted financial system (with undercapitalized banks and securities markets), and an inefficient system of state-run firms.

Finally, the González government faced little pressure from its left to embark on drastic changes. During the early post-Franco years, the PCE, following a course that was if anything more moderate than the Socialists', lost much of their support and fell to internal bickering and breakup. The major labor unions, as well, had experienced declines in membership and militancy beginning in the late 1970s. Electoral logic suggested that the PSOE had little to lose by moving to the center.

In domestic policy, the González government has focused on the economy, specifically on a strategy designed to help domestic firms become competitive as Spain "rejoined Europe." That strategy has featured a macroeconomic policy with three core elements. The first has been an attack on inflation, in which the government, in addition to employing classic measures such as budget-deficit reduction (including cutbacks in social security) and tight monetary policy, has sought to restrain wage demands. The main mechanism for the latter, especially during the first four years, was an incomes policy based on peak-level *concertación* between the government, the main labor organizations, and the employers' association. However, the labor unions, including the Socialists' "sister" confederation, the General Workers Union (UGT), became increasingly disillusioned with the government's austerity policy, ultimately breaking with the government and leading a massive general strike in December 1988. This hostility has continued into the 1990s, with another general strike being called in May 1992.

Second, the government has sought to attract foreign capital by offering an array of credits, low interest rates, tax breaks and other inducements. These incentives produced the desired result, giving Spain the highest rate of capital inflow in Europe during the 1980s. Finally, the government has attempted to reduce Spain's unemployment rate, the EC's highest, by encouraging early retirement, recruitment of idle labor and greater labor market "flexibility" (e.g., use of provisional, renewable six-month contracts).

In addition to these general measures, the González government has enacted a two-pronged program to boost industry. First, the government has sought to reform the largely unprofitable public industrial sector, mainly by reorganizing and privatizing parts of the Instituto Nacional de Industria (INI), a state agency that oversees some seventy manufacturing and service firms with over 215,000 employees. Second, the government in 1984 enacted an ''industrial reconversion'' plan to restructure eleven distressed sectors including steel, shipbuilding and textiles. Although there was considerable local resistance designed to save the 70,000 jobs slated for elimination, the government persisted in implementing most of its program.

González's economic policies have produced mixed results. On the positive side, with an average annual GDP growth rate of 3.5 percent between 1983 and 1991, the Spanish economy surpassed the EC average of 2.6 percent. The government can rightfully claim to have achieved its central aim: the fostering of a business environment that welcomes foreign capital and encourages greater market efficiency among Spanish firms. On the other hand, problems remain, especially in unemployment and inflation. Although the former has been sizably reduced—from a high of 21.1 percent in 1985 to 16.0 percent in 1991—it remains nearly twice the EC average. Inflation (6.3 percent in 1991) also continues to outpace the EC average (5.0 percent). Most alarmingly, the rapid growth that was achieved in the late 1980s proved impossible to sustain because of growing budget and trade deficits. This prompted the government in 1991 to enact a restrictive monetary and fiscal policy, which has further alienated working-class supporters.

In addition to the economy, other major domestic concerns have included regionalism and education. The 1978 constitution, in responding to demands for greater regional autonomy, pledged to decentralize governmental authority, and the Suárez government quickly granted ''historic communities'' such as the Basque country, Galicia and Catalonia new statutory powers. By 1982 this process had led other regions, having no particular historic or cultural claims to autonomy, to also press for new powers. Although González had supported this autonomy process while in opposition, once he took power his ardor cooled. He has generally sought to moderate the rate and scope of further decentralization, a position that has caused friction between his government and the newly energized regional governments.

In the area of education, the government sought, through the 1984 Maravall law (so named for the education minister), to standardize the curriculum for all primary and secondary schools, public and private, receiving state aid. Among other things, this law banned mandatory religion classes in Church-run schools receiving state assistance. Since virtually all Catholic schools are state-subsidized, Church officials viewed the law as an infringement on religious freedom and sponsored massive protests, which were supported by right-wing parties. The government refused to buckle, however, claiming that the measure would democratize school administration.

Foreign policy under González has reflected the same moderation and reversal of past positions as has domestic policy. While in opposition, González and the Socialists espoused a mildly anti-American, "Third Worldist" policy, for example, actively opposing Spain's entry into NATO and endorsing the Nicaraguan Sandinistas and other Third World nationalist movements. At the same time, however, González favored closer ties with the European stalwarts of NATO and strongly backed EC membership. Once in power, he had to face the contradictions of such positions. How could Spain pull out of NATO (which it had only joined in the spring of 1982), while embracing the European Community?

As we have seen, González's answer has been to pursue European unity at the price of abandoning his anti-NATO stance. In seeking to conciliate both the generally anti-NATO left (including many members of his own party) and the pro-NATO right, he called for a referendum to decide Spain's NATO membership. The referendum, held in March 1986, was carefully worded so as to favor continued membership but under conditions that would reassure leftist opponents (e.g., no nuclear weapons would be allowed on Spanish soil, and U.S. troops would be gradually removed from Spain). The vote itself—53 percent in favor of continued membership versus 40 percent opposed—was a resounding victory for the government, which had strongly campaigned for the measure.

Since that time, González has consistently aligned himself with pro–Atlantic Alliance, pro-European unity leaders such as François Mitterrand and Helmut Kohl. The only question about his continued commitment to the European unity process during the 1990s is whether the Spanish economy can withstand the monetary stresses caused by Germany's high interest rates. For example, during the September 1992 crisis within the European Monetary System, Spain was forced to devalue the peseta. But there is little doubt that González views European integration as the chief vehicle for Spanish economic development and democratic legitimation.

The next electoral test for González and the PSOE was scheduled for October 1993. Returned (although narrowly) to office for an unprecedented fourth term, González can rightly claim a record of historic achievement, for he has taken his country squarely into the European mainstream after decades (if not centuries) of isolation and ostracism. He has safeguarded the consolidation of democracy, while fostering a favorable environment for private sector growth. On the other hand, critics can charge, also rightly, that he has done so by abandoning any pretense to socialist values of solidarity and equality, relying instead on criteria of market efficiency. Thus his legacy as a "progressive" leader is likely to be long debated. What few will contest is that Felipe González, both in opposition and in power, has influenced domestic political life more profoundly than any other figure in post-Franco Spain.

BIBLIOGRAPHY

Gillespie, Richard. *The Spanish Socialist Party: A History of Factionalism.* Oxford: Clarendon Press, 1989.

Maravall, José. *The Transition to Democracy in Spain.* London: Croom Helm, 1982.
Payne, Stanley G. (ed.). *The Politics of Democratic Spain.* Chicago: The Chicago Council on Foreign Relations, 1986.
Preston, Paul. *The Triumph of Democracy in Spain.* London: Methuen, 1986.
Share, Donald. *Dilemmas of Social Democracy: The Spanish Socialist Workers Party in the 1980s.* Westport, Conn.: Greenwood Press, 1989.

W. RAND SMITH

H

JÖRG HAIDER (1950–) took over the leadership of the Freedom Party of Austria (FPÖ) in 1986 and has become the most controversial figure of contemporary Austrian politics. His rise to influence, in particular by increasing the electoral base of the FPÖ by more than threefold—to a high of 16.6 percent in 1990—has seriously undermined the position of the two established mainstream parties, the center-left Social Democratic Party (SPÖ) and the center-right Austrian People's Party (ÖVP). The success of Haider and his party must be seen in the context of anti-establishment pressures from the far right in a number of Western European countries. And it is exactly the issue of "how right is Haider really?" that polarizes public opinion in Austria.

Jörg Haider was born in Bad Goisern, in the province of Upper Austria, on January 26, 1950. Haider's father was an active National Socialist who left Austria for Germany and in 1933 joined the Austrian Legion (Österreichische Legion), a group that used Bavaria as an operational base against Austria. After the Nazi occupation of Austria in 1938, Haider's father returned to Austria and served as chief administrator for youth affairs (*Gaujugendverwalter*) in the province of Upper Austria, at that time renamed Upper Danube by the Nazis.

The young Jörg Haider studied law at the University of Vienna, completing his dissertation in 1973. Afterward he worked as a university assistant at the Institut für Staats und Verwaltungsrecht, also a unit of the University of Vienna. In 1976, when Haider was in his mid-twenties, a scholarship was offered to him for study in Toronto. However, his wife was pregnant and their economic circumstances were precarious. By this time, Haider's rhetorical talents were already well-known, and Mario Ferrari-Brunnenfeld, the FPÖ party leader in the southern Austrian province of Carinthia, offered Haider the job of provincial party secretary, a position Haider held until 1983. That year, Haider himself succeeded Ferrari-Brunnenfeld as FPÖ party leader in Carinthia. In retrospect, Ferrari-Brunnenfeld judged his appointment of Haider to have been a serious mistake.

The FPÖ had been founded in 1955, the "third party" in the Austrian political system behind the SPÖ and ÖVP. It grew mainly out of the VdU (Verband der Unabhängigen, i.e., Independent Union) and stood clearly outside the consensus of Austria's political mainstream. The FPÖ began as an antisystem party and targeted former Nazis as its primary electoral base. However, under the leadership of Friedrich Peter (1958–1978), the FPÖ successfully began to break out of its isolation and move to the center. Bruno Kreisky, the influential leader of the SPÖ (1967–1983), encouraged the FPÖ's move to the center and sought to establish an SPÖ-FPÖ partnership to squeeze out the ÖVP.

In the 1980s, two crucial developments occurred in Austrian politics. The dominance of the two established catchall parties, the SPÖ and the ÖVP, began to erode, as the Austrian electorate began to swing to the right. The year 1983 marks an important watershed: In general elections, the SPÖ lost its absolute majority and formed a "Small Coalition" with the FPÖ. At the national level, the FPÖ, under the leadership of Norbert Steger (1979–1986), had begun the process of trying to transform itself into a truly centrist liberal party. But in 1983, Jörg Haider also took over the leadership of the FPÖ in Carinthia province, and he quickly proved himself to be an exponent of the right wing.

Carinthia province, in the south of Austria, had always been one of the most important regional bases for the FPÖ, going back to the *Kärnter Abwehrkampf* in the aftermath of World War I, when the German-speaking population of Carinthia developed an anti-Slavic reflex from fears of being taken over by Yugoslavia. A severe political struggle developed between Steger and Haider over the future of the FPÖ, carried out to a large extent through the mass media.

The "Reder case" was typical of this struggle. In it, Walter Reder, member of the Waffen-SS in World War II, was sentenced to life imprisonment after being held responsible for the massacre of the Italian town of Marzabotta, where 1,800 people were killed in October 1944. In January 1985, Reder was released and flown to Austria. The Austrian minister of defense, the FPÖ's Friedhelm Frischenschlager, welcomed Reder personally at the airport, causing a storm of political protest. Haider, nonetheless, judged Frischenschlager's action to have been "excellent" (*vorbildlich*).

While Norbert Steger tried to put the FPÖ on a liberal track, its electoral base was in decline. The FPÖ suffered a series of provincial losses from 1983 to 1985, and opinion polls forecast an all-time low of 3 percent of the vote if national elections were to be scheduled. Against this national trend, Jörg Haider had been able to stabilize and reinforce the FPÖ's position in Carinthia. Under his leadership, in the provincial elections of 1984, the FPÖ's electoral support increased to 16 percent, up from 11.7 percent in 1979. These results strengthened his position against Steger. Their conflict escalated to an open showdown at the FPÖ party conference in Innsbruck in September 1986. With a margin of 57.7 percent, Haider defeated Steger and became the new FPÖ leader (*Bundesparteiobmann*).

Haider's victory, however, exacted a political price. In June 1986, the SPÖ's Franz Vranitzky became the new Austrian chancellor, or head of the federal government. Vranitzky had strong feelings against Haider, whom he regarded as too far right. Vranitzky decided to call an election for November 1986, in the process disbanding the ''Small Coalition'' with the FPÖ. In January 1987, a ''Grand Coalition'' of the SPÖ and ÖVP was formed.

Nonetheless, under Haider's leadership, the FPÖ had improved its position during the 1986 elections, climbing to a national level of 9.7 percent of the vote. As party leader during the campaign, Haider followed a line of directly and aggressively attacking the incumbent government, coloring his attacks with strong streaks of populism. This strategy gained him electoral support, but, on the other hand, also forced him into a classic dilemma: The more radically populist Haider behaved, the more electoral support he earned, all the while diminishing the chance that a political party would be willing to form a coalition with him.

In March 1989, provincial elections were held in Carinthia, and their outcome caused a shock wave. The SPÖ lost its majority in the province's parliament, and the ÖVP was relegated to a third-place finish. With 29 percent of the votes, the FPÖ finished a clear second. By forming a coalition with the ÖVP, Jörg Haider achieved his greatest political triumph thus far. In May 1989, he was sworn in as governor of Carinthia.

This series of events illustrates one of Haider's main strategies for the FPÖ: Overtake the ÖVP at the national level as the leading nonsocialist ''bourgeois party'' within the center-right/right spectrum and then form a coalition with the ÖVP, but with the FPÖ as the dominant partner. In November 1991, this scenario was repeated in provincial elections in Vienna.

Jörg Haider's rise to power marks the victory of the right wing over liberal groups within the FPÖ. Surveys of the mass public's left/right political perceptions clearly document that, since 1976, the FPÖ has shifted from the center-right to a position clearly to the right of the ÖVP. However, the question that divides public opinion in Austria is precisely *how far right* is Haider really?

There are two interpretations. The first is that Haider is primarily a populist, always ready to moderate his politics if he sees coalition opportunies. The second interpretation argues that Haider has a hidden agenda, pretending to be a populist while actually standing very far to the right. Some observers outside Austria, such as members of the Socialist group in the European Parliament, call the FPÖ a ''Nazi Party'' (Reymonds Dury) and speak of Haider's politics as ''Yuppie Fascism'' (Glyn Ford).

It is a tricky proposition to assess how far right Haider is. Haider himself is very quick to sue in court anyone who calls him a Nazi, as illustrated by the trial of Irmtraut Karlsson who labeled the FPÖ a ''Nazi party.'' When asked directly in interviews, Haider refers to the Nazi concentration camps as ''mass murder.'' In February 1992, the FPÖ also supported in parliament the passing of the *Verbotsgesetz* law, which tries to regulate and suppress neo-Nazi activities more effectively. On the other hand, Haider has made statements that possibly indicate a far-right bias. In an interview on Austrian television, August 18, 1988,

Haider said, ''You know as well as I that the Austrian nation was a miscarriage, an ideological miscarriage [*ideologische Missgeburt*].'' And on June 13, 1991, in the provincial parliament he commented on Nazi Germany this way: ''In the Third Reich they had a proper employment policy, something even your government in Vienna is not capable of [*Im Dritten Reich haben sie ordentliche Beschäftigungspolitik gemacht, was nicht einmal ihre Regierung in Wien zusammenbringt*].'' In addition, Haider has also met with extremely right-wing politicians, such as the leader of the Austrian NDP (Nationaldemokratische Partei/National Democratic Party), Norbert Burger, in 1987.

In an interview with the author on September 1, 1992, Haider was confronted directly with the question of positioning himself on an ideological left/right axis. Haider did not give a clear answer; instead, he used the adjective ''center forward'' (*mitte vorne*), emphasizing that on security issues the FPÖ stands ''more to the right,'' whereas on social issues it is ''more to the left.'' Asked to comment on national socialism and the interwar period, Haider replied that history always demands a differentiated analysis and rejected any ''simple yes-no or black and white scheme.'' He also maintained that such a historical and scientific evaluation of national socialism should not be the topic of a political discussion.

Many observers agree that if Jörg Haider had been expelled from the FPÖ by Norbert Steger in the mid–1980s, and forced to create his own national party from scratch, he never could have developed such a strong electoral base so rapidly. Such a party would have been clearly defined as far-right, thereby facing serious constraints. Instead, however, Haider managed a ''right-wing coup'' within the FPÖ, and he continues to ''misuse'' the FPÖ to send ambiguous political signals, taking full advantage of the fact that the FPÖ was a well-integrated entity in Austrian political culture, which voters had long gotten used to.

Jörg Haider's political momentum is derived from several forces. Most important, it is animated by an antiestablishment thrust. Throughout the postwar period, Austria can be described as a consensus society, permanently compromising between the interests of the two major catchall parties, the SPÖ and the ÖVP. At the center of this consensus arrangement lies the *Sozialpartnerschaft* (social partnership), a complex network of formal and informal corporatist patterns controlled by the two major parties. With the Haider-FPÖ, this established arrangement is seriously challenged.

Another important resource for Haider is his anti-immigration position. With the fall of the Iron Curtain and the opening of borders to the East, immigration flows into Austria have vastly increased, creating new problems, such as a perception of increased crime. This has created an overall political climate of *Ausländerfeindlichkeit*, or a public opinion reflex against foreigners. Haider demands that immigration be cut back. In addition, Haider has benefited from a general opinion and electoral swing to the right, compared to the period of SPÖ dominance in the 1970s. And not to be underestimated is the image that

Haider tries to cultivate as the ''yuppie politician,'' young, dynamic and on the attack. To understand Haider's concept of policy making, it is important to realize that he never focused on crafting a new party program, but instead emphasized the creation of new political images—of himself and of the FPÖ—using to a large extent the mass media as a crucial vehicle. Like Schönhuber and the Republikaner in Germany or Le Pen and the Front National in France, the Haider-FPÖ is a movement fed by similar processes.

In 1989 the Austrian government applied for European Community membership, but linked this application to a national referendum once the EC has accepted Austria's application in the mid–1990s. Although the FPÖ traditionally regarded itself as ''the European party'' (as recently as the last FPÖ party program in 1985), Haider has turned his party around on this important issue. As some observers interpret a ''no'' recommendation for the referendum would be a logical consequence of Haider's populistic behavior, thus enabling him to translate anti-EC sentiment into votes for the FPÖ. Going even further, Haider wishes to abandon Austria's neutrality and wants to join NATO and the Western European Union.

Following his comment on the ''proper employment policy'' of Nazi Germany, Haider suffered his most serious defeat in June 1991. As the result of a joint SPÖ-ÖVP move in the provincial parliament of Carinthia, Haider was replaced as provincial governor by Christof Zernatto, an ÖVP member. However, Haider again managed a comeback in the second half of 1991 when the FPÖ achieved important electoral gains in three provincial elections, most significantly in Vienna.

In 1992, Haider multiplied his attempts to persuade the ÖVP to leave its coalition with the SPÖ in order to form a new ''Small Coalition'' with the FPÖ. In this, Haider backed the ÖVP twice on important issues: In May 1992, Thomas Klestil of the ÖVP won the presidential election, and in June, Franz Fiedler, also of the ÖVP, was approved by parliament as the new director of the Austrian Rechnungshof, a legal body that monitors the public administration's budget.

In the long run the FPÖ and Haider will be confronted by serious challenges. Even if the momentum of the FPÖ has not yet crested, it will encounter ''natural growth limits'' that function as thresholds. So the FPÖ must again consider coalition politics if it wants to influence Austrian government policy directly. Either Jörg Haider must become more moderate, or he runs the risk of staying chronically isolated. And a strategy of defiant isolation could possibly endanger Haider's own position within the FPÖ, exposing him to possible leadership coups. But Jörg Haider has not yet exhibited the qualities of a status quo politician.

BIBLIOGRAPHY

Bailer-Galanda, Brigitte. *Die neue Rechte: Jörg Haider—ein Politiker der neuen oder ganz alten Art?* Vienna: Zukunft, 1990.

Campbell, David F. J. ''Die Dynamik der politischen Links-Rechts-Schwingungen in

Österreich: Die Ergebnisse einer Expertenbefragung.'' *Österreichische Zeitschrift für Politikwissenschaft* 21(2): 165–79 (1992).
Goldmann, Harald, Hannes Krall, and Klaus Ottomeyer. *Jörg Haider und sein Publikum: Eine sozialpsychologische Untersuchung*. Klagenfurt: Drava, 1992.
Luther, Kurt Richard. ''Die Freiheitliche Partei Österreichs,'' in Herbert Dachs et al. (eds.), *Handbuch des politischen Systems Österreichs*, 247–62. Vienna: Manz, 1991.
Scharsach, Hans-Henning. *Haiders Kampf*. Vienna: Orac, 1992.
Stirnemann, Alfred. ''Gibt es einen Haider-Effekt?'' in Andreas Kohl et al. (eds.), *Österreichisches Jahrbuch für Politik 1991*, 137–86. Vienna: Verlag für Geschichte und Politik, 1992.

DAVID F. J. CAMPBELL

CHARLES HAUGHEY (1925–) has sometimes been called the ''Houdini of Irish politics'' because of his ability to escape from tight political spots. His critics often compared Haughey's leadership style to that of an American ward boss. Like a ward boss, Haughey knew how to use patronage and personal loyalty to gain political power. Also like a ward boss, Haughey was willing to compromise with his opponents to achieve Fianna Fail's policy objectives.

In particular, Haughey suppressed his strong nationalist feelings and worked with a British government headed by Margaret Thatcher during some of Northern Ireland's darkest days. He seemed willing to do what he thought best for the nation without regard for his own preconceived opinions on a given subject. While Haughey accomplished much good during his career, bringing innovative social, cultural and economic programs to Ireland, he also always seemed to have a knack for finding trouble. His image as a scandal-plagued leader began with the arms scandal of 1970, was perpetuated by his hands-on approach to government and was reinforced by the simultaneous presence of Fine Gael's Garret FitzGerald on the Irish political stage.

Charles Haughey was born into a strong nationalist family of modest economic means. The Haughey family had deep roots in Derry and his father had been an IRA gunrunner and soldier for the Irish Free State during the 1921–1925 civil war. The young Haughey was educated at University College, Dublin, and took a law degree at the King's Inns. He demonstrated his nationalist passions early on when he helped incite a riot by burning a Union Jack to protest its being flown over Trinity College on V-E Day 1945.

After college Haughey built a fortune based on real estate speculation and his accounting practice. During this period, he married Maureen Lemass, daughter of the Fianna Fail activist Seán Lemass. When Seán Lemass became Fianna Fail leader and succeeded Eamon De Valera as prime minister in 1959, Lemass would become one of the driving forces behind Haughey's rise to leadership in the party and eventually to the premiership.

Haughey was first elected to the Dail in 1954 and quickly rose in the party structure. He served as minister for justice, minister for agriculture and minister for finance in various Lemass governments. He then became senior minister to

Prime Minister Jack Lynch in 1966, but his continued political progress was slowed by a series of events in his personal life.

In 1970, Haughey's political career almost ended with the arms crisis, which involved allegations that Haughey had conspired to illegally ship weapons and cash to the Irish Republican Army (IRA). Much later, in 1993, a BBC documentary would assert that "four secret bank accounts were set up by then–Finance Minister Charles Haughey." Neil Blaney, Fianna Fail minister for agriculture at the time, explained the plot by saying: "We didn't help to create the Provisional IRA but we certainly would have accelerated, by what assistance we could have given, their emergence as a force." The plan, Blaney said, was to send Irish troops into Ulster as "the home army entering home territory." Some evidence indicates that, during sworn testimony, Haughey lied about his role in the scheme. These charges were to haunt him throughout his career and seemed to make the public more willing to believe subsequent accusations against him than might otherwise have been the case.

Even though he had avoided a criminal conviction in the arms case, Haughey's political career seemed finished as a result of it. He had been asked to resign from the government during the scandal, but had refused, only to then be fired by Prime Minister Lynch. His display of insolence earned Haughey the lasting emnity of the Fianna Fail establishment and forced him to adopt a grass-roots approach toward regaining high office in the party. And his efforts in this regard proved so successful that Jack Lynch could not ignore them. As a result, Haughey was chosen minister for health in 1975 and again in 1977. Haughey would then become prime minister himself as the result of a backbench rebellion against Lynch. In what has been characterized as a "moment of great irony," Haughey achieved what he had always aspired to, without himself having much to do with it.

Haughey's rise to prominence reflects the very traits that would mark his tenure as prime minister. First, he seemed to be a man who understood how to gain and expand his hold on political power. Second, Haughey understood how to communicate with the party rank and file the over the heads of the party establishment. He also put to use his talents at communication with the general public. Third, Haughey always seemed comfortable walking a fine line between being a "man of the people" and being a member of Ireland's political elite. Fourth, he was deeply committed to the principles of Irish nationalism. (This commitment would subsequently color his dealings with the Thatcher government on the Northern Ireland question.) Fifth, as Haughey's career progressed, it became clear that he was very pragmatic, allowing himself to deftly change positions on controversial isssues. Finally, he seemed to demonstrate a remarkable penchant for either being involved in scandals or surrounding himself with individuals who were involved in unsavory activities. These six traits mark Haughey's political ascent, his stint as Fianna Fail leader and his tenure as prime minister.

Haughey's strong nationalist leanings led many in both the North and the

South to believe that he would be inflexible in his approach to the Northern Irish question. His policy toward Northern Ireland seems, however, to have been filled with the same pragmatism manifest in his domestic policies. On the one hand, Haughey was shrewd enough to use the Northern question to advance his political career at home; on the other hand, he was pragmatic enough to adopt a more moderate stance abroad. Some argue that his position on Northern Ireland both enhanced and undermined his political career. As the London *Sunday Telegraph* at one time asserted: ''Charley was a victim, among other things, of time warp. He was the old breed, a rogue who flamed up the Ulster issue for votes.''

Haughey also knew how to deal with the British government on the Northern question and could sense when it was inappropriate to use the issue for political purposes. He sometimes claimed to have a ''special relationship'' with Mrs. Thatcher that he said put him in a better position to negotiate with her than Fine Gael's Garret FitzGerald, this despite the fact that it was FitzGerald who usually espoused a moderate line and Haughey who espoused the more militant line toward the British.

There is no doubt that he knew how to play the Northern Irish card to improve his political fortunes. For example, Haughey attracted global attention when he called Northern Ireland ''a failed political entity.'' Such statements may have played well within Fianna Fail and among Haughey's likely voters but did little to reassure Ulster's Unionists about Haughey's plans for Northern Ireland. Unionists came to see Haughey ''as the hard man of Irish politics,'' cunning and insistent that there be one Ireland for one island. His strong nationalist stance fit the Fianna Fail profile and helps explain his popular appeal, as well as his quick rebound from the arms crisis.

In 1981, Haughey became a prisoner of events during the hunger strikes and his government fell amid public fears that he would not be flexible enough to negotiate with Margaret Thatcher. Because his political fortunes seemed to be as tied to events in Ulster at least as much as they were to anything within the Irish Republic, he often seemed to be cursed: Given Garret FitzGerald's more moderate stance toward the British government's activities in Ulster, every time events flared there, the Irish electorate seemed to reject Haughey while embracing FitzGerald.

But while Haughey may have spoken with a loud nationalist voice about Northern Ireland, his dealings with the British government were an exercise in political pragmatism. At the same time that his government was beating the drums for a united Ireland, it was also developing an agreement to sell gas from the Kinsale fields to a leading Northern Irish gas company, Belfast Gas. Even though many of Belfast Gas's consumers did not agree with Haughey's vision for Ulster's future, they nonetheless constituted a superb market for the Irish Republic's natural gas resourses. Such pragmatism toward the British always shone through when he addressed Irish-American groups about the Northern Irish problem. Those who expected either stirring exhortations in favor of nationalist paramilitary organizations or a recitation of the hard nationalist line were always left disappointed. Irish-Americans were usually presented with Charles Haughey, the statesman, rather than Charles Haughey, the rogue extremist.

Political pragmatism and realism also marked the way Haughey handled Anglo-Irish relations during the 1982 battle over the Falklands. Given Ireland's history, a strong nationalist would have openly and aggressively supported the Argentinian side. Haughey appeared to personally do so, but his public remarks were always tempered, staying well within the bounds of Ireland's policy of strict neutrality. Ireland's complex relationship with Britain and the domestic political climate provided further incentives for moderation. Haughey seemed to realize that his personal opinions would help neither his nor the nation's political fortunes.

Haughey's reaction to the Anglo-Irish agreement shows how he could rail against an idea as leader of the opposition then, following a reversal in political fortune, implement the very idea that he had railed against. He initially argued, with great force, that the agreement was unacceptable, his objections to the pact being based on traditional nationalism, mainly that it legitimated the partition of Ireland. Taking the nationalist hard line, he backed the New Ireland Forum's call for a unitary state on the island. He also suggested that the Irish and British governments create a conference to "formulate new constitutional arrangements which would lead to uniting all of the people of Ireland in peace and harmony." He augmented his attack on the agreement by arguing that the agreement violated Articles 2 and 3 of the Irish constitution. It may have been easy to level such charges but, because it seemed most people in Ireland supported the agreement, Fianna Fail never pursued this line of attack in court.

After all this, however, when it became clear that his position as opposition leader would not allow him to block the treaty, that Ireland was under great international pressure to sign the agreement and that, moreover, the treaty was quite popular at home, he gave up the fight. Quite ironically, the FitzGerald government soon fell, and the task of enforcing the pact fell to Haughey and Fianna Fail.

As to economic policy, while Ireland had always been plagued by a struggling economy, the country enjoyed some of its best years under Haughey governments. The same kind of political pragmatism and realism observed in his rise to power and his foreign policy is also apparent in Haughey's approach to the economy.

While Haughey spent most of his public life advocating strong state intervention in the economy, his later years saw him shift toward the kind of free market approach Margaret Thatcher had championed in Britain. This conversion probably had as much to do with Ireland's budget woes, high unemployment rate and high emigration figures as much as it did with a philosophical change of heart. It took a great deal of political and intellectual courage to press for the draconian spending cuts and sweeping privatization programs that Haughey came to advocate during the middle 1980s. He was well served by his political instincts, however, because, even though individual cuts were seldom popular, the package as a whole enjoyed a great deal of public support.

Perhaps Haughey's most innovative economic proposal involved turning Ireland into a tax-free zone for creative artists. The aim of this scheme was to keep Irish artists at home, to lure major artists to Ireland from abroad and to create employment by developing the kinds of support industries that a large art colony would generate. At the same time, the government worked to lure American, Japanese and European high technology firms to Ireland. These efforts provided some new employment, especially in chronically depressed areas, but at the price of diminishing the nation's tax revenues. While Ireland received some jobs in exchange for tax concessions, much of the profits generated through this kind of foreign investment were returned to the corporations' nations of origin.

Despite economic innovations promoted by Haughey's government, Ireland's 20 percent unemployment rate remains among the very highest in the European Community, while during the 1980s, Ireland experienced a wave of emigration unlike any since the 1950s. Neither innovative political leaders nor full integration into the European Community has been able to solve Ireland's intractable economic problems. The Haughey economic record is therefore difficult to assess because Ireland has always been characterized by a problematic economy that makes prosperity seem relative. At worst, Haughey's economic policies may have had only modest lasting impact; at best, they were at least put to the test.

The policy area dearest to Haughey's heart, however, was social policy, and he spent most of his career arguing for the creation of a large welfare state in Ireland. In this, he advanced a number of innovative programs that also happened to be politically popular. For example, his government provided the elderly with free telephones, free electricity and free travel.

His approach to the Family Planning Act of 1979 shows how Haughey was as pragmatic and politically oriented when making social policy as when pursuing other policy interests. The Family Planning Act made contraceptives available exclusively through chemists' shops, permitting their sale only to married couples in possession of a doctor's prescription. In addition, a chemist could refuse to fill the prescription if he so desired.

Haughey was the Fianna Fail minister responsible for this legislation, and he described its somewhat curious provisions as ''an Irish solution to an Irish problem,'' for in fact his plan legalized the sale of contraceptives without incurring the Catholic Church's full fury, along with the Church's ability to mobilize large segments of the electorate in opposition to an isssue. While Irish Protestants and family planning advocates may not have been fully satisfied with the outcome, given the prevailing moral and social climate in Ireland it was something they decided they could live with. The 1984 referendum on abortion would again show that Haughey was keenly aware of and willing to bow to prevailing political trends. The Haughey approach to social policy seems to have been to support ideas that reflected the majority of the nation's outlook and would not generate widespread opposition.

As party leader, the most curious thing about Haughey's rise to power was its happenstance. He had done a respectable job as a front bencher during the 1960s but had never been the party establishment's choice for the leadership. He responded to this rebuff and to the arms scandal by building his own political organization within the party. Like most Fianna Fail leaders, Haughey had a common touch. He was enormously popular with lower-class and rural voters. As a result, many of his ideas seemed aimed at these constituencies, and it is not surprising that the more urban and affluent segments of the electorate tended to take a much dimmer view of him. These groups described Haughey in terms that always focused on scandal and his ability to get into trouble.

The ''organization that Charlie built'' was cemented by his being a master of patronage. As the Knock Airport case shows, however, such mastery could sometimes lead to problems. In this particular case, Haughey had promised an airport to Monsignor O'Horan of Our Lady of Knock Shrine, located in Knock, County Mayo. While Haughey felt that the monsignor had asked for a small airstrip, the monsignor apparently believed he had received approval to build a full-fledged international airport in the nearby town of Kilkelly. Of course, one of the last things Ireland needed, most people believed, was another international airport. When construction bills began pouring into Dublin, government funding was halted. The affair became a political embarrassment; in the end, the airport was finished with private funds.

Haughey established his control over Fianna Fail by 1979 but did not finish rooting out his enemies until 1985. Through it all, he was never able to gain the full trust of either his own party or the general public. Some argue that public distrust of Haughey propelled Fine Gael to power and encouraged Desmond O'Malley to run for the Progressive Democrats in 1985. As the *Washington Post* (January 31, 1992) put it, the Progressive Democrats consisted of ''members of Haughey's ruling Fianna Fail—soldiers of destiny—who were disgruntled over what they described as corruption and dishonesty during his reign.''

The movement of Progressive Democrats reflected the internal dissension raging within Fianna Fail. The party had been badly divided for more than twenty years prior to the split and much of the party's division centered in some way around Haughey, who had in any case risen to power out of a three-way division within Fianna Fail. As a result, of course, he had to spend much of his time seeking to maintain his internal support. Because he never fully dominated Fianna Fail and was plagued by a string of scandals, the stage was set for his political downfall.

That it took ten years for a wiretapping scandal to undo Haughey is not so surprising, as Fianna Fail has a long tradition of loyalty to its leader regardless of the prevailing circumstances. The scandal that finally did Haughey in was an echo of the ten-year-old ''Liffeygate'' affair: In 1982, illegal wiretaps were placed on the phones of two political journalists. When this story broke in 1983, Fianna Fail Justice Minister Sean Doherty accepted responsiblity for ordering the taps and in 1984 claimed that Haughey had known nothing about them. Haughey also denied the charges but many in his own party and in the electorate did not believe him. As one of the wiretap victims explained, "Charles Haughey always knew. It was his business to know."

At the same time, a number of other accusations were floating around Dublin about Haughey and other Fianna Fail members' behavior. Some were accused of insider trading during the privatization of the state-owned sugar company. There was also a scandal involving the beef processing industry, and the resignation of Telecom Eireann's chairman amid accusations that the company had purchased property that he partially owned. Faced with this landscape of scandal, the possibility of an internal challenge and the distinct likelihood of defeat in the event of a general election, Charles Haughey resigned in early 1992.

While Charles Haughey is a major figure in modern Irish politics, it is difficult to evaluate his performance in office. Many of the most interesting events in his career deal with Fianna Fail politics or ethics problems. However, to focus on these alone would be to ignore the innovative social, economic and foreign policies that Haughey governments pursued. Haughey was a political and policy pragmatist, a man who, in becoming larger than life, created very real enemies and became plagued by a series of seemingly endless scandals. He was done in by an accumulation of events that had taken place over an entire career. In this, the Liffeygate affair seemed to convince many Irish voters that their worst fears about Haughey had been true all along. Once this change in Irish public opinion had taken place he did what any good soldier would do and stepped away from Fianna Fail.

What is most striking about Charles Haughey's career is his marked understanding of politics. Here was an individual who knew what the voters wanted and regularly found ways to deliver; his career was consequently advanced. He used political processes like an American ward politician, building an organization based on personal loyalty and policy pragmatism. This was not a usual pattern in the parliamentary system of the Irish Republic. Haughey seems to have possessed a basic political ideology of pragmatism that made him flexible on most issues. As a result, it should not be surprising that he was successful and controversial at the same time. Given the way he climbed to power, it should also not be surprising that he was involved in a number of scandals. Charles Haughey was in Ireland what many children of Irish emigrants became in America: a compassionate but flawed politician.

BIBLIOGRAPHY

Coleman, Doyle. *Man of the People: A Portrait of Charles J. Haughey.* Cork, Ireland: Mercier Press, 1986.

Dwyer, T. Ryle. *Charlie: The Political Biography of Charles J. Haughey.* Dublin: Gill and MacMillan, 1987.

Feighan, John. *Codename Operation Rogue: A Study of the Vilification of Charles J. Haughey by the British Secret Service.* Dublin: Mercier, 1984.
Holland, Jack. *The American Connection: U.S. Money, Guns and Influence in Northern Ireland.* New York: Viking, 1987.
Joyce, Joe. *The Boss: Charles J. Haughey.* Dublin: Poolebeg Press, 1983.
O'Malley, Padraig. *The Uncivil Wars: Ireland Today.* Boston: Little, Brown, 1984.

KENNETH COSGROVE

ERICH HONECKER (1912–1994) ruled the German Democratic Republic (GDR) from 1971 until the collapse of his communist regime in 1989. Honecker's successful management of the construction of the Berlin Wall in 1961 won him admiration both in the GDR and in Moscow. He gained the post of first secretary of the Socialist Unity Party (SED) in 1971 and set out to foster economic growth within a system of centralized ownership. Succeeding years brought international recognition for the GDR's apparent ''socialist economic miracle.'' Honecker presided over the relative normalization that relaxed inter-German ties during the 1970s. After Gorbachev's rise to power in Moscow, Honecker led the conservative allied opposition to the new Soviet policy of openness and reform. Erich Honecker also achieved worldwide prominence for his country's sports teams, a policy he developed as a practical means to enhance the GDR's international stature.

Honecker was born in 1912 to a working-class family in what later became West Germany (the Federal Republic of Germany). He came to his communism through his father, Wilhelm, a Saar miner and political activist. The mines in the Saar were controlled by Baron von Stumm, an industrial magnate and severe authoritarian. After World War I, the region was ceded to France, effectively exchanging von Stumm's harsh rule for French military occupation. This environment lent credibility to Wilhelm Honecker's theme of proletarian exploitation. In 1922, at age ten, Erich Honecker joined the Spartacus League (a communist youth organization) and four years later entered the Communist League of German Youth, a direct organ of the German Communist Party (KPD).

When Honecker entered the youth league in 1926, it had already been transformed by Stalin's campaign to reorient all communist parties to the Soviet model. Thus Honecker had little experience with the more independent ways of the KPD before 1926. His socialization was Stalinist, and he accepted the party's policies readily. After two failing years as a farmer, Honecker became an apprentice roofer under his uncle, later working for him. This arrangement gave him time for an active Communist Party life. By 1928 he was leader of his local youth league branch.

The party sent him for basic education in Marxist doctrine and youth organization as soon as he became a local leader. In 1930 he was dispatched to Moscow for a year of study with other German youth leaders at the Communist Youth International School. Upon his return he became a full-time Communist Party functionary.

Honecker thus entered professional politics in Germany at a time of growing unrest. When he became political director of the Saar Communist Youth League, the Social Democratic Party (SPD) was the paramount enemy of the KPD. The next year, in 1932, the two parties put aside their differences to battle the rising tide of national socialism. It was too little and much too late. Adolf Hitler seized total power after his appointment to the chancellorship, and Erich Honecker went underground.

Because he was little known to the Reich, Honecker was sent from the relative safety of the Saar region to Essen in the more perilous Ruhr area, where he was made political director for the region. He worked underground, using an alias, trying to forge a united front among religious, social democratic and communist groups. Honecker was then sent home to work on behalf of the party in the Saar plebiscite. The vote went heavily for renewed union with Germany—against the KPD's opposition. Honecker, rising faster in an ever more desperate party, was summoned to Prague by the party's exiled leadership. There he was made youth secretary for Greater Berlin, but this was work with few prospects. In December 1935, Honecker was arrested along with six comrades and sentenced to prison in Berlin.

Honecker's decade in prison was a source of revolutionary pride for him, but that view was not shared by his fellow prisoners. He was aloof, did not participate in revolutionary cells in the prison and by 1937 was even made a "trusty," allowed to work outside the prison. He escaped from one such work detail in the spring of 1945 and then waited for the approaching Red Army. He was later reproved by the party's central committee for his failure to include others in his escape.

Honecker's experience in youth organization propelled him into a supervisory role in the KPD's effort to recruit young people in Berlin. He worked tirelessly. In 1946 he was named president of the newly formed, supposedly nonpartisan Free German Youth (FDJ). Honecker maintained the facade of nonpartisanship, but in fact worked exclusively to build the FDJ into a communist organization. During his tenure, he managed to have responsibility for sports organizations placed under the FDJ umbrella. Inside the organization, he would tolerate no opposition. By 1950 the party accepted him as a candidate member of the politburo, principally in recognition of his work with the FDJ.

Honecker's six years of candidate membership in the politburo strengthened his position and his ability to use the FDJ for his own career. He was a trusted assistant of Walter Ulbricht, the founding first secretary of the Socialist Unity Party. Both Ulbricht and Honecker were acutely aware of the drain of talented youth from the GDR. Many of the brightest and best educated walked west in Berlin. The result was a drive inside the FDJ that amounted to a militarization of the organization. The FDJ was to be the mobilizing vanguard of communist German youth, and FDJ units were dispatched to shore up sagging elements of the people's police.

The continuing flood of refugees out of the GDR prompted purges within the party. Honecker survived, and may have even had a hand in organizing the expulsions. In 1953 he divorced Edith Bauman and married Margot Feist, an FDJ functionary. It was about this time that Stalin died, leaving Honecker and Ulbricht both shaken. Their insecurity led to still another purge. During the workers' uprising of June 17, 1953, a faction of the politburo tried but failed to oust Walter Ulbricht. Honecker had remained loyal to his patron; as a result, his career was furthered.

The FDJ's performance, particularly during the workers' uprising, led to growing party criticism of Honecker. His close ties to Ulbricht, however, safeguarded his position. In mid–1955 he embarked on a year in Moscow at the Soviet Communist Party training college, a rite that became a requisite for full membership in the politburo. Upon his return he became the functionary responsible for state security—just in time to face revolts in Poland and Hungary.

Once again Honecker toed the Soviet line. He became closer still to Walter Ulbricht, standing by him as an internal party revolt brewed. Honecker helped to quell this rebellion and was promoted to full membership in the politburo in 1958. He took charge of security for the SED, a key post. While in 1958 the number of refugees fleeing the country fell to its lowest level, the porous border remained a fundamental challenge to the regime. When more citizens continued to flee to the West in 1959 and 1960, the party resolved to take action. Ulbricht petitioned Moscow and the Warsaw Pact for permission to build a wall in Berlin. They refused. Ulbricht stirred up more unrest, and refugee totals soared. Ulbricht went back to his allies in 1961 and won permission for his wall.

Erich Honecker was put in charge of this project, and the barrier was erected in the dead of night on August 13, 1961, with Honecker overseeing every detail. The wall generated revulsion in the West, but Honecker's star rose rapidly in the SED with this success and the absence of significant repercussions. The wall provided a means to contain the GDR's most talented citizens for service to the nation. Subsequent economic growth in the late 1960s then emboldened Ulbricht to challenge the USSR's ideological purity.

The Soviet leadership was distinctly unenthusiastic about Ulbricht's lecturing, particularly because the Kremlin was interested in pursuing opportunities for détente arising from West Germany's "Ostpolitik," but the process was blocked by Ulbricht's intransigence on Berlin. On April 3, 1971, Honecker and Ulbricht met with Leonid Brezhnev in Moscow. Shortly thereafter, Honecker replaced Ulbricht as first secretary of the SED, and the Quadripartite Agreement on Berlin went forward.

Honecker's years at the helm of the SED were dominated by the struggle for international acceptance and economic growth. The principal instruments for international recognition were sports and technical assistance to Third World states. The drive for economic growth was centered on the creation of *Kombinate,* or combines. These were large vertically integrated industrial production systems. They combined the advantages of central, hierarchical control while retaining more autonomy and flexibility in the lower echelons of the supply and production systems. The system also allowed Honecker to eliminate almost all private ownership of businesses until world economic pressures in the late 1970s and early 1980s led to a renewed willingness to tolerate it. In 1985, 30,000 licenses were granted to small-scale entrepreneurs by Honecker's government.

The remarkable success of the GDR in international sports attracted tremendous attention—and questions. The apparent achievements of the combines won admiration throughout the communist bloc—even in Moscow. Honecker managed these gains with a politburo drawn largely from his old allies in the FDJ. Harsh, even brutal, treatment of dissidents continued, but most citizens enjoyed a slightly more open system, particularly regarding official tolerance of GDR citizens who watched West German television broadcasts.

The advent of Mikhail Gorbachev in 1985 brought new challenges to an aging Honecker. He saw in Gorbachev the twin dangers of weakness and social reform. Honecker led the still-Stalinist states of Eastern Europe in their opposition to the new Kremlin policies. But Gorbachev prevailed. Hungary adopted reforms in spring 1989 that even went beyond *perestroika* and *glasnost*, dismantling with great fanfare its own ''iron curtain'' along the border with Austria. Honecker, ill and aloof, did not sense the danger. When thousands of GDR citizens made their way to Hungary for vacation that summer, they found an open border. This was the trigger that eventually brought down both Honecker and the GDR. The total number of East German refugees in 1988 was 39,845. In 1989 it jumped to almost 349,000. During the late summer and fall of 1989 demonstrations for reform and the freedom to travel reached unprecedented levels. Almost 200,000 marched against the regime on October 16, 1989. Erich Honecker resigned his position on October 18. He retreated to the background as his colleagues watched the system collapse around them. Fearing arrest, Honecker entered a hospital on a Soviet military base near Berlin. He was then spirited to Moscow on March 13, 1990.

In Moscow, Honecker was protected by Mikhail Gorbachev, the leader he had openly criticized. The failure of the Moscow coup and the rise of Boris Yeltsin clearly put Honecker at risk. He fled to the Chilean embassy, calling in a favor he had granted after the fall of Allende in 1973. Erich and Margot Honecker spent 232 days in the embassy, constantly seeking asylum in the diminishing number of still-communist regimes. All the while, German leaders pressed Chile to give Honecker up. By July 29, 1992, German pressure succeeded. Honecker was too costly a guest. He was sent to Germany to face trial for manslaughter in the cases of forty-nine would-be GDR émigrés. His wife flew to Chile, where their children live. German courts subsequently released him on grounds of his poor and deteriorating health. He then joined his wife in Chile, where he lived in modest circumstances and near obscurity until his death in 1994.

It was a remarkable end to a career that epitomized the modern communist functionary. Erich Honecker did not belong to the pioneering, pathbreaking generation of communists. Nor did he come to communism with the fervent idealism of many other Germans in the 1920s. He was born into communism. There is no sign that he ever questioned his father's strict adherence to the cause, and Honecker's rise to leadership was always through the second echelon. Like many other East European communist leaders in the 1980s, Honecker ascended to power in communism's bureaucratic era.

Socialism's collective consciousness was lost on Honecker. He long had the reputation of a selfish man with a ruthless capacity to get ahead at the expense of others. Almost every turn in his career came to him as the default candidate: His breaks within the communist movement during Hitler's early years of power came to him precisely because he was unknown and unremarkable. In prison he shunned his comrades. While committed comrades such as Robert Havemann organized political cells and fashioned an elaborate communication system, Honecker worked to gain the favor of guards who controlled the privilege of outside work details.

During the early postwar days, Honecker had the good fortune to be the only loyal communist with significant experience in youth work and in building cadres. Even while he was building his empire in the FDJ, Heinz Lippmann described him as a "functionary with an inferiority complex." He took credit for others' work while he toiled tirelessly to create his power base in the FDJ. These qualities attracted party leader Walter Ulbricht, who needed a loyal and unremarkable lieutenant. In 1957, when Ulbricht faced a particularly strong faction opposing him within the party, he deliberately elevated Honecker to the politburo in order to shore up his own position while avoiding the risk that Honecker would pose a threat.

Erich Honecker rose on the strength of his loyalty and his work, but both of these qualities resulted in a grim and oppressive style of leadership. Honecker was loyal to communist authority, centered first and foremost in Moscow. Because he had no compunction about shifting positions radically when the party changed its mind, he was an ideal lieutenant for Ulbricht and the Kremlin. Once he assumed control, Honecker accepted normalized relations with West Germany, as long as the Soviets supported him.

His principal political concern as first secretary was to eliminate domestic threats to his government. He installed his own team in power, including his wife. Dissidents were discouraged with even greater fervor, if not with public fanfare. Older challengers of the regime were stripped of their children and their jobs. *Republikflucht,* the "crime" of leaving the country without authorization, became a capital offense. All private businesses and farms were nationalized. Central control was paramount in the Honecker era.

The same level of amoral commitment attended Honecker's pursuit of glory for the GDR in sports. Competitions were held throughout the country to find the best potential athletes among the GDR's children. These boys and girls were taken away to the country's athletic factories, a mixture of the most advanced training and illicit pharmacology. The GDR's prodigious success in international competitions was a product of public policy and extraordinary governmental support.

The East German economy was one of Honecker's proudest achievements. But like almost the whole GDR, however, this too was a facade. Unable to afford oil at world market prices, Honecker directed that several villages be removed so that the soft brown coal under them could be strip-mined. The combine system brought central control, but not the economic gains that Honecker touted. In fact, the economy of the GDR was highly dependent—to the tune of 5 percent of its GNP—on subventions from West Germany. Honecker accepted increasing normalization with the West because it brought in desperately needed cash. Yet he failed to see that the Bonn policy of "small steps" would undermine his regime at its foundation. As the sister city agreements, family visits and organizational contacts increased, the lies of the GDR leadership were exposed. When the regime collapsed, Western specialists were astonished to find primitive industrial plants, no genuinely competitive technology and seriously neglected infrastructure. The GDR was an economic Potemkin village.

Honecker's leadership was corrupt, coercive and in the end untenable. There was never much evidence of a life of the mind in Erich Honecker. His handpicked successor, Egon Krenz, found Honecker completely unnerved in October 1989 by the stream of refugees and the waves of demonstrations. At a politburo meeting in the midst of this crisis, Honecker wanted to conduct routine business. When dissidents stormed the regime's elite, sealed living compound outside Berlin, they found the Honecker house to be a model of bourgeois domesticity. Erich and Margot Honecker's lives bore no connection to the revolutionary fighter Honecker claimed to be. Even in exile, Honecker was hardly heroic. He complained that he should be paid a pension for his years of service to Germany. Desperate to find a haven, he petitioned every remaining communist country, but even North Korea would promise nothing beyond medical care. When faced with inevitable extradition and trial, Honecker threatened to expose secret arrangements with West German politicians.

Erich Honecker was a product of a system that demanded total obedience, purging creative talent that refused to fall behind the rigid party line. It was a system that rewarded loyal followers as long as they posed no threat to the current leadership. In the long run, such a system is an almost fail-safe formula for mediocrity. In the GDR, Honecker combined his mediocrity with a ruthless disdain for opponents and virtual contempt for the people he claimed to serve.

BIBLIOGRAPHY

Work by Honecker:

From My Life. Oxford: Pergamon Press, 1981.

Other Works:

Glaessner, Gert-Joachim (ed.). *Die DDR in der ära Honecker.* Opladen: Westdeutscher Verlag, 1988.

Gotz, Hans Herbert. *Honecker, und was dann?* Helford: Busse Seewald, 1989.
Lippmann, Heinz. *Honecker and the New Politics of Europe.* New York: Macmillan, 1972.
McAdams, A. James. *East Germany and Détente.* Cambridge: Cambridge University Press, 1985.

RONALD A. FRANCISCO

J

JOHN XXIII (ANGELO GIUSEPPE RONCALLI) (1881–1963) was leader of the Roman Catholic Church from 1958 until his death in 1963. As pope, he was responsible for convening the Second Vatican Council in 1959 to ''modernize'' the Church against great resistance from within. He approved of the ecumenical movement and demonstrated his commitment to it by receiving Archbishop Fisher of Canterbury in 1960 and inviting Patriarch Athenagoras I of Constantinople to attend sessions of the Vatican Council.

Within domestic Italian politics, John XXIII sought to prohibit Italian bishops from interfering with local elections, and he contributed to the Christian Democratic Party's ''opening'' toward the Socialists. Moreover, although Catholics were forbidden to vote for Communists and while he did not lift the excommunication of followers of the Communist Party, he did receive in private audience the daughter and son-in-law of Nikita Khrushchev.

In international affairs, his Ostpolitik opened Vatican diplomacy toward the countries of Eastern Europe and to the Eastern churches. He authored eight encyclical letters, the most famous of which are *Mater et Magistra* (1961) and *Pacem in Terris* (1963). Although his reign as pope was relatively brief, John XXIII's influence over the Catholic Church worldwide was overwhelming. And in that capacity, his role as a world leader was also very significant.

Angelo Giuseppe Roncalli was born on November 25, 1881, in the village of Sotto il Monte in the extremely Catholic province of Bergamo. He was the fourth child and first son of Battista Roncalli and Marianna Mazzola, who were modest farmers. From them he learned the love for simple things, as well as the wisdom typical of farm people. From these roots, he evolved into an accomplished diplomat and became the most loved pope of the 20th century.

Early in his life Roncalli expressed a desire to enter the priesthood and began studying toward that goal. In 1892, at the age of eleven, he entered the seminary in Bergamo, where he distinguished himself with his academic achievements. He was also known there for his amiability and gift for singing, subsequently being named choir master.

At the age of nineteen Roncalli was already in his third year of theology but was too young to be ordained a priest. He left Bergamo for Rome to continue his studies at the College of St. Apollinaire. There he met and developed a long-standing friendship with Ernesto Buonaiuti, the founder of Italian modernism. While in Rome he was also drafted into military service, thus being forced to interrupt his studies. In 1903, he returned to Rome for the investiture of Pius X; in December of that year he received the diaconate. Roncalli then went on to earn his doctorate in theology in 1904 and was ordained into the priesthood that year at the age of twenty-three.

Roncalli wished to continue his studies by pursuing a degree in canon law, but instead he was appointed secretary to the newly named bishop of Bergamo, Monsignor Giacomo Maria Radini-Tedeschi, who was considered a staunch activist of Italian social Catholicism. The influence of Monsignor Radini-Tedeschi on the young Roncalli was enormous, the former discovering in the latter more than a mere secretary, but a spiritual son. Roncalli in turn had found the model for his priestly life.

In these years Roncalli's interests widened significantly. In 1905 he traveled abroad for the first time, accompanying Monsignor Radini-Tedeschi to France. In 1906 he began recording all documents related to the 1564 visit to the Bergamo diocese by St. Charles Borromeo. In executing this task, Roncalli became acquainted with Monsignor Ratti, the future Pope Pius XI. It was during this period that he also began opening his mind to the new social trends and ideologies identified as "modernism"—so much so that Roncalli found himself having to deny accusations of having embraced the movement which had been condemned by Pope Pius X as a heresy.

When Italy entered World War I, Roncalli left Bergamo to return to the army, serving first as a medic and then as a chaplain. When the war ended, he was charged by Bergamo's bishop with the care of youth both within and outside the seminary. Then in 1920, Benedict XV—who as Giacomo della Chiesa had been a good friend of Radini-Tedeschi—noticed the young priest, calling Roncalli to Rome in 1920 to serve as national director of the Organization for the Propagation of the Faith. In 1925, at the age of forty-four, Roncalli was made titular archbishop of Areopoli (later to become Mesembria in the province of Emimonto) by the new pope, Pius XI. Shortly thereafter, Pius XI named the new bishop apostolic visitor to Bulgaria, an appointment that began Roncalli's long and successful diplomatic career.

Roncalli arrived in Sofia on April 25, 1925, to find the country on the brink of civil war. Trying to improve the condition of Catholics in Bulgaria, he worked hard to maintain friendly relations between the Vatican and King Boris III—who in 1930 married Princess Giovanna of Savoy, daughter of the Italian king, Victor Emmanuel III. In 1931, Roncalli was named apostolic delegate. In 1935, he left Bulgaria for Istanbul, where he was to be Vatican envoy responsible for both Turkey and Greece.

The warm, compassionate, yet stern bishop who had arrived practically unnoticed in Sofia ten years earlier was bid a solemn farewell upon his departure. During his tenure in Bulgaria, the diplomatic credo that evolved was a simple one: Roncalli believed that minor issues should be relegated to a secondary position in order to guarantee success on major issues.

In Greece and Turkey, he found much more work to do, and he immediately set to work. By the time World War II began, Bishop Roncalli had succeeded in reorganizing the Catholic communities and their network of activities in both countries, so much so that the Holy See charged him with coordinating communication between Italian troops abroad and and their families. A strong believer in the brotherhood of races and religions, Roncalli personally organized a network to secure the safety of the persecuted. Counting upon his diplomatic status and the outrage that would occur were anything to happen to him, Roncalli concentrated on protecting women and children, especially Jews. His humanitarian activities during World War II were widely recognized in both Turkey and Greece, so much so that Damaskinos, the Orthodox metropolitan of Athens, could not help but hug and kiss him.

His empathy for others did not go unnoticed in the Vatican, and in 1944, Bishop Roncalli was appointed papal nuncio to Paris. Once again, his diplomatic and personal skills were put to the test, since in France he found a divided and struggling country which kept looking in hatred to the past rather than in friendship toward the future. Moreover, the Church itself was not held in the highest esteem, since it was widely thought to have supported the Vichy government of Marshal Pétain. In this regard, the newly appointed nuncio was asked to recommend to Pius XII the removal from office of thirty French bishops accused of collaboration with the Vichy regime. Roncalli's response was to temporize, studying each case on its own merits. He eventually concluded that the majority of them had been accused upon hearsay rather than valid proof. In the end, twenty-seven of the accused bishops remained in office.

In France, Roncalli carefully observed new doctrinal and pastoral developments within the French Catholic Church but never directly interfered in the French Church's affairs, thereby avoiding a number of confrontations. His approach played well in France and he became widely loved and esteemed throughout the country.

In 1953, Roncalli was made cardinal and sent to Venice. Roncalli welcomed the assignment, regarding Venice as the ideal location for a man who had been uprooted from the northern regions of Italy to be sent to work in both the East and the West. For him, Venice was the link between the two, and Venice enshrined the life he had given to the Church. Finally, the Venice assignment was for him an opportunity to concentrate on pastoral care, which had been his original vocation.

Pius XII died on October 9, 1958, and Cardinal Roncalli left for the conclave in Rome never to return to Venice. After the eleventh ballot, on October 28, 1958, a world watching on live television for the very first time saw white smoke leave the chimney of the Sistine Chapel and learned that Angelo Giuseppe Cardinal Roncalli had become pope and would henceforth be called John XXIII.

From his first appearance on the Vatican balcony it became obvious that this pope would not be just a "transitional pope," as had been widely speculated. Nor was he to be like his predecessors, somewhat distant from everyday Church citizens. This was to be a pope who loved people and loved being with people, and John XXIII quickly became the most loved pope of the 20th century. Five years later, as he spent the last three days of his life in agony, the whole world followed on radio, television or in person at St. Peter's Square in the vain hope of a medical miracle. If John XXIII was ready to die, as he himself had said a few days earlier, the world was not yet ready for him to do so. On June 3, 1963, John XXIII lost his battle with cancer, and people the world over felt they had lost a family member.

John XXIII was deeply influenced by his own personal life experience and by that of his generation. Thus he was a rare combination of both revolutionary and reactionary beliefs and of both doctrinal and pastoral commitment. Throughout his life he strived to put into practice the wisdom of the farmer, a wisdom founded on simple things. Yet somewhat paradoxically, this approach brought revolution to the Catholic Church in complex, not simple ways. John XXIII demonstrated throughout his life that, while not denying the past, he had no nostalgia for it. He thus set forth to modernize the Church by bringing it back to its pastoral origins, all the while not ignoring the political role the Church itself could play during the Cold War period. For John XXIII, the Second Vatican Council was a necessary if painful revolutionary process.

It is in this light that the granting of the private audience to Khrushchev's daughter must be seen. The threat of the Berlin Wall in 1961 spurred the pope to improve relations between the Kremlin and the Vatican. It was likewise this same conviction that led him to intercede with the Soviet leader during the Cuban missile crisis. It is not surprising, therefore, that while he never lifted the excommunication of communists imposed by his predecessor, he also forbade Italian bishops from meddling in national politics. This move allowed the Christian Democratic Party (DC) to open toward the left, forming a coalition with the Socialist Party. Conservatives in the Vatican and in the DC strongly resented the pope's conciliatory attitude toward communist regimes, as well as his innovations within the Church structure. Italian conservatives also feared his "domestic" agenda, which included a reform of the Roman Curia.

At a very problematic and crucial juncture in world history, John XXIII projected clear and coherent beliefs, preaching the interdependence of the world community and the equality of mankind regardless of race or creed. In the former, it was he who broke with the traditional Vatican rule limiting the College of Cardinals to seventy; he increased its size to eighty-five and named the first African (Monsignor Lauream Rugambwe from Tanganyika), the first Japanese (Monsignor Peter Tatsuo Doi of Sendor) and the first Filipino (Monsignor Rufino I. Santos) in the history of the Church.

John XXIII also encouraged Catholics to take part in ecumenical movements, and he established the Secretariat for Promoting Christian Unity, inviting representatives of other faiths to attend as observers the working sessions of the Vatican Council. Due to both the efforts of two observers from the Russian Orthodox Church and John XXIII's intercession, the leader of the Ukrainian Church, Archbishop Joseph Slipyi of Lwow, was released from a Soviet prison and allowed to return to Rome.

To the Roman Catholic Church, the pontificate of John XXIII stands out almost like a true Copernican revolution: The church turned away without nostalgia from the counter-Reformation and inwardly rediscovered itself as the people of God, while outwardly exhibiting a feeling of solidarity with the world. John XXIII distinguished between ideologies and social programs. Doctrinal objections were no longer permitted to interfere with cooperation if the latter could improve the overall condition of humankind. He differed from his predecessors in his strong belief that the world could still be influenced toward good.

John XXIII understood that the papacy was a political institution as well as a religious one and that political considerations would perforce determine the orientations of the Church. Albeit not having been trained for Church politics, he learned from his experience and was much more personal in his approach, thus allowing Catholics to leave their isolation and encouraging them to join with all men of good will in pursuit of the common good.

Some claim that John XXIII was a reformist who, in exile for over thirty years, dreamt of his ideals. Others argue that he was a shrewd traditionalist who adapted to changing circumstances. Still others say that he was a slightly superficial extrovert who merely set in motion major events, such as the Vatican Council, which then inevitably took their own course. Whatever one's convictions in this regard, twenty years after his death, John XXIII remains a legend of almost mythical proportions in both Church history and Italian politics.

BIBLIOGRAPHY

Allegri, Renzo. *Il Papa che ha cambiato il mondo.* Rome: Reverdito, 1988.

Holmes, J. Derek. *The Papacy in the Modern World.* New York: Crossroad, 1981.

Klinger, Kurt. *A Pope Laughs.* New York: Holt, Rinehart and Winston, 1964.

Nicora, Alberigo Angelina, and Alberigo Giuseppe. *Papa Giovanni per la pace nel mondo: Messaggio cristiano e impegno politico.* Rome: Cinque Lune, 1985.

Vaillancourt, Jean-Guy. *Papal Power.* Berkeley: University of California Press, 1980.

MARIA ELISABETTA DE FRANCISCIS

JUAN CARLOS I (1938–), king of Spain since November 22, 1975, has contributed decisively to his country's transition to democracy, which put an end to almost four decades of authoritarian rule under General Francisco Franco. On coming to the throne, he instigated a series of reforms which led to the dismantling of the Francoist political system and the adoption of a democratic constitution in December 1978. On February 23, 1981, it was largely his personal intervention which foiled a military coup organized by a small group of officers who had taken the government and the Chamber of Deputies hostage. As constitutional monarch, Juan Carlos has played a major role in forging a new international role for Spain, becoming one of Europe's most respected heads of state.

Juan Carlos de Borbón y Borbón was born in Rome on January 5, 1938, the son of Don Juan de Borbón y Battenberg and Doña María de las Mercedes Borbón y Orleans. In April 1931, his grandfather, King Alfonso XIII, had been forced off the throne and into exile by a coalition of left-wing and reformist parties which subsequently proclaimed the Second Spanish Republic. In July 1936 the more conservative sectors of Spanish society, led by elements of the armed forces, rebelled against the democratically elected government of the Republic, thereby initiating a bloody three-year-long civil war. King Alfonso XIII backed the uprising wholeheartedly, and his heir, Don Juan, was only narrowly prevented from taking up arms on behalf of the Nationalists by their leader, the allegedly monarchist General Franco. However, the latter failed to restore the monarchy after the defeat of the Republic in April 1939, in view of which Alfonso XIII abdicated in favor of Don Juan in early 1941.

With Italy at war, the Spanish royal family was forced to seek refuge in neutral Switzerland, where Juan Carlos later attended boarding school until 1948. By 1943, Don Juan had come to the conclusion that the Allies would never allow Franco to remain in power after the defeat of Nazi Germany and Fascist Italy, which had provided substantial aid to the Nationalist camp during the Civil War. In view of this, in 1945 he issued a manifesto which presented himself and the parliamentary monarchy he hoped to establish as the only viable alternative to either Francoist authoritarianism or Republican chaos. Franco never forgave him, retaliating in 1947 with the Law of Succession, which proclaimed Spain a kingdom and empowered Franco to appoint a successor of his choice, either as regent or as king.

Juan Carlos soon became a pawn in a cat-and-mouse game played by Franco and Don Juan until 1969. Following a decisive meeting between these two in 1948, it was decided that Juan Carlos should continue his schooling in Spain. In the summer of the following year, however, Don Juan's relations with Franco deteriorated further, with the result that Juan Carlos remained at his father's side at Estoril, near Lisbon, until 1950. After he completed his secondary education, in 1954 it was agreed that Juan Carlos should spend the next four years at Spain's three military academies, even though Don Juan had originally intended him to study abroad. After a third and final interview held in 1960, Juan Carlos embarked on a two-year course at Madrid University, where he was greeted with hostility by antimonarchist elements and supporters of the rival Carlist dynasty within the Franco regime.

In 1962 Juan Carlos married princess Sophia, daughter of King Paul and Queen Frederica of Greece, and at Franco's invitation took up residence at La Zarzuela, a large country house on the outskirts of Madrid. During these years

Juan Carlos and his family lived an extremely uneasy and vulnerable existence. Franco was characteristically ambiguous as to his intentions, allowing rival candidatures to the throne to proliferate while refusing to discard the possibility of appointing a regent. This was done so as not to antagonize any of the regime's competing factions while at the same time ensuring their loyalty to the dictator. What was more, Don Juan refused to accept that he himself had been discarded for good, placing his son in an increasingly awkward predicament.

In the mid–1960s, Franco came under growing pressure both from within the regime and from abroad to appoint a successor. This was advocated by those who favored the regime's continuity as much as it was by those who looked forward to a gradual evolution toward a more democratic system of government. The former regarded the appointment of a successor as the best way of ensuring that Franco's death would not automatically spell the demise of his regime, while the latter saw it as a means of encouraging him to delegate power and perhaps even stand down altogether. Those who did most to convince Franco of the need to appoint a successor without further delay, notably his alter ego, Admiral Luis Carrero Blanco, generally favored the first of these outcomes.

When Franco finally offered to appoint him successor, Juan Carlos was torn between a son's loyalty to Don Juan (to whom he was also heir) and the possibility of finally restoring the monarchy, albeit on the general's terms. Had he turned down the offer, Franco would have found another candidate, possibly his own cousin, Alfonso de Borbón Dampierre, who enjoyed considerable support within the regime, or named a regent instead. Without his father's consent, and in keeping with the Law of Succession, in July 1969 Juan Carlos was finally proclaimed Franco's successor, in return for which he swore to uphold the fundamental laws of the regime.

As prince of Spain (a non-Bourbon title intended to underline the creation of a new monarchy), Juan Carlos attempted to remain above the political fray while seeking to increase his popularity among ordinary Spaniards. His formal duties were relatively few, and his main occupation was to absorb the information provided by his numerous visitors—as many as 120 a month in 1970. These visits no doubt heightened his awareness of the growing demand for change in Spanish society, a demand he had begun to detect while at the university.

Foreign travel provided an additional source of enlightenment. In the course of his frequent travels abroad, he acquired firsthand knowledge of a number of monarchies and was able to compare the parliamentary model (in its British or Japanese versions) with more autocratic varieties (as seen in Iran, Saudi Arabia or Ethiopia). More important, Juan Carlos was able to meet the major Western leaders of the day, notably Presidents Nixon and Ford of the United States, Pompidou and Giscard d'Estaing of France and Scheel of Germany. Indeed the existence of a successor proved most convenient to Western governments who were anxious about Spain's future but found Franco's regime distasteful, for they could cultivate the future king without appearing to court Franco.

Events in other southern European countries also proved instructive. In 1968,

Juan Carlos's brother-in law, King Constantine II, was forced to flee the country after having failed to stand up to the colonels who had taken power a year earlier. Democratic opinion never forgave Constantine for his weakness, and in 1974 Greece declared itself a republic. This reinforced the lesson Juan Carlos had long since learned from Alfonso XIII's connivance with the Primo de Rivera dictatorship (1923–1931) to the effect that constitutional monarchs who allow the armed forces to subvert constitutions are merely postponing their own downfall. Events in neighboring Portugal, moreover, provided dramatic evidence of what could happen to authoritarian regimes incapable of reforming themselves.

Franco's plans for Juan Carlos became somewhat clearer in June 1973, when he finally appointed Carrero Blanco prime minister, the first person ever to hold this position in the regime and widely regarded as the person chosen by Franco to guarantee continuity after his death. In the event, the Basque terrorist organization ETA thwarted these plans by assassinating Carrero Blanco in December of that year. He was succeeded by Carlos Arias Navarro, who in February 1974 unexpectedly announced a series of reforms allegedly aimed at democratizing political life. Although he never saw eye to eye with the prime minister, Juan Carlos supported these measures wholeheartedly in the hope that they would allow the more pragmatic, forward-looking sectors of the regime to organize themselves with a view to participating in a more open and competitive political system. Much of the Arias Navarro program, however, was stillborn.

In July 1974 Franco became seriously ill, forcing Juan Carlos to become temporary head of state, something he resisted with all his might out of fear of becoming unduly compromised. The prince was fortunate not to have to endorse any major decision, however, and by September the general was well enough to resume office.

In view of Arias's failure to implement his program, Juan Carlos stepped up his contacts with both regime reformists and anti-Francoist opposition leaders. The latter had tended to dismiss him as a somewhat inane puppet figure and were generally reluctant to acknowledge the possibility of a democratizing process led by the monarch from within the regime. Some, including the Communists, preferred to toy with the idea of enlisiting Don Juan's support against his own son, a notion they soon had to abandon. In fact, some have argued that, by becoming increasingly hostile to Franco in the wake of Juan Carlos's appointment, Don Juan helped to reconcile the opposition to the notion of a parliamentary monarchy, thereby facilitating his son's future task. On the eve of Franco's death, however, the monarchy had few genuine adherents among the major opposition groups, and support for Don Juan merely served to undermine Juan Carlos.

Franco became terminally ill in mid-October 1975, once again forcing the prince to become temporary head of state against his will. In early November, Arias Navarro abruptly resigned in protest at Juan Carlos's failure to inform him of a meeting with senior officers at which he discussed ways of dissuading

Don Juan from formally challenging his claim to the throne. After much pleading, the prime minister withdrew his resignation, though not without strengthening his position in the process. After a series of desperate operations, Franco finally expired on November 20, and Juan Carlos was formally invested king of Spain two days later. The virtual absence of Western representatives at the general's funeral contrasted sharply with the presence of numerous heads of state and government at the king's proclamation on November 27.

Juan Carlos came to the throne imbued with several basic ideas. The most important of these was that the Franco regime, whatever its achievements, could not outlive its founder, and this for a number of reasons. First, the regime's legitimacy had its roots in the Civil War, and its survival stood in the way of a genuine national reconciliation. Second, the political institutions created by Franco over the years lacked any genuine life of their own because they had never been allowed to develop. In order for the monarchy to survive the general's departure, it would have to acquire a new legitimacy of its own, and Juan Carlos had long since concluded that this could only be democratically based. Finally, a growing number of Spaniards regarded the regime as an obstacle to the nation's continued socioeconomic development. More specifically, Spain had been excluded from the European Community on account of the nondemocratic nature of its political system, and the king was determined that his country should once again play a leading role in European affairs.

Juan Carlos and his advisers faced the daunting task of transforming the existing political system while respecting the Francoist legal order, including its own mechanisms of reform. A blatant transgression of the constitution on his part would have released institutions such as the armed forces from their duty to obey him, thereby rendering him largely redundant. On the other hand, the opposition's program—which included the formation of a provisional government, elections to a constituent assembly, and a plebiscite to determine the institutional issue—was hardly designed to guarantee his continuity in office. His own survival demanded that he prevent either camp from winning the upper hand, all the while paving the way for genuine democratic reform.

Juan Carlos was initially unable to appoint a prime minister of his choice, but at least succeeded in inducing Arias Navarro to include a number of reformist ministers in his new cabinet. More important, he was able to appoint his former tutor Torcuato Fernández Miranda to the presidency of the Cortes (parliament) and the Council of the Realm, a position which gave him considerable control over both the legislative process and the selection of the next prime minister.

The first six months of Juan Carlos's reign were marked by a sharp increase in labor unrest—largely instigated by the illegal trade union organizations—as well as the emergence of a powerful proamnesty movement and a heightened demand for home rule in Catalonia and the Basque country. The Arias government, which had promised a gradual democratization of the political system, reacted to this challenge with a combination of repression and appeasement, a policy which satisfied nobody. In view of his prime minister's reluctance to deal with the opposition, the king was forced to descend into the political arena himself, personally reassuring some of the more moderate political leaders. This situation began to endanger the monarchy itself, however, and after delivering a speech to a joint session of the American Congress in which he openly committed himself to a Western-style political system for the first time, in early July 1976 Juan Carlos finally dismissed Arias and replaced him with Adolfo Suárez, a young minister and former Francoist apparatchik.

The situation which ensued has sometimes been compared to a theatrical production of which Juan Carlos was the impresario, Fernández Miranda the author and Suárez the leading actor. Fernández Miranda's answer to the king's dilemma took the form of the Law for Political Reform providing for the election of a democratic assembly, which was approved by the Francoist Cortes in November 1976 and subsequently endorsed in a referendum, as required by the existing provisions for constitutional reform. Suárez then turned his attention to the opposition, which agreed to participate in the elections scheduled for June 1977 in return for measures such as the legalization of political parties and trade unions, a broader amnesty and the dissolution of the Movimiento (the Francoist single party).

Juan Carlos feared that a left-wing victory would destabilize the transition process, and therefore encouraged Suárez to form his own electoral coalition, Unión de Centro Democrático (UCD), which narrowly failed to win an absolute majority. This result enabled UCD to have a major say in the ensuing constituent process, while preventing it from imposing its views entirely. The constitutional issue closest to the king's heart was, of course, the future of the monarchy itself. While the Communists had effectively acknowledged the institution in return for their highly controversial legalization in April 1977, the Socialists continued to demand some form of democratic decision on the matter until their republican amendment was defeated in the Cortes in May 1978.

Although the monarchy never was put to a referendum, Spaniards indirectly legitimated the institution in December 1978 by endorsing the new democratic constitution, which defines the political form of the state as a parliamentary monarchy. The king acquired the dynastic legitimacy which had initially eluded him in May 1977, when Don Juan recognized him as the rightful king of Spain, a decision later ratified by the constitution, which pronounced him the legitimate heir of the historic dynasty.

The largely symbolic role ascribed to Juan Carlos by the 1978 constitution is not unlike that performed by most of his counterparts in other European monarchies. As head of state, he has the task of arbitrating and moderating the regular workings of the political institutions. Under the guidance of the legislature and the executive, the king summons and dissolves the Cortes, calls for elections, proposes and appoints the prime minister, and sanctions and promulgates laws. He also exercises supreme command of the armed forces, though it is the government which dictates defense and military policy.

The king has nevertheless paid special attention to the armed forces, often using the annual military celebration of January 6 both to offer encouragement and to remind them of their constitutional duties. In this respect, the monarchy may be said to have acted as a bridging institution, allowing the armed forces to transfer their loyalty from one political system to another, without being unfaithful to their past.

Unfortunately, the king's exhortations have not always been heeded. On the evening of February 23, 1981, shortly after Suárez's resignation, a detachment of Civil Guards, acting in collusion with army units in Madrid and Valencia, took the government and the Cortes hostage just as the latter was about to vote in a new prime minister, Leopoldo Calvo Sotelo. The coup's organizers cleverly claimed to be acting with the king's consent, and it was only after numerous telephone conversations with senior officers that Juan Carlos was able to dispel this impression, thereby aborting the coup. The king's dramatic early-morning broadcast informing the Spanish public that the constitution had been upheld won him the lasting gratitude and respect of most Spaniards, including many who had hitherto accepted the monarchy with great reluctance.

In 1982, the formation of a moderate Socialist cabinet led by Felipe González with a solid majority in the Cortes was greeted with relief by the king. The Socialist electoral victory put an end to several years of weak UCD governments unable to respond to challenges posed by internal party strife, economic crisis, military unrest and Basque terrorism. As the constitutional monarch of a consolidated democracy, Juan Carlos has settled down to a more conventional role, in which he exercises the right to be consulted, the right to encourage and the right to warn.

Democratization has brought in its wake the creation of a quasi-federal system which has largely met the demands of the various Spanish regions, including those with distinct languages and cultures of their own. In this context, the king has emerged as a most effective advocate and symbol of an increasingly decentralized, multicultural Spain, as exemplified whenever he addresses the Catalan, Basque and Galician populations in their own languages. Admittedly, a small minority of Spanish citizens refuse to regard him as their legitimate head of state, as was made painfully clear during his first official tour of the Basque country in early 1981. In spite of this, the king has undoubtedly contributed to making the Spanish state more attractive to those who initially continued to associate it with the Franco regime. In Spain, as in Belgium, the monarchy's role in resisting centrifugal forces would in itself appear to justify a hereditary head of state.

Juan Carlos and Sophia, both of whom speak all the major Western European languages fluently, have also become Spain's most effective representatives abroad. In the early days of his reign, the king played a decisive role in obtaining Western support for the democratizing process, a task in which he was sometimes aided by other European monarchs. Juan Carlos attributed a great deal of importance to the external dimension of Spain's return to democracy and took an active interest in the process leading to membership in the European Community in 1986. Although he was always in favor of Spain joining NATO, a decision adopted in 1982 and only ratified by the Socialists in 1986 after submitting the matter to a referendum, he did not allow his personal preferences to interefere with government policy.

The king has also played a major role in injecting new life and meaning into Spain's hitherto largely rhetorical relations with Latin America, where he enjoys considerable prestige as a champion of democracy. During his visit to Argentina in 1978, with the military junta firmly in power, the king spoke out forcefully in defense of democratic values and institutions. Five years later, in Uruguay, he made his visit conditional on being allowed to see the leaders of the outlawed opposition parties, many of whom came to regard this event as a turning point in their struggle against their military rulers. More recently, the king has played a major role in the institutionalization of the Ibero-American Community of Nations. Given Spain's earlier role in the Americas, it is ironic but also curiously fitting that the monarchy should have become the ideal vehicle for the contemporary nation's reencounter with its former colonies.

The monarch has also enjoyed a high profile in Spain's traditionally close relations with the Arab world, putting his personal ties with a number of rulers to excellent use. Surprisingly, perhaps, this has not prevented him from making an equally substantial contribution to relations with Israel, which only established diplomatic relations with Spain in 1986, and with the long-forgotten Sephardic diaspora. By expressing interest and respect for the non-Catholic religions and cultures which played a decisive role in Spain's past, the king has helped to advance the cause of religious tolerance and pluralism.

The esteem in which the monarchy is held by Spaniards is largely the consequence of Juan Carlos's performance in the exceptional circumstances of the country's transition to democracy. Additionally, it reflects the skill with which the king and queen have adapted the institution to the country's current needs and tastes. The Spanish royal family benefits from a modest civil list, pays taxes, has little property of its own and barely associates with aristocrats and grandees. What is more, the royal couple complement each other admirably: While Juan Carlos feels more at home on a yacht than in a concert hall, the reverse is true of Sophia.

In Spain, the transition to democracy has brought in its wake the emergence of a new collective identity, which Juan Carlos personifies. The Spanish monarchy reflects back to the country an image of itself that it not only identifies with but admires, because the king and queen embody an image of Spain—modern, tolerant and cosmopolitan—which Spaniards find deeply flattering to themselves. In other words, in Spain as elsewhere, the monarchy is a mirror which enables ordinary citizens to admire themselves. Although it will not be easy for Juan Carlos to transmit his personal prestige and moral authority to his heir Prince Felipe (1968–), there is reason to believe he has succeeded in guaranteeing the institution's continuity.

BIBLIOGRAPHY

Carr, Raymond, and Fusi, Juan Pablo. *Spain: Dictatorship to Democracy*. London: George Allen & Unwin, 1979.

Gilmour, David. *The Transformation of Spain: From Franco to the Constitutional Monarchy*. London: Quartet Books, 1985.

Powell, Charles T. *El piloto del cambio: El Rey, la monarquía y la transición a la democracia*. Barcelona: Planeta, 1991.

———. *Juan Carlos I of Spain*. London: Macmillan, 1994.

CHARLES T. POWELL

K

KONSTANTINOS KARAMANLIS (1907–   ), a conservative politician, has been an integral part of the Greek political structure for half a century, spanning all the major events of postwar Greek politics. He was elected a deputy in 1935 as a member of the Laikon Komma (Popular Party) and again in 1936. He entered ministerial office for the first time in 1946 as a minister of labor and followed as minister of transport (1948), minister of social welfare (1948), minister of defense (1950) and minister of public works (1952). In 1955 he was appointed by the king to the post of prime minister.

Karamanlis subsequently formed his own party, the Ethniki Rizospastiki Enosis (National Radical Union), won three elections (1956, 1958, 1961) and served as prime minister until June 1963. Following a narrow defeat in the November 1963 elections, Karamanlis left Greece for self-imposed exile in France. He ended this exile in the summer of 1974, when he returned to Greece and again took the oath of prime minister, amid dramatic events due to the ill-fated coup in Cyprus, the ensuing invasion of northern Cyprus by Turkish troops and the fall of the military regime in Greece. He regrouped his old party under the new name of Nea Dimokratia (New Democracy), won two elections (1974 and 1977) and served as prime minister until 1980. In May 1980 Karamanlis was elected president of Greece; he was reelected to the same post in May 1990. His term expires on May 5, 1995.

Karamanlis, the first of eight children, was born on March 8, 1907, in the Macedonian village of Proti, in the northern region of Greece. At the time of his birth, Proti was under Turkish occupation. Karamanlis became a citizen of the kingdom of Greece at the age of six when Proti was liberated during the Balkan Wars of 1912–1913. Greek politics at that time were highly unstable, primarily because of coups, countercoups, dictatorship and friction from the ongoing dispute over the monarchy versus the republic.

His father, George Karamanlis, was a schoolmaster and later a successful tobacco farmer. Politically, he was known to be a strong nationalist and a royalist. He often carried on his nationalistic activities against both the Turks and the Bulgarians, for which he was imprisoned several times. His father's political activities reportedly constituted the early beginnings of Karamanlis's long apprenticeship in politics.

Karamanlis received his primary education in Proti and his secondary education in the neighboring towns of Nea Zichni and Serres and later in the capital city of Athens. He entered the University of Athens in November 1925 and received his law degree on December 13, 1929.

In the course of his studies in Athens, Karamanlis reportedly attended parliamentary debates and reflected frequently on contemporary political events within and outside Greece. His assessment was that Greek politics lacked continuity, responsibility, tolerance and reason. In response, he developed a conservative perspective on politics generally. He yearned for political stability. Consistent with his conservativism, achieving and maintaining political stability meant preserving the status quo. Predictably, Karamanlis resolved his own concerns over the issue of the monarchy versus the republic by choosing to be a royalist.

Following completion of his studies, Karamanlis returned to Serres in northern Greece, served four months with the nineteenth Infantry Regiment, and started his law practice. In the general elections of June 9, 1935, Karamanlis stood as a candidate and was elected a deputy for the Laikon Komma in his native prefecture of Serres. Deputy Karamanlis was in office for about six months when the prime minister, Panagis Tsaldaris, and his government, were overthrown by militant royalists who sought an immediate restoration of the monarchy.

In new elections in January 1936, Karamanlis was reelected to parliament, a victory that was followed by a setback. On August 4, 1936, Ioannis Metaxas, the prime minister, using the pretext of communist danger, convinced the newly restored King George II to dissolve parliament, to suspend parts of the constitution and to grant him emergency powers. Parliament did not meet for the next ten years, delivering a blow both to democratic political development in Greece and to Karamanlis's political career.

Karamanlis returned to Serres and resumed his law practice. In the years ahead, in addition to dictatorship, Greece suffered economic depression, war with Italy, foreign occupation by Germany, Italy and Bulgaria and a bitter civil war that resulted in untold suffering for the country. Also during the same time, Britain's influence in Greece diminished significantly and the United States emerged as Greece's new chief protector through the Truman Doctrine.

Karamanlis's political career resumed its forward momentum when he was reelected deputy for the Laikon Komma in Serres in the general elections of March 1946. Between 1946 and 1955, he served in four different cabinet posts, one of which he occupied twice. In the future, when he was dropped from a ministerial position, he was able to fall back on his seat in parliament.

In November 1946, Karamanlis was appointed minister of labor in the Tsaldaris government (Tsaldaris being the leader of the Laikon Komma). Because of government restructuring, however, he held the portfolio for only about three months, a term too short to deal effectively with the recovery problems created earlier by the war with Italy and foreign occupation and which at the time were made worse by the civil war in progress.

Appointed minister of transport in May 1948, in a coalition government under Sophoulis, Karamanlis energetically sought and secured American support for his reconstruction programs. He stayed in this cabinet post for only six months, but he succeeded, through effective use of American aid and legislation, in making major contributions to Greek infrastructural recovery, among them the expansion of the road network and public services into remote areas of the country and improvements in the electricity supply in Thessaloniki and Athens.

As minister of social welfare, a post to which he was appointed in November 1948, Karamanlis dealt directly with the problems of war victims; these were the most challenging problems of the recovery process yet to face him. Once again, through effective use of relief funds—both Greek and American—he made extensive trips to areas with affected populations and organized the preparation of clothing, shelter, food, medicine, fuel and security for the many hundreds of refugees and war-wounded. His success was so great that he not only survived a reorganization of the Sophoulis government in January 1949, but the Ministry of Health was also temporarily added to his principal social welfare portfolio. Subsequently, a bill he had drafted earlier "on the coordination of measures for the remedy of all categories of needs of the victims of the bandits" was passed by the government, became law and was implemented almost immediately.

In August 1950, Karamanlis was appointed to represent the Laikon Komma as minister of defense in the precarious coalition that was formed under Venizelos following the general elections of March 5, 1950. His term at defense lasted only seven weeks but he succeeded in making his mark both through new legislation and limited American funds. Specifically, Karamanlis dealt with the logistics of preparing the Greek force for Korea, responded to revived guerrilla activities in northern Greece and, in a gesture of respect for the military's corporate interests, increased allowances to soldiers and promoted legislation addressing housing issues for officers. He also took the opportunity to express concerns over Bulgarian threats to divert the course of the River Evros in eastern Macedonia.

Soon thereafter, Karamanlis returned to being an ordinary deputy as a result of yet again government restructuring. About the same time, the Laikon Komma, having previously shown signs of disintegration, was replaced by a new party, Ellinikos Synagermos (Greek Rally), led by the former commander in chief, Alexandros Papagos. Karamanlis became a member. Following the general elections of September 1951, Karamanlis declined an offer to represent the Greek Rally as minister of defense in the coalition government that emerged under Plastiras and Venizelos. He returned, however, to the post of minister of public works in the Papagos government following Ellinikos Synagermos victory in the general elections of November 1952. In the meantime, Greece became a member of NATO in February 1952 and Karamanlis married Amalia Kanellopoulou on July 2, 1952.

As before, as public works minister, Karamanlis undertook, supervised and saw to completion an extensive recovery program of infrastructural facilities, industry, communications, utilities and public services. A measure of Karamanlis's competence was Papagos's move to add the ministry of communications to his primary responsibilities late in 1954. A year later, fate and circumstances converged to give Karamanlis and his ascent to power a major boost.

On October 4, 1955, Papagos died. The following day, King Paul, in a surprise move, designated Karamanlis for the premiership and asked him to form a government. Karamanlis was then forty-eight years old, quite young according to the age standards of Greek politics. Thus Karamanlis, the relatively young deputy from the Macedonian countryside, was catapulted into prominence.

At this point, Karamanlis formed a new party, Ethniki Rizospastiki Enosis (ERE, i.e., National Radical Union), won three triumphant elections of his own (February 1956, May 1958 and October 1961) and served as prime minister until 1963. Of the three elections, the first bore the distinction of resulting in a council of ministers that included, for the first time, a woman, appointed minister of social welfare, the same post that had been instrumental in establishing Karamanlis's reputation earlier. The third elections, however, were clouded by allegations of fraud. Although the claims of neither side were ever entirely proven or disproved, the opposition made extensive use of these allegations to attack Karamanlis, urging the king to dismiss him.

Be that as it may, Karamanlis as prime minister provided modern Greek history with the longest continuous term in office and with valuable lessons on political development based on continuous and coherent political institutions. Supporters pointed with pride to the eight continuous years in office and to the party's principles, which they claimed remained consistent throughout the years.

Karamanlis also proved to be one of the very few enthusiastic modernizers in Greek history. He set forth to modernize Greece through rehabilitation of its industry, major cities, tourism, communications and economic stability, through reform of public life and through Greece's accession to the European Community (EC). All of these were met with various degrees of success, thus fulfilling to a large degree Karamanlis's goal of integrating Greece more closely into Western Europe. As prime minister, he also devoted considerable time and energy to issues of foreign policy and security.

With respect to foreign policy, by the time Karamanlis became prime minister, the Cyprus issue had acquired dramatic dimensions, and it required an immediate solution. The essence of the issue consisted in the movement among Greek Cypriots for self-determination and union with Greece, on the one hand, and the movement among Turkish Cypriots for partition of the island, on the other hand. This situation led to numerous outbreaks of violence in Cyprus and to a steady deterioration of the relations between Greece and Turkey, respective protectors of the Greek and Turkish populations on the island.

Karamanlis adopted Greece's point of view on the Cyprus issue: self-determination for the island and union with Greece. Turkey supported the Turkish Cypriot demands for partition of the island. The conflict was complicated further by Britain (suspected of favoring partition), which had annexed the island in 1914.

Karamanlis sought unsuccessfully to win international support for Cypriot-Greek union from both within and outside the Western Alliance. He was probably aware of the compelling fact that because alternative scenarios favoring union were not adopted earlier, his options were now limited. In the end, a compromise was reached between Britain, Greece and Turkey which led to the establishment of an independent, unitary republic of Cyprus in 1960. The compromise agreement dashed Greek hopes for union and Karamanlis was severely criticized. Some of his own ministers defected in protest. In response, he went to the king, offered his resignation and sought dissolution of the parliament. The elections of 1961 confirmed his party's majority and gave him a fresh and strong mandate. Controversies were soon to follow, however, which, according to detractors and supporters alike, may not have diminished the significance of his accomplishments but did tarnish his reputation—at least for the time being.

In May 1963, Grigorios Lambrakis, a deputy of the Eniaia Dimokratiki Aristera (United Democratic Front), was assassinated by two extreme rightists during a peace march in Thessaloniki in northern Greece. Subsequent investigations showed that the assassins were connected with government officials in high places. Karamanlis, although not personally implicated, bore some responsibility as head of the right-wing government in question. The opposition, in particular, pointed to the Lambrakis tragedy as an example of left-bashing that had ostensibly long been practiced by all right-wing governments in Greece.

Also in 1963, Karamanlis's relationship with the royal family, already strained in the early 1960s, started showing fresh signs of deterioration. For various reasons, including a dispute with the royal family over whether a state visit to London should or should not have taken place, Karamanlis resigned on June 11, 1963, claiming that he no longer had the king's confidence. He left temporarily for Zurich, but returned in time to prepare for the subsequent general elections.

Karamanlis's ERE was defeated in the general elections of November 1963. For the first time ever, Karamanlis would have been in the position of opposition leader, an interesting notion given his own ideas on responsible opposition and its absence from Greek politics. Karamanlis, however, went into self-exile in Paris. An opportunity was thereby lost to observe whether and the extent to which a successful former prime minister would build a responsible opposition force based on principles of continuity and coherence. Perhaps there is some truth to claims, made both by supporters and detractors, that Karamanlis disliked being in the opposition, or that he would not be an effective opposition leader.

On April 21, 1967—following confrontations between the king and his prime minister and long periods of constitutional crisis and caretaker governments—a group of colonels seized control of the Greek state, less than a month before scheduled elections. An aborted countercoup by the king forced the royal family to leave Greece. From his self-imposed exile, Karamanlis repeatedly served as the focus of conservative opposition to the military regime until its downfall in 1974. Karamanlis then returned to Greece in the summer of 1974 to lead the first postjunta civilian government. The transition from a military to a civilian regime was remarkably smooth, an indication that both the military and civilians were ready for a return to civilian government. Karamanlis subsequently established a new party, Nea Dimokratia (New Democracy), won two elections (November 1974 and November 1977) and served as prime minister until 1980. A popular referendum held on December 8, 1974, abolished the monarchy and a parliamentary republic was established in its place.

After the restoration of civilian government, Karamanlis succeeded in reversing the damage caused by the military regime in areas such as Greece's traditional relations with Western Europe and the United States, the economy and political institutions. He also directed immediate attention to disputes with Turkey over Greek and Turkish minorities living in each other's countries, the continental-shelf rights in the Aegean Sea and the division of Cyprus.

Karamanlis's crowning achievement was the accession of Greece to the European Community (EC). It was the result of hard bargaining and a process that consisted of several landmarks, including the opening of formal negotiations with the EC in 1959, the signing of the Association Agreement between Greece and the EC in 1961, Greece's application for full membership in the EC in 1975, the signing of the Accession Treaty between Greece and the Community in May 1979 and the accession of Greece to the EC as a full member in January 1981. Thus a major political objective of Karamanlis's political career, to integrate Greece more closely into Western Europe, was accomplished. Today, efforts to bring Greece further into line with the requirements of the EC's program for political and monetary union enjoy the support of all major political parties. Moreover, the Greeks are said to be among the strongest supporters of a United Europe.

Konstantinos Karamanlis was elected to the presidency of the Greek republic in May 1980. According to his constitutional role, he was expected to be above politics. However, he was reportedly maintaining strong influence over the conservatives and acting as a restraining influence on Andreas Papandreou, the leader of the Greek Socialist Party, the Panhellenic Socialist Movement. Papandreou headed Greece's first Socialist government, coming to power on October 18, 1981. Contrary to expectations, Prime Minister Andreas Papandreou did not support President Karamanlis for a second term. Karamanlis was reelected to the presidential post, however, in 1990, when Nea Dimokratia had returned to power.

As an historical figure, Karamanlis will be remembered in various ways: as one of Greece's most respected statesmen, as the conservative politician who did a great deal to strengthen Greece's political and economic ties to the West, as the leader who gave Greece periods of unprecedented political stability and restored Greek democracy after the military regime collapsed in 1974, and as the politician to whom the credit belongs for Greece's accession to the European Community—an immense legacy under any circumstances, especially the turbulent ones of Greece's postwar political history.

BIBLIOGRAPHY

Woodhouse, C. M. *Karamanlis: The Restorer of Greek Democracy.* New York: Oxford University Press, 1982.

KOSTAS MESSAS

URHO KEKKONEN (1900–1986) was elected president of Finland in 1956 by a majority of a single vote (out of three hundred grand electors). He was reelected to that office in 1962 and again in 1968. In the 1962 election, he was reelected with difficulty, the outcome of the election being chiefly a result of a foreign policy crisis ensuing from Soviet intervention in Finnish internal affairs amid the presidential campaign. By 1968 Kekkonen had reestablished his primacy in Finnish politics and was reelected once again to the presidency triumphantly.

In 1973, because of developments in Finnish foreign policy, he announced his decision not to run for reelection to the presidency. However, he was persuaded by the major political parties to accept an extension of the mandate he had received in 1968. By passing the so-called exception law, the Finnish parliament voted in 1974 for the extension of his term of office for another four years. In spite of the fact that by 1976–1977 Kekkonen had begun to show repeated signs of mental fatigue, he was renominated for the presidency by all the major political parties for the election of 1978, and he was then elected by an overwhelming majority. However, due to his mental decrepitude he was unable to stay in power for his full final term. In 1981 his inability to handle the tasks of head of state was finally recognized, and he resigned from the presidency in the same year. Kekkonen died five years later.

Urho Kekkonen was perhaps the most significant political leader of Finland, for he came to the fore of Finnish politics at a time when there was an urgent and inescapable need to redirect Finland's foreign policy after its wars against the Soviet Union in 1939–1940 and 1941–1944. Working as prime minister alongside the aging president, Juho Kusti Paasikivi, Kekkonen contributed to the development of a policy designed to keep Finland out of the quarrels between the big powers. This policy included both the pursuit of neutrality and, somewhat contradictorily, a treaty of mutual assistance with the Soviet Union.

After his election to the presidency, he forcefully defended and implemented this so-called Paasikivi-Kekkonen line. He believed in personal diplomacy and took care to cultivate personal contacts with Soviet leaders, who always looked upon him with great respect. Gradually Kekkonen became a sort of father figure to the Finnish people, a man who safeguarded the security and stability of the country. He institutionalized the national consensus on foreign policy. Any attack on him was regarded as an attack on Finnish foreign policy, thereby an attack on the vital security interests of the nation. His impact on the political culture of Finland was immense: He demanded and received obedience and submission. He was both feared and respected, in that order.

Urho Kekkonen was born in Pielavesi in Finland, the son of a work manager. He was an extrovert and an active young person, eager to be accepted and to exert influence. He received his bachelor of laws degree in 1928, then worked as a lawyer in a municipal organization and defended his doctoral dissertation in public law in 1936. In his youth he was a national champion-level athlete, and he remained a sportsman throughout his life, always maintaining an interest in the outdoors. Well into his old age, he regularly went fishing, hunting and skiing. Kekkonen's devotion to physical training also assumed political and organizational dimensions: For example, after leaving active sports competition, he chaired the Olympic Council of Finland from 1938 to 1946.

As a student, Kekkonen was active for several years in student politics and was already known during this period for his skills and persuasiveness as a debater and writer, much engaged in attempts to strengthen Finnish unity and working against the spread of communist ideas and influences. At one time he was closely associated with the Academic Karelia Society, a student movement which was originally formed to promote Finnish unification, although it later developed semifascist characteristics.

In the early 1930s, Kekkonen began to launch his political career. He became active in the Agrarian Party, soon attaining a prominent position within the party apparatus. In 1936 he became a member of the Finnish parliament and was appointed in the same year to the cabinet, serving as minister of justice. When the cabinet resigned, he became minister of the interior in the next government.

During the period of war against the Soviet Union, he did not hold any ministerial portfolio, but after the wars, his views on foreign policy and relations with the Soviets evolved somewhat, and Kekkonen returned to the government, serving as minister of justice in 1944–1946. Then from 1948 to 1950, he was speaker of the Finnish parliament. In the presidential election of 1950, he challenged the incumbent president, J. K. Paasikivi, as candidate of the Agrarian Party. He lost.

From 1950 to 1953, Kekkonen then headed four consecutive cabinets as prime minister. After a brief detour in 1954 as minister of foreign affairs, in the same year he resumed the prime ministership, staying in that post until elected president of Finland in 1956.

By the force of his will, he was able to establish a presidency characterized by much personal influence alongside a government, headed by a prime minister, which was responsible to parliament. This "semipresidential" regime introduced a certain dualism into constitutional and political life. However, this dualism operated in practice in different ways. The practical authority exercised by Kekkonen as president did not necessarily correspond to the formal powers invested in the presidency. Sometimes dualism between the presidency and the prime ministership was a fiction, with the president clearly supreme, whereas at other points it operated in a real sense with an effective division of authority between president and prime minister.

Finland is certainly among those semipresidential systems that combine both formal and real authority: The authority of the Finnish president is paramount in terms of formal powers and is quite impressive also in terms of real authority. However, the extent to which real authority answers to formal authority in Finland has also, of course, fluctuated. Some Finnish presidents have extended their activities to a wide range of matters and issues, being unable, however, to act independently from other important political institutions and actors. Others have adopted more limited roles, restricting their activity to a certain area of policy and upholding their right to be preeminent in that area.

However, Urho Kekkonen was the most pronounced example of a third type: As president, he was both active and influential in a broad range of policy areas and he was capable of steering others rather than being steered by them. Quite often in the comparative politics literature, Finland is classified as a presidential regime. While this classification is, in fact, incorrect, it was obviously informed by Kekkonen's tenure as president.

In order to understand the variations in presidential power in Finland, one needs to consider a number of factors. Some relate to the personality of the incumbent president—Kekkonen in particular—others to the conjuncture of daily politics, which may or may not invite presidential intervention. Still other factors relate to onetime events of great significance that upset political routines and call for forceful action. All these factors were operating during Kekkonen's tenure: He was an active and engaged person, richly endowed with personal ambition. The life span of a cabinet government was usually short during his time in office, as the parliament was plagued by unstable minority coalitions, especially when crises in the relations with the Soviet Union emerged in 1958–1959 and again in 1961–1962.

The most important factor to consider, however, is the link between foreign and domestic policy. Years ago, the American president John F. Kennedy, in a celebrated description of how foreign policy relates to domestic policy, declared that the line between the two policy sectors was in fact like a line drawn in water.

This phrasing catches an essential aspect of the Paasikivi-Kekkonen approach, which prescribed that foreign policy must take precedence over domestic policy and, therefore, that decisions in the field of domestic policy must be adjusted and subordinated to decisions in the field of foreign policy. The influence exercised by the foreign policy leader in this respect must, to employ another aquatic metaphor, spread out like rings in water. This is precisely what happened in Finland during the postwar period. Foreign policy power was transformed into domestic policy influence: Kekkonen, the foreign policy leader, became the central figure in domestic politics as well.

The interplay between what is foreign and what is not also explains why a clear and uncontroversial picture of Urho Kekkonen's leadership has not emerged. Two intertwined threads run through his lifework, and they convey rather different messages about the character and success of his leadership.

It cannot, on the one hand, be denied that he was a successful leader in the field of foreign policy. When in 1975 Finland hosted the Conference on Security and Cooperation in Europe, the country had come a long way indeed from the timid, cautious and degraded international position it had been banished to in the wake of World War II. Even Kekkonen's most stubborn opponents must admit that this was a remarkable achievement. On the other hand, it is true that the methods employed by Finland and Kekkonen did not always fit with Western observers' expectations about correct neutrality. Finland was frequently said to have submitted to the political domination of the Soviet attitude; in the late 1950s, the term *Finlandization* was introduced in the international discourse to describe the policy of countries that adjust to Soviet wishes.

The fact remains, however, that in implementing the Paasikivi-Kekkonen line, Finland gradually widened its spheres of activity and freedom. Finland joined the Nordic Council in 1956, became a member of the United Nations in the same year, joined the European Free Trade Area in 1961, had its neutrality acknowledged by the United States, England and France in 1961–1962, joined the OECD in 1967, concluded a free trade agreement with the EC in the early 1970s, and so on. By the end of the 1970s, Finland was a part of the Western European economic system with firm ideological, political and cultural ties to West, although, of course, it still faced the strategic dilemma of being situated in an area of vital importance for Soviet security.

The fundamental premise of Kekkonen's foreign policy strategy was based upon a lesson well learned: In times of crisis, Western countries are not to be depended upon. During the wars with the Soviet Union, Finland had received from the West sympathy but no support, words but no guns. The West had abandoned Finland. The protection of the country's national interest, therefore, had to be built upon friendly relations with the Soviets.

On the other hand, however, Kekkonen's foreign policy strategy never called for Finland to be a part of the Soviet Union. To the contrary, Finland was to remain an independent nation, fundamentally different from countries in the communist camp. The implication of this strategy was the pursuit of a policy of strict neutrality, leaning neither toward the West nor the East, but also implying, at the same time, that the Soviet Union had nothing to fear from Finland and nothing to gain from attempts at turning Finland into a satellite.

The cornerstones of this strategy were to be, on the one hand, the Treaty of Mutual Assistance, signed with Moscow in 1948 and renewed in 1955 and again in 1975, and, on the other hand, the notion that building relations with the Western world presupposed that Soviet confidence in Finland could be maintained. In other words, the degree of freedom that Finland could enjoy in structuring its place in the Western world was a function of the country's ability to convince Soviet leaders that Finland would not turn against them.

To be sure, in Finland the objection was often raised that Kekkonen went too far with the Soviets in terms of concessions, thus unduly damaging Finland's image in the West. Much the same result, it was claimed, could have been achieved with a less compliant and humble attitude vis-à-vis the Soviet Union.

While it is impossible to demonstrate the validity of this claim, it is clear, however, that Kekkonen enjoyed the confidence of Moscow to a greater degree than any other Finnish politician. He was thus able to profit from his special relations and frequent contacts with the Kremlin establishment. In 1960, the Soviet leader Nikita Khrushchev even declared that whoever was for Kekkonen was for friendship with the Soviet Union and that whoever was against Kekkonen was against friendship with the Soviet Union.

However, there were certainly limits to Kekkonen's complaisance and ingratiation with the Soviets. He did not hesitate to react negatively when the Soviets overstepped what Kekkonen viewed as the bounds of reason, nor did he hesitate to explain the strategic rather than ideological nature of Finland's efforts to build and maintain good relations with its eastern neighbor. In a much-quoted speech to the Soviet leadership in 1960, he declared that even if all the rest of Europe were to become communist, Finland would stick to its system of government. And when during the 1970s the Soviet Union displayed an ambition to draw Finland closer to the Soviet Bloc—discussing, for instance, possible joint Finnish-Soviet military exercises, Kekkonen firmly rejected the Soviet approach.

Tensions in Finnish-Soviet relations did in fact provide Kekkonen with opportunities to demonstrate his agility in foreign policy, while also serving as a stage upon which foreign policy considerations could spill over into Finnish domestic politics. In the autumn of 1958, for example, the Soviet Union imposed diplomatic and economic sanctions against Finland to indicate its displeasure with the fact that the Communists had been kept out of the Finnish cabinet even though they had been victorious in parliamentary elections. Soviet pressure caused the cabinet to resign, and the crisis was only resolved after talks between Kekkonen and the Soviets in Leningrad in January 1959.

However, Kekkonen's success in this instance did not consolidate his personal authority. He was still challenged by domestic opponents. To finally disarm his critics, another Finnish-Soviet crisis was needed. In the autumn of 1961, in the wake of the Berlin crisis and in the midst of a presidential campaign that was unfolding quite unfavorably for Kekkonen, the Soviet Union insisted on military talks with Finland in accordance with the Treaty of Mutual Assistance. Again, Kekkonen traveled east and met with Nikita Khrushchev in Novosibirsk, convincing Khrushchev that military talks were unnecessary, indeed that they would work against Soviet interests. Relief in Finland was enormous, and Kekkonen was able to capitalize upon the incident, easily winning the presidential election.

Since consistency is regarded by many as a political virtue, Kekkonen's supporters have taken great pains to emphasize the straight-arrow nature and the coherence of his leadership. However, this argument does require some impressive logical somersaults and a considerable amount of indulgent interpretation. For example, the assertion that throughout his career Kekkonen worked for national unity is often substantiated by a reference to his decision in 1966 to accept the Communist Party as a cabinet partner: Kekkonen himself declared his intention to integrate the Communists into Finnish society. More cynical observers would note Kekkonen's long overdue debt of gratitude to the Communists, who by a skillful strategic operation had ensured his election to the presidency in 1956, as well as his pugnacious will to manipulate the political field to his own advantage.

As a person, Kekkonen provoked mixed feelings as well: He was loved and respected by many and he was hated by many. This was reflected in his leadership, which was dualistic and relied on a system of sanctions and rewards. His striving for national unity also sometimes employed strange methods: While supporting some, he would condemn others to wandering in the political wilderness. He was quick to classify political parties in terms of their so-called dependability in foreign affairs, and he was equally quick to deny cabinet positions to parues that did not please him in this respect. More often than not, these parties were those who found it hard to accept his leadership style and his conception of domestic politics. The role he played in initiating and maintaining a severe split in the Social Democratic Party (SDP) in the late 1950s and the early 1960s is not fully documented, but it is quite clear that decimating the main party to oppose him worked to Kekkonen's advantage and was magnified by his unvarnished efforts to recuperate SDP deserters.

As his position became secure and as he grew older, Kekkonen's inclination toward a dictatorial manner took on more drastic and unveiled expressions. Into descriptions of parliamentary life in Finland, the term *whip parliamentarism* was introduced to describe the rough methods he used to bypass normal procedures, intervening in the practices and prerogatives of other political institutions. For instance, in 1976 Kekkonen broke a strike of railway traffic controllers by stating that he would refuse to approve any parliamentary bill that met the strikers' demand for a reduction in the retirement age.

Kekkonen also began to use somewhat unorthodox, informal means for shaping and controlling the political process. He wrote streams of letters both praising and criticizing politicians, bureaucrats, editors, managers and private individuals, and the contents of these letters were made publicly known. He surrounded himself with networks of informers and messengers, who kept him abreast of developments within different segments of society, all the while circulating intimations of his will and intentions. Such hints were received by sensitive ears: By the 1970s, compliance with Kekkonen's wishes in politics became almost total. Some adapted and obeyed out of a belief in the blessing of his leadership, others out of opportunistic expectations, still others out of the fear of reprisals.

Two images of Kekkonen therefore emerge. In the one, he was a patriot and a statesman, acting in the best interests of the nation, heavy-handed with his opponents only out of necessity. These latter clearly did not fully understand the realities of power and complexities of Finland's international position. These critics had to be mastered, educated and prevented from damaging the common cause. In this view, Kekkonen stands out as a leader with a special capacity to promote the country's security, fearlessly prepared to ensure the domestic conditions necessary to a successful foreign policy.

In the other image, Kekkonen was, by contrast, a shrewd and unscrupulous politician who consciously overstated the risks involved in Finland's geopolitical situation and did so in order to magnify his own role and importance. He calculated, according to this view, that if he was regarded as indispensable to the handling of Finland's fateful foreign policy dilemma, he could, on the one hand, secure the continuation of his rule, and, on the other hand, discredit his opponents and keep them out of powerful positions. In this view, Kekkonen stands out as a leader who devoted great energy to his own political career and who did not hesitate to invoke foreign interests in his strategy, bypassing normal democratic and parliamentary procedures whenever necessary.

Both images are probably to some extent both true and false. In Finnish public opinion, however, the darker view has became more prevalent. Certainly, Urho Kekkonen is much less appreciated in Finland today than he was during the 1960s and 1970s. In some respects, the Finnish political system has even taken notice of the Kekkonen experience, adopting measures designed to check similar developments. For example, the Finnish parliament amended the constitution to limit the president to a maximum of two terms.

Pertinent questions are also now asked about the substance of Kekkonen's relations with Soviet leaders, recent research findings even suggesting that Kekkonen was actively involved in inviting the two Soviet intrusions into Finnish politics which stabilized and confirmed his leadership, although there is still as yet no undisputed proof of this. The fact that the international context surrounding Finnish foreign policy has changed almost completely during the late 1980s and early 1990s has likewise contributed to a certain disparagement of Kekkonen's achievements. On the other hand, however, the political experiences of the Cold War period are still recent enough to obstruct a completely unprejudiced view of Kekkonen's balancing between the realities and temptations of power. The final chapter on Urho Kekkonen, therefore, has yet to be written.

BIBLIOGRAPHY

Works by Kekkonen:

Neutrality: The Finnish Position. Speeches. London: Heinemann, 1970, 1973.

Finnlands Weg zur Neutralität: Reden und Ansprechen. Herausgegeben von Tuomas Vilkuna. Düsseldorf und Wien, 1975.

Gedanken eines Präsidenten. Düsseldorf: Econ, 1981.

A President's View. London: Heinemann, 1982.

Other Works:

Arter, David. ''Kekkonen's Finland: Enlightened Despotism or Consensual Democracy?'' *West European Politics* 2 (1981).

Hakovirta, Harto. *East-West Conflict and European Neutrality*. Oxford: Clarendon Press, 1988.

Jakobson, Max. *Finland: Myth and Reality*. Helsinki: Otava Publishing Company, 1987.

DAG ANCKAR

PETRA KARIN KELLY (1947–1992) cofounded the German Greens' ''antiparty party'' in 1979 and was a major spokesperson and theoretician for the Greens internationally. Her popular appeal was pivotal in winning election of the first Green representatives to the West German parliament (the Bundestag) in 1983; she secured the seat for Nuremberg, holding it until 1990.

A leading international peace and human rights activist, she was awarded the Alternative Nobel Prize in 1982 by the Right Livelihood Foundation in Stockholm, Sweden. Committed to civil disobedience, she introduced the traditions of Gandhi and Martin Luther King to Germany during the Cold War. In 1991 the *Sunday Times* of London placed her on its list of ''1000 Makers of the Twentieth Century.'' *Wiener* chose her in 1992 as one of the twenty-five most prominent ecology activists in the world. Kelly espoused an alternative paradigm of politics (''ecopax''), emphasizing holistic ecological thinking, nonviolence and participatory democracy.

Although most readily associated with the Greens, Kelly's leadership was more extensive and complex than just the party. She represented a critical opposition to the ''false gods'' and destructive behavior of established politics generally, as well as the vision of an alternative social order. Her values expressed the spirit of postmaterialism, and she was perhaps the single most important leader of that post–World War II generation to challenge the credibility of the Western democratic ''civic culture.''

She came of age during the 1960s. While sympathetic to the ''counterculture'' concept of the New Left, she rejected, from her perspective of civil disobedience, the New Left's radical disobedience. Similarly, Marxist class conflict was unacceptable to her. With her Kantian-like commitment to moral ends through moral means, Kelly uncompromisingly denounced all violence. She, therefore, vehemently disagreed with left-wing fundamentalists (*Fundis*) of the Greens who proposed ''selective violence'' (for example, against property). Kelly never accepted the idea of an ''irreconcilable enemy,'' believing that the powerful, entrapped in their own web of violence, are themselves in need of liberation. While her intellectual roots had been planted on the European left, they grew well beyond both the old left and New Left.

Contrary to leaders whose reputations have been built through established political offices, Kelly—though she served as a parliamentarian and was elected speaker of the Greens—achieved her fame primarily through the power of her ideas. She might be called an ''entrepreneurial'' leader, for part of her ''antipolitics'' genius was to create the organizational vehicles needed to promote the alternative cause. Of these initiatives, the Greens' ''antiparty party'' received special attention because it became an electoral force.

Kelly's message was unequivocal and urgent: Status quo politics is morally bankrupt and deadly. Humankind's very survival is at stake. Greedy, violent power elites—legitimized and protected by the sovereign state they selfishly run—wreak unbridled havoc and destruction with their competitive power scrambles. The rights and lives of others are trampled underfoot by the ''structural violence'' manifested in the self-serving state apparatus and by physical violence. Poverty, as analyzed by Kelly, results directly from such ''structural violence.'' Violence against others, especially against women, in turn, releases violence against the natural environment. (The relationship between violence against women and that against the environment was the foundation of Kelly's ''ecofeminism'' concept.) Abuse of human and ecological rights are two sides of the same coin.

Kelly's alternative was ''ecological peace'' (''ecopax''), which emphasizes the interconnectedness and life-enhancement potential of the global processes constituting the natural system of life. Ecopax requires learning to think and act holistically (in terms of interconnectedness) and peaceably (in terms of life enhancement). This ''rethink'' produces an ''outer ecology,'' protecting the environmental context of this interconnectedness, and an ''inner ecology,'' promoting identification with the spiritual dimensions of life. The sunflower, Kelly's choice for the Greens' logo, captures her vision of ecopax. Growing straight and strong, in tall ''solidarity'' clusters, it beams life and hope through its sunlike visage.

Her ''antipolitics'' objective was, therefore, to undermine elite power by exposing the human and ecological damage produced through structural and physical violence. As a civil disobedient, she attempted to raise mass consciousness by transforming situations of abuse into public issues and by mobilizing nonviolent resistance (for example, sit-ins) to policies of abuse.

Information and publicity were thus crucial to Kelly's efficacy as an ''antipolitics'' leader. The primary task being to communicate information, her support system consisted of media connections and all the technical accoutrements of modern mass communications. This information age leadership was more individualistic, spontaneous, mobile and broadly based than conventional organizational leadership. She was brilliantly adept at using the media, this skill being referred to as her ''American style.''

The crucible of her leadership was the west Bavarian town of Günzburg, where she was born on November 29, 1947. Thirty-six years earlier, Josef Mengele, who later became the infamous Nazi concentration camp ''doctor'' known as the ''angel of death,'' had also been born in Günzburg. The fact that she came from the same town as Mengele made a strong impact on Kelly.

Convinced that the silence of the fearful had greatly strengthened the Nazis, Kelly became the avowed enemy of silence in her own lifetime. Insisting upon remembrance, she pushed for restitution to forgotten Nazi victims, including the Basque cultural-religious center, Guernica, razed by Nazi *Blitzkrieg* bombing. Campaigning since the 1980s against mainland China's genocidal assault upon Tibet, she implored that ''we must not be silent.'' (She was the foster parent of a Tibetan girl.) Her ''antipolitics'' assumed the character of a mission in which she became the instrument of the angel of life.

Kelly was, undoubtedly, not only a political but a vital spiritual force in this regard. Educated as a child in a Roman Catholic convent school, she at one time considered becoming a Dominican nun. She preserved this spirituality at the heart of her political mission. However, believing that the Church did not honor its principles in its stand on women's rights and in its passivity on world poverty, she ultimately quit the Church in 1980, writing a letter of explanation to Pope John Paul II, as was characteristic of her style.

Behind her sense of mission also lay a personal tragedy. In 1970 her stepsister, Grace, died of eye cancer at the age of ten. The loss was profound for Kelly. She subsequently founded the Grace P. Kelly Foundation for Children especially to fund a humanistically designed clinic called the ''Children's Planet.'' Grace's death, linked to environmental poisoning and excessive radiation, propelled Kelly by her own admission into the antinuclear, ecological movement.

Her years in the United States gave structure to her mission. In 1959, following the second marriage of her mother, Marianne, to John E. Kelly, a lieutenant colonel in the American NATO forces stationed in Germany, Kelly moved with her family to Georgia, then to Virginia and Washington, D.C. (Having been abandoned by her biological father when she was seven, Petra dropped her birth name, Lehmann, in favor of the Kelly surname. She was not, however, officially adopted.) While attending American University's School of International Service, earning a B.A. degree in 1970, she became politically involved. Working as a volunteer for Hubert Humphrey, she developed a close relationship with him, in spite of disagreement over the Vietnam War. (Humphrey organized a memorial mass for her sister, Grace.) Her work, however, for Robert Kennedy's 1968 presidential campaign was the chief catalyst.

Through Kennedy, she came into contact with the civil rights movement, learning therefrom of civil disobedience. She now found the means to translate moral protest into social action. Following in the footsteps of Gandhi and Martin Luther King, Kelly resolved to take civil disobedience to unknown territory, her own native Germany. In Germany, then the dividing line of the Cold War, Kelly saw the confluence of the world's life-threatening forces—great power hegemony and confrontation, the arms race and resulting ecological devastation—and took her stand.

Her years in America also opened up a transnational vista for her that continued to expand. She spent a year (1970–1971) at the University of Amsterdam, earning a master's degree in political science, and returned the next year to teach as a Woodrow Wilson scholar at American University. In 1972 she joined the European Community staff in Brussels as an administrator for social and health policy and remained there until 1981, traveling frequently to Germany (much to the detriment of her health) to work in the Citizens' Initiative Movement for Environmental Protection (BBU) and in the evolving Greens' movement.

Her resulting intellectual foothold, embracing several cultures, encouraged her in comparative analysis. Grasping the interdependence of the global village as a chain of cause-effect national relations, she began framing issues of peace as well as human and ecological rights with an international perspective. The threat to humankind being universal, she rallied against national self-containment, claiming there can be no "partial survival," no "small death." She was, therefore, a European federalist, though she feared a developing "two-tier" Europe of rich and poor states.

While she was based in Germany, Kelly's leadership had worldwide ambitions and repercussions. Her protests recognized no national boundaries, topically ranging from Morocco's occupation of the Western Sahara to apartheid, Sakharov's Kremlin-imposed exile, Western companies in Bhopal and the Persian Gulf War. She involved herself in struggles on behalf of ethnic minorities across the world, such as the Australian aborigines and the native North Americans, and she was affiliated with the Unrepresented Nations' and People's Organization (UNPO), founded in 1981 in The Hague. Criticized by some Greens for her "distracting" internationalism, Kelly interpreted this "nationalizing" of the German Greens as a sexist-inspired attack upon her involvement in the struggle for universal women's rights.

By 1972 the essentials of her alternative thinking were in place. Still receptive to conventional politics, she thought her political home lay with West Germany's Social Democratic Party (SPD), formally joining it that same year. The SPD's Willy Brandt, then chancellor, especially caught her imagination. As the erstwhile Nazi Resistance fighter, Brandt struck a common chord. Moreover, his Ostpolitik, in its recognition of two German states and renouncing of claims to the Oder-Neisse territories of present-day Poland, corresponded with her own peace aspirations, as well as her denouncing of German reunification as a desirable goal.

The eventual fall of Brandt to a spy scandal and his replacement by Helmut Schmidt as chancellor presented Kelly with a *crise de conscience*. She believed in the SPD but considered Schmidt a betrayal of the party's principles. The decisive issue was the "double track" policy of NATO, promulgated in 1979, to station land (Pershing II) and cruise missiles in Europe, especially in Germany. Schmidt urged cooperation with NATO. The die was cast; Kelly left the party in 1979, writing an explanatory note to Schmidt.

Leaving the SPD inaugurated a dramatic, new phase of leadership for Kelly. Emotions ran high in Germany over the NATO policy. Kelly rode the crest of this sentiment in co-initiating the Krefelder Appeal protesting the Pershing missiles. (The protest was written by Gert Bastian, a former Bundeswehr general who resigned his commission in protest against nuclear overkill, joined the

Greens and became Kelly's closest confidant.) By 1980 the appeal had over five million signatures as opposed to the 700,000 for the Dattelner Appeal organized to support Schmidt. NATO policy did not budge, however, and Kelly regarded this as her gravest defeat. With the appeal, nonetheless, she helped create a forum on political policy that had never before existed in Germany. She also became an instantaneous public figure.

Fortuitously, too, elections for the European Parliament (EP) were scheduled for June 1979. Anticipating these elections, Kelly, politically homeless after leaving the SPD, turned her attention to the Greens movement. At the historic conclusion of a two-day Greens conference in Frankfurt, on March 18, 1979, Kelly announced the formation of the Greens' "antiparty party." She made it clear that the Greens were different. They would not participate in coalitions to shore up "bankrupt" conventional parties (though the Greens' realist wing on the right advocated collaboration with the SPD), and they would not pursue "politics as usual."

What followed was a decade of meteoric success. Although the Greens did not win any European parliamentary seats in 1979, they enjoyed a startling victory in the 1983 Bundestag elections, gaining twenty-seven seats. This spectacular breakthrough led to rampant speculations that the Greens would replace the Free Democrats (FDP) as the third strongest parliamentary party and thus become a likely coalition partner. In 1984 this speculation seemed on the verge of reality. The Greens captured 8.2 percent of the German vote for the European Parliament, while the FDP lost all its EP seats, failing to meet the 5 percent minimum threshold.

During this period, Kelly also organized two dramatic protests. In Nuremberg, now her parliamentary constituency, she undertook a program of "symbolic action." In February 1983, the city—symbol of Nazi abuse of power and the judgment against the Nazi regime in the war crimes trials—hosted the "Green Tribunal against First Strike and Mass Destruction Weapons in West and East." The tribunal put nuclear powers on trial and found them guilty. Then, in the following "hot autumn" of 1983, Nobel laureate Heinrich Böll linked hands with Petra Kelly to form a human chain stretching one hundred kilometers from Stuttgart to Neu Ulm in protest against nuclear weapons.

The decade of the 1980s established Kelly as a popular and formidable "antipolitics" force. She was not, however, without controversy. In the Cold War fever, her antinuclear politics, including the promotion of Germany as a nuclear-free zone, stepped on some Western political toes. Nevertheless, in her 1987 Bundestag campaign, she reaped 17 percent of the vote, the average Green candidate barely rising above the 5 percent minimum threshold. These were the years of rising expectations in the face of Gorbachev moves for *glasnost*. Indeed, Kelly and her Greens entourage would visit with Gorbachev in the Kremlin. The "new politics" of the Greens prospered.

On December 2, 1990, it all collapsed. In the first all-German elections to the Bundestag after unification, the Greens lost all their seats. For most commentators, the Cold War's demise deprived the Greens of issues. Had Greens issues, however, really disappeared in a world of post-Chernobyl and post–Exxon Valdez? Was peace no longer an issue in a so-called new world order characterized by increasing arms transfers and regional conflicts? Or had the euphoria surrounding Kohl as "unification chancellor" clouded the voter's perception of these issues?

Kelly faulted factional dissension within the Greens for the downfall. Presented by the media as a party in disarray, the Greens did not impress the voters with a clarity of purpose. Principled but nondoctrinaire, Kelly remained outside the infighting. Jealous of her prominence, however, warring Greens made Kelly their scapegoat, much to their own eventual detriment.

To complicate matters, she refused, in defiance of Greens "antileader" rules, to rotate out of her parliamentary seat at midterm in 1985 in favor of a substitute Green. Denied her 1984 request for exemption from rotation, charged with leadership ambitions and censured, Kelly steadfastly held to her seat until 1990. In the spirit of civil disobedience, she challenged rotation, charging it impeded the continuity of parliamentary work and deprived voters of favored, duly elected representatives. As a member of the prestigious foreign relations committee, Kelly, in 1985, was in the midst of getting a resolution passed condemning Germany's transfer of arms to Cambodia. Following the rotation issue, Kelly's Nuremberg constituency gave her a resounding vote of confidence by reelecting her in 1987.

After 1990 the Greens lost valuable parliamentary office space, access to vital information and the irreplaceable opportunity to influence the political process firsthand. From this searing experience, Kelly learned that it was essential to have "one foot in parliament and one foot outside." Parliamentary experience matured her thinking on leadership and the importance not only of opposition but of policy making. Indicative of her approach, she regarded her greatest victory in the Bundestag to be resolutions she proposed condemning China's Tibetan policies. These were all passed unanimously, with no abstentions. The first resolution in 1987 (following a public forum Kelly organized for the Dalai Lama in Bonn) represented an implicit criticism of Chancellor Kohl's visit to Tibet under Chinese auspices that same year.

Writing an open letter to the Greens in 1991, she stressed the Greens' need to perfect policy-making skills and to develop a commensurate professional division of labor. Among other organizational reforms, she urged dropping the rotation rule, establishing a media relations unit and developing a "think tank" of experts. Having no intention of accepting 1990 as the ultimate political verdict, Kelly made these recommendations with an eye on the 1993 Bundestag and 1994 European Parliament elections. Kelly's leadership had matured.

Tragically, however, on October 20, 1992, the body of Petra Kelly was found lying in the bed of her Bonn home. She had been shot once through the temple with a .38 caliber Derringer pistol at point-blank range. In the corridor outside the bedroom lay the body of Gert Bastian, who had been similarly shot. The bodies were badly decomposed, but the approximate date of death was established by the police as about October 1. The official police report lists the deaths as the murder of Petra Kelly by Gert Bastian and his subsequent suicide. No note was found, and no motive was deduced.

Memorials were held for Kelly and Bastian throughout the United States, where she, especially, had a wide following. At this time, skepticism remains about the official report and calls are being made for an independent investigation.

Petra Kelly was called the Joan of Arc of the peace movement, for her leadership was visionary, saintly and heroic. She regarded the introduction of civil disobedience to Germany as her most important political contribution, and she came to symbolize the conscience of a ''new'' Germany. Her death created an unmistakable void. It remains to be seen whether the Greens, demoralized by the tragedy and by their own internal conflicts, will find a sufficiently inspirational organizational force to heal their wounds and reinvigorate them electorally. Petra Kelly, however, leaves behind the vibrant legacy of her world-relevant ideas and, through them, her once charismatic leadership will find its enduring transcendence.

RUTH A. BEVAN

NEIL KINNOCK (1942–) was the leader of the British Labour Party from 1983 to 1992. His record as party leader was mixed. Electorally, he led Labour to two resounding defeats at the hands of the governing Conservative Party in 1987 and 1992. These elections were the last in a series of four consecutive defeats which have kept Labour in opposition since 1979. On the other hand, however, Kinnock saved his party from disintegration and displacement by the Alliance (Social Democrats and Liberals) as Britain's second major party. He accomplished this by ending Labour's decade-long internal warfare between left and right factions and by modernizing the party's policies and organizational structure.

Neil Kinnock was born on March 28, 1942, in Tredegar, South Wales. Tredegar was a mining village in the Rhymney Valley, an area which was the birthplace of Welsh socialism, steeped in a tradition of political radicalism. Like many of their neighbors, most of Kinnock's male relatives were coal miners and socialists. His father, Gordon Kinnock, was a miner, later a steelworker, active in local labor politics. His mother, Mary Howells, was a district nurse whom Kinnock characterized as ''a very radical socialist with a Christian tradition.'' During school holidays, she would take young Neil with her on rounds so that he could experience firsthand the poverty of his community. Kinnock was a committed socialist at fourteen, and he joined the Labour Party a year later. His greatest lifelong inspiration was Tredegar's native son, Aneurin Bevan, the famed left-wing politician known for his fiery oratory.

Kinnock's political career began as a student at University College, Cardiff, where much of his time was spent as an activist in various left-wing causes. It was in the course of his political activities that he met his future wife, Glenys Elizabeth Parry, a student at Cardiff who shared his partisan background and progressive sentiments. They were married in 1967.

After graduating in 1966 with a bachelor's degree in industrial relations and history and a teaching diploma, Kinnock worked as a tutor-organizer with the Workers' Education Association, an adult-education charitable organization run jointly by trade unions and the Department of Education. In 1968 he became the political education officer of the Bedwelty Constituency Labour Party. A year later, despite a number of disadvantages (his youth, his relative inexperience in Bedwelty politics and his strong left-wing orientation), Kinnock was nominated the local party's prospective parliamentary candidate. Bedwelty was a safe constituency for Labour, so he easily won a parliamentary seat in the June 1970 general election, even though the Labour Party lost nationally. When Kinnock took his seat as one of the youngest members in the House of Commons, almost every aspect of his life to that point (family, childhood, education, marriage, job, social life) had revolved around the Welsh labor movement and socialist politics.

During the period of Edward Heath's Conservative government (1970–1974), Kinnock remained an obscure, neophyte backbench member of the opposition. He associated with the left wing of the Parliamentary Labour Party (PLP), joining the Tribune Group and the Campaign for Labour Party Democracy. Easily reelected in Labour's narrow victories of 1974, he served briefly as parliamentary private secretary (PPS) to Michael Foot, the left-wing employment minister in the 1974–1979 Labour government.

However, Foot called him ''one of the worst PPSs in history,'' and his heart was clearly not in the job. Kinnock feared that participating in government would preclude him from criticizing the cabinet on such issues as economic policy and the devolution of legislative powers to Wales and Scotland. He consequently turned down offers of junior ministerial positions, especially after his wife warned him that the party leadership was merely trying to silence him. Kinnock felt most comfortable cast in the role of left-wing rebel. In a highly symbolic (and photogenic) gesture, for instance, he ostentatiously boycotted the 1977 state opening of Parliament because of the Labour government's intention to increase public expenditures for the royal family.

A number of his Labour colleagues in Parliament considered Kinnock to be something of a lightweight, due to his verbosity, inattentiveness to detail and tendency to commit political gaffes. Nevertheless, he won their grudging admiration—while also further alienating the party leadership—by his effective opposition to the government's plans for Welsh devolution (a measure prompted by the then-minority Labour government in its attempt to stay in power by securing the support of nationalist M.P.'s).

But if Kinnock was not well liked within the parliamentary party, he was becoming increasingly visible and popular among grassroots party activists because of his speaking performances on television and at party functions. He was in much demand as a speaker before constituency party groups, enabling him to cultivate a network of personal supporters outside Parliament. This paid rich dividends, for he was elected by constituency party activists to Labour's national executive in 1978, thereby securing a place on the national political scene. The following year he was again easily reelected to Parliament, despite the national victory of Margaret Thatcher's Conservative Party.

Immediately following Labour's 1979 defeat, Kinnock's patron Foot persuaded James Callaghan, the party leader, to appoint Kinnock to Labour's shadow cabinet as education spokesperson. Kinnock's acceptance of this offer was a watershed in his political evolution, signifying not only advancement to a front-bench position within the parliamentary party but also an initial break with his erstwhile allies from the left wing.

At that time, the left was campaigning to remove the power of appointing the shadow cabinet from the party leader and to allot all its positions by election of the PLP. Kinnock was also the deciding vote in the party's national executive to reject a left-wing motion to remove the party leader's final say over the party electoral manifesto. He further alienated the left when he refused to commit himself as Labour's future education minister to the restoration of education cuts then being proposed by the Thatcher government. His most decisive step came in 1981 during Tony Benn's left-wing campaign for deputy party leader, when Kinnock led several members of the Tribune Group in abstaining on a crucial runoff ballot of the party's electoral college, thereby allowing the right-wing candidate to win by a razor-thin margin. Hailed by moderates as "the man who saved the Labour Party" from Bennite domination, his action was vilified by the left as one of betrayal by an ambitious schemer who wanted to undermine the strength of his main rival on the left.

From 1979, and especially after the election of Foot as Labour's leader in 1980, Kinnock successfully adopted the mantle as principal defender of the party leadership and proponent of party unity. He was, as the *Sunday Times* put it, "the left-winger every right-winger loves." But as the country approached the 1983 general election, Labour was in deep disarray. After a decade of growth, the left wing had reached its zenith within the party, and its influence over Labour's positions on economics and defense placed the party clearly outside the political mainstream of Britain.

This increasing power of the Labour left precipitated an intraparty civil war, resulting in the defection of many on the party's right to the newly formed Social Democratic Party in 1981. The SDP joined the centrist Liberal Party in an electoral alliance that threatened to replace Labour as the major opposition to the Thatcher government. Labour's leader, Michael Foot, was both ineffectual and miscast, and the mismanaged 1983 campaign only reinforced the party's image of incompetence, division and extremism. During this campaign, Kinnock delivered blistering personal attacks against Mrs. Thatcher, a move which alienated uncommitted voters, but endeared him to Labour partisans. The outcome was a foregone one in any case. With only 28 percent of the national vote,

Labour had its worst showing in an election since 1918, and the party had only narrowly beaten the Alliance parties for second place.

The contest to succeed Foot as party leader began almost immediately after the 1983 debacle. Kinnock was the obvious candidate from the ''soft'' left faction of the party. The division of the Labour left into ''hard'' and ''soft'' factions emerged as a result of the 1981 Bennite challenge to the party leadership. The hard left was committed to radical socialist policies, such as the alternative economic strategy and unilateral nuclear disarmament, as well as to decentralizing decision-making authority within the Labour Party. Even more extreme, some advocated ''extraparliamentary opposition'' (i.e., illegal mass action) to resist the policies of the Thatcher government. The hard left generally argued that only through a more vigorous radicalism could the Labour Party win back its traditional working-class supporters and thereby arrest its electoral decline.

The ''soft'' left shared many of the hard left's policy positions, especially on the economy and defense, but its commitments were tempered by a realism reflecting the electoral and global constraints in which Labour and Britain found themselves. Kinnock described his strategy as ''socialism by plod,'' often stating that ''idealism is the energy of socialism and realism the means to carry it out.'' He was contemptuous of the ideological pretensions of ''saloon bar revolutionaries'' and of the empty ''gesture politics'' of many on the hard left who, unlike himself, were not from working-class backgrounds. Kinnock, and the soft left generally, realized that socialist policies could only be enacted by a Labour Party in power, and power could only be won by appealing to a wider and more moderate electoral base than the party now possessed. As for the right wing of the party, it shared the soft left's electoral realism, but rejected the party's left-wing orientations toward economics, defense and intraparty decision making.

Kinnock's candidacy for the leadership was helped along by several factors. He had the early support of Foot and a number of the largest trade unions. Benn's defeat in the general election removed his major challenger from the Labour left. Kinnock's grassroots network was also crucial, given the 1981 change in the party's procedure for choosing its leader, vesting authority in an electoral college dominated by votes from constituency parties and trade unions. His lack of ministerial experience in the 1974–1979 Labour government meant that he was not associated with its failures, and he thus represented a new generation of leadership. Perhaps most of all, the electoral humiliation of 1983 convinced many on Labour's left that the party needed to return to Britain's political center of gravity. At the same time, many on the party's right felt that Labour needed a leader from the acceptable left who would highlight the party's differences from the Social Democrats, then in ascendance.

Kinnock's message to his demoralized party during the leadership campaign was also reassuring: Nothing, he argued, was fundamentally wrong with the party or its policies. Only the divisiveness of the 1970s and 1980s (especially Benn's quixotic campaign in 1981) and an inadequate presentation of the issues to voters had led to electoral defeat. At the 1983 Labour Party conference, Kinnock was elected leader on the first ballot with an overwhelming 71 percent of the electoral college vote.

As leader, Kinnock sought to reverse Labour's declining electoral fortunes by extirpating the influence of the hard left in the party, but his initial efforts were derailed by the year-long national coal miners' strike begun in March 1984. The strike placed Kinnock in a difficult political position. He believed that the miners were justified in their opposition to Thatcher's pit-closing policy, which had precipitated their walkout. However, he was upset that Arthur Scargill, the militant president of the miners' union, had not consulted the rest of the labor movement and—in disregard of union rules—had not conducted a ballot of members before calling the strike.

Kinnock also found repugnant Scargill's revolutionary syndicalism, which viewed the strike as an extraparliamentary blow against the Thatcher government and parliamentary democracy. Kinnock was also disturbed by the violence on the miners' picket lines, which was, at least in part, caused by the union's tactics. But support for the strike was official Labour Party policy and a political litmus test for the British left. Kinnock therefore could not, and did not, unequivocally dissociate himself from Scargill or the strike until rather late in the day. The strike revived embarrassing memories of Labour's inability to restrain its union allies (much as in the 1979 "winter of discontent" which led to the party's electoral defeat that year) and raised uncomfortable questions about Kinnock's moral courage and competence to govern.

Kinnock also faced challenges from two extreme left groups which had come to power in several Labour-dominated local councils. One of these was the "new urban left," a loose grouping of largely middle-class radicals whose ideology reflected the counterculture politics of the 1960s. By the early 1980s they had brought together ethnic minorities, feminists, single parents, the disabled, the homeless, welfare claimants, homosexuals and public employees into a diverse "community politics" coalition which governed in London and other cities. This group subscribed to a vision of decentralized and participatory "municipal socialism" that challenged the notions of "parliamentary socialism" held by Kinnock and the Labour Party's mainstream.

A second challenge came from Militant Tendency, a group of Trotskyite revolutionaries who adopted the tactic of "entryism" into the Labour Party. The group had captured the party organization in Liverpool, and it became the city's dominant political force when Labour won an overall majority in the city council in 1983. In 1984 Kinnock managed to undermine a campaign of illegal noncompliance organized by extreme left Labour local councillors against the Thatcher government's rate-capping legislation restricting local authority expenditures. In 1985, Labour suspended the activities of the Liverpool party and expelled its leadership. Over the next few years, the national party continued to purge members of Militant Tendency from its ranks and to exercise greater control over local party organizations dominated by the extreme (or ''loony'') left.

Kinnock's strategy for transforming the party required that he isolate and subdue its hard left. To do so, he used divisions in the Labour left to forge an alliance in the national executive between the soft left and the right against the hard left. The soft left continued to support his intraparty coalition as long as Kinnock stood firm on certain key issues, especially unilateralism. The right saw Kinnock as its only defense against the hard left.

Kinnock was also supported by many of the party's affiliated trade unions, which directly or indirectly choose two-thirds of the membership on Labour's national executive. Over the previous two decades, Britain's trade unions had become disenchanted with the party leadership because of attempts by the Wilson and Callaghan Labour governments to control strikes and wage increases. Their reduced support for Labour's right-wing leadership had been a major factor in the growing power of the Labour left. But now the unions were being decimated by the Conservative government's antiunion labor legislation and economic policies. The miners' strike fiasco clearly revealed the bankruptcy of syndicalism as a political strategy for opposing Thatcherism. Union leaders recognized that only a Labour government could protect their interests, but the 1983 election proved that the party was not electorally viable without the unified and moderate image that Kinnock wanted to achieve. The unions thus fell behind Kinnock, whose control of the party was cemented by late 1985.

In early 1986, Kinnock launched Labour's ''freedom and fairness'' campaign, which attempted to redefine the party's socialist commitments so as to incorporate popular aspects of the Thatcher revolution, such as the sale of council (public) housing and the widening of equity ownership from the privatization of state corporations. A central role in Labour's reconstruction was given to a new Shadow Communications Agency, which employed modern market research methods and advertising techniques to repackage and sell the party to voters. The target for this new campaign was the upwardly mobile, new working class, whose support, Kinnock argued, was essential to any future Labour victory. The party's new direction was criticized by the Labour left, however, as superficial ''designer socialism.'' It attacked Kinnock's ''electoralism'' (i.e., pursuing electoral victory at any price) for betraying Labour's long-standing, fundamental socialist principles. Kinnock's Labour Party, one left-winger wrote contemptuously, was merely the ''SDP Mark II.'' But Kinnock pressed on with his project to divest the party of its ideological baggage.

The party's third consecutive electoral defeat in June 1987 intensified the intraparty debate over its socialist orientation. Arguing that the outcome demonstrated the imperative for a thorough review of Labour's policies, in 1988 Kinnock prepared ''A Statement of Democratic Socialist Aims and Values,'' equating socialism with the extension of individual freedom rather than with more traditional themes of collectivism or social justice.

He also established seven policy review groups to reconsider and rewrite party positions in all major policy areas. These steps renewed charges of Kinnock's betrayal of socialist principles and of his intention to transform Labour into a social democratic party. The left therefore decided to mount a challenge to Kinnock with the candidacy of Tony Benn for the party leadership. The party was at that time facing a serious financial crisis and trailing badly in opinion polls. The sense of drift and malaise among party members was exacerbated by Kinnock's lackluster performance in Parliament and by his low personal popularity among voters. He was increasingly seen as remote and authoritarian, in part as a result of the way in which he was handling the party's policy review. During the spring of 1988, he had unilaterally hinted publicly at reversing long-time Labour Party commitments to public ownership of the means of production and to unilateralism, prompting resignations from Labour's shadow cabinet. Rumors circulated of a possible leadership coup from the right wing of the party, only to be scotched by Benn's challenge from the left. The choice between Benn and Kinnock—between the party's recent past and its hope for the future—was an easy one for the party. With 88 percent of the electoral college vote, Kinnock was able to claim his overwhelming victory as a mandate to continue the process of party reformation.

When it was published in the spring of 1989, the party's policy review actually included little that was new, tending to confirm the accumulations of incremental changes in thinking that had been developing over the past several years. Many of its ideas had been adumbrated in Kinnock's earlier speeches and writings. The new policies represented less a radical break with the past than a return to the party's more moderate positions of the immediate postwar period, before the rise of the Labour left in the 1970s and 1980s. The party turned away from commitments to extensive nationalization of industry, the economic nationalism of the "alternative economic strategy," unilateralism and withdrawal from the European Community. The review acknowledged the valuable role to be played by market forces in fostering a dynamic, productive and internationally competitive British economy (a view which Kinnock called "supply-side socialism"). It also emphasized that Labour sought to extend and improve individual choices in the consumption of private as well as public goods (which Kinnock called "socialist individualism").

The report signaled Labour's attempt to achieve a greater degree of autonomy from the trade union movement; it accepted much of Thatcher's statutory restrictions on the unions and remained silent on union shibboleths such as the preservation of trade union immunities which guaranteed "free collective bargaining." More generally, the review tried to reposition the party closer to those popular aspects of the Thatcher revolution which reflected the now predominantly affluent British voters' aspirations for themselves and their families. While not a dramatic departure, the policy review was nevertheless significant as a monument to Kinnock's victory over his party's left. It was overwhelmingly adopted at Labour's annual conference in October 1989.

Kinnock also moved to modernize the party's organizational structure in order to reduce the power of two intraparty obstacles to further party transformation. One obstacle lay in the control of constituency party organizations by grassroots party activists who exercised a great deal of authority, especially over the selection of parliamentary candidates. Reflecting changes in party membership starting in the 1960s, these activists were increasingly middle-class, ideologically motivated left-wingers who sought to challenge the national party leadership and to radicalize the party. Kinnock attacked their power in a number of ways. The party's national executive intervened in candidate selections to block the adoption of radical left-wingers in certain constituencies. In 1990, the party abolished the automatic reselection process which required sitting Labour M.P.'s to submit to a veto by constituency activists on their candidacy. That same year, Kinnock transferred the authority to make decisions about candidates from the local activists to the entire constituency party membership on the basis of one person/one vote.

A second obstacle to Kinnock's "new model party" lay in the power exercised by Labour's affiliated trade unions. Unlike other European socialist and social democratic parties, the Labour Party was founded largely by the nation's trade unions (in 1900) as the political agent of the labor movement, and it continues to be dominated by the unions, both financially and constitutionally. Labour's affiliated unions controlled 90 percent of the vote at the party's annual conference, and local union branches tended to dominate many of its constituency parties as well. Over time, the connection between the party and its unions became an electoral liability for Labour. Public approval for trade unions declined, and voters became wary of the party influence wielded by union leaders, reinforcing popular images of the party as old-fashioned and unresponsive to the interests of the broader, nonunionist electorate. Kinnock moved to reduce the voting strength of trade unions at the party annual conference and in the constituency parties, succeeding only partially before the 1992 election arrived.

The party was confident as it approached the general elections scheduled for April 1992. Opinion polls indicated that the policy review and organizational changes were having the desired result on the electorate. Other circumstances were also favorable for Labour: The SDP had faded into oblivion, dragging the Alliance with it; the country's economy had entered a recession in early 1990 and unemployment continued to climb; the Conservatives were unpopular because of the poll tax and were badly divided over Europe. Panicking at the prospects of an impending Labour victory, the Tories replaced Mrs. Thatcher with John Major, who postponed calling the election until virtually the last moment. Polls showed Labour leading throughout the campaign, and in its last week, the party held a victory rally in Sheffield. But the party was defeated for a fourth consecutive time. In the stunned aftermath of this defeat, Kinnock announced his decision not to stand again for the party leadership. In June 1992, amid an emerging intraparty debate over what went wrong, the party elected John Smith to replace Kinnock as its leader.

In some ways the 1992 election results might appear encouraging to Labour. Improving upon its share of the 1987 vote, the party continued its steady comeback from the disaster of 1983. But Labour was continuing to rely on declining social and regional constituencies for its votes. Its traditional supporters, perhaps, had returned to their party, but expanding groups of the electorate targeted by Labour and critical to its electoral success had not. The upwardly mobile, new working class of homeowners, employed in services or in the private sector, living in suburbs or new towns in the south of England, did not aspire to the values articulated by Labour, even after its reformation. By 1992 Kinnock had succeeded in restoring Labour to its postwar tradition of being a moderate, social democratic party; but by 1992 popular support for postwar social democracy had dramatically attenuated. Kinnock's achievement lay in re-creating a party oriented toward winning the elections of a previous generation.

For after World War II, a social democratic "settlement" emerged in Britain. This settlement between capital and labor, seeking to avoid the antagonistic relations of the interwar period, established a prevailing consensus on the fundamental conditions of capital accumulation and class relations in an industrial society. Among other things, this consensus included a commitment to maintaining full employment and the welfare state. These commitments, in turn, entailed substantial intervention by the British state through a mixed economy, government subsidies to private industry, economic planning, Keynesian demand management, greater public expenditures and transfers, and high taxation.

While the social democratic program was predicated on continued expansion of private capital, Britain's economic woes were increasingly evident by the 1960s. Both Labour and Conservative governments were forced to adopt measures to stabilize the national economy, including restrictions on trade union power and wage increases. These measures undermined the prevailing class compromise, resulting in ideological and class polarization that characterized British politics in the 1970s and 1980s. The dominance of Thatcherite neoliberalism in the Conservative Party and the growing influence of Bennite socialism in the Labour Party during this period were both manifestations of the collapse of Britain's social democratic consensus.

Kinnock succeeded in returning Labour to the social democratic mainstream, but it was no longer the same stream. Long-term changes in conditions for capitalist accumulation and in the British electorate made social democracy far less viable in the 1990s. The globalization of economic activity and the fiscal crisis of the state in advanced industrial societies have weakened states' control over national economies, thereby constraining the redistributive, welfare and full-employment policies of governments. At the same time, the decline of traditional manufacturing industries and the working class has undermined the social basis for social democratic politics. To some extent, ironically, these social changes are the result of the success of past social democratic policies. Kinnock's failure lay in the fact that the British voter no longer aspired to what even a moderate social democratic Labour Party had to offer. The record of the party during the Wilson and Callaghan governments continued to raise doubts about its ability to manage the economy. And even as the memories of these years faded, voters continued to reject Labour because of its social democratic proclivities toward increased public expenditure and taxation.

It is ironic that Kinnock's revitalization of the Labour Party might be the major obstacle to ending the rule of the Conservative Party in Britain. The Tories remained in power because the opposition was divided, assuring them a majority in Parliament as a result of Britain's first-past-the-post electoral system. Given the stability of the Conservatives' vote from 1983 to 1987 to 1992, the real contest in which Labour and the Alliance were engaged concerned who would emerge as the major opposition in British politics. Kinnock's transformation of Labour saved the party from the oblivion of third place, or worse. In doing so, he dominated the opposition with a party whose values and ethos derive from 1945, or even from 1900. His success precluded any potential realignment of the British left, as well as the emergence of a new partisan force which could more effectively challenge Conservative hegemony.

BIBLIOGRAPHY

Works by Kinnock:

The Future of Socialism. Fabian Tract no. 509. London: Fabian Society, January 1986.
Making Our Way: Investing in Britain's Future. Oxford: Blackwell, 1986.

Other Works:

Drower, G. M. F. *Neil Kinnock: The Path to Leadership*. London: Weidenfeld and Nicolson, 1984.
Harris, Robert. *The Making of Neil Kinnock*. London: Faber and Faber, 1984.
Hughes, Colin, and Patrick Wintour. *Labour Rebuilt: The New Model Party*. London: Fourth Estate, 1990.
Leapman, Michael. *Kinnock*. London: Unwin Hyman, 1987.
Seyd, Patrick. *The Rise and Fall of the Labour Left*. London: Macmillan, 1987.

JEFFREY FREYMAN

HELMUT KOHL (1930–) has led the German Christian Democratic Party (CDU) since 1973 and, as chancellor, has governed the Federal Republic since 1982. Since he remains at the center of German politics, it is impossible to come to a firm conclusion on his contributions. Yet, it is clear that he reached the high point of his career in 1990 when he became the first chancellor of a reunited Germany.

Thus, any evaluation of his chancellorship must distinguish between the years before the upheaval of 1989, the period of German reunification (1989–1990), and the period since. Before the fall of the Berlin Wall Kohl's critics pointed to his government's lackluster performance in addressing pressing policy problems and to his seeming inability to provide clear direction to his government coalition. In 1989 and 1990, Kohl forcefully took advantage of emerging opportunities and pushed German reunification along. By 1992, however, his image as a forceful leader had evaporated again, and he himself admitted mistakes in managing German reunification and, particularly, in estimating its true costs.

Helmut Kohl was born in Ludwigshafen, an industrial city in southwestern Germany, on April 3, 1930. His father worked as a civil servant for the Bavarian internal revenue service. Kohl was a young adolescent during World War II, spending the last months of the war in a Hitler Youth camp at Berchtesgaden. In 1950 Kohl finished high school with the *Abitur* certificate, and in the fall of the same year he enrolled at the University of Frankfurt. The following year he transferred to the University of Heidelberg, where he completed his university career with a dissertation in history, "Political Development in the Palatinate and the Rebuilding of Political Parties after 1945." In 1958 he began working for an iron foundry in Ludwigshafen, but within a year he took a new position with the chemical industry's trade association in his home state.

Kohl's political activities began rather early in his life. While he was still a high school student, he joined the Christian Democratic Party in 1946. In the 1950s he began to build a political base within the party in his home state *(Land)* of Rhineland-Palatinate. He won his first important party office in 1953. Six years later he became the youngest deputy in the *Land* parliament. At this time, Rhineland-Palatinate was governed by Peter Altmeier, also a Christian Democrat. By 1969 Kohl had succeeded in pushing Altmeier, who then was the longest-serving minister-president in the whole of West Germany, out of office. During Kohl's tenure as minister-president of Rhineland-Palatinate from 1969 until 1976, he established a record as a reformer and innovator. His policy innovations included administrative reform, the establishment of an ombudsman office and reforms in education and social policy. Kohl also modernized his own party. This record did not only further Kohl's own career but also provided opportunities for other politicians in the state, such as Norbert Blüm.

While Kohl himself advanced in 1969, the Christian Democratic Party overall suffered a defeat in the federal elections of 1969. Although the CDU remained the strongest single party, the Social Democrats (SPD) under Willy Brandt formed a new governing coalition with the Free Democrats (FDP). Since the Christian Democrats had governed West Germany since its founding in 1949, this was a traumatic event for the party. Yet, the reality of being an opposition party did not really sink in until the 1972 election, when the CDU/CSU again failed to displace the SPD-FDP coalition. In 1971 Kohl made his first unsuccessful attempt to become national party chairman. Two years later Kohl tried again and gained the office. In the years following his election, Kohl and his leadership group strengthened the party organization, including an expansion of the party's membership base.

In the 1976 election Kohl competed at the head of the CDU ticket against the SPD-FDP coalition led by the incumbent chancellor, Helmut Schmidt. The Christian Democrats significantly increased their share of the vote and regained their position as the largest single party, which they had lost in 1972. Nevertheless, the Christian Democrats fell short of a complete victory, and an acrimonious debate ensued between the moderate CDU leadership under Kohl and the more stridently conservative Bavarian sister party CSU, led by the colorful but controversial Franz Josef Strauss. While Kohl argued that the only realistic strategy for regaining power was to woo the Free Democrats away from the SPD, Strauss favored a strictly confrontational course symbolized by such campaign slogans as ''freedom or socialism.''

After the 1976 election, Kohl resigned as minister-president of Rhineland-Palatinate and moved to Bonn to be the CDU's opposition leader. In internal party conflicts, Kohl proved to be a more sophisticated tactician than his rival Strauss, but in the 1980 campaign Strauss, rather than Kohl, was the chancellor candidate for the CDU/CSU. Not surprisingly, Strauss lost the election. The Social Democratic victory proved to be short-lived, however. Although the re-elected chancellor Schmidt enjoyed wide personal popularity, he confronted mounting economic problems, criticism from his own party's left wing and increasing tensions with the FDP.

As a small party the FDP always faces the menace of the 5 percent minimum threshold clause under Germany's electoral law, and Schmidt's problems therefore endangered the FDP as well. On October 1, 1982, a majority of FDP deputies in the Bundestag formally switched sides and supported Helmut Kohl in a constructive no-confidence vote against the incumbent chancellor Schmidt. Kohl's strategy had finally paid off and he formed a coalition government between the CDU/CSU and the FDP. Although there had been nothing unusual, improper or illegal about this change of governments, Kohl came under strong pressure to seek popular approval of the change. Elections were held in March 1983 and returned Kohl's coalition to office.

Kohl himself provided a yardstick for evaluating his chancellorship when he called for a *Wende* (turnaround) after thirteen years of alleged socialist mismanagement. In foreign policy, the record of the Kohl government points more to continuity rather than sharp change. This was largely the result of the fact that foreign minister Hans-Dietrich Genscher, who had held the position since 1974, retained the foreign affairs portfolio under Kohl.

The first immediate challenge facing the new Kohl government involved NATO's highly controversial deployment of intermediate-range nuclear missiles on German soil in 1983. More generally, the Kohl government faced an international environment in which superpower relations had steadily deteriorated from the late 1970s through the first Reagan administration. To the disappointment of some U.S. officials, West Germany under Kohl continued to pursue a policy of détente and, to some extent at least, succeeded in insulating inter-German relations from the harsher climate of East-West confrontation in the early 1980s. In fact, relations between East and West Germany improved in the 1980s even before the Gorbachev years. At the same time, the ultimate goal of reunification assumed a more prominent place in Kohl's public speeches than in those of his Social Democratic predecessor. In West Germany's relations with the West, Kohl stressed that the Federal Republic was a reliable ally. Furthermore, Kohl built on the record of close Franco-German relations begun under former chancellor Adenauer by cultivating a personal friendship with French President François Mitterrand.

Domestically, one of Kohl's major priorities was to rein in public spending and reduce budget deficits which had increased significantly during the 1970s and early 1980s. This has to be seen in the broader context of the predominant intellectual and political climate of the 1980s. In the early years of the decade, "Eurosclerosis" was an often-used expression to describe Western Europe's long-lasting economic problems. In the view of conservative and liberal politicians in the Christian and Free Democratic parties, overcoming these problems required limitations on the government's role in the economy through a reduction and reorientation of government spending, privatization of state-owned enterprises, cutbacks in subsidies and changes in the labor markets.

Until 1989 the record of the Kohl government in this area was mixed. Budget deficits shrank from 1983 until 1986, but the government made only limited progress in its professed goals of subsidy reduction, privatization and deregulation. It is important to recognize, however, that Germany's Christian Democrats have always typically tempered free market rhetoric with other considerations, such as the social aspects of Germany's "social market economy."

Consolidating public finances also implied a retrenchment in social programs. Under the Kohl government some cutbacks occurred, including, for example, reductions in unemployment benefits for families without children and changes in financial aid for students. However, lean years for social programs had, in fact, begun as far back as the mid–1970s.

Many discussions of Kohl's leadership qualities focus not only on the substance of his government's policies but on his decision-making style. Both critics and supporters point to Kohl's highly developed instinct for power, particularly in regard to internal party maneuvering. Kohl has held virtually the whole range of possible party positions from local party chairman to district and statewide offices, as well as the national leadership position. Until 1992 most challengers paid dearly for rebellion against Kohl, usually disappearing into political obscurity.

In contrast to his predecessor as chancellor, Helmut Schmidt, Kohl never developed an acknowledged level of expertise in a particular policy area but remained comfortable as a generalist. According to all accounts, his preferred tool for keeping abreast of political developments is the telephone rather than reading lengthy memoranda. Both before and after reunification, Kohl has been criticized for being either unable or unwilling to provide clear direction to his squabbling coalition partners. Rather than decisively intervening when problems develop, his critics charge that he simply tries to sit out crises. Nevertheless, his critics almost always underestimate Kohl's willingness and ability to respond to direct threats to his own authority.

During Kohl's tenure as chancellor, the German political party system has undergone some important changes. From 1961 until 1983, only three parties were represented in the German Bundestag, the CDU/CSU, the SPD, and the small but important FDP. In 1983 a fourth party, the Greens, cleared the hurdle of the 5 percent minimum threshold clause, winning seats in the Bundestag. Since the Greens generally place themselves to the left of the Social Democrats, they posed more of a challenge to the SPD than to Kohl's Christian Democrats.

In the late 1980s, however, the Christian Democrats began to face an electoral threat in the form of the new anti-immigrant Republikaner Party and other extreme right-wing parties and groups. This presented the CDU with a dilemma. Acrimonious debates began within the party between politicians such as the former secretary general Heiner Geissler—who favored a centrist course and even speculated about Germany as a multicultural society—and the CSU, which wanted to move the party further to the right. In 1989 Kohl was an embattled party leader and chancellor, but developments in the former German Democratic Republic dramatically changed the course of German politics and may have saved Kohl's hold on office.

Neither Kohl nor any other West German politician controlled or even significantly influenced the breathtaking series of events which led to the fall of the Berlin Wall on November 9, 1989. Without attempting to account for the fall of the wall, one factor which contributed to the collapse of the East German regime in 1989 and which also played a role in later decisions on economic unification was the dramatic rise in emigration out of East Germany and the corresponding immigration into West Germany.

In May 1989 Hungary had first opened the floodgates by dismantling its border fortification with Austria. According to official FRG figures, in November 1989 over 130,000 East Germans moved to West Germany. On November 28, 1989, Kohl took the initiative and presented to the Bundestag his so-called ten-point plan on overcoming the division of Germany and of Europe. In this plan Kohl called for the establishment of confederal structures between East and West Germany with the eventual goal of creating a German federation. Subsequently, on February 7, 1990, Kohl went a step further and suggested immediate negotiations between the East and West German governments on creating a currency union.

The political rationale for a currency union was to send a "signal of hope" to the citizens of East Germany, thus encouraging them to stay rather than to migrate to the West and creating irreversible institutions supporting not only economic but also political unification. The so-called German economic, monetary and social union went into effect on July 1, 1990. Both the timing and its concrete modalities generated considerable public debate in Germany. One specific point of contention centered around the conversion rate of the East German ostmark into West German deutsche marks (DM). While the Kohl government favored a 1:1 conversion rate, the (West) German central bank, the Bundesbank, proposed a rate much less favorable to the East German currency. Taking into account not only wages, salaries and pensions but all other assets and liabilities, the conversion rate eventually chosen reflected a compromise between the government and the central bank.

As the East German communist regime unraveled in 1989, East Germany witnessed a proliferation of new political movements and political parties. Existing political parties, which had been aligned with the ruling communist Socialist Unity Party (SED), severed their ties to the old regime. On March 18, 1990, the first free elections were held in the GDR. Chancellor Kohl played an active role in the election campaign through personal appearances and, most important, by bringing together a number of conservative groups which competed in these elections under the label "Alliance for Germany."

Contrary to what some opinion polls had predicted, the "Alliance for Germany" achieved an impressive victory with 48 percent of the vote. According to survey results, Kohl's personal popularity in the East was high, but the Free Democrat and foreign minister, Hans-Dietrich Genscher, who had personal ties to the East German city of Halle, was even more popular. Supporters of the Alliance in East Germany voted for the party because they favored Kohl's strategy of rapid unification and because they regarded Kohl's Christian Democrats as more competent in bringing prosperity to the East than the Social Democrats or other groups.

From March 1990 on, events unfolded rather quickly. Internally, on July 22, 1990, the East German parliament, the Volkskammer (or People's Chamber), passed a bill reestablishing five states in East Germany: Brandenburg, Mecklenburg–West Pomerania, Saxony, Saxony-Anhalt and Thuringia. On August 3, 1990, East and West German negotiators concluded their work on the unity treaty, which contained detailed provisions for the application of West German law in eastern Germany. On August 23, 1990, the Volkskammer voted to accede to the Federal Republic of Germany in accordance with Article 23 of the (West) German Basic Law, which provided the quickest and constitutionally least complicated vehicle for reunification. The accession of the five new eastern German states became effective on October 3, 1990.

The external aspects of German unification primarily involved negotiations between the two German states and the four World War II Allies, the United States, the Soviet Union, France and Great Britain. The so-called two-plus-four talks ended with the signing of a treaty on September 12, 1990. Kohl himself played a prominent role in two of the most sensitive foreign policy issues tied to unification. First, Kohl initially waffled on the finality of the border between Germany and Poland. Although there was never any real doubt about the outcome of this controversy, Kohl's ambiguities were a response to the electoral threat from the nationalist Republikaner Party. Kohl also faced the task of gaining Soviet approval for German unification and for Germany's continued membership in NATO. On July 16, 1990, Kohl and Soviet President Mikhail Gorbachev reached an agreement on German NATO membership, a reduction in the size of Germany's armed forces, the phased withdrawal of Soviet forces from eastern Germany and German financial concessions to ease this process.

Kohl's performance in clearing all the legal and political obstacles to German unification in such a quick, smooth and decisive manner gave him and his party a clear advantage in the all-German elections of December 1990. He campaigned as the first chancellor of a reunited Germany, while his opposition in the Social Democratic and Greens parties was internally divided and unable to provide a convincing and coherent alternative to Kohl's course. Not surprisingly, Kohl's coalition of Christian and Free Democrats handily won the election, but the outcome did not represent a triumph for Kohl's CDU/CSU, which experienced its worst results since 1949. The only unambiguous winner was the Free Democratic Party. Since reunification, Kohl's Christian Democrats have suffered a number of electoral defeats in *Länder* elections. As a result of these developments, in 1992 only one western German state was led by a Christian Democratic minister-president.

To understand the drop in Kohl's popularity since reunification and to assess his leadership in implementing German reunification, it is essential to examine three challenges facing Kohl and the country as a whole. First, it proved relatively easy to unify the country's institutions, but the united Germany now faces the much more daunting task of overcoming social and economic divisions between an affluent West and a relatively impoverished East where unemployment effectively hovers around 30 percent. After unification, western Germany experienced a mild economic boom, while large parts of eastern German industry collapsed. Second, eastern and western Germany no longer constitute the frontline states of two opposing alliances, but united Germany is again the most populous and, given the disarray in Russia, the most powerful nation on the European continent, although it is clearly not a hegemonic power such as the United States was after World War II. Thus, Germany and its neighbors must redefine Germany's position in Europe and the world. Finally, in the past few years, Germany has been a magnet for refugees and other immigrants, at the same time as violent acts against foreigners have risen dramatically.

Regarding economic and social unification, the Kohl government has made some serious errors. Transforming a centrally planned economy, such as the East German one, into a market economy probably cannot be done without committing policy mistakes, but some of these could have been avoided. In former East Germany, the government owned virtually all enterprises. Massive expropriation of private property in East Germany had begun under the rule of the Soviet occupation authorities in the 1940s and continued after the establishment of the German Democratic Republic in 1949. Rather than looking forward, the unity treaty attempted to undo previous injustices by promising former owners restitution of their property instead of monetary compensation. At the insistence of the United States, Jewish property owners who had lost their property under the Nazis also benefited from this policy, but the Soviet Union and East German negotiators successfully demanded exceptions for the expropriation wave of 1945–1949. The economic consequences of this misguided policy have been to slow down the privatization of East German industry and to put up obstacles to Western investment in the East. To be fair to Kohl, however, it was not the Christian Democrats but the Free Democrats who had pushed for this policy.

Kohl himself is to blame for the unrealistic promises he made during the election campaigns of 1990. He promised East Germans that they would all benefit from German unification and that nobody would be worse off. Addressing West Germans, Kohl denied the need for tax increases and other sacrifices to pay for reunification. Such promises encouraged unrealistic expectations in the East and undermined the limited willingness of West Germans to share the wealth with their East German fellow citizens. The task of bringing living standards in eastern Germany up to western levels requires vast amounts of money for years to come. The resulting distributional struggles pit eastern against western *Länder,* and unions against employers and the government. Kohl failed to adequately prepare the country for these problems. While such behavior may be understandable in an election year, little has been done to correct this leadership deficit since the elections of 1990.

While Kohl's record in domestic policy has been uneven, Germany's foreign policies under his leadership have been largely successful, despite some occasional blunders. To dispel fears about increased German power and possible dominance of Europe, Kohl and other politicians in his cabinet have stressed that Germany saw its future within a more integrated Europe and that Germany's neighbors did not have to fear the rebirth of an expansionist Germany. Kohl's commitment to European integration runs through his entire political career, and in the 1980s and 1991 he invested considerable political capital in the European Community's "1992" project and in the even more ambitious goals of European political and monetary union as embodied in the EC's Maastricht Treaty.

Yet, while the mid-to-late 1980s experienced a trend toward convergence of Western European economic policies, the economic consequences of German unification have created tensions between Germany's domestic priorities, such as controlling inflation, and the repercussions of German monetary policy on the French, British or Italian economies. If popular apprehensions about loss of sovereignty in Denmark and France, as well as the turmoil in European currency markets of 1992 and 1993, are signs of things to come, Kohl's vision of a united Europe following the unification of Germany will fade.

The third broad challenge facing Germany, immigration policy, is both a domestic and foreign policy issue. In 1991 over 250,000 foreigners applied for political asylum in Germany, while an additional 220,000 ethnic Germans from Eastern Europe and the Soviet Union settled in the Federal Republic. In the context of 20th-century German history, the treatment of minorities in Germany also serves as a sign of the lessons Germans have learned from their past. The domestic political debate in Germany on immigration has so far exhibited an excessively legalistic focus. For example, Kohl and other politicians pretended that a solution to Germany's problems in this area depended on changes in Article 16 of the constitution, which guarantees the right of political asylum. Yet this overestimates the impact of legal changes on actual immigration patterns, and it ignores the point that xenophobic sentiments and acts may continue even in the absence of foreigners.

On balance, Kohl's record is best described as uneven, and assessments vary according to whether one focuses on his achievements as the chancellor of German unity or his successes and failures before and after reunification. Compared to his predecessors, no chancellor has been as deeply rooted in his party as Helmut Kohl. However, his dominance of the party may turn out to be a mixed blessing for Germany's Christian Democrats in the future, just as the party faced a difficult task of rebuilding after Adenauer's long tenure in office.

BIBLIOGRAPHY

Filmer, Werner, and Heribert Schwan. *Helmut Kohl.* Düsseldorf: Econ, 1990.

Lipschitz, Leslie, and Donogh McDonald (eds.). *German Unification: Economic Issues.*Washington: International Monetary Fund, 1990.

Pridham, Geoffrey. *Christian Democracy in Western Germany: The CDU/CSU in Government and Opposition, 1945–1976.* New York: St. Martin's Press, 1977.

Schmid, Josef. *Die CDU: Organisationsstrukturen, Politiken und Funktionsweisen einer Partei im Föderalismus.* Opladen: Leske and Budrich, 1990.

Sinn, Gerlinde, and Hans-Werner Sinn. *Kaltstart: Volkswirtschaftliche Aspekte der deutschen Vereinigung.* Tübingen: J. C. B. Mohr, 1991.

Smith, Gordon, William E. Paterson, Peter H. Merkl, and Stephen Padgett (eds.). *Developments in German Politics.* Durham, N.C.: Duke University Press, 1992.

CLAUS HOFHANSEL

JENS OTTO KRAG (1914–1978) was leader of the Danish Social Democratic Party from 1962 to 1972 and prime minister of Denmark from 1962 to 1968 and 1971 to 1972. At the time of his death he was characterized as one of very few great statesmen of an international stature to come out of Danish politics during the 20th century. This judgment has not yet been revised, even if many Danes have reacted negatively to the extension of the European Community's influence on Danish political and economic life through the provisions of the Maastricht Treaty. One of Krag's most recent biographers is arguably correct to conclude "that his Danish and thus also Nordic contribution to the European vision will preserve his position among the statesmen of the 20th century."

The outstanding contribution of Jens Otto Krag was to create and sustain in Danish politics a drive for joining the European Common Market. He was able to accomplish this by monitoring and manipulating the political situation in such a way that this major foreign policy decision would be made by the Danish cabinet with the consensus support of most of the parties in the Folketing (parliament). Denmark's entry into the EC would later be confirmed by a clear majority of Danish voters in a popular referendum. Krag personally orchestrated the many complex moves necessary to bring the country to this point, and as a final result, Denmark acceded to membership in the European Community on January 1, 1973.

Jens Otto Krag was born in 1914 in a provincial town in Jutland. His family was of very modest means, his father earning his living as a tobacconist. This poor family background did, however, not hinder the intellectually bright boy from graduating from the local gymnasium. In 1933 he then began studying economics at the University of Copenhagen.

By his teenage years, Krag had already become active in the youth organization of the Social Democratic Party. He pursued these activities during his university years, gradually emerging as a diligent and energetic young journalist and teacher in the labour movement. During this time, he was able to become personally acquainted with the leadership of the party and the trade unions.

After obtaining his university degree in 1940, Krag spent the war as a civil servant in a Danish government agency, beginning a promising and fast career. During this same period, he became a leading economic commentator for the labor movement. And he also became a protégé of Hans Hedtoft, the rising new star of the Social Democrats.

The national political debut of Jens Otto Krag occurred in 1944, when he was appointed secretary for a program committee set up by the party. As the Social Democrats were preparing themselves for politics in the postwar period, Krag became the driving force in this committee. The new party program that he developed introduced Keynesian ideas, proposals for nationalization and notions of "economic democracy"—a number of new and startling ideas in Danish politics. Although the defeat of the party in the 1945 election constituted an effective obstacle for turning these proposals into actual policies, the "Denmark of the Future" program became a landmark in Danish politics, and the name of Jens Otto Krag became both familiar and notorious in political circles.

In 1947 Krag was elected to a seat in the parliament. That same year, when he was only thirty-three years old, he was appointed minister of commerce. He served in this difficult position for the next three years. In 1950 he left the government of his own will and spent the following two years in Washington, D.C., where he served as economic attaché in the Danish embassy.

Returning to Denmark in 1952—and after some turmoil in his private life—he became a cabinet minister once again in 1953. From this point on—and until his final farewell to Danish politics in 1972—he served in all Social Democratic governments. During the 1950s, he held the ministerial portfolios for labor, economics and international economics, taking over in 1958 his favorite position as minister of foreign affairs. In 1962, the illness of the incumbent prime minister catapulted him into the highest political office, the prime ministership. He was at the same time also elected chairman of the Social Democratic Party.

When he ended his active political career in 1972, Krag had been a member of parliament for more than twenty-three years and had served as cabinet minister for eighteen years and as leader of his party for ten years.

Jens Otto Krag was not a typical leader in the Danish labor movement. He did not "spring from the people" as its leaders had traditionally. Furthermore, academic training and education were not an advantage to the politically ambitious in those days. In the case of Krag, these disadvantages were to some extent counterbalanced by his long service in the movement. In his younger days, his obvious writing talents and his knack for educating the cadres gave him access to the inner circles of the party. Several party leaders did, however, look on the upstart with some suspicion.

Krag would probably never have made it as far as the prime minister's office, if it had not been for the fact that his three predecessors had either died or otherwise left the office prematurely. His mentor, Hans Hedtoft, died unexpectedly from a heart attack in the mid–1950s. Hedtoft was succeeded by H. C. Hansen, another strong party leader with a traditional working-class background. Hansen, moreover, was not a great admirer of Krag, partly because he did not like the ambitious young academic and his decidedly bohemian behavior, partly because he probably also saw a rival in Krag, who early on took a strong interest in foreign policy, a field in which Hansen himself was more interested than in domestic affairs. It is noteworthy that both of these two political leaders were able to serve simultaneously as prime minister and foreign minister for considerable periods.

H. C. Hansen died from cancer in 1959 and was succeeded as prime minister by Viggo Kampmann, a brilliant economist who had served with distinction as a civil servant and then later on as minister of finance. A combination of an unstable personality and a severe heart condition did, however, cut short Kampmann's political career by 1962. This time, Krag seemed the logical choice, but he also actively exploited the full potential of this opportunity. In fact, Krag's personal attributes were suited to this particular political era: He was not a charismatic politician. As a public speaker he was not very memorable. And although he spoke foreign languages, he was never totally at ease during international negotiations—at least not during the early phases of his career. He could sound stuffy, and he definitely never got used to appearing on television. Krag was probably lucky that most of his political life took place before television had become the primary communications medium in Danish politics.

Krag did not make many friends—if any. A certain detachment and aloofness was characteristic of his behavior; these traits were often mistaken for arrogance. He was often characterized as "a closed book." "Impenetrability" was another term frequently used by his biographers. His eyes could turn into narrow slits when he was irritated, in which case no one could divine his thoughts. In public debates he could also be merciless and sarcastic. He became notorious for his comment "We are on Easy Street," which he uttered during a period of economic hardship in 1949. Later he remarked, "One has an opinion, until one gets a new one, right?" While on one level this was a bold and honest admission of a perennial truth about how political leaders think and act, on another level, his comments were easily misunderstood and misconstrued.

Given these problematic characteristics of Krag's personality and leadership style, how could he have become the undisputed leader of the Social Democratic Party, heading several governments, and even in opposition have been considered the central political figure in Danish politics?

He did possess a formidable command of his party, and he always had a keen eye for personal threats to his position as leader. But the complete answer to his rise to the very top of Danish politics must include the fact that Krag combined a cool intellect and an analytic mind with ruthlessness and a strong will. Jens Otto Krag was a shrewd and talented negotiator. On the one hand, he was not afraid of brinkmanship, but he also possessed a great ability to forge compromises. He was as a rule the best informed and the best prepared for such occasions. Early in his tenure as prime minister he proved himself a master of negotiation when in 1963 he negotiated the so-called unified solution. This agreement meant in reality the introduction of a modern incomes policy in Denmark. The political parties in parliament, the trade unions and the employers' association all in the end agreed on a compromise position on salaries, prices and taxes (as well as a great many other items)—hence the label. This political feat became a model for many other attempts to set incomes policies in Denmark.

Krag's experience from working many years in organizations of the Danish working class also gave him an edge in many social situations, when seeking a new political mandate, when control of organizational networks had to be reinforced or when it was time to purge organizations of his enemies. And his personal acquaintance with all the major European leaders and his close working relationship with most Danish top diplomats made him the undisputed key figure in matters of Danish foreign policy. But qualities such as intellectual ability, talent for performing in complex negotiations and ruthlessness do not by themselves make a politician a statesman of international stature. In the case of Jens Otto Krag it was his determined pursuit of a singular political goal that made the difference.

Denmark, of course, is a small state with an open economy and occupying a delicate geopolitical location on the map of Europe. On the one hand, the safety and well-being of Danish citizens depends heavily on the political and economic development of Europe proper. In this, Britain and Germany are the two major powers that count, especially in the face of Cold War tensions involving the Soviet Union. On the other hand, Danes are quite proud of their nation, and they cherish the "Danish Model," as they refer to their welfare state and its underlying ideology. Moreover, Danes exhibit some tendency to consider themselves better than their neighbors, even to the extent of valuing a self-sufficiency ethic that sometimes looks like isolationism—if such a term can be used at all with reference to a very small country with a very open economy. It was in this complex context that Jens Otto Krag pursued his political vision.

One of his predecessors, his mentor Hans Hedtoft, had managed to take Denmark from long-time neutrality to membership in NATO. Krag then concentrated on the economic aspects of foreign policy. Early on he saw that membership in the European Free Trade Association (EFTA) was at best only a temporary solution for Denmark and that a Nordic economic association, although having rhetorical appeal, was a blind alley. He believed that ''Scandinavism'' or ''Nordism'' were naive and romantic ideological constructs, belonging to the past. Denmark, being small and dependent on the major European powers, had first and foremost to cultivate and preserve close links with the United Kingdom, at the time Denmark's major trading partner.

Second, Krag had to decide how best to approach the forging of links with the continent, especially the six countries that had formed the European Economic Community in 1957. When the first Danish application for membership in the EC was sent off in 1961, Krag had already formulated the strategy that he would pursue over the next decade: Denmark would act together with the United Kingdom as much as possible. Yet this strategy was enormously complicated by British hesitations regarding the EC throughout the 1960s and then the complexities of negotiating the conditions of EC membership with the six original member states. As a result, Denmark had to keep options open for negotiations within EFTA as well as with the other Nordic countries.

Denmark's route to EC membership was long and difficult. Not only did Charles de Gaulle place obstacles in the way, but there was also growing opposition within Denmark and within the Social Democratic Party itself and some of the trade unions.

In 1972 the conditions for Denmark's accession to the EC were finally agreed upon, and a Danish parliamentary majority favored joining. However, the left-wing Socialist People's Party put up a fight, thus threatening the internal cohesion of the labor movement even more. In addition, a grassroots organization, the ''People's Movement against the EC,'' had been formed and was stirring up trouble over the question. Moreover, in the meantime, voters in neighboring Noway had rejected EC membership in a national referendum. It was Krag himself who decided to refer the Danish decision to a popular vote, and in spite of all this opposition, led the campaign to victory. No less than 90 percent of the voters turned out, and the victory was a clear one: On October 2, 1972, 63 percent voted to approved Denmark's membership in the EC.

The following day Krag surprised and shocked everyone, including the queen, who was in attendance, by announcing from the rostrum of the parliament that he wished to step down immediately from his position as prime minister and party leader. Within a few hours he had succeeded in convincing his Social Democratic colleagues to elect Anker Jørgenson as new party leader, hence prime minister. Thus Krag's ''abdication'' did not bring down the cabinet, it only relieved Jens Otto Krag of his responsibilities.

In abdicating Krag admitted that he had for some time been waiting for this moment in order to devote more time to the pursuit of his literary and artistic ambitions. While on his way up in Danish politics and later on as a busy political leader, he had found bits and pieces of time to paint and to write, especially his diaries and his memoirs, as well as a volume on the recent history of the Social Democratic Party. He now wished to do more along these lines.

Unfortunately, Krag was not very happy with his new life outside politics. He wrote some, but not much. For a while he taught political science at Aarhus University, but without much success. Later he was appointed to head the EC delegation in Washington, D.C. Apparently these jobs were not enough to fill the void created by his early and abrupt retirement from Danish politics at the topmost level. His last years were not happy ones, as human decay set in. Krag died from a stroke in 1978 at age sixty-three.

History adds three postscripts to the story of Krag's successful political career and his tragic personal end.

First, in the years that followed, other Danish politicians, including his successor, as well as many voters, did not see EC membership in the same perspective as Krag had. For them, the EC was primarily a commercially advantageous arrangement. But it was also considered to be the embodiment of a distant bureaucracy that interfered with the daily life and domestic political freedom of the Danes. Given this change of perception, it is understandable how a clear victory in favor of EC membership in 1972 could change to a narrow defeat of the Maastricht Treaty ratification twenty years later. In 1992 Krag had been dead for fourteen years. When in 1966 he was given the coveted Carolus Prize in Aachen, Germany, he had spoken about European integration as the major task facing his generation and about how European unity was a fundamental necessity. Yet even before his death, such high-flown rhetoric was considered misplaced in Danish political circles.

Second, a year after Krag ended his active political career, a parliamentary election resulted in a shocking defeat of all the traditional parties, including the Social Democrats. Neither the former prime minister nor his colleagues were able to explain what had gone wrong, as waves of populist protests moved through the electorate. The ''Danish Model'' came under attack and has been so ever since. While in recent years these populist protests have died down somewhat, it has dawned on Danish politicians that the very structure of the Danish welfare state, with its emphasis on large-scale, labor-intensive public institutions—and correspondingly high levels of taxation—do not fit well into the dominant European pattern. Could—and should—these developments have been predicted before 1972?

Third, the party which Jens Otto Krag controlled so effectively also soon fell upon hard times. His successor had to give up the prime ministership in 1982, opening a period of deep leadership crisis. In the meantime, the Danish Social Democratic Party was exiled to the opposition benches for a decade, as the party organization itself became seriously weakened. The party lost a considerable number of its members, and the internal unity of the party and the trade union movement became severely strained. When these subsequent developments are taken into consideration, it may be that in the long run Jens Otto Krag will stand out as the last of the ''old'' leaders of the once dominant Social Democratic Party. At the very least, one can conclude that Krag demonstrated his extraordinary political skills by ending his career exactly when he had reached the zenith, while the going was still good.

BIBLIOGRAPHY

Works by Krag:

Ling mand fra trediverne. Copenhagen: Gyldendal, 1969.
Kamp og fornyelse. Copenhagen: Fremad, 1971 (with K. B. Andersen).
Dagbog ved et Axsskifte 1971–72. Copenhagen: Gyldendal, 1972.
Travl tid, god tid. Copenhagen: Gyldendal, 1974.

Other Works:

Dansk Biografisk Leksikon, vol. 8: 229–34 . Copenhagen: Gyldendal, 1981.
Hansen, Soren (ed.). *J. O. Krag—som vi kendte ham*. Copenhagen: Fremad, 1978.
Kaarsted, Tage. *De danske ministerier 1953–1972*. Copenhagen: PFA & Odense University Press, 1992.
Rasmussen, Erik. ''H. C. Hansen, J. O. Krag og Udenrigsministeriet.'' *Historie*, 1982: 381–419.
Thorsen, Svend. *Folketinget i næ rbillede*. Copenhagen: 1974.

MOGENS N. PEDERSEN

BRUNO KREISKY (1911–1990) has arguably been the most significant Austrian leader since 1945, playing a prominent role in Austrian politics for most of the postwar era. Kreisky led the Austrian Social Democratic Party (SPÖ) to its greatest successes. As secretary of state, minister and federal chancellor, he held government positions longer than any other Austrian politician and had an enormous impact on the politics of his country. His role in international politics also went far beyond the significance of just Austria.

Bruno Kreisky was born on January 22, 1911, in Vienna to a wealthy Jewish family. His father, Max Kreisky, was an industrialist and his mother, Irene Kreisky (née Felix), was from a wealthy industrialist family as well. His great-uncle, Josef Neuwirth, was a liberal M.P. from 1873 until 1895 and an influential journalist and cofounder of the most important Austrian newspaper, the *Neue Freie Presse*. Although he became the leader of a working-class party, Kreisky had led a very upper-middle-class lifestyle and despised the *petite bourgeoisie*. Yet, according to close observers, he had enormous respect for working-class and other ordinary people. Kreisky listened to them very carefully and many of his domestic political initiatives as federal chancellor had their origin in talking with these people.

Kreisky became a socialist during his days in school. It was the political events of the interwar period—in particular the brutal police action following the burning of the Palace of Justice by a rioting mob in 1927—which were decisive for his political development. After completing school, Kreisky began to study law at the University of Vienna while intensifying his political activities. When the Social Democratic Party was banned following the short but sharp civil war in 1934, Kreisky engaged in clandestine activities for the party. In January 1935, he was imprisoned on suspicion of high treason because of his Social Democratic propaganda activities. During the ensuing antisocialist trial, it was his speech in defense of these activities that attracted international attention to Kreisky for the first time. In March 1936, he was found guilty of high treason and sentenced to one year of hard labor in prison. He was released from prison in June 1936 but banned from the university for two more years. He did not complete his law studies (Dr. Jur.) until 1938.

After the annexation of Austria by Nazi Germany in March 1938, Kreisky was imprisoned by the Gestapo until August of that year, then released only on condition that he leave Austria. With his international socialist contacts, Kreisky managed to emigrate to Sweden in September 1938. He stayed there until 1951, a period which was important to him both privately and politically.

In 1942 Kreisky married Vera Fürth, who came from an Austrian industrialist family, and their two children were born in Sweden. Kreisky earned his living by working for the Swedish Food Corporation. His political activities in Sweden included the chairmanship of the Club of Austrian Socialists and the Austrian Community. Unlike his political hero, the Austrian Marxist Otto Bauer, and the Austrian socialist emigrants to other countries, the Austrian community in Sweden sought the independence of a sovereign Austria after the war rather than inclusion of Austria in a democratic Germany.

Kreisky's political thinking was considerably influenced by his Swedish experience. This included support of neutrality in international relations and political pragmatism in domestic politics. From the Swedish Social Democrats, he learned that it is possible to change society qualitatively by introducing gradual changes step by step. He also learned that Social Democratic hegemony can be achieved if the bourgeois conservatives are internally split. This was important to Kreisky's political strategy once he returned to Austria.

In 1945–1946, Kreisky was an organizer of the Swedish relief program for Austria. From 1946 until 1951 he served as an Austrian diplomat in Sweden. Then after a few months as a civil servant in the Foreign Ministry in Vienna, Kreisky was appointed adviser to the newly elected federal president Theodor Körner in 1951. In 1953, he was appointed secretary of state (junior minister) in the Foreign Ministry and became foreign minister in 1959, when the SPÖ managed to take over this portfolio from the center-right ÖVP. He remained in this post until the breaking up of the ''grand coalition'' between the ÖVP and the SPÖ in 1966, following the electoral defeat of his party.

Parallel to his government career, Kreisky also advanced within the SPÖ. In 1956 he was elected to the party executive and won a parliamentary seat. In 1959 he became deputy party chairman. In 1967, Kreisky was elected party chairman in a hotly contested election. In the 1970 election, he introduced substantial party reform and was able to campaign on an appealing electoral platform. The SPÖ won a plurality of seats and Kreisky formed a minority government. In 1971, the SPÖ won a parliamentary majority, which it defended successfully in both 1975 and 1979.

As electoral leader, Kreisky was enormously important to achieving these victories. He interpreted his party's success in terms of a "voter coalition" between a large bloc of Socialist voters and 3 to 5 percent liberal, or Kreisky, voters. Because of his electoral effectiveness and his authority, he could exercise strong leadership in the party and the cabinet, and as both party chairman and federal chancellor, Kreisky was more powerful than any of his predecessors. In 1983, when the SPÖ lost its majority by a narrow margin, Kreisky resigned as both federal chancellor and party chairman. However, he remained active in domestic and international affairs until his death on July 29, 1990.

Before, during and after his time as federal chancellor, Kreisky was a politician whose influence exceeded the geographic boundaries of his country. World leaders found it useful to discuss international issues with him and made good use of his services as a go-between. In particular, Kreisky often served as intermediary between the West and the communist states. During his time as foreign minister and federal chancellor, Vienna was twice the host of summit meetings between the American president and the leader of the Soviet Union. In addition, Kreisky also actively promoted the Council on Security and Cooperation in Europe (CSCE), and from 1976 until 1989, he served as vice president of the Socialist International.

Throughout his career, Kreisky exercised enormous influence upon Austrian foreign policy in his positions as presidential adviser, secretary of state, foreign minister and federal chancellor. From the beginning, he was important to introducing and shaping Austria's policy of permanent neutrality. Kreisky was one of the first to see neutrality (following the Swiss model) as a means of winning back sovereignty after ten years of Allied occupation (1945–1955), and he persuaded his own reluctant party accordingly. As foreign minister, he placed great stress on the continuity and predictability of Austrian foreign policy.

Kreisky's security concept for Austria was based on its being widely recognized as a neutral and respected member of the international community. Besides neutrality, this included an international role for Austria and good personal contacts with the most important world leaders. In order to increase Austria's international role, Kreisky worked to establish Vienna as the third center for United Nations activities behind New York and Geneva.

Kreisky was also one of the first in his party who recognized the need to bring Austria closer to the European Community (EC), which during the 1960s was referred to as "the capitalist bloc" by the chairman of the Austrian Social Democrats. Nevertheless, Kreisky placed qualifications on how this should be achieved. Unlike the Social Democrats' coalition partner, the conservative Austrian People's Party (ÖVP), Kreisky did not believe that membership or a separate Austrian treaty with the EC would fulfill Austria's commitment to neutrality as outlined in the State Treaty of 1955. Rather, he favored a multilateral treaty between the EC and the European Free Trade Association (EFTA), of which Austria was a member. The failure of the conservative ÖVP government of 1966–1970 to work out terms of a bilateral association treaty between the EC and Austria eventually permitted Kreisky's conception of EC-Austria relations to triumph. Under his chancellorship a multilateral treaty between the EC and EFTA was signed in 1972 establishing a free trade zone.

Kreisky was influential in shaping Austrian party politics, in particular during his terms as chairman of the SPÖ (1967–1983) and federal chancellor (1970–1983). Within the SPÖ, he managed to draw the party away from its dogmatic positions, thereby enlarging its appeal. Under Kreisky's leadership the Social Democrats adopted a new basic party program in 1978 which, despite some leftist jargon, turned away from the idea of nationalizing industry. He also improved the party's relationship with the Catholic Church. These were strained because of the Social Democrats' anticlerical stand during the interwar period and the Church's clear stand against the party. Under Kreisky's chancellorship, the question of state financing for Catholic schools was settled in the Church's favor.

The first years of Kreisky's own government in the early 1970s were mainly devoted to modernizing and democratizing the country. During this period, he reformed the electoral system, the universities, the army, the broadcasting system and the criminal and family codes, as well as introducing industrial codetermination.

Many of these reforms did nothing more than acknowledge societal developments and were therefore based on broad public support. These included the recognition of the equality of women in the family, the possibility of divorce even when one spouse opposes it and the withdrawal of state sanctions against adultery, homosexuality and abortion. Electoral reform reduced barriers for entry to parliament. A 1975 law for the first time officially recognized and legitimated the activities of political parties. State subsidies were introduced for the parties and their vehicles of political education, and in order to maintain pluralism of the press, state subsidies for newspapers were provided for in 1975. Other reforms increased the participation of societal groups in decision making within institutions such as the university, the broadcasting system and firms.

Several of these reforms had a significant impact on Austrian politics. The 1970 reform of the electoral law reduced the biases against small parties and parties with a mainly urban support base. This reform helped not only the SPÖ but also the Austrian Freedom Party (FPÖ), a smaller center-right group, in turn helping to protect an SPÖ minority government. For Kreisky's long-term strategy, informed by his Swedish experience, was both to ensure the survival of the FPÖ (therefore maintaining division in the nonsocialist camp) and to have a "special relationship" with it in order to use it as a potential coalition partner should the SPÖ fail to win a majority on its own. This eventually happened in 1983, although it did not ultimately lead to the results envisaged by Kreisky. State subsidies for political parties, in addition to helping all parties generally, were also designed to give the small parties an extra boost. Therefore they had the effect of reducing the FPÖ's dependence on subsidies from industry, which might have endangered cooperation between it and the Social Democrats. Finally, the reform of the broadcasting system was aimed at making it more friendly toward the government.

Kreisky's governments contributed considerably to the growth of the welfare state. Social insurance and pension systems were expanded so that they eventually covered almost the entire population. Paid holidays for blue- and white-collar workers were extended from two to five weeks under the Social Democrats; these groups also benefited from other expansive social welfare measures. Free schoolbooks and free school transport were introduced, and the educational sector was considerably expanded, greatly increasing the number of Austrians receiving a university education.

As federal chancellor, Kreisky had to face economic recessions following the oil crises of 1974 and 1981. Having been personally affected by social misery and the political crisis caused by mass unemployment in the 1930s, Kreisky saw the struggle against unemployment as the central goal of his government. By practicing unprecedented deficit spending, by maintaining high levels of employment in the nationalized industries and by expanding the public sector, his unemployment policy was very successful: Austria's unemployment rate remained among the lowest in the Western world.

However, in the early 1980s high international interest rates forced Kreisky to reduce deficit spending while facing increasing resistance within Austria to the high costs of this policy (especially high rates of taxation and a large public debt). Consequently, unemployment had increased to more than 3 percent—which for Kreisky defined the threshold of full employment—when he resigned from office in 1983.

After his resignation Kreisky continued to fight against unemployment. He chaired the international Kreisky Commission of academics and politicians, which drafted a program, published in 1989, for full-employment in the 1990s. As a consequence of Kreisky's full-employment policy, Austria still has one of the lowest unemployment rates among countries in the 1990s. This achievement is, nonetheless, offset by the rapid buildup of state debt under Kreisky and the lack of industrial adjustment to international markets, particularly in the nationalized sector.

Kreisky's interest in international affairs went well beyond Austrian foreign policy. From the 1960s Kreisky was interested in the Middle Eastern conflict. For Kreisky, being Jewish was a question of religion rather than race. Because he was an agnostic, he regarded his Jewish background as irrelevant, and he explicitly rejected the notion of having any special loyalty vis-à-vis Jews or the state of Israel. He was one of the first Western politicians to establish good contacts with Arab leaders.

His actions in this regard did generate controversy. For example, in 1973, there was a terrorist attack in Austria on Jewish emigrants from the Soviet Union. In order to secure the release of the hostages, Kreisky agreed to a terrorist demand that an emigration camp run by the Jewish Agency be closed down, although he did not put into question Jewish emigration in general from the Soviet Union via Austria. Nevertheless, Kreisky was severely criticized by Israel for his decision, although this may also have been due to the fact that Jewish emigrants from the Soviet Union were no longer channeled exclusively to Israel but were free to choose any country as their destination.

In 1974, 1975 and 1976, Kreisky led fact-finding missions of the Socialist International (SI) to Israel and the Arab countries. In 1977, the SI published its proposal for peace in the Middle East. In 1978, it organized a meeting of Kreisky, Willy Brandt, Anwar Sadat and Shimon Peres in Vienna. To a certain extent these activities prepared the ground for the Camp David agreement between Israel and Egypt, although Kreisky was critical of the actual outcome. He considered the Palestinian problem to be the central issue of the Middle Eastern conflict, believing a solution to the conflict to be impossible without the involvement of the Palestinian Liberation Organization (PLO).

Kreisky increasingly tried to use his influence to make the PLO an acceptable actor in the Middle East. In October 1979, in a speech before the United Nations, Kreisky argued that the PLO was the legitimate representative of the Palestinian people. However, Kreisky's endorsement of the PLO was severely criticized by Israel, and it was not shared by most Western nations. In Austria, he was criticized by the main opposition party and the press and was only lukewarmly supported by his own party. A few years later, however, Kreisky's analysis has been accepted by many of his former critics, including many Israelis. Perhaps Kreisky's most important impact on the Middle Eastern conflict was his contribution toward the deradicalization of the Arab countries and the Palestinians. In his many contacts from the early 1960s, Kreisky contributed to their readiness to accept the existence of Israel and to replace terrorism with more civilized political tactics.

During the last years of his government, Kreisky became increasingly involved with the developing countries. In 1978, he demanded a Marshall Plan for the Third World and he was among the initiators of the 1981 United Nations North-South Conference in Cancún, Mexico. Kreisky was also the most outspoken critic of American policy vis-à-vis Central America during the Reagan administration. This position not only caused him problems with the United States but also within Austria. The press and the opposition claimed that Austrian interests would be better served by staying out of these matters and maintaining good relations with the United States. Paradoxically, moreover, Kreisky's championing of Third World needs was not backed up by his policies: Although during his chancellorship he did increase aid for development, Austria remained among those Western nations which spent the lowest proportion of their national income on aid.

Kreisky described himself as a man "between the times." He was born under monarchy, then formed politically by the First Republic during the interwar period. His political career took off in the Second Republic of the postwar period. Like many Austrian politicians, he learned lessons from the intense class conflict and the breaking down of democracy in the period between the two world wars. But his long stay in Sweden and, more generally, his sensitivity to developments in other countries which might be relevant to Austria gave him a very special approach to politics.

Politics was clearly Kreisky's great passion (he had turned down the opportunity to become an industrialist in Sweden), and he was widely regarded, by friend and foe alike, as an extremely skillful politician. He was indeed a master of raising new ideas, developing initiatives, doing the unexpected, finding the right words for a particular audience, attracting media attention and dividing the political opposition. It was these qualities that led to his enormous electoral successes. However, Kreisky was more than a skillful party politician. Despite his pragmatism, he maintained a vision of a good society, and in many respects he was the modernizer of Austria. What is more, Kreisky also viewed politics in its international dimensions. Often his analyses of international affairs were ahead of their time. What is remarkable about his accomplishments is that as a politician from a small country, he had little more than persuasion and his international reputation to use in the implementation of his ideas.

BIBLIOGRAPHY

Works by Kreisky:

Aspekte des demokratischen Sozialismus. Munich: List, 1974.

Neutralität und Koexistenz. Munich: List, 1975.

Die Zeit in der wir leben: Betrachtungen zur internationalen Politik. Vienna: Molden, 1978.

Das Nahostproblem. Vienna: Europaverlag, 1985.

Zwischen den Zeiten. Berlin: Sieder, 1986 (Memoirs, vol. 1).

Im Strom der Politik. Berlin: Sieder, 1988 (Memoirs, vol. 2).

Other Works:

Amerongen, Martin van. *Kreisky und seine unbewältigte Gegenwart.* Graz: Styria, 1977.

Bielka, Erich et al. (eds.). *Die Ära Kreisky: Schwerpunkte der österreichischen Aussenpolitik.* Vienna: Europaverlag, 1983.

Lendvai, Paul, and Karl Heinz Ritschel. *Kreisky: Porträt eines Staatsmannes.* Vienna: Paul Zsolnay, 1974.

Reimann, Viktor. *Bruno Kreisky.* Vienna: Molden, 1972.

Wistrich, Robert S. "The Kreisky Phenomenon: A Reassessment," in Robert S. Wistrich (ed.), *Austrians and Jews in the Twentieth Century.* New York: St. Martin's Press, 1992.

WOLFGANG C. MÜLLER

L

JEAN-MARIE LE PEN (1928–) has become one of the most important leaders of the resurgent extreme right in Europe during the past decade. Indeed, it can be argued that Le Pen has helped to reinvent the politics of the far right for post–Cold War Europe. As the president of the French National Front (FN) since its founding in 1972 he has skillfully blended the issues that have traditionally concerned the extreme right in France—church, family and modernization—with the new social issues of the 1980s: immigration, law and order, and national identity.

Since 1983, Le Pen has consistently attracted a national electoral following of over 10 percent of the voters, a percentage that increased to 14 percent or more in the presidential elections of 1988 and the French regional elections of 1992. Perhaps more important, the rhetoric of the National Front has had a broad impact on the issues that have dominated French politics during the past decade. By 1992, over 30 percent of French voters claimed to ''agree'' with the ideas of Le Pen (particularly regarding immigration and law and order), and the electoral pressure of the party has ensured that these ''ideas'' have been high on the political agenda (particularly the agenda of the established parties of the right), despite the fact that the National Front has never held a national ministry and that Le Pen has never held national office. Electoral success has also enabled the National Front to build a substantial national party organization, as well as a network of officeholders at the subnational level through which the party exercises considerable bargaining leverage over the decision-making processes of subnational governments. Le Pen's electoral success in France has also lent support to blossoming movements of the far right throughout Europe.

Throughout this period, Jean-Marie Le Pen has consistently defied predictions of his own political demise. Neither changes in the electoral system (in 1988), nor numerous political gaffes committed by him, nor splits in his party, nor attempts by the established parties of the right to isolate the FN nor attacks by the media and established political figures has served to reduce the electoral support for the National Front. Growing distrust for more established political parties combined with the very real concern over the issues consistently raised by Le Pen among the electorate have enabled him to maintain his popular support.

This success is all the more remarkable because it defies the political patterns of the French Fifth Republic. Le Pen is neither an upstart nor an established political figure. Most successful politicians of the right have built their political careers through a combination of party networks, office holding and old school ties, and those on the left have tended to emerge from the more established party networks or from the trade union movements. Le Pen has been an active politician far longer than most French political leaders, but he is a veteran of a long line of failed and discredited political movements. As we shall see, the movement of Le Pen from the peripheral world of the extreme right to center stage of French politics has not occurred through his abandonment of his political roots, but rather through the greater acceptance of and enhanced importance of the world of that periphery at the center of French political life.

Jean-Marie Le Pen was born in Brittany in 1928, the son of a modest family of small farmers and fishermen. Like most children from his region and background, he attended Catholic schools and regarded Marshal Pétain, the leader of the collaborationist Vichy regime, as a national hero. Nevertheless, as a sixteen-year-old in 1944, he reflected the complex loyalties of many of his contemporaries when he joined a local Resistance group and fought briefly against the retreating Germans. He would later say that he thought that he took more risks than many others who had made political or literary careers from their experiences during that period.

At the time of the Liberation, he quickly became an anti-Gaullist and an active anticommunist. His anti-Gaullism, he would argue, was based on de Gaulle's refusal to reconcile with Pétain and to recognize that the "hero of Verdun" had acted honorably and for the good of the country. His anticommunism emerged from the bitter experience of postwar purges and trials.

By the time he entered the Faculty of Law in Paris in 1947, the main lines of his political commitments were formed, but in Paris these commitments became better defined. A street brawler and effective speaker, he quickly became a leader of one of the numerous far-right fringe groups and the president of a law student association. During this period between the end of World War II and the deepening of the French war in Indochina, Le Pen was a militant, active in street demonstrations and confrontations with the left. In 1953, before completing his law degree, he volunteered as a paratrooper to fight the communists in Indochina. His battalion arrived too late to relieve the French garrison at Dien Bien Phu, and, he claims, at that moment he pledged to devote his life to politics.

After the loss of the French war in Indochina in 1955, Le Pen returned to Paris. He arrived after the war in Algeria had begun, and on the eve of the legislative elections of 1956, just in time to be drawn into the electoral politics of Poujadism. The UDCA (the "Poujadist" movement) was first organized in 1953 as a populist, antitax protest movement by farmers and small shopkeepers.

It spread most rapidly in areas that traditionally voted for the left and was frequently supported by the Communist Party in many localities. However, by 1955, the leadership of the movement had become strongly antileft, anti-Semitic (a prime minister of Jewish origin, Pierre Mendès-France, was in office during the last six months of 1954) and strongly in favor of maintaining Algeria as an integrated part of France.

Le Pen became a candidate and a principal spokesman for the Poujadists and in 1956 was elected deputy from Paris, the youngest deputy elected that year. When the National Assembly was reorganized after the elections, he was chosen president of the small Poujadist parliamentary group. During his time in the Assembly, Le Pen became well-known for his vituperative attacks against the left and his formulation of the issues to which he would be committed during his political career: law and order, the threat of communist subversion, the danger posed by immigration and a passionate defense of French Algeria. Although Le Pen's rhetoric more or less defined the fringe world of the extreme right, neither the Poujadists nor Poujade met his expectations. He was able neither to hold the Poujadist group in the National Assembly together nor to convince Poujade to lead a movement to maintain French Algeria at any cost. In the end, after barely six months, Le Pen temporarily resigned from the National Assembly and rejoined the army.

He signed up for six months with his old Foreign Legion regiment, in time to take part in the invasion of Suez at the beginning of November 1956 and then go on to Algeria, where he remained until the summer of 1957. He was later accused of having engaged in torture during interrogation of a prisoner in Algeria. These accusations were based on two police reports that were divulged in 1962. Le Pen has always denied that he personally engaged in torture, but has also defended the need to use torture under certain circumstances. When he returned to his seat in the National Assembly in June 1957 (he now sat among the ''unaffiliated'' deputies), he made it a point of defending the more questionable actions of his comrades in arms (*les paras* of the parachute division) and, by implication, his own.

In 1957, Le Pen organized a small fringe group, the National Front of Soldiers (FNC). He spent the summer on the beaches campaigning first for the retention of French Algeria and then for a candidate in a by-election, a Muslim who supported French Algeria. During this campaign he lost the use of his left eye in a fight and for years afterward wore an eye patch that accentuated his reputation as a street-fighter and marginal political activist.

Le Pen was reelected to the National Assembly in 1958 as a deputy from Paris, part of a wave of deputies elected on the right after the Fifth Republic was established. He remained in the National Assembly until 1962, when he began to move into a political career pattern that might have led to his advancement within the traditional parties of the Fifth Republic. He became an influential member of the National Assembly's Committee on National Defense and was responsible for the defense budget. However, when an insurrection against de Gaulle's government broke out in the streets of Algiers in January 1960, Le Pen openly supported the rebellion, thus effectively ending his influence in the National Assembly. He opposed the "revolt of the generals" in Algeria thirteen months later, but also strongly opposed until the end the recognition of Algerian independence.

His electoral fate was tied to that of the members of his parliamentary group, the Center of Independents (CNIP), which rapidly lost strength as right-wing voters flocked to the Gaullist banner in 1962, 1967 and 1968. By 1962, he seemed to be politically isolated, without a political party, bitterly supporting a lost cause. During the decade between 1962 and 1972, Le Pen continued to pursue his political goals while earning his living as director of a small record company that issued such "hits" as "Songs of the German Revolution, Men and Deeds of the Third Reich" (for which he would be fined and given a suspended sentence in 1968). In the run-up to the presidential campaign of 1965, he became secretary general of the Support Committees for Jean-Louis Tixier-Vignancour, a well-known right-wing lawyer who had been minister of information during the Vichy regime and had defended General Salan at his trial for the 1961 revolt of the generals. But Le Pen was even too extreme for Tixier (who got 5.3 percent of the vote in the first round of the 1965 presidential elections). Indeed, following the election, Le Pen and his allies were excluded from the Support Committee and for several years remained largely outside the ferment of rearguard right-wing extremism.

By 1969, however, movements of the extreme right had been given a boost by the reaction to the student movement of 1968 and by de Gaulle's resignation from the presidency. The National Front, created in 1972, represented an uneasy alliance of the traditional, "revolutionary" extreme right of the New Order, which was essentially opposed to the existing republic, and the allies of Le Pen, who were willing to work within the existing order. The leaders of the New Order saw their role as the "motor force" of an enlarged popular alliance of extreme-right forces that would ultimately create a new revolution: "The Revolution consists in totally destroying the old regime [the Fifth Republic] and putting into place the New Order . . . whatever the cost." Le Pen became the first president of the National Front, the model for which was an Italian neo-fascist party, the MSI.

The new alliance represented a considerable success in bringing together militant right-wing sects that had opposed each other with some vehemence, but within a year the New Order had been dissolved by the government, and Le Pen and his associates took control of the organization. In 1974, the former militants of the New Order had reorganized as the New Forces Party (PNF), setting up an internecine battle within the extreme right that endured until 1981. During this decade of competition, Le Pen succeeded in bringing into the National Front a variety of small neo-fascist and even neo-Nazi groups and personalities and developed an enduring alliance with the fundamentalist Catholic movement led by Cardinal Lefebvre. Nevertheless, the electoral fortunes of both competitors went from bad to worse. In the presidential elections in 1981, neither Le Pen nor his adversary was able to secure the necessary signatures from local officials to gain a place on the ballot. In the elections that followed, both parties combined secured far less than 1 percent of the vote for the few candidates they were able to run, less than half their level of support in 1973.

In a political universe dominated by four large, well-organized political parties, there seemed to be no room and no support for what appeared to be a political party that represented ideas and politicians whose time had long since past. In the 1970s, the increasingly consolidated parties of the center-right continued to hold governmental power, as they had since 1962, leaving no room for the marginalized extreme right. Nor was there room in the opposition. The consolidated Socialist and Communist left, organized around a Common Program for Government, posed an increasingly effective electoral challenge to the center-right.

Voter support for both government and opposition parties continued to grow in the 1970s, indicating that French voters were less inclined than they had been in the past to desert established political parties for marginal protest movements of either the left or the right. In May 1981, François Mitterrand, the Socialist candidate, won the French presidency; a month later the Socialist Party gained a clear majority in the National Assembly, and, for the first time in the history of the Fifth Republic, a government of the left (Socialists and Communists) was formed, supported by an overwhelming majority in the National Assembly. Thus, there was every indication that the movement (and the ideas) represented by Jean-Marie Le Pen was simply a hangover from ancient history.

However, since 1981, Le Pen has managed to outdistance his rivals within the extreme right, to gain a considerable electoral following, and, as a result, become a pivotal actor in current French politics. Far from ancient history, the ideas of the extreme right have become an integral part of the current political debate and have influenced the political agendas of the established parties of both the right and the left.

In 1983, Le Pen ran for the city council in the twentieth district of Paris, gaining 11.5 percent of the vote on the first ballot (compared with 2 percent by the FN list in 1977). Under the circumstances, this electoral loss was widely perceived as a political victory. In the June 1984 elections for the European Parliament, the National Front list headed by Le Pen attracted almost 10 percent of the vote, and in opinion polls FN sympathizers increased from 18 to 26 percent. This electoral breakthrough was confirmed by the results of the 1986 legislative elections, with a vote for the National Front of almost 10 percent, more votes in metropolitan France than the Communists.

The results of the first round of the 1988 presidential elections confirmed an apparent stability of the National Front electorate at the national level. Ninety percent of the FN voters of 1986 remained loyal to the party candidate, Jean-Marie Le Pen, a percentage that was not matched by any other party. This time the shift of votes from the parties of the established right was far more substantial than it had been in 1986. About 1.7 million voters of the right moved from these parties (15 percent), which when combined with smaller shifts from the left (mostly from the Socialists) and others from smaller parties and new voters, gave Le Pen 4.4 million votes (14.4 percent of the total), 63 percent more than the FN had attracted in 1986. Electoral support declined by about 30 percent in the legislative elections that followed in 1988, but this rose once again to 14 percent in the regional elections of 1992.

It is therefore reasonable to argue that the National Front has become an established political party that generally attracts between 10 and 14 percent of the vote. At the national level, the party has not been able to translate this support into parliamentary representation, but at the subnational level, the National Front has gained a wide network of offices in local, departmental and regional governments. As a result of the 1992 regional elections, for example, the National Front held the balance of power in nine of the twenty-one metropolitan regions of France and in six of them was ultimately responsible for the establishment of a governing coalition of the right. It has used these offices and this enhanced bargaining power to influence policy and to build more substantial party organizations.

How then can we understand this emergence of Le Pen and the extreme right during the decade of the 1980s? One place to begin is the diminishing public support for all established political parties that first became evident in the late 1970s. After several years of rising unemployment and declining economic growth (following two decades of economic expansion), popular approval for all established political parties began to decline. This trend was accentuated by the policies of economic austerity imposed by the Socialist government in 1982, on the eve of local elections in 1983. Although surveys showed declining support for the government, they also indicated little confidence in the established parties of the right that spoke for the opposition.

During most of the post–World War II period, the strongest manifestation of opposition to government policy had generally been the vote for the French Communist Party, the largest party in the country under the Fourth Republic (1946–1958) and the largest party on the left until the mid–1970s. However, the Communists were now part of the government and in any case had been steadily losing credibility (and voter support) since the late 1970s. The decline of the Communist Party strengthened the position of the Socialists in the short run, but severely weakened the left in the long run and opened up new opportunities on the right. However, because voters clearly lacked confidence in the politicians they had rejected in 1981, space was opened for ''new'' political forces, in the sense that voters were more willing to vote for issues rather than ideology, ignoring established party commitments. On the left, the Green parties clearly benefited from this voter volatility, and on the right, the National Front was the chief beneficiary.

Into this changing political environment stepped Jean-Marie Le Pen. Le Pen's ability to focus the attention of voters on two interrelated issues—the dangers of immigration and law and order—proved to be more effective in this fluid environment than it had been in the 1970s. Relatively few voters cared deeply about these issues in 1982–1983, but a large proportion of those who did were now willing to vote for him and the National Front. Le Pen's surprising electoral success and his ability to use the media to fully exploit that success gave him sudden national attention. The weakness of the established parties of the right and their vacillation between ignoring the National Front and forming coalitions with it in order to combat the Socialists magnified the power of both the party and its leader. Moreover, the challenge of Le Pen forced other parties to place the issues of the extreme right—immigration and law and order—higher on their own political agendas than they were otherwise inclined to do. This process increased both Le Pen's support and his opposition.

Thus, by the end of the decade, without governmental power but with an increasingly committed constituency within the right and a political party with growing roots throughout the country, Le Pen had made the program of the extreme right part of the national agenda in France. He continued to attract voters who cared deeply about questions of immigration, law and order, and, increasingly, national identity. What was less recognized, however, was that the very debate that he and his party provoked vastly increased the number of people who cared about such issues but who voted for other parties.

The future of Jean-Marie Le Pen is partially related to the conditions that facilitated his rise in French politics: high levels of unemployment, the lack of public confidence in established political parties, the marginal importance of the National Front for the electoral and governmental success of the right, the importance of the media in political life and the saliency of immigration as a political issue. All of these conditions are likely to endure in the foreseeable future, and Le Pen will continue to exploit all of them to enhance his political position. The irony of Le Pen's success is that issues and skills that had been honed in the hothouse atmosphere of the far right have proven to be quite relevant for at least limited success in the 1990s. The politics of the past seem to have become those of the future.

BIBLIOGRAPHY

Works by Le Pen:

Les Français d'abord. Paris: Carrère-Lafon, 1984.

La France est de retour. Paris: Carrère-Lafon, 1985.

Also, see his articles in the newsletter *La Lettre de Jean-Marie Le Pen.*

Other Works:

Birenbaum, Guy. *Le Front National en politique.* Paris: Balland, 1992.

Dumont, Serge. *Le Système Le Pen*. Anvers: EPO, 1983.

Jouve, Pierre, and Ali Magoudi. *Les Dits et les non-dits de Jean-Marie Le Pen.* Paris: La Découverte, 1988.

Mayer, Nona, and Pascal Perrineau (eds.). *Le Front National à découvert.* Paris: Presses de la Fondation Nationale des Sciences Politiques, 1989.

Rollat, Alain. *Les Hommes de l'extrème droite*. Paris: Calmann-Lévy, 1985.
Roussel, Eric. *Le Cas Le Pen*. Paris: Lattès, 1985.
Taguieff, Pierre-André. *Le National populisme*. Paris: Le Seuil, 1989.

MARTIN A. SCHAIN

SEÁN LEMASS (1899–1971) was Ireland's prime minister from 1959 to 1966. Despite a relatively brief reign at the head of Irish government, he is widely regarded as one of the architects of modern Irish society. The secret to his enormous influence lies in many years of diligent service for—and leadership in—Ireland's most successful political party, Fianna Fail.

Lemass was born in 1899, while Ireland was still under the political control of Great Britain. He came of age politically in 1916, making a small contribution to the failed Easter Rebellion of that year. When Ireland broke free of British rule in 1922, the contours of Irish political debate were cast for the rest of the century. The creation of the "Irish Free State" required the political separation of the twenty-six counties of southern Ireland from the six counties of Northern Ireland. The decision to "partition" the island, leaving Northern Ireland under British rule, was then, as it is now, extremely controversial. Its immediate effect was to create a deep and bitter division among southern leaders previously united in the struggle against the empire. That division ultimately resulted in civil war. Lemass was on the side of those who fought partition, and therein began the political affiliation that would bring him to the highest level of power in Irish politics.

To understand his career one must begin with Ireland's sole "founding father," Eamon De Valera, who organized opposition to the treaty of 1922 that partitioned Ireland. De Valera went on to fight and lose a civil war over partition. He then turned defeat into victory by organizing the Fianna Fail party, molding it into the single most important party machine in modern Irish politics. De Valera, once described as a "messianic leader," came to embody the very idea of Irish independence in the 20th century. Throughout most of his remarkable career in Irish politics, De Valera had Seán Lemass at his side. In revolutionary times, Lemass served as De Valera's minister of defense. When De Valera became prime minister, he depended on Lemass to develop the fundamentals of Fianna Fail economic policy. Lemass needed De Valera to deliver the votes; De Valera needed Lemass to deliver the goods.

Lemass first assumed government office as minister of industry and commerce in 1932. He was just thirty-two then and was the youngest government minister in Europe. The protectionist policies he pursued then were largely the result of two factors, worldwide depression and the ongoing tension in relations with Great Britain. De Valera's vision of a self-sufficient and independent republic was quickly translated into agricultural and industrial policies designed to protect native products by minimizing foreign competition. In terms of economic performance, some of these policies worked and some did not. In terms of political performance, lingering antipathy toward Britain (Ireland's largest trading partner) ensured support for the party line.

The economic cold war with Britain proved costly to Irish agriculture, as British markets were difficult to replace. Ironically, protectionism did little to help Irish farmers, whose devotion to De Valera and Fianna Fail had been unswerving. On the industrial front, Lemass had more success. He established close relations between the government and labor unions; his Conditions of Employment Act has been described as a "worker's charter."

Lemass adopted a corporatist approach to economic planning as early as the 1930s. His first instrument of economic policy was the creation of state-sponsored bodies (more accurately called semistate bodies). These are public authorities, often endowed with regulatory functions, whose governing board is appointed by the minister of a sponsoring governmental department. In legal terms, they are statutory corporations. Some produce goods, others regulate activities, others aid in planning, development and research. Technically they are autonomous, free from control by the parliament. They function as satellites of the government, working in the "outer edge of the public sector." They provide a forum for leaders of both public and private sectors to set the course for development by mutual agreement.

Today, there are at least one hundred of these bodies, each exercising substantial influence on a wide variety of economic and social affairs (e.g., developing the tourist industry, maximizing commercial turf production, running the national airline). By 1979, they provided 9 percent of all employment in the nation. The economic patterns set out by Lemass in the 1930s permeate all Irish public policy today.

During World War II, obvious political considerations prevented the deployment of Irish resources to protect British sovereignty. During this period, therefore, De Valera set Ireland on a course of strict neutrality in foreign policy. This policy allowed some opportunity for economic development. Lemass was successful as minister of supplies simply by steering a course that avoided economic collapse. He also experimented with new economic initiatives, as with the creation of a truly national transportation system.

In the postwar years, Lemass came to realize that isolation from powerful Western economies would, in the long run, hurt the nation. A high rate of emigration, often seen as the cornerstone of Ireland's relations with the Western world, returned in the 1950s. Emigration presented a major challenge to the government. For while Western Europe was enjoying a postwar economic boom, Ireland's economic growth was very slow. For those under thirty years old, the 1950s were the time to leave. Approximately 20 percent of that age group had left Ireland by the end of the decade. For some of the younger age groups, the emigration rate was close to 40 percent.

In domestic Irish politics, a government's success was measured not only by employment rates, economic growth and so on, but also by low emigration figures. High rates of emigration in the 19th century could be traced to British colonial policies and/or disastrous agricultural conditions. High rates of emigration in the independent Irish republic of the 20th century appeared to be the fault of Ireland's own government. One cannot underestimate the centrality of the emigration issue in Irish politics during the 20th century. Lemass once commented—referring to chronic emigration and problems of productivity—that Ireland might face a "situation in which the very disappearance of the race was a possibility that could not be ignored." Indeed, the issue of emigration continues to be a particularly powerful and emotive one in Irish politics today.

Struggling with the emigration problem, Lemass understood that agriculture would always be central in the Irish economy. However, developments in agricultural technology meant that farms would expand in size while employing fewer people. Minimizing emigration required new job opportunities. New jobs could only come from a competitive industrial and technological base. In a nation with limited natural resources, the development of such a base depended entirely on an open relationship with British, European and American economies. By the end of the 1950s protectionist policies were, therefore, more or less extinct. Free trade and integration with the world economy were high on the agenda, and export markets appeared to offer the greatest potential for economic expansion and lower emigration rates. Seán Lemass was quick to understand (and to act on) the principle that foreign trade and foreign capital were central to Ireland's future. Every government since the 1950s has followed the same principle.

For some, free trade, especially free trade with Great Britain, was a daring move for an Irish politician; for Lemass, it was the only way that made sense. His nationalism, unlike De Valera's, had few traces of the melancholia, insularity and inertia that haunts the Irish psyche.

It was by unanimous agreement that the higher echelons of Fianna Fail chose Lemass to replace De Valera as prime minister in 1959. The choice was no surprise: Lemass had exercised extraordinary influence on the government even before his appointment as deputy prime minister in 1945. Moreoever, De Valera's age and worsening health had substantially reduced his capacity to govern for at least a decade. Thus De Valera was elected to the largely symbolic post of president, while Lemass, after thirty years of devoted service, finally reached the most powerful political office in the nation. His term lasted seven years.

Before most others, Lemass recognized that Ireland's membership in the European Community (EC) held great potential for industrial and agricultural growth. Despite his best efforts, however, Ireland did not gain membership in 1961, when the EC was only four years old. His goal would not be achieved until 1973, some two years after his death.

Lemass enjoyed a virtual monopoly on Ireland's economic policy from the 1930s to the 1960s. His most important contribution was the "First Program for Economic Expansion" written in 1958. This proposal made it clear that the protectionist policies which had dominated the early years of the republic had to be abandoned. Industrial expansion, exports and foreign investment would be encouraged. These policies, when put into practice, proved to be particularly effective; economic growth occurred rapidly in the early 1960s, reaching twice the projected rate. At various times, Lemass had worked to create a national road network, the merchant marine, the power company and the national airline. The expansion of the 1960s sparked a period of profound social and cultural change in Ireland and stood in stark contrast to the stagnant and harsh climate of the previous decade.

Ironically, Fianna Fail did not win overall parliamentary majorities while Lemass was prime minister. The party remained in government because opposition parties were so divided that they could not agree on workable coalitions. It remains all the more remarkable that Lemass achieved as much as he did under these difficult political conditions.

A shift toward the corporatist approach to public policy is one of the central legacies of Lemass's tenure. Corporatism here refers to the procedure by which "economic decisions are discussed and agreed upon between the state and the major employers and the trade unions bodies." While Irish economic policy remained essentially under the control of the government, the extent of private sector participation in planning expanded dramatically. While that change was partly the product of 20th-century economic challenges, it was also a reflection of the pragmatic, performance-oriented, managerial philosophy that permeated Irish government under Seán Lemass.

One significant consequence of this innovation in government policy was a decline in the responsibility and authority exercised by the Dail, the lower house of parliament. This consequence did not disturb Lemass. As one commentator put it, "Lemass himself had little confidence in the capacity of the average Dail member to contribute intelligently to economic decision-making."

Lemass also provided the bridge between two generations of Irish political leaders. The first was a generation whose ideology was built out of their experience with the independence movement in both rebellion and civil war. Nationalists above everything else, they were "politicians by accident." The second generation consisted of young, aggressive, professional politicians; like Lemass they were less ideological, more pragmatic and keenly aware of the significance of economic policy. As Lemass once put it: "We do not work on the basis of theory. We work always on the basis of the best method of getting the job done." This second generation remains the backbone of Irish government today. Lemass identified his goals with these words: "The historical task of this generation is to *consolidate the economic foundations* of our political independence" (emphasis added). This stands in clear contrast with De Valera, who had repeatedly emphasized two national aims: the ending of partition and the revival of the Irish language (Gaelic).

The seven years of Lemass's leadership were truly a transition period for Fianna Fail. Many of Ireland's most important ministers in the latter 20th century made their names under his regime. But the groundwork for this transition had been well laid. In the late 1940s, Lemass had overhauled the party organization, guaranteeing for future generations of Fianna Fail candidates an efficient and responsive party machine. Charles Haughey, Ireland's most illustrious, not to say notorious, party leader of recent times, was appointed parliamentary secretary and later minister of agriculture by Lemass. The fact that Haughey was his son-in-law actually made the appointment quite difficult for Lemass. He asserted at the time that, in his role as father-in-law, he had advised Haughey not to take the job. To his credit, Lemass carefully avoided showing any support for Haughey in the leadership battle that emerged in 1966.

Like many leaders inspired by a vision of unprecedented progress, he met resistance in established bureaucracies. He came to see the civil service as a reservoir of inertia that had to be spurred into an active role in Ireland's growth. He went so far as to encourage departments to think of themselves as "development corporations." As one commentator put it, Lemass "changed the concept of Ireland from that of an ageing Cathleen Ní Houlihan to that of Ireland Inc."

Lemass recognized that long-term planning was essential to stable and positive economic conditions. Those conditions could, in turn, reduce the emigration problem and foster closer ties between Great Britain, Northern Ireland and the Republic. In that eventuality the potential for a resolution of the partition problem would be greatest.

Long-term planning, the cornerstone of all these developments, required radical change in the attitudes of Irish civil servants. Lemass set the Irish civil service on a new course, urging a complete reversal of deeply held beliefs about the role of government. He rejected the development of an adversarial relationship between business and bureaucracy, insisting that both sides were "partners in a common adventure."

Lemass is also unique in that he took the initiative to seek a closer relationship with Northern Ireland. He was the first Irish leader to visit the prime minister of Northern Ireland, then Terence O'Neil, in Belfast. This initiative, though it produced little real change, reflected a commitment on his part to open, sincere and friendly dialogue. It was a distinct departure from the overt suspicion and distrust that marked prior diplomatic contacts. His statement that "unity has got to be thought of as a spiritual development which will be brought about by peaceful persuasive means" captures the Lemass approach perfectly. It also contrasts sharply with the more bombastic rhetoric used inside and outside Fianna Fail on this most explosive issue.

Lemass, in his rhetoric and in practice, sought a new understanding of Irish nationalism. He redefined Ireland's path in the world, emphasizing international ties, economic growth, foreign trade, industrialization. He did not partake of the obsession with a melancholy past that often dominates Irish political debate. He took no solace in romantic visions of Ireland's rural life, commenting once that "my favorite Irish scene would be a big square factory brimming over with workers in dungarees."

When Seán Lemass died from heart disease in 1971, his passing was keenly felt by all who took pride in Ireland's development in the 20th century. Many believed that if he had come to power earlier the nation would have seen more extensive and progressive changes. As the editors of the *Irish Times* noted, "He came to power too late—he left power too early."

BIBLIOGRAPHY

Bew, Paul, and Henry Patterson. *Seán Lemass and the Making of Modern Ireland.* Dublin: Gill and MacMillan, 1982.

Coogan, Timothy Patrick. *Ireland since the Rising.* New York: Praeger, 1966.

Farrell, Brian. *Chairman or Chief: The Role of the Taoiseach in Irish Government.* Dublin: Gill and MacMillan, 1971.

———. *Seán Lemass.* Dublin: Gill and MacMillan, 1982.

Gallagher, Michael. *Political Parties in the Republic of Ireland.* Manchester: Manchester University Press, 1985.

Schmitt, David E. *The Irony of Irish Democracy.* Lexington, Mass.: Lexington Books, 1973.

JEROME O'CALLAGHAN

RUDOLPHUS (RUUD) LUBBERS (1939–   ) is without doubt the leading Dutch politician of the 1980s and early 1990s. Serving three terms, Lubbers not only holds the longest tenure of any prime minister in the history of the Netherlands, but is also one of Western Europe's most durable and successful political leaders. In a country as Calvinist and egalitarian as Holland, people do not very often get excited about political leaders. Yet many Dutchmen, whether among his political friends or enemies, agree that Lubbers is a politician of extraordinary stature.

Who is this "Sunday child in politics," as he is frequently called, extremely successful in domestic Dutch politics and widely expected to either succeed Jacques Delors as president of the European Commission or accept another important international position? The answer is complex.

Ruud Lubbers was born the sixth child and third son of a relatively wealthy Roman Catholic family on May 7, 1939, in Rotterdam. His father, Paulus Johannes Lubbers, himself the son of a guest-house keeper and book and cigar dealer, was director of Lubbers Hollandia Engineering Works. His mother, Wilhelmine Karoline van Laack, was the daughter of the well-known master of a river vessel.

Lubbers received his first education at the Jesuit-led Sint Canisius College in Nijmegen, going on to study economics at the Netherlands School of Economics (the predecessor of Erasmus University) in Rotterdam, where he graduated *cum laude* in 1962. His main interest at the time was in monetary affairs, and the subject of his master's thesis was the relationship between productivity and the balance of payments. After finishing his studies, and while still serving in the army, he married Maria (Ria) Emilie Josepha Hoogewegen, the daughter of a Rotterdam lawyer, with whom he eventually was to have two sons and a daughter.

Lubbers seems originally to have contemplated an academic career, but when his father died suddenly in 1963, he decided to become secretary to the management board of Lubbers Hollandia Engineering in order to help his older brother, Robert (Rob) Marie, with the business. Two years later, he was appointed codirector of the family company. In the meantime, he had been named treasurer, then president of the Young Catholic Employers Association, which later—under his chairmanship—was to merge with the Young Protestant Employers Association to become the Young Christian Employers Association.

This merger was part of a more general ''depillarization'' process which characterized Dutch politics and society during this period. The Netherlands had long been the prototype of what political scientists Hans Daalder and Arend Lijphart have called a ''pillarized'' country, with separate organizations for Catholics, Calvinists, socialists—and to a significantly lesser extent, the liberals—across almost all sectors of social and political life. But as a result of increasing individualization and secularization in Dutch society of the 1960s, these pillars began to crumble, though thus far they have not completely disappeared. On the contrary, important areas like education, broadcasting and health care, despite these changes, remain more or less segmented.

In the early 1970s, Lubbers also served as chairman of the Catholic Association of Metalwork Employers and was a board member of the Netherlands Christian Employers Federation. In his capacity as member of the Council of the Federation of Mechanical and Electrical Engineering Industries (Federatie Metaal en Elektrotechnische Industrie, or FME), he among other things participated in complicated collective agreement negotiations for the metal industry. Finally, in 1970, he joined the Programs Advisory Council of the Catholic Broadcasting Association (Stichting Katholieke Radio Omroep, or KRO).

Together with his wife, Lubbers became a member of the Catholic People's Party (Katholieke Volkspartij, or KVP) in 1964. Between 1966 and 1968 he was, his business career notwithstanding, involved in activities of the Christian Radical group within this party. This group was a reaction to the allegedly antisocialist stance of the Catholic Party after the collapse of the center-left coalition in October 1966. However, when this group broke away from the KVP to become the Political Party Radicals (Politieke Partij Radikalen, or PPR), Lubbers decided to remain with the KVP. In 1970, Lubbers was elected to the eighty-one-member Rijnmond Council (Openbaar Lichaam Rijnmond) in his hometown of Rotterdam. The council's main task was to coordinate the policies of the various municipalities in the harbor area in and around Rotterdam. Lubbers became his party's principal spokesman for economic affairs in this body.

Somewhat unexpectedly, three years later at age thirty-four, Lubbers was nominated by the KVP parliamentary leader, Frans Andriessen, to the office of minister for economic affairs in the center-left coalition led by Joop den Uyl, a Social Democrat. Because he was the minister who most directly faced the domestic consequences of the international oil crisis, Lubbers appeared regularly on national television. Among other things, he worked to persuade the Dutch of the importance of simple energy conservation measures, such as lowering thermostats and closing window curtains at night. Lubbers soon became a well-known public figure. Other measures taken by the den Uyl cabinet during this period included the introduction of car-less Sundays and petrol rationing. During his four years as economic affairs minister, Lubbers also introduced legislation to stimulate private investment and to introduce capital growth sharing.

To his disappointment, Lubbers did not continue as minister in the center-right van Agt cabinet formed in 1977. Instead, he became senior deputy parliamentary leader of the newly formed Christian Democratic Appeal (Christen-Democratisch Appèl, or CDA). The CDA was a federation formed by the KVP and the two main Protestant parties in the Netherlands, the Calvinist Anti-Revolutionary Party (Anti-Revolutionaire Partij, or ARP) and the Dutch Reformed Christian-Historical Union (Christelijk-Historische Unie, or CHU). The federation then resulted in a formal merger of the three parties in 1980. This fusion is generally considered to be the most important development in the post–1945 Dutch party system and demonstrates that, although organizational and other changes have occurred, pillarization thus far has not disappeared completely in the Netherlands.

In the autumn of 1978, Lubbers had been elected parliamentary leader of the CDA. In this capacity, he contributed significantly to the merger of the ARP, CHU and KVP, especially through his patience and persistent pursuit of compromise, both between the van Agt cabinet and the parliamentary CDA and between the several factions of the highly divided parliamentary party itself. At the time, the parliamentary CDA was divided into both confessional groups (Anti-Revolutionary, Christian-Historical and Roman Catholic) and into left and right wings. The price Lubbers had to pay for this role of almost permanent mediator was the initial image of a woolly-mouthed, rather colorless politician. Later, the term *Lubberiaans* would find its way into the Dutch language to describe a manner of speaking without revealing much.

Lubbers remained parliamentary leader of the CDA until November 1982, when he was sworn in as prime minister after Andreas van Agt suddenly decided to leave Dutch national politics. From November 1982 to July 1986 and from July 1986 to November 1989, he presided over the first and second Lubbers cabinets, two center-right coalitions of Christian Democrats and the liberal-conservative People's Party for Freedom and Democracy (Volkspartij voor Vrijheid en Democratie, or VVD). In 1989, he was reappointed to lead a third Lubbers cabinet, a center-left coalition of the CDA and the Labor Party (Partij van de Arbeid—PvdA).

One of the most remarkable features of this period is that one and the same Christian Democratic politician was able to work successfully in successive coalitions with Social Democrats, Progressive Liberals (Democraten '66, or D'66) and Radicals in the 1970s, the conservative Liberals during most of the 1980s and, once again, the Social Democrats in the 1990s. Of course, in part this was made possible by the fact that the CDA is, like the Catholic People's Party before it, the pivotal party in the Dutch political system. The Netherlands traditionally is a country of political minorities, therefore necessitating coalitions. Since 1917, when the present system of proportional representation was introduced, it has proven virtually impossible to form a (national) coalition without the Catholics first, the Christian Democrats later.

In 1982, Lubbers inherited an extremely difficult economic situation, although it was a situation to which he himself had also contributed as CDA parliamentary leader. During the first van Agt cabinet from 1977 to 1981, Lubbers had opposed a number of proposed expenditure cuts and other fiscal measures, in part because he did not judge the Dutch political climate to be ripe for these measures, in part because of pressures from the influential left wing within the parliamentary CDA, in part because of the traditional rivalry between him and van Agt. As a result, in 1982 Lubbers faced a huge budget deficit of about 6 percent of Holland's gross national product (double the present European Union norm) and a high unemployment rate of some 12 percent of the working population.

To cope with this economic crisis, Lubbers's first cabinet moved quickly to enact a "no nonsense" austerity program, which significantly cut government expenditures and social welfare benefits, including unemployment compensation, and reduced the minimum wage. Perhaps the most drastic provision in the austerity package, however, was the 3 percent cut in public sector salaries. Britain's prime minister, Margaret Thatcher, reportedly complained to Lubbers that this measure was disastrous for her reputation as the Iron Lady! In preparing the package, Lubbers collaborated extensively with, among others, fellow Christian Democrats such as Onno Ruding, the minister of finance, and Jan de Koning, minister for social affairs and employment. Resistance in Dutch society to these austerity measures was fierce and widespread, especially among the various trade unions, although in the end largely unsuccessful.

Revitalizing the Dutch economy had hardly begun when the Lubbers cabinet faced the potentially even more controversial issue of the deployment of forty-eight Pershing II and cruise missiles in the Netherlands, which was scheduled to take place sometime during 1986 according to NATO's so-called dual track decision of 1979. Alone among its European partners, the Dutch government had failed to make an absolute commitment to this deployment. Opposition to the plan from the relatively powerful Dutch peace movement—which organized two huge protest marches in Amsterdam and The Hague, as well as a petition signed by a fifth of Holland's 14.5 million inhabitants—was especially strong.

The situation was rendered even more complicated, however, by the fact that Lubbers also faced substantial dissent over the issue within his own Christian Democratic Party, in part due to the participation of some of the main Dutch churches in the peace movement. On June 1, 1984, the Lubbers cabinet—very much in accordance with one of the traditional "rules of the game" in Dutch politics as defined by Daalder and Lijphart—reached agreement on a plan to postpone the final decision until November 1, 1985. If, in the meantime, the Soviet Union were to reduce the number of its SS–20 missiles to 378, then the

Netherlands would not deploy the cruise missiles. Not surprisingly, in November 1985 Lubbers was obliged to announce that the Soviets had not met this condition. In the end, however, the Netherlands did not actually deploy the Pershing II and cruise missiles, because of the intermediate nuclear forces treaty concluded by the United States and the Soviet Union in December 1987.

A third and final controversial issue confronting the first Lubbers cabinet was euthanasia. Lubbers's own position on the issue appeared to be somewhat more liberal than that of his own Christian Democratic party, illustrating his more or less pragmatic approach to politics—not, however, unprincipled. Again, postponing the decision was the basic strategy adopted. This time it would take until 1991 before a compromise could be reached: Euthanasia would remain in the penal code, but only when serious doubt existed as to the ''carefulness'' of the doctor should a case come before court.

Having taken relatively unpopular stands on the controversial issues of the depressed economy and the stationing of nuclear weapons on Dutch soil, the CDA seemed to have little prospect of winning the general election scheduled for May 1986. But Lubbers, paradoxically, appeared to have become very popular with Dutch voters despite his advocacy of unpopular policies. Vigorously defending his economic record, especially, Lubbers waged a very personalized campaign, asking the electorate in effect to let him finish the job. His personal popularity, what Dutch political observers have called the ''Lubbers effect,'' carried the CDA to a surprising landslide victory, achieving a margin of nine seats in the Dutch Second Chamber (Tweede Kamer). Although the liberal-conservative VVD lost nine seats in these same elections, it also remained in the government.

The second Lubbers cabinet, comprised of the CDA and the VVD, set out three goals: to reduce unemployment to 500,000 (from an all-time high of almost one million in 1984), to reduce the state budget deficit to 4.6 percent of GNP, and to prevent the collective tax burden from increasing. In spring 1989, however, the cabinet collapsed prematurely because of a revolt staged by a majority of the Liberal members of parliament. The specific proposals to which Joris Voorhoeve, the Liberal parliamentary whip, objected were the ending of tax breaks for automobile commuters and an increase in excise taxes on fuels. Both measures were part of a newly announced National Environment Plan aimed at cutting pollution by some 70 percent by the year 2010. Apart from environmental politics, however, the collapse was probably at least as much caused by frictions and personality clashes both between and within the ruling parties. More specifically, Lubbers was accused by many Liberals of playing too dominant a role in coalition politics. One of the reasons for this, however, was that the Liberal minister for economic affairs and vice premier in the second Lubbers cabinet, Rudolf de Korte, was not really a match for the experienced Lubbers.

In retrospect, it is not certain whether Lubbers was all that unhappy with the collapse of his second cabinet in 1989. After all, he had been arguing in public for quite some time that after a period of economic austerity measures, renewed attention would have to be paid to social policies. Shortly after the downfall of his cabinet, moreover, he presented a so-called ''Agenda for the Future,'' which targeted issues such as the environment, integration of minorities, crime, and political and administrative reform. It is quite possible, indeed likely, that he saw better prospects for carrying out this agenda in a coalition with the Labor Party. The latter, after a twenty-year period of polarization and a change in political leadership (the former chairman of the Federation of Dutch Trade Unions, Wim Kok, replacing Joop den Uyl), had become more moderate. After parliamentary elections, in which a rather unfortunate VVD lost further ground while the CDA managed to maintain its 1986 level of support, a coalition was formed between Christian Democrats and Social Democrats, with Lubbers once again prime minister. In power through the early 1990s, this coalition faced a number of problems, including the necessity for new austerity measures because of international economic and monetary turmoil.

The conclusive impact of Lubbers on Dutch politics cannot be completely measured, if only because his political career is generally considered to be far from over. Nonetheless, his own party, the CDA, the Dutch political system, the country as a whole and the international environment have all been affected by his political leadership.

Lubbers's impact on the CDA, to begin with, cannot be easily overestimated. As we have seen, during his years as CDA parliamentary leader, Lubbers contributed significantly to the formal merger of the ARP, CHU and KVP in 1980, doing so by being a permanent mediator between the various confessional and socioeconomic factions. Under his political leadership the CDA was thus transformed from a highly divided and uncertain alliance of three rival parties, which seemed destined to further decrease in size and influence, into a relatively cohesive and self-confident unitary party dominating Dutch political life. Clearly, Lubbers succeeded in becoming increasingly popular both with his followers and with (Liberal and other) voters well outside his own CDA's rank and file, despite, or perhaps because of, his advocacy of tough policy measures. His pragmatic approach to politics, mentioned earlier, was also instrumental in this. As a result, his Christian Democratic Party was able to maintain its pivotal position in a period of depillarization and secularization.

As far as the political system is concerned, the first Lubbers cabinet, especially, can be said to have at least temporarily changed executive-legislative relations in the Netherlands. Increasingly, the governmental parties in parliament saw their principal task as one of keeping ''their'' cabinet in power. The price that had to be paid for this was increasingly strict party discipline as well as far fewer opportunities for opposition parties to influence government policies. After a period of unprecedented polarization and politicization in the 1960s and the 1970s, the traditional businesslike character of Dutch politics was reemphasized.

In this, Lubbers came to resemble more a British prime minister, like Margaret Thatcher, or a German chancellor, like Helmut Kohl, than a traditional Dutch prime minister, who, because of the multiparty system and coalition cabinets, is no more than a *primus inter pares*. But Lubbers made it a habit of presiding in person over virtually all the meetings of both the plenary council of ministers and those of the various cabinet committees and was early on assisted by a small but highly competent staff of civil servants. Increasingly, Lubbers's office inside the parliamentary complex in The Hague became the place where many of the most important decisions were made, rather than in parliament itself. As a result, within the CDA itself the prime minister, not the parliamentary party leader, became the most powerful figure.

Finally, during his ten years in office, former Dutch minister for foreign affairs Hans van den Broek, recently named European commissioner, engaged in an almost continuous power struggle with Lubbers over who was to bear primary responsibility for foreign policy. This may turn out to be the only structural change to Dutch political decision making during the Lubbers era, caused as much by the process of European integration as by Lubbers himself.

The impact of Lubbers on the country as a whole is widely perceived to have been substantial as well. In particular, his economic record is impressive. In 1992, unemployment in the Netherlands was 7 percent of the working population (down from 12 percent in 1982), while the budget deficit was approximately 3.5 percent of gross national product (down from 6 percent in 1982).

In retrospect, perhaps Lubbers's greatest domestic achievement, however, was restoring public confidence following years of political, social and economic turmoil. The atmosphere of gloom and doom that the Netherlands knew in the early 1980s, especially during the second and third van Agt cabinets (1981–1982), quickly faded away after he had taken over. Part of the explanation for this lies no doubt in the fact that the rigorous austerity program of the first Lubbers cabinet, as well as the new political doctrine his Christian Democratic Party was developing at the time, corresponded remarkably well with the general political climate.

In fact, one could argue that to a considerable extent Lubbers and his cabinet were carried along comfortably by the neo-conservative tide which swept Western Europe and the United States during the 1980s and which brought to power politicial leaders such as Ronald Reagan, Margaret Thatcher and Helmut Kohl. The CDA in the 1980s proclaimed that the only way to finance an increasingly costly welfare system was to move away from the "caretaker state" toward what it initially called a "caring society" and later called a "responsible society," consciously borrowing a concept developed within the World Council of Churches in the 1940s and early 1950s. In the "responsible society" people themselves were to take more responsibility for providing social services in order to relieve a bankrupt and overloaded government.

This concept, with its strong reliance on volunteers, has frequently been labeled "nostalgic" and "moralizing." In reality, critics claimed, the policies of the first Lubbers cabinet were rather insensitive toward the unemployed and less well-off and helped to widen the gap between rich and poor in Dutch society. Although to some extent this may indeed have been the case, it can also be argued that in the long run this was the only way to overcome economic problems which dated as far back as at least the early 1970s. As the economic recovery made progress, Lubbers then began to focus more on several great reforms—of health care, the fiscal system, the judiciary and decentralization of the central government. While it is too early to pass final judgment, Lubbers did seem to be less successful in these admittedly complicated and time-consuming operations.

Finally, the impact of the Lubbers era on the international environment has been limited, simply because the impact of a small country such as the Netherlands is limited no matter who its political leaders of the day. Taking this factor into account, however, Lubbers probably achieved the maximum that could be achieved. One example is the surprise proposal which he launched on June 25, 1990, on the first day of the European Summit in Dublin, for a European Energy Community, designed to both help the former Soviet Union financially and give Western Europe access to Russia's huge fossil fuel reserves. In December 1991, the European Energy Charter was signed in The Hague by representatives of some fifty countries.

Another prominent example is the Treaty of Maastricht, of which Lubbers and van den Broek were two of the principal authors. Like his Christian Democratic Party, Lubbers strongly favors further European integration. At the same time, however, he believes that it should be decided on a sector-by-sector basis whether it is more sensible to make policy on a European level or on a national level. (But then, the principle of subsidiarity, which has in the meantime become one of the main principles underlying European cooperation, is not so accidentally of Roman Catholic origins.) Finally, Lubbers (as well as Foreign Minister van den Broek) has also been important in the Netherlands' consistent support of NATO, even though NATO's dual track decision in 1979 has led the Dutch to be a slightly less faithful ally than during the 1950s and 1960s. Neither Lubbers nor van den Broek thinks that a choice has to be made between strengthening European integration and the maintenance of the security relationship with the United States in the Atlantic Alliance.

So who is Ruud Lubbers? In spite of a small number of recent Dutch-language books on him, surprisingly little is known about Lubbers personally, except perhaps that from time to time he enjoys a good game of hockey. He talks little about himself in interviews, claiming that readers would not be much interested. Partly because of this, even in his own party, he is not loved so much as respected. Of course, Lubbers could be depicted—as he often is—as a workaholic, an early riser at his desk in The Hague before the morning commute starts, not returning home until late in the evening. He is also, clearly, a pragmatist, someone who thinks through at least ten possible solutions for each single problem. Finally, as his main ''handicap,'' one could mention his past as a businessman. On several occasions during the last twenty years, usually with elections approaching, he has been accused of directly or indirectly benefiting his family company, in which he still has a financial interest.

But, although there may be some truth to each of these characterizations, they somehow do not seem to constitute the whole story. Probably a more important clue to his complex personality lies in his (post–Vatican II) Catholicism. Of course, the Roman Catholic faith plays no direct role in his public life. Depending on his audience, however, Lubbers regularly invokes the meaning of Christian inspiration in politics, claiming to be inspired most by Roman Catholic political philosophers, such as Henri Bergson (1859–1941) and Pierre Teilhard de Chardin (1881–1955). Religious faith does play a prominent role in his private life, providing him with, among other things, a moral philosophy and a strong ethical belief in equality, not unlike other figures in the Dutch social-Catholic tradition—Charles Ruijs de Beerenbrouck, Carl Romme, Jozef Cals or Marga Klompé—not unlike, moreover, someone like Jacques Delors.

Whether or not Lubbers will succeed Delors as president of the European Commission, one thing is certain: His powers of diplomacy, developed in the intricacies of the consociational democracy that is still the Netherlands, in combination with his religious and political ideals and the five languages he speaks more or less fluently (Dutch, English, French, German and Spanish), make him a likely candidate for the position or, for that matter, any other job where he would have to deal with the challenge of keeping national and European political leaders on the road to further European economic, monetary and political unity.

BIBLIOGRAPHY

Work by Lubbers:

Samen onderweg: Over democratie, christendom en samenleving, economie en internationale vraagstukken. Utrecht: Het Spectrum, 1991.

Other Works:

Joustra, Arendo, and Erik van Venetië. *Ruud Lubbers: Manager in de politiek.* Baarn: Anthos, 1989.

Tijn, Joop van, and Max van Weezel. *Inzake het kabinet-Lubbers.* Amsterdam: Sijthoff, 1986.

HANS-MARTIEN TEN NAPEL

JOSEPH LUNS (1911–) dominated Dutch foreign policy for nineteen years as minister of foreign affairs (1952–1971). After withdrawing from Dutch politics, he was appointed secretary general of NATO (North Atlantic Treaty Organization). He stayed at NATO until 1983, remaining in Brussels after his retirement from public life. By far, the most significant part of Luns's career were his years as foreign affairs minister. By the 1960s, Luns, a tall, extroverted diplomat who traveled widely on behalf of his small country, came to be regarded Mr. Holland himself.

Luns was born in Rotterdam on August 28, 1911, one of five children. His family was Catholic and sent him to a Jesuit high school in Amsterdam, where they had moved. He then finished his last few years of high school at a private institute in Brussels. After graduation, he returned to the Netherlands and studied law at the Universities of Leiden and Amsterdam.

In 1939, Luns entered the Dutch foreign service and was sent to Switzerland. A few months later, World War II broke out, and in 1941 the Dutch government-in-exile (London) asked him to look after Dutch interests from unoccupied Portugal. After the war, Luns traveled to New York to join the Dutch delegation at the United Nations. In 1952, the government recalled him and he was appointed minister without portfolio (charged with foreign affairs along with the foreign minister). However, two men heading the ministry of foreign affairs caused considerable friction, and Luns made it clear that he would only stay if he were appointed minister of foreign affairs. That finally happened in 1956.

Luns enjoyed such a long ministerial career thanks to his membership in the Catholic Party, which dominated Dutch politics until 1973, and owing to his own personal popularity. In particular, Luns is known for his practical jokes and witty repartees. Numerous publications, containing collections of his speeches and meetings with famous and not so famous people, attest to his sense of humor. Luns's view has always been that humor and jokes are part and parcel of the political discourse.

Undoubtedly, his easygoing manner and ability to see the comic aspects of serious events made him an extremely popular man in the 1950s and 1960s. The same cannot be said for his later years as secretary general of NATO. Many people accused him of immaturity, superficiality and even senility. This reassessment of Luns's personality partly reflected a generational split in Dutch political thinking. Younger voters and foreign affairs specialists held quite different, less hawkish, opinions about the Soviet Union and East-West conflict than Luns, who came of age during the height of the Cold War and never shook his dark views of communism and the Soviet Bloc. In the end, Luns was a man who provoked strong feelings. Some loved him; others hated him.

Luns, in his years as the Netherlands top foreign affairs official, held a number of strong opinions about his country and its role in world politics. For Luns, the Netherlands was not simply a small, marginal actor in world politics. As evidence, Luns liked to mention that 115 countries in the UN have a lower national income than the Netherlands, 95 have fewer inhabitants and 25 a smaller territory.

Of course, Luns was realistic and knew that the Netherlands had no exclusively independent role to play in NATO or East-West relations. His working assumption, however, was that the Netherlands was an important trading nation, belonging to the ten richest countries in the world and providing considerable foreign aid to less developed countries. Nonetheless, even Luns recognized that the Netherlands' security policy could not evolve on its own and ought to rely on the continued superiority of American nuclear arms and on a visible American military role in Europe. Whenever European leaders mentioned the possibility of establishing an European nuclear defense umbrella, Luns would vehemently oppose such a course as dangerous and irresponsible. Any such development would impair, he argued, the alliance with the United States, would accelerate the arms race and harm East-West relations. The position of the Netherlands, and Luns, was unequivocally clear: Europe should rely on the United States for its defense.

As minister of foreign affairs, Luns pursued a unambiguously pro-American, Atlanticist policy. He feared an erosion of U.S. commitment to Europe and did not wish to give the Americans a pretext for withdrawing from Western Europe. These strong pro-American views inevitably brought him onto a collision course with President Charles de Gaulle of France, for one of de Gaulle's major preoccupations in the 1960s was to circumscribe American influence in Europe. In this effort, France blocked British membership in the European Community because it considered Britain to be nothing more than a front for American power. Similarly, under de Gaulle, France attempted to exploit the institutions of the European Community to create a European base for France's global political ambitions. In both of these issues, Luns held opposing convictions, never hesitating to oppose de Gaulle's long-term objectives.

Unlike de Gaulle, Luns repeatedly argued for admitting Britain to the European Community. Luns's reasoning reflected three major concerns. The first was the Atlanticist leaning of the British foreign policy establishment, which dovetailed neatly with the Netherlands' confidence in a nuclear defense system financed and maintained by the Americans. Second, Luns, who came from a liberal-conservative political background, strongly believed that the entry of Britain would strengthen the free trade character of the European Community, militating against its more protectionist tendencies. The third motive was linked to creating a better balance between larger nations. Two closely cooperating bigger states, like France and Germany, could easily ignore the interests of the smaller states. Britain's accession to the EC was seen as a counterweight to a Franco-German partnership.

In 1962, Luns also opposed de Gaulle's plan for political unification and an extension of NATO's sphere of operations to areas outside the North Atlantic and Western Europe. Although the initiative came from the French, Konrad Adenauer, chancellor of the Federal Republic of Germany, in his desire to placate the French, endorsed de Gaulle's attempt to exclude Britain from the EC and to stall further progress toward genuine political integration. To that effect, the French floated a plan that would have eliminated the political independence of EC institutions, making them responsible for purely administrative and technical operations, and shelved enlargement (admitting Britain) permanently. Luns rejected these proposals on four grounds: (1) the French idea of an intergovernmental union would fatally weaken the supranational powers of the European Community; (2) a political bloc would form inside NATO that would result in a schism with the United States; (3) Britain *should* be a member of both the new defense union and the EC; (4) the political union embodied in the Treaty of Rome (the EC) should further develop in supranational directions.

Adenauer never forgave Luns for vehemently opposing a plan which he had wholeheartedly endorsed. At the European summit in Paris, in 1960, Luns's list of objections provoked Adenauer to mutter, loud enough for Luns to hear, that it was outrageous for a young fellow like Luns to oppose him. In response, Luns mumbled to his neighbor, equally audibly, that it was outrageous for an old fellow like Adenauer to engage in foreign policy. While Adenauer never got to like Luns, the latter was in the end justified in his objections because other EC member states decided to oppose the French plan as well and respectable Europeanists also turned against the proposal. Interestingly, many Dutch commentators spoke admiringly of Luns for having stood up against de Gaulle for the sake of the supranational ideals.

A far more difficult moment in Luns's career as minister of foreign affairs came with the New Guinea crisis of 1961–1962. The roots of the West New Guinea (West Irian) dispute date to the Round Table Agreement of 1949, when the Netherlands granted independence to Indonesia. According to the agreement, the question of administrative control over West New Guinea was to be resolved within one year of the signing of the treaty. Subsequent negotiations failed and relations between Indonesia and the Netherlands worsened.

By 1960, passions in both countries ran so deep that they threatened the postwar stability of the Pacific area. The Soviet Union supported Indonesia's claims, which resisted all attempts to grant New Guinea its own statehood or self-determination and which regarded any continued Dutch presence as an intolerable vestige of colonialism. Although the Dutch had no economic or security stakes in New Guinea and while hardly any Dutch citizens lived in this largely unknown territory, the loss of the island was seen as the final severance of Dutch ties with the East Indies, thereby provoking considerable psychological and irrational resistance. In this, Dutch governments continued to cling to an utterly unrealistic view in which they presented themselves as the guardians of the Papuan people until the local population was ready to govern itself. Much of this Dutch rhetoric was highly moralistic and disguised an emotional reluctance to let go of the last bit of Dutch territory in East Asia.

In 1960, Indonesia nationalized Dutch economic interests, broke diplomatic ties and mobilized the nonalignment movement against the Netherlands. President Sukarno of Indonesia ordered complete mobilization and repeatedly threatened to invade New Guinea. Small naval skirmishes took place in waters off New Guinea beginning in January 1962. In the Netherlands, opposition to the official government position began to increase and both the Dutch business world and left-wing members of parliament hoped to see Luns removed from the foreign ministry, arguinig that he obstructed a peaceful resolution of the New Guinea dispute. However, as Luns's negotiating tactics reflected unanimous cabinet policy, the prime minister did not bow to these pressures to fire Luns.

What brought the dispute to resolution, apart from the threat of further escalation, was the decision of the Kennedy administration to support Indonesian claims. American negotiators told the Dutch that the United States would not come to the defense of the Netherlands in case of war with Indonesia; Indonesia was then awarded control over New Guinea on its terms.

At the last moment, Luns tried to save the situation by proposing a plan to transfer New Guinea to the United Nations, which would hold it as a trusteeship until the Papuans were ready for self-determination. For the Netherlands, UN control would have blocked a possible transfer of New Guinea to Indonesia. The plan, however, was voted down at the General Assembly and quickly shelved. The transfer to Indonesia was expeditiously completed after the failure of the Dutch plan at the UN.

The New Guinea crisis hurt Luns and the Netherlands. The Dutch government refused to acknowledge that it could not defend either ethically or politically its claims on New Guinea in the long run. Its emotional attachment obstructed a rational, balanced course of action which would have guaranteed a better future for the Papuans. The conflict took the lives of Dutch soldiers, sacrificed the livelihood of Dutch citizens in Indonesia, and consumed inordinate amounts of time and attention throughout the Dutch foreign affairs establishment.

In interviews years later, Luns claimed that the Netherlands did not lose much by giving up New Guinea, and he is right. However, for years, the Dutch government fought tooth and nail against Indonesian plans for New Guinea. The issue of how to keep Indonesia away from New Guinea dominated foreign policy from 1949 until 1962. In retrospect, Luns claimed that his failure in the New Guinea dispute was of no national importance and that the Netherlands lost a battle for the principle of self-determination. But this battle for a moral principle preoccupied Luns and his government for close to twelve years. More embarrassing yet, as soon as the Netherlands withdrew from its last East Asian territory, all interest in the Papuans disappeared. New Guinea was forgotten and never mentioned again, as if Luns and his countrymen tried to forget everything by pretending nothing had ever happened. Two years later, in 1964, Luns visited Indonesia, establishing relatively cordial relations between the two countries.

Although the New Guinea issue constituted a black page in Dutch foreign relations, Luns's domestic standing was not irreparably hurt by it. Instead, criticism of his foreign policy only began to mount toward the late 1960s as social groups and political parties on the left increasingly questioned his conduct of foreign policy. The Vietnam War galvanized younger voters and turned foreign policy into an intensely political issue. Many younger observers complained about the lack of democratic oversight in foreign affairs and of Luns's unabashedly pro-American, Atlanticist orientation. Luns also alienated many Catholic voters, among his strongest supporters, because he opposed publicly liberalization measures introduced by the Vatican. With his standing in the Netherlands deteriorating and having to fight off ever more articulate opponents, Luns was relieved to move to NATO in 1971. Fortunately for Luns, his reputation in the foreign press was still very high. Commenting on his appointment as NATO secretary general, the *New York Times* concluded that Luns exerted an influence far out of proportion to the size and strength of his country. He served as NATO secretary general until 1983.

Ironically, Luns's departure to Brussels and NATO did not mean an end to political controversies at home. In fact, in this second career, Luns suffered from a sharp decline in popularity, and his influence on politics waned. Events partially beyond his control contributed to this loss of influence and standing in the Netherlands and world affairs. But it was also his personal behavior and opinions that undermined his lustrous career.

Among the events beyond Luns's control was the victory of the Dutch Labor Party in the 1973 elections. In the Labor Party, left-wing politicians exerted considerable influence and labeled Luns an archconservative, Cold War leftover who was out of touch with new trends in world affairs. The left's dislike of Luns took on extreme forms in 1974 when students nearly attacked him physically on the street. He had given a public lecture at the faculty of economics at the University of Rotterdam and was able to escape unharmed only because of a large bevy of police officers.

Luns's relations with Dutch governments, however, did not improve after the reelection of conservative-led cabinets. Throughout the 1970s and early 1980s, the once popular foreign minister was perceived by many members of parliament and voters as arrogant, childish and out of tune with the new spirit of détente and disarmament. Luns never hesitated to counter his critics, although his verbal combativeness only added to the disenchantment of many of his compatriots with the Dutch secretary general of NATO.

The 1979 NATO decision to deploy 108 Pershing II and 464 cruise missiles in Western Europe brought the question of NATO's very existence to a boil in the Netherlands, especially since 48 missiles had been designated for deployment on Dutch soil. In fact, many citizens in the Netherlands, as well as Belgium, Britain and Germany, feared getting caught in a "limited" nuclear skirmish between the Soviet Union and the Americans. Churches, left-wing parties and citizens' groups organized themselves to put pressure on national governments to renege on their agreement to accept the deployment of these missiles. In the Netherlands, churches were at the forefront of the issue, helping significantly to found the peace movement. With churches at the forefront against official NATO policy, the Christian Democratic Party, successor to the Catholic Party, to which Luns had belonged, was itself severely divided on the question. Many party members were active in the peace movement, and the party leadership hesitated to make a firm commitment to move forward with the missiles' deployment. The Dutch government therefore postponed a final decision about stationing the missiles on Dutch soil until 1984, finally acquiescing in 1985. (In the event, upon the conclusion of an intermediate nuclear forces treaty between the Soviets and the United States, the missiles were not deployed on Dutch soil.)

During this whole period, Luns was unrelenting in his criticism of Dutch government coalitions, displaying a total lack of understanding of the profound electoral dilemmas faced by the Christian Democratic Party. He castigated and reprimanded the Dutch government for underestimating the Soviet threat, for misunderstanding the valuable contribution of medium-range nuclear missiles for NATO's defense strategy and for yielding to the pressure tactics of uninformed citizens and groups.

However, even those favoring the missiles' deployment found his hectoring unwarranted and misplaced—precisely because it confirmed in the eyes of the peace movement the deepest suspicions about NATO and the United States. Peace movement leaders branded Luns a militaristic leader who would willingly sacrifice Western civilization for the sake of deterring the Soviet Union. Not only were members of the peace movement and the Christian Democratic Party disenchanted with Luns, other European member states of NATO also felt that Luns was the wrong man to deal tactfully with the legitimate questions and powerful message of the peace movement. His doctrinaire anti-Soviet views only reinforced anti-NATO views in the opposition. Certainly, by the late 1970s, European leaders of NATO believed that Luns should resign to make room for a younger, more sophisticated secretary general who understood the philosophical and emotional reaction of many voters against the concept of "limited" nuclear warfare.

But NATO's dilemma during this period was that Luns liked his job and European governments had no good pretext for forcibly removing him. Many subtle hints and outright pleas for his voluntary retirement did not convince Luns to exit gracefully despite his advanced age. Finally, he did leave the NATO post in 1983 after having overstayed his welcome for close to five years. Not surprisingly, he and his wife remained in Brussels, feeling more at home in Belgium than in their native country. His years at NATO clearly minimized his considerable achievements as Dutch minister of foreign affairs. All in all, while Luns was an important minister of foreign affairs in the Netherlands, he proved to be a second-rate chief executive of the Western defense alliance.

BIBLIOGRAPHY

Akkermans, Hans. *Eigenwijs vredesbeleid: Vredesbeweging and veiligheidsbeleid in Nederlands*. Amsterdam: SUA, 1983.

Eichenberg, Richard C. "The Myth of Hollanditis," *International Security* 8: 143–59 (1988).

Lijphart, Arend. *The Trauma of Decolonization: The Dutch and West New Guinea*. New Haven, Conn.: Yale University Press, 1966.

Rochon, Thomas R. *Mobilizing for Peace: The Antinuclear Movements in Western Europe*. Princeton, N.J.: Princeton University Press, 1988.

Silj, A. *European Political Puzzle: A Study of the Fouchet Negotiations and the 1963 Veto*. Cambridge: Harvard University Press, 1967.

Steenhorst, René. *Joseph Luns*. Amsterdam: Teleboek, 1985.

Voorhoeve, Joris J. C. *Peace, Profits and Principles: A Study of Dutch Foreign Policy.* The Hague: Martinus Nijhoff, 1979.

Wels, C. B. *Aloofness and Neutrality: Studies on Dutch Foreign Relations and Policy-making Institutions*. Utrecht: H & S, 1982.

PAULETTE KURZER

M

HAROLD MACMILLAN (1894–1986) was prime minister of Britain from January 1957 to October 1963, bringing the Conservative Party from the depths of the Suez War fiasco to the heights of the smashing 1959 general election victory that raised doubts about whether the Labour Party would ever again control the British government.

Macmillan's family operated the famous publishing firm founded by his grandfather and carrying the family name. In his early life, the most significant influence was his American-born mother, who had great expectations for him and his older brother Daniel. Macmillan followed Daniel to Eton and Oxford, never graduating from the latter, and then enlisted in the army. As a Grenadier Guards officer in World War I, he was wounded three times; his final injuries forced his return to Britain for a three-year convalescence. This wartime experience had a profound, lifelong impact on him.

After recuperating, he returned to the service and was posted to Canada as aide to the duke of Devonshire, then governor-general. There Macmillan met the duke's daughter, the Lady Dorothy Cavendish, whom he married in 1920. Their marriage brought Macmillan into the higher ranks of the aristocracy and concluded his military career.

After a brief stint in the family publishing house, he was elected to the House of Commons from Stockton-on-Tees, a district in the north of England that he had narrowly lost in 1923. The poverty of his constituency, which he represented until 1945 except for two years following a 1929 election defeat, complemented by his wartime service with working-class soldiers, gave Macmillan a lifelong commitment to the disadvantaged.

Although hampered by a weak speaking style that he struggled to overcome, Macmillan criticized much of British government policy in the interwar period. Moreover, his criticism was not restricted to speeches. Beginning in 1927, he was either author or coauthor of various pamphlets and books that advocated a progressive, almost socialist orientation for British government. The most important of these was his 1938 book, *The Middle Way*. The mainstream of the

Conservative Party, of course, found Macmillan's proposals disturbing. Not trusting him, they regarded him as not just the typical ineffective backbencher, not just a member of the party's lowest tier, but worse, a maverick.

Macmillan's views on defense policy during this period also became controversial, much like Winston Churchill's. Although he would differ with Churchill on independence for India and the abdication of Edward VIII, as the 1930s proceeded Macmillan joined Churchill as an outspoken critic of the Conservative government's defense policy. Both men found the responses of Conservative prime ministers Stanley Baldwin and Neville Chamberlain to the military buildup of Nazi Germany to be insufficient.

Never part of the inner circle that met frequently with Churchill, Macmillan was nonetheless remembered when Churchill returned to cabinet office. Soon after Churchill became prime minister in May 1940, he sent Macmillan to the Ministry of Supply as parliamentary secretary (junior minister).

Insignificant then, this was the first step in a long climb to the top of British politics. Under three supply ministers, Macmillan proved to be an indefatigable administrator before leaving in 1942 to become under secretary at the Colonial Office, where he was also parliamentary spokesman for the colonies. Then in late 1942, he was named minister resident at Allied headquarters in Algiers. This proved to be a crucial step in his journey to the top of British politics. Close observers, whether American such as Robert Murphy, or British such as Richard Crossman, concur that his performance in North Africa was brilliant. Although the locale was clearly an American sphere of primacy, Macmillan's influence was substantial, extending well beyond the strong friendship he developed with the American commander, General Dwight D. Eisenhower.

For example, Macmillan's fluent French was invaluable in mediating the rivalry between Henri Giraud and Charles de Gaulle as they competed to be recognized head of the Free French forces. Of these two generals, President Franklin Roosevelt preferred Giraud, as Churchill also often did. Macmillan, assigned the task of getting the two Frenchmen to work together, recognized de Gaulle's superior political skills and greater support among his countrymen and eventually persuaded Allied leaders to endorse de Gaulle.

During this period, Macmillan began to demonstrate a number of unexpected qualities: a buoyancy that inspired those with whom he worked and a willingness to take risks, whether by ignoring an order that he considered unwise or by taking bold initiatives when lacking directives from above. Yet, all the while he gave credit for any successes to his American colleagues.

In November 1943, Macmillan was given the additional responsibilities of United Kingdom high commissioner in Italy, and he moved his operations to Naples. The next month he was appointed resident commissioner for the central Mediterranean, and he took an active part in persuading Italy to surrender and then in creating a new Italian government. During this period, his associates were predicting, at least in their diaries, a future prime ministership for him.

In these multiple roles, Macmillan's powers were vast, although temporary.

He was not only instrumental in resolving key matters in Italy, but his responsibilities extended to crises in Yugoslavia, Lebanon, Syria and Greece. In November 1944, he was appointed head of the Allied Commission in Italy. This civilian organization replaced the military Allied Control Commission that he had often criticized. Then as German forces withdrew from Greece and civil war ensued there, Macmillan went to Athens, where he mediated among the former Resistance groups, managing to achieve a cease-fire. The new Greek government was structured as Macmillan proposed, with Churchill initially opposed.

At the end of World War II, Macmillan had a remarkable record but one that was not readily visible to the public. He had proven to be an effective, innovative administrator, exercising powers more broadly than he probably ever would again. His leadership was not restricted to the hypotheticals proposed by a backbench outsider, but had been tested in practice. And his numerous achievements were often accomplished against the advice of others. He was deliberately self-effacing, giving credit to associates. Nonetheless, those close to him recognized the crucial impact of his efforts.

In the first six months after the war, Macmillan's career resembled a roller-coaster ride: Appointed to the cabinet as secretary for air, he lost his Stockton seat in the July general election, but was then returned to the House of Commons from Bromley in Kent with a comfortable November by-election victory.

Now a member of the shadow cabinet, Macmillan became the Conservative spokesman on industrial policy. In that role, he criticized Labour Party efforts to assert greater government control over economic and social matters. These Labour policies were similar to those that he had advocated in the 1930s, but now he attacked them as being unrealistic, inefficient and ineffective. At the same time, he actively participated in drafting his own party's Industrial Charter, part of the Conservative program to project a new image after the crushing electoral defeat of 1945.

A Conservative victory in the October 1951 election returned Churchill to power. Despite his desire for a higher post, Macmillan was named minister of housing, directed by the party manifesto to build 300,000 new houses a year, a figure then deemed unattainable. For an aspiring leader, these prospects were dismal. Assuming his new post, Macmillan knew nothing about housing, his top civil servant was inept, and the economic situation was worse than his party had claimed in the campaign. Overall government policy concentrated on restraining government spending. Nonetheless, Churchill gave housing high priority, feeding it resources while starving other programs. Bolstered by this and the recruitment of new key aides, as well as through his own cunning, tact, flamboyance and determination, Macmillan surpassed the 300,000 goal in 1953.

This record, despite doubts about his often stiff mannerisms, brought Macmillan to his party's front ranks. Whereas the audience for his wartime efforts had been small, now it was nationwide. Three years at Housing were followed by six months as minister of defense. Anthony Eden then replaced Churchill as prime minister and made Macmillan foreign secretary. This post, one he cherished, was in fact his greatest disappointment. Eden, thrice foreign secretary with over a dozen years there, dominated foreign policy. Macmillan's role was hollow, reducing him essentially to a figurehead. But he did address a few notable issues: the Baghdad Pact, Cyprus, the movement toward Western European unity and the defections of the spies Guy Burgess and Donald Maclean.

Despite the limitations upon him in the Foreign Office, Macmillan was disappointed when, after only nine months, he was appointed chancellor of the Exchequer (finance minister). There he was faced with one of the periodic economic crises that afflicted Britain throughout the 20th century. His first budget message was well received, despite an unusual innovation, the premium bond, a modified lottery. Free of Eden's constant oversight, Macmillan exhibited strong leadership at the Treasury.

But it was not those duties for which he would be remembered in this period. To the contrary, his principal role was as a member of the inner circle that planned the Suez War. He shared with Eden the view that the seizure of the Suez Canal by Gamal Abdel Nasser of Egypt was a prelude to Nasser's encroachment on other territories throughout the Middle East, similar to what Adolf Hitler had done in Europe in the 1930s.

Not only was Macmillan the leading hawk on Suez, he assured Eden that the United States would stand by Britain if it took military action against Nasser, confirming this assessment through personal meetings with President Eisenhower and the American secretary of state, John Foster Dulles. Although Macmillan was one of the few British officials that worked well with Dulles, the chancellor misread both Americans on the Suez issue.

When the Suez War began in late October 1956, Macmillan was a principal defender of British aggression. But after the United States brought pressure on the British pound and British access to oil supplies—sunken ships in the Suez Canal cut off customary routes—Macmillan was the first in Eden's inner cabinet to advocate British withdrawal from Egypt. He never backed off from his support for Eden's attempt to overthrow Nasser, but when the attempt was clearly failing, Macmillan moved quickly to endorse removal of British forces. As chancellor of the Exchequer, he was in the best position to realize the vulnerability of the British economy to American threats.

While Eden had always been an excellent second in command, he was a failure as prime minister. Macmillan, however, was the opposite. Arguably, his service under Eden was the least effective of his numerous terms in public office. But as prime minister, he was soon labeled ''Supermac.''

Upon succeeding Eden as prime minister, Macmillan's prospects were bleak. The Suez venture was revealing, for it demonstrated the dependency of Britain on American backing. Given the national despondency over Suez and a shaky economy, Macmillan's tenure as prime minister did not look likely to be lengthy or auspicious. Had the Tories erred in not picking his rival, Richard A. Butler?

At 10 Downing Street, the British prime minister's residence, Macmillan promptly exuded confidence and enthusiasm, inspiring his colleagues and the public. He welcomed the challenge before him, as he had those of World War II. His cabinet retained several members from Eden's, including advocates and opponents of the Suez decision. He elevated or brought into leadership posts several young Conservatives, such as Edward Heath, Reginald Maulding and Iain Macleod, who would form the core of party leadership for the next two decades.

Macmillan proved to be a sound judge of personnel and was a superb chair of the cabinet. (A notable exception was his purge of the cabinet in 1962, one of the few instances in which he panicked.) His experience, preparation and intellect exceeded those of his colleagues. But unlike some other prime ministers, he encouraged his cabinet to offer their views and weighed them carefully in his ultimate decisions.

During his term as prime minister, Macmillan's foreign policy rested upon three poles: the United States, the Commonwealth, which replaced the British Empire, and Europe. Immediately, he moved to restore the special relationship with the United States. This would be a theme of his tenure; moreover, he was better equipped than anyone to do this, building initially upon his acquaintance with Eisenhower, and later upon remote ties between his family and John F. Kennedy's. He also benefited from the latter's admiration for the British and his willingness to accept Macmillan as an elder adviser. With Anglo-American relations once again firm, Macmillan won American backing for economic aid to Britain, aid that was partially responsible for the atypical British economic prosperity of the late 1950s.

As during the war, Macmillan was acutely aware that Britain was the weaker partner in this special relationship, but he was confident that his nation could be the Greece to America's Rome. In that role, he sought to serve as a mediator between the Soviet Union and the United States, which he believed to be too rigid in its posture toward Moscow. In pursuing this goal, Macmillan labored incessantly to arrange a summit between the two superpowers. More than three years of personal diplomacy to this end was aborted on the eve of the 1960 Paris Conference when Nikita Khrushchev backed out upon Eisenhower's refusal to apologize for the flight of the American U–2 spy plane that the Soviets had shot down over their territory. Despite this setback, Macmillan's endeavors were instrumental in achieving the first nuclear test ban treaty and what eventually became Soviet-American détente.

The Commonwealth was another focus of his foreign policy. On his 1958 world tour he became the first prime minister to visit India, Pakistan, Ceylon (Sri Lanka), Australia and New Zealand. The trip was a great public relations success, however unexpected and incongruous, given the ordinarily stiff Edwardian figure of the prime minister, which was now exposed to various exotic native ceremonies, cuisine and costumes. But Macmillan was exhilarated by this journey.

However, his enthusiasm for Britain's multicultural ties did not blind Macmillan to demands for independence from throughout the former empire. Unlike Churchill, Macmillan sought to accommodate rather than be compelled to grant independence. In 1960, speaking to the parliament of South Africa, the site of European imperialism's worst excesses, he summarized his approach in one phrase, "a wind of change sweeping across Africa." This attitude encompassed those British territories outside Africa, as well. This policy and the actions he took to implement it proved binding on his successors.

It was with the third foreign policy pole, Europe, that Macmillan was least effective. He was an early advocate of European unity, but like Churchill he was ambivalent and imprecise about Britain's place in that scheme. He chose to stand aside when the Treaty of Rome, creating the Common Market, was signed soon after he came to office. To join would weaken British links to America and the Commonwealth, be contrary to British public opinion and run counter to centuries of British sentiment that Britons were a community distinct from the continent.

There was also doubt about whether the Common Market would succeed, a not unlikely suspicion given the long history of animosity between the original six signatories. But by the turn of the decade, the economies of the six were booming while Britain's briefly robust one began to sag. Macmillan reversed course, applying for Common Market membership in 1961. Ironically, France's de Gaulle, who might never have become president of France without Macmillan's sponsorship in World War II, vetoed Britain's application in 1963.

While Macmillan's most visible achievements were in foreign policy, he pursued a delicate balance between that and domestic issues. To ease pressure on the budget, he cut defense costs by ending conscription and stressing the nuclear option, which was not without complications. Conservative leaders, especially Macmillan, were said to have lost the opportunity to put the British economy on a sound basis in the 1950s. That ignores the pressures from an electorate demanding an end to the deprivations of the interwar period, World War II, and to continued rationing of consumer products. No other prime minister solved Britain's economic woes.

Macmillan's last year at Number 10 was marked by controversy: the John Profumo scandal, the Vassall case and the defection of Guy Burgess to the Soviet Union. Events seemed beyond Macmillan's control as pressure mounted for him to step aside. Prostate surgery brought his resignation that year. He retired from the Commons in 1964.

Macmillan's personality was complex, even contradictory. Devoutly religious, he was also fatalistic. Several times he was on the verge of leaving public life. He endured frequent spells of depression, but overcame an innate shyness to demonstrate, as prime minister, a theatrical debating style that devastated his foes. As Macmillan noted, his rise to Number 10 was fortuitous: If Hitler had not come to power, Churchill would not have been prime minister, and Macmillan would likely have left the House of Commons or remained on its backbenches.

His last months in office were the nadir of his leadership, but he later received high marks for his record. He presided over Britain's strongest economic period after 1945, and laid out the policies that granted independence to Britain's remaining colonies while initiating a thaw of rigid Cold War attitudes. Macmillan ranks with Clement Attlee and Margaret Thatcher as the most able prime ministers of the postwar era; his was clearly one of the brightest stars in the British political firmament during this period.

BIBLIOGRAPHY

Works by Macmillan:

The Middle Way. London: Macmillan, 1938.

Autobiography: (London: Macmillan) Vol. 1, *Winds of Change 1914–1939*, 1966; Vol. 2, *The Blast of War 1939–45*, 1967; Vol. 3, *Tides of Fortune 1945–55*, 1969; Vol. 4, *Riding the Storm 1956–59*, 1971; Vol. 5, *Pointing the Way, 1959–1961*, 1972; Vol. 6, *At the End of the Day 1961–1963,* 1973.

The Past Masters: Politics and Politicians. London: Macmillan, 1975.

War Diaries: Politics and War in the Mediterranean, January 1943—May 1945. London: Macmillan, 1984.

Other Works:

Fisher, Nigel. *Harold Macmillan: A Biography.* New York: St. Martin's, 1982.

Horne, Alistair. *Harold Macmillan*, 2 vols. New York: Viking, 1989.

Sampson, Anthony. *Macmillan: A Study in Ambiguity.* London: Allen Lane, 1967.

THOMAS P. WOLF

GEORGES MARCHAIS (1920–), as secretary general of the French Communist Party (Parti Communiste Français, PCF), has played an important role in French political development ever since the inception of the Fifth Republic in 1958. His political career includes two very distinct phases. In the 1970s, he led the most powerful opposition to post–de Gaulle conservative governments. During this period, Marchais spearheaded an effort to renovate and to adapt the PCF to developments in French society. In the 1980s, while France was governed by the Socialist François Mitterrand, Marchais emerged as the increasingly controversial leader of a declining party which had lost nearly two-thirds of its voters and had become, in a span of only ten years, an almost marginal political force in the country.

Georges Marchais was born on June 7, 1920, to a working-class family in Normandy, a conservative region of northwest France. His father died when Georges was ten. He received a religious upbringing from his mother, a practicing Catholic. Marchais attended local public schools until the age of fifteen, when he left for Paris and became an apprentice in a small manufacturing company. He later worked as a skilled laborer in an aeronautics firm. At this point, he was not a union member nor, by his own admission, was he interested in politics. For Marchais, the social upheaval which surrounded the Popular Front government of the 1930s was not, as it was for thousands of other young workers, the impetus to political or trade union involvement.

Neither did the German occupation of France spur him to political engagement. Too young to be drafted, Marchais stayed in Paris at the beginning of the war and married in 1941. To this day, it is unclear why he left Paris in 1942 to work in Germany, although he has often been criticized for doing so. In any case, one thing is certain: Georges Marchais was not among the many Communists who fought the Nazi occupiers and thereby gained a personal stature independent of the party. For the rest of his political career, this would be a source of embarrassment. To reinforce his standing as a Communist leader, he would frequently invoke his humble origins and the fact that he was a ''real'' worker, but he could never claim to have been a part of either the Popular Front or the Resistance, the two great movements which assumed mythical status and became permanent historical reference points in French political life.

The exciting historical circumstances surrounding the Liberation inspired many Frenchmen to become involved in public life. Marchais, who had found a steady job at a company in suburban Paris, became a member of the Confédération Générale du Travail (General Workers' Confederation, CGT), a Communist-dominated union. One year later, he joined the PCF, which at that time enjoyed significant political power and prestige in France. With a membership of 800,000, the PCF held considerable sway over the union movement. In the November 1946 parliamentary elections, the Communists won 5.4 million votes (roughly 30 percent of the electorate) and held 182 National Assembly seats. Several Communist leaders, including the party's general secretary, Maurice Thorez, held cabinet posts between 1945 and 1947.

Marchais said that he joined the PCF to protest the eviction of Communist ministers from the coalition cabinet headed by the Socialist Ramadier. This event marked a critical moment in French political history. The two major leftist parties split and a period of isolation for the PCF began. This isolation was later accentuated by the rising importance of the Cold War and independence movements in Indochina and Algeria.

Georges Marchais thus had his first experiences as a union and political activist in an atmosphere full of tremendous social and political tension. His personal energy gained him attention in the PCF and in 1952, he was chosen to become a full-time official with the Paris regional steelworkers' union. From this point onward, he quickly rose in the party's ranks: He became an alternate member of the central committee in 1956 after being promoted to secretary of the South-Seine Federation (composed of local party organizations in the suburban areas south of Paris). Three years later, he became a permanent member of the central committee and an alternate member of the Politburo. At this point, he left his union activities to devote himself completely to party work. In 1961, he moved to the top of party hierarchy as a permanent member of the Politburo and party secretary, a key position in the organization.

Marchais owes his rapid rise in the party at least partially to the support of

Maurice Thorez. Thorez first noticed the young activist's work during meetings of the South-Seine Federation, where both were members. His experience as both a trade union and a political activist, as well as his origins as an ''authentic'' laborer also probably worked in Marchais's favor. During this difficult period punctuated by dissent and expulsions, however, a systematic rise in the party hierarchy, such as Marchais's, also required conformism and unquestioned loyalty to the party line.

Marchais's ascent occurred during a very difficult period in the French Communist Party's development. Khrushchev's denunciation of Stalin's crimes and the repression of the Hungarian uprising in 1956 disillusioned many activists and intellectuals, who ultimately chose to break with communism. Two years later, de Gaulle ushered in the Fifth Republic, striking another hard blow to the party. In the 1958 parliamentary elections, the PCF lost roughly one-third of its voters and more than two-thirds of its seats in the National Assembly.

Under these conditions, Georges Marchais's task as the person responsible for the party's administration and operations was especially hard: Despite repeated Gaullist victories, he had to inspire party activists with hope and dynamism. Marchais approached this challenge with perseverance and energy. As a reward for his efforts, he became the party's number two man when Maurice Thorez died in 1964. Marchais would have retained this post longer had not the new secretary general, Waldeck Rochet, left his position suddenly in 1970 due to serious illness. Marchais became assistant secretary general and subsequently became secretary general in June 1972 at the age of fifty-two. He had nearly unanimous Politburo support.

His promotion was well received in Moscow and in the Communist International, where Marchais was already well-known, having traveled extensively in socialist countries and meeting most communist party leaders between 1960 and 1972. In 1964, he led a PCF delegation to Moscow to ask its ''brother party'' for an explanation of Khrushchev's forced resignation. In November 1968, Marchais met with Brezhnev to express the French Communists' disapproval of Warsaw Pact intervention in Czechoslovakia.

In domestic politics, Marchais developed and implemented the Communists' new political strategy, which had been adopted at the seventeenth party congress in 1964, just a few months before Thorez died. The Communist Party proposed a stable political coalition between itself, the Socialists and other small parties on the Left, entailing not only electoral alliances but also unified policy programs. In the year he became PCF secretary general, Marchais and François Mitterrand, the Socialist leader, signed the ''Common Program of Government,'' which marked an historic turning point in French politics. The product of long negotiations, this document symbolized the reconciliation of the two major left-leaning parties and presented voters with a coherent political platform. The Common Program contained a number of radical reform proposals, including government decentralization and nationalization of the country's largest companies. For Communists, the program aimed to establish "advanced democracy," that would be the first step toward socialism.

Under Marchais's leadership, the PCF undeniably underwent a renewal both in terms of doctrine and party operations. The party abandoned the old Leninist concept of "proletarian dictatorship," instead defining a "democratic and peaceful path" to a "socialism in French colors," all the while respecting fundamental French liberal traditions. Both the "events" of May–June 1968 and the conflicts that followed encouraged the revision of Marxism in this French context. Communist intellectuals went to work analyzing new social trends; the party's journals and publishing house produced a number of studies that revisited issues of capitalism, economic crisis, social classes and movements.

At the same time, the PCF distanced itself from the Soviet Union. The party issued increasingly pointed criticisms of Brezhnev's policy, and Marchais suspended all direct contact with the Soviet leader between 1974 and 1980. He met instead with Enrico Berlinguer and Santiago Carrillo, leaders of the Italian and Spanish Communist parties respectively, in Madrid in 1977. This initiative, which the Soviet party loudly rejected, aimed to define the outlines of "Eurocommunism" as distinct from the Soviet model.

The political climate of the 1970s was generally favorable for the left in France. The PCF enjoyed relative success in both national and local elections and its leader became better-known among the populace. Marchais's humble origins, populism, ultrapatriotism and inexhaustible energy were much appreciated as they surfaced in the political debates and "shows" that amounted to media-sponsored cockfights. Marchais won a seat in the National Assembly in 1973 and headed the PCF list for the 1979 European Parliament elections. He was also the party's candidate for president in 1981.

His presidential candidacy marked simultaneously the apex of Marchais's political career and the beginning of a much less glamorous period punctuated by a series of failures that led the PCF into its spectacular decline. In less than ten years, the party lost more than half its voters. Today, after the collapse of communism in Eastern Europe, the PCF, founded in 1920, sees its very existence questioned. Marchais himself certainly is not the singular cause of this disaster, which has its origins in broader historical and social trends. Still, Marchais's management of the PCF surely contributed to the beginnings of its demise and made it impossible for the party to reform and update itself as the Italian Communists were able to do.

Marchais forced a number of intemperate changes in the party's strategy. On the eve of the 1978 parliamentary elections, for example, Marchais broke with the Socialists, mercilessly attacking his former allies. Voters who in 1981 supported the Socialist Mitterrand from the first round in order to ensure a victory of the left had not taken easily to the PCF's abrupt about-face three years earlier. The party received only 20.7 percent of the vote in the 1978 contest; Marchais won 15.5 percent in his 1981 presidential bid. Marchais then blandly endorsed Mitterrand for the second round of the 1981 race.

After three years of denouncing the Socialists' "turn to the right," but upon Mitterrand's victory in 1981, the PCF leadership decided to accept the offer of cabinet positions. The party gave nearly unconditional support to its own ministers but at the same time criticized the government's austerity policies. This gave the public an impression of incoherence and indecision on the part of the PCF. When the party decided to pull out of the Socialist cabinet in 1984, it was already too late: Having stood by as the Socialists pursued two years of austerity, the PCF lost the support of that part of the electorate hit hardest by unemployment and salary freezes.

The party's sudden change in its policies toward socialist countries—as radical as its domestic policy reversals—also alienated activists and PCF voters. Beginning in 1978, Marchais and the party leadership launched a rapid reconciliation with socialist leaders which was enthusiastically endorsed at the party's twenty-third congress in 1979. Having visited Nicaragua and met with Fidel Castro, Marchais was in Moscow in 1980 when the Red Army invaded Afghanistan. He had gone to sign a mutual declaration with the Soviet Communist Party which, while recognizing the PCF's reservations with respect to some aspects of Soviet power, withheld criticism of Soviet foreign policy. The French public was particularly shocked to hear the PCF leader, after a long meeting with Brezhnev, justify Soviet intervention in Afghanistan on live television from Moscow.

During the same period, the PCF remained relatively complacent in reaction to General Jaruzelski's imposition of martial law in Poland. French Communists at first hailed Mikhail Gorbachev's reform efforts in the Soviet Union, but they became increasingly critical; the PCF ultimately considered his failure to be the consequence of his having abandoned socialist principles. These ill-conceived policy positions demonstrated that the PCF was out of touch with the Eastern European situation during this time and was ill prepared for the revolutions looming on the horizon.

Moreover, Marchais had instituted a number of changes in the party's political strategy without consulting or even informing PCF activists. Each of his decisions provoked a wave of protest leading to the formation of various dissident groups within the party. A number of Communist mayors also initiated their own battles with the party leadership. Marchais was only able to retain his position by vigorously applying the principles and practice of "democratic centralism" and by maintaining the support of party regulars heading PCF regional federations.

Within the space of a few years, Marchais had lost much of his popular, media-based support. He conveyed the image of a stubborn and unpredictable leader, clutching on to his position despite his advanced age, spouting a rhetoric rendered completely devoid of meaning by communism's worldwide collapse. Finally, recognizing his loss of popularity, he decided neither to run for president in 1988 nor to head the PCF list in the 1989 European elections. Finally, in 1994, he stepped down from his position as general secretary.

As a political leader, Georges Marchais is among neither the theoreticians, the revolutionaries nor the builders of "new societies." He could easily have been one of the "organization men," an ordinary manager who retires quietly and in peace. By virtue of an historical irony, communism's demise conjures up parallels between Marchais's political destiny and that of a ship's captain, tragically alone on a sinking vessel.

BIBLIOGRAPHY

Work by Marchais:

Le Défi démocratique. Paris: Grasset, 1973.

Other Works:

Harris, André, and Alain De Sedouy. *Voyage à l'intérieur du parti communiste*. Paris: Editions du Seuil, 1974.

Robrieux, Philippe. *Histoire intérieure du parti communiste*, 5 vols. Paris: Fayard, 1980.

Tandler, Nicolas. *L'Impossible Biographie de Georges Marchais*. Paris: Albatros, 1980.

JEAN-YVES NEVERS
Trans. by Lynne Louise Bernier

WILFRIED MARTENS (1936–) led nine governmental coalitions and was prime minister of Belgium longer than anyone else in this century. During his time in office, he managed a crucial period in constitutional change that transformed Belgium from a unitary to a federal state. He also led a shift in Belgian economic policy and was an ardent supporter of a unified Europe, leading to talk of him as a possible candidate for the presidency of the Commission of the European Community. And he addressed the emotionally intense issue of immigration and minorities in Belgium.

Wilfried Martens was born in 1936 in a rural community in East Flanders. His parents were small farmers who did not own their land, and his father died when Martens was seven. Martens was often ill and at the age of fourteen contracted rheumatic fever, which caused heart damage eventually requiring surgery in 1983. He was identified early on as an exceptional student and was encouraged to continue his education, first at a Catholic preparatory school and then at the Catholic University of Louvain (Flemish).

The extension of Martens's studies had two important effects on him: First, in preparatory school, he decided to replace his East Flanders dialect with standard Dutch, demonstrating his identification with the Flemish movement and affirming his attachment to the values of a broader Flemish/Dutch culture. Second, while at the Catholic University of Louvain, Martens became active in Catholic and Flemish student organizations and made many contacts in Catholic-Flemish intellectual and political circles.

Martens began to draw public attention in 1957 when, as president of the Flemish Youth Committee, he organized a march to protest the lack of a Flemish presence in the 1958 Brussels world exposition, and subsequently he was arrested while protesting the opening of the exposition. Then in 1961 and 1962 he organized marches on Brussels in support of federalism for Belgium. These demonstrations caused the French-language press to label him an extremist. Thus Martens began his political career in the streets and in public squares and meeting halls—outside the established political parties. From his student days through the completion of a law degree in 1960 and into the beginning of a legal practice in Ghent, the main organizational focus of Martens's political activities was the Flemish National Movement.

Martens began to focus on party politics in 1964. In many ways it would have been logical for him to join the Volksunie, the Flemish nationalist party, especially since he had served on the executive board of the Flemish National Movement. Instead, in 1965, Martens joined the Christelijke Volkspartij (CVP), the Christian democratic party that was dominant in Flanders and the strongest party in Belgium. He developed many contacts with CVP elites and ran, unsuccessfully, as a CVP candidate for parliament.

In 1965 he also received a staff position with Pierre Harmel, then presiding as prime minister over a Christian Democratic–Socialist coalition government. From this point on, Martens began a rapid rise in the party. He held additional staff positions in CVP-led coalitions, was twice elected president of the CVP youth organization (1967 and 1969), was elected president of the CVP (1972) and in 1974 was first elected to parliament.

As party president Martens organized the CVP's 1974 electoral campaign, producing the party's greatest success since 1958. This ''presidential''-style campaign focused on Leo Tindemans as the party leader. The result was two successive Tindemans-led government coalitions and a period of close cooperation between Tindemans and Martens.

This cooperation broke down, however, during the second Tindemans government. Although the conflict between the two men was complex, perhaps the most important dispute between them was over the so-called Egmont Pact, a six-party agreement that Tindemans had negotiated as a major step toward Belgian federalism. As sharp differences of opinion concerning the Egmont Pact arose within the CVP, personal tensions developed between Tindemans and Martens. Tindemans's unexpected and, for many, perplexing resignation as prime minister in 1978 opened the door for Martens to become prime minister in the new government formed in 1979.

Between 1979 and 1991 Belgium had ten coalition governments. Martens was prime minister in nine of them. (The only one he did not lead was a very short-lived Christian Democratic–Socialist coalition in 1981.) Martens's first four coalitions between 1979 and 1981 represented efforts at Christian Democratic–Socialist cooperation with brief participation in 1979 (Martens I) by the Francophone Democratic Front (Front Démocratique des Francophones—the dominant party in Brussels) and by the Liberals in 1980 (Martens III). Three coalitions with the Liberals (Martens V–VII) covered most of the period from 1981 to 1988. The final phase of Martens's leadership came when the CVP returned to a coalition with the Socialists, first in association with the Volksunie

(Martens VIII) in 1988 and then, as the broader coalition fell apart, with the Socialists alone (Martens IX) in 1991.

Negotiations to form the Martens VIII government took nearly six months, from the December 1987 elections to May 1988. Relative gains by the Socialists in these elections and relative losses by the CVP created pressure to include Socialists in the new government. But Martens had declared that he would not be prime minister in a government with Socialists. He also suggested that for personal reasons (among other things, the illness of a family member), he wished to scale back his political activities. The negotiations to form a new coalition were therefore largely conducted by Jean-Luc Dehaene, who had been Martens's associate since the latter's CVP youth days and had served in previous Martens governments.

After discussions with party leaders and with the king, however, Martens agreed to accept the prime ministry. Yet the Martens VIII coalition came apart in September 1991 when the Volksunie members of the government resigned in a clash over a division of economic resources between Wallonia and Flanders. The government lived on briefly as a Christian Democratic–Socialist coalition (Martens IX) which lacked the two-thirds majority needed to pass important pending legislation. Meanwhile, elections in November 1991 produced losses for the CVP, the Socialists, the Liberals and the Volksunie, while environmental parties and the right-wing Flemish Party gained. In 1992, Dehaene managed to form a new coalition government. Martens was not a member of it, having "retired" to the Belgian Senate.

Wilfried Martens played a major role in restructuring the Belgian state. His career exemplifies the shift from seeing federalism as a threat to seeing federalism as a solution. He moved from being viewed as an "extremist" agitator for Flemish demands to a manager of constitutional change. And he brought his party along from serious hesitation about federalism to an enactment of federalist reforms.

In Belgium, federalism became a solution to a structural problem. The country had been created as a unitary state composed of two distinct cultural and linguistic communities. Politics and society were dominated by French speakers who saw Flemish demands for cultural recognition and political equality as a threat to the unity of the state and as demonstrating questionable loyalty. Moreover, the German occupation during both world wars tried to use the Flemish movement for its own purposes.

After World War II, the Flemish region became economically and demographically stronger than Wallonia, where the coal and steel industries had begun to decline. Correcting the political imbalance between the two regions, meeting long-standing Flemish demands and recognizing the new economic status of Flanders all required substantial change in the Belgian system. In both regions, individuals increasingly proposed federalist solutions to these problems.

A number of factors, however, complicated the adoption of federalism in Belgium. First, a federal structure in Belgium must take into account both the existence of regions in a geographic sense and communities in a cultural sense. Second, Brussels, the national capital, is a largely French-speaking city surrounded by Dutch-speaking Flanders. The growth of Brussels, fueled in part by its role as the center of European Community institutions, has complex implications for linguistic boundaries. Third, hard political decisions must be made about allocating national resources between a growing Flanders and a declining Wallonia. Fourth, the regions have different dominant political parties: the CVP in Flanders, the Socialists in Wallonia and the Francophone Democratic Front in Brussels. Finally, complex procedures for amending the Belgian constitution require that parliament pass a declaration of intention to amend specific articles, that a new parliament be elected and that the new parliament then pass the amendment by two-thirds majority. Amendments therefore depend on both elections and coalition formations.

As early as 1958, Martens declared that the survival of the Flemish as a people necessitated self-government. In 1962 (when he was twenty-five) at a conference held by the Flemish National Movement, he outlined an extensive proposal for what he later called "unionist federalism." The language boundaries, he argued, should be strengthened to provide a regional base for the cultural communities. The Flemish and Walloon communities should have their own legislatures. The component states of such a federation would require cultural autonomy and some control over taxation. And Brussels would become a federal region, dependent on federal authority and limited in its territorial base. The CVP leadership responded coolly to this proposal, calling it impractical and a source of division within the Flemish community.

The evolution from the CVP's cool reception to Martens's early proposals to support for the major constitutional modifications of 1988 involved several changes in orientation. Historically the Flemish movement had emphasized cultural recognition, demanding that Dutch language and culture have equal status in Belgium with French. The first of Martens's proposals for unionist federalism reflects this orientation. Indeed, much relevant legislation of the 1960s instituted linguistic laws giving recognition to Flemish culture.

By the 1970s, nonetheless, Flemish leaders began to focus on the economic advantages to having greater regional autonomy. Consequently, their emphasis shifted from linguistic laws to broader economic and political concerns. The pragmatic basis for Flemish support of federalism thereby expanded. And while CVP leaders still expressed some reservations about federalism, at the very least they wanted to provide moderate alternatives to more radical proposals for federalism and autonomy than were being discussed.

In the 1970s, constitutional revisions led by the CVP took an important step forward, formally recognizing the existence of the cultural communities. These were given limited decision-making powers through cultural councils. Geographic regions were also recognized and given their own limited legislative powers. These constitutional amendments also required Flemish-French parity in the composition of the government.

Another major step forward toward federalism seemed about to occur in 1977 with the negotiation of the Egmont Pact under the leadership of Leo Tindemans. The agreement clearly articulated the idea of a state with three main levels of decision making: a central government, three communities (French- and Dutch-speaking communities, as well as the small German-speaking community) and three regions (Flanders, Wallonia and Brussels city). Tindemans's abrupt resignation from the prime ministry in 1978 came during the debate on legislation to implement this pact. At this point, Martens became the key player.

The first three Martens governments struggled to rework the Egmont Pact. In 1980, legislation was passed which more clearly established the decision-making institutions and powers of the regions and communities. Important questions about the status of Brussels remained unresolved, however, and debate continued about how much legislative power the regional bodies should have over education, the economy and taxation. There were also calls for a system of tax sharing to give the new institutions a stronger financial base. Nonetheless, Martens qualified the decisions of 1980 as substantial progress that established parliaments and executives for both Flanders and Wallonia.

After 1980, Martens felt pressed to shift the energies of his government from regionalization to the growing economic problems facing Belgium that plagued the Christian Democratic–Liberal coalitions of the 1980s. Subsequently, however, attention was forced back to the issue of federalism by the peculiar issue of Voeren/Fourons, a French-speaking municipality that had been shifted to the Dutch-speaking side of the language boundary in 1962. In Voeren/Fourons, the French-speaking mayor began to flout the law by mounting a media campaign to have his town returned to the Walloon region. In this, the mayor was supported by Walloon Socialists who saw the issue as a means to strengthen their political position.

As divisions over the issue arose within the governing coalition, the government resigned, setting the stage for the 1987 elections, the entry of the Socialists into the Martens VIII coalition and the constitutional revisions of 1988. In the end, the long negotiations to form the Martens VIII government provided an arena to resolve many issues left hanging in 1980. Regional governments gained control over education and expanded their powers into other arenas, such as infrastructure, and Brussels received a separate set of regional institutions. The portion of tax revenue going to the regional governments was increased, and other structures and procedures were established to deal with conflicts between levels of government, such as cooperation on economic issues. Shortly after this extraordinary breakthrough, however, the Martens VIII coalition fell apart in a dispute over the granting of government contracts and licenses that would have produced different levels of benefit for Flanders and Wallonia. At that point, the process of regionalization was still not complete, but Belgium had become a federal state.

The Belgian experience in creating a federal structure has been suggested by some as an example for other multiethnic states to follow. The establishment of decision-making structures based on cultural community and separate from structures based on territory is a particularly creative response to problems that seem intractable elsewhere. Martens played an important role in creating these structures—within his party, in interparty negotiations and within the government. The final result bears a strong resemblance to what he proposed in 1962, unquestionably a considerable achievement.

Yet success in instituting federalism in Belgium depended on a relative cultural homogeneity that existed at the beginning of the process and on a tradition of interparty negotiations to form government coalitions. Other multiethnic states do not commonly enjoy these favorable conditions. And even though 1988 saw a major breakthrough in federalism for Belgium, the collapse of Martens VIII over the allocation of economic benefits between the regions shows that Belgian leaders must still learn to make difficult decisions within the federal framework.

Federalism in Belgium clearly took place in the context of economic changes. The Belgian economy is characterized by strong external links and depends on foreign trade. Moreover, much Belgian economic activity is in the hands of multinational corporations. In the 1970s, the oil shock and world economic crisis hit Belgium with great force. Unemployment and inflation reached disturbingly high levels, and some multinationals shifted their investments out of Belgium. Labor unrest during this period also threatened the pattern of labor-management consultation that had developed during the 1960s.

Government efforts to restructure the economy and create new jobs added to growing budgetary deficits that became the focus of political contention in the 1970s and 1980s. Calls for wage moderation and limits on government spending stimulated new political tension. The declining economic base in Wallonia intensified the political problem. Labor unrest was stronger there and enjoyed clear expression through the Walloon Socialist Party, which dominated the region's politics. In economically stronger Flanders, on the other hand, economic neoliberalism was gaining support within the CVP. The Christian Democratic–Socialist coalitions of the 1970s and early 1980s struggled to find common ground bridging these differences.

Supported by elements in the CVP, Martens had been shifting his economic orientation. In 1969 he had drawn attention by calling for the formation of a progressive front. By 1981 the Martens V coalition with the Liberals moved toward a neo-liberal program in response to economic problems. Generally, fear of unemployment created a climate conducive to policy change, and the Liberals provided willing coalition partners to such a program.

Three times coalition governments received special powers from parliament to act on economic issues. The dramatic beginning was an 8.5 percent devaluation of the Belgian franc in February 1982, a decision made after consultation with the International Monetary Fund and Belgium's European Community partners. This devaluation was coupled with a temporary wage and price freeze. Various other steps followed, all aimed at building profits as a way of strengthening the economy. The system of indexing welfare benefits to the cost of living was modified, and limits on welfare benefits were introduced. Laws on labor contracts were also changed in ways that arguably strengthened the position of employers by creating new forms of contractual relations.

Opponents of these policies saw them as favoring profits over wages and saw actions taken during the same period to reorganize police powers as part of an antilabor approach. By 1985, however, Martens could argue that his policy shift had produced measurable improvements in the economy. Elections that year brought six additional parliamentary seats to the CVP. Yet by 1991 and the end of Martens's last government, Belgium was still faced with serious economic problems. Austerity measures and the structure of the social security system were still being debated, and the Belgian deficit as a percentage of GNP was the highest in the European Community.

How Belgium responds to its economic problems depends heavily on the development of the European Community. Martens played an active role in the EC in two ways. First, as a member of parliament and CVP leader he worked to promote cooperation among European Christian Democratic parties and to articulate positions that bring together the left and right wings of the Christian Democratic spectrum. In 1976 he was a cofounder of the European People's Party, the organization that groups together Christian Democrats in the European Parliament. He became president of the party in 1990.

Second, as prime minister Martens played a direct role in European Community politics. At first he appeared weak relative to other European heads of government. He did, however, obtain acceptance of the 1982 devaluation, and his stature in the organization grew. He also responded forcefully to British Prime Minister Margaret Thatcher's 1988 attack on European cooperation. For a time there was talk of making him president of the European Commission. However, Martens's prospects for a more prominent personal role in European institutions were weakened by the need to defend Brussels's position as the political center of Europe against French ambitions for Strasbourg.

Martens took an important first step in another policy area: the status of immigrants. As in other Western European states, Belgian immigrants have become the focus of highly emotional concerns. Racist appeals have gained power in the context of economic problems and areas of urban decline. To make things worse, immigrant policy must take into account the cultural differences of Belgium itself. In 1989 Martens selected Paula D'Hondt, a CVP senator and former government minister, to serve as royal commissioner for migrant policy. D'Hondt produced a massive study that provided reliable information on immigrants and outlined a set of policy proposals.

Here Martens's contribution has been to define the issues, for the election of 1991 suggests how far these issues were from being resolved by the end of his last coalition. In that election, the right-wing Flemish Party had emphasized anti-immigrant themes, and Belgian voters rewarded it by increasing the party's parliamentary seats from two to twelve. Leaders across the political spectrum in Belgium were deeply struck by these results. The D'Hondt report could provide a basis for action if this concern can be changed into a political consensus.

Wilfried Martens provided Belgium with an important continuity of leadership in a difficult time. The restructuring of the state that he contributed to is an impressive accomplishment for the country as a whole and for all those who worked on it. How Belgian federalism will function, however, remains interwoven with unresolved economic and social issues and with the evolution of Belgium's European context.

BIBLIOGRAPHY

Work by Martens:

Een gegeven woord. Tielt: Lanoo, 1987.

Other Works:

de Ridder, Hugo. *Omtrent Wilfried Martens.* Tielt: Lanoo, 1991.

Delmartino, Frank. ''Regionalization in Belgium,'' *European Journal of Political Research* 16 (1988).

Hooghe, Liesbet. *A Leap in the Dark: Nationalist Conflict and Federal Reform in Belgium.* Western Societies Program Occasional Paper Number 27. Ithaca, N.Y.: Cornell University, 1991.

Lagasse, Charles-Etienne. *Les Institutions politiques de la Belgique et de l'Europe.* Brussels: Editions Ciaco, 1990.

Peterson, Robert L., and Martine M. De Ridder. ''Government Formation as a Policy-making Arena,'' *Legislative Studies Quarterly* 11(4) (1986).

Witte, Els, Jan Craeybeckx, and Alain Meynen. *Politieke geschiedenis van Belgie van 1830 tot heden.* Antwerp: Standaard Uitgeverij, 1990.

ROBERT L. PETERSON

PIERRE MENDÈS-FRANCE (1907–1982) is considered certainly one of the greatest statesmen of the French Fourth Republic (1946–1958). As prime minister from June 7, 1954, to February 5, 1955, he personally conducted the country's foreign policy, leading to a peace treaty ending France's involvement in the Indochina war. Other significant actions included beginning Tunisia's path to independence and overseeing the rejection in parliament of the controversial European Defense Community (EDC) Treaty. He also presided over the opening stages of the Algerian conflict, though after the fall of his government he remained a vocal critic of subsequent French governments' handling of the affair.

Mendès-France was much more than a foreign policy activist, however, and in many ways his legacy owes more to the impact of his economic and political ideas on the evolution of the French non-Communist left than to particular foreign policies of his seven-month government. His influence was felt mainly through his ability to articulate a philosophy of renewal, for the state as well as for the economy. Many of his principles, which could be characterized by the term *social democracy*, as well as many of his followers and fellow travelers, were represented in the Socialist governments under President François Mitterrand in the 1980s and early 1990s. Mitterrand himself served as Mendès-France's interior minister.

Pierre Mendès-France was born in Paris in 1907, the son of a textile merchant from Limoges. Although Jewish in ancestry—his family ancestors had left Portugal in the 1500s during the Inquisition—he was entirely secular in both personal and public orientation. Mendès-France displayed a high intelligence early on, accelerating his move through the educational system. He obtained his baccalaureate at fifteen and went on to graduate from the elite Ecole des Sciences Politiques (School of Political Science) in June 1925. He also finished his law school courses at the Faculty of Law in June 1926, entering the Paris Bar in that year at nineteen years of age, the youngest in France. Complementing his educational efforts, he was also a political activist. During this period of turbulent and politicized student activities—from both the left wing and the right wing—Mendès-France joined the Republican and Socialist University Action League, becoming its secretary general in 1927. He also joined the Radical Party, the oldest political party in France, quickly aligning himself with its left wing, known as the Young Turks.

Mendès-France formally entered political office as a Radical deputy from the Eure, in Normandy, in May 1932, becoming the youngest deputy in France. Two years later he was elected mayor of Louviers, also in the Eure. In 1938, Socialist Prime Minister Léon Blum appointed him to his first ministerial post, undersecretary of state for the Treasury, making him the youngest minister of the government.

It was during this period that Mendès-France criticized the first Blum cabinet of 1936 on economic grounds. His arguments displayed not only his grasp of national and international economic dynamics (he had written both a critique of Raymond Poincaré's economic policy and a treatise on international finance) but also his commitment to break with convention and pursue paths considered politically unpopular, for instance by calling for a swift devaluation of the franc at the beginning of the Popular Front government in 1936 rather than a continuation of the commonly accepted deflationary policies of prior governments.

Later, in the second Blum government, in which he was then a minister, Mendès-France's economic ideas had crystallized into a dynamic interventionist plan (he was greatly responsible for importing Keynesianism into French economic discourse). His plan encompassed such elements as price controls, a two-year suspension of amortization of the public debt and levies on capital up to 17 percent. Adopted by the Chamber of Deputies, it was opposed by the Senate, provoking the fall of Blum's second government.

With the onset of World War II and the fall of France to German forces, Mendès-France fled to French North Africa with other army and air force units. He was arrested by the Vichy government and tried for desertion. He escaped to England, however, and joined the Free French forces led by Charles de Gaulle. During the latter years of the war, he flew in a dozen bombing raids and then became part of the immediate post-Liberation government under de Gaulle.

In the early postwar period, he participated in the founding of several international organizations and, in 1944, served as the French representative at Bretton Woods. He was also elected to the executive commissions of the IMF and the World Bank in 1945 and helped launch the United Nations Economic and Social Council (UNESCO). Mendès-France left de Gaulle's government over a dispute concerning the appropriate economic policy for rebuilding the nation after the devastation of war. Mendès-France had introduced a plan for positive government intervention, which implied a good deal of economic rigor, but de Gaulle sided instead with his finance minister, Pleven, opting to float a loan and adopting a generally more laissez-faire orientation.

Now outside of government, but still a Radical Party deputy and chair of the National Assembly's finance committee, Mendès-France developed a reputation as something of a Cassandra during the early 1950s because of his criticism of French Indochina policy, which he combined with an economic critique. In 1953 he came within thirteen votes of acquiring the prime ministership, kept from it primarily by Communist deputies. During the 1954 Dien Bien Phu crisis in Vietnam, French negotiations stalled, the government fell and the French president, René Coty, asked Mendès-France to again try to form a government. On June 18, 1954, he secured the required constitutional majority, one of the largest ever of the Fourth Republic, after a dramatic speech in which he gave himself a deadline for arriving at a peace treaty.

Mendès-France was prime minister for little over seven months, and on February 5, 1955, he lost the confidence of the National Assembly, having angered too many entrenched interests which feared his reformist orientation, for example, the powerful wine industry. After the parliamentary elections of 1956, in which the Republican Front (primarily Socialists, Radicals and some independents) made considerable headway, Mendès-France returned to government as a minister without portfolio under the Socialist, Guy Mollet. Four months later, again on principle, he resigned from the government, unhappy with Mollet's handling of the increasingly violent situation in Algeria.

Opposing de Gaulle's creation of the Fifth Republic in 1958, as well as his referendum on a popularly elected president in 1962, Mendès-France spent most of the 1960s in the political wilderness. At the urging of friends and supporters, he was elected again to the Assembly in 1967 from Grenoble and immediately carved out for himself a position as a rational and moral critic of the Gaullist government. During the "events of May" in 1968, he sided with several of the student organizations, at least to the extent that he acknowledged publicly their legitimate criticisms of the regime.

During a brief turn of events at this time, François Mitterrand, the symbolic head of the democratic left, announced that in the event of a political vacuum he was ready to assume leadership of a government and Mendès-France would be his choice as prime minister. In the subsequent parliamentary elections that year, which represented a law-and-order backlash to the May events, Mendès-France narrowly lost his seat. Until the end of his life, Mendès-France never returned to elected office or served in a governmental capacity. However, he remained active as a critical voice on many issues, especially Arab-Israeli affairs.

Mendès-France had a long political life, even though his time in actual government service—as a prime minister or other cabinet minister—was relatively brief. His impact on wider political dynamics, however, was noteworthy. The overarching concern of Mendès-France throughout his political career was the modernization of France. In this regard his significance for the political left, especially the Socialist Party during the 1980s, was primarily as an intellectual and organizational forerunner in the attempt to rejuvenate the non-Communist political left as the instrument of this modernization.

Mendès-France inspired a generation of young and intelligent high civil servants and technocrats, many of whom later became members of the Mitterrand Socialist government. By the mid-1950s, the new newsweekly *L'Express,* founded by Jean-Jacques Servan-Schreiber, had become the unofficial organ of ''mendèsisme,'' a general intellectual and policy orientation aimed at breaking with convention and introducing new patterns of economic policy making, notably democratic planning for productive investment. Mendèsisme also stressed a new organizational configuration for the left in France, one that would be able to reach majority status. In this regard, the necessity for a new relationship with the ostracized Communist Party was recognized. Mendès-France never convinced the Communists, however, that his vision of social democracy included a privileged position for them or a fundamental change in capitalism. The technocratic nature and composition of his movement, as well as its weak links to the labor movement, contributed to his ultimate failure to unify the left.

From 1955 to 1957, Mendès-France briefly had the opportunity to translate his ideas into action, that is, beginning to modernize and rejuvenate the left. On May 4, 1955, he became leader of the Radical Party, and until his resignation two years later in spring 1957, he attempted to mold it into the vehicle by which to put into practice his plans for modernizing French politics. The Radical Party, even to supporters of his at the time, represented an odd choice of political party to carry out his plans, for it was one of the most undisciplined, in terms of parliamentary cohesion in voting, and was comprised of a traditional middle-class base. A party of loosely organized units of local notables rather than a tightly structured mass party, it seemed far removed from the traditional circle of Mendès-France supporters, characterized as they were by their urban, ''new middle class'' socioeconomic status.

Nevertheless, Mendès-France chose the party of which he had been a member since the age of sixteen and began to refashion its organizational rules in order to eventually take on the party's independent-minded parliamentarians. In the end, party splits, intransigence on the part of Radical M.P.'s, and the inopportune scheduling of parliamentary elections in 1956 all led to his failure to reshape the Radical Party. Too few changes in party statutes and internal organization, the inability to emphasize more the role of party militants (generally pro–Mendès-France) and, finally, a preoccupation with principles and policy rather than with day-to-day activity in precincts and party headquarters led Mendès-France to recognize that further efforts would only lead to the marginalization of what was left of the Radical Party.

In a sense, Mendès-France's goal was to build a modern social democratic–type party, along the lines of the Swedish or West German social democratic parties. But as long as the existing Socialist Party (the SFIO) and the Communist Party eyed him suspiciously while jealously guarding their electorates, a French party of the social democratic type was doomed. Still, his stress on revitalization of the French economic and political systems inspired many of the young men around him to pursue these goals later on. When the SFIO finally collapsed in 1969, many of those who built the new Socialist Party (Parti Socialiste) along with François Mitterrand and later became government ministers in the 1980s were first introduced to "transformational" political activism by Mendès-France. Mitterrand had been his interior minister, Foreign Minister Claude Cheysson had been his chief of staff, Defense Minister Charles Hernu a Radical Party "mendèsiste," and so on.

Eventually, Mendès-France left the Radical Party, joining in the "migration" or "bleeding" from the major parties of the Fourth Republic that took place during the 1960s. One major phenomenon that occurred was the "club movement," the founding of small political organizations engaged in debating the changes then remaking the social and economic landscape of France, for example, migration from rural areas to cities, state-led mass production industrialization, and so on. Although refraining by and large from electoral activities, some of the more notable clubs did produce policy positions that eventually found their way into the new Socialist Party.

Emerging out of this same frustration with the established parties—and like the clubs, an organization characterized more by the power and attraction of its ideas rather than organizational clout—was the Unified Socialist Party (Parti Socialiste Unifié, or PSU). The PSU was itself made up of several clubs, and Mendès-France's final political affiliation was with this party. Having been excluded from the Radical Party in early 1959 for joining with Mitterrand and others in an attempt to "institutionalize" the opposition to the new Gaullist Fifth Republic by forming the Union of Democratic Forces, Mendès-France joined a breakaway group from the SFIO, the Autonomous Socialist Party (PSA) in late 1959. In April 1960, the PSA and several other groups merged to form the PSU. Mendès-France kept out of the new party's organizational decisions, yet the prestige of his adherence was a definite plus for the small party. By the late 1960s, the national secretary of the PSU was Michel Rocard, later to become a prime minister under Mitterrand in the late 1980s and perhaps the best exemplar of mendèsisme in the Socialist Party.

Overall, Pierre Mendès-France was one of the towering figures of the French Fourth Republic, a regime that did not particularly lend itself to strong leaders.

The irony of his long experience and efforts to renew France and the political left was that his most important, concrete actions came in the realm of foreign policy, rather than in domestic economics and politics. Still, he came to embody the determined effort to transform the splintered and quarrelous factions of the left into a modern and disciplined tool to lead in the revitalization of the French economic and political system. He opposed de Gaulle in 1958 for many reasons, but a primary objection was the displacement of parliament in French democracy by what he considered to be a potentially authoritarian office, the presidency.

Especially during the episode of his attempt to re-create the Radical Party and until his retirement from politics in 1968, Mendès-France also associated with and maintained links to French political youth movements, as his oblique participation in the events of May 1968 attest. He came to symbolize during the 1950s the spirit of renovation, especially during the worst crises of the Fourth Republic. "Movement" versus "limits," "rigor" versus "laxity" were slogans that characterized his participation in the major events of France extending from the 1930s to the 1960s. Surrounding him during the 1950s were the young men who would later be given the full potential to govern, attempting to finally realize his ideals of democratic planning and modernization of state and society. Mendès-France died in 1982, having witnessed the election of the Union of the Left to national office. In terms of intellectual debts, the Socialist governments of the 1980s owed much to Mendès-France as the trailblazer for what they would eventually accomplish.

BIBLIOGRAPHY

Work by Mendès-France:

A Modern French Republic. London: Weidenfeld & Nicholson, 1963.

Other Works:

Lacouture, Jean. *Pierre Mendès-France.* New York: Holmes & Meier, 1984.

de Tarr, Francis. *The French Radical Party: From Herriot to Mendès-France.* New York: Oxford University Press, 1961.

ROBERT LADRECH

KONSTANTINOS MITSOTAKIS (1918–) was prime minister of Greece from 1990 to 1993. Although Mitsotakis has not served in office as extensively as some of his predecessors—such as the conservative Konstantinos Karamanlis or the socialist Andreas Papandreou—his political activities in various capacities have greatly contributed to Greece's domestic and foreign policies. Successful in politics at a young age, Mitsotakis's first encounter with responsibilities in a national government came in 1951 when he was named deputy minister of economics at age thirty-two. Since, he has always been involved in Greek politics, either as a member of government—having held numerous ministerial posts—or as a member of the opposition. In his career, Konstantinos Mitsotakis frequently preached centrist ideologies but also often found himself serving ideologies that were more conservative than he would have liked to admit.

Mitsotakis's involvement with public life began much earlier than his involvement with the national government. He participated actively as a young officer in resisting the invasion of the German army in the Balkan Peninsula in the early 1940s. Later, on his native island of Crete, he became a leading figure in the island's local resistance against the German occupation army. He was arrested twice by the Germans and sentenced to death. In the first instance he escaped execution due to a general amnesty, in the second because of an exchange of prisoners that was agreed to between Allied headquarters in the Mediterranean and the German military command.

Subsequently, Mitsotakis participated in another Greek political drama, the civil war. This civil war lasted until 1949, five years after the German occupation forces had withdrawn. Although the civil war affected every corner of the country, in some parts of Greece the conflict was nonetheless somewhat less severe than in others; this depended greatly on the political leadership of the various local groups fighting against each other. The conflict on Crete was by far much milder than that on the mainland. Here, Konstantinos Mitsotakis's leadership contributed to minimizing the bloodshed. His centrist approach to the issues, which were the focal point of the opposing camps' hatred of each other, kept that hatred from reaching levels that it was to reach in the rest of Greece.

Konstantinos Mitsotakis was born on October 18, 1918, in Halepa, a suburb of the city of Chania on the island of Crete. Mitsotakis's political roots are associated with the greatest of political figures in modern Greek politics, Eleftherios Venizelos: His grandmother was the great politician's sister. Although this fact alone is highly significant in Greek politics, where family ties count for much, nevertheless the Mitsotakis family was extremely active in politics even before Venizelos became famous. Mitsotakis's grandfather and other members of his family were extensively involved in politics, mainly because of the revolutionary fervor that dominated the island of Crete in the late 1800s. Crete was then a dominion of the slowly disappearing Ottoman Empire, and a number of well-known citizens of the island fought hard to unite Crete with the rest of Greece—among them the Mitsotakis family. Thus, Konstantinos Mitsotakis not only made a political name for himself but his family roots are deeply political in every sense of the term.

Mitsotakis's first years of education took place on his native Crete, in Halepa and in Chania. His university education was completed at the University of Athens, where he studied law and graduated in 1940, just a few months before the Greek-Italian war broke out.

The decade that followed was one of the most difficult ones in modern Greek history. First, there was the occupation by the German and Italian forces. Second, almost immediately after the end of occupation, the long and bloody civil war erupted in Greece. It is not surprising that events of the 1940s shaped the political behavior of the younger generation of political leaders, who later became leaders of present-day Greece. Konstantinos Mitsotakis was no exception. His involvement in both World War II and the Greek civil war played a determining role in his ideological formaton. In both, he preferred taking conciliatory positions on controversial issues. This conciliatory approach to politics would eventually earn him a number of insulting epithets. He was variously accused of being an apostate, disloyal and a traitor.

Mitsotakis's active national political life started in 1946 when he was elected for the first time to the Greek parliament at age twenty-seven. In 1951, when thirty-two, he was appointed deputy minister of economics in the government of Sophocles Venizelos. This appointment should be characterized as significant because it trained the young Mitsotakis for other ministerial responsibilities in subsequent governments in the 1960s. Most important, however, it established his political credibility within the opposition parties to which he would belong for almost ten years.

From 1952 to 1963, the conservatives, under the leadership of Konstantinos Karamanlis, clearly dominated politics in Greece. The opposition consisted of a number of strong political leaders, among them George Papandreou, and represented mainly centrist ideological tendencies, at least in theory. Mitsotakis became one of the leading spokesmen of this opposition.

In the early 1960s, the Center Union Party was formed out of these opposition groupings. In fact, the Center Union was mainly constituted by a conglomeration of distinguished leaders whose ideological convictions were nonetheless unclear. Judging from political events that followed in the 1960s, one could assume that the political personalities who formed the Center Union Party differed substantially from each another in terms of ideology. Some of them could just as easily have been members of the ERE (the National Radical Union Party), Karamanlis's conservative movement. Others could just as easily have been members of leftist parties. Although much of his political rhetoric was quite centrist, in fact, Konstantinos Mitsotakis's tendency was most inclined toward the right wing of the Center Union, as his behavior in the decades that followed was to demonstrate.

In November 1963, the Center Union Party won the general election, and Mitsotakis was awarded one of the most prestigious ministries, economics. The party had run on a platform of social justice, restructuring the country's infrastructure, and most important, national education. But all these policy areas required a great deal of economic resources, shifting existing economic resources into new areas and in general reprioritizing the goals of the country.

The Ministry of Economics was of course largely implicated in realizing these goals. As economics minister during this period, Mitsotakis earned a reputation for being a good manager in addition to regularly voicing his commitment to fulfilling the Center Union Party's electoral platform. In its short life (November 1963-July 1965), this George Papandreou government would, under the circumstances, achieve a number of its objectives (though far from all of them), with Mitsotakis playing a large role in the government's affairs.

But Greek politics changed radically in the years between 1964 and 1967, and Mitsotakis's political behavior during this period marked both his career and Greek political developments for the subsequent twenty-five years. As we have seen, the Center Union Party was not a cohesive party. The various leaders within it fought each other for the party's leadership at every opportunity presented to them. Mitsotakis was no exception to this rule.

In July 1965, a major opportunity for leadership change arose when the simmering conflict between King Konstantinos and Prime Minister Papandreou came to its peak. The king dismissed Papandreou from the premiership and asked several leaders of the Center Union Party to form a new government. After many attempts, a new government was successfully formed, supported by some members of the Center Union and some members of the opposition. That government was led by Stephanos Stephanopoulos, and Mitsotakis was again a leading figure, becoming the minister of coordination, a very significant post.

The question here revolves around the significance of Mitsotakis's participation in a government that clearly did not enjoy popular support. While it is difficult to assess what would have happened had Mitsotakis remained loyal to Papandreou, his defection from the party leader had several important consequences. First, a majority of Center Union voters lost confidence in Mitsotakis (who until then had been considered the rising star in Greek politics), as well as in other leaders who participated in this new government. This loss of confidence stemmed from the electorate's sharp feelings of betrayal. With the instigation of both leaders from the left and Papandreou's loyalists within the Center Union, thousands of Greeks manifested their frustrations in the streets of the large cities in Greece.

This problematic change in government not only raised constitutional questions but also led to political chaos in the country. Between 1965 and 1967, popular demonstrations of discontent and anger never ceased. Mitsotakis himself explained that he knew upon leaving the party for participation in the new government that he did not have the support of the people and that this would damage his political career. But he feared, he said, that the Greek monarch would use the army to abolish representative democracy. Mitsotakis argued that to salvage whatever was salvageable in Greek democracy, Papandreou's confrontational approach must be avoided. This argument, of course, was quite consistent with Mitsotakis's ideology of conciliation.

Later developments would obviously prove that Mitsotakis had been seriously mistaken, for what he wanted to save was not, ultimately, saved at all. On April 21, 1967, a month before scheduled parliamentary elections, a military coup took place which sent Greece into seven years of dictatorship. Mitsotakis's defection from the Center Union had had an indirect but very important impact on the military takeover of the country, for, since Greek voters believed their political rights to have been betrayed by Mitsotakis and other "apostates," the popularity of both George and Andreas Papandreou was running extremely high as the May 1967 election approached. It was this popularity of the Papandreous' which caused the army to move. With a junta in firm control of Greece, most politicians were either exiled or left politics entirely forever. Of course, there were also those who cooperated with the junta. As for Mitsotakis, he went into exile, resolving to prepare for his eventual political comeback. His departure from Greece during the dictatorship demonstrated to a degree that he was more dedicated to democratic principles than his political enemies credited him with being.

With the restoration of Greek democracy in 1974, Mitsotakis returned to Greece as did other exiled leaders. Political events of the 1960s greatly influenced the universe of Greek politics that emerged after the dictatorship fell in 1974. The Center Union Party fragmented into a number of smaller parties, and Karamanlis's ERE changed its name to Nea Democratia (or New Democracy). In all this, Konstantinos Mitsotakis's political future looked very dismal. But developments would demonstrate that Mitsotakis was not only able to make a credible comeback, but that he would also be able to play a role of the highest importance in Greek national politics. Joining the ruling conservative Nea Democratia Party under Karamanlis's leadership, he became minister of coordination in 1978 and minister of foreign affairs in 1980. In 1984 he became leader of the Nea Democratia and in 1990 his party won the general election and he became prime minister.

What contributed so much to Mitsotakis's political success, especially when so many thought his political career to be doomed after the political turmoil of 1965? At least two factors come to the fore in assessing Mitsotakis's political comeback. The first is his political ideology. His insistence on taking a middle-of-the-road approach made him seem desirable at times when the politics of hostile confrontation seemed to prevail. When he became prime minister in 1990, his archrival Andreas Papandreou's political capital was fading. The Papandreou government's legacy of very heavy public debt, along with Papandreou's confrontational approach to foreign affairs, made Mitsotakis's milder approach seem to be a tonic to Greek voters. The second factor lies in Mitsotakis's sheer persistence. No other politician in a comparable position would have insisted and persisted as Mitsotakis did. By waiting for the right time and the right circumstances, Mitsotakis was able to reach the top of Greek politics.

Nonetheless, the program of severe economic austerity that Mitsotakis felt compelled to follow during his tenure as prime minister, along with a worldwide recession that worsened Greece's domestic economic situation even more, brought Andreas Papandreou and his Greek Socialist Party back to power in the general elections of 1993. Mitsotakis was also the victim of internal divisiveness within his own Nea Democratia Party. A young ''maverick'' within the party, Antonis Samaras, split from Mitsotakis, forming his own party, called Political Spring. The split deprived Mitsotakis of his parliamentary majority and forced elections to be held seven months early. In them, Papandreou won an absolute majority of 170 seats in the 300-seat parliament.

Although Konstantinos Mitsotakis served little more than three years as prime minister of Greece, he had great influence on Greek politics. In domestic affairs, he tried to reduce state spending and the public debt. In addition, Mitsotakis reduced inflation, helping to bring the drachma into line with the proposed criteria of European Community monetary union by the end of 1999.

In terms of foreign policy, he has always been a supporter of Greece's membership in the European Community. When he became a member of Nea Democratia, he took an active role in supporting Karamanlis's pro-EC policies. As for relations with Turkey, Mitsotakis has taken mainly a stance of negotiating differences between the two countries. This line has improved Greece's image among NATO members and with the United States, which has worked hard to avoid direct confrontation between Greece and Turkey. As soon as Mitsotakis became prime minister, relations between the United States and Greece improved considerably.

In general, the same can be said of relations between Greece and other European Community members. Usually, Mitsotakis went along with the main decisions of the majority of other EC member states. In addition, Mitsotakis was a full supporter of the Maastricht Treaty for greater monetary and political union in the European Community, a fact that makes him one of the most pro-Europeans in the EC. His pro-NATO and pro-EC positions have been welcomed positively by Greece's allies, although the lingering dispute over rights to the name *Macedonia* by the previous Yugoslav republic has been a somewhat bumpy detour in Greece's foreign relations with its allies.

Overall, Konstantinos Mitsotakis is a leader who has displayed great political skills. His mistakes in the 1960s did not keep him from coming back and, under a new ideological banner, reaching the peak of the Greek political pyramid. During his term as prime minister, he was able to identify weaknesses in Greek economic policy and devise reasonable remedies, although these did not bring the desired results soon enough. He performed well in foreign policy, drawing Greece closer to the European Community and the Atlantic Alliance. Although turned out of office in 1993, Mitsotakis can take comfort in the fact that not many now expect his successor, the aging socialist Andreas Papandreou, to dramatically reverse much of his domestic and foreign policies.

BIBLIOGRAPHY

Demetrakos, Demetres. *Kostas Mitsotakis: Apo ten antistasi sten politiki 1918–1961* (*Politike Biographia*), Tomos A. Athens: Papazeses, 1989.

Diamantopoulos, Thanasis. *Kostas Mitsotakis: Apo ton anendoto ste dictatoria 1961–1974* (*Politike Biographia*), Tomos B. Athens: Papazeses, 1989.

CHRIS BOURDOUVALIS

FRANÇOIS MITTERRAND (1916–), fourth president of the French Fifth Republic, is, with Charles de Gaulle, the most important political figure in contemporary French history. Mitterrand's political apprenticeships occurred during the Resistance and Fourth Republic years (1940–1958). He then turned in the 1960s to reconstructing French socialism and, more broadly, France's divided left. He was elected president as the Socialist candidate in 1981 and became the first Fifth Republic president to be reelected in 1988. Mitterrand's presidency is remarkable for the contrast between its initial resolute leftism and subsequent reversal of directions.

François Mitterrand was born in Jarnac, a small village in the Charente area of France's southwest, on October 26, 1916, one of eight children in a middle-class Catholic family. His father was a stationmaster and his mother a cultivated and avid reader from whom Mitterrand acquired early on an enduring love of literature and books. The family's moderately conservative political leanings were passed on to the children even though the young Mitterrand, in Catholic boarding school, was more interested in letters than in politics. These predilections survived Mitterrand's migration to Paris in the 1930s to study law and politics, despite the background of left-right political polarization and turmoil of the Popular Front years.

Mitterrand's political baptism came in World War II. Mobilized into military service, he was wounded, captured and imprisoned in the early days of the German invasion in 1940. Activism inside German prison camps and a successful escape to the Vichy zone after several attempts led Mitterrand to a position in the Vichy civil service. He was even awarded the *francisque*, a high Vichy honor. While working officially on the problems of ex–prisoners of war, Mitterrand began to lead a double life, first as a supplier of forged papers to the Resistance and then, under the name of Morland, as an active Resistance leader. Mitterrand's Resistance activities involved working intelligence networks among prisoners of war and may have contributed to a certain closed and private approach to politics which observers later remarked. His Resistance work also brought Mitterrand into contact with General Charles de Gaulle, contacts which, from the outset, were fraught with conflict.

Upon the Liberation, Mitterrand was tapped for an important administrative post, but his differences with de Gaulle barred him from immediate high political office. He turned briefly to journalism, where his literary and polemical gifts served him well. In 1946 his half century of elective office began with election to the National Assembly. He quickly assumed a leadership role in a small center-left political group and, at the record young age of thirty-one, became minister for veterans' affairs. The Fourth Republic, however, was characterized by highly unstable parliamentary majorities. Mitterrand, in control of a political grouping whose support was constantly needed, was thus able to embark upon a remarkable career. When the balance of parliamentary power shifted from center-right to center-left in the mid–1950s, in governments led by Pierre Mendès-France and, later, the Socialist leader Guy Mollet, François Mitterrand became a pivotal figure, serving as colonial affairs minister, interior minister and justice minister.

These positions, which placed Mitterrand on track to become prime minister, also put him at the center of the difficulties which would bring the Republic to its end before he could reach this goal. In particular, as Algeria was legally a part of metropolitan France, any disorder in Algeria fell under Mitterrand's purview. In this, Mitterrand usually played a progressive role in the agonizing governmental debates about the Algerian question, but he was nonetheless officially responsible, both collectively as a member of the cabinet and through his own ministries, for many terrible policies of repression in Algeria, including the systematic use of torture.

Mitterrand's ministerial years in the Fourth Republic refined central elements of his political style. Fourth Republic governments were always high-stakes political games. To stay in power, ministers had to learn how to balance party affiliations, electoral prospects, principles and personal ambitions. Mitterrand became an acknowledged master of such equations and a connoisseur of France's electoral geography. Any politician who reached maturity in these years clearly reveled in manipulating power. By the end of the Fourth Republic, public doubt already existed about whether Mitterrand's principles were the point of departure or the product of such Florentine maneuvering.

Mitterrand was one of a very select group of top Fourth Republic politicians who opposed both the transfer of power to General de Gaulle and the advent of the Fifth Republic in 1958. In retrospect, there is great irony in his position. The Gaullist constitution magnified the powers of the French presidency and greatly reduced those of parliament. Mitterrand opposed these changes vehemently, but as president he would later embrace them with great enthusiasm. At the time, however, his lonely opposition, plus the major change in political balance brought by Gaullism to the detriment of the French non-Communist left, pushed Mitterrand into the political wilderness.

Mitterrand had been a centrist in the left-right spectrum of the Fourth Republic, more committed to matters of civil liberties and the rule of law than thorough social reform. The changed circumstances of the Fifth Republic—whose parliamentary, and later presidential voting rules polarized politics—made centrism an unpromising posture. Mitterrand thus had to reposition himself on the left side of the spectrum in order to relaunch his career.

Mitterrand's first opportunity arose in the period prior to the first direct presidential elections in 1965. After protracted negotiations, the leadership of the non-Communist left was unable to reach consensus on a candidate to oppose de Gaulle. At this point, Mitterrand—the representative of a small group of loyalists called the Convention for Republican Institutions—emerged as a last-minute compromise. Mitterrand's solid performance in the campaign discomfited de Gaulle, who was forced to campaign seriously in order to win the runoff. Mitterrand thus reemerged from political exile as a first-ranking figure. Perhaps the central reason for Mitterrand's success was his willingness to be a candidate of "left union" who refused overt anticommunism.

From this critical moment, Mitterrand developed the complicated strategy which would ultimately make him president of France. Its first element was that the French Socialist Party had to be remodeled with Mitterrand at its head, a task which would test all of the future president's maneuvering skills. Simultaneously, this renewed Socialist Party had to enter into electoral and programmatic alliance with the Communists, who at that time consistently held over 20 percent of the French vote as well as the core of France's labor movement. Here Mitterrand reasoned that by carefully entering into coalition with the Communists he could actually reduce their strength to the benefit of the Socialists. Finally, this alliance had to be effective enough to endow François Mitterrand with the political and electoral momentum to carry him to a presidential victory.

The multidimensional success of this strategy was undoubtedly Mitterrand's greatest achievement. His conquest of the Socialists and the renewal of the Parti Socialiste (PS) took less than a decade after 1965. Mitterrand's domination of the PS was consecrated in 1971 at the Epinay congress. This new PS was an ingenious organization which allowed the conflictual coexistence of different political tendencies within a federal organizational structure. This apparatus allowed Mitterrand to manipulate the internal balance of forces in order to maintain his position. Simultaneously the plethora of different left approaches coexisting inside the party constrained the endemic divisiveness of the non-Communist left.

Such a flexible political tool was important for Mitterrand's great gamble to enter into coalition with the Communists. Sealing the alliance involved adopting many of the Communists' broad programmatic outlines for domestic reform, as well as their general political rhetoric. A deal—major foreign policy differences excluded—was reached in 1972. From this point, Mitterrand's strategy banked on a general electoral shift toward the "united left" and its presidential candidate, Mitterrand. The bulk of this shift, primarily coming from the "new middle classes," would go toward the Socialists. Here the internal pluralism of the PS would allow it to appeal in a number of different directions at once. In this way, growing Socialist strength would progressively undermine Communist ability to influence the coalition and, eventually, undercut support for the Communists more generally.

This path to ultimate success was not an easy one. Mitterrand lost the 1974 presidential election to the center-right candidate Valéry Giscard d'Estaing by a minuscule margin (a shift of less than 1 percent of the vote would have brought him victory) and the unified left which he led then lost the 1978 legislative election. In consequence, Mitterrand faced serious challenges from within the PS by those who opposed the coalition with the Communists. Moreover, the Communists themselves, faced with the growing relative electoral power of the PS, started to pull back. Nonetheless, triumph finally came in the May 1981 presidential election, when Mitterrand defeated the incumbent Giscard and ended the right's two decades of dominance over French politics. Putting his presidential powers to use right away, Mitterrand then dissolved the right-wing parliament, allowing the left, led by the Socialists, to win an absolute majority.

Mitterrand, who had only learned how to "talk Socialist" in the 1970s, came to power in 1981 presiding over a coalition, including Communists (in government for the first time since 1947), endowed with a program calling for "rupture with capitalism" and the energetic construction of social democracy in France.

The package included extensive nationalizations, enhanced government economic planning, redistributive fiscal and budgetary policies, major reforms in industrial relations to strengthen the legal position of workers and significant decentralization of the French state. The approach generally assumed that solutions to unemployment, flagging international competitiveness and social inequalities could be solved by an activist government backed by enthusiastic popular support and mobilizing available national resources.

The first Mitterrand government, under Prime Minister Pierre Mauroy, quickly set out to implement most of this program. The public sector in France reached unprecedented size, and reforms of all kinds were legislated. The international context, marked by a global recession largely induced by the new Reagan administration's determination to wring inflation out of the American economy, proved inhospitable, however. French inflation, persistently higher than its more prudent neighbors', rose even further. Budget deficits deepened, Keynesian stimuli caused a wave of imports and led to severe balance of payments difficulties, and the franc developed chronic weaknesses. A rash of austerity programs was then abruptly implemented by finance miniser Jacques Delors in 1982–1983. The left's ambitions to gain greater independence from the Americans in international affairs—symbolized by Third-Worldist rhetoric—were also deflated in this brief period.

Mitterrand's movement back toward a new economic and international realism properly began with a major crisis of the franc in early 1983. At this point, the French government faced a clear choice between leaving the European Monetary System in order to continue with Socialist reforms or sticking with Europe and charting a new course in domestic policy. Mitterrand chose the second approach. While Prime Minister Mauroy continued to claim that nothing fundamental had changed, his ministers energetically began to promote the new program of economic austerity within the framework of European monetary institutions. France would pursue this line for the rest of the Mitterrand presidency. From this point on, therefore, Mitterrand's fate would depend upon success in negotiating three great turns, in economics, international affairs and politics.

After 1983, in the economic realm, the new policies involved accepting the fact that rapid economic globalization made social democracy in one country no longer feasible. Inflation was therefore squeezed down to German levels, Europe's lowest, the franc was made rock-solid and firms were strongly encouraged to do whatever was needed to achieve international size and flexibility. The overarching new goal was to use state leverage, largely through monetary and market mechanisms, to prod firms toward international competitiveness. Specific measures chosen included a public sector incomes policy, de-indexing wage growth from inflation, allowing firms to begin shedding labor and to restructure on a grand scale, strong efforts to lower social overhead costs and decrease the state's tax bite, and policies to increase profit levels at the expense of wages in the distribution of national income. During this period, Mitterrand's governments also worked to reform France's capital market, creating in turn a mini-boom on the Paris bourse.

This economic shift, which moved France into 1980s orthodoxy, was tied to basic foreign policy changes. In this realm, any ''socialist'' distinctiveness after 1981 was quickly abandoned. Mitterrandist France did not have the means to do more than surrender to the realities of a renewed Cold War and arms race while retaining limited foreign policy autonomy in those regions of the world, largely ex–French colonial areas like Africa and the Middle East, where it defined special interests. Changed economic policies also prompted Mitterrandist France to begin a decisive turn toward Europe, allowing Mitterrand therefore to assume de facto coleadership of the European Community (EC) with Helmut Kohl of Germany. This shift, symbolized after 1985 by the activist European Commission presidency of Jacques Delors, made a renaissance of the European Community possible, starting with the 1985 white paper on completing the single market, the Single European Act signed in 1986 and the subsequent ''1992'' program for full market integration within the EC. At stake in this, from Mitterrand's point of view, was the consolidation of the European Community as a third pole of market economic success and political power coequal with North America and Japan.

The new policy outlook, both domestically and internationally, could no longer sustain the Socialist position in France's traditional left-right ideological and programmatic polarization. The Socialists were no longer committed to anticapitalism, statism and redistribution, which had been the bread and butter of their earlier appeals. Rather, they had become mild social democrats. Structuring a plausible new appeal became an urgent task, if only for electoral reasons. It could only be based upon arguments about the Socialists' managerial superiority over the right—the Socialists presented themselves as ''modern'' in contrast to the right as ''archaic''—in France's new quest for international economic competitiveness. This appeal was augmented by reference to the Socialists' greater compassion and sensitivity to popular concerns as demonstrated by their attachment to the welfare state, education and the more general needs of the less well-off.

Mitterrand's new economic course beginning in 1983—accepting economic globalization, promoting restructuring of French industry in the interests of competitiveness and a monetarist ''competitive deflation'' to German levels in order to solidify the franc—undoubtedly had many positive effects. Important sectors of French industry became better prepared to fight it out internationally; many French firms became much leaner and meaner. The problem was that change in the international economy plus upheavals in France's immediate European environment produced a meager harvest.

The recession of the early 1990s was as severe as that of the latter 1970s. Moreover, it came after many years, most of them presided over by François Mitterrand, when France's earlier commitment to near-full employment was significantly eroded. Official unemployment figures in 1992–1993 were well over

10 percent (slightly higher than the EC average), with much higher real joblessness masked by various stopgap labor market policies.

Chronic un- and underemployment, moreover, produced serious demoralization among younger people and the pain and pathologies associated with widespread social marginalization. To the degree to which such marginalization disproportionately touched immigrant, non-European residents of France it encouraged cultural conflicts and nativist racism. In more general terms, the last years of the Mitterrand presidency saw a France in which income, wealth and opportunity were more unequally distributed than they had been before 1981. Evidence of this was inescapable, even amid the splendors of Paris. France's great capital—undoubtedly enhanced by a program of ''grand projects'' promoted by Mitterrand, like the new Louvre, the Arche de la Défense, the City of Science at La Villette, the Bastille Opera and the new ''Très Grande Bibliothèque'' (literally ''very big library,'' officially named the Bibliothèque de France)-was also rife with the newly homeless and destitute.

The fate of Mitterrand's grand international strategy, built around renewed Franco-German collaboration and a renaissance of European integration, was quite as ambiguous. The major axis for new French initiatives following upon the left's great domestic policy shifts in 1982–1983 was Europe. And, in fact, the European Community expanded its ambitions tremendously after 1985, largely with French support, building on the enormous initial mobilizing power of the Single Market/1992 program. Success followed success until the unparalleled events of 1989.

The fall of the Berlin Wall in that year and the end of the Cold War proved disorienting both for France and the EC. German unification—which Mitterrand himself greeted with public skepticism, the first in a number of diplomatic *faux pas* which would later include failure to back Gorbachev in the August 1991 coup attempt—proved tremendously costly to the Germans and, by implication, the European Community. Moreover, the ex-communist societies of Central and Eastern Europe did not easily flower into capitalist democracies, to the chagrin of France and everyone else. Post–1989 Europe came to be symbolized by the Yugoslav tragedy, to which Franco-German differences of appreciation contributed greatly. In other areas, the Gulf War divided the EC and revealed the limits of French influence. Finally, the onset of recession coincided with adoption of the Maastricht Treaty for greater European monetary and political integration, for which Mitterrand spared few efforts. This combination reinforced nationalism and anti-EC feelings in many EC member states, including France itself. The September 1992 French referendum on ratification of the Maastricht Treaty, called by Mitterrand, was an indicator of the low level of success of Mitterrand's international programs, since the Europe option had been unquestionably their central axis and Maastricht its turning point. In the French referendum, the treaty was barely approved.

It was in the third area, that of politics, that trouble was deepest. The failure of the new government's ''left'' period after 1981 cost it considerable popular support, symbolized by massive mobilizations in 1983–1984 against its plans to reform the educational system. The compression in living standards and the rising unemployment which followed the Socialists' turn to economic realism cost the government even more. The right was thus able to reestablish its electoral majority as early as the local elections of 1983. Another electoral consequence was the beachhead established on the extreme right by the racist National Front.

Mitterrand's first seven-year presidential term would outlast that of the 1981 left parliamentary majority by two years (a full legislative term in the French system being only five years) and, from 1984 onward, when the Communists left the majority, it was clear that for the first time in the Fifth Republic there would be "cohabitation" between a president of the left and a parliamentary majority of the right. Anticipating this, Mitterrand changed the electoral law to proportional representation for the 1986 legislative elections, a maneuver which staved off the worst, but at the cost of awarding the National Front greater credibility and allowing it a strong presence in parliament.

However, Mitterrand was able to manage cohabitation with the right between 1986 and 1988 with great skill, and he won reelection in 1988 against prime minister Jacques Chirac by a margin of 10 percentage points. Mitterrand succeeded in part by positioning himself resolutely in the center of the political spectrum and, more importantly, by putting himself forward as a reassuring figure of continuity. "Tonton" (an affectionate reference to an uncle in French) became his public nickname. Moreover, Mitterrand's success occurred against the background of evident divisions on the right between the mainstream Gaullists and centrist Giscardian parties on the one hand and the National Front—which had done well in the first presidential round—on the other, as well as divisions within the mainstream right itself. Mitterrand's 1988 reelection may have been his most striking, and arguably last, demonstration of political virtuosity.

Mitterrand's second term was characterized by a deepening of political problems caused by abandoning the Socialists' earlier clear leftist identity. After the 1988 presidential election Mitterrand flirted briefly and unsuccessfully with an opening to the political center and then dissolved the two-year-old right-dominated parliament. That the Socialists were unable to achieve a majority in these 1988 legislative elections—being forced then to depend on Communists and maverick centrists for their majority—was an indicator of the difficulties to come. The tranquillity of the next three years of government under Prime Minister Michel Rocard was greatly helped along by the return of economic growth for the first time since the 1970s. Rocard's successors, however, were less fortunate. Edith Cresson, chosen by Mitterrand in 1991 to capitalize upon her status as the first female prime minister in French history, faced darkening economic circumstances ineptly. Pierre Bérégovoy, after 1992, demonstrated greater political skills, but was obliged to pursue what had become resolute monetarism—

the so-called strong franc policy—into a deep recession. His government was thus held responsible for record levels of unemployment.

The legislative elections of 1993 were the lowest point of the Mitterrand presidency. The Socialist Party received fewer than 20 percent of the vote, and the left more generally suffered its worst results in modern history. These 1993 elections demonstrated the perceptiveness of electoral specialists, who had for some time been pointing to a rise in individualism in the French electorate at the expense of ideological and party loyalty. Above all, the left and the Socialists had been cut down because of the abrupt policy shift away from traditional leftist appeals which had been engineered by President Mitterrand. The electoral law multiplied the moderate right's 45 percent support into four-fifths of the seats in parliament and created a new period of cohabitation in the worst possible circumstances for Mitterrand. These elections also provided new evidence of a fragmentation of party groups more generally, demonstrated in a Green vote grounded as much in political confusion as in commitment to ecology. The elections also sustained the racist National Front at 12-plus percent.

Short-term exploitation of divisions on the right in the mid–1980s and the brief economic recovery later on in fact covered up the long-term political damage to the left. The election results of 1993 demonstrated clearly that the new appeal of post-Mitterrand Socialists as competent, realistic and humane managers of a new France afloat in dangerous international waters was hopelessly inadequate. Repeated scandals involving campaign funding, as well as the "contaminated blood" issue (it became clear that in the mid-1980s then-Prime Minister Laurent Fabius and his team had knowingly allowed HIV-contaminated blood to continue to be used in French hospitals), also demonstrated that Socialist elites had become cynical and complacent in their long period in power. Looming over everything else was François Mitterrand, a president whose maneuvering capacities made him appear, in time, as inscrutable, too clever by half and ineffective. By 1993 Mitterrand's popularity ratings were the lowest on record of any president of the Fifth Republic.

François Mitterrand is a paradoxical figure. Having carefully constructed a new Socialist political identity for himself in the Fifth Republic and built a new political instrument to carry it, he was elected president of France. Once president, however, both Mitterrand and his party very quickly renounced this identity and dismanted the instrument. Mitterrand found himself presiding over, and promoting, a vast process of change in France's domestic life and international position, but in both realms the changes were totally different from those which he had proposed prior to his election.

Mitterrand has in fact been a president of transition, obliged to manage multiple and basic reorientations in French politics and society. As his long career moved toward its close, the results of his presidential work as manager of basic transitions were mixed at best. His popularity had vanished. His Socialist Party was weakened, perhaps beyond repair. France itself was in a precarious state. By definition, however, changes of the magnitude which Mitterrand has confronted take much longer than two French presidential terms to make their logics clear. Perhaps, with time, his record will be reevaluated in a more positive light.

BIBLIOGRAPHY

Works by Mitterrand:

Le Coup d'état permanent. Paris: Plon, 1964.
Ma part de vérité. Paris: Fayard, 1969.
L'Abeille et l'architecte. Paris: Flammarion, 1978.
Ici et maintenant. Paris: Fayard, 1980.
The Wheat and the Chaff. New York: Seaver, 1982.

Other Works:

Favier, Pierre, and Michel-Martin-Roland. *La Décennie Mitterrand*, 2 vols. Volume 1, *Les Ruptures*, Paris: Seuil, 1990; Volume 2, *Les épreuves*, Paris: Seuil, 1991.

Giesbert, Franz-Olivier. *François Mitterrand ou la tentation de l'histoire*. Paris: Seuil, 1977.

Ross, George, Stanley Hoffmann, and Sylvia Malzacher (eds.). *The Mitterrand Experiment*. New York: Polity/Oxford, 1987.

GEORGE ROSS

GUSTAV MÖLLER (1884–1970) belongs to the second generation of political leaders in the Swedish labor movement. His most important positions were as secretary of the Social Democratic Party from 1916 to 1940, as minister of social affairs from 1924 to 1926 and again, with a minor interruption, in the years from 1932 to 1951. As party secretary for more than three decades, he was second in the Social Democratic hierarchy and had primary responsibility for the organization of the party. In his position as social affairs minister for more than twenty years, he was the political architect behind Sweden's universal and extensive social insurance system.

Gustav Möller came from very humble conditions in southern Sweden. His father was a blacksmith who died when he was three months old, and he was raised by his single mother, who died when he was fourteen after a grim struggle to provide for her children. About his mother, Möller at the end of his political career wrote that ''one can certainly have worse sources of inspiration and motivation for one's politics than a lively desire to take care, so far as one can, to prevent a destiny like my mother's.''

Gustav Möller's political leadership is important because of the role he played in the Swedish Social Democratic Party, generally considered to be the most successful reformist labor movement in the world, both electorally and in terms of political outcomes. Since 1932 Sweden has had a Social Democratic prime minister for fifty-four out of sixty-one years (1932–76 and 1982–91). For that success, there have been two general explanations advanced: First, some scholars argue that social democratic parties come in various forms—for example, the British, the Latin-European and the German-Scandinavian—whose historical relations differ between the party, the unions and the state. As party secretary during what might be called the "formative years," the question is what role Möller played in forming the party and its relation to the union movement.

Other scholars, however, argue that it is the relation between policies launched by social democratic governments and their electoral support among different social groups and classes that explains the variation in different social democratic parties' electoral successes. In this view, in order to attract enough votes to reach government power, social democratic parties must model their policies so as to appeal not only to the shrinking industrial working class, but also to the growing class of white-collar and traditional middle-classes voters.

Accordingly, social democratic party strategists face a difficult dilemma. They can restrict themselves to traditional working-class questions. While this makes it difficult to reach the requisite electoral support (given the existing class structure), at the same time it is easier for the party to stay united behind a traditional working-class ideology.

Alternatively, the party can attempt to broaden its electoral base by opting for policies designed to attract white-collar workers and the middle class. This strategy might well achieve broad support and government power, but it risks diluting the party's once pure working-class ideology, thereby creating strong internal tensions within the party. According to some, the steepness of this tradeoff varies between countries (depending, among other things, on the organization of the labor movement) and explains the variation in the success of different social democratic parties. The Swedish Social Democrats have been held up as the master among social democratic parties at finding the best possible balance in obtaining such cross-class support. What role did Möller play in reaching this balance?

Finally, there is the role of ideology in social democratic politics. Here, two approaches compete: In the one, the pragmatic, nonideological character of Swedish social democracy is stressed. In the other, the importance of its Marxist ideological heritage is emphasized. With Möller, to what extent did his concentration on practical reforms cause him to forget the ideological—in this case the socialist—dimension of the party?

Before becoming party secretary, Möller had been active in the Social Democratic youth movement, where he fought against its revolutionary tendencies. The struggle against anarchists and Bolsheviks continued after Möller was named party secretary in the very tumultuous year 1916. In a series of articles between 1915 and 1920 in the party's theoretical journal, Möller developed an argument against the antidemocratic forces within the labor movement based on the idea that a revolutionary upheaval would hurt production, aggravate poverty and create an electoral majority against the Social Democratic Party. Möller based his argument on the failed revolution in nearby Finland. His preferred strategy was to secure democracy, reach compromise with other political forces (mainly the Liberals) and pursue what he called "illusion-free" politics. By this he meant that the Social Democrats "must carry out the most precise possible investigations of *all* the preconditions for Social Democracy's advance and for the possibility of implementing its program. In that way we act in the best interpretation of the spirit of Marx, the great realist.''

An example of illusion-free politics concerns the possibility of redistribution. Using available statistics, Möller showed that even if the income and capital of the privileged classes were evenly distributed, this would not in any significant degree increase the living standard of the working class, because the latter was too large in relation to the former. While Möller never lost sight of socialization of the means of production as the main future goal for the labor movement, he argued that the most important goal was to eliminate widespread poverty by (1) increasing production and (2) establishing a system of universal social insurance.

One of the problems with socialization which Möller emphasized was the danger of bureaucratization. Möller argued that there was no point in socialization if its main effect were to increase the power of state bureaucrats. Through intense debate and propaganda activities along these lines, he managed to isolate the revolutionary groups within the party. Ideologically, the idea was that socialism should not be established at the price of democracy. The result of Möller's and others' uncompromising line was that the revolutionary groups left the party in 1917 shortly *before* the Bolshevik Revolution in Russia, thereby securing the reformist and democratic character of the Swedish Social Democratic Party.

During the 1920s, the Social Democrats formed two minority governments. Both times the party had to resign (in 1923 and in 1926), partly because of the lack of a unified political strategy and partly because it could not coordinate its strategy with the unions' activities in industrial disputes. In 1928, for the first time the party lost badly in an election where the question of socialization had dominated. These events became important lessons for Gustav Möller. From 1928 on, together with his long-term collaborator Per-Albin Hansson, who had become party leader in 1926, he successfully launched a strategy to change the party and its relation to the union movement.

According to Möller, the union movement had to leave its free and neutral position behind in the conflicts between Social Democrats, communists and syndicalists. Instead, unions should adapt their activities to the party's political strategy. In practice, this meant two things. One was to roll back the strong communist influence in the union movement and secure Social Democratic hegemony—at least at the top. The second was to centralize union organization and, especially, gain control over the strike weapon. Union strategy had to be coordinated with party strategy if the labor movement was ever to become a dominant political force. To achieve this, Möller and Hansson began to reform the party and change its relation to the unions after the 1928 election defeat.

The Social Democratic Party that took power in 1932 was a very different organization than the party that was defeated in 1928. To use the party theoretician Panebianco's terminology, it had changed from a ''loose,'' more or less fragmented movement, into a ''hard,'' much more unified organization. No longer did the party leadership confront strong political factions, and it had succeeded in subordinating the unions' activities to the party's political strategy. To a large extent, this was Möller's work, and it was a prerequisite for making the party the "natural," hegemonic party of government in Sweden for the coming five decades.

The number of social reforms launched by Gustav Möller during his two decades as head of the Ministry of Social Affairs are too numerous to mention. As we have seen, one of Möller's basic ideas was to launch a system of social insurance that would lift the working class from poverty and insecurity. A working class struck by continuing economic hardship and social insecurity could not be expected to command production when the time came. The problem, besides financing of course, was how to do this without (1) subordinating citizens to the power of a state bureaucracy (the Bismarckian system) or (2) stigmatizing recipients of social assistance as inferior citizens.

Here, Möller launched some important new ideas. Foremost, he introduced the notion of social policy as a citizen's right. In his own words, "In so far as it is possible social benefits should be provided as a *general right of citizenship*; the system should cover all needs that do not result from self-created economic difficulties; the system should contribute to the *equalizing of incomes*. . . . Our aim has been and remains that social benefits should not be restricted to just wage-earners or any other social group. We want to have *people's insurance*, not workers' insurance."

Universal schemes—such as flat-rate pensions, sickness compensation and child allowances—would not stigmatize the recipients because every citizen was to be a recipient; neither would they increase bureaucratic power because no discretion would be left to bureaucrats; nor would they be delegitimized because of fraud because rules of eligibility were simple and precise. In short, Möller was astutely aware of the delegitimizing effects that poor implementation of good intentions could have and of the need of formulating policy so to attract the greatest possible electoral support for the party.

Moreover, as reforms were directed to the whole population rather than merely the industrial working class, increased electoral support for the party could be expected. This was especially important for Möller because he was one of the first to realize that the "development of the productive forces" would not automatically make the industrial working class the majority in society. On the contrary, if the party was to maintain its electoral strength it was important to attract support from the growing "middle class" of white-collar employees.

In some areas, where means testing could not be avoided because of the very nature of the social reform in question, Möller still mistrusted the established Swedish bureaucracy. To implement such reforms, he either turned to the less bureaucratic local municipalities or created new types of nonbureaucratic public or corporatist organizations. Of several, two are worth mentioning. When an unemployment insurance scheme was introduced in 1935, Möller paid much attention to the question of what institution would be given the task of implementing the scheme. Unemployment insurance is problematic because in each case it has to be decided whether the unemployed person (1) does in fact belong to the workforce, that is, unemployed through no fault of his or her own; and (2) the kinds of jobs an unemployed person can refuse without losing the insurance benefit. These are questions that cannot be regulated centrally because they defy precision. Instead, discretion must be given to the local agency responsible for implementing the scheme.

By skillful strategic maneuvering in the parliament, Möller succeeded in establishing a system in which the unemployment scheme would be implemented not by a public bureaucracy, but by union-run unemployment funds. The right to the insurance was thereby in practice connected to union membership, and union officials were given implementation powers over the scheme. In addition, Möller deliberately constructed this scheme in such a way as to ''force workers into the unions.''

The importance of this can be shown by figures from the 1980s about degrees of unionization in Western capitalist democracies. There is indeed great variation between 12 percent (France) and 86 percent (Sweden) among these democracies. Most important in this case, however, is that the countries among the top five have the same union-run system for unemployment insurance as Sweden, while all the countries below them have government-run schemes. While this factor does not explain all variation in union strength, statistical analysis shows that countries with an unemployment insurance scheme managed by the unions have about 20 percent higher levels of unionization than the rest. In this case, it is thus possible to show that Möller in fact created a part of the future strength on which his own political power was based.

Möller also launched the closely related active labor market policy during the late 1930s. Even though the economic depression was formally over, so-called islands of heavy unemployment still existed in specific trades and/or areas. To deal with this problem, Möller wanted to establish a governmental institution which, instead of handing out cash benefits to the unemployed, would deal with the problem more actively through such means as vocational training, help in relocation of the workforce, temporary relief works, state orders to industry and so on.

The problem Möller faced was that the state institution that had previously dealt with these matters during the 1920s had totally lost legitimacy among the organized working class, partly for having at times forced workers to act as strikebreakers, partly because of the very low pay and harsh conditions at its so-called labor camps. It was the inability to get parliamentary support for changing this organization (called the Unemployment Commission)—especially in its ability to force workers to act as strikebreakers, thus striking at the very heart of the unions' power—which forced the Social Democratic minority government's bitter resignation in 1926. Against this background, Möller faced a difficult task in organizing an active labor market policy.

While he could not get a parliamentary majority behind disbanding the Unemployment Commission in 1932, he was able to establish a parallel system which he controlled directly from his ministry, thereby also ensuring that the policy would be implemented in a much more prounion manner. During the rest of the 1930s, the old Unemployment Commission was then starved of resources, funds instead being directed to Möller's new program. At the beginning of 1939, disguising it as a wartime crisis commission, Möller established a new labor market authority.

In contrast to the previous commission, which had been a stronghold for anti–Social Democratic bureaucrats, the new labor market board was organized to give the parties sympathetic to workers and the unions a dominating influence. Both the leadership and personnel at the middle and "street" level were recruited from the union movement. This was not done as a way of rewarding people who had contributed to the party's electoral campaign. Instead the idea was that the policy in question could not be implemented by relying on traditional Weberian rules and regulation. Rather, it was necessary to have people in the implementation process who knew the political goals behind the policy and who were personally committed to the program. This policy continued during and after the war, leading to the establishment of nothing less than a Social Democratic cadre organization. Möller believed that this new policy, which demanded a great deal of discretionary decision making at the implementation stage, could only work if the major "target group"—the unions—were given control over the organization.

The creation of this labor market board was typical of Möller's combination of ideological commitment and interest for organizational details. The organization, known as AMS (Arbetsmarknadsstyrelsen), has since the 1950s been at the heart of what has been named the "Swedish model," implementing the active labor market policy under the direct supervision of the union movement. In its reliance upon "active" measures to combat unemployment, Sweden is still in a unique position among Western capitalist democracies.

The organizational strength of the Swedish working class and the electoral strength of the Social Democratic Party during the postwar era was thus to a large extent created by Möller's reforms of labor market and social policy during the 1930s and 1940s. Social and labor market policy was not only seen by Möller as "policy" per se, but as a way of strengthening the very forces upon which the Social Democratic Party based its strength, especially the blue-collar unions. In addition, the creation of a "hard" party from 1928 to 1932 has certainly made the Swedish Social Democrats an unusually united and coherent party compared to many, if not most, of its sister parties.

As a social reformer, Möller never considered the welfare state an alternative to socialism. Although the organizational problems that he had raised during the late 1910s were never to be solved, he continued to believe that social policy reforms, no matter how extensive, were not the ultimate goal of the party. In 1944, he argued openly for maintaining the Marxist heritage in the party program and he took a firm stand in the Swedish debate against diluting the party's ideology. Throughout his political career, Gustav Möller had a firm knowledge of and a living interest in Marxist theory. He was one of the founders of the Society for Marxism in 1916, a sort of study group for Social Democratic intellectuals. What is especially interesting in this context is that when the Social Democrats entered the government in 1917, Möller persuaded the Society to try to combine theoretical Marxism with the administrative issues of governance mentioned above.

In 1946, party leader Per-Albin Hansson suddenly died and the question of succession came up abruptly. In the struggle for party leadership, Möller clearly overrated his support. Being second in the party and, according to one biographer, more than anyone else personifying the party for the broad masses, he did not see any serious contenders. By underestimating the demand for a generational change in the party's parliamentary group, and by underestimating the opposition from other ministers to his rather expensive social reform program, he lost the battle over the leadership of the party in 1946 to the young Tage Erlander. Embittered, he stayed in the government until 1951 when a coalition between the Social Democrats and the Agrarian Party was established.

Möller's strength as political leader was his unique combination of advanced theoretical analysis with politics as praxis. Although extremely successful in both structuring the party and its policies to advance the future of the movement he served, the irony of history is of course that he never saw the realization of socialism. One could also argue, of course, that his very success in building an extensive and generous welfare state prevented the realization of his more far-reaching ideological goal. The younger generation in the party that took over in 1946 was more interested in securing the gains that had been achieved in social policy than in experimenting with democratic socialism.

BIBLIOGRAPHY

Works by Möller:

''Den sociala revolutionen,'' *Tiden* 10: 241–56 (1918).

''I Socialiseringsfrågan,'' *Tiden* 11: 188–92 (1919).

''Socialiseringsproblemet,'' *Tiden* 12: 97–105 (1920).

''The Swedish Unemployment Policy,'' in *The Annals of the American Academy of Political and Social Sciences*, Vol. 197, 47–71, 1938.

''De planerade socialreformerna,'' *Tiden* 38: 70–85 (1946).

''Svensk socialpolitik,'' *Tiden* 44: 391–99 (1952).

Other Works:

Pontusson, Jonas. *Limits to Reformism.* Ithaca, N.Y.: Cornell University Press, 1992.

Rothstein, Bo. ''Managing the Welfare State: Lessons from Gustav Möller,'' *Scandinavian Political Studies* 8 (3): 151–70 (1985).

———. ''The Success of the Swedish Labour Market Policy: The Organizational Connection,'' *European Journal of Political Research* 13: 153–65 (1985).

———. *Den socialdemokratiska staten.* Lund: Arkiv Förlag, 1986.

Schüllerqvist, Bengt. *Från kosackval till kohandel.* Stockholm: Tiden, 1992.
Tilton, Tim. *The Political Theory of Swedish Social Democracy.* Oxford: Clarendon, 1990.

BO ROTHSTEIN

ALDO MORO (1916–1978) was one of the most prominent politicians in Italian postwar politics. Elected to the Constituent Assembly in 1946, he was subsequently reelected to the Italian parliament until his tragic death, murdered in 1978 by Red Brigade terrorists. Head of the Christian Democratic Caucus of the House of Deputies in 1953, he became secretary general of the ruling Christian Democratic Party (DC) in 1959. Five times prime minister in relatively long-lasting governments, several times minister (notably of foreign affairs), at the time of his death Moro was president of the Christian Democratic Party.

Like many Christian Democrats of his generation, Moro began his political career as a leader in Catholic organizations—the only ones allowed to survive under fascism. From 1939 to 1942, he served as national chairman of the Federation of Catholic University Students (FUCI). Later, from 1945 to 1946, he became president of the Catholic Action Movement for University Graduates. In the meantime, Moro graduated in law and in 1947 won the chair in penal law at the University of Bari.

A very prolific writer in Catholic publications before actively entering politics, Moro played a significant role in the drafting of the new Italian constitution and was for a time identified with the group of young Catholic professors (*professorini*) gathered around Giuseppe Dossetti (later vice-secretary of the DC) and Amintore Fanfani (later secretary of the DC and six times prime minister). A controversial figure in his party and in Italian society, Moro's purely political achievements are many and significant. On the other hand, his performance as a government leader, especially as prime minister, while not yet having been subjected to serious scholarly scrutiny, still cannot be considered in an entirely favorable light.

A devout Catholic, Moro believed that it is the task of Catholicism to identify the values to be pursued by a Christian in politics. It is then the task of political activity to identify political solutions most appropriate to the implementation of those values. While never inclined to overtly antagonize the Catholic Church, the Vatican, or the pope, Moro did claim full autonomy and independence in the political field, even when the pope was as close a friend of his as Paul VI. Therefore, Moro encountered much opposition from within the ranks of the Christian Democratic Party itself, particularly among those who wanted to utilize Catholic principles and the Vatican's positions to buttress their own vested interests and power. Moro's paramount political goal was to shape and preserve a party with a Christian inspiration, but not expose it to the domination of the ecclesiastical community. He strived for a party capable of interpreting and leading a dramatically changing Italian society. In this, Moro won several battles. It remains very doubtful, however, whether he also won the war.

His first really major political achievement was the formation of a governmental coalition which included the Italian Socialist Party (PSI) in 1962. At the time, the Socialists had been disengaging themselves from a "unity of action pact" with the still pro-Soviet Italian Communist Party (PCI). The PSI represented some segments of the reformist working class, of the progressive middle class and of the intellectuals. Moro believed that the consolidation of a democratic regime in Italy could better be pursued by expanding the governmental coalition to include the PSI, all the while taking care to isolate the PCI in order to contain its political influence.

Always worried about the fragility of Italian democracy, Moro aimed at the gradual enlargment of the Italian republic's democratic foundations. In a lengthy speech at the DC's party convention in Naples in 1962, Moro succeeded in convincing a rather reluctant party to accept this so-called opening to the left. In this, Moro was able to bring a united party to this reconciliation with the center-left, contrary to the Socialists, who suffered a serious split.

Unfortunately—and for reasons that were not under Moro's control—the center-left was far less reformist in its orientation than had been widely expected. The Socialist split fatally weakened the coalition, while powerful domestic and international forces opposed it. Massive capital flights made it difficult to introduce deep reforms in the economic system. Many Christian Democrats continued silently or vocally to sabotage the center-left. The alliance with the Socialists, considered by Moro essential for the consolidation and growth of Italian democracy, was declared "not irreversible" by Fanfani, his traditional nemesis within the DC. A coup d'état—probably well known in advance within some high political and governmental circles—was blocked at the eleventh hour. Finally, Moro himself proved to be an obstacle to a dynamic reformist effort.

Prime minister in three successive center-left governments from December 1963 to June 1968, Moro presided over a loss of reformist élan. His proud claim—"I have governed and do govern in the spirit of the center-left, putting the lay soul and the Christian soul of the country together in a strong progressive push"—is revealing of his strong preference for the politics of coalition making rather than the politics of reform. In all likelihood, it was his very style of politics and his conception of Italian democracy that prevented him from being an innovative and powerful government leader. Indeed, Moro's outstanding ability was expressed above all in his capacity to persuade his friends and foes and to mediate among conflicting interests and objectives.

It would be unfair to say that Moro liked political maneuverings inside the corridors of power. To the contrary, though in somewhat complicated and convoluted prose, Moro never disguised either his purposes or his goals. In a faction-ridden Christian Democratic Party, Moro was not a faction leader until he finally recognized the necessity of creating a tiny faction in order not to be completely excluded from intraparty decision-making processes. This faction never constituted more than 10 percent of the party's delegates.

This development occurred in 1969 when the DC's dominant faction, the *dorotei*, not only emptied the center-left governing formula of most of its reformist content, but also attempted to definitively rid the party of Moro's influence. However, Moro defended his place in the party, his ideas and his vision in a speech of rare force, mincing no words, clearly denouncing the party for its mistakes and calling errant party members by name.

This short-lived reformist phase of the center-left was, however, still bearing some fruit. In particular, Italian society had become freer and more exacting. Moro's vision had been prescient, but his policies inadequate. In the students' and workers' movements, he saw a transition from a vertical society with power concentrated in a few organizations, above all in the major political parties, to a horizontal society with power diffused and dispersed. This evolution made a strong center-left coalition even more necessary in order to prevent the confrontation he feared between a coalition guided by the Communist Party and one led by the Christian Democrats. In his opinion, Italy was and remained a problematic democracy, for a great ideological gulf separated the PCI from the DC, a gulf characterized by a polarization of ideas and values and by the PCI's reluctance to fully accept a democratic framework, as well as by its persistent ties with the Soviet Bloc.

In this context, the increasing complexity of Italian society and an explosion of new, unprecedented demands for political, socioeconomic and cultural change could not be easily accommodated in a narrow and shortsighted government sphere. In Moro's view, the immobilism of the center-left and its rejection of what he called the ''strategy of attention'' toward the Communist Party were wrong and counterproductive. Yet his strategy toward the PCI was unfortunately soon superseded by a strategy of terrorism, first on the right wing, mounted by neo-fascists with support from some disloyal sectors of the Italian secret services, then on the left wing, initiated by splinter groups within the Communist Party who rejected its parliamentary stance. In this period, Moro suffered his gravest political defeat.

Moro was the party's candidate in the presidential election of December 1971, when a large majority of his own colleagues, as well as some former allies from the center-left coalition (especially the Republicans), with the decisive support of the neo-fascists, preferred the DC baron Giovanni Leone to him. Ironically, Leone would later have to resign the presidency in the wake of the Lockheed bribery scandal just one month after Moro's murder by the Red Brigades. Moro's never-announced candidacy was doomed by accusations that he was willing to give a greater role to the PCI, perhaps even to include it in a government, were he to be elected president.

Following this defeat, Moro's influence in Italian politics plummeted to its lowest point ever. The center-left lay in ruins and was replaced by a center-right coalition led by Giulio Andreotti, serving his first term as prime minister. Though Moro remained in the government as minister of foreign affairs—a prestigious though powerless office—his political career seemed clearly on the wane.

There is no satisfactory assessment of Moro's tenure and performance at the foreign ministry. Traditionally, in postwar Italy, the Ministry of Foreign Affairs has been a kind of parking space for senior statesmen, those who have been prime minister, or for rising political stars, those who will become prime minister. On the other hand, Italian foreign policy had never been conducted very actively. Subordinate to the Atlantic Alliance and quite passively pro-European, Italian foreign policy was shaped by Italy's dependent relationship with the United States. In only one area did Italian policy makers seem to be willing to act independently: in their Mediterranean policy toward Arab states, especially the oil-producing countries. Predictably, this was a sore point in relations with the U.S. Department of State.

Moro's tenure as minister of foreign affairs was characterized by an attempt to gradually reduce Italy's subordination vis-à-vis the United States and to obtain more of a free hand in the Mediterranean, an area considered vital to Italian interests. No tangible results ensued, except, perhaps, some deep suspicions against Moro on the part of several top American policy makers, in particular Secretary of State Henry Kissinger. Allegedly, Kissinger had already been incensed by Moro's supposed willingness to open a dialogue with the PCI.

The disastrous defeat of the official Christian Democratic position on the abortion referendum (the DC favored repealing the abortion law) produced an upheaval in the DC. Moro returned to office as prime minister, presiding over his fourth government (November 1974–January 1976). Though his government was officially only a coalition with the Republicans, unofficially it also relied on the Socialists.

Another major electoral defeat in 1975 removed the Christian Democrats from the local governments of almost all the important Italian cities. This catastrophe finally obliged the DC's leadership to proceed to an agonizing reappraisal of the strategy followed for ten years by the *dorotei.* In a sharp and bitter confrontation with the party establishment, Moro succeeded in creating an alternative majority within the party and electing his close collaborator, Benigno Zaccagnini, to the office of DC secretary general.

Zaccagnini's honest face, coupled with a serious and credible threat of the Communists—supposedly on their way a relative majority—clearly played a decisive role in the June 1976 national elections. Moro saw two winners in the results of these elections: the DC, which had survived the challenge by retaining its relative majority, and the PCI, which had considerably increased its votes, thereby becoming a full-fledged coprotagonist on the Italian political scene. Still, Moro rejected the offer of an historic compromise made by PCI Secretary Enrico Berlinguer. Once again, Moro recognized both the novelty and the unavoidable complexity of the political landscape, trying to guide his party and Italian society through it without traumatic consequences.

A new "third phase" of Italian politics—after the first phase of *centrismo* (a four-party centrist alliance from 1948 to 1960) and the second, center-left phase (a four-party alliance including the Socialists from 1962 to 1972)—was clearly being inaugurated. For Moro, the ultimate goal was the implementation of full democracy (*democrazia completa*) in Italy wherein all political forces would have access to governmental participation, alternating in power. This goal was, however, a distant one whose outcome was not necessarily inevitable.

In the meantime, faithful to his conception of politics, Moro bought time. Elected president of the Christian Democratic Party, he decided to devote all his great bargaining skills to the formation of a government led by Giulio Andreotti, a government acceptable for lack of good alternatives to both the Socialists and the Communists and one floating on a sea of abstentions. Nobody doubted that Moro was again in charge of Christian Democratic strategy.

Indeed, he was engaged in a process not dissimilar from the one that had led him in his celebrated ''opening'' to the Socialist Party, to the center-left. In order to succeed, however, Moro wanted and needed a unified party, explaining why he refused to lead the government himself. Instead, he opted for the appointment of Andreotti, who represented a guarantee to the Vatican, to moderate segments of the DC electorate, and to the state apparatus. This is also why, in a spirited speech, he defended the party from accusations leveled against it for its involvement in the Lockheed scandal. ''We will not allow you to try us,'' he proclaimed to the left in parliament. To Moro, the overriding political imperative was to preserve the DC as a countervailing force in the face of the left's advance.

Aldo Moro was a Christian Democrat essentially because he believed in the role of a Christian party in Italian politics. Moreover, in the 1970s he also felt a deep obligation to maintain the unity of the party in order to withstand the Communist challenge and to prepare for the third phase of Italian politics. Both within and outside the party, his power was limited, but his prestige was great. His critics were many, but his political triumph was achieved when he was able to convince many doubters that it was indispensable for them to vote for an Andreotti government that would also be supported by the Communists.

The paradox of the Italian political system was that the two sides could not work together because they represented two so different, contrasting views of Italian politics and of the international system. Yet in a democracy as fragile as Italy's, it was impossible for the opposition to perform its role in an uncompromising manner. Such opposition would destabilize democracy. For Moro, the imperative of the new politics was simple: Sign a careful truce and wait cautiously for new developments. The very day Andreotti's government—enjoying the parliamentary support of the Communists—was to be inaugurated (March 16, 1978), Aldo Moro was kidnapped by the Red Brigades.

In the fifty-five days of his imprisonment, Moro fought desperately for his life. He resorted to all his persuasive abilities to convince the Red Brigades to release him and the authorities to bargain with the Red Brigades. In vain he sent letters to his ''friends'' within the DC, to his family, to his closest collaborators, to Bettino Craxi, secretary general of the Socialist Party, to his longtime friend Cardinal Montini, now Pope Paul VI. A heated debate developed over whether these letters had been, in fact, written under duress. An even more heated debate developed over what approach to take in the crisis, although a quick declaration was made that there would be no bargaining over the hostage Moro.

Today, no one would doubt the legitimacy of Moro's letters, even when some of them drew unflattering portraits of prominent Christian Democrats, such as Andreotti, Cossiga and Taviani, for during his "people's trial," he never revealed information of any importance, much less state secrets. But his efforts did not save his life. Too weak, too insecure, too inefficient, the Italian state could not afford to bargain with the Red Brigades for an exchange of "political prisoners." Also, the Red Brigades could not afford to free Moro, the most militant among them having decided well in advance to kill him.

Moro's murder marked the high point of Red Brigade strength. At the same time, it produced a major rift in the organization and among other elements of left-wing terrorism. More important, Moro's murder brought to an abrupt end the third phase of Italian politics. Left-wing terrorists had thus achieved at least one of their goals: preventing the Communist Party from "betraying" the working class by joining in a government with the Christian Democrats. Some argue that Moro's aim was not to bring the Communists into a government at all. Instead, his unavowed long-term goal was to wear down the PCI, keeping it midstream, reducing its electoral following and blunting its reformist inclinations. After all, critics and apologists agreed, this is exactly what Moro had shrewdly accomplished with the Socialists.

Whatever the third phase of the Italian political system was to be in Moro's vision, it is difficult to believe that he was not committed to reinforcing the foundations of fragile democracy in Italy. In particular, he sought to oblige the PCI to fully accept the rules of a democratic regime and Italy's international commitments. However, not only has "enlargement" of Italian democracy not been achieved, but, as Moro feared, the Christian Democrats have drifted to the right without a discernible strategy, losing votes, blurring their identity, lacking any clear vision of the future. Indeed, Moro had intimated that the future was no longer in their hands. There is no assurance that, had Moro lived, Italy would have achieved full democracy. But there is no doubt that Moro's death impoverished Italian politics for many years.

BIBLIOGRAPHY

Works by Moro:

L'Intelligenza e gli avvenimenti: Testi 1959–1978. Milan: Garzanti, 1979.

Scritti e discorsi, Vol. 1, 1940–1947; *Scritti e discorsi*, Vol. 2, 1951–1963. Rome: Edizioni Cinque Lune, 1982.

Other Works:

Baget Bozzo, Gianni, and Giovanni Tassani. *Aldo Moro: Il Politico nella crisi 1962–1973.* Florence: Sansoni, 1983.

Cicerchia, Annalisa (ed.). *Aldo Moro: Stato e società.* Rome: Presidenza del Consiglio dei Ministri Dipartimento per l'Informazione e l'Editoria, 1990.

Drake, Richard. *The Aldo Moro Murder Case.* Cambridge: Harvard University Press, 1992.

Moss, David. "The Kidnapping and Murder of Aldo Moro," *European Journal of Sociology* 22(2): 265–93 (1981).

Various Authors. *Moro, la Democrazia Cristiana e la cultura cattolica.* Rome: Edizioni Cinque Lune, 1979.

Wagner-Pacifica, Robin Erica. *The Moro Morality Play: Terrorism as Social Drama.* Chicago: The University of Chicago Press, 1986.

GIANFRANCO PASQUINO

P

JUHO KUSTI PAASIKIVI (1870–1956) was most important in Finnish politics for having succeeded in guiding Finland toward a policy of neutrality after World War II and in preventing the Soviet-supported Finnish Communists from taking power. In this, Finland was an exceptional example in the postwar period, for it was the only Western neighbor contiguous to the Soviet Union able to preserve intact its constitution and democratic system. To use George F. Kennan's expression, ''Containment'' succeeded with Finland.

Juho Kusti Paasikivi was born into a poor country family in south Finland. Only with the help of his relatives was he able to go to school and then continue his studies at the Universtity of Helsinki. He was Finnish-speaking by origin, and therefore it was natural for him to join the Finnish (Conservative) Party. Later he became a leading activist in that party.

Initially, Paasikivi planned an academic career; his main interests were history, languages and jurisprudence. And although Finland's relations to Russia started to deteriorate dramatically at the end of the 19th century (Finland had been part of the Russian Empire as a grand duchy since 1809), Paasikivi maintained an interest in Russian language and history, studying in Novgorod and acquiring a very good knowledge of Russian culture. While he never did, in fact, became a professional historian, later, as a politician, Paasikivi would gain much benefit from this knowledge.

After completing his dissertation in jurisprudence in 1901, Paasikivi was appointed assistant professor at the University of Helsinki. His future career as a teacher and researcher seemed to be clear. But despite this very auspicious beginning of an academic career, after five years as a professor he was appointed director of the Finnish Treasury. Moreover, during the years 1907–1913, he was twice elected member of parliament. As a member of the Finnish Party, Paasikivi supported compliance with Russian political demands, setting the young ambitious politician apart from the activists demanding Finnish independence. Finally, difficulties with the Russian administration led him to withdraw from politics altogether.

When the Finnish parliament approved the declaration of independence on December 6, 1917, Paasikivi proved to be a firm monarchist. His aim was to establish a German prince on a Finnish throne. When appointed prime minister, he still believed that imperial Germany would win World War I, and he therefore based his policy on German political and military support. The Finnish civil war then broke out in January 1918, and with the aid of German troops, General Mannerheim and his "White Guards" crushed the "Red Guards" supported by Russian Bolshevik troops. German troops stayed on in Finland but when imperial Germany collapsed in November 1918, this German orientation was terminated, and Paasikivi's Senate was forced to resign.

For some years Paasikivi remained aside from domestic politics, but when peace negotiations began with the Soviet Russians in Tartu, Estonia, the Finnish government again called on his knowledge of Russia, appointing Paasikivi leader of the Finnish delegation to these talks. Seizing an advantageous political situation, Paasikivi succeeded in obtaining a relatively good peace treaty: Finland retained the same borders as it had had during the grand duchy period and was also given additional territory for access to the seaport of Petsamo. However, Paasikivi's political opponents accused him of treason for failing to get the Soviet Union to cede another territory, East Karelia, to Finland.

In 1934, at the age of sixty-four, Paasikivi retired from his post as director of the board of a large Finnish bank, Kansallis-Osake-Pankki. At this time, he was a well-known political figure in Finland, but was certainly not yet a "statesman."

As in the rest of Europe during this period, a radical right-wing movement was increasing its political influence in Finnish society. This process also occurred within the National Conservative Party (the successor to the earlier Finnish Party). When Paasikivi was elected the Conservative Party's leader, he immediately set about to counterattack against the right-wing radical faction which had developed ties with the German Nazis. During the first half of the 1930s, Paasikivi became a leading figure in the struggle of democratic political parties against the right-wing totalitarian movement.

Thus, from the mid-1930s, Paasikivi was increasingly involved in the shaping of Finnish foreign policy. This was to become the main field of his life's work. In the Finnish Party, and in its successor the National Conservative Party, Paasikivi represented a moderate attitude toward the so-called language question. Close ties to Scandinavia, and especially to Sweden, were an important element in Paasikivi's political thinking. For this reason he was appointed the Finnish minister to Stockholm in 1936, his main task being to secure a defense alliance between Finland and Sweden. The Finnish parliament had, in fact, declared a "Scandinavian orientation" to be Finland's official line in foreign policy.

However, the Winter War, which broke out on November 30, 1939, was to prove that Paasikivi and the Finnish government had not succeeded in their so-called Scandinavian orientation. Finland, in fact, found itself isolated. Prior to the war, Paasikivi had gone to Moscow three times as the head of a Finnish delegation. He had recommended that Finland make concessions to the Soviets, but the incumbent foreign affairs minister rejected the idea, attempting to avoid the fate of the three Baltic republics. The Finnish people stood behind the government's policy, apparently afraid that Soviet demands would intensify.

Without any declaration of war, the Soviets attacked Finland. The Finnish government resigned, and the Risto Ryti government was appointed. Paasikivi served as a minister in the Ryti government, as well as a member of the so-called war cabinet. He also took part in the peace negotiations of March 1940.

However, instead of being given a portfolio in the post–Winter War government, Paasikivi was sent to Moscow as the chief Finnish envoy. Gradually he became disenchanted with the government's policy and began to feel that he was no longer being kept sufficiently informed of affairs by either the prime minister or the foreign minister. Thus he was not even aware of the pro-German orientation of the government's foreign policy that had already been adopted by autumn 1940. He believed that the government's political line jeopardized the development of peaceful relations with the Soviet Union, so he decided to resign.

For practical reasons, Paasikivi had to remain in Moscow until May 1941. Then, only a few weeks after he returned home, Finland joined the Germans in war against the Soviet Union. Paasikivi remained without a political post throughout the duration of the "Continuation War" from 1941 to 1944.

At the beginning of the German invasion of the Soviet Union, Paasikivi considered a German victory to be the likely outcome of the conflict. This was quite typical of his realpolitik way of thinking. But by winter 1942 he had become convinced that Germany could not win. Later he came to be regarded as one of the intellectual leaders of the so-called "peace opposition." Nevertheless, he avoided making his position known publicly, remaining loyal to the government and to president Ryti, to whom he was the closest political adviser. His only official task during the war was to lead the Finnish delegation in peace contacts with Moscow. None of these negotiations came to anything, and the war continued for another six months.

Paasikivi reappeared on the Finnish political stage soon after the war ended in September 1944. In a totally new political context, he enjoyed wide approval both among all the Finnish political parties and in Moscow. Although Marshal Mannerheim had been elected president of the Finnish Republic in August 1944, his health deteriorated rapidly during the course of the 1944–1945 winter, and Paasikivi effectively served as head of state. Before the parliamentary election in the spring of 1945, Paasikivi publicly demanded that old "war politicians" withdraw from politics and give way to "new faces." After the election, he formed his second government, which was based on a coalition of "three big parties," the Agrarians, the Social Democrats and the Communists.

Immediately after the signing of the Moscow truce, the Allied Control Commission arrived in Helsinki. Russians dominated the commission, British officers being essentially outsiders. At this time, the condemnation of so-called war criminals became a very delicate and problematic public issue. In this, Paasikivi had to bow to Soviet pressure for war crime trials, but fortunately the proceedings took place in Finland instead of Moscow. The former president, Ryti, was sentenced to ten years' imprisonment. Six other ex-ministers received shorter sentences. Shortly after this, Mannerheim retired from the presidency, and Paasikivi was formally elected president of Finland.

In the 1947 Paris Peace Congress, Paasikivi attempted to renegotiate more favorable peace conditions for Finland but to no avail. Finnish borders stayed as they were at the end of the war, and war reparations remained severe ($300 million in gold). Moreover, at the end of 1947 Stalin sent a letter to Paasikivi proposing that Finland and the Soviet Union sign a "treaty of friendship, cooperation and mutual assistance." This was a frightening omen because the same process in Czechoslovakia was already leading to Communist domination. In response, Paasikivi made a counterproposal to Stalin's proposition. Paasikivi's proposal was neither formally nor practically similar to treaties the Soviet Union had already signed with other socialist countries. For example, it did not provide for automatic military cooperation between the two states.

At the end of the 1940s, Paasikivi had hardened his attitude toward both the Finnish Communists and the Soviet Union. He dismissed the Communist interior minister and then in the spring of 1948 ordered a heightening of readiness of the Finnish army and police so as to demonstrate to the Soviet Union that what was going on in Czechoslovakia could not be replicated in Finland.

In 1948, Paasikivi also appointed a Social Democratic minority government, excluding the Communists from it. He never again accepted Communists in any government.

At every opportunity, Paasikivi distanced Finland from the Soviet Union (while also isolating the Finnish Communists), thereby very skillfully guiding Finland toward neutrality through these politically dangerous postwar years. His tenure as president ended when he retired in 1956. He died not long afterward during the same year. During the final year of his presidency, the Soviet Union closed its military base at Porkkala near Helsinki, and Finland became a member of both the United Nations and the Nordic Council.

During his wide-ranging career, Paasikivi's greatest advantage was his broad knowledge of both Russian and classical culture. Better than most of his contemporaries, he was able to situate current political problems in the perspective of their historical background. He was also very good at analytical thinking. He could therefore reliably analyze current events, using his insights as a basis for practical political decisions. Paasikivi's recently published diaries clearly show this process taking place. Among Western statesmen overall, Paasikivi easily had the greatest knowledge of Russian culture, politics and way of life.

As a political negotiator, Paasikivi was both very skillful and courageous. In negotiations with Stalin and Molotov—both very difficult opponents—whether in autumn 1939, winter 1940 or spring 1944, Paasikivi was undaunted. He was usually receptive to a sensible compromise, but never to surrender.

Paasikivi also had an exellent ability to place distance between himself and other people, exhibiting all the while an air of natural authority. This helped him, for example, in difficult negotiations with the Russians. His appearence was also imposing, for he was a large man with a severe countenance. Later as president of the Finnish Republic, he was also very authoritarian. Consequently, Paasikivi was respected by both his subordinates and his opponents.

But while Paasikivi was very authoritative, he never tried to dominate parliament politically. In negotiations with the Russians, he often used this fact as a tactic against his opponents, making reference to the Finnish parliamentary system whenever Russian demands went too far. In this, Paasikivi was both a smart tactician and a man of principle, rendering his policies flexible while remaining consistent. And although he always attempted to understand Russian interests, Paasikivi was, nonetheless, intellectually tied to the West. Especially important to him were relations with the other Scandinavian countries.

But Paasikivi was also a man of violent temper and a very difficult colleague. In this sense, he was quite rigid and inflexible, and conflicts often resulted. In his realpolitik, he was often too pessimistic. Following Bismarck, he believed only in big power politics in international relations. But the vigorous defense by the Finnish army in the Winter War (1939–1940) demonstrated that Paasikivi was incapable of understanding the enormous power of idealism in a small nation. Paasikivi based too much of his thinking on the assumed dominance of Finland by those countries which seemed to be most powerful at the time. This led him to his misguided reliance on imperial Germany in 1918, to pessimism in autumn 1939 in the face of the Soviet threat and to an overestimation of German strength in 1941.

Although Paasikivi retained his intellectual abilities into old age, during the 1950s he begn relying too heavily on Prime Minister Urho Kekkonen (later a president of Finland). He failed to see that Kekkonen's political principles were totally different from his own.

Paasikivi's greatest importance in Finnish domestic policy was, as we have seen, his prevention of the right-wing movement taking power in the Conservative Party at the beginning of the 1930s and his isolation of the Finnish Communists after World War II. Internationally, his most significant achievement was to prevent Finland from becoming part of the Soviet-dominated Socialist Bloc. His policy of ''containment'' succeeded for Finland.

BIBLIOGRAPHY

Works by Paasikivi:

Paasikiven linja (Paasikivi's Line), 2 vols. (Speeches), 1956.
Muistelmia sortovuosilta (Memoirs from the Years of Russian Oppression), 2 vols. 1956.
Toimintani Moskovassa ja Helsingissä 1939–41 (My Political Activity in Moscow and Helsinki, 1939–41), 2 vols. 1958.
Päiväkirjat 1944–56 (Diaries 1944–56), 2 vols. 1985–86.
Päiväkirjat 1941–44 (Diaries 1941–44), 1991.

Other Works:

Hakalehto, Ilkka (ed.). *J. K. Paasikivi Suomen politiikassa.* 1970.
Ikonen, Kimmo. *Juho Kusti Paasikivi: Linjanrakentajan tie 1870–1941.* 1986.
Polvinen, Tuono. *J. K. Paasikivi,* 2 vols. 1989–1992.

MARTTI TURTOLA

OLOF PALME (1927–1986) was one of the 20th century's most important Swedish politicians, known throughout the world for his commitment to development and equality in the Third World.

Palme came from a family rooted in the landed and commercial classes of Sweden, Finland and Latvia. As such, he grew up in an upper-class environment characterized by many contacts with the outside world. His father, Gunnar Palme, who died at age forty-four from a heart attack, was director of the family's insurance company in Sweden and was active in conservative politics. His mother, Elisabeth, was the daughter of a professor of agriculture in Riga, Latvia, a descendent of a line of German-Balt officials and landowners. She grew up in a turbulent era for the Baltics, characterized by Russian suspiciousness of Germans, Red revolutionaries' hatred of landowners and the efforts of the Latvians themselves to limit the influence of German speakers. Soon after beginning medical studies in Germany, Elisabeth was forced to return to Riga and follow her mother, who had been deported, into the interior of Russia. The daughter was allowed to emigrate to Sweden in 1915, and she married Gunnar Palme one year later.

Although most of Palme's family and upbringing were characterized by conservative political views, he inherited from his mother a stern work ethic and commitment to social causes, as well as a certain distance and shyness in personal relations, a simplicity of habits and modesty of needs and a good memory that sometimes lent itself to grudges and irreconcilability.

As a child, Palme was short of stature, and this tendency to be smaller than his peers was exacerbated by the fact that he began school a year earlier than normal. As a boy, he was very competitive and athletic and fought a great deal. Nonetheless, intellectually, he was an early developer who devoured books, was interested in learning and very quick-witted.

The decade between Palme's graduation from private boarding school and the beginning of his employment in 1953 as private secretary to the Swedish prime minister, Tage Erlander—paving the way for his involvement in politics—was characterized by his search for a professional identity and a niche in life. He completed his military service in the cavalry and was promoted to the rank of reserve officer. He tried his hand at journalism and was employed, unsalaried, at the country's major conservative newspaper, where his mother had connections. He won a stipend to study at Kenyon College in the United States and succeeded in obtaining his B.A. there in one year. He enrolled at the Faculty of Law of the University of Stockholm in fall 1948 and subsequently received his B.L. degree. And he played with the idea of seeking a post with the Swedish Foreign Ministry, given his considerable linguistic abilities (as a child, he grew up speaking Swedish, German and French) and knowledge of foreign countries.

For many years, activism in Swedish student unions served as a springboard for young people with social and political aspirations. This certainly was the case with Olof Palme. He was recruited by the National Organization of Swedish Students (SFS), where he played a very active international role in resistance to the main communist-dominated international student organization. In the spring of 1952, he was elected SFS chairman and in that capacity made good use of opportunities to be seen in public and to conduct discussions with Swedish government officials.

During this period, Tage Erlander, the Swedish prime minister, was looking desperately for a qualified personal secretary. Several people are thought to have drawn his attention to Palme, who by spring 1953 had resigned as SFS chairman and gone to work on the defense staff. To Palme's great surprise, the prime minister approached him and offered him the job.

By this time, Palme had already developed pronounced social democratic sympathies. His leaning toward the left and away from his family's conservative political values had evolved gradually. In subsequent years, Palme would explain this development in his political views with reference to a variety of events, ranging from his childhood on the Latvian estate of his grandparents to his years in a boarding school for the wealthy. The formative experiences he most often referred to included a heated domestic political debate over new tax legislation proposed by the Social Democrats, and above all, the new way of looking at Sweden he acquired during his stay in the United States. There he witnessed the stark contrast between the "haves" and "have nots." Palme's leaning toward the left was bolstered by a journey he made to Asia in 1953, prior to his employment with Tage Erlander. The experiences of that trip, on which he witnessed poverty and destitution, became the fertile soil in which his lifelong commitment to the Third World was to flourish.

Throughout his political life, Palme would be reminded—especially by those from nonsocialist circles—of the contradictions between his upper-class background and his sympathies for the organized workers' movement. The spiteful labeled his conversion pure opportunism. It was considered shrewd to join the party that dominated Swedish politics at that time—as if a multitude of other careers had not been available to an individual with Olof Palme's talents and background. But he eased into his life's calling gradually and by coincidence, and the political positions he occupied did not mean he was cut off from the environment from whence he had come. In these respects, Olof Palme was similar to Lisbet Beck-Fries, whom he met for the first time on a skiing trip in the mountains in 1953, and whom he married in 1956. She, too, came from an aristocratic family and had, in the course of her psychology studies, gone through a political development similar to her future husband's.

The period from Palme's first post in the government to his elevation to prime minister and party leader covered sixteen years. It was characterized both by continuous, intensive collaboration with Tage Erlander and by the gradual broadening and reinforcement of Palme's own political standing. Palme had an unusual relationship to Erlander, who was his senior by more than a quarter of a century. The young man who was originally employed as an efficient secretary with linguistic abilities very soon became the prime minister's confidant and right-hand man. Palme and Erlander became inseparable and thrived in each other's company. They were also similar in many ways: quick-witted, quick-tongued, unconventional and slightly bohemian. They both had wide interests and were open to new ideas, as well as being pragmatic and obsessed by politics. The propensity to worry and periodic melancholy of the elder was balanced by the younger man's greater optimism and feeling that things could be taken care of. In Erlander, Palme had found himself an older man to admire, to like and to learn from. What blossomed between them was almost a father-son relationship.

In this period, Palme became an important domestic and international adviser to the prime minister, and by 1963, he was made minister without portfolio. During the years leading up to his own election as prime minister, he became a part of the small circle of ministers—the informal inner cabinet—that the aging Tage Erlander relied upon so much. Palme was minister of communications in 1965–1967 and minister of education in 1967–1969.

During the early years, Palme evinced special interest in two policy areas: education and foreign policy. Palme's first official assignment in education policy was to chair a commission set up in 1959 to devise a new student financing system. This assignment was followed by others. Palme's interest in education matters culminated in two years as minister of education. One of his persistent themes there was the continual emphasis of education's role in a broader social and economic context. He repeatedly stressed the values of democracy, classlessness and equality. In different ways, Palme tried to contribute to the phasing out or minimization of status differences and barriers between different sorts of education. He became involved in adult education and continuing education, and he judged research from the point of view of its social utility. The student unrest of the late 1960s also occurred during Palme's tenure as education minister. In May 1968, he leapt unafraid into a debate with protesting students in the student union building they were occupying in Stockholm, expressing considerable sympathy for their demands for increased student influence.

Palme's special interest in foreign policy and international affairs also became evident early on. During the early 1960s, Palme worked with a commission dealing with aid to developing countries. At that time, as he often would do subsequently, he referred in speeches and addresses to his own experiences traveling through Southeast Asia in the early 1950s: Children had run after him for block after block begging for money. Men and women lay apathetically by the wayside, their stomachs swollen with hunger. Palme's words and deeds in this regard created an image of him as the conscience of the world and as a foreign policy leftist.

For example, in a speech given in the summer of 1965 to a conference of Christian Social Democrats, he proclaimed: "It is an illusion to believe that demands for social justice can be met with violence and armed force. It is very hard to win people's commitment with promises to defend a freedom that they have, in reality, never enjoyed." The speech was clearly aimed at the United States, which at that point was stepping up its presence in Southeast Asia. It aroused protests both in official circles in the United States and from the political opposition in Sweden.

Moreover, Palme's tone hardened gradually. Throughout the late 1960s, in speeches that resonated with protest, he spoke of oppression and poverty in the Third World and of the justification of demands for national freedom and social liberation. In February 1968, Palme led a march through the center of Stockholm, accompanied by the North Vietnamese ambassador to Moscow. Among the controversial things he said on that occasion was that the American role in Vietnam had developed into a threat to democratic ideals, not just in Vietnam but in the world as a whole. To protest, the United States recalled its Stockholm ambassador, and several politicians from Sweden's nonsocialist parties hardened their criticism of Palme as a foreign policy actor. Accusations rained over him for having allowed himself to be influenced by the leftist wave that was washing over Sweden at the time, thereby jeopardizing Sweden's traditional policy of neutrality.

Palme's criticism of American Vietnam policy reached a crescendo three years after he took office as prime minister. Shortly before Christmas 1972, he penned a statement regarding the intensified American bombardment of Vietnam. In it, he stigmatized what was happening in Vietnam as torture and outrage. It could, he claimed, be compared with such other historical atrocities as Guernica, Oradour, Babi Yar, Katyn, Lidice, Sharpeville and Treblinka. The American reaction to this assault was even stronger than before. A newly appointed Swedish ambassador to the United States was declared *persona non grata* in Washington, and at home, too, many were shocked by Palme's tone. At the same time, however, petitions against the American bombing of Vietnam were circulating throughout the country and had been signed by over two million Swedes.

Palme's early commitment to the Vietnam question contributed to his being viewed, in the 1960s, as a spokesman for a younger generation that was characterized by anti-Americanism and leftist tendencies. However, Palme was not really an anti-American. He criticized American government policy, but he also continued, as he had since his years as a student in the United States, to feel at home in an American setting, following American politics and reading American books and journals. Nor did Palme particularly identify himself with the left wing of the Social Democratic Party. But his involvement in the Vietnam issue highlighted his tendency to express himself both drastically and emotionally.

Palme thus became the focus of highly charged attention both within Sweden and abroad before he even became prime minister.

Public speculation as to the possibility of Palme becoming prime minister and leader of the Social Democratic Party had, indeed, begun early. Palme stood out as the representative of a new Social Democratic generation, and from early on he enjoyed the support of the Social Democratic Youth League. Apparently, however, he pushed aside thoughts of the party leadership for a long time and was neither as willing nor as eager to succeed Erlander as many presumed. However, those of the middle generation who had been mentioned as possible candidates dropped out and the only ones to remain in the end were Palme and Finance Minister Gunnar Sträng, who was nearly as old as Erlander. Sträng, too, proved unwilling to succeed Erlander and, in a ringing speech, expressly declined the nomination at the September 1969 Social Democratic Party conference: ''Our party shall not elect a party leader and prime minister for a short interregnum. If there is a young man who possesses all the desirable qualifications and an older man who has some of those qualifications, everything speaks in favor of the younger one being elected.'' Olof Palme was voted party leader by acclamation.

He took office at a time when the Swedish Social Democratic Party was thought to be invincible. In the general election one year earlier, the party had won over 50 percent of the votes. Palme's closing speech to the conference that elected him took the form of an intensive plea for the continued construction of the ''strong society'' that had grown through the 1960s, making it clear, with these words, that he would be carrying on in the social democratic tradition of reform. If anything, the pace of reform would accelerate: The values dominating the late 1960s—equality, democratization, internationalization—would be reinforced. Palme took office at a time when Sweden, as an advanced welfare state, had come to be viewed by many outside the country as a model for the world to follow.

The image of Sweden as the land to envy would change during Palme's first seven years as prime minister, as a result both of problems that washed over the country from abroad and of changed political circumstances at home. The job of party leader and prime minister thus became considerably more difficult than it had been before.

One difficulty lay in Sweden's changing economic situation. International competition intensified. The system of fixed exchange rates collapsed. Central Swedish industrial branches went under. Growth in Swedish productivity declined. And then the international oil crisis occurred. Sweden found itself, like others, in a situation of high inflation accompanied by economic stagnation.

Another difficulty that afflicted Palme as prime minister was a considerably different parliamentary situation than that which had prevailed in earlier decades. One year after he took office, the first elections were held to a unicameral parliament that had replaced the century-old bicameral system in Sweden. In its design, the earlier system tended to favor large parties such as the Social Democrats. In the 1970 election to the new parliament, however, the Social Democratic Party's share of the electorate dropped to 45.3 percent and in the 1973 election to just 43.6 percent. During the 1970–1973 period, the Social Democrats, together with the Communists, still had more seats in parliament than the three nonsocialist parties put together, while during the latter period the socialist and nonsocialist parliamentary blocs had exactly the same number of seats each. Sweden had gotten itself into a peculiar "equilibrium parliament," with many issues being decided by the drawing of lots. Further complicating Palme's position as prime minister, the three nonsocialist parties displayed a greater inclination to act in concert than ever before.

A third difficulty faced by Palme during the 1970s, finally, was the heightened profile of a new dimension in Swedish politics—the Greens. One manifestation of this was a newly found concern over technological advances, particularly nuclear power as a major source of energy. Palme, on the other hand, had always shared the belief of the previous generation in nuclear power as a clean energy source. Toward the end of his tenure, and under pressure from Center Party leader Thorbjörn Fälldin and other prominent Center Party members, the issue became one of the most controversial in Swedish politics, dividing the Social Democrats as well as the country.

As a consequence of these and other difficulties, Palme sought to lead the Social Democrats toward more formal cooperation with some of the nonsocialist opposition parties. But attempts to cooperate with them and with private industry were also rendered difficult by Palme's own personality. Throughout his career he exhibited traits of both the inside problem solver and the outside agitator. Ever since his days as a student leader, Palme had been a practical sort: His wished to arrive at compromises and decisions. At the same time, he was also a celebrated orator. His often caustic and emotive rhetoric could send shivers of pleasure up and down the spines of the converted, but could also alarm and repel others, thereby making compromise more difficult.

During the difficult days of the equilibrium parliament, however, Palme did manage, in many matters, to demonstrate his ability to solve problems and patch together compromises. Among other things, roundtable talks with the opposition were convened. During one of these, in the spring of 1974, a comprehensive agreement was reached with one of the nonsocialist parties, the Liberals, on economic policy.

Palme's achievements during his first term as prime minister were of different kinds. On the international level, he contributed to perceptions that Sweden spoke with a fearless, often loud voice in the world community. At the beginning of his first term in office, Europe was the focus of his international interest. At that time, he entertained hopes that it would be possible for Sweden to enter the Common Market. In the late winter of 1971, however, Palme and other members of his government concluded that Swedish foreign policy—traditionally neutral—could not be combined with the security policy ambitions which the European Common Market began to evince at that time.

In the domestic political realm during his first period in office, what Palme did—apart from his duty to strive for traditional social democratic values for the greatest possible levels of employment and for the continued construction of the welfare system—was above all to effect a series of reforms in the area of working life. Measures were taken to improve working conditions, to reinforce security of employment and to develop workers' participation in management. These measures were widely commended. At the same time, however, they contributed to the further strengthening of the Swedish trade unions—in public debate, reference was often made to "corporatization"—just as they contributed to the creation of a climate in which the Swedish blue-collar trade union confederation (LO) could push for what were known as "wage earner funds," a surplus profit tax administered by funds with strong trade union representation. This proposal was to bring Palme considerable trouble.

Palme's relations with the blue-collar federation had been good in his early days as party leader. But when the LO congress of 1976 passed a resolution pressing for a variation of the wage earner funds that was far too extreme in the eyes of the Social Democratic Party, it exemplified the deterioration in teamwork between the government and the trade union movement. It was also this question which, together with the nuclear power issue, actively contributed to Olof Palme's becoming, in the autumn of 1976, the first Swedish Social Democratic leader in forty years to be forced into opposition.

In the period between 1976 and 1982, three nonsocialist parties held a majority of their own in parliament. They did not, however, succeed in governing together during the whole six-year period. Palme, in opposition, attacked the government with particular severity for various kinds of "incompetence" during the years they governed jointly. Ever on the offensive, he also tended, in keeping with traditional Social Democratic strategy, to couple his attacks against the government with charges of being divided in its daily work. He himself played an active role on three especially important occasions, when divisions between the non-socialist parties became particularly apparent.

On the first occasion, during August 1978, when the nonsocialist three-party government split over the issue of nuclear energy, it was largely thanks to Palme that one of the coalition partners, the Liberal Party, was subsequently able to form a government on its own. He did so by persuading his own parliamentary forces not to vote against the speaker's proposal for a Liberal prime minister, but to abstain instead. However, although he hoped that this government, brought into being with the help of the Social Democrats, would pave the way for closer cooperation between his party and the Liberals in the lead-up to the 1979 election, the strategy backfired. The Social Democrats lost in 1979, and a new nonsocialist three-party government came to power.

On the second occasion, Palme helped to bring about a nonsocialist split over the referendum on nuclear power that was held in the spring of 1980. Within a few days after the March 1979 nuclear accident at Three Mile Island in the United States, Palme decided that the Social Democrats should push for a referendum on nuclear power in Sweden. He was deeply affected by what had happened in the United States. He also knew that his own party was divided over nuclear power, but feared that the issue could overshadow interest in other important political matters at a later stage. The referendum, which was held some six months after the new nonsocialist coalition came to power, threw into sharp relief both the cooperation that had developed between the Social Democrats and Liberals, and the sharp divisions within the nonsocialist ranks.

On the third occasion, Palme wholeheartedly accepted the work done by the spokesmen for economic matters in his party in reaching agreement on taxation policy between the Social Democrats and two of the three nonsocialist governing parties. The incumbent government fell and was succeeded by a two-party ''bourgeois'' coalition. Palme witnessed the coalition's disintegration with satisfaction.

Although having lost power, the Social Democratic Party continued to rally around Palme as party leader throughout the years in opposition, in spite of some internal dissension regarding his perceived aloofness and incessant travels abroad. Other party members, however, expressly defended his commitment to international affairs and viewed it as the continuation of Social Democratic ideological traditions.

His international activities certainly multiplied. Palme was a member of Willy Brandt's commission on relations between industrialized and developing countries. He served as vice president of the Socialist International, an organization which, by the end of the 1970s, had increasingly taken on global dimensions. He was made chairman of the independent international commission for disarmament and security issues, which was formed in 1980 in response to aggravated international tensions. Known as the Palme Commission, it had seventeen members from East and West. Finally, Palme also acted as a special Middle East envoy of the UN secretary general, with the assignment of attempting to persuade Iran and Iraq to negotiate peace, although his efforts were unsuccessful.

During his years in opposition, Palme linked domestic policy considerations to foreign policy with increasing passion. Those values thought desirable and worth striving for within a country he saw as worth attempting to establish in the world community as a whole: Palme believed in working for democracy and for open dialogue between those with different views toward the ends of solidarity and equality. Nor in his speeches at home in Sweden did Palme neglect to weave in international perspectives in arguments pertaining to related domestic affairs. In the end, while out of power during this period, he was absorbed by his many activities on the global stage.

Palme's second period in office as prime minister from 1982 to 1986 was to be very different from his first. The first time, Palme had been pushed forward by others. Now he was hungry to return to power. The first time he had been very young, imbued with success and very energetic. Now he was somewhat scarred and often impatient.

Sweden's situation in autumn 1982 was also different from that of thirteen years earlier. Whereas during Palme's first period as prime minister, he essentially followed the program of the previous Erlander governments, this time his principal task was to pull Sweden out of a severe economic crisis. By and large, most of what the government set out to do was accomplished in the three or so years in which Palme once again served as prime minister: The government granted production elbow room and rolled back the budget deficit, all the while maintaining the basis of the Swedish welfare state, although caution was exercised in the introduction of new reforms. However, this, too, was a minority government, and relations between it and the nonsocialist opposition were strained.

First, the issue of wage earner funds continued to sow the seeds of dissension. Although a watered-down version of the idea was finally adopted by parliament late in 1983, the issue cast a shadow over the economic policy Palme had been trying to conduct with private industry and the nonsocialist opposition.

Second, Palme and the government had difficulties with their own supporters. Tensions between the party and the trade union confederation heightened in the 1980s, evolving into a sort of ''war of the roses'' within the Swedish labor movement. As party leader, Palme was motivated to hold the movement together and arrive at compromises between the different interests within it, but at the same time was irritated by the LO's attempt to control the SDP.

As a person and politician, Palme continued to be controversial until his death, never becoming the beloved elder statesman that his mentor Tage Erlander ultimately came to be. During these final years, particularly harsh criticism emanating from conservative quarters was leveled at his foreign policy, criticism that had dogged Palme ever since his involvement in the Vietnam issue: He readily condemned oppression in countries far removed from Sweden while expressing himself with considerably more caution with respect to the communist dictatorships in the immediate vicinity. Granted, Palme sought to establish businesslike relations with the then-superpower Soviet Union—always open to dialogue. Nonetheless, he did not excuse or overlook the flaws in the Soviet system. Early on he had clearly established his anticommunism, in particular based upon his own experiences of ruthless communist attempts to take over international student organizations. He retained this stance throughout his political life as a politician even if, when it came to the ''liberation'' of developing countries, he tended to view communist experiments somewhat more generously.

Palme's active political career was brutally interrupted on February 28, 1986, by his as yet unsolved murder in downtown Stockholm. He died shortly after his fifty-ninth birthday. Reactions around the world to Palme's assassination took an already shocked Sweden by surprise. Until then, neither his followers nor his opponents in Sweden had fully understood how well-known he had become throughout the world. Palme was widely viewed outside of Sweden as a symbol of aspirations for understanding and peace between East and West, North and South, and for the right of small states to self-determination.

By the end of his life, Palme had, more than any other Swedish politician, brought the world and its problems into Swedish daily life and through his actions, made Sweden known in the outside world, particularly in developing countries. Through Olof Palme, Sweden was internationalized. Ironically, the way he died illustrated Sweden's increasing convergence with the rest of the world. What other countries had previously experienced had now happened in Sweden: A man of good intentions met a tragic, early death.

BIBLIOGRAPHY

Elmbrant, B. *Palme.* Stockholm: Författarförlaget Fischer and Rye, 1989.
Richard, S. *Le Rendezvous suédois.* Paris: Stock, 1976.
Ruin, O. "Olof Palme," in *Svenskt Biogratiskt Lexikon.* Stockholm, forthcoming.
Strand, D. *Palme igen? Scener ur en partiledares liv.* Stockholm: Norstedts, 1980.

OLOF RUIN

ANDREAS GEORGE PAPANDREOU (1919–) is one of the three or four most important leaders of modern Greece, along with Eleftherios Venizelos, George Papandreou and Konstantinos Karamanlis. At present he is the best-known politician inside as well as outside Greece. His premiership from 1981 to 1989 produced changes in Greek policies at both national and international levels, and in 1993, his Greek Socialist Party regained a parliamentary majority, returning him to the premiership. In social affairs, his performance has been exceptionally active and positive; in economic policy, his record is decidedly mixed and not very impressive.

Andreas Papandreou combines two essential characteristics for successful Greek political leaders. One is to come from a traditional political family and the other is to be well educated. He is the son of George Papandreou, known in Greece as the father of democracy, and he is a distinguished scholar, educated as an economist at Harvard University. While at the beginning of his political career, his success could be attributed mainly to his famous father, later, as a mature politician, Andreas Papandreou has put his own seal on Greek politics.

Andreas Papandreou was born on February 5, 1919, on the island of Chios. His father, George Papandreou, was the son of a Greek Orthodox priest from a small village in the Peloponessus region of Greece. Andreas's primary and secondary education was completed in Greek schools. He then went to law school at the University of Athens (1937–1939).

The decade of the 1930s was one of the most formative periods of his life. In 1936 a right-wing coup d'état took place in Greece under the leadership of Ioannis Metaxas. In response to the Metaxas's dictatorship, Papandreou joined a resistance group. In 1939 he was arrested and tortured. Upon his release, he emigrated to the United States, where he pursued his academic career, enrolling in 1940 at Harvard and receiving his doctorate in economics in 1943. He then joined the U.S. Navy, became an American citizen, and married an American citizen, Margaret Chant.

During his previous decade in Greece, Papandreou had been surrounded by political passions, which were as high there as they were all over Europe. But his establishment in the United States brought calm to his political life. He began to see politics more from an American perspective than from a European.

However, his passion for politics was reawakened by Adlai Stevenson's 1952 Democratic presidential campaign. After Stevenson's defeat by Eisenhower, Papandreou became chairman of Stevenson's committee in Minnesota, although Papandreou's political background as a young student was much more left-wing than any liberal faction within the American Democratic Party. His involvement with the party's politics can thus be interpreted in two ways: Either the Democratic Party was the only political organization in the United States remotely close to his own political views, or his radical views had been tempered in the United States, becoming compatible with moderate Democratic ideology.

Papandreou's stay in the United States, along with his academic successes there, paved the way for his political comeback in Greece. While in the United States, he worked as an instructor at Harvard University and was named an associate professor of economics at the University of Minnesota. He also taught at Northwestern University and at the University of California, Berkeley. At Berkeley, he held the chairmanship of the Department of Economics from 1956 to 1959. In 1959 he returned to Greece for one year to study the Greek economy with the support of Guggenheim and Fulbright fellowships. This year was a turning point in Papandreou's life. It marked the end of his academic career in the United States and the beginning of his political leadership in Greek politics.

The end of the Greek civil war in 1949 established a new era in Greek politics, one of conservative democracy. When Andreas Papandreou arrived in Greece in 1959, the conservative party in power, under the leadership of Konstantinos Karamanlis, was well entrenched. Karamanlis's principal opponent was Andreas's father, George Papandreou. Nonetheless, to general surprise, Karamanlis asked Andreas to head a center for economic research. He accepted.

The new realities of Greek politics reawakened Papandreou's old leftist ideological convictions. While his father was a politician with unshaken liberal democratic principles, he had often been forced to compromise in his long political career. It took the father sixty years to finally declare what he called his "anendotos agonas" (unyielding fight), becoming more defiant of rightist politics. Andreas, on the other hand, was an uncompromising politician from the very beginning. In 1964, he was elected to the Greek parliament, mainly because he was the son of George Papandreou, leader of the Center Union Party and Karamanlis's archrival.

Andreas Papandreou entered Greek politics in a period of extreme political and social change in Europe. This was especially true in Greece, where the wounds of the Greek civil war had not yet healed. Strong animosities between left and right were evident in every aspect of Greek political life. By the end of the 1950s, Karamanlis, leader of the ERE (National Radical Union Party) had begun to lose popular support. In the 1958 elections, the left managed to more than double its strength. While Karamanlis and the conservatives also won the 1961 elections, allegations of fraud were brought by the opposition parties, paving the way for the end of Karamanlis's government.

Election fraud, the involvement of foreign governments in domestic Greek politics and the assassination of a leftist Greek deputy led to the opposition's victory in elections held in 1963 and 1964. During this turbulent period, Andreas Papandreou refined his political ideas and began to formulate the future policies that he would put into practice when given the opportunity.

As a member of the Center Union government during this time, Andreas Papandreou was the most ideologically radical among his colleagues in both economic and foreign policy. The Greek economy had improved considerably during the 1950s and early 1960s, yet it was still by no means as developed as the other Western European economies; it was still in need of restructuring in order to lay the foundations for modernization. Being both the only trained economist among the new government's members and the new prime minister's son, his influence soon became apparent.

The economic policies that Andreas recommended to his father's cabinet were well received by neither his party's leaders nor the opposition. Some of his recommendations were too leftist and threatened the economic interests of the Greek political establishment. Thus, Andreas Papandreou came into conflict not only with the opposition but also with his own party. His insistence in restructuring the economy and the educational system earned him many enemies, although for him restructuring was essential to modernization and the ability of Greece to catch up with the rest of Europe.

As to foreign policy, Andreas Papandreou was similarly radical and, more important, nationalistic. The most important foreign relations issue for any Greek government regardless of its ideological makeup is the Cyprus issue, especially because it inevitably involves Turkey, the traditional enemy of Greece. Andreas Papandreou joined his father on this issue in taking a more independent position from the NATO allies as to how this problem should be solved. This stand independent from NATO (and the United States) brought intense wrath upon him from his opponents within the government, among the opposition and from the monarchy.

Perhaps the Cyprus problem contributed the most to the destabilization of Greek politics in the 1960s, eventually bringing an end to Greek democracy. It also reinforced Andreas's radical and nationalistic attitudes. When he and his father were "summoned" to Washington by President Lyndon B. Johnson for discussion of the Cyprus issue, Johnson informed them that either the Greek government would accept an American-sponsored solution or the United States would not be able to protect Greece in the event of a Turkish attack.

To this ultimatum, Andreas Papandreou replied that he would seek assistance elsewhere, implying the Soviet Union. This act by itself had an extraordinary effect on Greek foreign policy and on Andreas's political future. Subsequent events related to the Cyprus issue led him to resign from his position in the government, freeing him to become more personally active in seeking solutions directly with the Cypriot government, military figures and other political forces. This independence from his father's government, however, earned him a reputation as conspirator against Greek democratic principles.

Andreas Papandreou's leftist ideology, his nationalistic attitudes regarding the Cyprus problem and his growing popular support between 1964 and 1967 culminated in a coup d'état by a group of military officers that put an end to Greek democracy on April 21, 1967, a month before scheduled elections. The campaign leading up to these elections had signaled that Andreas Papandreou was gaining unprecedent popular support. By almost all accounts the military officers took action in order to prevent Andreas from gaining further political power. After the coup, Papandreou was arrested and imprisoned by the military government. After several months of confinement, he was released and sent into exile.

His seven-year exile (the number of years it took the military to hand power back to civilians) had a profound impact on Papandreou's life. During it, he never ceased to work for the overthrow of the Greek dictatorship. As soon as he left Greece in early 1968, he began to organize other Greek exiles and Greek emigrants, putting together one of the most active antidictatorship movements in or outside Greece. The movement was called the Panhellenic Liberation Movement (PAK).

To Papandreou, PAK provided the basis for an effective struggle against dictatorship, encompassing members from all the Greek diaspora—from Australia to Canada, from the United States to Sweden. PAK also provided Papandreou with the organizational structure and personnel for the political party he was to form upon his return to Greece in 1974. When democracy was restored in Greece that year, Papandreou thereby had an organization in place with which to contest the elections. And since many of PAK's leaders had experience in other Western democracies, their ideas were more modern than those of the average Greek politician, whose experience was acquired strictly in the Greek environment. This factor alone enhanced Papandreou's credibility later on when his Socialist Party positioned itself as a party of *alaghi* (change).

Ironically, it was the Cyprus issue that brought Papandreou back to Greek politics, for in 1974 the Greek junta mishandled the issue by overthrowing the legitimate Cypriot government and replacing it with another that better suited the junta's objectives. The incident provoked Turkey's invasion of Cyprus, and the junta, unable to effectively handle the invasion, stepped down, calling back a number of politicians from exile; among them was Papandreou.

Papandreou's position on the Cyprus issue, however, had always been different from those who thought that the problem could be solved through the NATO alliance. The 1974 Turkish invasion of Cyprus seemed to prove his point: NATO stood by and watched the invasion without any attempt to stop it. Papandreou played upon this event subsequently, using it to ascend to political leadership in Greece.

When Papandreou returned to Greece in 1974, he surprised almost everyone by founding his own party, the Panhellenic Socialist Movement (PASOK), rather than becoming part of the Center Union Party's leadership. Papandreou's PASOK differed from other Greek political parties in that it was composed of very few old political names and most of its leadership had a technocratic background. These characteristics were well received by the majority of the electorate, simply because—as Papandreou made clear—the party had no intention of returning to politics as usual. Papandreou, in fact, organized the party in such a way as to give a great deal of authority to leaders at the local level.

Although Papandreou did not win the first election after his return from exile, as time went on it was clear that he was the only leader who had a program for change and his popular support increased. Between 1974 and 1981, *alaghi* (change) became his party's slogan.

Alaghi meant a number of things to Papandreou: change in economic affairs, change in social affairs, change in foreign affairs. In the 1977 parliamentary elections his party improved its position dramatically, jumping from 13 to 25 percent of the vote. The 1981 elections finally brought Papandreou to power. His party captured 48 percent of the vote and an absolute majority in the parliament.

From 1974 to 1981, Papandreou went through a steady evolution in his ideological thinking, moving from the far left slowly toward the center. For example, in 1974 he vehemently opposed Greece's membership in NATO and the European Community. He also sought good relations with the Soviet Bloc and with the Arab countries of the Middle East. But his stands on these issues moderated. Before being elected prime minister in 1981, he had promised to conduct a referendum in Greece on membership in the European Community. Similar changes occurred with regard to NATO and American bases in Greece.

In campaigning for office, Papandreou had promised to transform the Greek economy from a developing to a developed one. In striving for this, he followed two major paths. First, he tried to shift investment from the large industrial centers to the countryside. Second, his government became heavily involved in assisting private investment in peripheral areas. Shifting investment away from large cities like Athens and Salonika reflected Papandreou's ideology of decentralization.

But decentralization, for Papandreou, was necessary in politics as well as in economics. In order to implement his program of economic decentralization, he restructured local administrative governments, making them much more active. The concept of decentralization was important because it addressed one of the most intractable problems facing the Greek economy, the overpopulation of the large cities.

However, the policy of decentralization was not very successful because as soon as Papandreou came to power, investment slowed considerably, a response on the part of the wealthier classes to his socialist approach to the economy. Thus Papandreou's dream of creating a more vibrant economy with the participation of the state did not go very far in the face of an uncooperative investment community.

Nonetheless, his initiative to diminish the income gaps between rural and urban populations obtained positive results. Through new legislation and with the assistance of the European Community, he improved the working and social conditions of Greek farmers. In particular, the government assisted farmers in establishing cooperatives in order to improve agricultural production. In addition, the government dramatically improved social benefits to farmers. But in order to achieve these objectives, Papandreou's government borrowed large sums of money, further spurring the high rates of inflation that already existed when he was elected in 1981.

High rates of inflation and a large government debt led Papandreou to reverse course in 1985 and declare a policy of austerity This reversal met part of its objective, chiefly by reducing inflation from 23 percent in 1986 to 13 percent in 1988. But the economy's growth severely slowed as a result.

It was in social policy that Andreas Papandreou had the most impact on Greek politics. For example, divorce laws were liberalized, and pensions for the elderly were provided. His government also legislated equal opportunity for women and legally abolished the institution of dowry. But perhaps Papandreou's greatest social contribution was the national health system, a government-funded and -operated health system that was one of his most debated social initiatives, being extensively criticized by the opposition and the medical community. Papandreou insisted, however, that health care for every citizen, rich and poor, was fundamental, and he never gave up this objective.

Overall Papandreou's foreign policy was independent and highly nationalistic. His greatest concern was relations with Turkey. In disputes between Greece and Turkey over the navigational, mineral and air rights to the Aegean Sea, as well as the Cyprus problem, Papandreou took nationalistic, independent stands. He first sought to strengthen Greek armed forces by equipping them with modern weapons. It was obvious that he was concerned to prevent any attack from Turkey. In addition, he believed that in diversifying its military weaponry, Greece would become less vulnerable to foreign dependency.

Papandreou was very suspicious of Greece's NATO allies and especially of the United States. This suspicion led him to announce his ''dual track'' foreign policy. Although Greece would ''remain allied with NATO, nevertheless, friendship and cooperation should be sought elsewhere as well.'' In following this policy, Papandreou made extra efforts to built special relations with Arab countries, and he became close friends with various Soviet Bloc countries.

This close relationship with the Soviet Union angered almost every Western ally. Papandreou was most criticized by the American government and his European Community colleagues when he failed to denounce the Soviet government for having shot down a South Korean passenger airliner in 1983. Papandreou's foreign policy also opposed American military bases in Greece. Their removal became one of the main issues of his foreign policy, although in 1983 his government signed an agreement with the Americans to extend their operation to 1989.

This change in Papandreou's position was not the first to occur in his foreign policy. Before becoming prime minister, he likewise promised to withdraw Greece from the European Community (EC), but instead renegotiated the terms of Greece's relationship with the EC. Similarly, although he had repeatedly denounced any meeting with Turkish President Ozal, he adapted to changing circumstances, agreeing to meet in 1988.

In 1989, due to a number of scandals that plagued his government and his party, Papandreou lost the general elections. This loss, however, did not inhibit him from becoming an active leader for the opposition. His leftist ideological positions continued to be present in all political debates, although his extremism has been tempered. For example, he now favors greater European Community cooperation and also talks about the unification of Europe, a drastically different position from that he had held in the 1970s.

Furthermore, Papandreou was able to make Greece visible in world affairs during his premiership. Together with the late Indian prime minister, Rajiv Gandhi, Argentine president, Raúl Alfonsín, Mexican president, Miguel de la Madrid, Tanzanian president, Julius Nyerere, and the late prime minister of Sweden, Olof Palme, Papandreou formed the "Group of Six" and won worldwide recognition in 1985 for the "Delhi Declaration." The main objective of the group was to influence the two superpowers to peacefully negotiate the reduction of nuclear armaments.

Overall, Andreas Papandreou elevated Greek political life from the politics of mere charismatic leadership to the politics of popular participation, although arguments to the contrary are abundant. To a certain extent he achieved his goals but not to the degree that his supporters expected. After his loss in 1989, he continued to lead the socialist party that he founded, continuing to interject his person into politics and remaining defiant of his opponents. In 1993, this aging Greek warrior was returned to power. In poor health and facing a sick economy, his new government will likely pursue fairly moderate foreign and economic policies. With the demise of communism since his last term in office, moreover, Papandreou faced a radically and rapidly changing world order. In all this, Papandreou has clearly tempered his opposition toward the Western Alliance, while his tone has become more conciliatory than it was in the 1960s, 1970s and 1980s.

BIBLIOGRAPHY

Works by Papandreou:

Fundamentals of Model Construction in Macro-Economics. Athens: Public Information, 1962.

Democracy at Gunpoint: The Greek Front. New York: Doubleday and Company, 1970.

Man's Freedom. New York: Columbia University Press, 1970.

Paternalistic Capitalism. Minneapolis: University of Minneapolis Press, 1972.

Other Works:

Chares, Manos. *Vaseis NATO kai PASOK: Andrea esy ta Protoeipes*. Athens: Ekdoseis Aletheias, 1983.

Karangos, Sarantos I. *Ecce Homo: Ho Mythologikos Mandyas tou k. Andrea Papandreou: Politika arthra*. Athens: Ekdoseis Gutenberg, 1990.

Karetsos, Kostas S. *Hellas sten peripeteia tou tholou paichnidiou tes exousias kai tes allaghes, 1963–1983*. Athens: Ekdoseis Status, 1984.

Mardas, Kostas E. *He Ellada sta dichtya ton vaseon: Apo to Dogma Truman ston Andrea Papandreou*. Athens: Ekdoseis Kastaniote, 1989.

CHRIS BOURDOUVALIS

GEORGE PAPANDREOU (1888–1968) is unique in politics, at least for those countries characterized by democracy during a major part of their history: While he is unanimously considered by historians and public opinion to be one of the three or four dominant politicians for two centuries of Greek political history—and his reputation posthumously continues to grow—he rarely actually exercised political power. During a half-century-long political career, he presided over the Greek government little more than a year and a half. And while he assumed his first ministerial portfolio in 1922 and was vice prime minister for five years, the different political parties that he led throughout his life almost always achieved only very mediocre election results.

Papandreou's political renown is therefore due to other factors than holding office: (1) At the beginning of the 1960s, he reunified the center-republicans after three decades of division and fragmentation. (2) Under his leadership, the Center Union Party, an organization that was ideologically heterogeneous but nonetheless politically cohesive, displaced the long-governing Conservative Party from power after a long and bitter political struggle. (3) As prime minister, he was removed from power by a constitutionally questionable royal decree, and the public viewed him as the victim of a plot. This contributed to making the elderly leader the most popular politician in Greece for some time. Moreover, Papandreou was perhaps the most eloquent parliamentary leader Greece has ever known; certainly he was one of the greatest orators of modern Greek politics.

Son of a modest country Orthodox priest (''pope''), Papandreou was born in 1888 in a small village near Patras. A prodigal student, he remembered vividly his early impoverished days; this pushed him subsequently to be particularly concerned with education policy. Almost every time he joined a government cabinet, he would choose the education ministry (even when holding other portfolios, including the premiership). During his career he consistently crusaded for free public education.

Having graduated from university with a law degree, he turned as a postgraduate student to a study of Marxist ideas, which were highly fashionable at the time. Papandreou saw no contradiction between Marxism and his deep sense of patriotism, which he continued to hold very dear. During this period, he interrupted his doctoral studies in political science in Berlin in order to serve in the Balkan Wars (1912–1913).

Papandreou returned to Berlin upon the wars' conclusion. While visiting the German capital, the Greek prime minister, Eleftherios Venizelos, noticed the articulateness of the young Papandreou. From 1915 to 1920, he served successively as prefect, director of the Ethnarque political office, and governor of the Aegean Sea islands.

The "military revolution" of 1922, brought about by the Asia Minor disaster, led to Papandreou's appointment as minister of the interior. Not wanting, nonetheless, to assume responsibility for the execution of royalists convicted as responsible for the Asia Minor disaster by the revolutionary court, Papandreou did not take office until the day after the executions. About the same time (1922–1923), he permitted hundreds of thousands of political refugees to settle in the Athens metropolitan area with the idea that they would tip the balance in future elections away from the royalist governments of 1920–1922 and in favor of the Venizelist partisans. The refugees were convinced that the royalist governments were responsible for their disadvantaged condition; the majority-rule electoral system in place at the time would render their electoral weight decisive.

As minister of national education in one of the last Venizelos governments (1932–1934), Papandreou approved the construction of approximately three thousand modern school buildings. Subsequently, and after Venizelos's retirement from political life, Papandreou founded his own party in 1935. It was initially known as the Democratic Party, then as the Social Democratic Party after the war and finally as the George Papandreou Party beginning in 1950. In the meantime, during the Nazi occupation of Greece, Papandreou succeeded in drawing the attention of the British to his analysis of the Greek and Balkan political situation, and with their approval, he was named president of the Greek Council in Exile.

Being very skilled at political maneuvers, Papandreou was able to convince the Greek Communist Party (KKE), one of the principle actors in the Greek Resistance movement, to join the government. As a result, after the liberation of Greece, the country was ruled by a government of national union.

Unfortunately, civil war erupted three months later when hostilities broke out between nationalist forces, supported by the British, and the Communists and their sympathizers. Papandreou was forced to resign his office and was therefore not a part of the various alliance governments who were finally able to prevail over the rebels. The existence of this common enemy—the Communists—led Papandreou to gradually moderate his traditional antiroyalist outlook. With the 1946 referendum on the return of the king, for example, Papandreou's official position called for a "no" vote, but he argued it so tepidly that his republican friends were dismayed and many commentators interpreted his attitude as supportive of the royal cause.

Subsequently in 1950, as vice prime minister in a tripartite centrist government, Papandreou vigorously opposed the liberation of Communist prisoners proposed by the incumbent prime minister. Nonetheless, in spite of his identification with the vindictive climate of the period, Papandreou failed in his bid for reelection as deputy. (In fact, his party lost every one of its parliamentary seats.) Consequently, in 1952 he was forced to collaborate electorally with the conservatives in order to regain his parliamentary seat as an independent. Gradually, he returned to his familiar political haunts in the nebulous center, but it was clear that a long political ''exile'' had begun for him, which lasted until the early years of the 1960s.

However, by the end of 1961, Papandreou had succeeded in reunifying the various and disparate forces of the center under his leadership. He did so by founding the Center Union Party, a flexible and ideologically heterogeneous organization whose initial conception called for it to be administered by a collegial board presided over by a chair.

Many factors lay behind the creation of this new party, which included different factional leaders whose relations with each other were very tense. First, the political center had been out of power for so long that to prolong such a situation any further would have surely destroyed the clientele links between centrist politicians and their electoral bases.

Second, the 1958 elections (which took place before the founding of his new party) made the ''Democratic Left,'' a cover for the illegal Communists, the largest opposition party. All the political class, therefore, including the monarchy, felt the pressing need for the creation of a new bourgeois party independent of the ruling conservatives. In this, the political class sought a mainstream party that could assure a change in the party in power without fundamentally questioning the social order established after the civil war.

Third, the international climate, changed by the election of John F. Kennedy to the American presidency, favored ''liberalizing'' political experiments in many of the smaller Western countries. Fourth, the right demonstrated a remarkable lack of scruples in manipulating the electoral system so as to divide its adversaries. Paradoxically, however, this had the opposite effect, leading to a movement of unity in the mainstream opposition. Finally, the political, monetary and economic stability of the 1950s led to a considerable improvement in the Greek standard of living, which in turn created a demand for more democratic forms of politics, such as periodic changes in the governing party.

In addition, Papandreou was made president of the new Center Union Party because of his combative political temperament, his great talents as orator and the support that he enjoyed among foreign powers. This latter factor was due to his progressively more liberal democratic political stance in combination with a ferocious anticommunism: He seemed to be, in short, the man of the moment. His advanced age, moreover, was also considered an advantage. Given that many other politicians aspired to the leadership of the party, including the incumbent prime minister, Papandreou was not perceived as a long-term threat to others' political ambitions.

Nonetheless, the new party did not immediately demonstrate a cohesion and viability that augured well for its long-term future. Personal rivalries within the party combined with a number of ideological divisions. Some conservatives, who had never successfully advanced their cause within the ruling conservative National Radical Union Party (ERE), coexisted very uncomfortably with others who were social democrats. Only with the elections of October 1961, which took place little more than a month after the founding of the Center Union, did the party manage to establish and consolidate a clear identity.

These elections, characterized by fraud and violence, completely recast Greek politics. A government proposal designed to indirectly suppress potential voters of the left was implemented in such a way by the police authorities as to apply equally to supporters of the center. In fact, instead of dissuading leftist participation at the polls, the law was implemented by the police authorities in such a way as to pressure voters to support the ERE. (Papandreou had been informed of the government's proposal by Prime Minister Karamanlis and apparently had agreed to it.)

The ERE ''won'' a smashing victory amid evidence of rampant electoral fraud. Seizing upon this occasion and the high emotions of public opinion, Papandreou called on the government to erect a monument to the ''unknown voter.'' For two years subsequently, he led an unrelenting campaign against the incumbent government, arguing that it was both illegitimate and illegal. During this period, even King Paul, not wanting to be identified with a prime minister seen as more and more corrupt, contested and authoritarian, indicated clearly that he favored a change in the political party in power.

In addition, thanks to Papandreou's relentless campaign, the Center Union began to consolidate itself, and as his popularity grew, so did his hold on the leadership of the party. Originally named as chair of the executive committee, a collegial body, Papandreou quickly transformed his role into one of an absolute, unchallenged chief. And yet, or perhaps because of this, as soon as the day after his electoral triumph of 1964—he obtained 53 percent of the vote—internal problems, battles and factional infighting within the victorious party came into broad daylight. The ambitions of the new prime minister's son, Andreas Papandreou, who had just begun his political career, also played a major role.

Finally, George Papandreou was forced to submit his resignation in summer 1965 after he had asked to hold simultaneously the prime minister and defense minister portfolios. The young King Constantine refused to sign the necessary decree, mainly because it was alleged that Papandreou's son Andreas was suspected of organizing a plot within the armed forces (the Aspida affair). In this, the king committed a serious tactical error, permitting George Papandreou to legitimately claim himself to be victim of a plot, thus redeeming his tarnished reputation. Upon Papandreou's resignation as prime minister, the king ignored the deep-seated democratic custom of turning to the majority party in parliament, in this case Papandreou's Center Union Party, for the new head of government. Instead, the king named himself prime minister.

A long political crisis followed, culminating in 40 out of 172 centrist deputies leaving the Center Union Party and forming a government which, thanks to the tacit support of the conservative ERE, obtained a vote of confidence in the parliament. This group was known as the ''Apostates.'' (It is revealing of the authoritarian and personal character of the center's leadership that the ''Apostates'' counted among their number some of the most eminent elected and ministerial officials of the center.)

In the face of what was widely viewed as a victimization of him by royal machinations which were supported by the Greek ''oligarchy,'' Papandreou recovered an immense level of popularity beyond anything ever seen in Greek politics. For more than a year, he violently attacked the king and the ''royal government.'' Nonetheless, he eventually came to conclude that prolonging the crisis would jeopardize the survival of democracy, so in autumn 1966 he reconciled with both the king and the head of the parliamentary conservatives.

Yet it was too late. The three men could no longer control the political situation. In April 1967, lower-ranking officers bypassed the ruling class and established a military dictatorship which would last more than seven years. Papandreou would not live to see democracy restored to Greece. He died an octogenarian in October 1968, hated by some, adored by most others, and considered by all to be the man who embodied the democratic ideals of the 1960s but who was not able to capitalize upon the political opportunities presented to him near the end of his life. And for many commentators, if that other eminent political figure of Greek centrism, Sophocles Venizelos, suffered from the fact that he was the son of his father, Eleftherios, George Papandreou's chief problem was that he was the father of his son, Andreas.

When very young, Papandreou had been a defender of Marxist-socialist ideals. Subsequently he became a close collaborator and follower of the great liberal-republican leader Eleftherios Venizelos. Papandreou then also became the leader of many different small ''personal'' parties for more than twenty-five years before becoming the ''grand federator'' of the whole political center near the end of his life. During this very long political career, Papandreou was always forced to adapt his tactics and his discourse to changing circumstances. He was alternately the ferocious enemy of the right and their occasional ally, as well as taking both hard-line and more moderate stances vis-à-vis the monarchy. He was also always ready to violently attack tomorrow his allies of yesterday.

Yet in spite of these numerous about-faces, he always held to an ideological foundation that remained relatively unchanged over the course of fifty years in political life. There were four principal elements to Papandreou's ideological worldview:

First, he always exhibited a concern for social welfare and a constant search for social compromise. A ''dose'' of socialism—at least insofar as he himself defined the term in the postwar period as generous treatment of the needy classes by the bourgeois state—seemed to him to be indispensible for the healthy functioning of the liberal capitalist system. Indeed, some nationalizations of firms and services was not excluded by his ideology insofar as they occurred in sectors where the laws of free competition did not pertain. Finally, one of his constant concerns was reducing the inequality of opportunity for the young.

Second, Papandreou always exhibited a deep suspicion regarding "big capital," and this dislike was always present in his political discourse. He often disputed even the patriotism of Greek capitalists.

Third, his anticommunism, perhaps the corollary of his nationalism, was always, and especially after 1944, intransigent and unrelenting. Of all the prominent figures of the center, including those nearer to the center-right, it was Papandreou who resisted most vigorously any tactical rapprochement with a left dominated by the illegal Communist Party. While the great defender of political democracy (which he preferred to see as social democracy), he nevertheless rarely opposed nondemocratic measures when used against the Communists, whom he viewed as the avowed adversaries of democracy. It was not by chance that at the conclusion of the Greek civil war, his party was the only one to be relatively overrepresented among military and police officers in votes cast.

Finally, Papandreou considered himself to be a sort of Gulliver among the Lilliputians and rarely showed much concern for democratic forms and procedures within the various political parties that he led. Indeed, his leadership style within his parties was most often quite authoritarian. During the whole period in which he led his own parties, this style led to few alliances with other mainstream politicians of the center—which explains his generally poor electoral results, although he was generally regarded as the most brilliant of centrist politicians. And when he became the head of the Center Union—a unified party but characterized by confederal structures, aiming to become one of the poles of an emerging bipartisanism and including many former prominent government officials among its number—Papandreou was unable to preserve the unity of the movement for very long.

As to Papandreou's philosophy regarding international relations and foreign affairs, he had always been a partisan of a unified Europe, which he conceived of as social democratic. Only such a Europe, in his view, would have the moral authority capable of resisting the seductiveness of the Soviet Union and communism. Political liberalism would be the unifying element of this cohesive West, in which the Anglo-Saxon world, by its vocation and for historical, geographic, military and economic reasons, would be the natural leader.

Greece's place in this world order would always be beside its traditional Western allies. Moreover, only the strength of this alliance could ensure the territorial integrity of Greece. But Papandreou had no illusions about this relationship: In fact, he was convinced that only a community of interests—founded in the actions of the great powers—could guarantee allied assistance to his country. Therefore, each time he judged it necessary for the national interest, he was prepared to distance himself from the Western Alliance. This was the case, for example, in 1964, when he refused the solution proposed by the United States on the Cypriot question, thereby significantly angering the Johnson administration.

Along the same line, and in spite of his unremitting anticommunism, Papandreou was convinced that Greece's geographic position did not permit it to enjoy the luxury of tense relations with the Soviet Union and other Eastern European countries. He held to this conviction independently of fluctuations in Soviet-American relations. He even envisioned, while prime minister, making an official visit to the Soviet Union, an initiative that provoked near hysteria among the conservatives, leading them to accuse Papandreou of being the Greek Kerensky.

While these reactions led Papandreou to renounce his plan for a diplomatic overture to the Soviet Union, they did not dissuade him from following a policy of considerably increasing commercial and economic relations with Eastern Europe during the seventeen months of his term in office. Some commentators of the period also thought that mysterious interests—negatively affected by a policy that could render the country economically dependent on the Soviet Union and thereby politically vulnerable to it—worked to overthrow the Papandreou government. Such speculation proved unfounded when the succeeding "Apostate" government followed exactly the same policy vis-à-vis Eastern Europe. To the contrary, it is clear that by the time Papandreou was forced out of office, he had lost most of his domestic and international allies. While talented at motivating mass publics, particularly at political rallies, for example, he proved incapable of efficiently managing a political party, a government or a country. This incapacity to manage was as responsible for his demise as was any "plot" on the part of his adversaries.

This son of a rural Orthodox priest from the Patras region was without doubt one of the most notable Greek political figures in the postwar period. Even his adversaries recognized in Papandreou a remarkable politician. Every time he participated in a coalition government, for example, he obtained more ministerial posts for his party than its parliamentary representation would have justified. And whenever a large number of parties cooperated for electoral purposes, Papandreou was given the leadership of the alliance, even though he often headed the smallest party of the lot.

While he was clearly a charismatic individual, a great orator, a highly talented parliamentarian, a cultivated intellectual and a courageous man, Papandreou never succeeded at *governing*. He preferred politics. The political word as opposed to political action was his real strength. Moreover, he felt more at ease in the opposition than in the government. Of his governing achievements, only education reform would prove historic. But the quality of his political discourse places him directly in line with Thucydides.

BIBLIOGRAPHY

Work by Papandreou:

Keimena, 1913–1942. Athens: Mpiris, 1963.

Other Works:

Anastassiadis, Georges. *Politevma kai kommatikoi skimatismi stin Ellada, 1952–67*. Salonica: Paratiritis, 1991.

Anastassiadis, Georges, and Paul Patridis (eds.). *Georgios Papandreou, i krisi ton thesmon, i kommatiki skimatismi kai o politicos logos: Messopolemos—Apelefierossi—Metapolemica chronia—Dictatoria, 1915–1968*. Salonica: University Studio Press, 1990.

Koressis, Constantin. *Georgios Papandreou: I zoi tou*, 3 vols. Athens: Planitis, n.d.

Netas, Victor-Fatsis Jean. *Epigrammatica kai amimita tou G. Papandreou*. Athens: Papazissis, 1975.

THANASSIS DIAMANTOPOULOS
Trans. by David Wilsford

R

JULIUS RAAB (1891–1964) was one of the most prominent leaders of post–1945 Austria. As federal chancellor, he was responsible for the decisive breakthrough of 1955, when Austria reached agreement with the Allied powers over its political future: In exchange for a commitment to permanent neutrality, Austria, after ten years of occupation by the Allies, was awarded its full sovereignty. In this and other accomplishments, Raab was the main architect of Austria's international position during the decades of the Cold War in Europe.

Raab also had great impact on domestic affairs in Austria: As one of the founders of the Austrian People's Party (ÖVP—Österreichische Volkspartei) in 1945, he stood for a flexible compromise between Catholic-conservative traditions, which his party was built upon, and pragmatic relations with the Social Democratic left. In the 1950s, as Austria stabilized its economy, political system and international status, Raab was a key figure exhibiting extreme pragmatism and great authority in both domestic and international politics.

Julius Raab was born on November 29, 1891, in St. Pölten, Lower Austria. His father was a master builder, a profession his son also learned and practiced for many years. Raab's family background was Catholic and middle-class, and he was deeply rooted in it. After graduating from a Catholic high school in Lower Austria in 1911, Raab enrolled at the Technical University in Vienna and joined one of the best-known of the traditional Catholic fraternities, ''Norica.'' Political careers within the Catholic-conservative camp (or ''pillar'') were usually strongly promoted by membership in such fraternities.

Before Raab could finish his studies in engeneering, World War I began. Raab, already a reserve officer in the Austro-Hungarian army, fought on the Russian and, later, the Italian front. In 1918, after the Austrian defeat, Raab left the army as a first lieutenant and returned to the university. During his studies, he became involved in local politics in Lower Austria and married Harmine Haumer in 1923.

However, Raab left the university before graduating because of the death of his father in 1925 and the beginning of his political career. In 1927, he was elected to the Austrian parliament, the Nationalrat, representing Lower Austria for the Christian Social Party. As a member of parliament from the dominant party of the ruling rightist coalition, Raab also became active within the ''Heimwehr,'' a politico-military arm of the Christian conservative right. In 1928, he was appointed leader of the Heimwehr for Lower Austria. Inside the Heimwehr, he advocated maintaining a strong alliance with the Christian Social Party and opposed those who argued for a more independent stance. In 1930, in the last free elections to the Austrian parliament before the war, Raab was reelected as a Christian Social M.P. once again.

In 1933, he joined the Fatherland Front (Vaterländische Front—VF), the all-encompassing political monopoly that the Christian Social chancellor, Engelbert Dollfuss, tried to establish as a substitute for political parties. After the civil war of February 1934 and after the proclamation of the authoritarian *Ständestaat* (or corporate state), Julius Raab was active in different capacities for this semifascist regime. In 1938, he became minister for commerce in the last cabinet of Kurt Schuschnigg, four weeks before German troops entered Austria.

During the seven years of the *Anschluss*, a term referring to Nazi Germany's annexation of Austria, Raab was not allowed to be active in politics. Although he was known to be an enemy of the regime, he was never imprisoned, and he stayed in touch with his Catholic-conservative friends, thinking about and planning for Austria's future after the defeat of the Germans, even though he never became actively involved in the Austrian anti-Nazi Resistance.

In 1945, Raab was made a member of the provisional government that was proclaimed by the ''antifascist'' parties after the liberation of Vienna. He was one of the founders of the Austrian People's Party, successor to the Christian Social Party, and he became chairman of the ÖVP's business league (Wirtschaftsbund), representing employers' interests. After the elections of November 1945, Raab became chairman of the ÖVP party group in the Austrian parliament. But his main power base became the presidency of the newly founded Federal Chamber of Commerce in 1946. In this capacity, Raab was responsible for the establishment of the ''social partnership''—the institutionalized cooperation between employers (represented by Raab) and employees (represented by labor unions).

In 1951, Raab became chairman of the ÖVP itself and, in 1953, federal chancellor, presiding over a coalition government composed of the People's Party and the Social Democratic Party (SPÖ). This arrangement, known as the ''grand coalition,'' dated from 1945. As chancellor, Raab strongly favored a clearly free market orientation and less state intervention in the economy.

But his main interest came more and more to be foreign policy. Despite his conservative background, Raab successfully established excellent relations with the Soviet Union. His government used the first period of détente, after Stalin's death, to bargain for the State Treaty, which reestablished Austria's sovereignty. Raab headed the Austrian delegation to Moscow which was able to reach agreement with the Soviet authorities in April 1955. The State Treaty was then signed in Vienna on May 15, 1955, by the foreign ministers of the four Allied powers (the United States, the Soviet Union, the United Kingdom, France) and Austria. The occupying troops left Austria, and the Austrian parliament declared Austria to be permanently neutral.

Raab's national and international prestige had reached its peak. In 1956, he and his party did extremely well in general elections: The ÖVP almost gained an overall majority in parliament, and Raab stayed on as federal chancellor. But he kept to his policy of cooperation with the SPÖ in the face of some strong intraparty criticism. Raab believed this coalition to be the best basis for international stability as well as for domestic reconciliation. As part of this domestic cooperation, Raab and Johann Böhm, the Social Democratic president of the Austrian Federation of Trade Unions (ÖGB), founded the Joint Commission on Wages and Prices in 1957. This commission became the core of the "social partnership," the cornerstone of the Austrian style of neo-corporatism.

That same year, Raab suffered a heart attack. This marked the beginning of his political decline. In the 1959 general elections, the People's Party lost three seats and the Social Democrats gained four. Despite growing critisism from within his own party, Raab insisted on continuing with the grand coalition. In 1960, he was replaced as party chairman and, in 1961, as chancellor by Alfons Gorbach.

During his last years, Raab was once again active as president of the Federal Chamber of Commerce and in 1963 ran for the ceremonial office of federal president, an election by popular vote. But he experienced a bitter defeat, losing by a wide margin to the Social Democratic incumbent, Adolf Schärf, who had been first elected in 1957. Raab's health was obviously poor, and the presidential campaign brought his condition into the open. He died on January 8, 1964.

Above all, Julius Raab is a chief example of the Christian conservative camp's political continuity over many years against a backdrop of great change. Born into the old empire of the Habsburgs and influenced in his formative years by political Catholicism, Austria's most influential bourgeois tradition, Raab fought for the Austro-Hungarian Empire on different fronts throughout World War I. Like other young Austrian officers, he was deeply influenced by this experience. This generation of officers then took over Austrian politics in the 1930s: Engelbert Dollfuss, chancellor, dictator responsible for the civil war of 1934, murdered during a Nazi uprising in the same year; Kurt Schuschnigg, Dollfuss's successor and victim of Nazi blackmail in the spring of 1938; and, finally, Julius Raab, Dollfuss's follower in Lower Austria and Schuschnigg's minister in 1938.

But Raab was able to surivive the disasters of the interwar period both politically and physically. In 1945, he was one of the key figures in the restructuring of the Christian conservative movement. In pre–1934 Austria or, especially, during the authoritarian state from 1934 to 1938, which called itself "Christian," relations between Church and state had not been strained. Nonetheless, Raab stood for a new approach between Christian conservatives and the

Catholic Church, a sort of friendly distance in which bishops tried to avoid direct involvement in party politics. While Raab represented the politicians, who came from the politically active Catholic organizations like the fraternities, he also exemplified the trend toward more autonomy between politics and Church. While he was always known for his personal piety, he did not define his political attitudes in terms of the Church's doctrines. After 1945, he formulated and implemented policies without checking with the Church.

Raab was a pragmatist—especially after 1945—distinctly different from the ideologues who led Austria into the catastrophes of 1934 and 1938. Raab was a leader who did not care very much about intraparty democracy or participation from below, but he did have an instinctive feeling for balances of power and therefore for the necessity of compromise.

This sensitivity to compromise made him the architect of Austria's post–1945 political culture. He preached the gospel of consensus among the major parties and insisted on governing in coalition with the other main force in Austrian politics, the Social Democrats. And he forged consensus among the major economic interests and became one of the founders of Austria's social partnership. He was a symbol of "consociational democracy," the pattern of reconciliation of former enemies by elite compromise. He was also a symbol of the capability to adapt by learning. In the 1930s Raab had been a leader of the antidemocratic Heimwehr, enemy to everything and everyone defined as being on the left. After 1945, Raab became the main partner of that very same left. He had learned the lessons of civil war and world war, of authoritarian rule and totalitarian dictatorship.

This ability to bridge seemingly huge differences helped develop his international influence. As a traditional conservative, he was able to be more flexible toward the Soviet Union than the SPÖ. Whereas the latter was always forced to demonstrate its differences from communism, the conservative Raab never had to be afraid of being criticized as "soft on communism." This enabled him to respond more openly to the first post-Stalinist overtures of the new Soviet leadership in 1954 and 1955. While some within his party criticized what they viewed as his anti-American leanings, Raab replied that "it does not make sense to pinch the Russian bear's tail," one of his most celebrated remarks.

This pragmatic openess made it possible to build upon these new Soviet overtures to start a period of international détente. The Austrian State Treaty was the most significant result of this first relaxing of tensions in the postwar period of East-West conflict. Austria, of course, was the main beneficiary of this brief period of mellowing between the superpowers.

Within the framework of the traditionally highly ideological Austrian political system, Raab's pragmatic flexibility was something of a phenomenon. But at the very same time, he was also representative of a political style that was bound to decline. Most telling, Raab was never able to master the modern mass media for his own political purposes. Unlike Bruno Kreisky, a Social Democrat of the next generation who dominated Austrian politics in the 1970s, Raab very much preferred small audiences, backstage bargaining and informal dealings to mass appeals through the electronic media. While his political beliefs were definitely anchored in the postwar era, his political style remained stuck in the old fashioned ways of pre–1938 politics.

In this, Raab strongly underestimated the importance of mass media for contemporary politics. He used a daily paper—the *Wiener Tageszeitung* (founded in 1947), later renamed the *Neue Österreichische Tageszeitung*—as his personal organ. But the paper had a small circulation, and the link between Raab and it was an obstacle to a better relationship with other, much more important media. And when the first Austrian television program was broadcast in 1955, Raab did not realize the impact this new medium would have on public opinion. He agreed to let the Social Democrats oversee state television because he thought of television as a kind of toy.

This attitude was exemplified by Raab's "no nonsense" approach to the media. His language was extremely sober, and he never tried to use the media for communicating with the people or for creating a certain atmosphere. He dealt with the media as he did with politics in general: like a small entrepreneur in a small business.

Upon his death, Raab became a symbol: for Austria's international neutrality as the main instrument for maximizing its security; for reconciliation between the two major parties, bound together by the mutual reminder of the 1934 civil war; for social peace through political moderation, expressed by institutionalized cooperation between business and labor; for the economic boom of the 1950s, the so-called Austrian economic miracle; and for the successes of the ÖVP, although the party was voted out of power in 1970, remaining in the opposition until 1986. Julius Raab became part of the nostalgic vision that present-day Austria sometimes indulges itself with: He stood above all for the unwavering optimism that characterized the early postwar era.

BIBLIOGRAPHY

Works by Raab:

Verantwortung für Österreich. Vienna: Virtschaftsverlag, 1961.
Selbstporträt eines Politikers. Vienna: Europa, 1964.

Other Works:

Brusatti, Alois, and Gottfried Heindl (eds.). *Julius Raab.* Linz: Trauner, n.d.
Reichhold, Ludwig. "Einführung," in *Selbstporträt eines Politikers.* Vienna: Europa, 1964.
Ritschel, Karl Heinz. *Julius Raab.* Salzburg: Reinartz, 1975.

ANTON PELINKA

KARL RENNER (1870–1950), Austrian politician and statesman, is unique in Austrian political history for he was twice a founding chancellor of the Republic of Austria, once after World War I (the first Austrian Republic) and again after World War II (the second Austrian Republic). Renner was also well-known beyond Austria as a political thinker, a theorist on nationalism and the role of the state, and a scholar of sociology and the Marxist doctrine.

Karl Renner was born on December 14, 1870, the eighteenth child of a small-peasant family in Untertannowitz (Dolni Dunajovice), a southern Moravian village near today's Austrian border. The abject poverty of his childhood, the public sale of his parents' homestead and his parents' end in the poorhouse were decisive formative experiences for him, explaining his lifelong devotion to social questions. After completing his secondary education, Renner moved to Vienna, where he served in the military, studied law at the university and met his wife and lifelong companion, Luise. Renner then became a civil servant at the Library of Parliament.

His scientific interests soon found expression in his essays on nationalism and other basic questions of the old Austrian Empire and on statehood in general. With these and other contributions, Renner became one of the best-known representatives of the scientific school of Austrian Marxism, to which the Social Democratic Party leader Otto Bauer, the philosopher Max Adler and the economist Rudolf Hilferding belonged as well. But rather than pursue an academic career, Renner went into politics and rose to prominence within the framework of "social democracy." In the first elections held under general and equal suffrage in 1907, he was elected to the Reichsrat, one of the houses of the multinational Habsburg Empire's parliament.

World War I destroyed the harmony and cohesiveness of the friends who made up the Austrian Marxist school and who had supplied the Social Democrats with brains and programs. What had until then been only latent differences between inner members of the circle became clear and manifest divisions within the party itself. The left wing of the party, represented by Otto Bauer, Max Adler and Friedrich Adler, the son of the party's founder Victor Adler, protested against involvement in the war. On October 21, 1916, Friedrich Adler went so far as to assassinate the Austrian minister-president, Count Stürgkh, in an ultimate, dramatic antiwar gesture.

Renner, on the other hand, supported the prowar position of the Social Democratic leadership. He did so not because he was a nationalist and a militarist—as his opponents accused him of being—but because he was convinced that it was impossible to break out of the logic of the nation-state, and thus out of the logic of war itself, without an international peace authority having adequate coercive powers.

In fact, Renner believed in the virtues of the multinational state, as the Austrian Empire exemplified, almost beyond its eclipse, quite in contrast to Social Democratic leftists who had begun to accept the downfall of the old Austrian Empire while simultaneously developing a taste for the strengthening forces of nationalism. Renner did not regard the triumph of nationalism in the formation of states as historic progress. Instead, he turned against the *Souveranitätsdogma* (dogma of sovereignty), which was tearing the community of nations apart and severely fragmenting it.

History often fancies irony and paradox: One of the whims of Austria's historical development was that it was this Karl Renner, who had fought desperately until the very last for the preservation of the multinational empire, who presided over the creation of a new, single-nation state. The Republic of Austria came into being through the exodus of the non-German nations, especially the Hungarians and the Czechs, from the old Austrian Empire in October and November 1918. Renner stumbled into the role of first Austrian chancellor.

The events of 1918 which led to the proclamation of the Austrian Republic on November 12 politically and constitutionally resembled a fairly amicable transition, a "changing of the guard," between the last imperial government, under the guidance of Heinrich Lammasch, a professor of international law, and Renner's new government. It was not a revolution in the real meaning of the term. There was no bloodshed and no resistance from the old regime, although the downfall of the empire felt psychologically like a revolution. Nonetheless, the transition was peaceful.

Renner was the first head of government in the new republic, a coalition between the Social Democrats and the conservative Christian Social Party. This government lasted from November 1918 until June 1920. During this time, Renner was also the leader of the Austrian delegation to the peace negotiations in St. Germain. Subsequently, he took the foreign ministry portfolio from Otto Bauer because of Bauer's position supporting Austrian union with Germany.

Yet even Renner was, like most other mainstream Austrian politicians, in favor of union with Germany as the logical, historically inevitable solution for the problems facing the new Austrian state. Because Austria was small, it was thought, it did not dare hope to exist autonomously. However, not only was Austrian union with Germany prohibited by the peace treaty of St. Germain (some called it a peace diktat), but the treaty also imposed territorial losses on Austria. Instead of adhering to the principles of national self-determination proclaimed, ironically, by President Wilson of the United States, the treaty took away from Austria the Alpine region of the South Tyrol and the German-speaking regions of Bohemia and Moravia. As small compensation Austria received a part of the former Deutschwestungarn (Germanic West Hungary), now called Burgenland (where, in fact, Renner's wife came from). The more that this shrinking of Austria increased the resentment of Austrians, the more that union with Germany appeared to be the logical solution. But the Allied powers would not permit it.

After Renner had completed this historic mission as chancellor and foreign minister, he withdrew from the political front lines. He not only disapproved of the peace treaty's terms regarding Austria, he opposed the polarization that overcame Austrian domestic politics and led to the early collapse of the coalition government and to sharp conflict between political camps. The political Catholicism of the Christian Social Party, which formed the so-called *Bürgerblock* (bourgeois bloc) governments from 1920 onward, found its greatest expression in the Catholic prelate, Ignaz Seipel. The radical wing of the Social Democrats, whose bastion was in "Red Vienna," was led by Otto Bauer and the Viennese mayor, Karl Seitz. Karl Renner, who even in this early period had been a man of reconciliation and social balance, earned little praise from either his political opponents or his own camp. As political consensus broke down, both sides proved unwilling to maintain the coalition which they had agreed upon in 1918. Everything was a squabble, including how to interpret November 12, 1918, the founding day of the republic. One side rejoiced, the other mourned, showing that the republic and parliamentarism did not enjoy the protection of any political consensus over fundamentals. Under these circumstances Renner did not have the stomach to fight these polarizing tendencies, especially those within his own party, and he retired from his leading role in state and party in 1920, returning to private life.

There, he devoted himself to his literary work, writing important papers, and also did leading work with the so-called consumer cooperative societies. He saw these as the third element of a "labor movement trinity" (*Dreieinheit der Arbeiterbewegung*) and he vigorously supported them. (The other two elements of Renner's trinity were the Social Democratic Party and the trade unions.) During this period, he also founded the Workers' Bank (Arbeiter-Bank) and served as its first president. This bank was conceived of as a counterpart to the "bourgeois" banks and was to be operated in the interests of workers.

But even during this period of relative political inactivity, which lasted ten years, Renner kept raising his voice against the ongoing polarization of Austrian politics. He did so, for example, at the Social Democratic Party convention in 1927, after civil disturbances in July of that year resulted in considerable bloodshed. These were the same events which inspired the Nobel Prize winner Elias Canetti to formulate his theories on the psychology of masses. These signs of the time already signaled the coming storm against democracy. In them, Renner did not only hold to account the actual participants in these tragic events—hundreds of casualties resulted when the police shot into the crowds of demonstrators—but also his very own party, which had been constantly inciting the masses, leading them to a dangerous explosiveness.

In April 1931 Karl Renner was elected president of the Nationalrat (National Assembly), the main chamber of the Austrian parliament, and thus came back to the front row of politics. It is an irony of history that the very Karl Renner who was an inspired democrat and parliamentarian should have provided the pretext for the dissolution of the parliament by Chancellor Engelbert Dollfuss, who had long demonstrated authoritarian tendencies and had prepared specifically for a return to authoritarianism. In the session of March 4, 1933, Renner resigned his Assembly presidency at his party's request when conflict between government and opposition became particularly intractable. The two Assembly vice presidents did likewise, thus creating a situation which seemed legally untenable, but which could have, with a little goodwill, been resolved in favor of continuing democracy. But goodwill was missing on the government's side, not least out of fear of the National Socialists, who, after all, then assassinated

Chancellor Dollfuss in the putsch of July 1934. Therefore, instead of mounting a common front against national socialism, the two main political camps in Austrian politics remained incurably separated, eventually paving the way for the loss of Austrian independence in March 1938 when German troops marched in. Austrian democracy, which had been built on unstable foundations from the very beginning, did not stand the test of 1933–1934.

Renner spent the eleven years during which democracy was banished in a kind of inner exile at his house in Gloggnitz in Lower Austria. Apparently, he did not feel called to revolutionary activity and resistance. During this period, he refrained from political comments and activities, with one notable exception, which has been interpreted again and again as opportunism and, even, treason. For this, he was and is still often resented. On April 8, 1938, he declared in the daily *Neues Wiener Tagblatt* that he would vote yes in the forthcoming plebiscite on Hitler's plan to annex Austria. This declaration was understood by many of Renner's followers as his request that they vote yes along with him and it struck many of them as a betrayal.

It was without doubt a political mistake, and the incident casts a shadow on Renner's lifework. Nonetheless, Renner most likely made his declaration because he regarded the *Anschluss* (Hitler's annexation of Austria) as historically inevitable and he wished to protect the Social Democrats and others from persecution by the Nazis. After all, Otto Bauer had also made a similar declaration from his exile in Paris. Besides, in an interview in the London magazine *World Review*, Renner both explained the reasoning behind his decision to vote yes and dissociated himself from national socialism more vigorously than he could ever do in Vienna at that time. In any case, Renner was convinced that he would again play a role in politics after the collapse of the Third Reich. In effect, he bought some peace from the Nazis, who then ignored him if for no other reason than that his only daughter was married to a Jew and therefore, according to Nazi logic, his whole family was Jewish kin.

When Austria was liberated in 1945, Renner went to Soviet headquarters in Gloggnitz on behalf of Austrians seeking protection. While there, in fact, he was presented to Stalin, who designated him for a leading political role. Originally, Renner had seen his task to be one of reconvening members of parliament in his capacity as its last president. Instead, however, Renner was appointed first chancellor of the provisional government. As chancellor, he made the first official statements on April 27, 1945, proclaming Austria's independence.

Unlike in 1918, the political class and the Austrian people were quite happy to form (to revive really) their own state. However, the postwar Austrian state was divided into four zones of occupation and ruled by four powers. In this, however, Renner did not at all play the role Stalin had intended for him as accomplice to Soviet plans. These were aimed at developing Austria into a "people's republic" along the model of Eastern European states or at the very least into a permanently divided country much like Germany. But he confounded these Soviet intentions, which had never been openly stated, by insisting on becoming not only head of government in the Soviet zone but of Austria as a whole and by insisting on early elections, which were to enable the Austrian people to legitimate Renner's government.

The outcome of the elections brought about a devastating defeat for the Communists and a victory for democratic forces. Unlike 1918, these latter finally managed to come together in a strong coalition. In this way, Renner not only put a stop to Soviet designs on Austria, but also positively influenced the early Cold War by placing limits on the expansion of communism in the heart of Europe. On December 20, 1945, Renner was elected by both houses of parliament to be the first head of state (president) of the postwar Republic of Austria. As chancellor and as president, his vision in this early postwar period set down much of the course for Austria's future.

At the end of his life, he returned to the ideals of his youth and adapted them to the present. Prior to World War I, he advocated changing the Austrian multinational state into a "democratic national federal state" according to the Swiss model. After World War II, by contrast, he looked to Switzerland as the model of international neutrality that should be adopted by Austria. In a way, neutrality proved to be a bridge for the Soviets, permitting them to decide to give Austria its full freedom in 1955 by agreeing to the terms of the State Treaty, although this might not have been accomplished even a year later after the 1956 Hungarian revolt.

Although Renner did not live to see the fruit of his efforts in the Austrian State Treaty, he did live long enough to observe with satisfaction that democracy had won a victory in Austria over both forms of dictatorship, fascism and communism. He also lived long enough to see Austria begin to develop from a liberal to a social welfare state, a tendency which he had always supported and which he addressed specifically in a programmatic speech at the first postwar congress of the Austrian trades union movement in 1948.

As a theorist of the state, Renner is of paradigmatic importance. As early as World War I, he was describing the "economization of state power" and the "intransigence of the state on the economy." He also argued that the state would become the lever of socialism. In his classic 1929 work, "The Institutions of Private Law and Their Social Functions," he demonstrated the changes that the Roman-law notion of private property had undergone and the limits that the right of an owner's free disposition of his property had experienced over the course of time. Renner wanted to involve the state more directly, replacing private capital where it had become superfluous or had harmful consequences.

But early on Renner also warned against the Bolshevist tendency to disturb the economy through political manipulation, even destroying it. He warned against the excesses of nationalization, which his Marxist colleagues considered the solution to all problems. In 1929, for example, he argued that "general socialization is general nonsense" (*Generalsozialisierung ist Generalunsinn*). Renner also warned against terrorism and anarchism, as well as against state socialist illusions. Nonetheless, he supported the modern welfare state and thought the liberal *Nachtwachterstaat* (''night watchman'' state), which Lassalle had scoffed at, to be in decline.

Renner's posthumously published sociological work, especially, shows him to be an unswerving enemy of every sort of totalitarianism and a passionate advocate of democracy. His understanding of democracy was not that of simple majority rule but rather stressed protection of minority and basic human rights. However, in some ways he was clearly too optimistic, as *Die Nation: Mythos und Wirklichkeit!* (The Nation: Myth and Reality), written between 1935 and 1937, shows. In it, Renner argues that the historical climax of nationalism occurred in World War I and that a victory for internationalism was imminent. Sadly, he was mistaken.

Karl Renner's ideals of peace and justice are as relevant today as ever. But even though his ideals were balanced by a remarkable pragmatism, even he underestimated the obstacles on the way to achieving them.

BIBLIOGRAPHY

Works by Renner:

Pseud. Rudolf Springer. *Der Kampf der österreichischen Nationen um den Staat.* Leipzig and Vienna, 1902.

Marxismus, Krieg und Internationale. Stuttgart, 1917.

Die Dreieinheit der Arbeiterbewegung. Vienna, 1928.

An der Wende zweier Zeiten: Lebenserinnerungen. Vienna, 1946.

Mensch und Gesellschaft: Grundriss einer Soziologie. Nachgelassene Werke Band 1. Vienna, 1952.

Wandlungen der modernen Gesellschaft: Zwei Abhandlungen über die Probleme der Nachkriegszeit. Nachgelassene Werke Band 3. Vienna, 1953.

Other Works:

Hannak, Jacques. *Karl Renner und seine Zeit: Versuch einer Biographie.* Vienna, 1965.

Leser, Norbert. ''Karl Renner,'' in *Die österreichischen Bundespräsidenten, Leben und Werk,* 122ff. Vienna, 1982.

Loewenberg, Peter. ''Karl Renner and the Politics of Accommodation: Moderation versus Revenge,'' in *Austrian History Yearbook*, vol. 22, 35–56. University of Minnesota, 1991.

Pelinka, Anton. *Karl Renner zur Einführung.* Hamburg, 1989.

———. ''Karl Renner—A Man for All Seasons?'' in *Austrian History Yearbook*, vol. 23, 111ff. University of Minnesota, 1992.

NORBERT LESER

MICHEL ROCARD (1930–) occupies a unique and often paradoxical place in contemporary French political life. He is a party leader who does not like political parties, a Socialist who does not believe in a strong state, and a philosopher noted for nonideological pragmatism. He has been a candidate for the French presidency three times, but won only 3.6 percent of the vote in 1969 and dropped out early in the contests of both 1974 and 1981. He has twice resigned from high office, first as minister of agriculture in 1985, second as prime minister in 1991. He has long been considered a likely successor to Socialist President François Mitterrand, but if he achieves that goal it will be contrary to Mitterrand's own wishes.

Rocard has at times been the most popular politician in France, and his policies during his three-year stint as prime minister (1988–1991) are generally acknowledged to have achieved considerable success, yet his career has been haunted by recurrent defeats, including his failure to win reelection as deputy to the French National Assembly in 1993. A principled pragmatist, a Protestant believer in a nation of Catholics and secularists, a problem solver unafraid to tackle any task, Michel Rocard appears to accept both victory and defeat with the same stoic certainty. The complex and varied turnings of his career and persona may help explain the affection that many French voters—more appreciative of an interesting puzzle than of simpleminded and no longer credible campaign rhetoric—continue to feel for him.

Michel Rocard was born on August 23, 1930, in Courbevoie, a suburb northwest of Paris. His family was part of the small (approximately one million) Protestant minority in France. His father, Yves Rocard, was one of the scientists who helped invent the French atomic bomb, and the son was expected to pursue a career in science as well. However, at the age of seventeen, while his father was abroad, Rocard dropped out of the intensive math course in which he had obediently enrolled at the elite lycée Louis-le-Grand and enrolled instead in the National Foundation of Political Science. This manifestation of independence met with the expected parental fury, and relations between father and son remained strained for many years thereafter, despite the latter's success first at "Sciences Po," then at the prestigious Ecole Nationale d'Administration (ENA) and finally in government and politics.

While in school, Rocard was active in left-wing student politics, and the conditions he observed in his first civil service post—as an inspector of finance in Algeria during that nation's struggle for independence—strengthened his leftist convictions. He joined the Socialist Party (SFIO) first, and then shifted to the Unified Socialist Party (PSU), a small splinter group that broke away from the SFIO when the latter supported de Gaulle's return to power in 1958. In 1967, Rocard became the leader of the PSU and in 1969 he was its candidate for president (winning 3.6 percent of the vote). Later that year he won a seat in the National Assembly on the PSU ticket, representing a district in the Yvelines, a department immediately to the west of Paris.

In 1974 the PSU, still a very small party to the left of the traditional Socialists, also split apart, largely thanks to Rocard, who led its larger and more conservative faction back into the Socialist Party, which was then in the throes of a dramatic reorganization led by François Mitterrand. In 1981, with Mitterrand having failed twice as the party's candidate for the French presidency (in 1969 and 1974), Rocard decided to run himself and began to campaign on a more moderate market-oriented form of socialism that he had come to believe in.

However, as soon as Mitterrand announced his own candidacy—which was ultimately victorious—Rocard withdrew.

Rocard was eventually rewarded in 1983 with the post of minister of agriculture, but resigned two years later, saying he could not support the president's decision to adopt a system of proportional representation for the legislative elections slated for 1986. Rocard argued, correctly, that such a system would help the smaller parties, including the extremist National Front (FN), Jean-Marie Le Pen's far-right racist and anti-Semitic party. Others claimed he quit because when Mitterrand decided to move the government closer to the market-oriented system favored by Rocard, he had chosen a younger moderate, Laurent Fabius, not Rocard, to replace his first prime minister, Pierre Mauroy.

Once again, Rocard began campaigning for the presidency, looking to 1988, and once again he announced his withdrawal as soon as Mitterrand announced his own candidacy for reelection. As in 1981, Rocard campaigned aggressively for his archrival, who won a second term with relative ease. This time Rocard was rewarded, as he believed he deserved, with the prime ministership.

However, in the legislative elections held shortly after Mitterrand's reelection, the Socialists won only 276 seats in the 577-member National Assembly, thereby forcing Rocard to rule with 13 votes short of an absolute majority. Although the opposition was unlikely ever to garner the 289 votes needed to bring him and his government down, the absence of a majority meant that throughout his tenure in office non-Socialist votes or key abstentions had to be attracted from either the 27 Communists or the 271 conservatives in the Assembly. Furthermore, this legislative election had been marked by the lowest voter turnout (71.1 percent) in a second round of French parliamentary voting since 1945.

Despite this undeniable absence of a mandate, a world economy which confounded hopes for an easy resolution of domestic problems, serious difficulties abroad and the necessity of serving a president whose trust and friendship were as limited as his powers were great, Rocard achieved considerable success during his term in office. Inflation was brought down to around 3 percent and the franc became, at least for a time, one of the most solid currencies in Europe. Investment in industry doubled, and 800,000 new jobs were created (not enough to reduce the rate of unemployment, however, as new job seekers were even more numerous). Although social unrest and strikes continued, particularly in the educational and hospital systems, the number of working days lost per year because of strikes fell to the lowest rate in thirty years and wage increases were largely kept within the rate of inflation.

To a certain extent, such policies were simply imposed on Rocard by the status of the world economy: So long as leading nations such as the United States, Germany and Japan followed anti-inflationary austerity programs, other nations had little choice but to do the same in order to maintain their international competitiveness. More impressive was Rocard's ability to combine such policies with important social reforms during his premiership. One such reform was the adoption of the *revenu minimum d'insertion*, or guaranteed minimum income for all legal residents of France. Those who receive this income also benefit from retraining and rehabilitation programs designed to help them become self-supporting in the future. A second program, the *crédit-formation*, was instituted to make it possible for workers to go back to school for further training without incurring financial hardship. Public housing for the poor was also improved, and the handicapped and the aged received new benefits. Rocard also pushed through a new law allowing for the suspension of all civic rights—including voting or running for office—for anyone convicted of serious racist or anti-Semitic offenses.

Rocard's reforms of the public administration were impressive, as well. The postal and telephone system was significantly reformed, as was the regulation of the judicial professions. Key reforms were also adopted in the financing of political parties and campaigns, while other reforms were initiated in the penal code and in regulations governing the terms of psychiatric internment. An important reform in the funding of the French social security system was the introduction of the *contribution sociale généralisée* (CSG), a new tax to be paid by those above a certain income level in order to meet the growing costs of health and old age pension benefits.

In the French quasi-presidential system, the president has dominant responsibility for foreign affairs, but as prime minister, Rocard was active in this domain as well. An early key accomplishment was the successful resolution of the long-term dispute over the future of New Caledonia, a French territory in the Pacific where the ferocity of those who struggled for independence was matched and often surpassed by those whose interests were strongly tied to metropolitan France. Rocard personally supervised the design of a compromise plan which won easy if lukewarm approval in a national referendum (only 37 percent voted, but those who did voted overwhelmingly for its acceptance) and brought peace at last to the long-embattled island.

The French have long been committed to maintaining their role as ally, "not vassal," of the United States, and Rocard ably seconded Mitterrand's continuation of this policy. He has always supported the idea of France's independent nuclear strike force (the *force de frappe*), as well as France's membership in NATO's political (but not military) structures. While in office he endorsed France's participation in the Persian Gulf War of 1991, but insisted that the objectives of the war be limited to the liberation of Kuwait. At the conclusion of those hostilities, he proposed an international conference to create new conditions of mutual trust and confidence between Israel and the Palestinians.

In general, Rocard's approach to the Middle Eastern dilemma was typically pragmatic and nonideological: While he never ruled out an independent Palestinian state, at the same time he insisted that all possible solutions be explored, including a possible Palestinian-Jordanian confederation. On the difficult question of French arms sales, he urged that France find other means to maintain a positive balance of payments, and he supported arms negotiations that could have the effect of reducing the market for French weapons. Rocard gave ardent support to the idea of a stronger Europe, including the creation of a common security policy and a common defense policy, but in accordance with his usual approach to problem solving, he always insisted that the best way to move toward that end was to endorse the idea generally rather than to propose a single, specifically French solution.

Overall, Rocard's approach to governance is to work hard and systematically on selected tasks that he believes can be accomplished, while keeping a watchful idea on other problems that interest him but which appear, for political or material reasons (or both), currently impossible to resolve. With the correct mix of gentle prodding and sympathetic inattention, perhaps the latter would gradually assume more manageable dimensions, eventually presenting themselves as candidates for action. As prime minister he maintained a very low profile, rarely appearing on television and coming off as utterly uncharismatic. He conveyed the image of a politician hard at work, solving day-to-day problems in a fashion one observer termed ''almost clandestine.'' When questioned on his approach, he admitted that while it was necessary to ''put on a show in politics'' in order to ''have a symbolic relationship with the public,'' doing so was not the same thing as ''managing the currency, straightening out the balance of payments or negotiating an exit from a strike.'' He made his preference for the latter kind of activity very clear.

Such a style earned him high points at the beginning of his tenure as prime minister. As time went on, he was occasionally accused of exaggerating the ills of the French economy in order to keep wages down and to spend less than was clearly needed to resolve serious problems of social unrest in the school system and in the suburban immigrant ghettos. By the end of his time in office, unemployment had risen to 2.6 million, 100,000 more than when he entered office. But in general his performance was widely praised, even in a business community not noted for its approval of Socialist endeavors.

It seems clear that what brought Rocard down in 1991, when Mitterrand demanded and received his resignation, was not the relatively limited popular discontent with his policies but rather a serious political scandal in which he himself played very little part. That scandal—a matter of illegal payments made to Mitterrand's reelection campaign in 1988 by Urbatechnic, a ''construction company'' that was mainly in the business of political fund-raising—seemed to implicate the president far more directly than Rocard: While Henri Nallet, who as justice minister ordered the investigating magistrate off the case, was indeed a member of Rocard's cabinet, he had more significantly served as Mitterrand's campaign manager in 1988.

However, prime ministers do not dismiss presidents in France, and Mitterrand was not the first French president to force the resignation of a popular and effective prime minister in order to distract the public from his own possible shortcomings. The president's efforts to distract were also subsequently apparent in his appointment of Edith Cresson as France's first woman prime minister to succeed Rocard. But Cresson proved to be poorly qualified, while the French press was unrelenting in its ferociously sexist denunciation of her mistakes. The net result was a further decline in Socialist fortunes.

Cresson's dismissal from the premiership in 1992 and her replacement by the more competent longtime finance minister Pierre Bérégovoy was too little, too late, and the Socialists went down to resounding defeat in the following year's legislative elections, a defeat so monumental it caused several party luminaries to lose their own long-held legislative seats. Among those swept from the National Assembly in the flood of irate opinion was Michel Rocard—whose efforts at personal raft building had consisted of little more than talk of possibly one day creating a new party.

The question of whether or not Rocard can salvage his presidential ambitions for 1995 must remain an open one and of course depends in part on the strength of his leading competitors. Within his own party these are Jacques Delors, the popular but electorally untested president of the European Community's Executive Commission, and former prime minister Laurent Fabius; on the right he can expect both former prime minister Jacques Chirac and former president Valéry Giscard d'Estaing to renew their own quest for the office.

However, Rocard's chances of becoming president also depend in part on his ability to make the French more clearly aware and supportive of the philosophy that stands behind his self-created image as a pragmatic problem solver. Presenting that image may fit his personality and may have itself exhibited a certain pragmatism while serving under a president like François Mitterrand, who would never have tolerated a showier style from a prime minister who was also a leading political rival. Nevertheless, Rocard is not a politician who simply moves from task to task applying the efficient management skills inculcated by ENA. As noted earlier, he chooses carefully what tasks he will undertake, and his choice is guided by more than just the likelihood of success.

Rocard's own books and his more thoughtful interviews reveal a well-thought-out left-of-center philosophy. His concern for the poor and underprivileged, in underdeveloped nations as well as in France, led him naturally to the Socialists and to a desire to use government as an instrument for improving social conditions. But he is not a strong party man, he does not believe in the natural goodness of social instincts and he is far from being an absolute egalitarian: For Rocard, socialism is "the collective wish for social justice, for less arbitrariness, for a reduction of inequality to a level that corresponds to the distribution of talents, risks and responsibilities."

And although Rocard believes in using government where needed, he is equally firm in his conviction that it must not be used where it is not needed. For him, individual freedom and a relatively free marketplace are essential ingredients for social and economic development, and an excessively strong state inevitably encroaches on these freedoms. This philosophy extends to the world at large: Rocard believes that stronger international law capable of imposing the rule of law on the world market must be developed in order to eliminate the worst ravages of unrestrained global capitalism, but he would leave that market otherwise as free as possible.

These carefully weighed and balanced beliefs are internally consistent and logically defensible, but they are not easily translated into the rhetoric of the political marketplace. It is a philosophy that may elicit respect, but is unlikely to arouse the mindless enthusiasms that so often determine the outcome of contemporary Western political contests. In the final analysis, the day Rocard has waited for so long may never come. On the other hand, the French have a reputation for being somewhat more resistant than other peoples to passing fads of political fashion, and Rocard may yet be able to command sufficient attention and respect to win the right to serve in the nation's highest office. "I am sure I will be president," he has said, "I just don't know when."

BIBLIOGRAPHY

Works by Rocard:

Le PSU et l'avenir socialiste de la France. Paris: Le Seuil, 1969.

Questions à l'état socialiste. Paris: Stock, 1972.

Le Marché Commun contre l'Europe. Paris: Le Seuil, 1973 (with Bernard Jaumont and Daniel Lenègre).

L'Inflation au coeur. Paris: Gallimard, 1975 (with Jacques Gallus).

Parler vrai: Textes politiques 1966–1979. Paris: Le Seuil, 1979.

A l'épreuve des faits: Textes politiques 1979–1985. Paris: Le Seuil, 1986.

Un pays comme le nôtre: Textes politiques 1986–1989. Paris: Le Seuil, 1989.

Other Works:

Bergouinioux, Alain, and Gérard Grunberg. *Le Long Remords du pouvoir*. Paris: Fayard, 1992.

Evin, Kathleen. *Michel Rocard: L'Art du possible*. Paris: Editions Jean-Claude Simoen, 1979.

Schneider, Robert. *Michel Rocard*. Paris: Stock, 1987.

KAY LAWSON

S

ANTÓNIO DE OLIVEIRA SALAZAR (1889–1970) ruled Portugal from 1932 to 1968, and his ideas dominated the country's politics even longer—from soon after the demise of the short-lived democratic republic in 1926 through the peaceful "revolution of the carnations" in 1974. As finance minister, starting in 1928, he stabilized Portugal's inflationary economy and eased it through the Great Depression. Then as premier, after 1932, he turned the military dictatorship into a constitutional authoritarian regime based on a hybrid of new corporatist and residual democratic institutions characterized by a Catholic conception of organic national interest. His "New State" was thus meant to steer a course between totalitarian fascism, then on the rise in Europe, and what Salazar considered to be the decadent democracies then collapsing all around him. That his political innovations built on Portuguese traditions instead of imported models accounts for the authoritarian regime's remarkable longevity.

During World War II, Salazar's skillful diplomacy balanced Portugal between neutrality and a traditional alliance with Great Britain, a combination that proved lucrative in both the short and long run. The caution so appropriate during wartime, however, became something of a liability afterward, as economic growth remained comparatively slow and Portugal continued to lag behind the rest of Europe in wealth and social development. Salazar's vision was perhaps most limited when it came to Portugal's anachronistic colonial empire. His stubborn, open-ended commitment to the status quo, in the face of both UN pressure and the expense of colonial wars, proved to be the corporatist regime's Achilles' heel, sparking a bloodless coup in 1974. Overall, few leaders have shaped their country's economics, domestic politics and foreign policy so profoundly for so many decades.

Salazar was born on April 28, 1889, to poor but deeply religious parents in a hamlet in the wine valley of Dão. From age eleven to eighteen, he attended a Catholic seminary. He never was ordained, but personally continued to live the ascetic life of a Seminarian. He studied law and economics at Coimbra University beginning in 1910, the same year that Portugal's democratic republic was proclaimed. He stayed on to teach political economy at the university, where he led a movement of Catholic intellectuals called the Academic Center for Christian Democracy (known by its Portuguese initials, CADC). Salazar regularly criticized the Republic as politically unstable, inflationary, anticlerical, and especially following the huge financial scandal of 1925, hopelessly corrupt.

During this time, Salazar is said to have been turned down for marriage by an upper-class girl. Despite his strong belief that the family was the nation's basic moral, social and political unit, he never did marry or have children of his own. After becoming premier, he would eventually adopt two female cousins of his lifelong housekeeper, Doña Maria, who in turn practically became a surrogate first lady. Salazar was elected to the National Assembly as a non-party CADC deputy for one term in 1921, but the experience so repulsed him that he became convinced political parties themselves were part of the republic's problem and should be banned, an opinion he never altered.

In May 1926, when the military overthrew the republic in a bloodless putsch, Salazar served as the dictatorship's first finance minister, but only for five days. He resigned as soon as the generals rejected his strict financial policies. Salazar was invited back in 1928 and finally granted the authority to implement these same tight pre-Keynesian economic policies. He promptly balanced the budget, put the currency back onto the gold standard and made the country self-sufficient in wheat production. Regarded as the regime's savior, Salazar began to exercise decisive influence in other policy areas as well, evident especially in two 1930 speeches that outlined his corporatist vision of government. Then in July 1932, President Carmona designated him head of government, or premier, the post he would hold for the rest of his life. Within a year, Salazar instituted a civilian authoritarian regime. His corporatist constitution was approved by plebiscite in March 1933 and followed by elections without opposition in December. The next elections would not be held until 1945. The most serious sign of opposition until then was the bomb that exploded near Salazar on July 4, 1947.

Salazar's "New State" was based on a nationalist reaction against the internationalism of both communism and fascism. Although it has been criticized as fascism without a fascist movement, the New State was not controlled by a mass party, it lacked a fully developed ideology and it never tried to mobilize its population—all hallmarks of fascism. Nor was Salazar's regime committed to rapid socioeconomic modernization. Portugal had a fascist movement, the blue-shirted National Syndicalists led by Rolão Prieto, but Salazar banned them in June 1934 for having too many foreign connections. Although Salazar did create a youth movement (called the Mocidade), a civil guard (the Portuguese Legion) and a single party (National Union), these institutions bore only a superficial resemblance to the corresponding institutions of Italian fascism and German national socialism. In contrast to both Italy and Germany, where fascist movements had founded new states, in Portugal the New State founded a movement with no independent life of its own.

For political principles to govern Portugal, where Catholic faith had been deepened by the Fátima vision in 1917, Salazar turned instead to the Catholic corporatism of the CDAL, drawing heavily on the encyclicals of Popes Leo XIII and Pius IX. These preached that the state should make itself responsible for social justice yet follow the principle of subsidiarity, that is, to undertake to do itself only that which neither market nor family could do alone. His Catholic political inspiration did not, however, extend to embracing Pius XI's commitment to the sanctity of individual human rights or the later liberalism of John XXIII's Second Vatican Council. Salazar believed that God, not the people, was the ultimate source of political power, that the common good, not majority will, was the source of political legitimacy, and that Christians had a duty to obey a government that respected the Church's spiritual sphere. In a 1940 concordat, Salazar restored the Vatican rights removed by the republic, but his relations with the Church were not entirely smooth. In 1958 the bishop of Porto was "encouraged" to leave the country for criticizing the government and he was not asked to return until 1969. Since Salazar vetted new appointments, the Vatican refused for eleven years to name a replacement.

Salazar's corporatist constitution preserved direct representation both in a popularly-elected president (until 1959) and in a popularly elected National Assembly, which was limited mostly to advising a premier who could rule by decree-law. But its great innovation was to set up an alternative advisory body, the Corporative Chamber, in which social groups rather than individuals were represented. This body reflected Salazar's conviction that the nation was not a pluralistic collection of atomized individual wills but rather an organic being composed of functionally specialized parts. Industrial and professional associations, merchants, financiers, workers, intellectuals, farmers and the Church were all represented in the advisory Corporative Chamber. Yet, with the power to increase spending vested solely in the executive, and most corporate representatives also appointed by the executive rather than elected by their corporations, Salazar's regime ended up less the viable alternative to traditional conceptions of democracy it claimed to be than a constitutional dictatorship of the premier himself.

Paternalism characterized the extensive practical limits on formal freedoms of speech, press and assembly, which Salazar felt were necessary to protect the nation's public opinion from dangerous ideas, both internal and external ideas. Since the family was considered the basic social unit, the right to vote was restricted largely to heads of families, although some women with college education and sufficient property could also vote. There was no right to strike; there were no independent unions. Instead, by 1956 the state was supervising all collective bargaining between corporations of businessmen and workers in all major industries. Membership was always voluntary in these corporations but the terms of the contracts they negotiated were binding on nonmembers as well.

In foreign policy, Salazar's greatest achievement was to keep Portugal neutral in World War II while reaping the benefits of allying with the winning side. This he achieved by preserving Portugal's traditional alliance with Great Britain, which dates back several centuries, even as he sold goods to both the Allies and the Axis until 1944. Only in 1943, after an Allied victory was in sight, did Salazar grant Britain base rights in the strategic Azores Islands. Portugal's economy thrived under this diplomatic balancing act, especially from the sale of wolfram, a crucial weapons-making material. After the war, Portugal received Marshall Fund aid (1947–1948), joined the NATO defense alliance (1949), and overcame a Soviet veto to join the United Nations (1955). Salazar could thus claim credit for recovering the international respect Portugal had lost under the republic.

Another achievement of Salazar's diplomacy was to help convince Spain to stay neutral in the war, even as it was signing the Comintern Pact with the Axis. Putting aside centuries of peninsular rivalry, in 1939 Salazar signed the Iberian Pact for mutual neutrality with Franco. Partly his calculation was that Portugal's sovereignty would be threatened by a communist regime in Spain, partly that Franco's authoritarian ideas closely resembled his own. So in 1938, Portugal became the first country to recognize the Franco government as the Spanish Civil War wound down.

In spite of the international postwar trend to decolonize, Salazar clung to a colonial empire that became more and more of a burden to a country of only 9.5 million people. From Macao in the Far East to Goa in the Indian Ocean to the African colonies of Angola, Mozambique and Guinea-Bissau, Salazar and his young foreign minister, Franco Nogueira, rebuffed UN demands—eventually included in a Security Council resolution of 1965—that Portugal grant its colonies independence. Insisting that each territory was an equal overseas province of Portugal rather than a subordinate colony—at least after colonial law revisions in 1951—Salazar tapped proud traditions dating back to Prince Henry the Navigator by insisting that Portugal was not just a small country in Europe. But in fact, less than 1 percent of the native colonial population could vote, and forced labor continued until another colonial law reform in 1961–1962.

The guerrilla wars of independence that began in Angola in 1961 (the same year in which India seized Goa) and spread to Guinea-Bissau in 1962 and Mozambique in 1964 soon forced Portugal to bear the heaviest defense burden in Europe—averaging 40 percent of the entire budget—in order to station 100,000 troops abroad. There was some irony in Salazar's commitment to such an unsustainable burden after having launched his career as finance minister in 1928 not just on a general financial conservatism but also on the specific demand that expenditures on the colonies be cut. After suffering a stroke in September 1968, Salazar was succeeded by former overseas minister Marcello Caetano, who doggedly pursued the colonial wars until the military's own frustrations with bleak prospects for eventual victory inspired junior officers to mount the ''captains' movement'' coup of April 25, 1974, which brought down Salazar's corporatist regime.

Perhaps ironically, Salazar's hybrid regime never fully displaced democratic institutions, a fact that may help explain how the antidemocratic revolutionary movement of 1974 could end up producing a democratic transition a year later—the first in what has become a wave of democratizations sweeping across southern Europe, Latin America and Eastern Europe in the past two decades. The National Assembly did not influence policy significantly during Salazar's lifetime, but under Caetano it began to provide a forum for liberal critics. Elections to the Assembly were never free, and direct presidential elections were suspended after a Salazar rival polled at least 25 percent of the vote amid fraud charges in 1958. But despite the proportionally small electorate and consistent voter registration irregularities, a unique window of pluralism opened for thirty days before every election. During that short time, political parties were permitted to organize and freedoms of speech, press and assembly were better respected. It is one of the many paradoxes surrounding Salazar that, by preserving these vestiges of the republic he claimed so thoroughly to reject, he may have contributed indirectly to modern Portugal's successful democratic transition.

On the whole, Salazar's influence on Portugal was unmatched during this century. A strong leader with a clear vision of where he wanted to take the country, he transformed Portugal from a country on the brink of political and economic chaos back into a productive economic and international actor. A single-minded vision of Portuguese national interest enabled Salazar to largely insulate his country from both the Great Depression and World War II. At the same time, however, this rigid vision and the caution it prescribed shut Portugal out of such benefits of the postwar world as rapid economic modernization, decolonization and democratization (and, therefore, European Community membership).

Salazar's legacy is therefore mixed. Portugal's social structure has changed the least, and its illiteracy has remained the highest (15 percent in 1970), of any Western European country, but its strategic international position has been recovered. The Portuguese colonial empire survived longer than any other Western power's, but in the end it dragged Salazar's corporatist regime down in mutiny and insurrection. Salazar's corporatist institutions successfully blocked both communism and fascism in Portugal for more than thirty years, but they also blocked individual human rights and a democracy that the Portuguese were far more prepared for than Salazar's paternal view of them could conceive.

BIBLIOGRAPHY

Work by Salazar:

Doctrine and Action (trans. by R. E. Broughton). London: Faber & Faber, 1939.

Other Works:

Braga da Cruz, Manuel. ''El Modelo político salazarista,'' in Hipólito de la Torre (ed.), *Portugal y España en el cambio politico, 1958–78*, 37–45. Mérida: UNED, 1989.

Caetano, Marcello. *Minhas memórias de Salazar*. Lisbon: Verbo, 1977.

Costa Pinto, António. ''The Salazar 'New State' and European Fascism,'' *European University Institute Working Papers in History* 12 (1991), Florence.

Kay, Hugh. *Salazar and Modern Portugal.* London: Eyre & Cambridge, 1970.
Lucena, Manuel de. "The Evolution of Portuguese Corporatism under Salazar and Caetano," in Lawrence Graham and Henry Makler (eds.), *Contemporary Portugal.* Madison: University of Wisconsin Press, 1979.

DANIEL V. FRIEDHEIM

POUL SCHLÜTER (1929–) has been one of the most significant political figures in Danish politics since World War II. In 1982 he became the first Conservative prime minister in Denmark since 1901; ten years later he was still in office. This in itself constitutes a remarkable feat in a Nordic welfare state mostly accustomed to Social Democratic governments. During Schlüter's tenure as prime minister, most Danish economic indicators have been considerably improved. At the same time, Schlüter has demonstrated remarkable political flexibility as a leader of nonsocialist minority cabinets consisting of two, three and even four political parties.

Poul Schlüter was born on April 3, 1929, in the town of Tønder in the southern part of Jutland, very close to the Danish-German border. His father, Johannes Schlüter, spoke German more fluently than Danish and had fought for the Germans in World War I, Tønder being in German territory from 1864 to 1920. But his experiences at Verdun accelerated a change in his father's own national identification from German to Danish. Coming from a modest social and economic background, his father gradually became a wealthy merchant. Poul Schlüter's mother, Else (née Holmskov), was the daughter of a prosperous farmer family.

The German occupation of Denmark from 1940 to 1945 was a stimulus for young Shlüter's interest in the world of politics. In late 1943 he joined the Conservative People Party's youth organization and became very preoccupied with the conflict between the Danes and the Germans. In the spring of 1945, when the local leader of the youth organization was driven into hiding by the occupation forces, fifteen-year-old Schlüter replaced him as the organization's chairman. As soon as the war was over, Schlüter became active in efforts to reconcile Danes and Germans.

In 1950 Schlüter became a member of the executive committee of the national organization for young Conservatives. In 1952 he became chairman of it despite a dispute with the leader of the Conservative People's Party (CPP). In 1954 he publicly attacked the leadership of the CPP for playing a too dominant role in the youth organization, but a year later the party's leadership succeeded in removing Schlüter from his position.

Schlüter was more or less politically inactive until he made a comeback in 1964, being elected to a seat in the Danish parliament (Folketinget). In the meantime, he had graduated in law from the University of Copenhagen in 1957 and begun practicing in 1960. While still a member of parliament in 1966, he ran for mayor in Gladsaxe, a suburb of Copenhagen which was a strong bastion of the incumbent Social Democrat. Schlüter ran a surprisingly strong race, and although he was beaten, he had clearly proven that he could appeal to voters. He then became vice-mayor.

But it was not until the early 1970s that Schlüter made his decisive breakthrough as a politician. At that time the traditional stability of the Danish party system was shaken by the emergence of the right-wing Progress Party under the leadership of the lawyer Mogens Glistrup. In the 1973 election, the Progress Party made a phenomenal electoral breakthrough by winning 28 seats in the parliament (out of a total of 179 seats), while the Conservatives were reduced from 31 seats to 16.

The Conservative People's Party had been part of a nonsocialist majority government from 1968 to 1971. While they had always appealed for tax cuts, during their participation in government during this period, the total level of taxation in Denmark had increased from 38 percent to 51 percent of GNP. These years also wore on some of the party's older leaders, and the remnants of the party soon divided into two conflicting camps, one oriented to the right wing, the other toward the center. In a fundamental struggle for power, the Conservatives nearly split apart.

Unlike most other outstanding personalities in the party, Poul Schlüter could not be identified with any of the rival factions. In early 1974 he was put forth as a compromise candidate for the leadership of the party. Soon thereafter, he became the undisputed leader of the party, playing the role of conciliator that was not untypical of him. But the party experienced new electoral disaster in 1975, when its representation in parliament once again was reduced, this time to a mere 10 seats. At the same time, Schlüter began to succeed in his efforts to renovate the organization and program. Voters rewarded his efforts with 14 total parliamentary seats in 1977, an additional seven in 1979 and another five in 1981. By then, the Conservative People's Party was the biggest non-socialist party in the Parliament.

But it still seemed to be a very unlikely prospect that Schlüter would ever become prime minister. The chance, however, came in 1982 when the Social Democratic minority cabinet, under Prime Minister Anker Jørgensen, decided to resign without calling a general election. Growing economic and financial problems combined with growing unemployment were too heavy a burden for a Social Democratic Party dedicated to the ideals of a welfare state with full employment. At the same time, however, the Social Democrats also relied on the traditional inability of the non-socialist opposition parties to cooperate together. On September 7, 1982, Schlüter found himself as prime minister heading a four-party minority cabinet, the so-called Four-leaf Clover cabinet. Furthermore, this government could count on the support from a fifth party, the Social Liberal party. Nevertheless, the cabinet had no parliamentary majority behind it, and its only chance to survive was the inability of the new opposition to cooperate, because the opposition included the Socialists and the Social Democrats, as well as the right wing Progress Party.

At that time very few, not even Schlüter himself, expected this cabinet to have a very long life span. The parliamentary foundations of the cabinet were not strong, and it seemed only likely to expect problems within a cabinet consisting of four parties facing the biggest single party, Social Democracy, in opposition. Last but not least, it had theretofore always proven impossible for these conservative parties to establish lasting cooperation.

But Schlüter's qualities were ideal for this kind of situation, calling for cooperation and compromises. He deliberately stressed his role as pragmatic leader of the entire cabinet rather than his role as leader of his own party. He was a brilliant mediator of cooperation within the cabinet, showing himself to be more of an open-minded and pragmatic man of the center than a dogmatic conservative. He also accorded the opposition a remarkable degree of influence in foreign and security policies. In many cases, he has been defeated by the opposition in the parliament without then resigning. This constitutes a new interpretation of Danish parliamentarism which has allowed the policy process to continue smoothly, although it does tend to reduce the distinctiveness of a cabinet's profile.

One of the main initiatives of Schlüter's cabinet was a program for modernizing of the public sector, including deregulation and privatization measures. In fact, this program was very much prepared by the previous Social Democratic government and was simply adopted and launched by Schlüter.

In the next few years, Denmark's economy improved and in the 1984 election Schlüter was rewarded: The Conservative People's Party won forty-two parliamentary seats with 23.4 percent of the total vote. Schlüter's succeeding governments subsequently handled a period of labor unrest in 1985 very well, leading to a relatively long period of peaceful labor relations. In 1986, a package of tax reform measures aimed at easing the marginal rate of taxation and improving savings. Another important event in 1986 was a referendum on the question whether Denmark should concur in the establishment of the EC's internal market by the beginning of 1993. Schlüter's recommendation was followed by 56.2 percent of the voters in spite of the opposition of the Social Democrats.

In 1987, however, new signs of cooperation problems emerged from the Four-leaf Clover cabinet. At the same time, the government was critized by the opposition for attacking the welfare state. After the September 1987 election Schlüter faced a loss of seven parliamentary seats, reducing his party's total to thirty-five. Surprisingly, however, the cabinet was reconstructed. The two smallest parties left the coalition, while the Social-Liberal Party joined it. From then on, the cabinet was formed by a three-party minority government.

In 1988 Schlüter personally seemed to shift farther toward the right wing in order to satisfy the Conservative Party's grass roots. At the same time, however, this supposed shift caused tensions within the cabinet, especially with the new coalition partner, the Social-Liberals. In the 1990 elections, the Conservatives lost another five parliamentary seats, while the Social-Liberal Party suffered such great losses that it was forced from the government. And although the Social Democrats were the biggest winners, with fourteen new seats and 37.4 percent of the total vote, they did not enjoy the same confidence from the small parties in the center of Danish politics as Schlüter did. Therefore, Schlüter was able to continue as prime minister, this time in coalition with just the Liberal Party under the leadership of the foreign affairs minister, Uffe Ellerman-Jensen.

The first years of the 1990s have not been the most successful for Schlüter's government. The June 2, 1992, referendum on the Maastricht Treaty on European monetary and political union resulted in a defeat of the treaty, although by a very narrow margin, despite a consensus among the political class that favored the treaty. Schlüter's salvation in this case was that the opposition Social Democrats this time had recommended the same position as the government. So the referendum's outcome weakened Schlüter's competitors, too. If this had not been the case, the government would clearly not have survived.

As it turned out, the Danish defeat of the treaty unleashed a number of repercussions in other EC member states, jeopardizing for a time the future of the Maastricht Treaty. After many months of complex negotiations over special clauses which would apply to Denmark, the Danes voted again on the treaty, approving it. One of the signficant by-products of the original defeat, however, was that it forced the eight political parties in parliament to put their divergencies aside, joining forces to reconcile the best possible position for Denmark in the EC with a proper respect for the referendum process.

Viewed in perspective, Schlüter has been a remarkable politician. Not only is he a political survivor, his long tenure as prime minister has also led to some remarkable changes. Denmark's economy and economic reputation have been improved, inflation has almost been eliminated, the Danish currency has been stabilized (although it, too, was the object of currency speculation within the European Monetary System in 1992 and 1993), a balance of payments deficit has been turned into a surplus and in general the Danish economy in the early 1990s has been considered to be among the strongest in Europe. The only aspect of the economy which has stubbornly refused to improve has been the rate of unemployment. Overall, an open economy like Denmark's is obviously very dependent on the international economic situation and is therefore influenced heavily by factors outside Denmark. For example, the reunification of Germany has caused a growing demand for Danish export products. Nonetheless, actions by the Schlüter governments, such as the tax reform of 1986, have also contributed to the stabilization of the economy.

The modernization of the public sector has also been a much-discussed theme during Schlüter's tenure as prime minister, but actual changes have not been very drastic. Few public institutions or enterprises have been privatized. The rate of growth in numbers of public employees has slowed, but there have not been reductions on the expected scale. One must remember that Schlüter's circumstances have been those of both a minority and a coalition government.

Schlüter's strength has been his ability to maintain these minority and coalition governments in office, thereby frustrating the Social Democratic opposition, which in spite of progress in the 1987 and 1990 elections have had their longest period in opposition since the first Social Democratic cabinet in 1924. As a sign of their frustration the Social Democrats in the spring of 1992 became engaged in an unprecedented internal power struggle which led to a replacement of their leader, Svend Auken, with a new leader, Poul Nyrup Rasmussen.

The reverse side of the coin has been the many compromises necessary to keep a diverse coalition together, as well as the necessity of accepting a foreign and security policy heavily based on the opposition's conditions. Despite the civil service's traditional extreme loyalty to any cabinet, no matter what ideological complexion it might have, there have been signs that the interaction between politicians and the civil service—in a parliamentary situation where the opposition in some policy areas has the same or even more influence than the incumbent government—has blurred the traditional lines of responsibility and bureaucratic ethics, alarming some observers.

Poul Schlüter should be viewed as a politician very typical of Nordic countries, which have often been labeled consensual democracies. In this political culture, compromise and flexibility are more important than ideological rigidity and rhetoric. In the Danish context, where there is a long-standing tradition of minority and coalition cabinets, these qualities are extraordinarily important. The political culture does not call for strong leadership but for flexible consensus makers.

In this regard, Poul Schlüter has an extraordinary political instinct; he is a gifted pragmatic politician. Schlüter has proven wrong the axiom in Danish politics that nonsocialist parties are unable to form lasting cabinets. He has proven wrong the axiom that a Conservative politician could not head a government. In all this, Schlüter has never been dedicated to an elitist version of Conservatism. Rather, he has always viewed his party as a party for the entire people, which undoubtedly has been a precondition for his success in a small, homogenous society. It is also obvious that he has never wanted to lead a frontal attack on the welfare state ideal as such. He is well aware that this is a hopeless cause in a country where surveys have shown that the ideals of the welfare state are highly appreciated. Yet he has also been able to satisfy hard-core conservative elements in his party when the situation necessitated this. Schlüter's talents have proved to be a very good fit for the requirements of consensual democracy in a Scandinavian welfare state.

BIBLIOGRAPHY

Works by Schlüter:

Ungkonservatismens idé. Copenhagen: 1952.

Den Lange Vej—fra nederlag til fremgang. Edited by Peter La Cour. Copenhagen: 1980.

Other Works:

Boelsgaard, Kurt. *Poul Schlüter—politikeren der samlede det borgerlige Danmark*. Copenhagen: 1984.

Fonsmark, Henning. *Schlüters Danmark: Historien om en politisk karriere*. Forthcoming.

Kristiansen, Michael, Thomas Larsen, and Michael Ulveman. *Poul Schlüter: En biografi.* Copenhagen: Spektrum, 1992.

TIM KNUDSEN

HELMUT SCHMIDT (1918–) was chancellor of West Germany from May 1974 to October 1982. Schmidt acquired a reputation as a superb economist, a powerful international statesman and a clever political strategist. His reputation is based upon his ability to guide West Germany's economy through two oil shocks relatively unharmed, as well as his diplomatic achievements in continuing Brandt's Ostpolitik (relaxing tensions between West Germany and its Eastern Bloc neighbors, particularly former East Germany, Poland and the Soviet Union). Schmidt's reputation as a crisis manager also derives from his handling of the Red Army Faction's terrorist activities during the 1970s, culminating in the abduction and slaying of Hanns Martin Schleyer, head of the Employers' Federation, and the highjacking of a Lufthansa flight to Mogadishu (Somalia) in October 1977.

However, Schmidt is also the first chancellor to be removed from power by a constructive vote of no confidence in the Bundestag. He was deserted in 1982 by his former coalition partner, the Free Democratic Party (FDP), over the issue of spending cuts and an enlarged budget deficit. Schmidt did not, despite the immense respect he earned outside of Germany, enjoy the best of relations with either his coalition partners or significant sections of his own Social Democratic Party (SPD).

Schmidt was born Helmut Heinrich Waldemar Schmidt on December 23, 1918, in Barmbek, Hamburg. His upbringing was, as he himself describes it, highly apolitical. His father was a teacher whose own father was Jewish (although the Nazi authorities never discovered this fact); his mother encouraged Schmidt's musical and artistic talents. He did well academically, graduating from high school in 1937. Drafted into the Reichsarbeitsdienst and the Wehrmacht, Schmidt became an officer in the antiaircraft defense division of the air force. Schmidt was first stationed in Bremen until 1940, then was sent to Russia in 1941. After a few months of active duty on the Eastern Front, Schmidt returned to Berlin in 1942 where he remained until 1944. Sent to the Western Front, Schmidt witnessed the collapse of Germany's army and became a British prisoner of war in April 1945.

Schmidt's interest in politics emerged while in prison camp, where he met a number of officers sympathetic to the Social Democratic Party. This rather late conversion to social democracy led to some tensions and difficulties with Social Democrats who had opposed Hitler, gone into exile or had been sent to concentration camps as a result of their opposition to the regime. Such Social Democrats were weary of newcomers like Schmidt who had served in Hitler's army. Nevertheless, while a student in Hamburg after the war, Schmidt entered the SPD when it was reconstituted in 1946. It was as a student that Schmidt made the acquaintance of Dr. Karl Schiller, a celebrated economist and soon-to-be

Hamburg senator for economics and transport. It was Schiller, a professor at the University of Hamburg, who offered Schmidt his first job (a quasi-political appointment) in the transportation ministry once Schiller was appointed to the Hamburg Senate.

Schmidt soon won a reputation as an energetic, efficient and imaginative city planner as well as a good public speaker on social and economic issues. He was asked to become a SPD candidate for a Hamburg seat in the 1953 election. Although he did not win the seat outright, Schmidt entered the Bundestag because he had been placed high enough on the party list. At the age of thirty-five, Schmidt had thus become a professional politician without, as he put it, wanting to become one.

Within his own party, Schmidt was somewhat of an outsider, since he expressed the view that social democracy needed to accept the armed forces. In 1953 the SPD was still committed to German neutrality, as well as being opposed to the reemergence of a military establishment. But since the party was in opposition, it could not hinder the Adenauer coalition government from creating the Bundeswehr. While Schmidt was supposedly the SPD's transportation expert, he earned his parliamentary reputation as ''Schmidt the lip'' (''Schmidt Schnauze'') as a result of a speech given in 1958 on the issue of nuclear weapons. Schmidt accused the governing parties of megalomania for wanting to equip the West German army with nuclear weapons, arguing instead for nuclear parity between the superpowers.

His career in the Bundestag appeared to have stalled by the end of the 1950s. Schmidt found himself in opposition to most of his SPD colleagues on the issue of defense and the armed forces. Schmidt also participated in reserve maneuvers in 1959, which alienated him from the mainstream of the party. He returned to local politics in Hamburg, but as soon as he had done so, natural catastrophe intervened and propelled Schmidt into the national limelight. During the night of February 16–17, 1962, a massive storm ravaged Hamburg, flooding the city. Without real authority or regard for it, Schmidt took control of over 40,000 soldiers stationed in or around Hamburg, an army of Red Cross volunteers and others, and orchestrated an immediate relief effort which is credited with saving over 1,000 lives and helping 18,000 people find shelter. Schmidt became known as a ''crisis manager.'' At this point, he was even more popular than Hamburg's most spectacular soccer star, Uwe Seeler.

Schmidt reentered the Bundestag in 1965, a considerably more well-known and powerful quantity than in 1953. By 1965 the Christian Democratic (CDU/CSU) government found itself in dire political straits brought about by a mild economic recession. Fearing political unrest, the CDU leadership offered the SPD the opportunity to become part of the government and formed the ''Grand Coalition.'' Schmidt became the SPD parliamentary party leader in 1967 and soon earned a reputation for toughness and impatience along with long-windedness. The SPD was confronted with difficult issues such as the passage of laws which provided emergency powers to the government that had formerly been held by the Allies. Many SPD activists and politicians opposed such legislation. After extensive discussion within the parliamentary party, it was Schmidt who enforced party unity in support of these laws.

Schmidt favored continued parliamentary cooperation with the CDU, but the party chair, Willy Brandt, had other ideas. In 1969 the Grand Coalition was dissolved, elections held and the ''small coalition'' between SPD and the Free Democratic Party (FDP) came to power. Schmidt not only disagreed with Brandt on the issue of cooperation with the FDP, which he mistrusted, but also on Brandt's strategy of opening up the SPD to the student protest movement, especially the leftist groups which had infiltrated the Young Socialists (JUSOS). Brandt campaigned on a platform of ''internal reforms'' and a foreign policy of détente; Schmidt disagreed with the extent of the first, although he wholeheartedly supported the second.

Brandt offered Schmidt a difficult ministry in 1969, defense. Not only was this a huge bureaucracy (some 15,000 employees in Bonn alone and responsible for another 650,000), but the ministry was also one of the most expensive and least popular among the German people, not least, of course, because of the general draft.

In order to avoid control by its bureaucracy, Schmidt developed an interesting leadership style. First he traveled around the Federal Republic listening to suggestions and complaints of German troops. He then formed a small circle of outside advisers and began an exhaustive consultation process yielding a number of reforms. Mandatory service was cut from eighteen to fifteen months; recruits were allowed to wear longer hair and beards; and, most important, middle and lower officer ranks were made more attractive to recruits by offering the opportunity to learn jobs and skills transferable to the civilian sector. Schmidt became a strong advocate of defense spending, particularly to support the presence of U.S. troops in Europe. Convinced that only a strong defense system including a major American presence would deter the Soviets and force them to the bargaining table, Schmidt advocated greater efforts on Europe's and Germany's behalf to fund U.S. troops.

Schmidt's position as minister of defense placed him in the center of the East-West confrontation and made him a powerful player in the foreign policy debate, not only in Germany but elsewhere as well. While supporting Brandt's efforts to normalize relations with Eastern Europe, particularly the Soviet Union and East Germany, he always stressed the importance of a good working relationship with the United States.

In an important contribution to *Foreign Affairs* in 1970, Schmidt outlined his arguments for the deployment of U.S. troops in Europe and offered to make a significant contribution to the modernization of American and NATO troops in Europe in order to counteract efforts in the United States to draw troops from Europe to Vietnam or even back to the U.S. in a ''new isolationism.'' At the same time, Brandt had laid the foundations for the Four Powers Agreement on Berlin, which reduced the difficulties imposed on travelers from West Germany to Berlin and East Germany, as well as bilateral treaties with Poland, East Germany and the Soviet Union that accepted current borders.

Yet, because Brandt's foreign policy was highly controversial and the SPD/FDP only held a slim majority in the Bundestag, the CDU leadership attempted to topple Brandt's government with a constructive vote of no confidence. Although the CDU ultimately failed, the margin of Brandt's victory in the vote was so slim that he felt that a new election ought to be called. The 1972 election results surpassed all SPD expectations: The party gained more votes than ever before and was, for the first time, the largest party in the Bundestag.

The 1972 election took place at the same time as Schmidt confronted another important choice. While Schmidt was expressing a desire to go into private business, Brandt offered him the position of finance minister. Karl Schiller, who had been the SPD's financial expert and federal minister of economics and finance under Brandt, had resigned in July 1972, ostensibly because he feared inflationary pressures as a result of a declining U.S. dollar and a rising deutsche mark. He had advocated budget cuts to control government spending.

Despite misgivings, Schmidt accepted Brandt's offer and became minister of finance. Apparently, Brandt was not in good health, and Schmidt felt that the SPD leadership group could ill afford another departure at this important juncture. Being finance minister also put Schmidt in contact with his French counterpart, Valéry Giscard d'Estaing. Schmidt, convinced that Europe needed to develop its own stable financial system after the collapse of Bretton Woods, worked toward this end through the development of a plan for a European monetary system with Giscard. These two finance ministers were to form not only a good working relationship but a friendship which was to shape the course of European events throughout the 1970s. Both were to become chief executives of their respective countries within a few weeks of one another.

Schmidt's reign as finance minister was hugely complicated by the first oil shock of 1973–1974. Willy Brandt had won the 1972 elections because of his foreign policy and his promises of internal reforms. The SPD/FDP government introduced a range of expensive reform policies from 1971 to 1972, such as higher family and living allowances, an increased pension plan, higher social security benefits and greater spending on education and science. When the oil crisis intervened in an otherwise rapidly expanding German economy, tensions over how to cope with the enormous rise in energy prices ran high not only between the political parties but within them.

The SPD, already racked with internal dissent from the "new left," experienced traumatic internal struggles over how to respond to the oil crisis. The "new left" charged that the leaders of the SPD and the unions were not prepared to challenge the capitalist system and were about to impose the costs of the crisis on "the workers." Schmidt insisted on cutbacks in social spending, as well as wage restraint on behalf of the unions. In 1973, the public sector unions launched a massive strike to obtain higher wages. Neither Brandt nor Schmidt was able to dissuade the public sector unions from their course. Failure to keep wages down, intraparty and intracoalition struggles over policy, failure to negotiate a European Community agreement on energy policy, the effects of the oil crisis and, finally, the discovery that an East German spy had been one of Brandt's closest associates led to Brandt's abrupt resignation from the chancellorship on May 6, 1974. Brandt proposed Schmidt as his successor.

On May 16, 1974, Schmidt was elected chancellor of West Germany by a majority of 267 to 225 Bundestag members. Although he faced difficult political and economic conditions, his decisions as finance minister in the two previous years laid the foundations for his success as chancellor, being credited for West Germany's extraordinary economic performance throughout the 1970s.

While most other European nations experienced stagnation, inflation and spiraling unemployment, Germany was largely spared from this vicious cycle. Of course, part of the explanation for Germany's economic performance has to do with factors largely beyond the control of political leaders, yet Schmidt had helped himself by insisting on a tighter monetary policy even before the oil shock. After the 1972 election victory, Schmidt reversed the expansionary budget policy of the previous two years (a feat neither of his predecessors had been able to fully achieve). As German exports shot upward and imports declined, West Germany was able to compensate for huge price increases in oil through its earnings abroad and savings at home.

West Germany's ability to escape the dire consequences of the first oil crisis were an important ingredient in Schmidt's electoral success of October 3, 1976. Despite bitter turmoil within the SPD, it and its coalition partner, the FDP, were able to hold onto a slight electoral advantage and a ten-seat majority in the Bundestag. The CDU did, however, control a majority of state (*Länder*) governments, thereby also controlling the upper parliamentary chamber (the Bundesrat) of the federal government.

The SPD's 1976 electoral victory was in large part due to Schmidt's popularity, which then took a severe beating shortly after the election. During the campaign, Schmidt promised that pensions would be raised. Within a few weeks of the election, however, the SPD/FDP government had to announce that a significant budget shortfall would necessitate the suspension of higher pensions for six months. Schmidt was reelected to the chancellorship on December 15, 1976, with the barest of parliamentary majorities and under the cloud of the so-called *Rentenlüge* (the pension lie).

The next four years of Schmidt's tenure were marked by foreign policy issues: The NATO two-track decision and the issue of the Soviet nuclear arsenal aimed at Western Europe, the difficult relationship with U.S. President Jimmy Carter and attempts to establish a European Monetary System and solidify the European Community all preoccupied Schmidt's chancellorship. The showdown with the Red Army Faction provided Schmidt with a remarkable success, although the price in terms of loss of life was high.

During this period, however, growing dissatisfaction with the SPD/FDP government's policy course within the SPD's activist base pointed to a gradual shift away from Schmidt's policy positions within the SPD. The 1976–1980 period was extremely difficult for Schmidt because none of the issues preoccupying him could be characterized as having been completely or successfully resolved. Each initiative was plagued either by unintended adverse consequences or international and national tensions or both.

During the early 1970s, a small segment of the student protest movement turned to a violent campaign against what it viewed as "enemies of the people." While at first its activities were restricted to bank robberies and arson, by the mid-1970s the Red Army Faction (RAF), also known as the Baader-Meinhof Gang, had graduated to kidnapping and assassinations of leading business and public figures.

After the first generation of terrorists had been captured and imprisoned, the remnants of the movement then attempted to use kidnappings as a means of freeing their comrades. In September 1977, the RAF kidnapped Hanns Martin Schleyer, the president of the Employers' Federation, in order to blackmail the German government into releasing eleven RAF members. When Schmidt refused to meet these demands, a group of Palestinians hijacked a Lufthansa flight to Mogadishu (Somalia) so as to exert even greater pressure on the Schmidt government. Schmidt, in consultation with the leaders of the various parties represented in the Bundestag, sent a special antiterrorist force to Somalia to free the hostages. After a successful rescue of the Lufthansa passengers, the Red Army Faction retaliated by assassinating Schleyer. Then, upon hearing of the Lufthansa plane's rescue, a number of RAF prisoners committed suicide in prison. While Schmidt had again lived up to his reputation as a skilled crisis manager, the decisions he had to make under these circumstances were surely not simple ones for him. The Schleyer murder did, however, represent the crest of the terrorist campaign in Germany.

A more long-term problem facing Schmidt was the gradual buildup of the Soviet intermediate-range nuclear capability in the form of the SS-20 ballistic missile. In Schmidt's view, NATO and the United States were turning a blind eye to this threat, which was aimed more at Germany than the United States, given these missiles' limited range. Schmidt's relationship with President Carter got off to a bad start when Schmidt called President Ford to congratulate him on winning reelection.

The relationship between Carter and Schmidt never improved much after that. Schmidt not only had reservations about American economic policy, which he viewed as having dire consequences for Europe, but also regarded Carter's foreign policy as suspect at best, naive and dangerous at worst. Drawing Carter's attention to the buildup of SS-20 missiles and the so-called backfire bomber on a number of occasions, Schmidt was rebuffed and ignored until the Carter administration and NATO reacted very sharply to the invasion of Afghanistan. While Schmidt had hoped to get the United States to negotiate a reduction of these two Soviet weapons systems, the United States and NATO now insisted on modernizing and upgrading their own nuclear arsenal in Europe. NATO's so-called two-track decision to introduce new weapons systems into Europe if the Soviets should fail to reduce their arsenal ran counter to Schmidt's own aims while nonetheless causing him grave domestic difficulties since it spawned the rise of a powerful peace movement in Germany, much of it originating in the SPD.

The emergence of the so-called new social movements (particularly the environmental and peace movements) is explicable only in the context of SPD/FDP government policies. The emergence of these movements led to the creation of the Greens Party in the late 1970s, which was to capture a significant portion of the SPD's electorate in the general elections of 1983 and 1987. After the oil shock of 1973–1974, the Schmidt government, which had favored nuclear power even before the oil crisis, now regarded nuclear power as the only viable alternative to foreign energy sources. Nuclear power was also backed by the German labor movement within as well as outside the SPD, but nuclear power was bitterly opposed by the SPD's new left. The government's acceleration of the nuclear power program caused a popular backlash not only from environmental groups but from citizens affected by the building of such plants in their own backyards. In addition to the antinuclear protest movement, Schmidt's attempts to maintain a balance of power between the U.S. and Soviet arsenals in Europe led to an invigoration of the peace movement, which opposed stationing Pershing and Cruise missiles in Germany.

By the late 1970s, Schmidt's energy and foreign policies had created a set of protest groups and movements which might very well have unseated him in the 1980 Bundestag elections. But because the CDU opted to nominate the arch-conservative Franz Josef Strauss as its chancellor candidate (a nomination which surely lost the CDU this election), Schmidt survived but at the expense of a much stronger FDP. Moreover, many potential Greens voters decided to support the SPD on the grounds that it represented the "lesser evil" in the choice between Schmidt and Strauss. Although Schmidt's overall majority in the Bundestag grew from ten to fifty-two seats, most of these gains were achieved by the FDP, which now began to impose its policy wishes on the SPD. Meanwhile, FDP leaders were starting to seriously consider a switch to a government coalition with the CDU/CSU.

The period from 1980 to 1982 witnessed a sea change in American and European politics. Schmidt's closest friend and ally, French President Giscard d'Estaing, lost his bid for reelection; Margaret Thatcher won power in Britain; Carter was replaced by Reagan in the United States. The second oil shock of 1979 hit a Europe whose economy was already slumping, unlike in 1973–1974, when the European economies were doing relatively well. Relations between the Soviets and the Americans went from bad to worse.

During this period, Schmidt found himself in extremely difficult intraparty, intracoalition and international situations. Within his party, critics from the protest movements attacked Schmidt's policies on NATO and the environment. While Schmidt still enjoyed the support of the majority of trade unions, their wage demands in a shrinking economic situation provided ammunition to the FDP politicians who advocated severe cuts in the welfare system to compensate for the rise of imports. The CDU/CSU leadership accused Schmidt of mismanagement because the German government ran a temporary deficit in 1981–1982, knowing that this was the issue on which they could attract FDP support. Internationally, the economic policies of the Reagan administration drove Europe into a deeper recession from which Germany still emerged relatively well but far from unscathed.

These pressures combine to explain the decision by FDP leaders in September 1982 to dissolve the coalition with the SPD. On October 1, 1982, the CDU leader, Helmut Kohl, won a constructive vote of no confidence in the Bundestag with the support of the FDP, thereby replacing Schmidt as chancellor. New elections were set for March 1983 which brought the CDU to electoral victory. The SPD, for its part, suffered an appalling electoral defeat, slipping back to results reminiscent of the 1950s. The Greens Party won over 5 percent of the popular vote, most of which came from the SPD. Particularly in the urban areas, the SPD lost a great many voters to the "new social movements."

Schmidt's legacy must be regarded as mixed. He disagreed fundamentally with Brandt's attempts to open the SPD to supporters of the initial student protest movement, which then became the foundation for the so-called new social movements of the late 1970s and 1980s. Schmidt clearly preferred to see the SPD as an ally of the trade union movement, particularly its more accommodative wing. He viewed social protest movement supporters as a nuisance to the SPD and did much to isolate and neutralize their role inside the party, which in turn contributed to the formation of the Greens Party.

Schmidt's position became increasingly isolated in the 1980s, especially once the SPD found itself in opposition and a new group of party leaders began to emerge at the regional and local levels. Schmidt's nuclear and foreign policy initiatives were rejected by the party after 1982, signaling a fundamental shift in the SPD's policy toward the environment, the peace movement and other issues raised by the social protest movements. In this sense, Schmidt undoubtedly lost his battle with the "new left" and the protest movement. He is not currently a leading figure within the SPD, but is editor of one of Germany's largest and most influential weekly newspapers, *Die Zeit*.

Yet, in other arenas, Schmidt's legacy is more enduring. He personified a type of leadership and authority which the SPD had lacked both in the Weimar and postwar period. Schmidt's leadership style—while not consensual and frequently seen as impatient—was highly authoritative and decisive despite the many institutional, organizational and political obstacles the coalition government faced throughout the period Schmidt was chancellor. Schmidt conveyed a confidence in decision making which eluded Brandt and reminded voters and negotiators of Adenauer. Schmidt proved that social democracy was capable of both managing a capitalist economy well and introducing important social and economic reforms. The considerable difficulties faced by Schmidt's coalition government—a worldwide economic slowdown, a political situation in which the opposition party controlled the upper chamber (Bundesrat), an FDP coalition partner ready to shift its allegiance, as well as grave internal splits in the SPD itself—in fact all underscore Schmidt's remarkable leadership qualities.

BIBLIOGRAPHY

Bölling, Klaus. *Die letzten 30 Tage des Kanzlers Helmut Schmidt.* Hamburg: Spiegel Verlag, 1982.

Carr, Jonathan. *Helmut Schmidt.* Munich: Knaur, 1987.

Graf von Nayhauss, Mainhardt. *Helmut Schmidt: Mensch und Macher.* Bergisch Gladbach: Luebbe, 1988.

Krause-Burger, Sibylle. *Helmut Schmidt: Aus der Nähe gesehen.* Düsseldorf: Econ, 1980.

Schmidt, Helmut, et al. *Kindheit und Jugend unter Hitler.* Berlin: Siedler Verlag, 1992.

THOMAS A. KOELBLE

MÁRIO SOARES (1924–) played a leading role in Portugal's transition from dictatorship to democracy following the April 1974 ''revolution of carnations''—so called for the flowers civilians placed in soldiers' rifle barrels during the leftist coup. As one of the country's most respected contemporary political figures, Soares staunchly opposed the dictatorship of António Salazar and Marcello Caetano, cofounded the Portuguese Socialist Party and helped ensure that moderate parliamentary democracy ultimately triumphed over a hard leftist regime. Along with others like Francisco Sá Carneiro and Ramalho Eanes, Soares was instrumental in successfully leading Portugal beyond the political uncertainties that dominated the postrevolutionary period. He championed democratic reform and the establishment of civilian control over the military. As a ''founding father'' of Portuguese democracy, Soares headed three governments as prime minister, led the parliamentary opposition for a time and from 1986 (his second term ends in 1996) has served as president of the Portuguese Republic.

Born on December 7, 1924, Mário Alberto Nobre Lopes Soares's well-to-do family provided a solid political orientation in liberal and republican thinking. His father served as a cabinet minister in the Portuguese republic of 1910–1926. Married to Maria Borroso in 1949, Soares served for a period as principal and taught in a private school his father founded. He received a degree in historical and philosophical sciences from the Faculty of Letters of the University of Lisbon in 1951 and then completed his law degree in 1957.

Soares's early legal practice overlapped with his political career. He defended many opposition leaders of the Salazar dictatorship. His own prerevolution activities included being a leader from 1946 to 1948 of the United Democratic Youth Movement (MUD), an antifascist but noncommunist group, serving in the 1949 election as secretary to presidential candidate General Norton de Mattos, being a member of the campaign committee for General Humberto Delegado in the 1958 presidential election and leading the opposition movement, Social Democratic Action, from 1952 to 1960. Soares himself ran as a Democratic Opposition candidate from Lisbon in the 1965 and 1969 legislative elections, the latter being considered one of the freest of the authoritarian regime.

Soares paid a high price for his opposition activities. The Salazar-Caetano regime imprisoned him twelve times, deported him to the island of São Tomé between March and November 1968, and exiled him to France from 1970 until the revolution in April 1974. Soares wrote extensively during his periods of exile and served as a lecturer at the University of Vincennes, at the Sorbonne and as an associate professor at the University of Higher Brittany, Rennes. Nonetheless, the authoritarian regime's ambivalence toward its opposition permitted Soares to return periodically to Portugal.

Soares's writing, speeches and other public opposition to the regime shot him to prominence once the revolution had succeeded. During this period, many civilian leaders presented strong credentials of opposition to both the past regime and to the revolution's hard left, along with a commitment to organizing a competitive party system: Francisco Sá Carneiro, who led the Portuguese Social Democratic Party (PSD) until his untimely death; Diogo Freitas do Amaral, who headed for a time the conservative Social Democratic Center Party (CDS); General Ramalho Eanes, who, as head of the armed forces, leaned toward the Communists but later founded the Democratic Renewal Party (PRD); and Soares as leader of the Socialist Party (PS).

Besides vehemently countering the Communist bid for hegemony as events unfolded in 1974–1975, Soares has also held many important positions in democratic Portugal: minister of foreign affairs from 1974 to 1975 (negotiated independence for Portugal's former colonies), minister without portfolio from March to August 1975, deputy in the Constituent Assembly in 1976, member of the National Assembly later that year, prime minister 1976–1978 and 1983–1985, and finally elected president of Portugal in March 1986 and reelected in January 1991. With the other leaders mentioned above, Mário Soares cautiously yet skillfully nudged the country toward liberal democracy. He effectively grounded his democratic challenge to extremism on his domestic popularity and international prestige.

The Socialist Party provided the platform for both Soares's prerevolutionary activities and his subsequent political career. In 1964, Soares and Salgado Zenha founded Portuguese Socialist Action in Geneva and transformed it into the Socialist Party in April 1973 in Bad Muenstereifel, West Germany. Despite attempts at moderation, the times generally made conflict unavoidable. Prior to the revolution, for example, the PS coexisted uncomfortably with the Communists as forces of opposition. Afterwards, Soares and the Socialists consistently disagreed with the Communists over the Armed Forces Movement's (MFA) military strategy.

Soares pushed the PS toward moderate socialism, an approach consistent with many Western European models of social democracy. Placing a greater emphasis on democracy than socialism, the party dropped all official references to Marxism at its third congress in March 1979. Seeking electoral competitiveness as a mass party, the PS's social policies remained vague and its economic programs focused on the private sector. Such an orientation raised criticism that the PS was made up of ''café socialists'' more comfortable in intellectual discussion in Lisbon's elegant coffeehouses than in governing.

The PS held moderate positions for several reasons, all linked in one way or another to Soares. First, the German Social Democratic Party (SPD) helped guide and strongly influenced Soares and the rest of the PS's leadership. Second, the PS's early membership was primarily young, cosmopolitan and urban, drawing heavily from Portugal's legal and academic elite. Unlike the Communists, the PS possessed no natural sociological or regional base and held only weak institutional links to the labor movement. Third, the PS unquestionably oriented itself toward Western Europe, remaining attuned to developments there and pursuing pro-European policies. Fourth, Soares had personally witnessed most of France's civil unrest of the 1960s.

While the PS provided Soares his greatest political asset, the Socialist International (SI) nurtured his ambition. His personal contacts through the SI since the 1960s and his stature as its vice president from 1976 reinforced Soares's position as PS secretary general (1973–1986) as well as providing the PS with credibility. Soares quickly became to socialism in Portugal what Willy Brandt was to it in Germany, Felipe González in Spain and François Mitterrand in France. Beyond Portugal's borders, Soares and the PS were one and the same. Soares parlayed this international standing into control over the party, helping to mold its European orientation and generating for the party a great deal of outside financial assistance.

Soares's leadership also produced internal controversy, deep divisions and accusations of ''baron-like'' behavior. His successful utilization of the party for his own political advancement often created political and ideological friction. He struggled constantly to maintain control of the party's internal tendencies. His resignation from the PS following his presidential election left a leadership vacuum and internal fragmentation to a party struggling to prosper beyond his heavy shadow.

Despite such conflict, Soares and the PS significantly contributed to the early development of democracy in Portugal through its moderating influence while a member of a series of provisional coalition governments. The April 1975 election to the Constituent Assembly, the first in democratic Portugal, openly revealed the Communists' weakness, as well as the PS's position as the strongest party at 37.9 percent. In July, Soares flexed his political muscles, leading the PS out of the fourth provisional government. During the next several months, the PS provided cover for many antigovernment demonstrations against the Communists and their fellow travelers in the following provisional government.

The Socialists again received a clear plurality in new elections in April 1976. Their electoral strength, staunch anticommunism, international standing and European orientation made them a logical choice to lead the next coalition government. Given his rejection of the Communists as a coalition partner and the distrust that dominated the relationship between Soares and the PSD's Sá Carneiro, Soares decided to go it alone. He formed a minority government in July 1976 with only the PS, deciding to focus on balancing internal party tendencies. Soares based this strategy on the continuation of problems within Portugal's party system characterized by irreconcilable differences among opposition parties. Indicative of such problems, first the Communists and then the PSD abandoned their noncoalition voting alliance so that the PS's minority government fell in December 1977. Soares later admitted this governing strategy to have been his greatest political mistake.

Soares's next move demonstrated his pragmatic approach to politics. Attracted by the PS's moderation, the CDS surprisingly joined the Socialists in a tactical government coalition, despite being strange political bedfellows—the PS still officially defining itself at the time as Marxist and the CDS with members linked previously to Salazar and Caetano's "Estado Novo" ("New State"). But as a political pragmatist, Soares knew this was the only possible party configuration. An even weaker, more constrained and predictably short-lived Soares II government thus replaced the minority Soares I government in January 1978. However, by July 1978 President Ramalho Eanes had concluded that the Soares II (PS/CDS) government had lost its majority in the Assembly. Despite efforts by the Council of the Revolution to keep Soares and the PS in power, President Eanes dismissed the government, thus winning this institutional confrontation.

As prime minister, Soares's troubles were also Portugal's problems. The Salazar-Caetano regime had laid no foundation for a modern economy, the MFA-supported governments had granted enormous wage increases, Portuguese industry was plagued with a decline in productivity and the huge influx of repatriates from the African colonies swelled the already large pool of unemployed. Prior conditions thus constrained the Soares governments, forcing restrictive economic policies which in turn cost them support. These governments therefore had to forsake moderate socialist policies for economic austerity, wage stabilization and the reversal of agrarian reforms in order to obtain International Monetary Fund assistance.

The Soares I and II governments did take many positive steps for Portugal. Despite the global recession, the austerity program generally succeeded, even if at a political price. On the diplomatic front, Portugal became the nineteenth member of the Council of Europe in September 1976 and signed the European Convention on Human Rights, and the Soares I government applied for membership in the European Community (EC). More important for a democratic Portugal, Soares's early governments provided time for the new democracy to mature, increasingly isolating the Communists and bringing the party system more into line with the more conservative views of the Portuguese electorate.

The constitutional reform of 1982 resolved many of the institutional problems left over from the "revolution of carnations." The party system and Portuguese coalitional politics nevertheless continued to produce government—as opposed to regime—instability. For a time after the Soares II government, the AD, a preelectoral alliance of the PSD and the CDS, temporarily ameliorated the situation, the Socialists no longer proving to be the only alternative, despite their remaining the single largest party. However, following the AD's breakup in 1982 and the election of April 1983, a PS-PSD coalition government was formed in mid–1983 and lasted until 1985. This Soares III government helped Portugal's struggling democracy to step temporarily out of its partisan quagmire, but the PS and Soares again paid a political price. As the junior partner, the PSD adroitly shifted blame for the government's austerity policy and a perception of government instability onto the Socialists. Outmaneuvering Soares, the PSD forced a new election.

The resulting parliamentary elections of October 6, 1985, proved important to Portugal for three reasons. First, for the first time since the revolution, an election produced a clear winner: Anibal Cavaco Silva's PDS won a majority, finally giving Portugal government stability as well as regime stability. Second, the election marked the temporary rise of a presidentially led party—the Democratic Renewal Party. A creation of outgoing President Ramalho Eanes, this party raised the prospect of a presidential party along the lines of the French Gaullist party and temporarily shifted political competition. Third, the election marked the end of Mário Soares's active role in government politics and focused his attention on a new goal.

The popularly elected presidency of the Portuguese Republic exemplifies the fact that in Portugal, as in many new democracies, politics is highly personalized: Names are generally more important than parties or policies. Despite limited formal powers, the Portuguese head of state has provided political continuity in a postrevolutionary Portugal that had seventeen governments in its first thirteen years. As President Eanes's second and final five-year term drew to a close, Soares sensed a long-awaited opportunity.

Soares' political life since the revolution epitomized the characteristics of a European head of state: a man of integrity, a defender of the republic and, important in Portugal, a strong anticommunist yet moderate leader. Soares had, however, developed a negative image in his last two years heading an unpopular government, a fact reflected in the PS's very poor 20.8 percent showing in the October 1985 elections. Despite this, two things favored Soares's bid for the presidency. First, he could count on the PS's support. Second, and probably more important, the Social Democrats initially had no candidate of their own. If he could survive the first round, Soares calculated he would win the second by turning the race into a left-right contest against the CDS's Diogo Freitas do Amaral.

Soares executed this strategy perfectly. Prior to the first ballot, the Communists squabbled about supporting ex–prime minister Maria de Lourdes Pintasilgo, who had a small but loyal band of supporters, or Francisco Salgado Zenha, President Eanes's handpicked candidate and former PS founder with Soares. The PCP ultimately chose the latter. Out of frustration, many Pintasilgo supporters campaigned for Soares. On the right, the only question was the PSD, since Freitas do Amaral had the clear support of the CDS. Anibal Cavaco Silva, the new PSD president, supported Freitas do Amaral when he agreed not to increase presidential powers beyond that of the 1982 revised constitution. This move to the right, however, drove some PSD members to support Soares.

Given these developments, Soares made it into the second round. Freitas do Amaral received 46.3 percent of the vote, Soares 25.4 percent, Salgado Zenha 20.9 percent and Pintasilgo 7.4 percent. Besides Soares's hoped-for second-place finish, this first round also marked two milestones for Portugal: the first election without a candidate from the military and the right's largest vote since the revolution.

In the second round, Soares, the consummate politician, strategically managed to draw votes ranging from the center to the far left by presenting himself as the left's candidate and even as the heir of the revolution. The Communists reluctantly supported this avid anticommunist as the "lesser of two evils" to avoid a victory for Soares's conservative opponent. This temporary union of the left was victorious—Soares won with 51.3 percent of the vote. On January 26, 1986, Mário Soares thus became Portugal's first civilian president directly elected by universal suffrage and the first civilian president in sixty years. Having reached the top, Soares resigned from the PS to give credibility to his promise to rise above party politics.

While this decision broadened Soares's appeal, it snubbed the Communists immediately after they had help elect him. He also offended the Socialists. When Soares was elected, the PSD led a minority government under Cavaco Silva. Silva's image and his advocacy of privatization and modernization, an economic upturn and Portugal's entry into the EC raised Silva's standing in the polls. Yet this minority government nevertheless fell in 1987 when the Socialists, the Communists and Eanes's PRD managed to marshal a vote of confidence against it.

To general surprise, instead of giving the left a chance to form a government, President Soares approved Cavaco Silva's call for new elections. Soares argued that the no-confidence vote had been ill prepared and that the left was too divided to rule. His decision elated the ruling Social Democrats given their favor in public opinion, leaving the left furious, for they had elected Soares. Many leftists called this a demonstration of Soares's true colors as a "closet conservative." Why did he do it? Politically, the move probably hurt former President Eanes's PRD more than it did the PS while also keeping the Communists isolated. More likely, Soares kept his preelection pledge of staying above party politics, truly believing Cavaco Silva was best suited to liberalize Portugal's economy in order to meet EC standards and to remove the last vestiges of leftist wording still in the constitution.

The PSD victory in the July 1987 election produced Portugal's first single-party majority government as well as *coabitação,* or cohabitation, between Cavaco Silva's right-of-center government and Soares as president. Despite personality and party differences, they have generally coexisted peacefully with smooth, albeit formal, relations. Unlike former President Eanes, Soares has gone to great lengths to cooperate with the government despite ideological disagreements, while Cavaco Silva has restrained the PSD's right wing. In May 1989, for example, Soares believed that this right-of-center government could decisively reform social and economic policy when it changed, with Socialist support, Portugal's constitutional commitment to socialism, reversing earlier nationalizations and rewriting labor legislation to permit management to dismiss employees.

Successful cohabitation, however, does not imply that Soares has hesitated to express his own views. Despite occupying a largely ceremonial post with no formal voice in foreign affairs and no longer being supreme commander of the armed forces, the Portuguese president does possess a limited veto and the power either to sign bills into law or send them to the Constitutional Court. Soares has sent only a modest number of laws to the Constitutional Court, for example, the Social Democrats' attempts to alter Portugal's labor laws.

He has also used the veto sparingly; for example, in 1986 he returned to parliament the revised autonomy statute for the Azores Islands. This statute would have permitted the use of the Azorean flag and anthem on an equal status with the Portuguese, but it was opposed by the military. In January 1990 Soares also sided with the military against the prime minister regarding changes in military pay and the professional career structure, which ended in the minister of defense's resignation. Later Soares contradicted government policy by proposing that Portuguese troops take part in the joint German-French European corps, and he independently called for a referendum on the Maastricht Treaty on European integration. In 1991, he strongly attacked political bias in Portugal's two state-run television channels, accusing them of partisanship, ''constant manipulation'' of the news and treating the government more favorably than the opposition parties. In 1992, he vetoed a decree drastically reducing the size of the Portuguese armed forces.

Soares's personal standing has increased the prestige if not the influence of the presidency. Moreover, Mário Soares seems comfortable with his presidential duties. For one thing, the job is clearly easier now given that Portugal is politically less divided and has a stronger sense of national cohesion, in part due to unprecedented economic prosperity, experiencing an EC-induced average growth rate surpassed only by Spain. The election of a PSD majority government in 1987 and again in October 1991 has meant that the power to name the prime minister has gone unused during most of Soares's presidency. In addition, Soares's personality appears highly compatible with the role of president. As prime minister, he was not always comfortable dealing with technical issues. Now, given the post's ceremonial character, Soares can devote much of his time to what he does best: listening, arguing, commiserating and joking in person-to-person contact with the full range of Portuguese people about their grievances, fulfilling his ceremonial functions without having to make tough policy decisions. As a familiar uncle figure, Soares has come to represent the Portuguese through hospitality, tolerance and coziness. His jovial and breezy style has made him a favorite regardless of one's political ideology. Frequently referred to affectionately as "Bochechas" (chubby cheeks) or "Uncle Mário," he has become a highly popular president and an undisputed elder statesman.

The best evidence of Soares's success as president is his reelection. In sharp contrast to the partisan nature and political maneuvering of the first election, on January 13, 1991, Soares won a second five-year term with 70.43 percent of the vote on the first ballot. As a master of the politician's "common touch," he drew support from across the ideological spectrum. The PSD even chose not to field a candidate against him. While he was elected in February 1986 basically only by the left, a large majority of the Portuguese electorate appears to have recognized that Mário Soares has in fact achieved his goal of becoming "the president of all Portuguese."

BIBLIOGRAPHY

Works by Soares:

Le Portugal Baillonné, 1972. Translated from the French as *Portugal's Struggle for Liberty*. London: Allen & Unwin, 1975.

Also:

As Ideas politico-socias de Teóofilo Braga. 1950.

Escritos politicos. 1969.

Destruir o sistema, construir uma vida nova. 1969.

Caminho difícil, do Salazarismo as Caetanismo. 1974.

Escritos do exílio. 1975.

Liberdade para Portugal (with Willy Brandt and Bruno Kreisky). 1975.

Portugal: Quelle révolution. 1976.

O Futuro será o socialismo democratico. 1979.

Resposta socialista padra o mundo em crise. 1983.

Persistir. 1983.

A Arvore e a floresta. 1985.

Intervençoes. 1987.

Other Works:

Bruneau, Thomas C., and Alex Macleod. *Politics in Contemporary Portugal*. Boulder, Colo.: Lynne Rienner, 1986.

Gallagher, Tom. *Portugal: A Twentieth Century Interpretation*. Manchester: Manchester University Press, 1983.

Graham, Lawrence S. "Redefining the Portuguese Transition to Democracy," in John Higley and Richard Gunther (eds.), *Elites and Democratic Consolidation in Latin America and Southern Europe*. Cambridge: Cambridge University Press, 1992.

Graham, Lawrence S., and Harry M. Makler (eds.). *Contemporary Portugal: The Revolution and Its Antecedents*. Austin: University of Texas Press, 1979.

Graham, Lawrence S., and Douglas L. Wheeler (eds.). *In Search of Modern Portugal: The Revolution and Its Consequences*. Madison: University of Wisconsin Press, 1983.

Lancaster, Thomas D. "Mediterranean Europe: Stabilized Democracies?", in Roy C. Macridis (ed.), *Modern Political Systems: Europe*, 7th ed. Englewood Cliffs, N.J.: Prentice-Hall, 1990.

Opello, Walter. *Portugal's Political Development: A Comparative Approach.* Boulder, Colo.: Westview Press, 1985.
Wiarda, Howard. *The Transition to Democracy in Spain and Portugal.* Washington, D.C.: American Enterprise Institute, 1989.

THOMAS D. LANCASTER

PAUL-HENRI SPAAK (1899–1972), one of Belgium's most prominent leaders for more than three decades, is most remembered for his role in international politics—especially in postwar European integration efforts—and his qualities of diplomacy and political oratory. In Belgian domestic politics, he was also known as a pragmatist (or worse, his opponents argued), often shifting positions with changes in the political situation.

Before World War II, as minister of foreign affairs and member of the Socialist Party, Spaak was an important advocate of neutrality for Belgium. After this policy failed, he sided with the Allies and became a strong opponent of Germany. During the German occupation of Belgium, he participated in the Belgian government-in-exile in London. After the war, he played an important role in the "royal question" (Leopold III's problematic return to the Belgian throne) and in the granting of independence to the Belgian Congo. After retiring from active participation in national politics, Spaak also endorsed a federal system for the unitary Belgian state.

During a long domestic political career, Spaak held the ministerial portfolios of Transport, Post, Telegraph and Telephone (1935–1936) and Foreign Affairs (1936–1938, 1939–1947, 1954–1957, 1961–1966). He also served as prime minister in a prewar government (1938–1939) and in governments after the war (1946, 1947–1949).

At the international level, he took part in the creation of several pathbreaking international organizations, such as the United Nations, NATO and the European Community (EC). He also played a prominent role in the early negotiations which eventually led to the creation of the ECSC (European Coal and Steel Community) and the signing of the Treaty of Rome, creating the European Economic Community and the European Atomic Energy Commission. In these roles, Spaak was one of the founding fathers of European integration.

Paul-Henri Spaak was born on January 25, 1899, in Schaerbeek, a commune of Brussels, part of a long line of politicians on his mother's side. (His father was a playwright and author of a number of famous plays, as well as being manager of the Théatre Royal de la Monnaie, one of the best-known Brussels theaters.) Spaak's mother was a Socialist member of the Belgian Senate whose own father had been a Liberal member of parliament before World War I. Moreover, Spaak was the nephew of Paul-Emile Janson, also a Liberal politician, who became prime minister before World War II. Today, Spaak's daughter, Antoinette, is also a member of the national parliament. She has chaired the Brussels-based Francophone Democratic Front Party (FDF—Front Démocratique des Francophones) and has represented it in the European Parliament.

In 1916, while trying to join the Belgian army fighting behind the Yser, the young Spaak was captured by the Germans and sent to a prisoners' camp in Germany. At the end of the war, he studied law at the Free University of Brussels. There he first became acquainted with Liberal students, then became a member of the Socialist Party, which at that time was called the Belgian Workers Party. He also led the Socialist student movement at the university.

After receiving his doctor of law degree in 1921, he opened a legal practice and became active in the Belgian socialist movement. During this time, he was known as an idealist. He promoted a policy program of reforms, antidespotic ideas and an alliance between intellectuals and manual laborers. He favored reform politics but with a democratic orientation and within the framework of existing institutions.

In 1926, when the Belgian Workers Party was included for the first time in a coalition government, Spaak became a partisan of revolutionary socialism. Turning his back on reformism, he began to call for Marxist-Leninist socialism. He protested against the established socioeconomic order, and he condemned war, which he viewed as a consequence of the logic of capitalism. Most radically, Spaak also advocated destruction of bourgeois society through violent revolution. With these beliefs, Paul-Henri Spaak started his career as an elected official, becoming a local councilman in the Brussels commune of Forest in 1926. In 1932 he was first elected to the Belgian parliament from Brussels.

Very quickly, Spaak became a prominent leader of the avant-garde wing of the Socialist Party, and he quarreled frequently with Emile Vandervelde, the great Socialist figure who oriented the party in a reformist direction rather than a revolutionary one. At the same time, as a trial lawyer he defended pacifists and anarchists before the courts. He also wrote for Socialist newspapers like *La Bataille Socialiste* (The Socialist Fight) and *L'Action Socialiste* (Socialist Action). Furthermore, at the 1933 Socialist International congress in Paris, Spaak pleaded for revolutionary conquest of power in society and supported a unified opposition to fascism by the socialist movement.

Spaak's views on the revolutionary role of the Socialist Party began to change a few years later under the influence of the Belgian Socialist leader De Man, who developed an important reform plan to redress the Belgian economy. This reformist orientation called for structural reforms through industrial nationalizations, a reinforcement of state authority in the economy and vigorous action against unemployment.

In 1935, while De Man was minister of public works, Spaak was appointed to his first ministry, Transport, Post, Telegraph and Telephone, in the Van Zeeland coalition government, composed of the Catholic, Liberal and Socialist parties. This government stayed in office little more than a year and was unable to implement most of the reforms that De Man called for and Spaak supported.

Spaak's shift from a revolutionary stance toward reformism was also accompanied by new support for the monarchy. Before his appointment to the government, Spaak had been a republican by principle. For him, it was logically inconsistent to be a democrat without opposing the hereditary monarchy. He became a monarchist of "reason" when he entered the government in 1935, arguing that the monarchy was the best regime for Belgium for two reasons: First, the monarchy assured the stability and continuity needed for parliamentary democracy. Second, the king played an important role as bridge between the two main linguistic communities of the country, the Dutch-speaking Flemish and the French-speaking Wallonians. (There is a third but much smaller Germanophone linguistic community in eastern Belgium as well.)

In the next elections, the Socialists and the Christian Democrats suffered electoral defeat. However, essentially the same coalition cabinet was formed, with Spaak receiving the Foreign Affairs portfolio for the first time. He kept this post in the succeeding government, as well, which lasted until 1938. In that year, he was named as the first Socialist prime minister of Belgium, while continuing to hold the Foreign Affairs portfolio. Spaak was only thirty-nine years old when he first served as prime minister.

In 1939, the cabinet changed again, the Socialists taking part in a government of national unity. In this government, Spaak continued to serve as foreign affairs minister. In that position, he advocated a foreign policy of neutrality for Belgium. This policy also reflected the views of King Leopold III, who was trying desperately to maintain the territorial integrity of Belgium through a formal declaration of neutrality. Spaak continued to push neutrality during the growing tensions between Germany, France and Britain. During this difficult period, he also advocated strengthening Belgium's military defense as a deterrent against potential aggressors. However, Belgium's neutrality did not prevent German troops from penetrating Belgian territory in 1940. Belgium then entered the war.

When the German ambassador to Belgium came to see Foreign Minister Spaak to ask that Belgian troops not resist the German invasion, Spaak related that he abruptly interrupted the ambassador by saying "Me first." He then accused the Germans of aggressive and criminal invasion against neutral Belgium and protested that no ultimatum, no note, no official communication had been presented by the Germans to the Belgian government. He finished his meeting with the German ambassador by affirming that the Belgians would defend their territory. This incident became a celebrated one in Belgian politics.

Several conflicts emerged between the monarch, Leopold III, and the government regarding the conduct of the war. As the military situation deteriorated and Belgian capitulation to the Germans became evident, the cabinet asked the king to leave the country for London. The king refused, preferring to stay in the country with his troops. Moreover, as Leopold was persuaded that the Germans would win the war, he argued against continuing the Belgian alliance with French and British forces, hoping to keep for Belgium the maximum possible autonomy.

The government, which by then had definitively rejected the neutrality policy and refused to capitulate to the Germans, went to France and then to London without the king. Spaak joined the government in London. In its exile, the cabinet decided to formally remove the king from the throne. In fact, the king lived in exile in Germany for four years.

While in London, Spaak held several ministerial posts: External Commerce, Work, and Social Care and Public Health. At the same time, he tried to create a new Belgian Socialist Party modeled after the British Labour Party.

In 1945, the government-in-exile returned to Brussels from London and resigned. A new national government was then created. Like other European governments, it was leftist-oriented. Spaak stayed on in the new cabinet, the only minister from the London government that did so. After being liberated by the Americans, King Leopold and his family took up temporary residence in Switzerland. The king affirmed his desire to return to Belgium as monarch. However, the government and the Socialist Party did not favor such a move, accusing the king of collaboration with the Nazis. The return of the king became an acutely controversial issue in Belgium known as the ''royal question,'' pitting those favoring the king's return to power against those calling for his abdication.

As prime minister in 1946—and again from 1947 to 1949—Spaak led the movement against the king's return to power. In parliament, he criticized the king's errors during the war. But after the elections of 1949 were won by Catholics, who favored the king, a popular referendum on the king's return was called in 1950 by the new Catholic-Liberal government. Fifty-seven percent of the country as a whole favored Leopold's return to the throne, but at the regional level, the Flemish supported the king's return by 72 percent and the French-speaking Walloons by only 42 percent. Upon the king's return to Belgium, a general strike broke out in Wallonia, involving many violent demonstrations, some ending in fatalities. In the end, Leopold yielded to public pressure and abdicated in favor of his son, Baudouin I. The latter reigned until his death in 1993.

After this turbulent interlude, Spaak again held the Foreign Affairs portfolio in cabinets involving coalitions with the Socialists. In this role, he led Belgium toward a foreign policy which placed it clearly in the Atlantic camp, very close to the Americans and the British. Moreover, Spaak's role in international politics became increasingly prominent.

While in London as a member of the exiled Belgian wartime government, Spaak worked constantly to improve Belgium's reputation, tarnished by the German occupation and the king's apparent appeasement of Hitler. In this, he worked to clearly situate Belgium in the Allied camp. Spaak's international reputation, however, mainly stemmed from his role in international organizations such as Benelux (the customs union comprised of Belgium, the Netherlands and Luxembourg), the European Community and NATO. Spaak was an especially important contributor to early attempts at European integration, such as the European Coal and Steel Community.

In 1945, Spaak was one of those instrumental in creating the United Nations and presided at the first general meeting of the UN. He was a strong proponent of exploring new ideas for world peace and promoting new forms of cooperation between states in the world system. In 1948, he gave his celebrated "fear speech." In it, he discussed the Soviet Union's aggressive confrontation with the United Nations, Western Europe and the United States. Spaak spoke of the fear inspired by the Soviets' attitude and reiterated the principles of peace and security embedded in liberal democracy.

During his international career, Spaak held important positions in a number of international organizations. Successively, he held the presidency of the United Nations General Assembly (1946), chaired the Council of Ministers of the Organization for Economic Cooperation and Development (1948) and presided over the first Consultative Assembly of the Council of Europe (1949). Between 1952 and 1954, Spaak was president of the newly formed Assembly of the European Coal and Steel Community (ECSC), the early forerunner of the European Community.

In 1955, Spaak continued his pursuit of an integrated Europe by chairing the commission in charge of studying the creation of the European Common Market. He thereafter became very active in the debates surrounding the Treaty of Rome, which created the European Economic Community and Euratom in 1957.

At the end of 1957, Spaak became secretary general of NATO in Paris. He also chaired the North Atlantic Council from 1951 until 1961. During this whole period, the Cold War, East-West relations and decolonization were issues of paramount concern. Spaak played a major role in redefining postwar politics in the international arena, be it on the European front through his constant pursuit of cooperation and Western European integration or on the world scene through his work with the UN and NATO.

In 1961, however, his party asked Spaak to come back to Belgian politics as it—and Belgium—faced a very difficult national and international political conjuncture. Domestically, the Socialist Party was deeply divided over important social movements; internationally, Belgium faced the crisis of decolonization of the Congo.

Spaak agreed to form a coalition cabinet with the Catholics, in which he served as deputy prime minister and minister of foreign affairs. This government stayed in office until 1965. During this period, Spaak played a very important role in the Congo question. The difficulties of the decolonization process had left a very negative image of Belgium in the international community, especially within the United Nations. Spaak succeeded in restoring Belgium's international image, while playing an important role in pacifying the Congo's explosive political situation.

Spaak stayed on as foreign affairs minister until 1966, when the Socialists were again relegated to the opposition. Spaak then distanced himself from his party, although he remained in parliament. But after a time, the split became more acute: In opposition, the Socialist Party opposed the presence of NATO in Belgium favored by the Catholic-Liberal government, even though Spaak outspokenly supported the government. Spaak voted against his party on the issue and then resigned his parliamentary seat in 1966. A few days later, Bell

Telephone MFG offered him a position on its board; he also became personal counselor to the president of ITT.

A few years after retiring from politics, Spaak made an important comeback into Belgian domestic politics in order to promote federalist ideas against the dominant unitary positions of the traditional Belgian parties, including his own Socialist Party. (Although, indeed, Spaak had previously defended the unitary state.) In the 1971 electoral campaign, he supported the new Brussels party—the Francophone Democratic Front—which quickly gained an absolute majority in Brussels and advocated the creation of a federal Belgium with three components, Wallonia, Flanders and Brussels, against the unitary state in which the Flemish had become dominant. This political debate was the final one in which Spaak was to be an important actor: He died in 1972.

Spaak played a major role in many issues of importance for Belgium. Twice he succeeded in restoring the international image of Belgium under very difficult circumstances, both during and after the war and with the Congo question.

But apart from these major political actions, Spaak's political career reveals many contrasts: In Belgian politics, Spaak was always very flexible, sometimes shifting his political positions quite markedly.

For example, between the two world wars, Spaak passed from humanist ideas to radical socialism, then to reformism and then again to more moderate views of society and politics. He also changed his position from one supporting neutrality for Belgium to one supporting Belgium as a closely allied member of the Atlantic community. Likewise, he changed from being a partisan of republicanism to a strong supporter of the monarchy. Toward the end of his life, he also advocated a federalism for the Belgian political system, after having long favored a very unitary Belgian state.

When criticized for his shifting political beliefs, Spaak always answered that it was political conditions that had changed. Nonetheless, he did recognize some mistakes. Maliciously, he liked to quote Talleyrand's words : ''Y a-t-il quelque chose qui prouve d'avantage ma fidélité que de rester fidèle à mon inconstance?'' (Does anything prove my loyalty more than remaining faithful to my inconsistency?)

Nonetheless, ''inconsistency'' was not so apparent in Spaak's internationalism, and it was to this domain that he devoted almost all of himself after the war. Here, he constantly gave primacy to integration in its various dimensions—territorial, economic (Benelux, the EC) and security (NATO). In this sense, by his substantial activities on the international scene, Spaak was certainly one of the main postwar architects of a more unified world. It is not surprising, therefore, that his memoirs, which are at once an important historical record and a masterful demonstration of the art of diplomacy, are almost entirely devoted to the great international events of his era.

BIBLIOGRAPHY

Works by Spaak:

Combats inachevés: De l'espoir aux déceptions. Paris: Fayard, 1969.
Combats inachevés: De l'indépendance à l'alliance. Paris: Fayard, 1969.

Other Works:

Outers, L. *Paul-Henri Spaak: Son dernier combat*. Brussels: Rénovation, 1972.
Smets, P.-F., and J. Goemaere (eds.). *La Pensée européenne et atlantique de Paul-Henri Spaak (1942–1972)*, 2 vols. Brussels: Fondation Paul-Henri Spaak, 1980.
Willequet, J. *Paul-Henri Spaak: Un homme de combats*. Brussels: Renaissance du Livre, 1974.

ANDRÉ-PAUL FROGNIER AND MICHEL COLLINGE

DIRK U. STIKKER (1897–1979) served the Netherlands in a variety of political and diplomatic capacities, transforming his savvy as a businessman into widely extolled leadership as social reformer, statesman and advocate for European cooperation. As social reformer and party politician, Stikker helped found the People's Party for Freedom and Democracy (1946). As statesman and Dutch foreign minister (1948–1952), he struggled with the delicate issue of Indonesian independence. As advocate for the Atlantic Alliance and a new unified Europe, he chaired the Organization for European Economic Cooperation (1950–1952) and was secretary general of NATO (1961–1964). He was, to borrow from the title of his memoirs, one of Europe's ''men of responsibility.''

Dirk Stikker was born on February 5, 1897, at Winschoten in the Dutch province of Groningen. His parents represented two traditions—banking and trade—that had historically endowed the Netherlands with its prosperity. His father, Uipko Obbo Stikker, came from a wealthy farming family but worked himself up as a banker, operating his own stockbrokerage firm. His mother, Ida Meursing, came from a shipping and merchant family, the seas long having been the lifeblood of Dutch trade with the East Indies. Stikker was educated in law at the University of Groningen, during which time he devoted his efforts to student government, the debating society and the courtship of Catherina Paulina van der Scheer, whom he married in 1922.

Following his father into the banking business, Stikker worked as a clerk in the Groningen Bank after receiving his LL.D. degree in 1922. After only a year he left for a 100-guilders-a-month ($40) post at the Twentsche Bank in Amsterdam, which he eventually parlayed into a position as regional managing director by the time he reached thirty. In 1935 Stikker changed direction, accepting the managing directorship of the Heineken Lagerbeer Brewery Company. There Stikker the brewer concerned himself primarily with Heineken's expansion and foreign interests, but he also developed a keen interest in business-government relations, to which he would devote so much of his later energies.

During the Nazi occupation of the Netherlands from 1940 to 1945, Stikker organized and chaired the Central Breweries Office, a confederation of Dutch breweries founded on the premise that single enterprises could never alone survive German interference. Designed to safeguard the integrity of Dutch business, the Central Breweries Office also provided Stikker a means to contribute to his country's underground resistance. Obliged by the occupiers to coordinate beer deliveries to German troops, Stikker and the Central Breweries Office managed to pass information on Nazi troop movements within the Netherlands to the exiled Dutch government in London. Brought together by the exigencies of occupation, Stikker and the leaders of the outlawed trade unions spent the war years thwarting periodic Nazi efforts to seize men and equipment.

Confident of an eventual liberation, Stikker, in concert with Dutch labor leaders, formulated secret plans to ensure productive relations between labor, business and government once the war ended. Their efforts came to fruition when, on the second day following the liberation of Amsterdam, Stikker announced the establishment of the Foundation of Labor (Stichting van den Arbeid). The Foundation of Labor compiled an impressive record of success, formalizing contacts between leaders of industry and labor, accommodating wage demands, diffusing strikes and achieving workplace reforms. Historians generally agree with Stikker's own assessment of the Foundation of Labor as one of the few gains of the war.

Somewhat unwillingly, Stikker allowed his devotion to Holland's postwar rebirth to draw him into the political arena. In 1945, his work with the Foundation of Labor earned him unsolicited appointments first to the National Advisory Board of the Dutch Provisional Parliament and then to the First Chamber of the Provisional States-General as an independent. Reluctant and without a political party, but in need of a vehicle to challenge what he saw as a confused and abusive postwar government, Stikker was persuaded by a breakaway faction of the Liberal Party to organize a new party in preparation for the 1946 elections. The Party of Freedom thus launched, it won nine seats in the Dutch parliament, three in the First Chamber (Senate) and six in the Second Chamber. Stikker the businessman became Stikker the party politician.

The Party of Freedom was short-lived, however, as Stikker sought to broaden the organization's base by merging in 1948 with the forces of Dr. P. J. Oud, a former Liberal-Democrat disgruntled with his group's lot in the Labor Party. Together, Stikker and Oud created the People's Party for Freedom and Democracy (Volkspartij voor Vrijheid en Democratie—VVD) with Stikker as president. Commanding eight seats in the 1948 Second Chamber, Stikker's new VVD played a pivotal role in the formation of the next government. In August 1948, Stikker assumed his party's one seat in Prime Minister Willem Drees's coalition cabinet, accepting the Foreign Ministry portfolio.

As a member of the Drees government, Foreign Minister Stikker's consuming interest lay in the search for an acceptable solution to the so-called Indonesian problem. For the Netherlands, as for most European countries, the toll of world war could be found not only at home but also in the far reaches of a once thriving colonial empire. Nationalism, fomented during the Japanese occupation of the Dutch East Indies, brought on a constitutional crisis in the Netherlands when Indonesian Republican forces under Mohammed Hatta refused Dutch efforts to resume colonial control over the country following the war. Indonesian attacks on Dutch nationals and Dutch "police actions" against Indonesian Republicans raised the stakes, as did ultimatums from the United States that Marshall Plan aid to the Netherlands was contingent upon speedy resolution of the colonial issue.

Stikker, determined that unconditional sovereignty should ultimately be transferred to the Indonesians but only if done so in an orderly fashion, deeply resented the outside pressure that interfered with his negotiations with the Indonesians. By the end of 1949 the Dutch had formally, if only reluctantly, transferred sovereignty to the Indonesians in exchange for a loose "union" of the two sovereign states which would ensure that Dutch interests there would be protected. Stikker came to believe that subsequent events, primarily Sukarno's abrogation of the Netherlands-Indonesia Union, vindicated his view that uninformed interference by outside parties had unwittingly sabotaged his efforts to achieve a lasting solution.

With the sphere of Dutch influence suddenly reduced, Stikker's focus during his remaining years as foreign minister turned to restoring the Netherlands' position within the context of European unity. Stikker represented his country in the fledgling Organization for European Economic Cooperation (OEEC), becoming in 1950 the chairman of the OEEC's Council of Ministers. Before resigning that position in 1952, Stikker had steered the OEEC's successful attempts at promoting recovery through the restoration of intra-European trade and the creation of a European payments system.

In 1952 Stikker relinquished his post as foreign minister, opting to exit from a government still reeling from its crisis with Indonesia and similar problems with New Guinea. Stikker himself lamented that he had tired of being his party's only representative in a four-party coalition where his policy positions frequently clashed with the majority view of the cabinet, in the parliament and even within his own party. At this time, Stikker quickly accepted an offer to become his country's ambassador to Great Britain, a position he held until 1958. From 1956 to 1958, Stikker combined his ambassadorial duties in London with those of ambassador to Iceland. When the British government chose not to sign the 1957 Treaty of Rome establishing the European Economic Community (EEC), Stikker saw little real need for his continued presence in London. Resigning his dual ambassadorships in 1958, Stikker was nonetheless talked out of retiring altogether by the opportunity to serve as permanent representative of the Netherlands to NATO and to the Council of the OEEC.

In NATO Stikker vigorously advocated Atlantic cooperation. Just as he had believed during the war that only an alliance of Dutch breweries could stand where individual enterprises would fall, so too did Stikker believe that during the deepening Cold War, Europe and America would have to forge a closer sense of community. Stikker labored to point out that the defense of Europe, especially in the age of nuclear weapons, had to be integrated and organized along the lines of agreed-upon strategic principles. Accordingly, he spoke out against efforts, like those of de Gaulle in France, to construct national nuclear forces outside the command and control of NATO. In 1961 Stikker agreed to become secretary general of NATO and chairman of the North Atlantic Council. Although the 1962 Cuban missile crisis found him ill in a hospital bed, Secretary General Stikker did earn acclaim with his mediation of the 1964 Cyprus crisis in which Greece and Turkey, both NATO members, had renewed their traditional animosities.

In July 1964 Stikker, his health failing, resigned as NATO secretary general. At the time most observers agreed that in his short tenure Stikker had played a key role in minimizing the fissures that by the early 1960s had begun to develop within the Atlantic Alliance. Stikker continued to work for international cooperation, serving as a consultant to UNCTAD in 1966. His book, *Men of Responsibility* (1966), is widely cited as an authoritative account of behind-the-scenes developments in postwar Dutch and European politics. Dirk Stikker died the day after Christmas 1979.

Critics have questioned neither Stikker's principles nor his philosophy of public service. Stikker the businessman valued prosperity, for his many enterprises, for his country and for Europe. He did not, however, place prosperity above social problems. His Foundation of Labor, born of his devotion to workers' rights and industrial peace, inspired similar attempts across Western Europe to ensure social welfare through formalized contacts between labor, management and government. Stikker the party politician valued democratic representation; he thus established the People's Party for Freedom and Democracy, hoping to remedy what he saw as an exclusionary and obsolete continuation of prewar party politics. Stikker the European valued common security, social and economic integration, and partnership between Europe and the United States. The confidence placed in Stikker by his contemporaries to lead NATO and the OEEC testifies to his leadership qualities. Overall, whether it was with the Central Breweries Office, the Foundation of Labor, the VVD, NATO or the OEEC, Stikker valued strong organization, for in organization he saw security against risk, be it the risk of outside invaders, intrusive government or nationalistic impulses.

Stikker did not, however, escape criticism or controversy. Indeed, he had his rivals and detractors. When he established a new political party, Stikker was criticized for creating a party too secular in its appeal. When he tried to address the crisis in Indonesia as foreign minister, Stikker's colleagues in the government and within his own party attacked him. Bitter fights with E. M. J. A. Sassen, the Dutch minister of overseas territories, over the principles of outright sovereignty, which Stikker favored, and federation, which Sassen preferred, resulted in contradictory and botched communications between The Hague and Batavia as well as creating the general impression in international circles of

Dutch ineptitude. Even P. J. Oud, who had helped Stikker found the People's Party for Freedom and Democracy and who was the party's parliamentary leader, assailed Foreign Minister Stikker for his attempts to transfer sovereignty over New Guinea to Indonesia.

The open rift with Oud represents perhaps the low point of Stikker's political career. In 1951 Oud orchestrated a vote of censure against the government, of which Stikker was a member. The vote failed, but having received an embarrassing no-confidence vote from his own party, Stikker resigned the cabinet. Stikker's colleagues in the cabinet also resigned *en masse*, bringing on a protracted cabinet crisis. C. P. M. Romme, leader of the Catholic People's Party, resolved the crisis by reconstituting the government, in which Stikker regained his Foreign Ministry portfolio. He also regained his party's tenuous support, but only after an eleventh-hour threat to leave the party.

Himself the frequent target of domestic criticism, Stikker later found his own voice as a critic in the international arena. His favorite target was de Gaulle's France. For Stikker, de Gaulle's efforts to distance France from its NATO allies to pursue its own mission and *grandeur* undermined the strength of the Atlantic Alliance. To Stikker, de Gaulle was a prima donna seeking attention for himself and for France at the expense of common security and regional progress. Stikker was especially outraged by de Gaulle's 1963 veto of British membership in the Common Market. In France Stikker saw a resurgent nationalism that had seemingly failed to learn the traumatic lessons of the previous half century.

Popular history will likely place Stikker in the second tier of postwar Western European luminaries. His name and accomplishments have not enjoyed the widespread enduring recognition of a Robert Schuman, a Paul-Henri Spaak or a Jean Monnet. Although he spent the better part of his eighty-two years in the political arena, Stikker disdained the publicity usually coveted by the career politician. Indeed, Stikker cultivated the image of a businessman driven to politics by a sense of duty but unencumbered by the politician's customary machinations. Avoiding lengthy stays in any post, Stikker never built a personal political fiefdom; instead, he jumped from profession to profession, from position to position and from problem to problem. By his own account he was unable to solve all the problems he tackled, and he admitted to losing interest in those issues he did resolve.

History must, however, credit Stikker with several signal contributions. Stikker, through his work with the Foundation of Labor, must be considered one of the pioneers of what is today called labor/business/government "concertation" or "neo-corporatism." Through his work in Dutch party politics, Stikker can be acknowledged as the founder of a competitive organization that generally ranks as the third-largest party in the Second Chamber. Through his work in government, Stikker should be singled out as one of the few genuine advocates of decolonization who foresaw the dangers inherent in a hasty transfer of sovereignty. Through his work in supranational institutions, Stikker deserves recognition for helping to create the early framework for European and Atlantic cooperation.

A man of both the Netherlands and of Europe, Dirk U. Stikker left a legacy whose ultimate value lies in the awareness he helped raise about the importance of the common interest over the individual interests of single nations. The subsequent successes of the European Community and NATO are in great part a result of his principles and passions.

BIBLIOGRAPHY

Works by Stikker:

''The Functional Approach to European Integration,'' *Foreign Affairs* 29(3): 436–46 (April 1951).

''1940–1945: De Wording van de Stichting van den Arbeid,'' in P. J. Bouman et al. (eds.), *150 Jaar Koninkrijk der Nederlanden*, 248–57. Amsterdam: De Bussy, 1963.

''NATO—The Shifting Western Alliance,'' *Atlantic Community Quarterly* 3:7–17 (Spring 1965).

Men of Responsibility: A Memoir. New York: Harper & Row, 1966.

Other Works:

Fursdon, Edward. *The European Defence Community: A History.* New York: St. Martin's Press, 1980.

Heller, Francis H., and John R. Gillingham (eds.). *NATO: The Founding of the Atlantic Alliance and the Integration of Europe.* New York: St. Martin's Press, 1992.

Van Raalte, Dr. E. *The Parliament of the Kingdom of the Netherlands.* London: Hansard Society, 1959.

Verkade, Dr. Willem. *Democratic Parties in the Low Countries and Germany: Origins and Historical Developments.* Leiden: Universitaire Pers, 1965.

WILLIAM M. DOWNS

FRANZ JOSEF STRAUSS (1916–1988) was one of the most prominent, though criticized, politicians in the Federal Republic of Germany since its creation in 1949. From 1956 to 1962, he served as minister of defense and was the driving force behind the reorganization of the West German army. From 1966 to 1969, he led the Ministry of Finance under Chancellor Kurt Kiesinger. In the mid–1970s, Strauss turned his concentration to the politics of his home state, Bavaria, and became its minister-president (governor) in 1978, a post he kept until his death in 1988.

In 1980, Strauss ran for chancellor as candidate of the Christian Democratic Party (CDU) but lost the election to the Social Democratic incumbent, Helmut Schmidt. After this defeat, Strauss made no more open attempts to seek national office in Bonn. However, he maintained a strong influence on national and international politics, the latter mostly characterized by foreign policy initiatives such as visits to China (1985), Syria (1986) and the Soviet Union (1987). These visits were regarded at the time as politically spectacular.

Strauss's political career began in the late 1940s. In 1948, he was named general secretary (party manager) of the Christian Social Union, the Bavarian sister party of the West German CDU. In 1949, Strauss gained a seat in the Bundestag, the newly elected West German parliament. This dynamic and ambitious politician was soon recognized by Chanceller Konrad Adenauer, who asked him to join his cabinet as a secretary for special tasks in 1953. In 1955, he took over the Atomministerium (Ministry for Nuclear Energy) before being named to his first really prominent political post as minister of defense in 1956.

During his six years in the defense ministry, Strauss gained recognition for his ability—only ten years after the end of World War II—to both reestablish the German army and to gain diplomatic approval for West German rearmament. His merits, however, were partly overshadowed by political scandals and attacks against his integrity, a situation that would follow Strauss throughout his entire political career and that finally prohibited him from ever becoming either chancellor or federal minister of foreign affairs, both positions which were his unspoken career goals.

Most prominent among these scandals was the so-called Spiegel affair in 1962. *Der Spiegel*, the leading German newsmagazine, had been criticizing Strauss for irregularities in the purchase of fighter aircraft from the American producer Lockheed. Then in 1962 the magazine published an article critical of NATO maneuvers in Spain. The West German government used this article as a pretext for initiating legal charges against *Der Spiegel*'s publisher and some of its journalists. A fact-finding committee later found that the state authorities had acted improperly—actions which, Strauss testified, he was not responsible for. His claim was proven false in at least one instance and, as a result, Strauss had to resign from his post as head of the Defense Ministry in October 1962.

In 1961, Strauss became chairman of the CSU, a leadership post that he kept until his death in 1988. The party usually received a good 60 percent of the Bavarian vote in federal elections, making it an important and unavoidable factor in all conservative coalitions in Bonn. Even after leaving Bonn in 1978, Strauss maintained a strong power base in national and international politics simply by being the CSU's party leader.

Four years after his resignation from the ministry of defense, Strauss again received a ministerial portfolio in the Grand Coalition government (1966–1969). Chancellor Kiesinger honored both Strauss's campaign support and his financial expertise by naming him minister of finance. Strauss formed a popular team with the Social Democrat Karl Schiller, who was minister of economics. Their programs led West Germany out of the mild recession it experienced in the mid-1960s.

In 1969, the conservatives lost the general elections and were sent into opposition for more than a decade. During the following years, Strauss was not only an outspoken opponent of Social Democratic Chancellor Willy Brandt's Ostpolitik (the policy of détente toward Eastern Europe), he also lobbied very aggressively against some members of the conservative camp. Though brilliant in rhetoric, his aggressive style and usage of defamatory vocabulary increasingly pushed him to the outer right of the conservative camp.

However, after CDU leader Helmut Kohl's defeat in the 1976 campaign, Strauss managed to be named the conservative nominee for the chancellorship in the 1980 general elections. Starting brilliantly, Strauss could not manage to control his temper during the second half of the campaign, falling back into old, bad habits. This was said to be a major factor in his defeat by the Social Democratic incumbent, Helmut Schmidt.

Two years before, Strauss had made a surprising but brilliant political move. He left national politics in Bonn to became minister-president of Bavaria, a position comparable to a governor's post in the United States. He gained wide praise by paving the way for Bavaria's development into a high-technology region, partly due to his power to attract defense and aviation industries to settle in the south. An avid pilot himself, he also became chairman of the supervisory board of Deutsche Airbus Industrie.

Apart from these activities, Strauss remained active and influential in international politics during the 1980s. He visited Tibet during a trip to China in 1987, met with the Soviet leader, Mikhail Gorbachev, in Moscow in December 1987 and—still subject to speculation by some—arranged large credits for East Germany in direct talks with Erich Honecker, head of the GDR.

Four years after Strauss's death, the new international airport in Munich was named after him, putting him in an exclusive circle with such political figures as Kennedy, de Gaulle and Dulles. Reactions to this honor are symbolic of Strauss's entire career: It seemed justified and appropriate to the Bavarian authorities but was little understood and roundly criticized elsewhere.

Strauss's most dominant political trait, next to his genuine political instinct for power and leadership, was his inabilitiy to form majorities outside Bavaria. His temper and political style always prohibited him from gaining broad, national acceptance as a politician, a fact which effectively barred him from becoming chancellor or minister of foreign affairs, as he so dearly wished.

BIBLIOGRAPHY

Works by Strauss:

Herausforderung und Antwort: Ein Programm für Europa. Stuttgart: Seewald, 1968.
Deutschland, deine Zukunft. Stuttgart: Seewald, 1975.
Die Zukunft gehört der Freiheit. Tübingen: Akademie für Politische Bildung, 1985.
Erinnerungen. Berlin: Siedler, 1989.

Other Works:

Engelmann, Bernt. *Das neue Schwarzbuch, Franz Josef Strauss.* Cologne: Kiepenheuer & Witsch, 1980.
Zierer, Otto. *Franz Josef Strauss. Lebensbild.* Munich: Herwig, 1978.
Zimmermann, Friedrich (ed.). *Anspruch und Leistung. Widmungen für Franz Josef Strauss.* Stuttgart: Seewald, 1980.

Zimmermann, Ulrich. *Unvergessen—Franz Josef Strauss das war sein Leben*. Passau: Neue Presse Verlag, 1988.

RALF BEKE-BRAMKAMP

ADOLFO SUÁREZ (1932–) has been one of the key political leaders in Spain in the last quarter century. His significance and importance lies in the role he played in creating the new democratic system that was established in Spain after General Francisco Franco's death in 1975. He was prime minister of the Spanish government from 1976 to 1981.

King Juan Carlos I of Spain appointed Suárez prime minister in July 1976, carefully doing so in strict adherence to the procedures of Franco's authoritarian political regime. Suárez and his colleagues quickly set to work to dismantle that regime, although many sectors of the population and parts of the political class questioned Suárez's appropriateness for the task, as he had been closely associated with the Franco regime, holding a number of official positions, such as civil governor in Segovia (1968), general director of Spanish state-run television (1969) and the last general secretary of the National Movement, the only party allowed under Franco's dictatorship. However, Suárez proved quite adept at the task, for, on the one hand, he managed to successfully legitimate the new, emerging regime in the eyes of many old Franco supporters while, on the other hand, also managing to shore up his credibility in the face of the former opposition. Both tasks were necessary to the successful reform of the fascist regime's institutional structures.

It is clear that the key to Suárez's leadership during this difficult transitional period—apart from his personal qualities and vision of the future—also lay to a great extent in the circumstances and problematic conditions of change in which his political career evolved. Pragmatic and innovative, Suárez was able to legitimate reform while defusing threats to order and stability. It is quite remarkable that such substantial transformation occurred peacefully, leading, moreover, to greater moderation in public opinion. Working to build consensus, dialogue and open debate over policy, during his term of office Suárez was able to preside over the first free elections in 1977, as well as a referendum in December 1978 which approved a constitution establishing democratic rights and institutions for Spain.

In all this, Suárez was careful to follow the established legal procedures of the dictatorship, managing to obtain Cortes (the Francoist legislature) approval of the Law for Political Reform a few months after he was appointed prime minister by the king. Thus a Francoist institution sanctioned this move, opening the way to political transition. Legitimacy was then formally transferred to the Spanish people by means of a referendum, as required under the Franco regime, which endorsed the new democratic assembly established by the Law for Political Reform.

Suárez's centrist views, reflected in his UCD (Union of the Democratic Center) and supported by a majority of Spaniards in two successive legislative elections (1977 and 1979), managed to defuse oppositionist breakaway tendencies and to legitimate reform in the eyes of a number of interests left over from the previous regime. Suárez was thereby instrumental in leading the way to fundamental change without significant disruption and trauma.

In this brilliant and delicate political transition, Suárez guided Spanish political reform through a number of crucial milestones: On April 1, 1977, he disbanded the National Movement's General Secretariat, of which he had been top leader. On April 7, he received the Soviet ambassador to Madrid. On April 9, he legalized the PCE (Spanish Communist Party). On July 28, 1977, Spain formally put forth its application to join the European Community (EC). On October 25, he brought all political and social forces together in signing the Moncloa agreements outlining a policy of economic austerity. On November 24, he brought Spain into membership on the European Council. In December 1978 he led the successful campaign for the referendum to approve the constitution. Finally, in elections of both 1977 and 1979, Suárez led the UDC to victory, each time finishing ahead of any other party formation.

Besides overseeing this rapid and remarkable transformation of the Spanish political regime, Suárez, as head of the government, undertook a number of other significant initiatives, such as legalizing unions and parties, granting amnesty, negotiating an electoral law, reforming the tax system and establishing the Statutes of Autonomy for Catalonia and the Basque country, as well as dissolving the corporatist unions, the National Movement and most institutions left over from Franco's regime. (He did not, however, succeed in breaking up the state-owned television monopoly.)

Quite important among these measures was Suárez's reformation of the heretofore highly centralized Spanish state in order to devolve more powers onto some regions. While leading the UCD, he favored ample regional powers and negotiated very pragmatically with regional nationalists the Statutes of Autonomy of Gernika (the Basque country) and Sau (Catalonia). These statutes were later approved in referenda of 1979 and 1980, respectively. Although Suárez lacked an overall design in his territorial conception of the state—being attacked at the time by many for being ''suicidal'' (vis-à-vis the interests of Spain)—the fact is that Suárez developed a political response to the needs of the periphery based upon certain regional autonomies that were welcomed by many.

Indeed, Suárez's centrist politics, quick action, clear goals and pragmatism helped to a great extent to prevent disruption and a vacuum in power. Suárez's role as one of the key figures in the Spanish transition to democracy is all the more significant when one recalls that Spain was in deep economic crisis during this period, all the while experiencing terrorism propagated by the ETA, GRAPO and other violent groups, and that claims from peripheral nationalist groups were becoming more and more vocal. At the same time, Suárez had to face growing pressures emanating from both revolutionary and reactionary elements of Spanish society in general.

Adolfo Suárez was born on September 25, 1932, in Cebreros (Avila) to a family of low social background. Given the date of his birth, he belonged to a generation that had not been implicated in the beginnings of Franco's regime (which dated from the 1936 uprising and the resulting Civil War). Nonetheless, his subsequent political career was tied to the National Movement (the party founded by Franco), and he held, we have seen, several offices in Franco's regime. Although some analysts have dwelled on his less than scintillating intellect and lack of distinguished academic background, on his relative denseness and fear for the "hand-to-hand combat" of parliamentary debates and on his relations with the press, everybody, nonetheless, recognizes his negotiating brilliance, his tenacity and capacity for work and his great personal charisma, with which he projected a progressive and reformist image and the credibility needed to carry out political transformation.

As to the foreign policy of his governments, it must be said that although he succeeded in obtaining international support for the Spanish democratization process and in normalizing Spanish foreign relations, his actions were nevertheless directed more toward continuity with Franco's foreign policy, rather than at fundamental change and construction of a new framework that would define Spanish foreign policy through debate on important pending matters.

Some argue that Suárez was not an esteemed leader in international circles and that, in spite of personalizing foreign policy, he lacked both sensitivity to foreign policy issues and an overall view of international relations. That very personalization, however, along with the diversity and lack of consensus within the UCD on foreign policy, contributed to his tendency to preserve the status quo inherited from the Franco regime, rather than striking out into bold, new foreign policy directions. Moreover, the necessities of consensus with other political forces in order to implement the transition to democracy also constrained Suárez from pursuing a clear, new foreign policy during his tenure in office.

Although Suárez did begin to define a new Spanish line with regard to Europe—Spain formally sought membership in the EC on July 28, 1977, and on November 24 of that year it was admitted to the European Council—an altogether different course was charted vis-à-vis the Spanish position regarding that other pole of Western Alliance, NATO.

Unlike the king, as well as many of his own UCD colleagues (in fact, it was his UCD successor as prime minister, Leopoldo Calvo-Sotelo, who finally brought Spain into NATO), Suárez avoided aligning Spain with NATO because he wanted to keep Spain a nonaligned country, intending to develop an autonomous "third way" toward Latin America and the Arab countries and avoiding involvement in the East-West confrontation. In fact, Suárez was always reserved toward the United States and later even blamed, in part, American pressure for his downfall.

Although it is usually said that his opposition to NATO had its origins in an agreement he reached with the PCE (Spanish Communist Party) when the latter was legalized and integrated into the democratic process, the fact is that Suárez was simply reluctant to accept a commitment to alignment with the West. Despite the fact that his UCD was reportedly in favor of the Atlantic Alliance, in the end the issue was never openly debated.

On the other hand, Suárez tried to make Spain into a bridgehead between Europe and Latin America. This is the setting for Suárez's trip to Cuba and Spain's status as an observer at the summit of nonaligned countries in 1978. He met with Fidel Castro, as well as with representatives from center parties and leaders from most of Latin America. He then followed up with a policy of cooperation and development with a clear Latin American orientation.

Finally, it must be mentioned that Suárez and his governments continued to follow the pro-Arab Franco line, maintaining very cordial relations with Yasir Arafat and with various leaders from the Middle East, while systematically refusing diplomatic relations with the state of Israel.

In Spain's new democratic regime, Suárez was closely connected to two political parties: the UCD (Union of Democratic Center), a coalition of parties, and the CDS (Social and Democratic Center), which he founded after the breakup of the first. But some argue that as a party leader during this period Adolfo Suárez had a too personalized view of political power and that he was not capable of constructing an ideological identity, thereby keeping him from being part of the ethos of any of the political parties and groups that he led.

The first, the UCD, was established as a coalition made up of fifteen small parties covering a fairly wide ideological spectrum, ranging from social democratic, democratic-Christian, liberal and conservative tendencies, as well as including small regional parties. There were also many independents, often linked to the old regime. These played an especially important role, however, as they maintained and controlled a dense network of local leaders and substantial sectors of the population. This helped mitigate the weak organizational substructure of the new UCD. Likewise, including independents helped to improve the coalition's integrating and reformist image.

Heading the government, Suárez managed to impose his leadership and control on the UCD under the banner of a vague populist ideology and, above all, under the flag of reformism, but the heterogeneity of positions, values and political goals in the coalition made unity of action difficult. However, although the coalition's ideological definition and, therefore, coherence was very weak, everyone still agreed on the way in which the transition to democracy had to be implemented, that is, through a path in between the "breakup" recommended by PSOE (Spanish Labor Socialist Party) and leftist forces, and the "continuity" recommended by parties such as the AP (Popular Alliance) and other forces from the old regime.

As long as the task of transition continued and election results were favorable to the UDC, friction was concealed. But Adolfo Suárez was not a party man and he had populist inclinations. He therefore tried to impose his personal style and own ideological view onto the other groups constituting the coalition. He even attempted to co-opt elites within the groups of his coalition, trying to change the UDC into a party with a personalistic focus—on him.

Suárez's personalized style of leadership caused strains that eventually disrupted the balance in internal power between the different political groups and leaders within the coalition. In addition to all that, Suárez's view of the party kept it from creating close links with social movements or groups. That is, there was no effective social network connecting the party with society. The split between conservatives and progressives within the reform movement led the conservatives to walk out, accusing Suárez of taking excessively left-leaning positions. The coalition that won two successive elections under Suárez's leadership (1977 and 1979) went into internal crisis, leading Suárez to resign in 1981. The coalition would dissolve in 1983, hardly a year after Suárez had left it.

Although the UCD was useful in joining Suárez to politicians who had democratic credentials, deepening his credibility and strengthening his leadership in the face of the awesome tasks of political reform, he failed to make the party into one capable of playing a sustainable role as a member of the democratic opposition. The leadership crisis, the absence of a political program and the factional war within its ranks put a quick end to the UCD.

But the crisis in the UCD and Suárez's downfall were not only a consequence of internal conflicts and dissension. Pressure and opposition from different forces—economic, religious, military and other—also contributed, to a great extent, to the disintegration of the ruling coalition.

For example, banking and business interests, through their powerful organization CEOE (Spanish Confederation of Business Organizations), began to support the creation of a "big right," in which they intended to combine the AP (Popular Alliance Party, led by Manuel Fraga) and the UCD's most conservative factions. The army, which had felt betrayed ever since the legalization of the Spanish Communist Party (PCE, at that moment led by Santiago Carrillo), also began an internal anti-Suárez campaign. The Catholic Church, in its turn, was fiercely opposed to reforms on divorce. The mass media, intellectuals and unions also withdrew their support. All this hastened the crisis building toward the UCD's breakdown, bringing on the demise of a larger center-right movement.

Overwhelmed by political paralysis and pressure, Suárez resigned the premiership on January 29, 1981; immediately thereafter, on February 23, he faced an attempted coup d'état by military officers during the parliamentary debate on his successor's investiture (a coup eventually faced down by King Juan Carlos). In November of that year, Suárez left the UCD's executive and in the summer of 1982 he left the UCD to found a new party, the Social and Democratic Center (CDS). This group was described as center-leftist and with it, he would only win two parliamentary seats in the 1982 elections, which the Socialist opposition (PSOE) won by an absolute majority.

Eventually, according to scholarly consensus, Suárez in power became an obstacle to long-term national interests, like stability and consolidation of the democratic system, whose very establishment had been led by him. In addition, he was no longer a well-respected leader in the eyes of the great powers in international circles.

Personally isolated both within and outside the UCD, Suárez soon became a symbol of the past. In spite of his work to demolish the Franco regime, his image could not avoid being tainted by his past in that regime. Moreover, in spite of the leftist tinge that he gave to the CDS, this was all but overwhelmed by the social force, ideological clarity and leadership of the much more successful Socialists.

Following the CDS's 1982 electoral disaster, Suárez and his new party obtained 5 percent of the parliamentary seats in the June 1986 elections. While this seemed to indicate a recovery of his presence in the center, the alliances and agreements he reached with the PP (Popular Party—formed by the AP and other sectors from the old UCD) and with the PSOE badly eroded his image in public opinion. In the 1989 general elections, the CDS all but collapsed, leading Suárez to relinquish his leadership of the party and withdraw from "active politics" in 1990.

BIBLIOGRAPHY

Coll Barricarte, Adolfo. *Adolfo Suarez, todos los cargos del presidente*. Barcelona: Ed. A. Coll Barricarte, 1979.

Figuero, Javier. *"La Empresa" que creó Adolfo Suarez*. Barcelona: Ediciones Grijalbo, 1981.

Meliá Pericás, Josep. *Así cayó Adolfo Suarez*. Barcelona: Editorial Planeta, 1981.

Morán Suarez, Gregorio. *Adolfo Suarez: Historia de una ambición*. Barcelona: Editorial Planeta, 1979.

Perez Diaz, Santiago. *La Caída de Suarez*. Madrid: Editorial Emiliano Escobar, 1981.

Sarasqueta, Antxón. *La Agonía del Duque: El enigma de Adolfo Suarez*. Madrid: Ediciones Temas de Hoy, 1991.

JOSÉ M. MATA AND FRANCISCO J. LLERA

T

MARGARET THATCHER (1925–) was Great Britain's longest continuously serving prime minister (1979–1990) since Lord Liverpool in the early 19th century (1812–1827). Moreover, Lady Thatcher was the first female prime minister and the first female leader of the Conservative Party in the history of Great Britain. She also was the first British prime minister to have a body of political thought and policies named after her: "Thatcherism" was a label for a variety of ideas and public policies on the conservative right, ranging from privatization of firms and services to a monetarist economic policy to traditional Victorian social values.

Widely regarded as one of the two strongest leaders of 20th-century Britain—the other being Sir Winston Churchill—Margaret Thatcher dominated the stage both domestically and internationally throughout her term in office. She presided over and helped to lead a renaissance in right-wing political ideas and significantly moved Britain away from its mixed economy in the direction of free enterprise. She also played a central role in lending support to leaders in Eastern Europe and the Soviet Union in their efforts to reject communism in favor of democracy and free markets, and she shaped much of the debate over the institutions and policies of the European Community. Since leaving office in 1991, Thatcher has continued to play an active role in both British domestic politics and international affairs as a member of the House of Lords.

Born in Grantham, Lincolnshire, in 1925, Margaret Thatcher's roots were humble ones. She often pointed out her lower-middle-class origins when claiming to speak with the authority of one who knew what the average Briton believed. Few leaders in modern times have attributed so much of their values, abilities and later successes to their early upbringing, and few have demonstrated such clear continuities in thought and conduct from childhood to adulthood.

Thatcher's father, Alfred Roberts, son of a shoemaker, was a grocer who had left school at twelve, while her mother, Beatrice Roberts (née Stephenson), daughter of a railway cloakroom attendant, was a seamstress. Devout Methodists who had met at church, they married, bought a grocery store and sub–post office and moved above their shop, where they reared two children, Margaret and her sister Muriel, in a flat with no running water and an outdoor toilet. This household—where ''cleanliness was next to godliness'' and order and precision were at the heart of everyday life—was the embodiment of Methodism. In later years, Thatcher enjoyed saying that at Number 10 Downing Street (official residence and office of the British prime minister), she was still living above the shop. By this, she meant to imply that she was running the nation's business along the same lines as her parents had run their household and business—long hours and balanced books.

Her father, by her own vivid accounts as well as those of people who knew her as she was growing up, was the formative influence in her life. He was an extremely well-read, civic-minded man who served as an alderman, later mayor, of Grantham, as well as justice of the peace. His daughter Margaret was his chief intellectual companion: He encouraged her voracious reading, and he engaged her in steady political conversation. She thoroughly absorbed his public service values and began working for political campaigns when she was ten. It is quite possible that Alfred Roberts and Methodism informed Thatcherism as much as did the doctrines of Adam Smith or Milton Friedman.

Unlike many of her Conservative predecessors and unlike many of her contemporaries in the party and her own cabinet, Thatcher was not a product of elite ''public'' (private) schools but rather of Kesteven and Grantham Girls School (public). She went on to Somerville College, Oxford, where she studied chemistry and, hence, ultimately, became the only British prime minister to have been a scientist—a background she later found useful in arguing with Ronald Reagan against the ''star wars'' strategic defense initiative and in attempting to persuade the international community of the importance of protecting the ozone layer.

At Oxford, unlike so many top Conservative Party politicians, Thatcher was not active in the Oxford Union, the exclusive debating club of young aspiring politicians, because women were not allowed to be members in those years. She did, however, become president of the Oxford University Conservative Association, where she gained political experience and began making the political contacts that would be important later on.

After leaving Oxford in 1947, she worked for five years in industry as a research chemist, and by 1950, she had run for Parliament, losing the election. In 1951 she ran again—and lost again. During this period, she also met and married an affluent businessman ten years her senior, Denis Thatcher, a Conservative like herself, who talked with her about politics, agreed with many of her political views and provided both the financial and emotional support for her career. Within the first several years of her marriage, she read for and was called to the bar, became a barrister specializing in tax law and gave birth to twins. By 1959, she had won the safe Conservative seat of Finchley in North London, which she represented until 1992 when she retired from the House of Commons.

In her early years in the House of Commons, Margaret Thatcher occupied a number of junior ministerial posts in the government and in the shadow cabinet. She began as parliamentary secretary (junior minister) to the minister of pensions and national insurance in the 1961–1964 government and then served in a number of shadow cabinet positions when the Conservatives entered the opposition: In chronological order, she held the shadow portfolios for Pensions, Housing and Land, Fuel and Power, and Transport, was the Conservatives' number two spokesperson for Treasury and, finally, held the shadow portfolio for Education. From 1970–1974, she was then Minister of Education in the Heath government.

In both her government and shadow positions, she broadened her knowledge and expertise and gained a reputation for being a formidable debater in the Commons and for being a master of detail. Her experience in both the government positions that she occupied prior to becoming prime minister had several lasting impacts. First of all, at Pensions she developed a lifelong low opinion of civil servants, most of whom she found uncreative, uninterested in argument and prone to offer a minister only advice he wanted to hear. At Education, she acquired a reputation for toughness when she boldly attempted to curtail the Labour Party's effort to make all state schools comprehensives. More important, she also acquired a reputation for ruthlessness for ending the school milk program for eight-to-eleven-year-old children. The epithet "Thatcher, the milk snatcher" followed her for the rest of her political career, suggesting an utterly heartless woman.

The depiction of Thatcher as a bloodless cost cutter in this period was to some extent the result of partisan exaggeration. Not only had it been Labour, while still in power, that had just a bit earlier ended the secondary school milk program, but also while Thatcher was at Education, she was a big spender. She exhibited few signs of the tight-fisted monetary and fiscal policy advocate who emerged over the course of the next decade. Furthermore, there was little evidence of the staunch advocate of free enterprise who would later attempt to make competitive capitalism a central tenet of Conservative Party thinking and policy. Her entire political career had in fact occurred in the context of the postwar political consensus in Britain in which the Labour Party and the Conservative Party had both subscribed to elements of the welfare state and to Keynesianism and in which the parties had seldom sought to reverse radically each other's key social and economic policies.

Few would doubt, however, that by upbringing and disposition, she believed in many of the values of free enterprise, especially such cornerstones as thrift, hard work and individual effort, and that she was disinclined toward a consensual style of decision making and governance. But it was not until about the last year of Heath's leadership in 1974 that her right-wing drift was beginning to emerge more clearly and even later than that before her diatribes against the postwar consensus were to make themselves heard.

In 1974, Thatcher became one of the first board members of a think tank, the

Centre for Policy Studies, started by Sir Keith Joseph. The group was loosely affiliated with the Conservative Party but financed by business. It was to become the font of much right-wing policy for the Thatcherites both in their opposition period and then in government. It was Sir Keith, upon the Conservative Party defeat in 1974, who announced his disenchantment with the policies of the last years of the Heath government. He subsequently became a chief critic of the postwar consensus and the leading Conservative exponent of tight monetary and fiscal policy and the virtues of free enterprise. And it was her long-standing friend, Sir Keith, who began to exert ever greater influence over Margaret Thatcher in these matters. Indeed, he was her tutor in her years as opposition leader and then during the early years of her government.

In fact, it was as a stand-in for Sir Keith that Margaret Thatcher became leader of the Conservative Party. In 1975, when the Conservatives were attempting to force Edward Heath to step down from the party leadership, Thatcher ultimately came forward to run against him only after Sir Keith, then the standard-bearer of the party's newly vocal right wing, removed himself from the contest. Among party insiders, although she was never considered a true contender for leader, she was viewed as a candidate who would seriously challenge Heath. In fact, she unseated him on the first ballot.

On the second ballot of the party's leadership contest, those perceived to be the true contenders entered the race. In this ballot, Thatcher faced four opponents who then fragmented the votes of the non–right wing, she emerging with an enormous victory for the right wing of the party. As commentators at the time noted, Margaret Thatcher's election as leader of the Conservative Party was an extraordinary surprise, owing much to good luck. But it was also more than just good fortune. Her ambition, diligence and keen political instincts, which would loom so large in her career as prime minister, had led her to take a chance as a dark horse on becoming a winner.

During the years as opposition leader, she became completely convinced that the chief cause of the economic ills of Great Britain had been generations of Labour Party socialism, both in terms of intervention in the affairs of business and in the creation of a vast system of social welfare, in conjunction with Keynesianism. This steady move leftward, she believed, had also been aided and abetted by the Conservatives themselves, who had either actively participated in or passively acquiesced in the increasing collectivism of modern Britain. In this view, the famed "British disease" was a socialist virus curable with a strong dose of laissez-faire. She believed that the way for the Conservative Party to revive its electoral fortunes was to end its participation in the politics of consensus and to adopt a free market ideology with economic and social policies reflecting that ideology. In turn, the way to revitalize the British economy was to infuse British culture with the institutions, principles and practices of free enterprise to create an enduring "enterprise culture" as a replacement for the "culture of dependency" created by socialism.

The effort to move the Conservative Party toward adoption of a laissez-faire ideology was one of the more dramatic departures of Margaret Thatcher from traditional Conservatism, which had always maintained that the Conservative Party was nonideological and, moreover, precapitalist. Although business interests had been prominently represented in the party throughout the 20th century, the Conservative Party has always possessed a strong antibusiness current arising from the fact that the earliest roots of the party lay in the Tory aristocracy and landed gentry. In addition, throughout most of its history, the Conservative Party had been dominated by the landed and other nonbusiness interests. Hence, Thatcher's task was twofold: To break the stranglehold of the Conservative patrician elite on the party's ideas and principles in order to secure the adoption of a free market ideology and then to convince the nation of the correctness of the ideology.

While leader in opposition, she set about developing this new Conservative creed under the tutelage of Sir Keith and with the help of numerous right-wing intellectuals, particularly from policy think tanks like the Institute of Economic Affairs, which had played a key role in Sir Keith's conversion. Though the shorthand for the ideology and policies might come to be called "Thatcherism," it is clear that she was not a singular pioneer or lone proponent of free enterprise ideas. Rather, she was part of a much broader movement of political thought which had begun sometime in the late 1960s and had already heavily influenced the first years of the Heath government. Nonetheless, it was Margaret Thatcher whose political and intellectual sagacity, in conjunction with her ambition, determination, and diligence, enabled her to articulate this ideology and bring it center stage both in Britain and worldwide.

Her first goal in office appears to have been the promotion of policies designed to create an environment hospitable to free enterprise rather than the creation of the enterprise culture itself. To this end, monetarism and union reform were the two policy areas to which the government devoted itself in the first term. She vigorously pursued monetarist orthodoxy in opposition to many members of her first cabinet and other senior members of her party, whom she dubbed the "Wets." Many of the Wets, though by no means all, had been from the ranks of the traditional patrician elite of the party and had been primary players in the postwar consensus. However, by the close of her first term, as the Thatcher cabinet prepared for the next election, the government had either abandoned its monetary goals or in any case missed them. Although Thatcher had maintained that she would make no "U-turns" with respect to the government's fundamental adherence to monetarism, the move away from it had already begun in her first term and had been finished by the end of her second term. However, it is also important to note in this connection that by about the same time, she had marginalized most of the Wets by removing them from the cabinet or accepting their resignations.

Her primary industrial relations legislation, designed to curb union power, was passed in 1982. This legislation included such provisions as the restriction of legal picketing to a picketer's own workplace, civil damages against unions of up to £250,000 for unlawful industrial action, government funds for union ballots concerning wage disputes and the need for four-fifths of the workforce to vote their approval by secret ballot for the introduction of a closed shop. This union legislation in combination with a general decline in union membership appears to have diminished the volatility of industrial relations compared to that of the period preceding the Thatcher years in the "winter of discontent." Certainly, British management has believed this to be one of the government's chief contributions to reinvigorating the capacity of British industry to increase its productivity.

The full-blown set of economic policies designed to usher in the enterprise culture did not by and large begin until the second term and, despite much derisory rhetoric concerning the welfare state, these focused primarily on the economy. Even though the 1979 party manifesto had championed denationalization, privatization only emerged as a clear policy priority in the final year of the first term and only became the centerpiece of the Thatcherite effort to create an enterprise culture in the second term. The Thatcher government over the course of time encouraged free enterprise by a number of policies which involved deregulation, paperwork reduction and contracting out of governmental services. But far and away the most important initiative involved the privatization of nationalized industries such as Britoil, British Telecom, British Gas, British Airways, Rolls-Royce, British Airports and BP. In addition, the government sold off other government-owned entities such as public utilities—namely, electricity and water—and most important of all, public housing. Between 1979 and 1989, the government received £23,479 million from its non-housing privatizations and £17,580 million from its sale of council (public) housing.

As part of its various privatization efforts, the government provided financial incentives for employees of nationalized industries to buy stock in their respective firms as they were privatized, and provided incentives to members of the general public to buy shares in industries scheduled to be privatized. Similarly, the government offered large inducements to residents of public housing to purchase their units and even increased these inducements later on in the third term. The government claimed that the logic behind the incentives for these purchases of shares and houses was that increasing share ownership among the British public would deepen their understanding of and investment in the free market system. Whether intended or unintended, however, one of the effects of the sale of council housing was to create more votes for the Conservative Party.

The breadth of shareholders did in fact widen in the short term but then appeared to narrow over the long haul as first-time investors discovered the logic of financial capitalism: Buy low—which they had done with the help of the government—and sell high. Thus, the strides made here will probably prove neither to be as great as the government claimed nor as small as the government's detractors maintained. The selling of public housing was especially popular with the British public and by most accounts a very successful policy, with the possible exception that the policy further weakened the mobility of the British workforce, whose immobility has traditionally presented problems for rationalizing the economy.

Certainly, critics rightly question whether any of these domestic economic policies will have been enough to make the British firm adherents of laissez-faire ideology and, therefore, to implant the enterprise culture permanently. It is especially important to note in this context that though the Thatcher government did undertake some reform of the social welfare system, the government did not succeed in any major overhaul or dismantling of social welfare's fundamentals. Only toward the very end of its tenure in office did the government attempt to reform the National Health Service by introducing a system of internal competition. And, significantly, the basic social welfare principle of universal entitlement to this service was in no way altered.

If the Thatcherites failed to make their mark on the social welfare system, they have, nonetheless, made a significant one on microeconomic policy. Her successor, John Major, has shown little inclination to alter the basic features of her microeconomic agenda, and, more important, the opposition Labour Party has acquiesced in or been supportive of many of these features. Thus, it may be the case that while Margaret Thatcher failed at consensual policy making, she did succeed in moving that consensus to the right.

Of course, the impact of free enterprise thought and policies developed during the Thatcher era has not been limited to Britain but has been enormously influential in countries throughout the world, capitalist and socialist alike. Such things as privatization and the selling of public housing to its occupants and increasing worker and citizen shareholding have inspired widespread interest in and adoption of these policies.

In addition, free enterprise economics has not been her only contribution to the discourse and policies of other nations. Thatcher—perhaps more than any other national leader of the postwar world, except in the United States and the former Soviet Union—has been at the center of foreign policy matters, an area about which she had virtually no experience when she first came to office. She learned on the job and did so quickly, for some of her chief foreign policy challenges and, hence, her achievements occurred in the first term.

First of all, after long questioning the wisdom of doing so, she accepted the advice of her foreign secretary and the Foreign Office professionals and helped to establish an independent Zimbabwe in 1980. Second, she sent Britain into war in the Falkland Islands against the forces of Argentine General Galtieri and won. This was a war which was immensely popular with the British public and which was widely credited with having turned the electoral tides in her favor in the 1983 election. Third, she presided over the negotiations for British return of Hong Kong to the Chinese in 1997. Fourth, she developed an abiding friendship with Ronald Reagan and in many ways re-created with him the transatlantic partnership of Winston Churchill and Franklin D. Roosevelt. This relationship with Reagan may ultimately have caused her problems in the European Community, where her counterparts often viewed her as too pro-American and not European enough. Fifth, she played a very supportive role in the international arena on behalf of Mikhail Gorbachev by encouraging others to recognize his sincerity and difficulties in attempting to end the Cold War and to promote *perestroika* and *glasnost*. The citizens of the former Soviet Union came to call her the "iron lady," intending it as a flattering sobriquet. Sixth, she became an outspoken critic of many of the possible pitfalls of the European Community, most notably in her famous Bruges speech in 1988, wherein she warned of the danger of a European superstate dominating Britain and other European nations from Brussels, suppressing their national identities.

It was her increasing anti–European Community stance that brought about the resignation of Sir Geoffrey Howe as foreign secretary and his attack on the prime minister for her lack of cooperation with the European Community. It was this major foreign policy issue in combination with the extreme unpopularity of the community charge, more commonly referred to as the "poll tax," that ultimately ended Thatcher's tenure as prime minister. The Conservative members of parliament came to believe that her intransigence with respect to both of these policies was a severe political liability. On November 22, 1990, they voted to replace her as party leader and, in effect, therefore, as prime minister. Thatcher was replaced by her chancellor of the Exchequer, John Major, who became prime minister.

In the final analysis, Thatcherism characterized not only a range of ideas and policies of the right but also a style of governance. The style accorded debate and disagreement a new central place in British public policy making and at its best stood for strong leadership and principled conduct. Both elements of this governmental style contributed to the success of much of Margaret Thatcher's agenda: She was willing to argue and fight for principle and to struggle to adhere to it. But the style, while at least temporarily dealing a blow to the consensual politics of the Conservative old guard and its cooperation with the Labour Party, also severely, and perhaps unnecessarily, alienated the old guard in the party as well as many others in British society. That style more than any other factor brought an end to the Thatcher era.

BIBLIOGRAPHY

Jenkins, Peter. *Mrs. Thatcher's Revolution*. London: Jonathan Cape, 1987.

Kavanagh, Dennis. *Thatcherism and British Politics*. Oxford: Oxford University Press, 1987.

Riddell, Peter. *The Thatcher Government*. Oxford: Basil Blackwell, 1983.

Weiner, M. J. *English Culture and the Decline of the Industrial Spirit*. Harmondsworth: Penguin, 1985.

Young, Hugo. *One of Us*. London: Macmillan, 1989.

Young, Hugo, and Sloman, Anne. *The Thatcher Phenomenon*. London: BBC, 1986.

CANDACE HETZNER

LEO TINDEMANS (1922–), one of the most powerful and popular politicians in postwar Belgium, is renowned as a leading European statesman in the tradition of his compatriot Paul-Henri Spaak. A member of the Monnet Action Committee for the United States of Europe (1960–1975), Tindemans is perhaps best known for his efforts while prime minister of Belgium to rejuvenate the European Community (EC) with his report on European Union. While the 1975 Tindemans report was not enthusiastically received by EEC member states at the time, many of Tindemans's ideas and proposals on a common foreign policy, a ''citizen's Europe,'' and institutional reform later served as a blueprint for the 1985 Single European Act and the 1992 Maastricht Treaty on European Union.

As prime minister (1974–1978), Tindemans sought constitutional solutions to Belgium's regional problems brought on by Flemish and Walloon demands for greater autonomy. While in office, he enjoyed the highest approval rating of any Belgian prime minister since 1935. In 1979, Tindemans was elected to the European Parliament (EP). He later left his EP post to serve as foreign affairs minister (1981–1989) in the Martens governments. During this period, he led a European-level effort to rekindle Middle East peace talks, directed Belgium's actions in the NATO dual track cruise missile deployment and helped preside over two Belgian presidencies of the EC. In 1989, he was reelected to the EP, later assuming the presidency of the EP's European People's Party in 1992. He continues to be a leading Belgian and European spokesman in international affairs.

Leonard Tindemans was born in Zwijndrecht, a suburb of Antwerp, Belgium, on April 16, 1922. He was the eldest of two sons of Frans, a skilled diesel mechanic, and Margaretha (Vercruyssen) Tindemans. Raised in the strong Flemish Roman Catholic home of his grandparents, Tindemans attended Catholic primary and secondary schools, where he was an exceptional student. Having learned how to read and write prior to his first day of school, Tindemans advanced to the fourth grade (Belgian *cinquième*) when he was only eight years old.

During his high school years, Tindemans became an active member of the St. Thérésia-Zwijndrecht troop of the Flemish Federation of Catholic Scouts. For the working-class boy from a small village, the scouts provided Tindemans with his first exposure to the outside world. An important event for young Tindemans was attending the World Scout Jamboree in Holland. Moreover, the scout training in leadership and teamwork piqued his interest in politics. It was during this period that Tindemans developed his ambition to be a diplomat. He believed, however, that a diplomatic career would not be possible, as his family background was too modest for a Belgian diplomatic corps comprised largely of nobility.

Tindemans's involvement with the scouts was reinforced in May 1940 with the German invasion of Belgium. Following the Belgian government's call for all men between the ages of eighteen to thirty-five to leave the country to avoid

Nazi imprisonment or forced labor, eighteen-year-old Tindemans fled to France with his scout troop. He returned to Belgium a few weeks later, however, when Hitler invaded France. Throughout the war, Tindemans found solace in the fierce anti-Nazi sentiment of the scouts.

The German occupation had a tremendous impact on Tindemans. The Nazi *Blitzkrieg* led to the loss of public rights for Tindemans and his fellow countrymen and women within a matter of weeks. More devastating for Tindemans, however, was the fact that his classmates were divided between resistance and collaboration. For a young man with diplomatic ambitions, the war provided Tindemans a cruel confrontation with world politics. It was this war experience which largely shaped Tindemans's future European ''faith'' in a larger construction of a United States of Europe.

Under the German occupation, Tindemans was permitted to continue with his studies from September 1940 until the end of the war. Because Nazi rule obliged him to attend the nearest school, Tindemans could not pursue his desired degree in political science granted at other Belgian universities. Instead, he received a degree in business and consular administration at St. Ignacius in Antwerp.

During this period, however, Tindemans's interest in world affairs was reinforced by a teacher of diplomatic history, Professor DeSchaepdrijver. The lectures and writings of DeSchaepdrijver made a considerable impression on Tindemans, who continues to cite the professor's works to this day. Following the war, Tindemans attended Ghent University, where he received a master's degree in economics. He later obtained a degree in social and political science in 1967 from the Catholic University of Louvain (KUL). Tindemans wrote his thesis on the political thought of Frans van Cauwelaert, the Flemish statesman and noted writer on international affairs, especially German-European relations. Like DeSchaepdrijver, van Cauwelaert remained a principal source of intellectual inspiration in Tindemans's life.

From 1946 to 1947, Tindemans spent much of his military service in West Germany where his fluency in English, Flemish, French and German enabled him to serve as a member of a multinational inspection team. Following his military stint, he returned to Antwerp, where he worked briefly as an insurance agent, and later as a journalist responsible for the economic page of the *Gazet van Antwerpen* newspaper.

Upon his successful completion of the first post-Liberation civil service exam, Tindemans entered the Belgian government in 1949 in the economic department of the Ministry of Agriculture. There he dealt with Benelux and General Agreement on Tariffs and Trade (GATT) issues. During the same period, Tindemans laid the groundwork for his career in politics with the Flemish wing of the Christian Democrat Party (CVP), a centrist party representing Roman Catholic middle-class and working-class interests. He founded the Young Christian Democrats group of Antwerp and edited a monthly magazine directed toward younger members of the party. In 1953, he left the Ministry of Agriculture to join the CVP's Study Center (CEPES) and from 1958 to 1966 served as the party's national secretary. In 1961, Tindemans was elected to the Chamber of Representatives—the lower house of Belgium's national parliament—to occupy the seat vacated by the death of Frans van Cauwelaert, his intellectual mentor. Tindemans served as deputy until 1989. Concurrently, he was also mayor of Edegem (1965–1978), a suburb of Antwerp.

Tindemans made his entrée into European and international politics in the early 1960s. He became a member of the Monnet Action Committee for the United States of Europe in 1960. Two years later, at the invitation of Henry Kissinger, he participated in an international seminar at Harvard University. From 1962 to 1968, Tindemans contributed regularly to the foreign affairs daily, *De Nieuwe Gids*. From 1965 to 1973, he served as secretary general of the European Christian Democratic Union (ECDU). In 1973, he was elected vice president of the organization. From 1966 to 1970, Tindemans was a professor of international relations at the Institut Supérieur de Formation Sociale. He returned to the teaching profession in 1976 as a visiting professor on the social sciences faculty at KUL. Today, Tindemans retains his position at KUL and writes prolifically on political thought, Belgian and European relations, and international affairs.

The turning point in Tindemans's political career occurred in June 1968 when he assumed his first cabinet post in Prime Minister Gaston Eyskens's coalition government. The government was formed in the aftermath of a four-month government paralysis resulting from the rise of Flemish and Francophone nationalism in the 1960s. This conflict culminated in the KUL language dispute. The Eyskens Social Democratic–Socialist coalition was the first Belgian government to provide for equal apportionment of cabinet posts between Flemings and Walloons, as well as the establishment of dual ministries for education, culture and community relations between the two language groups. Tindemans was asked to serve as the Dutch-speaking minister for community relations, a post that he did not desire but accepted nonetheless.

Known as a hardworking problem solver dedicated to his party, Tindemans was a natural choice for this sensitive position. Working closely with his French-speaking counterpart, Freddy Terwagne, Tindemans helped to develop a plan for the linguistic, economic and administrative decentralization of Belgium. This plan later resulted in the so-called third revision of the constitution in 1970–1971 which introduced profound changes in Belgium's governmental structure. While the reforms provided a framework for Belgian regionalization, they did not specify the details for its implementation. Parliamentary infighting and divisions within the Eyskens government over these reforms led to the dissolution of parliament in September 1971 and new elections two months later.

When a new Eyskens government was formed in January 1972, Tindemans was appointed minister for agriculture and middle-class affairs. Again, he was charged with a difficult portfolio given the emerging Common Agricultural Policy of the European Community. His tenure was short-lived, however, as the government collapsed in November that same year after linguistic and territorial issues provoked a split in the Social Democratic Party.

In January 1973, Edmond Leburton, a Walloon Socialist, succeeded in forming a grand coalition of Belgium's three leading parties—the Social Democrats, the Socialists and the moderately right-wing Liberals. Tindemans was appointed deputy prime minister as well as minister for the budget and institutional problems. The government fell a year later and King Baudouin named Tindemans the prime minister–designate, charged with the task of forming a new government. When Tindemans was unable to secure a viable coalition, he recommended and was granted dissolution of parliament and the calling of new elections.

In these March 1974 elections, Tindemans emerged as the undisputed national leader, having campaigned largely on his own name rather than on that of his party. However, he was neither able to reconstitute Leburton's grand coalition nor to form a working coalition with the Socialists.

One of the major obstacles in creating the governing coalition stemmed from Tindemans's views on federalism. He did not believe that federalism—dividing Belgium into two or three quasi-autonomous linguistic/cultural entities—would necessarily resolve the country's regional problems. For Tindemans, the unity of the Belgian state was imperative. In April, therefore, he settled for a minority cabinet with the Liberals. A majority government was then formed in June when the Walloon Union, a federalist party, agreed to take part. Tindemans immediately took steps to further conciliate the federalists by implementing a provisional regional law to set up regional councils in Flanders, Wallonia and Brussels that would advise the national parliament. However, he was not able to obtain the necessary two-thirds majority vote in parliament that would have invested the councils with legislative power. In August 1974, despite difficulties in resolving regional issues and interparty disputes, Tindemans enjoyed the highest approval ratings of any Belgian prime minister since 1935.

In the aftermath of the first oil crisis, the worsening economic situation in Belgium and the rest of Europe soon outweighed the Flemish-Walloon conflict in government priorities. In March 1975, the Tindemans government announced crisis measures that allocated a considerable amount of funding to create new jobs in public services. Two months later, Tindemans undertook a policy to control inflation and unemployment. He issued a decree freezing prices of key commodities, rents and public utility rates for a two-month period that was later extended to the end of the year. He also introduced measures to stimulate corporate growth by providing government aid for investments, reducing corporate taxes and easing credit restrictions. In October, the Tindemans government announced an additional twenty-five-point economic program designed to address the economic malaise. Despite these efforts, unemployment and inflation continued to rise. In 1977, Tindemans introduced an austerity program that included wage curbs and indirect taxes. These resulted in one-day protest strikes by labor unions.

In foreign affairs, Tindemans was largely occupied with NATO policy, the Conference on Security and Cooperation in Europe (CSCE) and relations with Zaire. In June 1975, the government belatedly announced that it would join other NATO allies in replacing the obsolete F-106 American aircraft with F-16 fighter planes. The decision angered many in the Belgian aircraft industry and Wallonia who had favored the purchase of the more costly French Mirage F-1 fighter from France. In CSCE matters, Tindemans regularly participated in top-level meetings among world statesmen in 1975 to discuss security and cooperation matters in Europe. In 1977, he was a signatory of the Final Act of Helsinki. In Africa, Tindemans sought to improve strained relations with Zaire by visiting the former Belgian Congo in September 1975. Tindemans also made official state visits to the People's Republic of China, the Soviet Union and the United States.

Tindemans's most highly regarded action during his tenure as prime minister was his attempt to rejuvenate the European Community in the 1970s through his Report on European Union. Concerned by the stalemate in European integration, Tindemans suggested in a December 7, 1974, radio interview that the European Community should undertake a top-level study to examine the potential creation of a European political union by 1980. The proposal was appropriately timed for the Paris meeting of EC heads of state and government a few days later, which invited him to draft a report.

In preparing the document, Tindemans studied previous recommendations for European unity and traveled to the nine EC member states where he met with government, industry and labor officials. In his forty-one-page report, *European Union: Report to the European Council*, Tindemans called on leaders of the member states to take action in common areas of economic, defense and foreign policies and to promote a "citizen's Europe." To improve the functioning of the community, he recommended the abolition of the Council's unanimous vote system and that the European Parliament be elected by direct suffrage. The report also promoted the notion of a two-tier approach in EC policy in which certain EC countries could move ahead on joint economic and monetary plans at a faster pace than others.

The Tindemans report received a lukewarm reception from the European Council, which was not yet ready to embrace such measures. In time, however, these leaders did agree to universal suffrage for the next EP election. Later, when a group of European-wide Christian democratic and centrist parties met to form a new European People's Party (EPP) in Brussels in anticipation of the mid-1978 EP election, Tindemans was unanimously elected its president—a position he held until 1985.

In March 1977, Tindemans was forced to call for new elections when two Walloon members of his cabinet refused to support a budget vote to protest the administration's failure to rescue the ailing Walloon steel industry. Running on the slogan "Tindemans more than ever," the prime minister received the most preferential votes ever received by a candidate in Belgium's parliamentary history. Yet Tindemans continued to be confronted by the Belgian regional problem.

He succeeded in forming a six-party coalition—including representatives from the federalist parties for the first time—by proposing a joint program of constitutional reform establishing permanent regionalization. Known as the Egmont Pact, this masterpiece of political accommodation envisaged five tiers of government with a special status accorded to Brussels. Despite careful negotiations, the pact collapsed when Tindemans failed to obtain the support of his own party, which viewed the Brussels portion of the plan as a concession to the Francophones. In August 1978, the "great expert in compromises" handed in his resignation to the king.

In resigning, Tindemans effectively decided not to fight the CVP over the Egmont Pact. It was believed that Tindemans, by forcing a new election, hoped to strengthen his somewhat diminished authority within the party and to promote his view on the future of the Belgian state. As a unitarist, Tindemans strongly believed that a move toward federalism would not be in the country's interest. Others in the CVP, however, did not share this stance. Wilfried Martens, the up-and-coming dynamic young leader within the party, supported more federalist actions ("unitary federalism").

Tindemans's actions proved costly. When elections were held in December to replace the caretaker cabinet, Martens was selected to head the new coalition government. For the first time in a decade, Tindemans found himself outside a cabinet. The most popular politician in recent Belgian history had been rejected by his fellow politicians. Somewhat ironically, Tindemans was then elected party president in 1979.

That same year, Tindemans turned his political aspirations to the European Community and was elected to the European Parliament. He became a member of the prestigious Committee on Economic and Monetary Affairs but was unsuccessful in his bid for EP president. Late in 1981, he resigned from the EP when called to serve as foreign affairs minister in the new Martens government. The prime minister had been pressured to appoint a politician who would have the depth of experience and European-level reputation needed to effectively lead during Belgium's six-month term as president of the EC Council of Ministers. Martens also wanted his party rival to share responsibility for the tough economic measures the government expected to issue. Tindemans, on the other hand, could not refuse the opportunity to pursue his diplomatic ambitions as minister of foreign affairs.

Tindemans played a leading role during his tenure in the Foreign Affairs Ministry (1982–1989). He arrived in office during a new low in EC-US relations based in part on controversy over the national gas pipeline in the Soviet Union and rising U.S. interest rates. At the June 1982 EC summit in Brussels, Tindemans advocated the launching of a new transatlantic dialogue with the United States. During this same period, Tindemans embarked on a major initiative to restart Arab-Israeli peace negotiations in a tour of the Middle East. He remained a key force in the promotion of an Arab-Israeli peace conference in the late 1980s.

In 1984, Tindemans launched a campaign to revitalize Benelux relations on the fortieth anniversary of the Benelux agreement. Fearing that the smaller countries in the EC could be undermined by the Franco-German axis, Tindemans sought to reinforce relations among the three countries by promoting coordination of Benelux positions prior to EC Council of Minister meetings. That same year, the Belgian government was forced to reckon with the NATO dual track decision to deploy cruise missiles. Faced with widespread domestic opposition, Tindemans undertook a series of consultations with NATO allies to find a politically acceptable way to adhere to the deployment schedule. In March 1985, the Belgian government agreed to uphold the NATO commitment—but not before Tindemans went to Moscow to encourage the Soviet government to take actions that might delay the initial sixteen-missile deployment.

In 1985, Tindemans helped to negotiate the Single European Act (SEA), which introduced significant changes to the EC Treaty of Rome—many of which were similar to those called for by Tindemans in his 1975 report. Two years later, he successfully directed another EC summit during which the heads of state and government agreed to end an EC deadlock over farm prices and reached a temporary agreement on a research framework program.

In 1988, to many observers' surprise, Prime Minister Martens kept Tindemans on in his newly created government. The two CVP men continued to have strong differences over budgetary concerns and regional issues. The wrangling over Belgian relations with Zaire proved to be the most contentious matter. Tindemans found that an increasing number of political decisions were taken outside of his control.

In June 1989, the day after he was elected again to the European Parliament, Tindemans resigned from the Martens government. Having turned his political ambitions to Europe, Tindemans openly campaigned for its presidency. Once again, his bid was unsuccessful as Egon Klepsch, a fellow Christian Democrat from Germany, won a fairly easy victory. Tindemans took over Klepsch's position as leader of the EPP. He remains one of the most visible and highly regarded members of the European Parliament.

Throughout his political career, Tindemans was viewed by the Belgian populace as an honest, hardworking, prudent individual who made decisions with care. He was the great compromiser, a politician that inspired confidence and respect. At the same time, Tindemans was not a passionate leader with a reputation for dynamism and novel ideas. Admirers called him trustworthy; opponents labeled him indecisive. Perhaps to a fault, Tindemans was also a dedicated party man. His personal nature would not permit him to make deals with party leadership. Yet, in his faithfulness to the party, he would agree to party positions with which he disagreed most. In the end, it was Tindemans's party that twice pushed him from national office.

Despite his important report on European union, Tindemans was never considered a dominating figure in European affairs. This reputation was due not only to his straightforward working manner, but also to the fact that he was from one of the smaller European countries. His steadfast devotion to the European Community and behind-the-scenes negotiations, however, cannot be overlooked.

BIBLIOGRAPHY

Works by Tindemans:

Een Handvest voor woelig België. Lier, Belgium: Van In, 1972.

Dagboek van de werkgroep Eyskens. Lier, Belgium: Van In, 1973.

Open Brief aan Gaston Eyskens. Tielt, Belgium: Lannoo, 1979.

Atlantische Europa: Frans van Cauwelaert en de Europese eenmaking. Louvain, Belgium: Davidsfonds, 1981.

Europa zonder kompas. Antwerp: Standard Uitgeverij, 1987.

Other Works:

de Winter, Noël. *Leo Tindemans: Les Ricochets d'un destin*. Paris: F. Nathan; Brussels: Editions Labor, 1980.

Lijphart, A. (ed). *Conflict and Coexistence in Belgium*. Berkeley: Institute of International Studies, University of California at Berkeley, 1981.

MARIA GREEN COWLES

PALMIRO TOGLIATTI (1893–1964) was the undisputed head of the Italian Communist Party from the mid–1920s until his death. He was the object of a veritable personality cult by party activists and was esteemed and obeyed rather than loved by other leaders of his party. Even his political adversaries admired his deep intellect and political intelligence.

Togliatti was a principal player on the Italian political scene in a period of many crucial developments. These included the rise and consolidation of fascism, the war on the side of Germany, the armistice with the Anglo-American forces and the struggle of the Italian Resistance movement. After the war a referendum established the Italian Republic with a constituent assembly, economic reconstruction got under way and Italy joined NATO. Finally, during the early 1960s, there was the advent of industrial expansion and the growth of consumption with the general transformation of Italian society and the Socialists' debut in government.

The Italian Communist Party (PCI) had in the meantime evolved from a small organization at its founding with a few thousand followers into a large popular party with more than a million card-carrying members and a greater than 20 percent share of the vote. During this period, the party followed the political line laid down by Togliatti. For a year early in the postwar period, from June 1945 to June 1946, he served in the government as minister of justice.

Togliatti was also a figure of international stature. For a number of decades he played an important role in the Communist International (CI). Admitted to the tight circle of Stalin's collaborators, he was made a member of the Comintern secretariat from 1934 until its dissolution in 1943. During the postwar period, he remained one of the Western leaders most consulted by the Soviet leadership. He always claimed to be both an original Marxist ideologue and a responsible national leader, free from foreign pressure. Nonetheless, his ideas and policies, while often the fruit of farsighted personal reflections, evinced, or at least sought to accommodate, the guiding principle of obedience to the internal and international needs of the Soviet Union.

From the beginning of his activity in the PCI, he realized that the events of the October Revolution could not be reproduced in Italy in the same way as in the Soviet Union or with similar consequences. He probably remained convinced of this until the very end of his life, and he often wavered between strict revolutionary discipline and the prospect of an ''Italian way'' toward socialism. However, when, as was inevitable, these two paths collided, he always chose to reinforce the iron link with Moscow.

Today Togliatti is recognized as one of the founding fathers of the Italian Republic. A leader of rare ability, he was also a model of political duplicity. In his own way, he was a tragic character. Almost thirty years after his death, he is still the subject of political debate in Italy. With Togliatti, historical evaluation and political judgment cannot leave moral questions out of the equation.

Togliatti was born in Genoa, in March 1893, to a lower-middle-class, very religious family. His father was an accountant and his mother was a schoolmistress. His father's work provided a relatively poor standard of living, and as a result the Togliattis were forced to move from time to time. Togliatti finished his secondary education at Sassari in Sardinia. In 1911 he won a grant that allowed him to matriculate at the University of Turin and to graduate with a law degree.

At that time, Turin was a very lively city, both culturally and politically. Large industrial complexes were established there, soon characterized by a highly unionized work force. At the university Togliatti met many socialist students such as Umberto Terracini, Angelo Tasca and Antonio Gramsci, with whom he was to spend a good part of his political career. He also joined the Italian Socialist Party (PSI) in 1914, but soon became disillusioned with it as he did not approve of its neutral stance at the outbreak of war. He subsequently enlisted as a Red Cross nurse.

In 1917 he returned to the PSI and began to contribute to different party newspapers. His true political apprenticeship, however, was to begin two years later with the founding of the journal *L'Ordine Nuovo* together with Gramsci, Tasca and Terracini. The Ordine Nuovo group performed an important role in preparing the ground for the birth of the PCI, which was to break away from the PSI in January 1921.

At this point, Togliatti did not yet hold a high-ranking position in the party. The true leader of the party during its first years was the Neapolitan engineer Amadeo Bordiga. He saw the Italian political situation in simplistic terms: Fascism was at the gates, and he believed that conditions were mature for a proletarian revolution. Intransigent and fractious, Bordiga refused to follow the policy guidelines laid down by the CI, which called for tactical collaboration with the Socialists. Because of this, Moscow ordered his removal in 1924.

Antonio Gramsci, in complete accord with the policy of a united front, was then nominated political secretary of the PCI. It was Gramsci who chose Togliatti as party representative to the CI. During this period, this was an extremely delicate position, given that the Soviets had shown that they intended to intervene directly in the internal affairs of the Italian Communist Party.

During this historical period, the Soviet Union was surrounded and threatened; as a result, Togliatti and Gramsci believed in the duty of revolutionary discipline. They also believed, however, that this obligation did not contradict the right to independently propose the best political analyses and strategies to be applied to Italy, a country already fallen into the fascist camp. Furthermore, while they admitted that the Soviet Communist Party had a permanent role within the International, they did not believe that this should impinge on the dignity of the other member parties.

During the first part of his stay in the USSR, which lasted from February 1926 to January 1927, Togliatti followed this policy in perfect accord with Gramsci. Of course, as long as the policies of the PCI coincided with those of the CI, Italian Communist Party leaders would not be in conflict. However, the moment of truth was about to arrive. During the spring of 1927, Togliatti moved to Paris, where the PCI, like all other antifascist Italian parties, had been forced to transfer its headquarters.

In Paris, Togliatti carried out the duties of sole party secretary. Gramsci had been arrested at the end of 1926 and imprisoned, and although he had not been put completely out of action by Mussolini, he refused to share any political responsibility with his old friend and fellow comrade. Their paths were to irredeemably part in October 1926 when Togliatti refused to pass on one of Gramsci's letters to Moscow in which Gramsci expressed his preoccupation with and reservations about the methods used by Stalin to wipe out the opposition of Trotsky, Zinovyev and Kamenev within the Soviet Communist Party. Gramsci realized at the time, both before and better than anyone else, that Togliatti was abandoning the common ideological and political ground that they had shared up until then.

Togliatti's tilt toward Moscow went a step further in the summer of 1928 when Bukharin and Stalin fought over the Soviet leadership at the sixth congress of the CI. Togliatti was closer to Bukharin's politics, but when he realized that Bukharin had been defeated, he did not hesitate to make a sudden about-face and abandon him.

The tenth plenum of the International was the congress which in July 1929 enshrined obedience to Stalin. On that occasion a new political catchphrase was launched for the affiliated Communist parties. There was no longer to be a "united front," but rather a "sruggle against social-fascism." The change signified that former Socialist allies would henceforth be considered part and parcel of fascist movements and governments.

Togliatti himself did not have any faith in the validity of this new tactic or in the political analysis behind it. Nonetheless, he adopted the new approach and publicly declared that all doubts and misgivings should cease in the face of the wishes of the International (read: Stalin). Togliatti expected the same compliance from PCI activists. Those who did not conform were isolated, like Terracini and Gramsci, in prison or were expelled with ignominy from the party, as with Tasca, Bordiga and the writer Ignazio Silone, to name but a few. By renouncing his own right to criticize and indeed his own freedom of thought, Togliatti was to achieve ever higher promotions within the Communist International hierarchy, indeed right to the very top with his election as secretary.

It would be too simplistic to put his motives down to ambition or desire for a career. Possibly, given Stalin's brutal means of physically eliminating any possible opponent or enemy, Togliatti had to consider saving his own skin. But even this explanation does not fully account for Togliatti's "Stalinization," and through him, that of the entire PCI, a process completed by the end of the 1920s and reinforced during the 1930s.

In fact Togliatti had very plain reasons for hewing to Stalin's line: First, given the general European crisis of the period, any hope of turning back the expansion of fascism and securing a future of peace and social justice for the peoples of Europe had to be entrusted to the Soviet Union. Any sacrifice, any renunciation, indeed any crime was legitimate to defend and reinforce the mother country of socialism.

Second, given the situation within the International and in the presence of a determined and ruthless Stalin, absolute leader of the communist movement, the Italians had constantly to conform, obey and even show fervor to save themselves as individuals and as a party. These expedients, while politically coherent and even understandable, given their historical context, led Togliatti to commit unforgivable deeds, ethically quite unacceptable. The Stalinist purges, the witch-hunt for the "enemies of the Revolution," the trials and ideological justifications given for the sentences, often death penalties, gave witness to the fact that Togliatti was not simply an enforcer of these acts, but also a person directly responsible for them.

This was so for the anarchists of the Spanish Civil War, where Togliatti worked from July 1937 to April 1939 as the envoy of the Communist International. Togliatti also acted against the leaders of the German, Yugoslav, Hungarian and Polish Communist parties and even against his own comrades in the Italian Communist Party who were living in Russia in those years. His second period in Moscow (1934–1937, 1939–1944) casts a long shadow over his whole political career and inevitably overshadows his merits.

Even his political successors admitted this, albeit rather late, somewhat vaguely and indirectly during Enrico Berlinguer's tenure as secretary of the PCI (1972–1984) and more explicitly after the birth of the Democratic Party of the

Left from the ashes of the old PCI in 1991. The reasons for such reluctance to engage in self-criticism, which still survive, are not only found in the traditional attitudes of parts of the Italian left but also in the two faces of Togliatti, one Stalinist and the other democratic and reformist.

Indeed, from 1933–1934, when the International opened its new campaign for the popular front, Togliatti returned to the subject of national paths to socialism and began to reflect on the value of democracy. It was only when Hitler took power that the social-fascist approach was abandoned.

In July 1935, for example, Togliatti drafted a report, along with Georgij Dimitrov, which was approved by the sixth congress of the Communist International. The report called upon all communists to fight with other anti-fascist forces to defend and reestablish democracy everywhere. This call to action was not only motivated by principle, but also by the international political situation of the Soviet Union, which was trying to move closer to France and Great Britain against Germany. Togliatti was one of the most credible and effective promoters of this new policy, making a fundamental contribution to creating a positive image for communist parties as forces for democracy, especially in France with the Blum government and in Republican Spain, threatened by the Franchists.

On the other hand, at the same time Togliatti was also sitting in judgment on Stalin's ideological tribunals, and the myth of the Soviet Union as sole bulwark against fascism was being perfected. After the Molotov-Ribbentrop Pact was signed in August 1939, Togliatti had to make a brusque about-face, abandoning his propaganda on democracy and brandishing the theme of the struggle against Anglo-French imperialism.

It was only after the German attack on the Soviet Union in June 1941 that the policy of a broad antifascist alliance was reinstated by the Soviet Communist Party and appeared in the directives of the Communist International. Under the pseudonym of Mario Correnti on Radio Milano-Libertà, a station which broadcasted clandestinely from Moscow, Togliatti made forceful speeches to Italian listeners, beseeching them to rebel against Mussolini. Then, in June 1943, Stalin disbanded the Communist International to prove his trustworthiness to the Anglo-Americans.

In practice, relations between the Communist Party of the Soviet Union and the other communist parties did not change. Nonetheless, this symbolic act was useful to Togliatti, who was able to return to the idea, often blocked before, of adapting socialist values to the particular historical, cultural and socioeconomic conditions of individual countries. On his return to Italy in March 1944, Togliatti portrayed himself as a crusader for the principles of national independence, freedom and democracy.

At this moment, Italy was undergoing a grave crisis. It had been split into two areas, the north being occupied by the Germans and governed by Mussolini's puppet government, the south having been liberated by the Allies and governed by the king and General Badoglio, who had signed the armistice on September 3, 1943. Civil strife broke out, however, when the antifascist parties, the PCI, the PSI, the Christian Democrats (Catholics), the Liberal Party (conservatives), the Action Party (liberal-progressives) and Labour Democracy (liberal moderates) all formed the Committee of National Liberation (CLN). This organization claimed to be the sole legitimate government in Italy, opposed to Victor Emmanuel III for his role in the rise of Mussolini.

In fact, by spring 1944 the CLN was clearly powerless, internally divided and not recognized by the Allies. Togliatti's intervention, however, rapidly changed this situation. In a speech made at Salerno he announced that the PCI was ready to collaborate with Badoglio, and he asked the other antifascists to put aside all doubts and quarrels. The liberation of Italy from the Nazis/Fascists was the first priority, he argued, and subsequently Italy could choose between monarchy and republic. He also stated firmly that the PCI would become a new party, open to all social groups, without prejudice regarding class, religion or ideology. Finally, he promised that Italian Communists did not have in the least the objective of a dictatorship of the proletariat, but rather would work for a "progressive democracy," that is, a lawful, pluralistic and multiparty state with a parliamentary government. If such a system fully respected democratic processes, the working class would obtain a central role.

The speech became known as the "turning point of Salerno," and its effects were important. By joining the Badoglio government, the parties of the CLN were fully recognized by the Anglo-Americans. For the PCI, the "turning point of Salerno," together with the massive role of its members in the ranks of the Resistance, legitimized the party as a governing force and earned it the approval of large and varied sectors of the population.

At the fifth congress of the PCI, its first legal one, in December 1945, Togliatti laid down his political program even more explicitly. He abandoned proposals for a planned economy, while underlining his commitment to social harmony and respect for law. Finally, he stated that he was convinced that economic reconstruction, the adoption of a new constitution and, generally, social progress and economic stability could only come about with a stable government based on a common understanding between the political parties enjoying the greatest popular support, that is, the Christian Democrats, the Socialist Party and the Communist Party.

For a year and a half, from December 1945 to May 1947, Italy was governed by an antifascist coalition in which these three parties had the greatest influence, and Togliatti kept the PCI within the limits he had set out. The day of the constitutional referendum, June 2, 1946, the votes collected by Communist campaigners were important in assuring the victory of republic over monarchy.

Clearly, Togliatti's greatest achievements were accomplished during this delicate phase of historical transition for Italy. It cannot be disputed that his party made a vital contribution to the broad democratic constitutional framework. Furthermore, it cannot be denied that he succeeded in stopping or at least limiting insurrections and unlawful protests carried out by some parts of the PCI.

Yet Togliatti had no intention of losing the trust of the PCI activists, most of whom were partisans of the Resistance, who had fought for the revolutionary dream. For this reason, he adopted his habitual double-faced policy. Thus he both condemned and repressed support for rebellion, while hinting that his policy was a matter of political necessity and that it masked his true objectives. And as if this were not enough, he allowed, or at least did not hinder, the party's military style of internal structure. This was not for revolutionary purposes, which he did not believe possible or even desirable, but rather for self-defense in case of an authoritarian takeover of the country, something which could not be altogether ruled out in the very earliest years after the war.

Togliatti's counterparts and especially his political adversaries noted these ambiguities. Industrialists and the Vatican put pressure especially on the Christian Democratic Party to break up the governing alliance with the left. Subsequently, the prime minister and leader of the Christian Democrats, Alcide De Gasperi, did so when he considered the moment to be ripe. Such an outcome, in any case, could have been forecast given the new context of the international Cold War.

From May 1947, Togliatti led a party which was permanently in the opposition. The exclusion of the Italian Communist Party from every subsequent postwar government (until the disintegration of the Soviet Union) was largely justified given Togliatti's policy choices after that date. On a national policy level, he refused to change the direction of the PCI and kept it within legal bounds, as for example during the acute tension which followed the attempt on his life on July 14, 1948. However, his total obedience to Moscow after the creation of Cominform in September 1947 belied the credibility of the formally democratic and reformist policies of the PCI and banished it to the political wilderness.

In the 1950s, Togliatti was convinced that world peace was threatened by American imperialism and that the only hope of salvation for mankind was the USSR. Indeed, Togliatti had no qualms in justifying a number of harsh authoritarian measures: the end of Western communist parties' autonomy, suppression of democracy and freedom in the Eastern Bloc countries, banning the Yugoslav leader Tito in 1948, the repression of the Hungarian revolt in 1956 and the sentencing of those who had inspired it.

However, Togliatti was surprised when Khrushchev denounced Stalin's crimes at the twentieth congress of the Soviet Communist Party, and he adopted a reticent profile. Togliatti considered this initiative by the Soviet secretary general to be badly timed and rash. From his point of yiew it would make the world more unstable and it weakened the image of the USSR, while the United States continued to increase its power. At that point even the Italian Socialist Party, which had been politically allied with the Italian Communist Party since 1943, distanced itself from Togliatti and began working toward becoming part of a coalition government with the Christian Democrats.

It was only in the very last years of his life that Togliatti seemed to recognize some errors of political judgment. In his ''Yalta Memorial,'' written only a few days before his death in August 1964, Togliatti formulated very clearly the ideas that each country had its own path to follow toward socialism and that there could be ''unity in diversity'' between the communist parties of the West and the East. In this, he summoned the courage to take a step forward, but still refused to cast doubt on the foundations of proletarian internationalism. For Togliatti, this eternal contradiction was never to be resolved.

BIBLIOGRAPHY

Work by Togliatti:

Opere, 6 vols. Rome: Editori Riuniti, 1973–1984.

Other Works:

Blackmer, Donald L. M. *Unity in Diversity: Italian Communism and the Communist World.* Cambridge, Mass.: MIT Press, 1968.

Bocca, Giorgio. *Palmiro Togliatti.* Bari: Laterza, 1973.

DiLoreto, Pietro. *Togliatti e la doppiezza: Il PCI fra democrazia e insurrezione 1944–1949.* Bologna: Il Mulino, 1991.

Sassoon, Donald. *The Strategy of the Italian Communist Party from the Resistance to Historic Compromise.* London: Frances Pinter, 1981.

Vacca, Giuseppe. *Gramsci e Togliatti.* Rome: Editori Riuniti, 1991.

MARINA TESORO

V

FRANZ VRANITZKY (1937–), leader of the Austrian Social Democratic Party (SPÖ—Sozialdemokratische Partei Österreichs) since 1988, became federal chancellor of the Austrian government in June 1986, at the head of an SPÖ-FPÖ coalition. Reacting to the right-populist shift of the FPÖ (Freedom Party of Austria) under its new leader, Jörg Haider, elected in September 1986, and to parliamentary elections in November 1986, Vranitzky linked the SPÖ to a "Grand Coalition" with the ÖVP (Austrian People's Party), the major nonsocialist party, located center-right, in January 1987. Since then Austria has been governed by a Vranitzky-led SPÖ-ÖVP coalition.

Franz Vranitzky was born in Vienna on October 4, 1937. His origins are rooted deeply in the blue-collar working class. In the late 19th-century the Vranitzky family migrated from Czechoslovakia, at that time part of the Austro-Hungarian Empire, to Vienna, the fast-growing imperial capital. Vranitzky's father was a foundry worker who developed very close ties to the labor movement. In reaction to a number of political events—the rise of fascism in the 1930s, the crackdown on Austrian parliamentarism and the implementation of the authoritarian *Ständestaat* from 1933 to 1938 by the conservative Christlichsoziale Partei (Christian Social Party)—Vranitzky's father became a communist, although later in life he converted back to socialism.

In 1938, when Franz Vranitzky was one year old, Austria was annexed by Nazi Germany (the *Anschluss*, which was supported by a large segment of the Austrian population). At that time, the Vranitzky family lived in very poor economic circumstances in a basement apartment of a house owned by a committed National Socialist. Vranitzky's father was drafted for service in World War II, and his mother carried on with the family during the war.

From these difficult childhood years, two interesting observations can be drawn for the later Franz Vranitzky: First, his family's strong anti-Nazi commitment developed in him a deep distrust of the far right. In this lie the roots of his distancing himself from the FPÖ under the leadership of the rightist Jörg Haider in the 1980s and 1990s. Second, in Vranitzky's successful career subsequently, one finds a typical example of a *sozialer Aufsteiger*—a ''self-made man''—who manages a breakthrough despite a low socioeconomic background.

Following the advice of one of his elementary school teachers, his parents enrolled Vranitzky in high school. He attended the Gymnasium Gablergasse in the seventeenth Viennese district, finishing in 1955. Afterward, Vranitzky studied international economics at the University Hochschule für Welthandel in Vienna, graduating in 1960. Later, while working full-time, he also decided to take a doctoral program, completing his dissertation in 1969.

In 1961, Vranitzky began work at the Austrian National Bank. In February 1962 he became a card-carrying member of the SPÖ. In that year he also married. Vranitzky stayed at the Austrian National Bank until 1970, when he was appointed by Hannes Androsch, at that time minister of finance in the SPÖ government, to a position in the ministry. Vranitzky worked at Finance until 1976 and then returned to banking: From 1976 to 1981, Vranitzky was part of the top management team of the Creditanstalt-Bankverein. From there, he moved to the Länderbank, where he became general director from April 1981 to 1984. In 1984, Vranitzky was called back into politics to serve as the Austrian finance minister.

For Austria, Franz Vranitzky represents a new and ''modern'' style of socialist. After a period of stability in the 1970s under the leadership of Bruno Kreisky (1967–1983), the SPÖ was faced with serious challenges in the 1980s. In the 1983 elections, the party lost its parliamentary majority and faced the necessity of coalition governance. In addition, the Austrian political agenda of the 1980s became reshaped by the impact of neo-conservatives (although not so significantly as in the Anglo-American countries). This shift, of course, did not work in favor of traditional socialist concepts.

Vranitzky's political task therefore was to adapt the SPÖ to this new political environment, bringing his party closer to a center-left orientation in order to improve its electoral competitiveness. In this, he was very successful, for in the 1986 and 1990 elections the SPÖ stabilized its position as the strongest party in Austria. This move toward the center was symbolically manifest in the decision to change the SPÖ label from ''socialist'' to ''social democratic'' in June 1991.

Moreover, in 1989 Austria applied for membership in the European Community and was admitted in 1995. In the long process of negotiating EC membership, Austria was required to make some changes in its constitution in addition to taking certain policy steps. As these changes required broad parliamentary support, there was not much room for any governing coalition apart from a center-oriented one, almost forcing the SPÖ and ÖVP to work together. And following the defeat of the Social Democratic candidate in the presidential elections of 1992, Vranitzky must once again concentrate on reinforcing the electoral competitiveness of the SPÖ.

In Austria the state and the banking industries are heavily intertwined. Nonetheless, Vranitzky's career path has been very unusual. Vranitzky has always had close ties to the SPÖ, but his early political career did not follow normal traditions. He did not come from the unions or other grassroots socialist movements. He preferred moving up through the top management of the Austrian banking system. Moreover, Vranitzky as manager, competent on economic issues, reflects precisely the image of the "new socialism" of the 1980s and 1990s.

Policy making with a professional managerial style turned out to be an effective calling card for a modern information society, where the selling of politics depends heavily on the mass media. In addition to his managerial image, Franz Vranitzky has benfited from a second advantage: His career was not too closely associated with the SPÖ, especially in the sense that he did not occupy a publicly visible position in the party bureaucracy.

In this, Vranitzky built up an image as "career hopper," along with the almost paradoxical situation of being publicly distant from his own party. *Manager* and *career hopper* are terms that successfully describe Vranitzky's political career, which has even earned him the label *Nadelstreif-Sozialist* ("pin-striped suit socialist"). As one observer reported to the author—in a play on words with the color red, symbolic for the socialist movement—Vranitzky is not red wine, but a pale rosé, at most.

Originally founded in the late 19th century as the Social Democratic Worker's Party of Austria, the SPÖ enjoyed its greatest successes under the leadership of Bruno Kreisky (1967–1983). From 1970 until 1983, there was a single-party SPÖ government. In the elections of 1971, 1975 and 1979 the SPÖ won an absolute majority of seats in the lower, dominant chamber of parliament, the Nationalrat, in the period 1971–1983.

The 1983 elections, however, brought new dynamics into the Austrian political system. The SPÖ lost its absolute parliamentary majority, its electoral support dropping from 51 percent in 1979 to 47.6 percent. Kreisky resigned as SPÖ party leader, leaving behind a twofold legacy. First, he initiated the SPÖ-FPÖ coalition, and second, he orchestrated the election of Fred Sinowatz as new federal chancellor (1983–1986) and SPÖ party leader (1983–1988). In September 1984 Sinowatz appointed Franz Vranitzky minister of finance. Political observers emphasize that it was Sinowatz, personally, and not Kreisky, who "discovered" Vranitzky in this crucial phase.

In the 1980s, the SPÖ was confronted with a series of challenges as the political environment became more complicated. Two general trends were apparent: First, the dominant position of the two catchall parties, SPÖ and ÖVP, began to erode. Greater electoral volatility and a growing tendency to vote for small parties implied that the "age of absolute majorities" in Austrian politics had come to an end. Vranitzky was keenly sensitive to this trend.

Second, the impact of the neo-conservative movement reshaped the Austrian political agenda. As elsewhere, the neo-conservatives criticized state intervention in economic affairs, and their critique caused market economy concepts to gain ground in Austrian public opinion. The image of the nationalized industries in Austria suffered a massive decline in opinion polls, and the idea of privatization won greater support. In this context it also should be mentioned that the *Sozialpartnerschaft* (Social Partnership), a corporatist network structure that mediates between the interests of the major parties and between the state and the private sector, came under some pressure, although a large majority still supports the *Sozialpartnerschaft* in principle. These trends put substantial pressure on the SPÖ, forcing it to adapt to the necessity of political coalitions and formulate a response to the neo-conservative critique.

In the mid-1980s, pressures on the SPÖ and its SPÖ-FPÖ coalition increased. The ÖVP position in opinion polls strengthened and, from December 1985 through much of 1986, it held a substantial lead over the SPÖ. Moreover, in the Austrian presidential election of June 1986, Kurt Waldheim, the ÖVP candidate, won overwhelmingly with 53.9 percent of the votes. At this crucial juncture, Sinowatz made a strategic calculation. He stepped down as head of the federal government and brought in Franz Vranitzky as his replacement. Vranitzky assumed office as federal chancellor on June 16, 1986. In September of the same year, the rightist Jörg Haider assumed the leadership of the FPÖ. With this development, Vranitzky decided to abandon the SPÖ's coalition with the FPÖ, and general elections were called for November 1986.

It was the first serious political test for Vranitzky and the outcome was quite surprising. Against the expectations of many observers and the predictions of opinion polls, the SPÖ won the 1986 election. While, indeed, the electoral base of the SPÖ declined to 43.1 percent (from 47.6 percent in 1983), the ÖVP finished with an even smaller share of the national vote, 41.3 percent (as compared to 43.2 percent in 1983). This "relative victory" of the SPÖ was explained by Vranitzky's own popularity. During this period, he enjoyed much higher approval ratings than his party, whereas the ÖVP, as a party, was supported by a higher percentage of those polled than its leader, Alois Mock.

In January 1987, a "Grand Coalition" was formed between the SPÖ and the ÖVP, with the SPÖ accorded the dominant position and Vranitzky continuing to serve as federal chancellor. This new center coalition was consonant with the mainstream of Austrian public opinion. In one poll, for example, 45 percent of respondents preferred this SPÖ-ÖVP Grand Coalition, 12 percent an ÖVP-FPÖ coalition, and only 15 percent a continuation of the former SPÖ-FPÖ coalition. Despite the objections of Bruno Kreisky, who still held a position as "honorary leader" of the SPÖ and favored continuing the SPÖ-FPÖ coalition, Vranitzky acted with great determination in putting together the Grand Coalition. This was one reason that the relationship between Kreisky and Vranitzky remained quite problematic until Kreisky's death in July 1990.

In all this, Vranitzky was clearly the SPÖ's "trump card" in the crucial 1986 elections, which it had been expected to lose. Internally during this period, and until 1988, the SPÖ followed a two-tier power distribution: While Vranitzky served as federal chancellor, Sinowatz continued to be party leader. Within the

SPÖ, there was still some concern regarding Vranitzky's banker image, and Sinowatz was able to maintain party cohesion, while assuring good communication between the SPÖ party apparatus and the government. However, building public popularity upon his electoral success, Vranitzky gradually increased his support base within the party, while Sinowatz's public popularity began to decline. In the end, Sinowatz resigned the party leadership and supported Vranitzky as his successor. At an extraordinary party conference, called in May 1988, Vranitzky was elected new party leader with 93.6 percent of the votes.

Beginning with 1986, Vranitzky succeeded in slowing the erosion of the SPÖ that had begun in the early and mid–1980s. The elections of 1990 were another crucial test, and they confirmed Vranitzky's approach. With 42.8 percent of the votes for the SPÖ, Vranitzky had managed to stabilize the SPÖ's electorate. At the same time, the ÖVP suffered its most severe setback, dropping to an all-time low of 32.1 percent, while the FPÖ expanded its electoral base to 16.6 percent, up from 9.7 percent in 1986.

This widened gap between the SPÖ and the ÖVP carried the implicit danger that the ÖVP might leave the center coalition, as its showing could be interpreted as a repudiation by the electorate. However, in December 1990 the SPÖ-ÖVP coalition was renewed for another legislative period, with Vranitzky continuing to serve as chancellor. Once again the mainstream of Austrian public opinion endorsed this arrangement. According to one poll, 54 percent of respondents wanted to see the Grand Coalition continued. Other possible coalitions found only marginal approval, with only 3 percent supporting an SPÖ-FPÖ coalition and 7 percent supporting an ÖVP-FPÖ coalition.

In these coalitions with the ÖVP, Vranitzky followed a policy mix of semisocialist and semiconservative approaches. On the one hand, he emphasized the necessity of market economy concepts; on the other hand, he argued that these should be embedded in the framework of a modern welfare system. For him, the functioning of the market economy should be smoothed out and made more efficient by incorporating the basic elements of social welfare. Whereas earlier socialist governments, such as those under Kreisky, did discuss the relative gains of a more or less market economy and the impact on social welfare, Vranitzky's message was very clear: Only a prosperous economy provides the necessary support for a social welfare system. Thus the logic of free market economics must be taken seriously.

Unemployment is a good example of Vranitzky's approach. For the pre-Vranitzky socialists, a low unemployment rate was the central axiom of policy making, even at the price of an increased national debt. With Vranitzky and the Grand Coalitions that he headed, a certain amount of unemployment, and even slight increases, were tolerable or even necessary for consolidating the budget. Indeed, budgetary discipline became a notably more important priority than before. In the period from 1986 to 1992, the Austrian federal debt was stabilized and inflation was brought under greater control. Unemployment, however, increased during the same period. In addition, nationalized industries and public enterprises in general were restructured, and some of them were privatized. In short, Vranitzky's governments followed a line of market economics injected with some ''soft'' socialism. Above all, as evident in his 1986 election campaign, one of his central issues was the modernization of Austria and its economy. Indeed, two Austrian political scientists, Fritz Plasser and Peter A. Ulram, have described Vranitzky's approach as the ''ideology of modernization.''

The process of becoming receptive to market economics was part of the streamlining program that Vranitzky designed for the SPÖ so that it could survive in a more conservative political environment. His basic political task was to increase the electoral competitiveness of the SPÖ against the nonsocialist parties. Opinion polls confirm that the public perceived that during the period 1976–1992 the SPÖ shifted from a left to a center-left party.

This perception also holds true within the SPÖ. In a culmination of this shift at the 1991 party conference, the SPÖ changed its name from the Socialist Party of Austria (Sozialistische Partei Österreichs) to the Social Democratic Party of Austria (Sozialdemokratische Partei Österreichs), but kept the abbreviation SPÖ. Franz Vranitzky was one of the main architects behind this decision, for in contemporary Western Europe the label *social democratic* is perceived as less left than *socialist.* Thus, in reaction to the neo-conservative agenda and a general decline of ''hard socialist'' concepts among public opinion, especially in the aftermath of the collapse of communism in Eastern Europe from 1989 to 1991, the logic of attracting votes leads increasingly to replacing *socialist* with the concept *social democratic.*

Nonetheless, the new ''social democratic'' image of the SPÖ could be interpreted in two ways: either aimed at a distancing of the party from traditional left-leaning socialism or a hearkening back of the party to its interwar history, when the Socialists called themselves *Sozialdemokraten.* These Social Democrats of the 1920s and 1930s, however, whose ideology was described as ''Austromarxism,'' were clearly leftist. In this, Vranitzky has indicated implicitly that with the label *social democratic* he did not want to revive older leftist concepts, but to draw a clear distance against too-left leaning ideas and policy approaches. During the thirty-second party conference, he refused to qualify the SPÖ as a ''left catchall party'' (*linke Volkspartei*). In addition, when asked directly by the author, Vranitzky emphasized that with *social democratic* he wished to underline the democratic traditions of the SPÖ.

This shift to the center-left by the SPÖ under Vranitzky has manifested itself on another crucial issue, that of Austria joining the European Community (EC). In July 1989, the SPÖ-ÖVP coalition government officially applied for EC membership. Several factors led to this decision. First, the EC single market, targeted for implementation by December 31, 1992, led to fears in Austria that it would be excluded from this market. Second, party elites within the coalition partner ÖVP had developed very strong pro-EC attitudes. Third, Vranitzky's assumption of the SPÖ party leadership marked the victory of the party's ''modernization wing'' over the more traditional Socialists. Part of Vranitzky's strategy in modernizing the SPÖ involved bringing the party onto a pro-EC path.

The SPÖ's shift on the EC also corresponded to changing Austrian public opinion. In a poll from 1988 the ''membership issue'' followed a clear left/right political cleavage: The more left the respondent was, the more he or she rejected the EC. In a comparable poll in 1991, the political equation had changed: SPÖ and ÖVP partisans supported EC membership the most, FPÖ voters were divided and supporters of the Greens kept their critical distance. Along a traditional left/right ideological continuum, this implies that it is mainly the political center which supports membership in the EC, whereas the left and right ''edges'' reject such attempts.

After evaluating Austria's application, the European Community agreed officially in July 1991 to begin membership talks with Austria in 1993. The issue of EC membership has shaped much of Austrian politics from the late 1980s into the early 1990s. Two aspects are central: First, joining the EC would require changes in the Austrian constitution. In Austria, constitutional amendments must be approved by a minimum of two-thirds of the Austrian parliament. Second, the Austrian government had decided, if membership is approved by the EC, to put the question to a national referendum. Opinion polls for the period 1987–1991 clearly showed that what was originally a large margin of support for EC membership had declined to a narrow lead for EC supporters.

For both Franz Vranitzky and the ÖVP, this evolution introduced a number of constraints, not allowing much room for maneuver in putting together political coalitions. Alternatives to the Grand Coalition did not appear very realistic or viable. The necessity of two-thirds parliamentary approval for constitutional amendments and of a majority vote in the referendum on ratification of EC membership linked the SPÖ and ÖVP tightly to each other. In all this, it was very difficult for Vranitzky to bypass the ÖVP. This holds equally true for the ÖVP and its coalition options regarding the SPÖ. Once the EC approved Austria's application for membership for 1995, the referendum could then take place. Until that time, much of Austrian politics had to follow, at least de facto, the logic of the ''Grand Coalition'' pattern. In addition to these factors, the rightist drift of the FPÖ and its unstable and populistic zigzag course under its leader, Jörg Haider, have also worked to stabilize the Grand Coalition. In the event, Austrian voters approved accession to the EC in late 1994.

Where Vranitzky has emphasized a different policy line from the ÖVP is the issue of Austria's neutrality, which it declared in 1955 as part of regaining its sovereignty from the Allied powers. In contrast to the ÖVP, which regards neutrality as incompatible with contemporary Europe, Vranitzky has been more cautious, at least in public discourse, on the question of how to deal with the neutrality issue.

In this respect, Vranitzky is also confronted with greater electoral constraints. Opinion polls show that SPÖ voters are the most ardent supporters of neutrality. Of course, de facto, with the collapse of Eastern European communism, European geopolitics have changed dramatically. Vranitzky and his coalition partner, the ÖVP, have therefore come perforce closer together. With the end of the Cold War era, Austria's neutrality must be redefined and readjusted. Here Vranitzky has spoken of embedding Austria and its neutral status in a "collective security system."

In 1992, the Austrian political climate became, once again, more complicated for Vranitzky and the SPÖ. The previous year, Erhard Busek was elected the new ÖVP party leader. Since then, the ÖVP has increased its electoral appeal significantly. During the presidential elections of April/May 1992, the candidate of the ÖVP, Thomas Klestil, overwhelmingly defeated his SPÖ opponent, Rudolf Streicher, in the second ballot with 56.85 percent of the votes. Then in June 1992, Franz Fiedler of the ÖVP was appointed by parliamentary vote, with backing of the FPÖ, the new director of the Austrian Rechnungshof, the agency that controls the state administration and its budgetary operations. And in municipal elections in the city of Salzburg in October 1992, the SPÖ lost severely.

Clearly, Vranitzky is challenged by several trends. First, the ÖVP has improved its electoral competitiveness. Moreover, with the assumption of the ÖVP's Klestil to the presidency, Vranitizky has lost the additional functions normally performed by the president which had fallen to him in the wake of the international community's boycott of the previous Austrian president, Kurt Waldheim. Second, the FPÖ has increasingly made overtures to the ÖVP to form a nonsocialist coalition against the Social Democrats. Third, while the SPÖ's movement toward the center under Vranitzky's leadership has captured some votes from the ÖVP, it has also alienated segments of the traditional SPÖ electorate. In the national elections of 1986 and 1990, the SPÖ lost most of its voters not to the ÖVP, but to the FPÖ. Assessing Vranitzky's problems, the magazine *Wochenpresse* has used the phrase "twilight of Vranitzky."

Nonetheless, opinion polls in the latter part of 1992 showed that Vranitzky still held a large margin of public approval against the ÖVP party leader, Erhard Busek, and the FPÖ party leader, Jörg Haider. Less positive for Vranitzky, however, was that he ranked second behind the new Austrian president, the ÖVP's Klestil. To again stabilize and improve the SPÖ's electoral competitiveness, Vranitzky has emphasized the necessity for internal party reform. One of the central issues has been his demand for introducing SPÖ primary elections, in which independents and non-SPÖ party members should also be eligible to participate. In principle, this reform was approved by the June 1991 party conference, but some SPÖ factions continued to resist this idea.

Overall, one must conclude that Franz Vranitzky and his policies successfully sustained the electoral competitiveness of the SPÖ during a period when socialist ideas faced structural disadvantages and had to be modified. What is perhaps most remarkable of all, the Austrian government is still headed by a socialist chancellor, Franz Vranitzky, even though nonsocialist parties have controlled a majority of seats in the Austrian parliament since 1983.

BIBLIOGRAPHY

Campbell, David F. J. "Die Dynamik der politischen Links-rechts-Schwingungen in Österreich: Die Ergebnisse einer Expertenbefragung," *Österreichische Zeitschrift für Politikwissenschaft* 21(2): 165–179 (1992).

Höbelt, Lothar. "S wie SPÖ: Sozialistisch, Sozialdemokratisch oder 'Sozial und demokratisch'?" in Andreas Kohl et al. (eds.), *Österreichisches Jahrbuch für Politik* 1986, 767–79. Vienna: Verlag für Geschichte und Politik, 1992.

Rauscher, Hans. *Vranitzky: Eine Chance*. Vienna: Ueberreuter, 1987.

Thurnher, Armin. *Franz Vranitzky im Gespräch mit Armin Thurnher*. Frankfurt am Main: Eichborn, 1992.

Ucakar, Karl. "Die Sozialdemokratische Partei Österreichs," in Herbert Dachs et al. (eds.), *Handbuch des politischen Systems Österreichs*, 210–26. Vienna: Manz, 1991.

DAVID F. J. CAMPBELL

W

KÅRE WILLOCH (1928–) has been one of the most prominent politicians in postwar Norway. As prime minister from 1981 to 1986, he was a distinctive influence on the country's political development. Under his leadership, Norway turned to the right, markedly liberalizing both financial and cultural policy. Banks and businesses were given more latitude, and the state broadcasting monopoly was abolished. Willoch won televised duels against his most important adversary, the Labor leader Gro Harlem Brundtland, winning important elections. But when the right-wing Progress Party in 1986 voted with Labor and the Socialist Left against the government's proposal to introduce economic cutbacks, Willoch resigned, leaving the premiership to his adversary, Brundtland.

Kåre Willoch was born on October 3, 1928, in Oslo. He obtained his university degree in economics in 1953, with the best grades ever given at the Department of Economics of the University of Oslo. Among his teachers were the Nobel Prize winners Ragnar Frisch and Trygve Haavelmo. In 1954 Willoch married the nurse Anne-Marie Jørgensen. Both his wife and their three children have influenced Willoch's political views, especially on social policy issues.

Willoch was employed by the Norwegian Association of Shipowners and later by the Norwegian Industrial Association. However, politics was soon to become his main occupation. He chose a different political orientation from that of his great-great-grandfather, Isaach Isaachsen, who became a member of the Jacobin Club during a stay in Paris. Isaachsen was elected to the Norwegian parliament in 1818, and he put forward a number of revolutionary proposals, which, however, gained little or no support. Willoch, a liberal-conservative descendant of this Jacobin, was to have far greater influence on Norwegian politics.

Willoch was elected a member of the Oslo City Council in 1951. He was elected a member of the Norwegian parliament, the Storting, in the 1957 election, at age twenty-nine becoming the youngest Norwegian M.P. so far. Willoch had become active in politics during the heyday of Norwegian social democracy. Under the leadership of Prime Minister Einar Gerhardsen, the Labor Party secured an overall majority in parliament during the whole period from 1945 to

1961. Nonsocialist parties did not represent a realistic government alternative. In the opposition, Willoch soon proved to be an intelligent politician.

In 1961, the Labor Party lost its parliamentary majority, rendering Prime Minister Gerhardsen dependent on the support of two representatives of the newly formed Socialist People's Party. Two years later the Gerhardsen government fell when the Socialist People's Party and the nonsocialist parties joined together in support of a vote of no confidence against the government based on its handling of a series of mining accidents at Spitsbergen. The Conservative leader John Lyng then formed a coalition government consisting of the four nonsocialist parties: the Conservative Party, the Christian People's Party, the Center (Agrarian) Party and the Liberals. Lyng appointed Kåre Willoch his minister of trade and shipping. But the Lyng cabinet could not obtain the confidence of the parliamentary majority, and Gerhardsen was reinstated as prime minister after four weeks.

The formation of the Lyng government, however, was to carry far greater political significance than merited by its extremely short life span. Namely, the nonsocialist parties had shown their ability to form a joint government. Gradually, the four parties also appeared more unified in parliament. Prior to the 1965 election, they declared their willingness to form a joint government if they returned to a parliamentary majority. Labor lost that election, and the nonsocialist parties formed a new coalition government, this time under the premiership of Per Borten from the Center Party. Again, Willoch was appointed minister of trade and shipping.

Borten the farmer and Willoch the academic did not get on very well—neither politically, socially nor culturally. Willoch did not favor government subsidies to the agricultural sector, and the logical, analytical and impatient minister of trade was increasingly annoyed by the prime minister's imprecise and slow leadership style. In 1970 Willoch left the government to become chairman and parliamentary leader of the Conservative Party. A year later, the Borten cabinet had to resign due to internal disagreement on Norway's relations with the European Community (EC).

Politically, 1972 and 1973 were two bad years for Kåre Willoch. In the fall of 1972, Willoch, an ardent EC supporter, was among the big losers when the majority of Norwegian voters rejected in a referendum the idea of Norway's membership in the EC. In the following year's election, the Conservatives, with 17.4 percent of the vote, suffered their second weakest showing ever. This electoral defeat was partly due to disagreement among the nonsocialist parties, which were unable to present a realistic government alternative, and partly due to competition from a new extreme right-wing populist party, the Anders Lange's Party (later called the Progress Party).

However, the 1973 defeat represented a turning point for the Conservative Party. In 1974 Willoch left the chairmanship of the party to Erling Norvik, continuing, however, as parliamentary leader. He was without doubt the dominant factor in the party's policy making. That the two conservative leaders were very different—the aloof and rather reserved Willoch contrasted sharply with the more charismatic, popular Norvik—might have caused problems, but politically they were very close, although Willoch was considered somewhat more conservative than Norvik. Together they were an extremely strong duo for the Conservatives. While the conservative wave that developed in Norwegian politics in the latter half of the 1970s must be seen against the background of an international trend, there can still be no doubt that Willoch and Norvik were independent contributing factors in the rise in Conservative support from 17.4 percent in 1973 to 31.7 percent in 1981.

The 1973 and 1977 elections both gave a parliamentary majority to the socialists. In 1981, however, the Labor prime minister, Odvar Nordli, resigned, partly due to health problems, partly due to pressure from members of his own party. Gro Harlem Brundtland was named to replace Nordli, becoming the first female prime minister in Norway. The following September she was to defend her position in a general election, and her opponent was Kåre Willoch, who had the support of the Conservatives as well as the Christian People's Party and the Center Party.

The 1982 election campaign was characterized by intense television duels between the two prime ministerial candidates, whom the mass media called by their Christian names Gro and Kåre. In these duels the opposition leader Willoch was invincible with his brilliant argumentation. Using his great store of quotations, he ruffled Brundtland's composure several times. The election became one of several defeats for Gro Harlem Brundtland, who had to hand the premiership over to Willoch. An attempt to form a coalition government consisting of the Conservatives, the Christian People's Party and the Center Party did not succeed, however. Instead, Willoch formed the first all-Conservative government in more than fifty years.

During coalition negotiations, the abortion issue created most of the difficulties. In 1978 Norwegian women had been granted the right to make their own decision on abortion during the first twelve weeks of pregnancy. In the Conservative Party, opinions were divided; there were strong defenders as well as opponents of self-determined abortion in the party. Willoch opposed the idea of reinstating a committee system to handle abortion applications. In 1980 the Conservative Party congress ruled that M.P.s would be allowed to vote their own conviction on the abortion issue. During the government negotiations in 1981, the Christian People's Party demanded that a new coalition government would have to introduce stricter abortion legislation, a demand Willoch could not meet. Consequently, the Christian People's Party, supported by the Center Party, decided not to join the new cabinet, although both parties supported Willoch as prime minister.

Gradually, the Center Party came to feel that they gained little in return for their support of the government in parliament. In the spring of 1983 the party insisted on joining the cabinet, and after a while the Christian People's Party followed. Willoch converted his Conservative government into a coalition government consisting of the three nonsocialist parties. Although Willoch would have preferred to continue with an all-Conservative cabinet, the numerous declarations of cooperation made prior to the 1981 election made it politically impossible for the Conservative Party to reject the other nonsocialist parties' demand for participation in the government.

The 1985 election became another contest between Kåre Willoch and Gro Harlem Brundtland. His three-party government lost its parliamentary majority, but with the Progress Party in a pivotal position, Willoch was able to continue as prime minister after the election. A substantial fall in oil prices in the spring of 1986, however, shook the economy of Norway, a significant oil-producing country. The cabinet had to propose financial cuts. However, the parliamentary majority, consisting of the Labor Party, the Socialist Left and the Progress Party, opposed cuts. Willoch refused to pursue an economic policy which in his opinion was reckless. In May 1986, therefore, Gro Harlem Brundtland was again able to assume the premiership, despite the fact that there was a nonsocialist majority in parliament. Willoch returned to parliament, where he became leader of the Committee for Foreign and Constitutional Affairs. In the fall of 1986 he declared that he would no longer be a candidate for the post of prime minister, and in 1989 he voluntarily left parliament.

Unlike his opponent, Gro Harlem Brundtland, Prime Minister Willoch considered domestic policy more important than taking an active part in international politics. But in 1987 he was elected chair of the International Democrat Union, an association of conservative and Christian democratic parties. Simultaneously, he was proposed by the Brundtland government as a candidate for the post of NATO secretary general to succeed Lord Carrington. Willoch, however, withdrew his candidacy when it became clear that the United States would support the West German candidate, Defense Minister Manfred Wörner. Both personally and politically, Willoch was well qualified for the job, but he knew that it would be unrealistic to believe that a candidate from a small country like Norway would be able to defeat the candidate of Germany, a far more important country in this context.

Many undoubtedly classify Willoch as a hawk in foreign and defense policy. He is interested in disarmament but has always believed that disarmament negotiations must be based on firmness and strength on the part of the West. Willoch strongly supported NATO's dual track decision to deploy American medium-range missiles in Europe if negotiations with the Soviet Union did not succeed in reestablishing nuclear balance. The resolution was supported by the Norwegian Labor cabinet, but the governing party was divided in this as well as other defense policy questions, like the issues of prepositioning of American military stocks in Norway and of Scandinavia as a nuclear-free zone. These disagreements within the Labor Party weakened it in the 1981 election.

In defense policy Willoch is undoubtedly a conservative. However, he is more than a conservative in the international sense of the term. Among other things, he has been more critical of Israel's policy toward the Palestinians than a number of other Norwegian politicians both in Labor and in the nonsocialist parties. Willoch calls himself liberal-conservative. On cultural and social issues he has liberal tendencies, clearly demonstrated by his stand on the abortion issue. He has also shown a greater degree of environmental consciousness since his days as prime minister.

Naturally, it is always difficult to compare ideological positioning on a left-right axis across different countries. Still, it is interesting to note that Norwegian observers disagree on whether to place Willoch on a par with the German Social Democratic former chancellor Helmut Schmidt or on a level with the present Christian Democratic chancellor Helmut Kohl. Seen in the context of American politics, Willoch is no doubt closer to George Bush among the Republicans than to Ronald Reagan. In the United States, he would probably be classified as a moderate Republican, but he could also be seen as a Democrat. Liberalization and deregulation, limitation of state subsidies and balance in government budgets are central aspects of Willoch's views on economic policy, but he is far more moderate than his former fellow prime minister, Margaret Thatcher. In Norway, Willoch was for a long time considered one of the more conservative figures in the Conservative Party. This view changed gradually, however, and Willoch came to be seen as more moderate. This can be explained by the general right-wing turn in Norwegian politics more than by a change in Willoch's own political views.

Willoch has also expressed his moderate views by sharply criticizing the extreme right-wing, liberalist policy advocated by the Progress Party. Willoch has no liking for that party, once characterizing its chairman, Carl I. Hagen, as a political savage. After the 1985 election, Willoch's cabinet became dependent on the parliamentary support of the Progress Party, but he did not enter into a formal agreement with it, mainly due to strong resistance from the Christian People's Party and the Center Party. But Willoch's own dislike of the Progress Party and its leader also contributed to the fact that his cabinet's relations to the Progress Party were never properly clarified. Willoch trusted Hagen's assurance that the Progress Party would not smooth the path for a Labor Party government. But, as we have already seen, the Progress Party contributed to the parliamentary defeat which led to the resignation of the Willoch government in the spring of 1986.

Willoch's moderate line must not be confused with lack of principle. Few Norwegian politicians have practiced such consistent and clear ideological politics during so many years as Kare Willoch. His politics were primarily characterized by a demand for balancing the public economy, as well as the wish to limit government involvement. He was no insincere politician trying to grab votes by making imprudent promises during election campaigns. In his memoirs, Willoch writes that although a party needs to have a solid election manifesto with a wide perspective, the most important thing is that the manifesto be correct. He was at least as preoccupied with not doing things wrong as with doing them right.

Willoch's political views defined clearly the limits of his willingness to make political compromises. More pragmatically oriented conservative politicians would have liked to see the Willoch cabinet continue governing even after a parliamentary majority opposed economic cutbacks in 1986. But it was impossible for Willoch to go on as prime minister and pursue a line of politics he considered irresponsible. Neither would he have accepted reservations regarding NATO resolutions, as the conservative Danish Prime Minister Poul Schlüter did when he was opposed by a parliamentary majority. Schlüter stayed on, whereas in a similar situation Willoch would have resigned.

Willoch's political firmness—some call it stubbornness—must be seen against the background of his great intellectual and analytical capacity. He had the ability to handle simultaneously a number of issues and details and to see the practical and fundamental consequences they might bring. Such qualities are undoubtedly valuable to a prime minister who is held responsible for mistakes his ministers make. But these qualities also caused a certain irritation, both among those ministers and in the parliamentary groups of the coalition parties. Nonetheless, he was highly respected, and there was never any doubt that he was a nonsocialist politician in a class of his own.

Kåre Willoch's political influence is perhaps best illustrated in comparison with Gro Harlem Brundtland. There can be no doubt that Brundtland has a far stronger profile than Willoch in international politics, first and foremost as the leader of the UN Commission on Environment and Development. On the domestic scene, however, Willoch has made a greater impact than Brundtland. The Willoch government left more permanent marks on Norwegian society than the three Brundtland cabinets together.

With the slogan "a more open society," the Willoch government implemented a series of liberalization and deregulation measures. For example, at the beginning of the 1980s Norway still had a state-run broadcasting monopoly. Willoch abolished this monopoly and legalized the establishment of local radio stations. Gradually, cable and satellite television were also allowed. The strict regulations governing shop opening times and the sale of houses were relaxed. A number of restrictions regulating banks and credit institutions were abolished. The government started privatizing industry, and the state-owned oil company Statoil was reorganized in order to curtail its power.

Taken individually, the reforms initiated by the Willoch government did not lead to a dramatic change in the Norwegian political system. Norway still has a mixed economy. But collectively the reforms led to a clear weakening of the elements of planned economy and a strengthening of the market-related aspects of Norwegian society. A number of changes have influenced the everyday life of Norwegian citizens. Moreover, the Social Democratic governments of Gro Harlem Brundtland have made no efforts to reverse the developments initiated during Willoch's premiership.

The Willoch government's deregulation efforts, however, also led to problems for Norwegian society. The situation became particularly problematic when banks and credit institutions were given a free hand. In their eagerness to increase their share in the rapidly growing loan market, the banks completely neglected the importance of security. When recession overtook the Norwegian economy, they suffered great losses. A number of large banks then needed assistance from the state in the form of loans and share capital. It is quite ironic that Willoch's liberalization measures in a sense led to a "socialization" of the Norwegian banking system.

At the beginning of the 1990s, the Norwegian economy is in great difficulty. By Norwegian standards, unemployment is at a record high, and a number of companies and families struggle against crippling debts. Willoch's political opponents place most of the blame on his liberalization efforts in the mid-1980s. His supporters, on the other hand, maintain that if the Willoch government had given way to the demands of the opposition leader at the time, Gro Harlem Brundtland, for increased public spending, the economic crisis would have been even deeper. It remains to be seen whether these problems are the temporary costs of necessary reforms or if these reforms placed Norway on the wrong track. Nonetheless, greater responsibility among the nation's bankers would have been more in line with Kåre Willoch's spirit—behavior that would have limited the adverse effects of the reforms implemented by Willoch's government.

BIBLIOGRAPHY

Works by Willoch:

Minner og meninger (Memories and Convictions). Oslo: Schibsted, 1988.
Statsminister (Prime Minister). Oslo: Schibsted, 1990.

Other Works:

Berg, Carl Johan. *Kåre Willoch, mannen og myten* (Kåre Willoch, the Man and the Myth). Oslo: Fabritius, 1978.

Nævdal, Bodil. *Dager efter dette: Et politisk portrett av Kåre Willoch* (Days to Come: A Political Portrait of Kåre Willoch). Oslo: Grøndahl, 1987.

Rommetvedt, Hilmar. "Norway: From Consensual Majority Parliamentarism to Dissensual Minority Parliamentarism," in Erik Damgaard (ed.), *Parliamentary Change in the Nordic Countries.* Oslo/Oxford: Scandinavian University Press/Oxford University Press, 1992.

Strom, Kaare. *Minority Government and Majority Rule.* Cambridge: Cambridge University Press, 1990.

HILMAR ROMMETVEDT

HAROLD WILSON (1916–) led the British Labour Party for thirteen years, won four out of five general elections, and served as prime minister for eight years, making him the most successful Labour Party leader. Wilson's meritocratic and managerialist vision inspired and unified the party in the early 1960s, yet his response to events in the 1970s did little to prevent the demise of the party and the postwar social democratic consensus. After leading the Labour Party to victory in 1964 and 1966, Wilson's 1967 decision to devalue the pound signaled the beginning of the diminishment of his authority and effectiveness, seen particularly in the failure of trade union legislation in 1968, the explosion of inflation in 1975, and the radicalization of the party. The postwar triumph of social democracy and collectivism gave way under Wilson to failures of economic policy, culminating in eras of neo-liberalism in the 1980s and the social market in the 1990s.

James Harold Wilson was born on March 11, 1916, in Milnsbridge, a village near Huddersfield in Yorkshire. His father, James Herbert Wilson, was an industrial chemist by trade, a nonconformist in religion and a radical liberal in politics. His mother, Ethel Seddon, was an elementary school teacher. In addition to his family's religion, scouting influenced the young Wilson, with trips to London and Australia and bouts of appendicitis and typhoid fever leaving their mark. Attending Royds Hall secondary school in Milnsbridge until 1932, when the family moved to Chester, he blossomed as a student at Wirral County grammar school, which enabled him to gain admission to Jesus College, Oxford University, in 1934.

At Oxford Wilson was a serious student with an affinity for liberalism. He focused on economics in a philosophy, politics and economics (PPE) honors program, getting the best first in PPE at Oxford in 1937. He won several academic prizes and joined the university liberal club. Staying at Oxford for postgraduate study, Wilson fell under the influence of William Beveridge, the liberal social reformer and academic. He worked on Beveridge's projects on unemployment and held temporary teaching posts at Oxford until war broke out in August 1939, when he volunteered for the civil service. On January 1, 1940, he married Gladys Mary Baldwin. Despite the war, he continued to work for Beveridge, at the Commission for Manpower after June 1940, the Ministry of Labour after December 1940, and the Commission on Skilled Men in the Services after June 1941.

Setting out to pursue a career in the civil service, Wilson joined the mines department of the Board of Trade as a statistical officer in August 1941, continuing on when it was reorganized as the Ministry of Fuel and Power in June 1942. He gained firsthand experience of industrial relations in the mining industry as joint secretary of the Greene board from June 1942 to July 1943. Briefly returning to the ministry, Wilson left the civil service in October 1944, hoping to return to university lecturing.

Meanwhile, Wilson moved into the Labour Party, influenced by the general secretary of the Fabian Society and senior miners' officials in the context of the opportunity afforded by the impending general election. Adopted by the Ormskirk constituency Labour Party in September 1944, Wilson advocated planning and the nationalization of coal. Heralding his 1945 election victory as an expression of the people's desire to see wartime organization extended to peacetime tasks, the new member of Parliament became a junior minister in the Ministry of Works, the youngest member of any British government since 1900. More civil servant than politician, Wilson dealt with housing until Prime Minister Clement Attlee appointed him to lead a delegation to a commission of the Food and Agriculture Organization in Washington in October 1946. In March 1947, he became secretary for overseas trade under Sir Stafford Cripps at the Board of Trade, negotiating trade deals with the Soviets.

On the basis of Wilson's reputation as an administrator and supported by Cripps and Hugh Dalton, Prime Minister Attlee promoted him to head the Board of Trade in September 1947, putting Cripps in charge of an enlarged economics ministry. Promoting the interests of trade and industry and observing Cripps's use of demand management and planning to promote export-led growth during 1948, Wilson became prominent in the summer and fall of 1949 when Cripps fell ill and a run on the pound in September led to a 30 percent devaluation. During the successful 1950 election campaign Wilson defended a mixed economy, though he soon resigned from the cabinet over proposed increases in rearmament spending, emerging as the junior political associate of left-winger Aneurin Bevan.

After Labour's defeat in the 1951 election, Wilson turned to journalism, to advising a firm of timber importers and to supporting the left-wing Bevanite faction of the Parliamentary Labour Party (PLP). Favoring public ownership on pragmatic grounds, Wilson maintained his success in the party's National Executive Committee (NEC) elections. Following another Labour defeat in 1955, Hugh Gaitskell became party leader and Wilson shadow chancellor of the Exchequer. In this post, Wilson expressed ambivalence about British membership in the European Economic Community (EEC), a preference for Cripps-style demand management, flexibility toward nationalization, greater planning and use of technology to generate growth, and nuclear disarmament.

Following Labour's third successive electoral defeat in 1959, Gaitskell insisted on moving to the right and Wilson gambled on a center-left, unifying, compromising strategy. Party battles over public ownership and unilateral nuclear disarmament diminished Gaitskell's leadership during 1960, although Gaitskell recouped by pulling the party back toward multilateralism in 1961. When Wilson topped the PLP elections in 1961, Gaitskell appointed him shadow foreign secretary. Focusing on EEC membership, Wilson attempted to satisfy supporters and opponents of entry, arguing that minimum conditions would have to be met before the party would commit to joining. Bevan's death in July 1960 put Wilson in charge of the left wing, and Gaitskell's death in January 1963 opened the door for Wilson's election to the leadership post. With the right divided, Wilson won the PLP vote by offering hope for a party revival. Promising unity, administrative competency and a greater use of science and technology, Wilson formulated his new socialist ideology, first in his speech on the "white hot technological revolution" at the 1963 party conference and then in his 1964 "New Britain" program.

Using television for the first time, Wilson led Labour to victory in the 1964 election, gaining a majority of five seats. Furthering the strategy of involving employers and unions in government policy, Wilson initiated a new planning department, in addition to new departments of technology, overseas development, Wales, and land and resources. An inherited balance of payments problem grew worse and was met with increased tariffs, given the priority of maintaining sterling as a reserve currency. Labour's opposition to nuclear weapons was quietly sacrificed, though Wilson faced parliamentary turmoil over Vietnam and Rhodesia. Despite reneging on electoral promises of increased pensions and lower prescription drug charges and bad publicity about his ''kitchen cabinet'' and private secretary Marcia Williams (after July 1974 Lady Falkender), Wilson's leadership enabled Labour to strengthen its position in the March 1966 election with an increased majority of ninety-seven, a first for a Labour leader. Intervening successfully in the seamen's strike, Wilson reacted to economic crisis in July 1967 with wage restraint and expenditure cuts, ruling out devaluation. Enacting tighter immigration controls despite objections by the home secretary, Roy Jenkins, he oversaw the liberalization of laws concerning homosexuality, abortion, divorce and theater censorship.

Despite the deflationary measures of July, a severe run on the pound in November provoked Wilson into devaluing the currency by 14 percent, ultimately a turning point in his career. The act left Wilson humiliated and signaled the beginning of his political demise. The ''new Britain vision'' gave way to the exigencies of defending the pound through expenditure cuts, tax increases dampening private consumption, and wage controls. Still, Wilson made important initiatives. He created superministries for labor, technology and environment (local government), set up a royal commission on the civil service in the hope of improving its management capabilities and started the Open University. The 1968 report of the royal commission on industrial relations led to *In Place of Strife*, outlining interventionist legislation aiming to reform trade unions by using statutory authority. Reflecting Wilson's view that unions were hampering economic growth, Barbara Castle led the government's effort, only to generate so much opposition from the unions, the PLP and Labour's NEC, that Wilson and Castle were forced to retreat.

The general election loss of June 1970 was another personal defeat for Wilson, diminishing his purpose and energy. Reelected party leader, he began writing about the Labour governments from 1964 to 1970. Profiting politically from the industrial conflict fostered by the Conservative government's trade union legislation and incomes policies, Wilson argued that Prime Minister Heath had agreed to join the EEC on unfavorable terms. When the NEC voted for a referendum on EEC membership, Wilson dropped his opposition on constitutional grounds. In a 1971 speech, Wilson repeated his view favoring a compact between government, industry and unions, in which voluntary wage restraint was facilitated by a social wage and price control in a context of full employment. Yet, he faced a leftward drift culminating in the 1973 program of the Trades Union Congress–Labour Party liaison committee, *Economic Policy and the Cost of Living*. This called for the state to promote industrial growth through public enterprise, a national enterprise board and planning agreements with large firms.

Trying to prevent the party from moving too far to the left, Wilson proclaimed a need for greater participation in a series of speeches in early 1973, but the ideological initiative had already been taken over by a coalition between left-dominated unions and party activists.

With the miners' strike leading to a general election on February 28, 1974, Wilson claimed that a social contract would facilitate policy making by gaining the cooperation of the unions. With less total votes than the Conservatives but more seats in the Commons, Wilson returned to office heading a minority government. He moved to mildly deflate an economy shocked by the rise in world oil prices, removed Heath's industrial relations act and placed Tony Benn at the Department of Industry to set up the national enterprise board, while undermining Labour's commitment to planning agreements. Working up proposals for legislation to extend union rights, prohibit sex discrimination, increase consumer protection, improve pensions and implement devolution, while getting the party to agree to a referendum on EC membership within one year, Wilson called a general election for October 10, 1974.

Gaining an overall majority of only four seats, Wilson formed his fourth government. During the campaign for the June 1975 EC referendum, he argued that membership would benefit Britain. As internecine conflict grew within the Labour Party, the prime minister mounted verbal assaults on the militant left and undercut the left by moving Tony Benn from Industry to Energy. During 1975 Wilson and Chancellor of the Exchequer Denis Healey attempted to defeat rising inflation. Wilson met the June 1975 run on the pound by deflating at home with a mix of tax increases, expenditure cuts and a voluntary incomes policy. He, however, seemed uninterested in the growing monetarist debate and was more concerned to avoid the evils of either devaluation or siege socialism.

To the surprise of most, Wilson announced his resignation on March 16, 1976, generating much controversy. But a number of factors explain his decision: physical and mental exhaustion caused by long hours of keeping up with government business, loss of control over the NEC, the disaffection of the Parliamentary Labour Party and economic policy failures, all this in conjunction with an absence of new ideas, the burden of Marcia Falkender's role in his administration and Mary Wilson's dislike of his public career. Taking a knighthood and staying in the Commons, the former prime minister wrote several books and chaired a royal commission on financial institutions. He also became a life peer in 1983 as Baron Wilson of Rievaulx. After 1986, Wilson rarely appeared in public, allegedly suffering from senile dementia.

Harold Wilson viewed politics as administration and himself as a successful administrator. This suited his personality. Wilson combined a penchant for hard work with a love of detail. He preferred facts to people, process to conviction, routine to extraordinary. Isolated but driven, he attained success through diligence. He feared that people, namely, cabinet rivals, the press and British intelligence agents, were conspiring against him, sometimes showing paranoia. Yet, he permitted trusted associates to criticize him harshly, particularly Marcia

Falkender. Being totally dependent on him, his closest advisers reinforced his isolation from the party and the country.

His view of politics also fit Britain's postwar collectivism. Believing that the state could improve societal management, Wilson gave consummate expression to the "corporatist bias" of the postwar years. Shunning big ideas and ideology, his socialism combined a vision of equal opportunity and managerial efficiency. His belief in collectivism was indebted to the wartime success of state intervention, and his efforts to articulate a socialist vision presented managerial tactics as political philosophy, in the fashion of the day. The white hot technology theme followed from the popularity of planning during the early 1960s, and advocacy of greater participation in the early 1970s reflected an emerging demand for industrial democracy.

A liberal in his early years, events positioned him on the center-left of the Labour Party. The first step followed from his resignation in 1950 over rearmament, leading to his identification as Bevan's successor. Next, as the promoter of the state's use of science and technology, he broadened the appeal of socialist planning, animating and unifying the party. Finally in order to hold the party together during the 1970s, Wilson played defensively, making concessions to the party left yet bowing to deflationary imperatives of domestic and international capitalism.

The failures of Wilson's governments derived from a breakdown of the managerialist formula of governing in the face of relative economic and political decline. The postwar collectivist solution to problem solving, state intervention and group incorporation, empowered unions, employers and consumer groups, while making government more accountable and vulnerable. This weakness was apparent in the 1967 devaluation and the 1968 failure to reform unions. These defeats were real, involving overt conflict. By the time that Wilson returned to office, governability had become the main issue confronting Britain's ruling class. In the 1974–1976 period, without authority and overwhelmed by pressures, defeats were endured without battle. Wilson failed to grasp the depth of the problem. After 1975 Margaret Thatcher offered an alterative future, ultimately more realistic than the left's siege socialism.

In foreign affairs, Wilson was a free trader and internationalist. The growth of Germany, France and the European Community imposed limits on British pretensions for economic prominence and autonomy. The hegemonic position of the United States meant that Britain had to adjust its policies in order to maintain American aid and goodwill, regardless of internal opposition. Wilson's close ties with Soviet leaders, dating from his trading missions at the Board of Trade, failed to yield benefits. In office, Wilson accepted Britain's self-image as a great power, never trying to reformulate the link between Britain's place in the world and her economic rejuvenation. This meant that Wilson defended the sterling as a reserve currency and was ambivalent about the EC, finally supporting Britain's staying in during the 1975 referendum. But Wilson's hesitancy gave no direction to the party and deepened the country's confusion about its future.

Wilson left the Labour Party in terminal decline. In some respects, Wilson made the party more like its European counterparts. The role of the leader became central, using television to emphasize personality, while orthodox doctrine was played down and modernized. He unified a party divided ideologically in the 1950s and won new support from middle-class and youthful voters. In other ways, however, the party defied modernizing trends. Its organizational and financial dependence on trade unions remained, while its constituency sections became conduits for militant activists that made the party the most left-wing in Europe by the early 1980s. This radicalization of the party took initiative and power away from the party leader. In the face of a crisis of governability, Wilson grew weary and opted out.

Overall, Wilson was an effective administrator and careerist whose fortunes ran out as the world in which he operated changed dramatically. His model of a mobilized wartime state effectively directing victory proved evanescent, when in peace self-interested groups usurped the authority and autonomy of the state. A brilliant and diligent workman, Wilson lacked the vision and commitment to rise to the 1970s' demand for a new kind of politics.

BIBLIOGRAPHY

Works by Wilson:

The Labour Government, 1964–1970: A Personal Record. London: Weidenfeld and Nicolson and Michael Joseph, 1971.

The Governance of Britain. London: Weidenfeld and Nicolson and Michael Joseph, 1976.

A Prime Minister on Prime Ministers. London: Weidenfeld and Nicolson and Michael Joseph, 1977.

Final Term: The Labour Government, 1974–1976. London: Weidenfeld and Nicolson and Michael Joseph, 1979.

Memoirs: The Making of a Prime Minister 1916–1964. With Brian Connell. London: Weidenfeld and Nicolson and Michael Joseph, 1986.

Other Works:

Morgan, Austin. *Harold Wilson.* London: Pluto Press, 1992.

Pimlott, Ben. *Harold Wilson.* London: HarperCollins, 1992.

JOEL D. WOLFE

LISTING OF SUBJECTS BY COUNTRY

AUSTRIA
Jörg Haider
Bruno Kreisky
Julius Raab
Karl Renner
Franz Vranitzky

BELGIUM
Baudouin I
André Cools
Wilfried Martens
Paul-Henri Spaak
Leo Tindemans

DENMARK
Jens Otto Krag
Poul Schlüter

FINLAND
Urho Kekkonen
Juho Kusti Paasikivi

FRANCE
Jacques Chirac
Michel Debré
Charles de Gaulle
Valéry Giscard d'Estaing
Jean-Marie Le Pen
Georges Marchais
Pierre Mendès-France
François Mitterrand
Michel Rocard

GERMANY
Konrad Adenauer
Willy Brandt
Ludwig Erhard
Hans-Dietrich Genscher
Erich Honecker
Petra Karin Kelly
Helmut Kohl
Helmut Schmidt
Franz Josef Strauss

GREECE
Harilaos Florakis
Konstantinos Karamanlis
Konstantinos Mitsotakis
Andreas George Papandreou
George Papandreou

IRELAND
Eamon De Valera
Garret FitzGerald
Charles Haughey
Seán Lemass

ITALY
Guilio Andreotti
Enrico Berlinguer

Bettino Craxi

Alcide De Gasperi

John XXIII (Angelo Giuseppe Roncalli)

Aldo Moro

Palmiro Togliatti

NETHERLANDS

J. M. (Joop) den Uyl

Willem Drees

Rudolphus (Ruud) Lubbers

Joseph Luns

Dirk U. Stikker

NORWAY

Gro Harlem Brundtland

Einar Gerhardsen

Kåre Willoch

PORTUGAL

António de Oliveira Salazar

Mário Soares

SPAIN

Santiago Carrillo

Francisco Franco

Felipe González (Márquez)

Juan Carlos I

Adolfo Suárez

SWEDEN

Tage Erlander

Thorbjörn Fälldin

Gustav Möller

Olof Palme

UNITED KINGDOM

Clement Attlee

Neil Kinnock

Harold Macmillan

Margaret Thatcher

Harold Wilson

COUNTRIES NOT INCLUDED

Andorra

Iceland

Leichtenstein

Luxembourg

Malta

Monaco

San Marino

Switzerland

The Vatican (cf. Italy)

CHRONOLOGY

1870–1950	Karl Renner.
1870–1956	Juho Kusti Paasikivi.
1876–1967	Konrad Adenauer.
1881–1954	Alcide De Gasperi.
1881–1963	John XXIII (Angelo Giuseppe Roncalli).
1882–1975	Eamon De Valera.
1883–1967	Clement Attlee.
1884–1970	Gustav Möller.
1886–1988	Willem Drees.
1888–1968	George Papandreou.
1889–1970	António de Oliveira Salazar.
1890–1970	Charles de Gaulle.
1891–1964	Julius Raab.
1892–1975	Francisco Franco.
1893–1964	Palmiro Togliatti.
1894–1986	Harold Macmillan.
1897–1977	Ludwig Erhard.
1897–1979	Dirk U. Stikker.
1897–1987	Einar Gerhardsen.
1899–1971	Seán Lemass.
1899–1972	Paul–Henri Spaak.
1900–1986	Urho Kekkonen.
1901–1985	Tage Erlander.
1907–	Konstantinos Karamanlis.
1907–1982	Pierre Mendès-France.

1911–	Joseph Luns.
1911–1990	Bruno Kreisky.
1912–	Michel Debré.
1912–1994	Erich Honecker.
1913–	Santiago Carrillo.
1913–1992	Willy Brandt.
1914–	Harilaos Florakis.
1914–1978	Jens Otto Krag.
1916–	François Mitterrand.
1916–	Harold Wilson.
1916–1978	Aldo Moro.
1916–1988	Franz Josef Strauss.
1918–	Helmut Schmidt.
1918–	Konstantinos Mitsotakis.
1919–	Andreas George Papandreou.
1919–	Giulio Andreotti.
1919–1987	J. M. (Joop) den Uyl.
1920–	Georges Marchais.
1922–	Leo Tindemans.
1922–1984	Enrico Berlinguer.
1922	Partitioning of Ireland.
1924–	Mário Soares.
1925–	Margaret Thatcher.
1925–	Charles Haughey.
1926–	Garret FitzGerald.
1926–	Thorbjörn Fälldin.
1926–	Valéry Giscard d'Estaing.
1927–	Hans–Dietrich Genscher.
1927–1986	Olof Palme.
1927–1991	André Cools.
1928–	Jean–Marie Le Pen.
1928–	Kåre Willoch.
1929–	Poul Schlüter.
1930–	Helmut Kohl.
1930–	Michel Rocard.
1930–1993	Baudouin I.
1932–	Adolfo Suárez.

1932–	Jacques Chirac.
1932–1968	Salazar rules Portugal.
1934–	Bettino Craxi.
1936–	Wilfried Martens.
1936–1939	Spanish Civil War.
1936	October 1: Franco invested at Burgos with the title of El Caudillo and becomes head of the national government.
1937–	Franz Vranitzky.
1938–	Juan Carlos I.
1938	March: Annexation of Austria by Nazi Germany.
	Portugal becomes first country to recognize Franco.
1939–	Gro Harlem Brundtland.
1939–	Rudolphus (Ruud) Lubbers.
1939	April 1: Spanish republican forces driven into an unconditional surrender.
1940–1945	Nazi occupation of the Netherlands.
1940	German invasion of France.
	June 18: De Gaulle broadcasts first of his appeals to the French to reject the armistice and continue the fight against the Nazis under his leadership.
1942–	Felipe González (Márquez).
1942–	Neil Kinnock.
1945–1955	Allied occupation of Austria.
1945	Parliamentary election produces a landslide for the British Labour Party.
1946	January: De Gaulle abruptly resigns as president of the provisional government.
	November: In French parliamentary elections, Communists win 5.4 million votes (30 percent of the total), gaining 82 National Assembly seats.
1947–1992	Petra Karin Kelly.
1947	Britain grants independence to India.
1948	Communist coup in Czechoslovakia.
	Finland signs the Treaty of Mutual Assistance with Moscow.
	First parliamentary elections of the new Italian Republic.
	April: Alcide De Gasperi leads Italy into NATO.
	End of Civil War in Greece.
	German Democratic Republic (East Germany) established.
	Konrad Adenauer elected chancellor of West Germany.

	New government declares Ireland a republic.
	The Allies accept the ''Basic Law'' as the basis of the postwar West German political system.
	The Netherlands grants independence to Indonesia.
1950–	Jörg Haider.
1950	March: Popular referendum held on the Belgium ''royal question.''
1951	Baudouin I sworn in as the fifth king of Belgium.
	European Coal and Steel Community established by France, Germany, Italy, Belgium, the Netherlands and Luxembourg.
	October: A Conservative victory returns Churchill to power.
1953	The French parliament refuses to ratify the Defense Community Treaty.
1954	Dien Bien Phu crisis for France in Vietnam.
	France defeated in Indochina.
	Restoration of West German sovereignty.
1955	Adenauer establishes diplomatic relations between West Germany and the Soviet Union.
	Austria commits to neutrality as outlined in the State Treaty.
	West Germany joins NATO.
1956	October: Nikita Khrushchev discloses the Soviet repression of the Hungarian uprising.
	November: Invasion of Suez.
1957	Spaak is named Secretary-General of NATO.
	Treaties of Rome signed by France, Germany, Italy, Belgium, the Netherlands and Luxembourg establishing European Economic Community and Euratom.
1958	Algerian crisis threatens the French Fourth Republic.
	Charles de Gaulle recalled to power.
	Michel Debré authors the French Fifth Republic constitution.
1959	John XXIII convenes the Second Vatican Council.
	Michel Debré named the French Fifth Republic's first prime minister.
	West German Social Democrats renounce more radical beliefs at the Bad Godesberg convention.
1960	Independence of the Belgian Congo.
	Santiago Carrillo becomes Secretary General of the Spanish Communist party.
1961	Revolt of the Generals in France.
	August: Berlin Wall constructed.
1962	Algeria receives its independence through the Evian accords.

1963	January: France and West Germany conclude the Treaty of Friendship and Cooperation.
	De Gaulle rejects the Limited Nuclear Test Ban Agreement.
	De Gaulle vetoes Britain's application for European Community membership.
	October 15: Adenauer resigns the West German chancellorship.
	Ludwig Erhard replaces Adenauer as West German chancellor.
1965	First direct presidential elections in France.
1966–1969	The Grand Coalition governs West Germany.
1966	De Gaulle makes an 11–day visit to the Soviet Union designed to encourage wide acceptance of his vision of Europe.
	De Gaulle withdraws France from NATO's integrated military command.
1967	April 21: A coup d'etat by military officers ends Greek democracy.
1967–1974	Dictatorship in Greece.
1968	Enrico Berlinguer strongly condemns the Soviet-led Warsaw pact intervention in Czechoslovakia.
	De Gaulle rejects the Nuclear Non-Proliferation Treaty.
	May: Worst outbreak of social unrest in France during post-war period.
1969–1974	Willy Brandt's term as chancellor of Germany.
1969	April: De Gaulle resigns the French presidency after his constitutional reform is defeated in a national referendum.
	British government dispatches troops to Ulster.
	Juan Carlos, eldest son of the pretender to the Spanish throne, named Franco's official successor.
1970–1983	Bruno Kreisky serves as Austrian federal chancellor.
1970	Willy Brandt travels to Moscow, East Germany and Poland for meetings with respective heads of government.
1971	Brandt awarded the Nobel Peace Prize.
	Joseph Luns is appointed NATO secretary-general.
1972–1984	Enrico Berlinguer serves as secretary of the Italian Communist party (PCI) until his death in June 1984.
1972	Norway votes against entrance into the European Community in a referendum.
1973	British government institutes direct rule of Northern Ireland from London.
	Ireland and Denmark accede to membership in the European Community.
	OPEC oil embargo.

1974–1982 Helmut Schmidt serves as chancellor of West Germany.

1974–1992 Hans-Dietrich Genscher of the Free Democratic Party serves 18 years as Federal Republic of Germany's foreign minister.

1974 April 25: Captain's Movement coup brings down Salazar's regime.

April: ''Revolution of Carnations'' in Portugal—so-called for flowers civilians place in soldiers' rifle barrels during leftist coup.

Greek Junta overthrows legitimate Cypriot government provoking Turkey's invasion of Cyprus.

Jacques Chirac appoints himself Secretary-General of the remnants of the Gaullist movement.

December 8: Popular referendum in Greece abolishes the monarchy and establishes a parliamentary republic.

1975 Margaret Thatcher becomes leader of the British Conservative Party when Conservatives force Edward Heath to step down.

November 22: Juan Carlos I invested as King of Spain.

1976 Bettino Craxi becomes the leader of the Italian Socialist party (PSI).

November: Spanish Law for Political Reform which provides for the election of a democratic assembly is approved by the Francoist Cortes.

1977 May: Egmont Pact becomes the cornerstone for the future transformation of the Belgian unitary state into a federal one composed of autonomous regions.

1978 Flemish and francophone wings of the Belgian Socialist Party split into two independent political parties.

March: Aldo Moro kidnapped and subsequently killed by Red Brigade terrorists.

New Spanish constitution adopted.

1979 ''Winter of discontent'' in the United Kingdom.

Petra Karin Kelly co-founds the German Greens ''anti-party party.''

1979–1990 Margaret Thatcher is Britain's longest continuously serving Prime Minister (1979–1990) since Lord Liverpool in the early 19th century (1812–1827).

1981 January: Accession of Greece to the European Community.

February: Military coup attempt in Spain.

May: François Mitterrand, a Socialist, wins the French presidency.

French socialists nationalize major industries.

Gro Harlem Brundtland becomes Norway's first female (and youngest ever) prime minister.

1982 Margaret Thatcher sends Britain into war with Argentina over the Falkland Islands.

Poul Schlüter becomes first Conservative prime minister in Denmark since 1901.

Spain joins NATO.

1983 NATO deploys intermediate-range nuclear missiles on German soil, engendering great controversy.

Election of the first Green representatives to the West German parliament (the Bundestag).

1985 Carrillo expelled from Spanish Communist party.

Mikhail Gorbachev assumes power in the Soviet Union.

White Paper on completing the single market of the European Community.

1986–1988 First experience in French Fifth Republic of "cohabitation" (president and prime minister from opposing political camps).

1986 European Community's Single European Act signed.

January: Spain and Portugal enter the European Community.

January 26: Mário Soares become Portugal's first civilian president directly elected by universal suffrage and first civilian president in 60 years.

February 28: Olof Palme assassinated in downtown Stockholm.

Jörg Haider takes over leadership of the Freedom Party of Austria (FPÖ).

June: Kurt Waldheim wins election to the Austrian presidency with 53.9 percent of the vote.

1989 November 9: The Berlin Wall falls.

1990 February: Dissolution of Italian Communist Party; reconstituted as the Party of the Democratic Left.

March 18: First free elections held in the German Democratic Republic.

July 1: German economic, monetary and social union goes into effect.

October 3: Accession to the Federal Republic of Germany of the five Eastern German states.

December: All-German elections.

1991–1992 Persian Gulf War.

1991 Disintegration of the Warsaw Pact.

June 18: André Cools brutally assassinated.

1992– Investigation of political corruption among Italy's elite known as "Clean Hands."

1992 Norway decides to resume whaling.

Petra Karin Kelly shot and killed in her home in Bonn.

June 2: Danish referendum on Maastricht Treaty on European Monetary and Political Union results in a defeat.

December 31: ''Deadline'' for full market integration in the European Community.

1993 Formal institution of federalism in the Belgian state.

1994 Georges Marchais steps down as French Communist Party leader.

INDEX

Boldface page numbers indicate location of entries.

CONTRIBUTORS

DAG ANCKAR is professor of political science at Abo Academy in Finland. He is president of the Finnish Political Science Association, past president of the Nordic Political Science Association and a member of the executive committee of the International Political Science Association. He is the author of books and articles in the fields of democratic theory, political institutions and the history of political science.

MARK BARTHOLOMEW (deceased 1994) was professor and chair of political science at the University of Maine at Farmington. His research and publications focused on the peace movement in Europe, the changing role of NATO and Western security, and the role of Willy Brandt in shaping the Socialist International.

RALF BEKE-BRAMKAMP holds a doctorate in political science and is a member of the senior staff of Bertelsmann, AG, Gütersloh, Germany. He is the author of *Die Drogenpolitik der USA, 1969–90* (1992) and a number of articles on drug control policy and utopianism.

FRANK BELLONI is professor of political science at Virginia Commonwealth University. He is the author of a number of articles on the Italian political system.

LYNNE LOUISE BERNIER is associate professor of politics at Carroll College, Wisconsin, where she teaches comparative and international politics. She has published a number of articles on decentralization and its local consequences in France.

RUTH A. BEVAN is David W. Petegorsky Professor of Political Science at Yeshiva University, New York. Specializing in ideological movements in Western Europe, she is the author of *Marx and Burke* and of numerous articles on the New Left and nationalism. She is currently at work on a political biography of Petra Kelly, at the request of Ms. Kelly before her death.

CHRIS BOURDOUVALIS is assistant professor of political science at Augusta

College, Georgia. He is the author of *Voting Behavior of Representatives in the European Parliament* (forthcoming) and has done extensive work on European Community and Greek politics.

DAVID F. J. CAMPBELL is a staff researcher at the Institute for Advanced Studies, Vienna. His current research focuses on comparative public policy, especially the issue of R&D funding in international perspective. Additional research interests include the concept of political swings in Europe and the United States and the historical development of the European Community.

MICHEL COLLINGE is a research assistant at the Catholic University of Louvain, Belgium. He has published articles in the fields of Belgian politics and nationalist movements.

KENNETH COSGROVE is visiting assistant professor at Ohio University. His research has focused on the politics of ethnic and foreign lobbying of the U.S. Congress, especially regarding the case of Ireland and Irish sympathizers in the United States. He served as a Carl Albert Fellow at the University of Oklahoma from 1987 to 1992.

MARIA GREEN COWLES holds a doctorate in international relations from American University, Washington, D.C. From 1991 to 1993, she was an SSRC-MacArthur Fellow on Peace and Security in a Changing World. Her research examines the rise and institutionalization of multinational corporate actors in the European Community of the 1980s.

ROBERT H. COX is associate professor of political science at the University of Oklahoma. He has published a book, *Between Bismarck and Beveridge* (1993), which examines the social politics of the Netherlands in the postwar period. He has also written extensively about the politics of the welfare state in Western Europe and Eastern Europe during the postwar period.

WILLIAM C. CROMWELL is professor of international relations and coordinator of European studies at the School of International Service, American University, and is an occasional visiting professor at the College of Europe in Belgium. He is the author of *The United States and the European Pillar* (1992) and a number of articles dealing with U.S.-European relations.

REBECCA DAVIS is assistant professor of political science at Virginia Polytechnic Institute and State University. She did her doctoral studies at Emory University, focusing on the elite recruitment of women to cabinet-level positions in Western European politics.

MARIA ELISABETTA DE FRANCISCIS holds a doctorate from the University of Connecticut and is presently assistant professor of Italian and comparative constitutional law at the University of Frederico II in Naples, Italy. She is the author of *Italy and the Vatican* (1989) and of a number of articles on Church-state relations in Italy.

MARTINE M. DERIDDER is a professional specialist in the Hesburgh Program in Public Service and assistant professor at the University of Notre Dame (Indiana). Her research interests include European integration, comparative public policy and the politics of Western European democracies. She has published articles on Belgian politics and government coalition formation in multiparty-systems.

THANASSIS DIAMANTOPOULOS is associate professor of political science at the Panteios University of Social and Political Sciences, Athens, Greece. He holds a doctorate from the University of Paris I and is the author of *Political Parties and Party Systems: Comparative Approach and Theory* (1988), as well as a number of studies of Greek politics.

DESMOND DINAN is associate professor of history and director of the Center for European Community Studies at George Mason University. He has written extensively on Anglo-French diplomatic relations, Irish foreign policy and the politics of European integration.

WILLIAM M. DOWNS holds a doctorate in political science from Emory University. He has served as a European Community Fulbright Fellow in 1992–1993 and as a fellow of the Center for International Affairs at Harvard University in 1993–1994. His research interests include internal party politics and government coalitions.

RONALD A. FRANCISCO is associate professor of political science and Russian and East European studies at the University of Kansas. His research concentrates on the interaction of domestic and international politics in Europe. His most recent book is *United Germany* (with Peter Wallach).

JEFFREY FREYMAN is professor of political science and chair of the Committee on International Studies at Transylvania University in Lexington, Kentucky. He is author of a number of articles on labor politics in Britain.

DANIEL V. FRIEDHEIM is the author of articles on democratic theory and the democratization of Portugal. He has just completed a doctoral dissertation at Yale University on regime collapse and the East German revolution of 1989.

ANDRÉ-PAUL FROGNIER is professor at the Catholic University of Louvain, Belgium, and head of the Political Science Department there. He has authored numerous articles on comparative politics in the fields of consociationalism, parliamentary studies, electoral behavior and cabinet decision making. He is presently a member of the executive committee of the European Consortium for Political Research.

CANDACE HETZNER is associate professor of business and public administration at Rutgers University, Newark, New Jersey. She has published a number of articles on British public policy and public administration. She is presently completing a book on Thatcherite microeconomic policy.

CLAUS HOFHANSEL is assistant professor of political science at Rhode Island

College. He is the author of a number of articles on German and U.S. foreign policies.

TIM KNUDSEN is associate professor of public administration at the University of Copenhagen. He is the editor of *Welfare Administration in Denmark* (1991) and author of a number of books and articles on Danish state building and welfare administration.

THOMAS A. KOELBLE is associate professor of political science and international relations at the University of Miami, Florida. He is the author of *The Left Unravelled* (1992) and a number of articles on electoral and party politics in Western Europe, as well as the problematics facing the left there. In 1991–1992, he served as a Research Fellow at the Center for European Studies at Harvard University.

PAULETTE KURZER is on the faculty of the University of Arizona. She is the author of *Business and Banking: Political Change and Economic Integration in Western Europe* (1993), as well as a number of articles on social democracy and monetary integration.

ROBERT LADRECH is associate professor of political science at Saint Mary's College in Notre Dame, Indiana. He is the author of a number of articles on social democratic parties and the dynamics of European Community integration. In 1992–1993, he served as a European Community Fulbright Fellow in Brussels.

THOMAS D. LANCASTER is associate professor of political science at Emory University. His research and teaching interests include comparative politics with a specialization in Western and southern Europe. Among his works, he has published *Politics and Change in Spain* and *Policy Stability and Democratic Change*.

KAY LAWSON is professor of political science and international relations at San Francisco State University and at the University of Paris (Sorbonne). She is the author of *The Comparative Study of Political Parties* (1976) and *The Human Polity* (third edition, 1993), and is the editor of *Political Parties and Linkage* (1980) and *When Parties Fail* (1988, with Peter Merkl).

NORBERT LESER is professor of social philosophy at the University of Vienna and director of the Ludwig-Boltzmann Research Institute for Austrian Intellectual History. A regular columnist for a Catholic weekly, he has authored and edited numerous books on political history and the history of ideas (*Genius Austriacus*, 1988). A *Festschrift* in commemoration of his sixtieth birthday appeared in 1993.

FRANCISCO J. LLERA is professor of political science and chair of the Department of International Studies and Political Science at the Basque Country University, Bilbao, Spain. He has published *Postfranquismo y fuerzas politicas en Euskadi* (1985), as well as a number of articles on Basque politics.

JOSÉ M. MATA is professor of international studies and political science at the

Basque Country University, Bilbao, Spain. He is the author of *Nacionalismo vasco radical: Discurso, organización y expresiones* (1993) and a number of articles on nationalism, political violence and Basque politics.

AMY G. MAZUR is assistant professor of political science at Washington State University. She is author of *Gender Bias and the State: Women's Rights at Work in France* (1994) and a number of articles on feminist policy formation in the postindustrial democracies.

KOSTAS MESSAS is adjunct professor of international studies at the University of Denver and at the Metropolitan State College of Denver. He is the author of forthcoming articles on democratization and civil-military relations.

MICHELE MICHELETTI is associate professor of political science at the University of Stockholm. She is author of *Organizing Interests and Protest* (1985), *The Swedish Farmers' Movement and Government Agricultural Policy* (1990), *Collective Action in Sweden* (1994) and *Understanding Organized Action* (1994). She has published a number of articles, as well, on collective action and Swedish politics.

WOLFGANG C. MÜLLER is associate professor of political science at the University of Vienna. He is coeditor of several books, including *Politics in Austria: Still a Case of Consociationalism?* (1992), and author of many articles and chapters on Austrian and comparative politics.

JEAN-YVES NEVERS is a researcher at the Centre National de la Recherche Scientifique at the University of Toulouse, France. His current research interests and publications include central-local relations, local government and urban politics.

JEROME O'CALLAGHAN is assistant professor of political science at the State University of New York at Cortland. He received a law degree in 1981 in the Republic of Ireland and a doctorate in 1988 from Syracuse University. His articles have appeared in a number of journals, including *Pace Law Review*, *Justice System Journal* and the *New England Law Review*.

L. MARVIN OVERBY is assistant professor of political science at the University of Mississippi. His published articles have appeared in the *American Political Science Review, Western Political Quarterly* and *West European Politics*, as well as a number of other journals. During 1983–1984, he studied in Ireland on a Thomas J. Watson Fellowship.

GIANFRANCO PASQUINO is professor of political science at the University of Bologna, Italy, and adjunct professor of political science at the Bologna Center of the Johns Hopkins University. He has written widely on Italian and comparative politics and coedited *Italian Politics: A Review*, vol. 7 (1992) and vol. 8 (1993).

MOGENS N. PEDERSEN is professor of political science and dean of social sciences at Odense University, Denmark. He is editor of the *European Journal of Political Research*, and he has published widely on legislative behavior, political recruitment, party systems, electoral behavior, the politics of research and higher education, and Scandinavian and Danish politics.

ANTON PELINKA is professor of political science at Innsbruck University and director of the Institute of Conflict Research, Vienna. He is author of *Social Democratic Parties in Europe* (1983) and *Kleine Koalition in Österreich* (1993). He is also coeditor of *Political Parties in Austria* (1989) and has published extensively in the field of comparative politics.

ROBERT L. PETERSON is associate professor of political science at the University of Tennessee. He has published a number of articles on the European Community and on Belgian coalition formation.

CHARLES T. POWELL is Research Fellow in Spanish Studies at St. Antony's College, Oxford, and a specialist in recent Spanish political history. His latest work, *Juan Carlos I of Spain*, was published by St. Antony's/Macmillan in 1994.

GARY PREVOST is professor of government at St. John's University in Collegeville, Minnesota. He is coeditor of *Politics and Change in Spain* (1985) and the author of several articles on Spanish social movements. He has also written extensively on the politics of Central America and the Caribbean, including *Cuba: A Different America* (1989), *The 1990 Elections in Nicaragua and Their Aftermath* (1992) and *Democracy and Socialism in Sandinista Nicaragua* (1993).

JÖRGEN RASMUSSEN is distinguished professor of political science at Iowa State University and is the executive secretary of the British Politics Group. He is author of *The British Political Process* (1993) and is coauthor of *Major European Governments* (eighth edition, 1991). His studies of British politics have appeared in British and American scholarly journals for the last thirty-five years.

HILMAR ROMMETVEDT holds a doctorate in political science and is research coordinator at Rogaland Research Institute in Stavanger, Norway. He is coauthor of *Parliamentary Change in the Nordic Countries* (1992) and author of a number of books and articles on Norwegian politics and policy.

GEORGE ROSS is Morris Hillquit Professor in Labor and Social Thought at Brandeis University and Senior Associate at the Center for European Studies, Harvard University. He is the author or editor of a dozen books on French politics, European labor and the European Community.

BO ROTHSTEIN is associate professor of political science at Uppsala University, Sweden. He has been a visiting scholar at Cornell University and Harvard University. Among his recent publications are "Marxism, Institutional Analysis and Working Class Strength" in *Politics and Society* (1990) and "Explaining Swedish Corporatism: The Formative Moment" in *Scandinavian Political Studies* (1992).

OLOF RUIN is Lars Hierta Professor of Government at the University of Stockholm. He is the author of a number of books and articles on interest organizations, higher education politics and governmental institutions. His latest book is *Tage Erlander: Serving the Welfare State, 1946–1969* (1990).

WILLIAM SAFRAN is professor of political science at the University of Colorado, Boulder. He is the author of *Veto-Group Politics* (1967) and *The French Polity* (fourth edition, 1991). He is also coauthor of *Ideology and Politics* (1979), *Comparative Politics* (1983) and *Politics in Western Europe* (1993), as well as numerous articles on French, European and ethnic politics.

MARTIN A. SCHAIN is professor of politics at New York University and is chair of the Center for European Studies there. He is the author of numerous books and articles, most recently on the problems of immigration and the far right in Western European politics. He is also coauthor, with Henry W. Ehrmann, of *Politics in France* (1993).

W. RAND SMITH is professor of politics at Lake Forest College. He has published *Crisis in the French Labor Movement* (1987), as well as numerous articles on labor and political economy in France and Spain.

CHRISTIAN SØE is professor of political science at California State University, Long Beach. He was born in Denmark and has studied at universities in Canada, the United States and Germany. He is coeditor of *The Germans and Their Neighbors* (1993), editor of the annually revised anthology *Comparative Politics* and author of numerous articles and chapters on party and coalition politics in Germany.

MARCUS STADELMANN is assistant professor of political science at the University of Texas, Tyler. He is currently at work on a book on the German Republican Party.

HANS-MARTIEN TEN NAPEL is lecturer in political science at Leyden University, the Netherlands. He is the author of *The Origins of the CDA: Towards a Unified Christian Democratic Party in the Netherlands, 1952–1980* (1992) and is currently engaged in a comparative study of the changing role of the judiciary in Western Europe.

MARINA TESORO is associate professor of contemporary history at the University of Pavia, Italy. She is author of *I Repubblicani nell'età giolittiana* (1979) and *Il Verde e il rosso* (1987), as well as numerous articles on Italian political parties and political movements of the 19th and 20th centuries.

MARTTI TURTOLA is professor of political history at the University of Helsinki and has served as editor in chief of the newspaper *Kouvolan Sanomat*. He is the author of "Erik Heinrichs: Mannerheim's and Paasikivi's General" (1988) and is currently at work on the authorized biography of the Finnish president, Risto Ryti.

ARISTOTLE TYMPAS is a doctoral candidate in the History, Technology and Society Program at the Georgia Institute of Technology in Atlanta.

LEONARD WEINBERG is professor of political science at the University of Nevada, Reno. He has been a visiting professor at the University of Florence, as well as a Fulbright Senior Research Fellow at that institution. His most recent book is *Encounters with the Contemporary Radical Right* (edited with Peter Merkl).

RUDOLF WILDENMANN (deceased 1993) was longtime professor of political science at the University of Mannheim, Germany, where he chaired a research institute. He is the author of a number of books and articles on parties, party systems and party government and is known particularly for his work on Ludwig Erhard.

DAVID WILSFORD is president and professor at the Institute for American Universities in Aix-en-Provence, France. He is the author of *Doctors and the State* (1991) and many articles on industrial and social policies in the advanced industrial democracies. Dr. Wilsford is currently working on a forthcoming book, *The Comparative Political Economy of Health Care*.

THOMAS P. WOLF is professor of political science at Indiana University Southeast and dean of the College of Arts and Sciences there. He is the author or coauthor of numerous articles on American, British and Japanese politics.

JOEL D. WOLFE is associate professor of political science at the University of Cincinnati. He is the author of *Workers, Participation and Democracy* (1985) and coeditor of *The Politics of Economic Adjustment: Pluralism, Corporatism, and Privatization* (1989).

STEVEN B. WOLINETZ is professor of political science at Memorial University of Newfoundland, Canada. He has written widely on Dutch and European political parties and has served as a Jean Monnet Fellow at the European University Institute in Florence for 1992–1993.

THOMAS C. WYLLER is professor emeritus of political science at the University of Oslo. He has published a number of books and articles on the policy processes and political system of contemporary Norway.

CYRUS ERNESTO ZIRAKZADEH is associate professor of political science at the University of Connecticut. He has published a number of books and articles and is currently working on a book-length study of John Steinbeck and the representation of class struggles in the United States during the 1930s.

ISBN 0-313-28623-X
90000>
EAN
9 780313 286230
HARDCOVER BAR CODE